How to

Get Into

the

TOP LAW

SCHOOLS

RICHARD MONTAUK

Prentice
Hall Press

Library of Congress Cataloging-in-Publication Data

Montauk, Richard.
    How to get into the top law schools / Richard Montauk.
        p.   cm.
    Includes index.
    ISBN 0-7352-0101-3 (paper)
    1. Law schools—United States—Admission.   I. Title.
KF285.M66 2001
340′.071′173—dc21

2001021691

Printed in the United States of America

10   9   8   7   6   5   4   3   2

ISBN 0-7352-0101-3

ATTENTION: CORPORATIONS AND SCHOOLS

Prentice Hall Press books are available at quantity discounts with bulk purchase for educational, business, or sales promotional use. For information, please write to: Prentice Hall Special Sales, 240 Frisch Court, Paramus, New Jersey 07652. Please supply: title of book, ISBN, quantity, how the book will be used, date needed.

 Paramus, NJ 07652

http://www.phdirect.com

Dedicated to three instructors, coaches, and role models who helped several generations of young people realize their potential:

Betty Edwards

Jack Edwards

Tom Gauerke

ACKNOWLEDGMENTS

I wish to thank those people who have been so helpful to the development and writing of *How to Get Into the Top Law Schools:*

First, the *admissions directors* at leading schools across the country who have been remarkably generous with their time and knowledge in discussing how admissions decisions are made at their schools. In particular, I would like to thank those I interviewed for this book and who have allowed themselves to be quoted at length throughout the text:

Elizabeth Rosselot (Boston College), Edward Tom (UC Berkeley/Boalt Hall), Michael Rappoport (UCLA), Andrea Sossin-Bergman (UCLA), Venetta C. Amory (Columbia), James Milligan (Columbia), Rick Geiger (Cornell), Dennis Shield (Duke), Robert Stanek (George Washington), Andy Cornblatt (Georgetown), Joyce Curll (Harvard), Kip Darcy (Hastings), Erica Munzel (Michigan), Kenneth Kleinrock (NYU), Don Rebstock (Northwestern), Janice Austin (Pennsylvania), William Hoye (Southern California), Faye Deal (Stanford), Shelli Soto (Texas), Anne Brandt (Vanderbilt), Albert R. Turnbull (Virginia), and Jean Webb (Yale).

Second, the *financial aid directors,* similarly generous with their time and knowledge regarding financial aid matters:

Dennis Tominaga (UC Berkeley/Boalt Hall), Veronica Wilson (UCLA), Alice Rigas (Columbia), Jane Deathe (Cornell), Kochie Richardson (Duke), Joyce Curll (Harvard), Katherine Gottschalk (Michigan), Stephen Brown (NYU), Don Rebstock (Northwestern), Janice Austin (Pennsylvania), Denise McGarry (Pennsylvania), Faye Deal (Stanford), Linda Alba (Texas), Juan Zabala (Texas), Jerome W. D. Stokes (Virginia), Louise DiMeo (Yale), and Zina Shaffer (Yale).

Third, the *career services directors,* for their insights regarding what employers value in recent law school graduates; what potential lawyers should know about law school, the profession, and themselves; and the current pay scales for different types of work in different locales:

Jean French (Boston College), Betsy Armour (Boston University), Jane Thomson (UC Davis), Karen Comstock (Cornell), Nancy Carver (George Washington), Abbie Willard (Georgetown), Susan Guindi (Michigan), Susan Gainen (Minnesota), Irene Dorzback (NYU), Kimberly Reed (North Carolina), Lisa Patterson (Notre Dame), Jo-Ann Verrier (Pennsylvania), Gloria Pyszka (Stanford), Susan Robinson (Stanford), Lisa Mead (Southern California),

Pam Malone (Vanderbilt), Steve Hopson (Virginia), Fred Thrasher (William & Mary), Jane Heymann (Wisconsin), and Theresa Bryant (Yale).

Fourth, *our clients,* from whom we have learned a great deal, and particularly those who have allowed their work to be reproduced in the book.

Fifth, *my colleague, Krista Klein,* whose expertise and hard work have contributed mightily to this volume.

Richard Montauk

How to Benefit Most from This Book

GETTING INTO A TOP SCHOOL IS THE HARDEST PART OF GETTING A TOP LAW DEGREE

Admissions directors at the world's top law schools admit that the hardest aspect of getting a degree from their schools is getting in. Getting through a top program may be demanding, but nearly 99 percent of the people who enroll get their degrees. At a school like Yale, however, only 6 to 8 percent of the people who apply are admitted. Of course, even more consider applying to the top schools than actually do so; the top schools routinely send out three, four, or five times as many applications as they have applicants. Those who dream of the top schools, but do not ultimately apply, are discouraged by the difficulty of gaining admission.

The reason it is so difficult to get into these schools is clear. The value of a law degree from a top school is immense. Graduates of the top schools earn salaries that are, on average, double or triple (or more) of what graduates from lesser schools make. There is even a pronounced difference in the earnings of graduates from the top-ranked and tenth- or twentieth-ranked schools. Increased salaries are not the end of the story. Greater career choice, increased job security, more interesting work, and numerous other benefits also result from a top law degree, so it is no wonder that so many people want to get into the best school they can manage.

Thus, it behooves you to do what you can to get into the school of your dreams. The first step is to make the best possible use of this book.

GETTING INTO A BETTER SCHOOL

The purpose of this book is to help applicants get into the best law school possible. Schools want candidates who will be successful lawyers of every stripe, legal journalists, administrators, and more. They assess a great deal of information to find them. Some of this is objective and quantifiable, such as a candidate's Law

School Admission Test (LSAT) score; whereas much of it is not, such as what a candidate intends to do in the future. The objective elements of an application, which can be termed a candidate's credentials, are obviously important. The subjective elements, however, are ultimately at least as important.

Harvard could fill its class with candidates from the world's top universities—people who graduated in the top 10 percent of their classes, have scores in the upper 160s or better on the LSAT, and so on. Of course it accepts people who fit this profile, but it actually rejects as many of them as it accepts. The point is that the very top schools are looking for more in their candidates than just good scores.

Schools admit people rather than scores. Schools look for leaders as well as for brilliant analysts—people who work well as part of teams, who are determined to make an impact, and who have thought carefully about how they want their careers to progress. Given a certain baseline of achievement, they will look at far more than someone's grade-point average or LSAT score, because those are simply inadequate predictors of leadership, teamwork, and other critical skills. Grade-point averages and LSAT scores also reveal nothing about how a candidate can enrich the learning experience of classmates by virtue of his or her work experience, extracurricular interests, and so on.

Schools do consider objective credentials, but only as a part of the total picture of the person. They use all of the information they get, including the essays candidates write, the recommendations submitted on their behalf, and, increasingly, the results of application interviews, to determine whether someone will be a successful law student and lawyer. *Especially at the very top schools, the "who" is more important than the "what."*

In fact, the personal statements and other essays, recommendations, and interviews are doubly useful for the schools. They not only show these leadership and other qualities, but also show schools how to interpret the so-called objective data. A grade-point average of 3.5 on a 4.0 scale means different things in different contexts. If a student has to work 30 hours per week at a demanding job, that performance looks better. Similarly, if the person is a gifted engineer but chose to take a lot of writing courses to improve a weakness, that performance again looks better. The only way that schools know how to interpret a grade-point average, let alone someone's work experience or aspirations, is by hearing what the applicant (and the applicant's recommenders) say about it. In other words, the personal statement and other essays, recommendations, and interviews not only present new information but also "frame" the objective data.

How to Get Into the Top Law Schools shows you how to maximize the value of your credentials by presenting them in the best way. It does this in several ways:

■ It shows what leading law schools are looking for in their applicants and exactly how they interpret the different parts of the applicant's folder.

■ It explains the nature of the admissions process, including showing who evaluates your application and how the final decisions are reached.

■ It explains and illustrates how you can (and should) improve your own marketing efforts—via your application essays, recommendations, and interviews—to increase your chances of admission at the schools you most want to attend.

The key is to develop your own *personal marketing strategy.* This must be comprehensive, because a disjointed couple of essays or a recommendation that is at odds with what you say about yourself, is the kiss of death for your application. To maximize your chances, you must take advantage of every opportunity to show how professional you are, and why *you* should be admitted.

This book will show you how to prepare applications that distinguish you from the rest of the applicant pool and show you in your best light. Admissions directors routinely note that only 10 to 20 percent of applicants market themselves really well. This gives you a great opportunity to improve your chances by learning how to do a professional quality application.

WHO SHOULD READ THIS BOOK?

This book is geared toward people who want to get into the best law school they can. Although the text is weighted toward getting into the very top schools, frankly, anyone who wants to improve his or her candidacy to any school, in the top 20 or not, would benefit from a thorough understanding of application strategy.

UNIQUE FEATURES

How to Get Into the Top Law Schools provides a thorough explanation of how you can get into the best schools possible. It guides you through each step of the process, showing at each point how to develop your own marketing strategy. It analyzes and discusses each element in a thorough, detailed fashion. The unique features include:

- Advice from over 20 admissions directors of the very top schools on every aspect of the applications process

  —Plus advice from the career services and financial aid directors, too

- Over 30 actual applicant essays representing

  —Successful applications to each of the country's top schools

  —Applicants from a wide range of backgrounds, ethnicities, work experience, and colleges (and majors)

- An in-depth look at the strategies available to you to minimize the cost of law school

  —The focus is on strategy, not how to fill out the form

- Detailed advice on how to write persuasive personal statements and other essays for maximum impact

- A first-of-its-kind analysis of law school interviews, a new and important feature of the admissions process at a majority of the top schools

- Solid advice on:

  —How to choose the right program for you

  —How to prepare for law school and how to get the most out of the program once you go

- A detailed timetable so you will know what to do when

- Complete explanations of what top schools look for in applicants, and how you can meet their needs

- Advice on what to do if you do *not* get into one of your top choice schools

HOW TO REALLY PROFIT FROM THIS BOOK

The key to maximizing the value of this book is to start the whole admission process early—earlier than you might believe necessary. As Chapter 6, "The Application Timetable," shows, it is ideal to begin the process more than a year before you expect to begin classes. Starting early, and using this book throughout the process, will allow you to complete strong, persuasive applications in the most efficient manner possible.

This book is designed to be used efficiently by people with radically different needs. Some will want to read it cover to cover; but many will want to dip into it for help on specific problems they face. Here are some suggestions for how to get the most out of the book, depending upon your own situation:

You Are in the Midst of Your Applications Now

If you have applications due in just a few weeks, you should read several core chapters of the book immediately to avoid making terrible mistakes. Chapters 5 and 7 show you how law schools will evaluate your applications, Chapter 8 shows you the basics of how to market yourself, and Chapters 9 and 10 show you how to think about addressing your personal statement and other essays. You will also want to read the analyses of specific essay topics that you are going to write about. In addition, if you have yet to choose your recommenders, or if they have not yet sent in your recommendations, read Chapter 11 to see how you can improve what they say. Before your interviews, which presumably will not happen until after you have filed your applications, you will certainly want to read Chapter 12 on interviewing. When you have time, read the other chapters, or the executive summaries of them, to understand the application process more fully. Part III, which covers the post-application period, is important reading for you after you have finished your applications.

WHAT IF ONE OF YOUR APPLICATIONS IS DUE IN A WEEK?

Do not panic! This book can get you up to speed fast. Before going any further in your applications, be sure to read the executive summaries of each chapter and read Chapters 7 and 8 thoroughly. Then consult the relevant essay discussions (concerning any topics you are working on at the moment) in Chapter 9 and look through the discussion of how to write a strong and persuasive essay. Also be sure to read Chapter 11 on recommendations before giving the "go-ahead" to your recommenders.

YOU ARE GOING TO APPLY TO SCHOOLS IN THE NEAR FUTURE

If you intend to apply to schools in the next several months, you will probably want to get an overview of the applications process by reading the executive summaries of each chapter now, plus Chapters 7 and 8, which will explain the fundamentals of what you want to demonstrate in your applications. Read the appendix to Chapter 6, "Application Timetable," to be sure that you do not miss the starting dates for important activities. Then read each chapter as it becomes relevant to your efforts, starting with Chapters 8 and 9, which will show you how to prepare for your essays.

YOU WILL NOT APPLY UNTIL SEVERAL YEARS FROM NOW

If you are not going to apply to schools for another two or three (or more) years, read Chapters 7 and 8 now. These will show you how best to ready yourself for admission, while you still have the opportunity to improve your credentials dramatically. Then read the appendix to Chapter 6, "Application Timetable," to determine when to start the process for keeps. Later on you can read the executive summaries of each chapter (about 15–18 months before you intend to go) to prepare for the application process itself.

YOU ARE NOT SURE THAT LAW SCHOOL IS FOR YOU

Read two chapters to start your assessment process. Chapter 1, "Why Go to Law School?" discusses appropriate and inappropriate reasons for attending law school, as well as some of the steps that all applicants should take to be sure that law makes sense for them. Chapter 2, "Looking at Law School," gives an overview of the law school experience, thereby offering you a chance to see in advance what you might be in for.

In general, some chapters will not be relevant to everybody. For example, people who have already done their research and determined which schools to apply to can happily skip Chapter 3, "How to Choose the Right School for You."

A FINAL NOTE: THE APPLICATION PROCESS
MAY PROVE HELPFUL (AS WELL AS PAINFUL)

Many applicants look upon the task of producing hundreds of details about their pasts, writing essays about intimate or obscure topics, securing recommendations from old professors and current bosses, and enduring interviews as a modern form of "death by a thousand cuts." They feel that it is trial enough simply to research the schools and figure out which ones would be appropriate for them, let alone to have to manage the data-, paper-, writing-, and time-intensive application process.

If that is your view, keep in mind that the application process, however imperfect it may be, encourages applicants to think seriously about where they want to go in their careers and in their lives, and how they are going to get there. Too few people do this at any point, let alone at this most appropriate of times. Applicants to law schools, whether they are still in college or have been in different careers for a dozen years, are highly likely to be right at the point where sensible decisions about these matters can yield a lifetime of benefits, and a failure to consider their options carefully can result in opportunities missed, opportunities that will not be offered again. Confronting such important career decisions might open doors you never even realized existed.

As Chapter 1 discusses in some detail, a very large minority—if not a majority—of those who attend top law schools end up sorry that they became lawyers. Do yourself a favor: Read that chapter and honestly evaluate yourself before committing yourself to the law.

ABOUT *DEGREE OF DIFFERENCE*

Founded by Richard Montauk in 1991, *Degree of Difference* (formerly *Education USA*) is a consulting firm that provides quality one-on-one service to individuals applying to professional schools (especially law and business), colleges, and other educational institutions. We help many hundreds of individuals each year plan their educational careers and complete successful applications to the top programs worldwide.

Degree of Difference provides a full menu of services for law school applicants.

OUR INDIVIDUALIZED CONSULTING

MATCHING APPLICANTS WITH LAW SCHOOLS

We begin the consulting process by learning about your past—your background, education, extracurricular interests, work experience, and the like—and your ambitions for the future. We help you to select the law schools that will be most appropriate for your needs and desires, and also ensure that your final list of target schools includes an adequate number of "stretches," "possibles," and "likelies."

■ *Note, too, that we advise some of our clients not to pursue a legal education (or at least not yet).* Some people are better off not going into law, either because law is not a good fit for them or because something else is simply a better fit than law would be. We urge such clients to explore their career options and help them to do so.

STRATEGIZING

We help you develop a coherent strategy to follow during (as well as before and after) the law school application process.

- We advise you on when to apply to school. Some candidates, for example, can improve their chances of getting into a top school dramatically with an additional year of interesting and substantive work, or well-planned community or civic activity.

- We help you develop a comprehensive positioning strategy. We show you how to market your strengths, account for or overcome your weaknesses, and best position yourself to enhance your candidacy.

- We teach you how to tailor your applications to each individual school.

- We help you make decisions regarding joint degree programs (and help you apply to the other, non-law program, as appropriate).

INTERVIEWING

Evaluative interviews are a relatively new part of the law school application process, yet they are being used by more and more of the top schools. We teach you how to approach your interviews with confidence and make a positive impression.

- We help you understand both your own candidacy—including how you compare with other applicants in a given school's applicant pool—and the schools to which you are applying.

- We show you what to expect in your interview and how to handle the most likely questions.

- We coach you on successful interviewing techniques, providing assistance not only regarding what to say but also regarding how to say it, what to wear, and how to act in a variety of formal and informal settings.

- We provide mock interview sessions.

SOLICITING RECOMMENDATIONS

Getting the most from recommenders is often one of the most difficult—and one of the most overlooked—tasks in the law school application process.

- We teach you how to look at your application in its entirety in order to determine what is most needed from your recommenders to fill in the gaps, enhance your strengths, and compensate for your weaknesses.

- We provide advice on how to approach recommenders tactfully, and how best to provide them with the information you would like conveyed in your letters of recommendation.

- We also assist your recommenders (if desired) to develop high-impact letters of endorsement.

COMPLETING APPLICATIONS

A sloppy or uninformative application will do you no good. We are happy to review any and all of your written materials to ensure that all the necessary information is well communicated and error-free.

- We review all of the written work, including application data forms; listings of extracurricular activities, community service write-ups, and job descriptions; and responses to short-answer and essay questions.

- We help you to write an appropriate résumé.

ESSAY WRITING

Writing personal statements and other essays is the area of greatest concern for most of our clients.

- We help you determine what subjects should form the basis of your personal statement(s). We also help you understand what should be communicated in addenda rather than in the main essays. We help you get the most out of your experiences and strengths.

- We help you craft themes in order to make your entire set of essays convey a set of consistent and solid messages.

- We edit essays and provide advice on essay structure and form, yet strive to do so in a way that retains a client's own voice, style, and personality.

Please note that we do not write essays for our clients under any circumstances.

HOW TO INITIATE A CONSULTING RELATIONSHIP WITH *DEGREE OF DIFFERENCE*

If you are interested in our consulting services, please contact us to discuss your current situation and goals—and how we can best help you. Some of our most successful clients sign up for our services one or more years in advance of actually applying for law school, in order to discuss long-term strategy and goals that should be addressed long before applications are put together. This way you will be best prepared to market yourself when the time comes.

On the other hand, plenty of clients come to us at a later stage in the game—at the beginning of the application "season" or even in the midst of doing applications. We are prepared to help you at any point in your application work and encourage panicked applicants who find themselves behind schedule to contact us for immediate assistance.

Please call us at one of our primary locations:

Degree of Difference, Inc.
2443 Fillmore Street, #330
San Francisco, CA 94115
Tel. (415) 273-1782
Fax (415) 567-1616
www.degreeofdifference.com

Degree of Difference, Inc.
126 Aldersgate Street
Barbican, London EC1A 4JQ
United Kingdom
Tel. (44) 20 76 08 18 11
Fax (44) 20 72 50 31 09

SEMINARS

We present, in both the spring and the fall, half-day and day seminars concerning law school admissions in major cities across the U.S. A typical seminar focuses on half a dozen critical issues. Each issue is introduced by a presentation that goes beyond the scope of this book. This presentation is followed by a question-and-answer session at which participants are encouraged to explore their own application concerns.

To find out the dates, locations, prices, and so on of upcoming seminars, please consult our Website.

CONTENTS

ACKNOWLEDGMENTS—v

HOW TO BENEFIT MOST FROM THIS BOOK—vii

ABOUT *DEGREE OF DIFFERENCE*—xv

Part I **INTRODUCING LAW SCHOOL**

1 **Why Go to a Top Law School?—3**
The Value of Going to a Top School—4
Financial Considerations—5
Should You Go to Law School?—6
Conclusion—20
Additional Resources—20

2 **Looking at Law School—25**
Typical Required Courses—28
Teaching Methods—29
Workload—31
Grading—32
Specialization—34
Courses Outside Law School—34
Joint Degrees—35
Publications—36
Student Body—37
Social Life—37

3 **How to Choose the Right School for** *You*—39
Know Yourself—and What You Want from a Law Degree—40
Research the Schools—40
Determine How Many Schools to Apply to—44
Avoid the Likely Pitfalls in Choosing a School—46
Final-Decision Criteria—47
Recommended Readings—47
Appendix I: Criteria for Assessing Schools—53
Appendix II: Visiting Law Schools—69

---

4 How to Use the Rankings—77

Using the Rankings—78
The Rankings—80
Other Rankings—89
Conclusion—94

5 The Admissions Process—99

"Rolling" Admissions—100
The Standard Admissions Model—100
The Use of Index Numbers—105
Admissions Outcomes—107

6 The Application Timetable—115

When Should You Apply—Early or Late in an Application Cycle?—116
How Long Will It Take to Do Your Application?—118
Application Timetable—119
Where Are Things Most Likely to Go Astray?—123
Using the Master Application Organizer—125
Appendix III: Application Organizers—127

Part II APPLYING TO LAW SCHOOL

---

7 Making the Most of Your Credentials—137

The Academic Record—138
The LSAT—146
Work Experience—157
Extracurricular, Personal, and Community Activities—165
Use Your Activities to Highlight Your Personal Side—169
Show Where You Are Headed—173
For International Students—176

8 Marketing Yourself—179

Creating a Marketing Strategy—180
Capitalizing on Your Strengths; Minimizing Your Weaknesses—187
Personal Statement Example—189
Fit In–Stand Out—191
Fashioning Your Message: Positioning—191

The Mechanics of Positioning: Using Themes—193
Conclusion—195
Appendix IV: Special Cases—199
Residency—199
Legacies—201
International Applicants: JD and LLM Degrees—203
Appendix V: Personal Organizer—209

9   Understanding Your Essay Options—215

Choice of Topic—216
Various Essay Topics Analyzed in Detail—217
Brief Notes on Additional Topics—232
Optional Essays—242

10   Writing Persuasive Essays—247

Getting Started—248
Planning—250
Reviewing the Elements of Good Writing—252
The Rough Draft—254
Editing Your Rough Draft—256
Giving Your Essays to Someone Else to Critique—260
Proofreading—261
Reusing Your Personal Statements—266
Further Reading—267
Appendix VI: Writing Résumés, Filling Out Forms, Including Extra Materials—269

11   Recommendations—277

Why Are Recommendations Required?—278
What Admissions Committees Learn from Recommenders—283
Who Should Write Your Recommendations?—285
How Many Recommenders?—294
Approaching a Potential Recommender—296
Increasing the Value of Your Recommendations—300
One-Size-Fits-All Recommendations—301
Making Sure Recommendations Are Submitted on Time—304
The Follow-up—304
Special Note for International Students—305
Employer Recommendation Example—305
Appendix VII: Recommendation Organizer—309
Appendix VIII: Recommendation Briefing Outline—311

12   **Interviews—313**

Should You Interview If Given the Choice?—316

Should You Interview If Requested To?—316

Before the Interview—318

The Interviewer—319

Interview Evaluation Forms—324

Knowing the School—324

Anticipating the Questions—328

The Interview Questions—329

Recollecting Your Thoughts During the Interview—335

Preparing to Describe Key Events—336

What Determines the Likelihood of a Given Question Being Asked?—337

Practice—339

Physical Preparations—340

During the Interview—343

How to Read the Interviewer—346

Your Question Time—347

Ending the Interview—348

General Rules for Interviews—349

Special Types of Interviews—351

How to Deal with the Incompetent Interviewer—353

After the Interview—355

Part III   ON THE ROAD TO LAW SCHOOL

---

13   **Responding to Wait-Listing, Denial, and Other Disappointments—361**

Responding to an Administrative Hold—362

Responding to Wait-Listing—362

Responding to Denial—367

Should You Ever Appeal a Denial?—368

Should You Reapply in the Future or Settle for a Lesser School?—369

Other Options—371

14   **Transfer and Other Options—373**

Transferring from an Institution Where You Have Been Admitted—374

Choosing the School You Will Transfer From—376

Begin a Degree Abroad—381

Complete a Degree Abroad—383
Participate in an Exchange Program or Become a Third-Year Matriculant—384
Use Another Law School's Career Placement Office—386

15 What to Do Once You Are Accepted—387

Deferral—388
Accepting Your Offer—391
Leaving Your Job—391
Finishing College—393
Preparing for Law School—394
Skills: The Bare Minimum—397

16 How to Get the Most Out of Law School—401

Time Management Is Your Biggest Responsibility—402
Preparing for Exams—404
Think Broadly about Your Career Development—405
Think Specifically about Your Career Development—407
Keep Stress Under Control—410
Don't Forget the Social Experience—411

17 Financing Your Law Degree—413

Calculating the Cost of Law School—414
Your Expected (Family) Contribution—415
Type of Financial Aid—418
Part-Time Work During Law School—429
Financial Aid Policies—432
Evaluating Financial Aid Packages—and Trying for More—444
Financial Strategies—448

Part IV APPLICATION ESSAY EXAMPLES

Application Essay Examples—455

Index—511

Part I

INTRODUCING LAW SCHOOL

1

WHY GO TO A TOP LAW SCHOOL?

— EXECUTIVE SUMMARY —

If you wish to go to law school, go to the very best one you can.
—The rewards of attending a top law school are compelling.
■
But do not go to law school until you have thoroughly analyzed:
Yourself
Law school
Law as a profession
Legal specialties and practice types that would fit you
■
Do not go to law school straight from college.
—You cannot understand your fit with the world of work
absent full-time work experience.

Once upon a time, a high school diploma was a sufficient credential to get a good executive job. Then, as more and more people went to college, a high school diploma was no longer enough to land an executive position. A college degree sufficed for a time, but as more and more people got MBAs and JDs, even a college degree was no longer sufficient to get most high-powered jobs. That was the case in the 1970s. Since then, the number of people getting such degrees has increased to the point that simply having such a degree is insufficient to get plum jobs; the *quality* of the law program has become determinative.

This does not mean you should necessarily go to law school (see the discussion later in this chapter). But if you do, you should go to the school with the best reputation you can manage.

THE VALUE OF GOING TO A TOP SCHOOL

As the number of JD holders in the world increases, so does the importance of getting a top-quality JD rather than just any law degree.

CAREER CHOICE

Some parts of the legal profession are virtually off-limits to graduates of lesser law schools. These include the major corporate law firms and high-profile government jobs as well as public interest organizations. The most desirable employers to work for, such as the major corporate firms, would no more think of recruiting at "Acme" Law School than they would of giving this year's profits to the Flat Earth Society. These firms look to hire the best and the brightest and they know that the best and the brightest are to be found at the world's leading law schools. The same is true in other legal fields, too. For instance, in a profession that is notorious for snobbery (regarding which law schools people attended), arguably the snobbiest employers of all are the public interest organizations.

STATUS

This category nearly speaks for itself. Whether for personal or business reasons, being a graduate of Yale conjures up entirely different impressions and reactions among people you encounter than does being a graduate of Acme Law. Status is partially related to the other items listed here, such as salary, but it also reflects the fact that Yale admits only people who are highly regarded to begin with.

CAREER FLEXIBILITY

The top law schools offer substantial geographic mobility to their graduates. Whereas lesser schools place few of their graduates outside their city or region, the top schools invariably send many of their graduates to firms across the country (and the world).

The benefits of going to a top school are not limited to your initial job upon graduation. If you decide to change employers, or even to change fields, the quality of your education will be one of the determining factors in your ability to make the switch successfully, and it will also determine how other people rate your chances (and whether they will risk hiring you). The alumni network, and your own personal network from law school, will also be important determinants of your ability to switch. With a strong network willing to help you, your chances are automatically better.

INCREASED PAY

The better the reputation of a school, the more its graduates earn. For example, the graduates of Harvard who enter the private sector will, in their first year, have median earnings of approximately $100,000. First-year graduates from the top dozen or two dozen schools can expect, on average, to earn 50 percent to 100 percent more than graduates from schools ranked nearer to number 50. This pay gap increases dramatically as one goes further down the rankings to those schools near the bottom of the 200 or so that grant law degrees in the United States.

It is important to note that the median salary of lawyers in the U.S. is below $70,000. Graduates of the top schools, however, earn more than that from the moment they start in private practice. In fact, lawyers at the leading firms have been making at least $140,000 in their first year out of law school.

INTANGIBLES

Many of the benefits of attending a top law school are intangible. For example, you will be spending three years of your life interacting with faculty and fellow students; you might well value having the smartest, most motivated group of faculty and fellow students you can. Indeed, given that many of the friendships and professional relationships you form at law school will continue for many years after school, you will derive pleasure from attending a top school long after graduation. By the same token, you will have the opportunity to work with and compare yourself to some of the finest minds in the country.

FINANCIAL CONSIDERATIONS

Getting a law degree represents an extremely large investment of money, as well as time and effort. The tuition for a three-year program may be $80,000 or more, and your income forgone may be double that. Books, computer, travel to and from the program, and other assorted expenses will add thousands more.

Is a law degree worth this large sum? Although not everyone will be financially better off from getting a JD, those attending the top programs are highly likely to be. The payoff to attending a top school is partly a matter of increased earnings. It is also a matter of increased career options, increased confidence that one can do a given job extremely well, increased security (no matter what happens there are jobs available for people from top schools), and increased status. It is therefore probably a mistake to view the decision to get a JD on a purely financial basis, despite the sums involved.

SHOULD YOU GO TO LAW SCHOOL?

This book is dedicated largely to the issues of helping you determine which schools would be best for you and showing you how to maximize your chances of gaining admission to them. A much more important question, however, is whether you should go to law school at all.

> Do not go to law school unless you are quite certain that you want to be a practicing lawyer (and you know the one or two fields that will best suit your needs) or you want to do something intimately related to legal practice, such as legal journalism.

A LAW DEGREE IS NOT A GENERAL PURPOSE DEGREE

The accepted wisdom is still that a law degree is the most flexible of degrees insofar as it will prepare you to do almost anything. This is utterly wrong. A law degree does nothing but teach you about practicing law. It does not teach you how to administer, nor does it teach you how to start a business (except in the narrow sense of how to file incorporation documents). The true multipurpose degree of today is the MBA, the skills from which would indeed help you in most fields.

IS LAW *SCHOOL* FOR YOU?

There is some correlation between those who most like law school and those who enjoy practicing law, just as there is between those who dislike law school and then dislike practicing law. The correlation, however, is not as strong as one might like. As a result, it makes sense to evaluate both law and law school independently.

Therefore, separate your decision into two parts: Consider first whether you are going to like law school. If you decide that the three years you will spend at law school will be the best three years of your life to date, then you need not have so high a degree of certainty that you will love the practice of law because at least the process of getting there will be enjoyable. On the other hand, if you determine that law school is likely to be a misery, you need to be dead certain that the practice of law is indeed right for you.

You can readily determine what law school will be like by spending time in law classes. You probably live near a law school. Approach the admissions department with a request to sit in on classes, or simply ask a professor for permission. Then follow one or two classes for an extended period. Do not just drop in once or twice. Instead, do the required reading and prepare for the class as if your grade (and life) depended upon it. Be sure to talk with other students about what they think of the process. (Note that the better the quality of the law school, the more representative and valuable this effort will be for someone who is potentially headed to a top school. Lower-tier law schools teach law in a different way, for a different purpose, and to a different group of students than do top schools.)

You might think you already have a fair idea of what law school will be like because you took political science or pre-law courses in college. Such courses, however, hardly even resemble true law school courses, so do not take your enjoyment of these as a sign that you will like law school.

Do not rely, either, on what is written or filmed about law school. You need to investigate it for yourself. If you do not go to this small amount of effort because you deem it to be too much trouble, you will deserve whatever you encounter later on!

IS LAW FOR YOU?

Law is not a single, unitary field; there are many different specialties within it, just as there are many different employers. Although there are certain personality traits that seem to fit most comfortably within law, the range is substantial. How, then, you might ask, can you sensibly investigate the field? Note, first of all, that you need to do two things. You need to understand your own interests, skills, and needs. You also need to understand what is on offer in law, and see whether the two provide a suitable match.

This book is avowedly not a career planning manual. It is important to note, though, that you should put yourself through the exercises that such manuals—and sophisticated consultants—require. The following is meant simply to sketch out (albeit extremely briefly) what types of analysis you will need to do and to provide you with a guide to the resources likely to help you.

UNDERSTAND YOUR OWN INTERESTS, SKILLS, VALUES, AND GOALS

It is important that you choose a career that matches your needs as fully as possible. It may be that no job will be perfect for you—giving you everything you might wish for, and fulfilling you completely—but ending up with one that is not at least a close fit inevitably leads to trouble. Many lawyers end up desperately unhappy, desperately wishing that they had chosen another field. The way to avoid such misery is to analyze your needs *before* you enter the field.

One starting point is to ask yourself and those who know you (family, friends, colleagues) what is likely to be most important to you in a career. What are your *interests*? Do you like to write, ride horses, travel, fiddle around in a laboratory? What do you have no interest in? You are, of course, most likely to enjoy a career that keeps you in touch with whatever areas or activities you enjoy.

What do you do well? Your inventory of *skills* is important for numerous reasons, one being that you will tend to enjoy whatever you do well, and vice versa, so entering a field that allows you to utilize what you do well is a good bet.

What are your *values*? At one level, this asks you to identify what causes you support—free speech, unfettered capitalism, environmentalism, and so on. At another level, this asks how you wish to live your life. Do you value time with your family more than being the highest paid associate in the office, for example? Both types of values should have a major affect upon your choice of career (and how you pursue your career).

What are your *goals*? What do you hope to accomplish in life, whether in the short term or the long term?

The resources listed below will provide you with a starting point for your self-analysis. Do not overlook the possibility of using a professional career counselor, but make sure it is someone who has substantial experience dealing with lawyers or would-be lawyers.

RESOURCES

Many professionals currently use the Myers–Briggs Type Inventory (MBTI) to analyze people's personalities and their likely fit with various jobs. The Keirsey Temperament Sorter (sunsite.unc.edu./jembin/mb.pl) provides an online scorable personality test based upon the MBTI.

These three books examine personality–job fit from the MBTI perspective:

Otto Kroeger and Janet M. Thuesen, *Type Talk at Work*

Jean M. Kummerov et al., *Work Types*

Paul D. Tieger and Barbara Barron-Tieger, *Do What You Are: Discover the Perfect Career for You Through the Secrets of Personality Type*

In *The Soul of the Law: Understanding Lawyers and the Law* by Benjamin Sells, a lawyer turned psychotherapist analyzes the key underlying issues that drive lawyers. (Recommended)

IT TAKES MANY YEARS TO GET OUT OF LAW (ONCE YOU ARE IN)

Deciding to go to law school is a risky decision that is surprisingly hard to reverse. Many people attend law school for lack of anything better to do or despite major misgivings. They do not drop out at the top schools, despite the fact that a large minority dislike law school itself. (Harvard's attrition rate is typically under 1 percent.) Those who dislike law school and those who are unsure of whether they are going to like practice (having not enjoyed their summer employment between years of law school) nonetheless enter practice. They console themselves in the first years of practice that the reason they dislike it is because they are simply at the bottom of the totem pole, learning necessary skills and establishing credibility. They assume that matters will improve. For those who find themselves still unhappy after three or more years, the natural instinct is to switch practice areas within the firm (if they enjoy their colleagues) or to switch firms (if they do not particularly care for their colleagues). This guarantees another few years of hoping that matters will improve.

Those who enter law are generally too goal-oriented to opt out; they will leave only when forced. It is only after half a dozen or more years that such lawyers will finally admit that they made the wrong career choice. They tell themselves that a law degree has at least prepared them to do anything. Unfortunately, they discover how untrue that notion really is. They talk with friends in other fields, headhunters who help lawyers find other employment, and so on. They learn that they will have to cut their salaries by two-thirds and be willing to start at the bottom of another field, unless they find a job closely related to law. (If they take a job closely related to law, such as being the executive director of a public interest organization, they still have to accept the salary cut.) Even if they are willing and able to take the massive salary cut involved in starting over—that is, they can give up their long-held professional identity (and their pride can handle no longer being a "professional"), despite their friends' and family's comments that they are wasting their degree, and their mortgage or law school loans do not require a substantial monthly payment—they find that the barriers to doing so are massive.

Employers value legal training only in lawyers. High-tech firms, traditional companies, and everyone else in business (and in innumerable other areas as well) do not believe that lawyers, uniquely, have been "taught how to think."

Nor do they find that lawyers have acquired any nonlegal skills worth paying for. Indeed, employers view lawyers as overly contentious, not very team-oriented, and very narrowly focused. Employers grant that lawyers (from top schools, at least) are probably pretty smart and willing to work hard. However, they also consider them to be damaged goods. They figure that such lawyers are running away from law rather than toward something else in particular. They also figure that because lawyers have so little background of relevance to choosing another field, they are likely to make another poor career decision the next time around, just as they did in entering law.

For those lawyers who wish finally to get the true multipurpose degree, an MBA, the outlook is also discouraging. The only lawyers able to get into top business schools are those who have had very substantial business experience along the way. Business schools value experience much more highly than do law schools, but they do not value a knowledge of product liability law, federal jurisdiction, or the like. Thus, lawyers with top GPAs and GMAT scores flop in the business school admissions game because they have wasted (by business school standards) their last eight or ten years.

This is not a pretty picture. The way to avoid it is simple: Learn in advance whether law and law school are for you.

It is a pity that law schools do not do what doctoral programs in other fields have long done: Give an intermediate degree along the way. If you wish to do a Ph.D. in economics, for example, but stop before completing your thesis, you will still get a master's degree. Law schools could do something similar, giving a master's in law after one or one-and-a-half years, which would be a good point at which you could assess whether law really made sense for you. Those who opted out of law would nonetheless have a fine-looking degree for their résumés, but would no doubt find it easier to leave at this point than to continue to invest heavily in a field that they might well already sense was not going to be what they had hoped.

**CAREER SERVICES DIRECTORS
DISCUSS SELF-ASSESSMENT**

It's extremely beneficial if a person has made some sort of self-assessment, looked inward and self-assessed his or her skills, interests, and values. It is important that these three coalesce. Fred Thrasher, Assistant Dean, Career Planning and Placement, William & Mary

Choose jobs, including part-time and summer jobs, as well as internships, to give you as much information as possible about yourself, the profession, or the world. Analyze important aspects, positive and negative, of all the experiences you've had. What did you like about being treasurer of a club, for example? Did you like preparing a financial statement each month, or analyzing the data, or did you just like the title?   Irene Dorzback, Assistant Dean for Career Counseling and Placement, NYU

People who come to law school should have given significant thought to who they are and what they want from law school. This means that they should have done a thorough self-assessment, have a good sense of self and know what they're good at.   Lisa Patterson, Director of Career Services, Notre Dame

Guidance programs in high school and college could do more to help students evaluate what they've done, what they've liked, and why certain activities appealed to them so that students have a frame of reference for determining their skills, interests, and values.   Irene Dorzback, Assistant Dean for Career Counseling and Placement, NYU.

WITHOUT FULL-TIME WORK EXPERIENCE, YOU CANNOT PROPERLY ASSESS YOUR NEEDS

It is very difficult to get sufficient understanding of what you do and do not like, let alone what the world of work is all about, without substantial work experience. Although you can eliminate some fields of endeavor as possible choices on the basis of your college and part-time work experiences, you are unlikely to get very far toward making a final choice. (Knowing that you dislike science does eliminate medicine from your future, but it does not help you choose among journalism, investment banking, and law.) Your twenties are the ideal time to sample the world of work, so take advantage of the opportunity.

You (and/or your parents) may be unwilling to take the risk that you will be unable to get into a worthwhile, rewarding, or prestigious position. As a result, you (or they) may feel the need to get into law school as soon as possible. This is wrong-headed for two reasons. First, your chances of getting into a good law school increase with real-world experience. (This is explored in detail throughout the rest of this book.) Second, the greatest risk is that you will have entered the wrong field and be unable to get out of it successfully. Therefore, do not rush into law school. Work for at least two years, in one or more serious jobs, after college. Make sure law school is an affirmative rather than a default choice.

CAREER SERVICES AND ADMISSIONS DIRECTORS
DISCUSS THE VALUE OF LIFE AND WORK EXPERIENCE

THE VALUE OF WORK EXPERIENCE BEFORE LAW SCHOOL

I encourage work experience, whenever possible. Law school is a very, very serious investment of time and money. It takes some time in a work environment to know who you are, what it is you want out of your work life.   Abbie Willard, Assistant Dean, Georgetown

Having had real experience helps students make more informed career choices; they have more realistic expectations of what the world is like.   Jane Heymann, Assistant Dean for Career Services, Wisconsin

Whenever I talk to pre-laws I urge them to work between college and law school. Almost regardless of what they do, it gives them a combination of sophistication, poise, maturity, and real-world experience.   Jane Thomson, Director of Career Planning, UC Davis

If all the top schools agreed not to accept applicants unless they had three-plus years of experience, it would probably work out better for everyone. The work experience would benefit applicants, who would better understand what they want with a law degree. As a result, it would really help career services directors, too. None of us wants to sit across from broken dreams, or a perception of law that was never checked out.   Irene Dorzback, Assistant Dean for Career Counseling and Placement, NYU

WAITING TO APPLY

Someone with a weak undergraduate record is well advised to wait to apply; the rule of thumb is about five years. Many require some time out to grow up as well as to accomplish something. They need to develop a sense of focus, time management skills.   Elizabeth Rosselot, Director of Admissions, Boston College

There is no penalty for waiting to apply to law school. I think there often is misplaced pressure from parents, however, to go to law school straight out of college.   Anne Brandt, Director of Admissions, Vanderbilt

Too many people apply to law school for lack of other ideas of what to do. You don't have to go to law school right out of college. I'm pleased that more applicants wait longer to apply now; they work for a few years on average and determine where they're headed. The older students tend to be more focused and are better able to handle the stresses of law school.   Faye Deal, Associate Dean for Admissions and Financial Aid, Stanford

Older, more experienced students seem to do better in class. They are often more dedicated and focused regarding why they are in law school. They have gained discipline and organizational ability, and are able to tackle school work more efficiently and well.   William Hoye, Dean for Admissions, USC

Students who've taken a break often are more motivated to take on the rigors of studying. They're usually excited about being back in an academic environment.   Kenneth Kleinrock, Assistant Dean for Admissions, NYU

We want to understand the applicant's motivation for studying law. We're very worried if someone is applying without knowing why they want to go to law school. Forty percent come direct from college. Too many of them don't know what they want to do, so they apply to law school. We worry a lot about that: It's a formula for misery for both the student and the law school. In that case I go into counseling mode and suggest a couple of years of useful experience.   Albert R. Turnbull, Associate Dean for Admissions and Career Services, University of Virginia

Most people who go to law school after time out are glad they took time out. Senioritis at college can be a real problem. You don't know what you want to do, which is frightening. You figure that you might as well hedge your bets, so you take the LSAT. If you do well, you apply to law school. If you get into a good school, you probably go. After all, it relieves the career uncertainty you've felt. Once you go, you commit yourself to finish. After you graduate—and almost everyone does—you'll end up practicing law for the next fifty years. The consequences to having senioritis are pretty serious.   Joyce Curll, Assistant Dean for Admissions and Financial Aid, Harvard

How Much Work Experience Is Preferable?

Ideally, an applicant would work for at least two years, and probably more, in an area he or she is interested in pursuing.   Susan Robinson, Associate Dean for Career Services, Stanford

There are a couple of reasons that work experience before law school is such a good thing. In terms of introspection and self-understanding, those with work experience are typically further along. Also, employers like to see a couple years of real-world experience.   Jo-Ann Verrier, Assistant Dean for Career Planning and Placement, Penn

I strongly believe that at least two years of work experience is greatly beneficial. Employers prefer someone who has had a couple years to mature and gain more life experience. Also, each year I analyze the class rankings. I routinely observe that people who have had several years of experience do better academically.   Kimberly Reed, Assistant Dean of Career Development and Placement, North Carolina

THE AFFECT OF WORK EXPERIENCE UPON YOUR MARKETABILITY

I've lobbied for years to not let anyone come to the law school who hasn't had work experience. Employers want people who can hit the ground running. Gloria Pyszka, former Director, Career Services Office, Stanford

The average age of our entering students is going up, and those with real-work experience are at an advantage in the job search. Betsy Armour, Director, Career Development Office, Boston University

Employers view work experience prior to law school very positively, particularly that deemed to be in "professional" settings. The only exceptions are when students have held multiple jobs for very short periods of time. Lisa Mead, Assistant Dean, USC

Interpersonal skills are crucial to success. Employers like to see that you've worked with a team, preferably in a professional setting. Susan Guindi, Director, Office of Career Services, Michigan

POOR REASONS TO ENTER LAW

Your parents want you to be a lawyer. Live your own life. If you are still being influenced to this extent by your parents, you are by definition not yet mature enough to choose a career.

You like to argue. Get married instead.

You are afraid to enter the workforce. Get a grip. Starting a first job is not nearly so difficult as starting college was. In fact, the consequences of failure are much less, too. If you are bounced by your first employer after a month, this need never even show up on your résumé. You will be able to gain other employment quite easily.

You do not know what else to do. If you are still at college or recently graduated, look at the career literature, discuss matters with friends and a high-quality career counselor (probably one in private practice rather than at college), and shadow people working in jobs that sound as if they might fit you. Do not worry that you might make a mistake. Your twenties are made for sampling. If you are substantially older, do all of the above, but focus your efforts on some in-depth career counseling, starting with an assessment of your needs and interests. In either case, do not feel you need to choose the exact right career immediately.

Each job you have should allow you, with suitable reflection and analysis, to understand better how you fit into the world of work.

You want to help people. This is a fine starting point, but practicing law is hardly the only way to help others. You should still want to find a career that will fit you; you will not be much use to others if you hate your career, in spite of being of benefit to others. (As is discussed below, most of those who enter law school intending to pursue public interest law careers do not actually do so. Thus, you may find yourself going in a different direction from that which you intended; this is not a bad thing, per se, but it does undercut the initial reason for going.)

You want to increase your options. Unfortunately, a law degree effectively closes many if not most non-law options (see the discussion above).

You want a glamorous field. Law may sound glamorous to those who do not know much about it, but it is actually a matter of very hard work, attention to detail, and working at the behest of others (partners, clients, et al.).

You want to enter a genteel profession rather than a business. Law is no longer an exclusive club whose members are guaranteed a good living without having to jostle one another and outsiders, too. Instead, it has become a cutthroat business. Firms go out of business, partners (not just young associates) are fired for not producing enough revenue—just like in any business. And, as in any business environment, lawyers need to manage their careers actively. (Check with lawyers to find out when they last revised their résumés in case they need to seek new employment.)

You want to make a lot of money. It is not terribly difficult to make money in law if you go to a top school and then enter a corporate practice. (Of course, it is not clear whether you are getting paid for one job or two, given the number of hours you will log.) Having said this, however, you risk failure if you find that you do not enjoy practicing law (or the type of law that pays particularly well). You also risk personal troubles if you force yourself to do something you dislike (especially for 80 hours a week). In addition, there are other ways to make a lot of money. In sum, this is a perfectly reasonable rationale for going to law school, but only if law will be a good fit for you in other regards.

You need another degree. There are some pretty interesting and valuable degrees other than JDs available.

CAREER SERVICES DIRECTORS DISCUSS POOR REASONS FOR ATTENDING LAW SCHOOL

Law school is the default option for those who are bright and don't know what to do.   Theresa Bryant, Executive Director of Career Development, Yale

Law school is the refuge for the liberal arts majors. They don't see a clear career path, so they opt for law school, believing that it will broaden their opportunities. That is definitely not the case.   Susan Robinson, Associate Dean for Career Services, Stanford

Some people call law school the liberal arts degree of the age, but it's not. Abbie Willard, Assistant Dean, Georgetown

WHAT ELSE COULD YOU DO WITH THREE YEARS AND $125,000?

Law school will take three years of your life and a lot of money. Before you commit to this, consider what else you might do. Here is just one possibility (there are an infinite number of others). Start by going to Central America to learn Spanish. If you live in a private home and are tutored individually for five hours a day, you will go from zero knowledge to absolute fluency within a year. (*Price:* about $700 per month, including room, board, and tuition.) After that, do a three-month cooking school course in Italy during the summer. (*Price:* about $10,000 for an expensive course, room and board included.) Then, do a master's degree in economics at The London School of Economics and Political Science. (*Price:* about $30,000, including room, board, and tuition.) Next, spend a summer as a tour guide cycling through France. (*Price: You* get paid for your effort.) Last, do another degree, perhaps in politics (The Fletcher School of Law and Diplomacy, for instance), perhaps in marketing (at HEC, the leading French business school, for example). (*Price:* maybe another $30,000–$40,000).

The net result of this odyssey: three years of exploring the physical world (Latin America, England, France, Italy); three years of exploring the intellectual world (fluency in Spanish, knowledge of Italian cooking, an outstanding master's degree in economics, and an outstanding degree in politics or marketing). *The price:* about $75,000, minus any earnings along the way. (Note the savings this represents compared with the total tab for law school.) If your parents are going to sponsor your law school effort, by the way, perhaps you should have them read this and consider what they could buy you for a lot less than law school might cost them. Whoever pays, are you sure that going into law—and working hard for three years at law school as a preliminary to working very hard as a lawyer—is your only option?

UNDERSTAND WHAT IS ON OFFER IN LAW

You can start your research by talking with lawyers you know or by examining books, such as those listed later, that describe law as a career. Once you have an overview of the field, however, you need to get beneath the generalities.

First, you need to investigate legal specialties (insofar as virtually no one is a generalist in law anymore). After your initial research, focus on two to four practice areas that appeal to you. Learn what personality types fit best with this area, what skills (general, such as public speaking, and specific, such as an ability to draft complex debt covenants) are necessary, what types of work fill up the day, and what are considered the best (and worst) aspects of the field. Read several of the professional journals in the field, cover to cover, for several months at a time. Once you have narrowed your interests to one or two fields, talk with a number of practitioners in each. Ask for permission to spend several days "shadowing" them, literally spending full workdays at their side, to learn what their work life is truly like. Be sure to ask, too, whether what you have seen is typical of their practices.

Second, understand what employment possibilities there are in the field. Examine the different types of employers (large firms, small firms, government agencies—municipal, state, federal—nonprofit organizations, and so on) for lawyers in the one or two specialties you have chosen. Learn the basics about each type:

- The focus of the work (at each level)
- Where they are located
- What hours are worked, and when (five days per week, on-call 24/7?)
- What the pay is at each level
- What it takes to advance to each level, and what percentage make it
- What those who leave end up doing
- How risky the employment is
- What the work environment is like (competitive, stressful, relaxed, dynamic?)
- The nature of one's colleagues (age, interests, training, skills, values, goals)
- The clients or interests represented

Compare and contrast the different employer types for whichever field interests you.

By the time you have gone through this exercise, you should know, for example, that criminal defense trial work and criminal appellate work may look nearly identical from the outside but are virtually unrelated in real terms. For instance, different personality types are attracted to each: Criminal defense lawyers like the courtroom action and derive some pleasure from being in touch with the more sordid aspects of humanity, whereas criminal appellate lawyers relish the intellectual challenges of their work but like to avoid the hurly-burly of direct contact with clients and the messiness of trials. The differences in how they get clients, how they charge, their reputations in the legal community, and a whole host of other matters are just as great.

One way to learn about law, of course, is to work as a paralegal in a law firm or other legal environment. You get a close-up view of lawyers going about their daily business; you also may perform some tasks that involve learning about legal research, writing, courtroom performance, and the like. Note, however, that firms often assign paralegals highly repetitive tasks that do not necessarily expose them to much of the firm's operations or let them see a variety of lawyers in action. If you choose to work as a paralegal, be sure that the firm you choose gives its paralegals a suitable exposure to the world of law (and then make sure you take full advantage of the opportunity).

PUTTING IT ALL TOGETHER

Once you have really explored one or two specialties and several employment options for each, compare the results with your analysis of your own skills, interests, values, and goals. Reconsider your options if the fit is not a close one.

FEW ENTERING LAW STUDENTS DO
SUFFICIENT CAREER RESEARCH

It is often claimed that students entering law school now do a pretty fair job of evaluating themselves and their career options. A quick look at one piece of data should dispel this notion. One of the truisms of law school admissions at the top schools is that half of those entering believe they will enter a public interest field, yet not even 5 percent do so. In fact, at most top schools the percentage entering public interest law is well *under* 5 percent. This means that over 90 percent of those who figured they were going into public interest law had done insufficient research about themselves and their career choices.

WHAT ELSE COULD YOU DO IF YOU DO NOT ENTER LAW SCHOOL?

The career literature regarding what jobs are on offer is nothing if not voluminous. If you are smart enough, and hard working enough, to get into a top law school, you also have what it takes to get a job in another field or in a related field.

Be an analyst at an investment bank or a research associate at a corporate strategy consulting firm. Be a reporter for a small-town newspaper. Choose something that appeals to you on its own, or because it will allow you to see close up the legal field you might wish to enter. If you like the field, and like what lawyers do in it, you will have learned something very valuable. If you do antitrust consulting work as an economist, for example, you may prefer to do what the antitrust lawyers do. On the other hand, you may stay on the economics side, or move on to something else entirely.

CAREER DISSATISFACTION

Every major survey done of lawyers in recent years—whether by the American Bar Association, the University of Michigan Law School, *California Lawyer* magazine, or others—has revealed a very substantial degree of career dissatisfaction. In every instance, a large minority of respondents has suggested that they would prefer to have entered another field. (This is in stark contrast to the results of studies of all workers, such as one by Rutgers University and the University of Connecticut, which found that 91 percent were happy with their work. What, one wonders, would the percentage have been had they not included lawyers?) In some cases, the most important reason for the dissatisfaction has been the lack of a suitable quality of life (interminable work, the need to be available to clients year-round, and so on); in other cases, it has been the nature of the work itself (dull, overly detail-oriented). This does not pertain only, or largely, to those who attended lesser law schools. In fact, there is a great deal to suggest that the graduates of top law schools are the most likely to feel intensely dissatisfied by their careers in law.

An interesting feature of the legal scene of recent years has been the publication of literally dozens of books cautioning people about the true nature of legal practice and the development of a mini-industry that helps practicing lawyers determine what they really want to do in life and another that helps them transition to other fields. The following books will give you a taste of this work. The Arron and Elwork books are particularly useful for understanding the realities of law practice.

Deborah Arron, *Running from the Law: Why Good Lawyers Are Getting Out of the Profession* (Highly recommended)

Amiram Elwork, *Stress Management for Lawyers: How to Increase Personal and Professional Satisfaction in the Law* (Recommended)

Kathy Grant & Wendy Werner/National Association for Law Placement, *The Road Not Taken: A Practical Guide to Exploring Non-Legal Career Options*

Donna M. Killoughey/American Bar Association, *Breaking Traditions: Work Alternatives for Lawyers*

**CAREER SERVICE DIRECTORS COMMENT
ON LAWYER DISSATISFACTION**

The number of Websites, studies, and support groups regarding lawyer dissatisfaction is extraordinary. This is very predictable because many of those people
did not know why they attended law school in the first place. They did not do, on
the front end of the process, the kind of self-evaluation that was called for.
Irene Dorzback, Assistant Dean for Career Counseling and Placement, NYU

A person cannot survive in this stressful profession without having an enthusiasm for law.   Susan Robinson, Associate Dean for Career Services, Stanford

---

CONCLUSION

Law is a fine field, but it is not for everyone. The risk that you will be one of the
large number who dislike it—and the cost and difficulty of getting out once you
are in it—should propel you to do substantial investigation before entering it. If
you choose law as a default choice, because you lack the common sense to try
something else or the nerve to enter the work world after college, you are setting yourself up for real trouble in the future.

If you do decide to enter law, learn as much as you can about the legal field
you intend to enter. As other parts of the book explain, this will help you to determine which law schools will be best for you; it will also help you to get the
most out of your law school experience, both in the classroom and outside. Last,
make sure you get into the best quality schools that you can. For help in that regard, read the rest of this book (or call for consulting assistance).

ADDITIONAL RESOURCES

Many of the books listed here are available from:

The National Association for Law Placement
1666 Connecticut Avenue NW, Suite 325
Washington, D.C. 20009–1039
Tel. (202) 667-1666
Fax (202) 265-6735
Web: www.nalp.org

Some of the key books listed in this chapter are currently out of print but are often available from libraries or law schools.

CONTEMPLATING LAW AND LAW SCHOOL

Susan Bell/American Bar Association, *Full Disclosure: Do You Really Want to Be a Lawyer.* Aims to explain the legal profession (and law school) to prospective law school students. Contains perspectives on a variety of legal practice areas. One chapter discusses the Myers–Briggs Type Inventory and its applicability to (budding) lawyers. (Recommended)

Richard W. Moll, *The Lure of the Law: Why People Become Lawyers and What the Profession Does to Them* (Recommended)

Law School Admissions Council, *So You Want to Be a Lawyer*

Mark Byers et al., *Lawyers in Transition: Planning a Life in the Law*

Scott Turow, *One L: An Inside Account of Life at Harvard Law School* (Overblown and out of date, but still amusing)

EXPLORING SPECIFIC AREAS OF LAW

American Bar Association Career Series: includes books on Admiralty, Civil Litigation, Entertainment, Government Jobs for Lawyers, Labor, Sports, etc.

National Association for Law Placement, *Guide to Legal Specialties.* Describes some 30 different legal fields.

Ronald Fox, *Lawful Pursuit: Careers in Public Interest Law*

Bradley M. Bittan, *The Public Defender Experience*

The National Association for Public Interest Law (*www.napil.org*). Good links to other public interest sites.

Harvard Public Interest Site (*www.law.harvard.edu/students/opia*). Excellent information about public interest law, plus good links to other public interest sites.

BEGINNING PRACTICE

Suzanne B. O'Neill and Catherine Gerhauser Sparkman, *From Law School to Law Practice.* A fine guide to what a new associate must do (well) in the first years of practice. (Recommended)

Mark Simenhoff, *My First Year as a Lawyer.* Lawyers in different types of law discuss their initial experience in practice.

Gary A. Munneke, *The Legal Career Guide: From Law Student to Lawyer.*

Note that the law schools interviewed for this book prepare a wealth of marvelous career materials. Once you have laid a reasonable foundation for your career decision-making, consider asking them what materials they might have to top off the information you have already accessed. You will benefit from their expertise; you will also learn something about which schools have the most professional career services operations—and which are most helpful regarding the fields you are exploring. This information will be helpful if you choose to attend law school and must decide which school to attend.

ADDITIONAL COMMENTS FROM CAREER SERVICES AND ADMISSIONS DIRECTORS

KNOWING WHY YOU WANT TO ATTEND LAW SCHOOL IS CRITICAL

You should enter law school not because you are fascinated with law, but with the *practice* of law. Gloria Pyszka, former Director, Career Services Office, Stanford

Our mission is to teach the basics, to help students find why they came to law school. At least half of them have no idea! Nancy Carver, Director, Career Development Office, George Washington

I talk to a number of prospective students whose reasons for wanting to attend law school are so ethereal. I want to say, "Take a deferral. . . . Go and *do* something." Gloria Pyszka, former Director, Career Services Office, Stanford

Imagine what it's like to feel stuck at the end of year one (of law school), knowing you're so in debt that you have no way out except to finish and get the best-paying job you can. Irene Dorzback, Assistant Dean for Career Counseling and Placement, NYU

Students need to be very purposeful, very strategic. Coming to law school simply because of a certain set of lofty ideals may eventually lead to a lot of unhappiness. Gloria Pyszka, former Director, Career Services Office, Stanford

People shouldn't head to law school unless they like serving—being in a position working with and for others, not for themselves—and actually want to practice law. Steve Hopson, Dean of Career Services, University of Virginia

We conduct a workshop at Admitted Students' Day to help prospective students explore a career in the law. We discuss what a law career entails . . . and integrating one's interests and passions into the decision to attend law school. We find that many don't necessarily want to practice law, so we discuss deferring their attendance until they have had the opportunity to engage in a more thorough self-assessment.   Irene Dorzback, Assistant Dean for Career Counseling and Placement, NYU

Ways to Learn about Law

If you want to learn whether you should become a lawyer, it's not a bad idea to do paralegal work. You might also shadow a lawyer for however long you can, or volunteer at a legal clinic, law firm, or government office. Take advantage of any resources on-campus. Sit in on law school courses. Go to panel discussions at law schools when alums speak about what they do. Talk with law school alumni who volunteer to help prospective lawyers or law students.   Faye Deal, Associate Dean for Admissions and Financial Aid, Stanford

Working as a Paralegal

Paralegal work is fine for those who want to find out if law is for them, but only some paralegal work is valuable as training. There is a massive difference between cataloguing documents in a warehouse and being, in effect, the second chair in litigation.   Albert R. Turnbull, Associate Dean for Admissions and Career Services, University of Virginia

I think that I'd advise anyone to consider working for a firm, not to learn legal substance, but to learn how firms work and understand what's involved in their future careers.   Robert Stanek, Director for Admissions, George Washington

Many applicants are paralegals. Paralegal jobs are not designed to prepare one for law school—nor do these jobs give a student a tactical advantage in law school—sometimes, however, paralegal jobs give you the opportunity to observe first hand the work of a lawyer in a specific area; similarly, you might get a sense of what is required of an associate in a law firm.   Kenneth Kleinrock, Assistant Dean for Admissions, NYU

Being a paralegal doesn't set you apart, so it doesn't help you get in. It does help you decide whether to be a lawyer, although it seldom gives you exposure to the wide variety of legal practices that you might wish to consider.   Elizabeth Rosselot, Director of Admissions, Boston College

Exploring Law as a Career

Students should have more than an inkling that they actually want to practice law, if not, preferably, some real exposure to it. The student who comes by default may question his or her decision—if not during law school, then after. Attending law school is not a "career" decision.   Fred Thrasher, Assistant Dean, Career Planning and Placement, William & Mary

The greatest problem I've seen is that students think, "I know that I'm only going to work in a big firm for a few years and then I'll figure out what I *really* want to do." That is the worst possible plan.   Susan Robinson, Associate Dean for Career Services, Stanford

No conductor ever asks if you want to be on his train. Unless people step off, ask themselves questions, interact with alums, take stock of the field, see whether it fits their specific needs, and so on, they may not ever figure out whether it's the right train to be on (or at least not for years and years). The first time people do this is when they go to work. Ten to twelve weeks of summer employment during law school, for example, is seldom sufficient. It takes time to sort out whether the source of dissatisfaction is the specific practice area, the city, the firm, the environment, or law as a profession.   Irene Dorzback, Assistant Dean for Career Counseling and Placement, NYU

2

LOOKING AT
LAW SCHOOL

— EXECUTIVE SUMMARY —

Both full-time and part-time programs are available.
—Yet there are relatively few top quality part-time programs.
■

The first year of the JD program is largely fixed,
but the second and third years offer flexibility.
■

Law schools use three basic types of instruction:
—Case Method

—Lecture

—Clinical Studies
■

The workload is generally heavy, especially for the first year-and-a-half.
—But note that you are the one who determines how much work to do.
■

Law schools offer highly flexible programs.
—You can specialize in any of several dozen fields.

—You can take (a few) courses in other parts of the university.

—You can do a joint degree.
■

Law school is not just about classes.
—Numerous social activities and publications beckon.

Law school has been a prerequisite for admission to the bar for approximately a century now. The initial assumption was that it was to provide training for someone without prior law study, so it was made a three-year degree, with the first year providing an introduction to the fundamentals of law. Although there have been innumerable changes in the typical program, it retains certain core characteristics. It is still, almost without exception, a three-year program (if done full time). It has a set of core courses that are required for all students. And it demands hard work.

In the last two or three decades, however, law schools have dramatically changed certain elements of their programs. For one thing, they have established clinical programs aimed to give students hands-on experience in the "practice" of law. This trend, harkening back to the informal apprenticeship method of law clerks in past centuries, provides needed balance to what are otherwise heavily theoretical curricula. For another, schools have followed the trends in legal practice to incorporate a more international focus, allow students to specialize in a particular area, and promote an interdisciplinary perspective.

Although the top law schools vary in the range of courses, clinics, and specialized programs they offer, they share a common approach to training lawyers. First-year students generally study seven subjects:

- Civil Procedure
- Constitutional Law
- Contracts
- Criminal Law
- Property
- Torts
- Legal Research and Writing

During the second and third years, the courseload in most law programs is entirely elective, with the possible exception of an independent writing project, Professional Responsibility course, or one of the core courses listed above (if it is given in the second year rather than the first). Despite this freedom, most schools expect that their students will select courses that require them to develop their research and writing abilities as well as substantive knowledge of major legal subject areas. During their second and third years, students also have the opportunity to gain academic credit through work done in a variety of clinical programs and internships.

This chapter is designed to give you a feel for what law school will be like in a full-time program. Part-time programs are similar in most regards, with the obvious differences caused by the fact that students are not spending all of their time in school. As a result, the first year is not so overwhelming and their social lives tend not to revolve around school.

FULL-TIME VERSUS PART-TIME PROGRAMS

For the past 10 years, approximately 17 percent of law students have been enrolled in part-time programs. Among the top programs, however, part-time law degrees are not commonly offered. The few examples, with the percentage of the student body enrolled in the part-time program, are:

Fordham	22%
Georgetown	21%
George Washington	15%
NYU	16%
Wisconsin	10%

The people who might find these programs attractive are likely to be older, with more experience, and may have family responsibilities that prevent them from attending a full-time program. Others are unable or unwilling to leave their current jobs and choose a part-time program as the only realistic means of furthering—or beginning—their legal educations. Others who could usefully consider a part-time program are those who have not yet explored law fully enough to be ready to commit to it, but who would like to "sample" a law school curriculum. They can take some courses while continuing to work full time. If they dislike law or law school, they can then quit without having dislocated their lives in the meantime. If they truly enjoy law and/or law school, they can continue in the program or transfer to another one. (For more information regarding the transfer decision, see Chapter 14.)

PROGRAM STRUCTURE

The structure of a part-time JD does not differ significantly from that of a full-time JD. The same core courses are generally required, although they may be taken in a slightly different sequence due to the scheduling difficulties that result from students' proceeding through the program at varying speeds. The number of courses that must be completed in order to graduate will almost invariably be the same.

ADVANTAGES

➤ If you are uncertain whether or not law school is the right move for you, you can sample law school without having to disrupt your life entirely.

► By maintaining your job, you can continue to receive a salary throughout the three-year program.

► You do not have to relocate for your studies.

► If your current work is related to the career you intend to pursue after law school graduation, you can often employ what you learn in law school on the job as you go. (Your studies may even be tax deductible—see the discussion in Chapter 17.)

► Ongoing relevant work experience may be drawn upon to enhance your performance in the law program.

DISADVANTAGES

► Part-time programs carry somewhat less prestige than do top full-time programs.

► You will not be able to commit yourself to your studies and to your classmates the way you could if you attended school full time. The result is that you will probably feel you have not gotten as fully to grips with many of your courses as you would have had you been a full-time student.

► The demands made by the combination of a full-time job and part-time study tend to be overwhelming, causing people to feel they are doing neither of these activities well. The possibility of handling both well, plus a rewarding personal life, is remote.

► Your job performance may suffer so much, due to the effort you must make for your classes, that you will not increase your responsibilities or salary as you would if you could devote yourself more fully to your job.

► Your company may not be pleased about your planning to subordinate your work effort for four to six years of school.

The bottom line is that a part-time course may make sense to the extent that your current job is very attractive to you and is of a type that would permit you to pursue a part-time program, and you are fortunate enough to have a top quality part-time JD program available in your area.

TYPICAL REQUIRED COURSES

Nearly all schools traditionally require the following courses:

Civil Procedure focuses on the rules that structure federal and state civil litigation.

Constitutional Law provides a general introduction to the U.S. Constitution's allocation of power among the branches of the federal government and to the limitations on the substantive powers of the government.

Contracts explores the nature and enforceability of promises and bargains, and the remedies available for nonperformance.

Criminal Law examines the general principles of criminal liability, the rules for enforcing punishment against those accused of criminal acts, and the rights guaranteed to those charged with crimes.

Property examines the philosophical and economic origins of property rights, the rules that govern the acquisition and transfer of property rights, and private and public means of regulation.

Torts explores the policies and rules of the private law system that provide compensation for injuries or damage to persons and property.

Legal Research and Writing introduces students to legal discourse through problem analysis, legal research, writing, oral skills, and legal citation. Students are introduced to the contexts for and processes involved in legal problem-solving and communication.

TEACHING METHODS

CASE METHOD

Most courses are taught via the case method in the first year of law school. (Some courses will be taught this way in the second and third years, whereas others will be taught via lecture or clinic.) Your reading for these courses will consist almost exclusively of a series of appellate cases, some long, some short. There will be no text—no book that gives an overview of the field and highlights what is most important within it. Instead, you will be expected to piece together the nature and structure of the field by reading a series of cases that focus on one legal point (or occasionally two). These points will not be aggregated for you. Thus, you must learn how to see the forest for the trees.

The accompanying classroom method requires substantial student participation. Instead of sitting back and taking notes on what the professor says, as you probably did in college, you will need to be alert to the direction the professor is taking. She will call upon students to answer highly specific questions about the required reading; she may also ask about the economic, political, societal, or other significance of the rules under discussion. If this is an aggressive attempt to grill students, it will be termed the "Socratic Method."

The Socratic Method is a misnomer when used in this context. Socrates asked his students questions to get them to understand and recognize the truths that they already had in their minds; inherent truths, if you will. The law school version of this has been distorted out of all recognition, focusing on not-yet-learned concepts rather than inherent truths. In the past, professors grilled students mercilessly on new or foreign concepts. (To see not altogether fanciful versions of this, watch *The Paper Chase* or read Scott Turow's *One L.*) There are still some unreformed Socratic Method types who "cold call" students—call on students who have not raised their hands or otherwise volunteered to answer—and seemingly delight in making them squirm. Most professors, however, have toned this down. The most common form of the still-feared Socratic Method involves professors warning a few students that during an upcoming class, they can expect to be called on, giving them plenty of advance notice (and incentive) to prepare the assigned cases well.

The form of the questions has not changed much over the years. The first student called upon regarding a given case is likely to be asked to give an overview of it: to state the court, parties, facts, issues, holding, and rationale behind a case. The follow-up questions may start by asking about the specifics of this case, but will soon venture afield into hypothetical matters. The professor will twist the facts of the case to determine what causes you to believe, for instance, that the court was right in its decision. "If the bus had not contained a bunch of convicts being taken away for execution but instead a group of nuns, would you still claim that the driver who rammed into it, killing three, should not be held liable?" "What if the driver was drunk at the time?" "What if the driver had not had a driver's license?" And so on.

One of the differences between this and the college-style lecture courses to which you are probably accustomed is that it is hard to take useful notes in such a class. Learning what is relevant for mastering the subject—and what will help you to ace the exam—is part of the first-year education process.

LECTURE

Many second- and third-year classes resemble the traditional lecture classes familiar to any American college student. (The general rule is that subjects depending more upon case law than statute are likely to be taught by the case method, whereas so-called statutory courses are more likely to be taught in a lecture format.) Lecture classes are less burdensome than case method courses insofar as there is no fear that the professor will call upon a student to grill him. Note-taking is also easier than in the case method classes, where one needs to be following every little nuance to be ready to answer highly specific questions. Instead, one can listen for major points and note them down, without fearing that he has missed the last thing said while writing a note, placing him in jeopardy.

CLINICAL STUDIES

The relatively recent utilization of clinical courses within law school curricula is an attempt to bridge the gap between theoretical instruction and the everyday work of lawyers. As "situation-based" teaching, clinical courses place students in actual or simulated circumstances that require them to address a client's problems.

Another, unspoken goal is to keep students involved in school and their classes through graduation. Most students in regular law classes have become bored and complacent by sometime in their second years; the change of pace offered by clinical education is one means of combating the problem.

The format of schools' clinical programs varies widely. Often, schools will have both "in-house" clinical programs and externship opportunities. The in-house clinics are more likely to be heavily supervised by faculty and administered in conjunction with a specific course. Clinical facilities centered outside the confines of the campus are supervised by staff attorneys and generally give students a bit more authority. Schools also offer "field placement programs," in which students receive academic credit for working in public interest organizations or governmental agencies under the supervision of a practicing attorney.

WORKLOAD

Top JD programs demand a remarkable amount of work. During the first year of a program (and particularly the first semester), the demands are especially great. There are several reasons for this. The first is that the schools are trying to teach critically important areas of law, plus an understanding of legal research and writing. There is a large amount to learn in such a short time, so the workload is inevitably high. (The second and third years are less intense, both because students have learned how to play the law school "game" and because they are taking elective courses suited to their interests and strengths.)

Another important reason for the time pressure is that the workload of a practicing attorney can be grueling. The JD program is structured to simulate that workload, so that students can be prepared for it later on. The excessive amount of work forces students to learn how to manage their time, one of the key skills a lawyer must acquire. Thus, a student will almost certainly have to learn to prioritize—to determine how to learn in the most efficient way.

So how demanding are these programs? They are so demanding that it is more appropriate to describe the amount of time a typical student is *not* working, rather than the other way around. Unmarried students typically take off one or two evenings per week, enough time each day for a physical activity, plus the occasional hour or two to relax. Married students generally spend a bit more time away from their books, but not a lot. Obviously even an understanding spouse and family are likely to be put out by this sort of schedule.

YOUR WORKLOAD IS UP TO YOU

For the average student, the first three semesters involve much more effort than the last three. Sometime during the middle of the second year, the average student opts out of the game—emotionally and academically. There are, of course, notable exceptions to this generalization. Those who are trying to make Order of the Coif, given to the top 10 percent of the class, may well keep pushing for top grades. The same is true for those whose employment fate will not be determined until (or after) the end of law school. Those who wish to teach law at a leading law school, for example, are likely to be given their first jobs elsewhere (perhaps clerking for a federal judge, working in a government agency, or teaching at a lesser law school). When it comes time for them to try to scale the heights of a top-tier law school, their law grades for each year of school are likely to be examined closely.

Students are in charge of their fate, of course, and can choose (within some limits) how much to study, but most do not recognize this until after the fact. As Chapter 16 discusses in detail, there are many ways to "do" law school. It is by no means necessary to read and brief every case, for instance, yet many students try to do so—at least during the first year. The level of uncertainty students face, given that almost none of them know enough about law school to be sure they can buck the crowd, means that a "groupthink" born of panic causes most students to put in extraordinarily long hours. Much of this work, if not most of it, is actually a waste of effort. To confirm this, ask students in their last semester what amount of the work they did in their first year was truly worthwhile.

GRADING

The difference between college and law school is nowhere more marked than in the grading. Most college courses involve at least a mid-term and a final exam; some involve a mid-term, a final, and a paper. Other courses involve multiple papers, multiple exams, or both. In nearly all first-year law school courses, however, the grade is based solely upon the single end-of-term exam. This exam is typically three or four hours long; it requires that you analyze a hypothetical case (or two or three) or a recently decided "real" case. Despite the nerve-wracking aspects of preparing for class each day, class participation is seldom graded. (Consequently, it is not worth torturing yourself over classroom performance. It is useful to impress fellow students and professors, but the most important means of impressing people is through your grades.)

Basing the entire grade upon one exam results in a great deal of anxiety for law school students. This is particularly true during the first year, of course, before students have adjusted to taking such exams, learned to study for them, and gained confidence that they will survive them.

CURRICULAR ORGANIZATION OF THE TRADITIONAL JD PROGRAM

The First Year

The first year is likely to be overwhelming unless you have had very good preparation for it, meaning that you have already had experience in a law related profession, or that you have taken the preparatory measures recommended in Chapter 15. There is so much work to do, so many new concepts to learn, that you are likely to feel you are drowning. Not only do you have a great deal to learn, you also have to learn *how* to learn. As time goes on, however, you will figure out how to cut through the massive amounts of case reading and detail and to focus on the key aspects. Most students feel that the first year (particularly the first semester) is infinitely more difficult than anything that follows.

The Second Year

The second-year curriculum is almost entirely elective, allowing students to tailor their courseload to fit their interests. The second year is hardly relaxed, however, due to the fact that students are spending serious amounts of time looking—and interviewing—for a summer job. They may also be lucky enough to be slaving away for law review or another school publication, or working part time.

The Third Year

The third year is more of a breeze. Students have grown accustomed to the Socratic Method, and many of the courses are just straight lectures in any event. In addition, many students are too occupied with part-time jobs or extracurricular interests to attend many of their courses anyway. A large number of students will find comfort in the fact that they have been offered jobs by the firms at which they spent their summers working. The result of so many students tuning out of course work is that those who remain engaged find it much easier to get good grades.

There is still a great deal of truth to the old law school adage that "in the first year they frighten you to death, in the second year they work you to death, and in the third year they bore you to death."

SPECIALIZATION

Just as the world of legal practice has become ever more specialized, so too have law schools tried to offer multiple courses in every popular (and not so popular) specialty. Whether this means traditional specialties such as labor law, or new ones such as any of the various corporate transactional areas, schools have tried with varying degrees of success to keep pace with the market. Some schools offer formal concentrations, akin to majors in college, but whether or not a school formalizes its offerings matters less than the availability of the appropriate courses and professors.

COURSES OUTSIDE LAW SCHOOL

Law schools have recently recognized that law is increasingly tied to other fields. This has been reflected in the increase in joint-degree programs they offer as well as the law schools' increased recruitment of professors with doctorates in other fields (in addition to their JDs). Unfortunately, these same schools are extremely ungenerous in the number of courses they permit law students to take for credit in other parts of the university. Thus, in law schools requiring approximately 30 courses in total, generally no more than two (or three, in some schools) may be taken elsewhere in the university.

This parochialism is particularly unfortunate in view of the way these same schools market themselves. Law schools routinely brag about all of the marvelous courses on offer throughout the university of which they are a part and make it sound as though it is a simple matter for one of their students to take advantage of these course offerings. Unfortunately, the reality fails to live up to the rhetoric. This is a policy sorely in need of modernization.

JOINT DEGREES

Joint-degree programs offer students the opportunity to study law and another field, more or less at one and the same time. A typical program, the JD–MBA, has students do their first-year at the law school (following the usual first-year law curriculum), their second year at the business school (following the usual first-year business curriculum), and their last two years taking a mixture of law and business courses. The time required to get the two degrees is four years, one fewer than would be required if the student did each degree separately. This saving of a year in study time is typical for joint programs, not just the JD–MBA. The integration of programs leads to this saving of time.

The top law schools now offer a full range of joint degrees, at both the master's and the doctoral levels. Yale, for instance, offers joint degrees with the schools of Forestry and Environmental Studies, Divinity, and Medicine, in addition to the more common arrangements with the School of Management and the Graduate School (meaning the usual departments such as economics, history, and the like). The University of Pennsylvania offers joint programs in business administration and other commonly pursued fields; it also offers joint programs in such unusual fields as bioethics, city planning, communications, and Islamic studies.

Although only a relatively small number of students pursues any of these programs (apart from the JD–MBA), the variety of programs on offer across the whole set of leading schools is truly impressive. Not every school offers a JD–MS Forestry or JD–MA Islamic Studies possibility, of course, so it is essential to research the specific degree options at each school.

A relatively new development is the opportunity to get two law degrees. Cornell, for instance, offers a chance to get both a JD and a Maitrise en Droit (French) or an M.LL. (German) degree at an affiliated European university. Students spend two years at Cornell followed by two years at the respective European university.

There are, of course, some potential disadvantages to doing a joint degree. Joint degrees generally require more time (and money) than a single degree.

Any sort of joint degree is also likely to limit the number of courses you can take that are totally unrelated to the two fields.

PUBLICATIONS

The top law schools have anywhere from a handful to a dozen and a half publications that are edited by students. Georgetown, for instance, publishes the *Georgetown Law Journal, American Criminal Law Review, Georgetown Journal on Poverty Law & Policy, Georgetown Journal of Gender and the Law, Georgetown Immigration Law Journal, Georgetown International Environmental Law Review, Law & Policy in International Business, Georgetown Journal of Legal Ethics,* and *The Tax Lawyer.* Despite the impressiveness of this listing, it is by no means inclusive of all of the many fields such journals cover.

The "law review" (called the "law journal" in Georgetown's case) is the flagship publication of each law school. It features articles by professors and practitioners, edited by second- and third-year students. Membership of the law review is immensely prestigious; being the editor-in-chief is extraordinarily so. At some schools, membership is determined by first-year grades: those with the highest grades are invited to join. At other schools, membership is determined solely through a writing competition: Prospective members write lengthy articles, with the best writers being invited to join. At still other schools, membership is determined by a combination of these two methods.

Being an editor of the law review involves as much hard work as it does prestige. Editors commonly put more time into their law review efforts than they do preparing for classes. The checking of citations ("cite-checking," in law school parlance), copyediting, and editing for substance combine to provide a formidable training in legal analysis and writing. Employers are by no means unaware of this. Indeed, many firms and agencies recruit primarily from law review ranks.

The other publications offer similar opportunities for learning, but at somewhat less rarefied levels. The competition to become an editor at these other publications tends to be much less intense than for the law review; the degree of competition varies according to the place of the specific journal in the clear, if informal, pecking order of the journals. Subject-specific journals, such as a labor law journal, offer the additional prospect of gaining subject-specific knowledge. As a result, the competition to gain prestigious and influential positions on them will likely be limited to those intending labor law careers.

STUDENT BODY

The student body at the top schools has changed considerably over the years. The ratio of men to women is commonly fairly equal; the percentage of women ranges from about 43 percent to 48 percent at typical schools. The percentage of minority students is climbing, having almost tripled in the last three decades. The percentage of international students, although still low, has increased dramatically in the last decade. Students come from a number of different educational and professional backgrounds. The percentage of students with work experience has overtaken that of the "traditional" applicant, the recent college graduate. Columbia, for instance, lists its entering class as containing: professional dancers and theatre managers; Peace Corps, VISTA, and military veterans; physicists, engineers, biochemists; management, computer, Website, trademark, and environmental consultants; professional musicians; editors and publishers; university professors and high school teachers; accountants and financial analysts; and human rights advocates.

Much of the learning experience in a high-quality program comes from your fellow students, who can give real-life insights into problems, based upon their recent experiences. The range of different jobs, industries, and educational backgrounds makes for a rich mixture of relevant experience to bring to bear in classroom discussions and study-group sessions. Whatever their work backgrounds, the different students have several things in common. They are invariably highly motivated as well as quite intelligent, and have been extremely successful in whatever they have done so far.

These are not just people you will work with, and compete with, during your time together in law school. You will form lifelong friendships with some of them and may well work for the same firm with some, too. Your law school colleagues represent your future network of contacts, the people who will be your clients and partners and sources of job information.

SOCIAL LIFE

Some suspect that the only way law students manage to have any social life at all is by sleeping very little. There is a lot of truth in this. The time pressure inherent in demanding programs ensures that only the truly energetic can manage a social or family life in addition to their studies (at least during the first half of the program). The bulk of law students, however, are energetic enough to live at least a moderately social existence.

Social life differs greatly from one program to the next. At all schools, however, student clubs and organizations will be the focus of substantial time and effort. Many of these are pre-professional clubs designed to educate students about the fields. An Environmental Law Society, for example, may hold forums at which participants in major disputes discuss their experiences and argue their points of view. In addition, it will help members get jobs in environmental law by inviting speakers and recruiters to visit and discuss the field—and their respective firms—with interested members. The leading schools tend to have a magnificent range of such clubs, covering everything from Criminal Law to Internet Law.

Not all student clubs are an extension of the job search. Many sports and activities can be found on a typical campus. These are likely to be open to spouses and even children. Like the pre-professional clubs, these offer the opportunity to demonstrate leadership and other desirable attributes, as well as energy and love of a given activity. Advocacy and action groups also abound. Examples include Civil Liberties Unions, Prison Legal Assistance Projects, and Volunteer Income Tax Assistance Programs.

Of course, not all student social life revolves around clubs. Student parties fortunately are a staple of law programs, with the excuse for holding one varying from the need to get away from studying when the pressure is greatest to the need to take advantage of the opportunity when the pressure is lowest. In addition, students find innumerable ways to enjoy informal activities with their fellow students and outsiders, although the more isolated campuses make interaction with nonstudents rather problematic.

3

How to Choose the Right School for *You*

— EXECUTIVE SUMMARY —

The first step in choosing a school is to know well what you
want from a law degree.

■

Researching the schools is a time-consuming, involved process.
—Start with the recommended guidebooks,
then investigate specific schools in depth.

—Consult the relevant rankings, but do not regard them as gospel.

■

Your search will not be complete until you:
—Visit the most likely choices.

—Check out these schools with leading employers in your chosen field.

■

Apply to an appropriate number and range of schools.

Your selection of a school should be driven by two actions: (1) analyzing your-self and your needs well enough to determine what programs will be most ap-propriate for you, and then (2) getting into the highest quality, best reputed of these programs.

It is essential that you really get to grips with both sides of this equation. Your reasons for getting a JD will help pinpoint which schools are right for you. You are likely to opt for the right program if you carefully analyze your own needs. By the same token, you are likely to choose the wrong program if you do only a cursory analysis of the different programs, depending largely upon their slick brochures or one-size-fits-all rankings.

KNOW YOURSELF—AND WHAT YOU WANT FROM A LAW DEGREE

Your decision to go to law school represents a milestone, and few decisions will equal this one in significance. You want to get it right. The starting point is knowing what you want to accomplish by getting a JD. Chapter 1 discusses some of the more common reasons for getting a JD. What are yours? Do you want to become the ACLU's leading appellate lawyer? Do you hope to become a spe-cialist in New York Stock Exchange rules and regulations, as well as securities law, so as to help countries adopting American-style stock exchanges? Do you want to be a commercial litigator for a major corporate law firm? Do you want to teach constitutional law at a leading law school?

Your reason for getting a JD will color your choice of schools. Your rela-tive ability—your strengths and weaknesses where law schools are con-cerned—will also help you narrow your choices. If you are among the country's top 5,000–10,000 candidates, you will probably focus your attention on the top 10 or 20 schools.

RESEARCH THE SCHOOLS

The process of choosing schools is likely to be an iterative one. As you under-stand better what you are looking for in a JD program, you will be able to choose programs that better meet your needs. As you research schools and learn what they have to offer, you may also change what you are looking for from a JD and thus what you will demand in a program.

STEP 1: DEVELOP GENERAL KNOWLEDGE ABOUT JD PROGRAMS

Before narrowing your search to a handful of schools, you should become acquainted with what the various JD programs have to offer.

1. Examine this chapter's discussion of several dozen possible criteria for choosing a school. This will introduce you to the wide range of factors that might be relevant to your choice of schools.

2. Read several of the publications devoted solely to the question of which school to choose. The best of the guides are listed at the end of this chapter, along with a brief description of their contents. These publications provide better overviews of the quantitative elements of the programs (such as the number of students and types of courses offered) than the subjective (such as what the schools do best).

3. You should also read the rankings produced by such publications as *U.S. News & World Report* to get a rough approximation of the reputation of the different schools. See Chapter 4 for more information on the different rankings.

STEP 2: START GETTING INFORMATION ABOUT SPECIFIC SCHOOLS

Your initial efforts should have generated a preliminary list of schools that might be appropriate for you. Now you should start to investigate these schools more seriously.

1. Start to determine which criteria are most important to you. Two criteria should weigh heavily in your thinking at this point. *What type of learning environment is best for you?* Some people need to get their adrenaline flowing through competition and fear. If so, there are a number of programs that should be ideal. For other people, these programs would be disasters because they learn best in collegial, supportive environments. If one of these environments would be much better than the other for you, be sure you know which schools fall in which category. *What subject(s) do you intend to focus on?* If you intend to focus on civil litigation, you may be safe going to any leading school, since they all offer numerous courses in it (although some of the leading schools are more famous for it than are others). If you intend to focus on international taxation, however, some schools will offer many relevant courses whereas others will offer one or none. In addition, you must *consider what additional criteria are particularly important for you.* The most likely criteria include location, size, teaching quality, mission, and cost.

2. Get information from the schools themselves. Have each send you its brochure, which will explain the school's philosophy, what it seeks in applicants, and what makes it noteworthy. (Do not, however, believe all that you read.) Ask for any recent newspaper and journal articles about the school that it

has on file. Examine any additional material the school provides, such as a CD/ROM. Visit the school's Website to gather further information. Either the brochure, the Website, or both should list what courses are currently on offer as well as detailed information about each member of the faculty.

3. Learn when you can meet the schools' representatives. They will travel to law school forums, which are gatherings held at cities around the United States and the world at which schools set up booths and relay information about their programs. The forums are convenient affairs for meeting representatives from a large number of schools, but they are sometimes too crowded and hectic to provide good opportunities for lengthy questioning of any one representative. Schools also send their representatives around the country, especially to leading undergraduate colleges, to do "dog-and-pony shows" to sell the programs to potential applicants. These sessions are often less hurried than the law school forums, thereby providing the opportunity to question representatives at greater length.

STEP 3: FOCUS ON THE SCHOOLS YOU FIND MOST APPEALING

By the time you have finished the first two steps, you should have a good understanding of which schools are most likely to meet your needs. It is now time to investigate these schools carefully.

1. Talk with each school's alumni to learn more about the schools. Schools are generally glad to give you the names of alumni living near you who have volunteered to discuss the respective programs. Recent alumni, in particular, can be good sources of information about the atmosphere of the school, its academic strengths and weaknesses, the ease with which they did (or did not) get a job in their chosen field, and the types of students who seem most pleased by their selection of this school.

2. Talk with a school's competitors to learn what the weak aspects of a school might be. (Take these comments with at least one grain of salt.)

3. Visiting the school is an important part of your research. There are a host of things you are unlikely to find out in any other way. Schedule your visit with the admissions office. They will make it possible for you to sit in on classes and meet students. You should by all means do this.

You should also talk with a representative group of students. If you attend this school, you will soon be spending all of your waking hours with people just like them, so be sure they are people with whom you would be comfortable. Do not limit yourself to those students the admissions office arranges for you to meet, because those who volunteer to do so may not be entirely representative of the student body. You can meet plenty of students just by going to the school's cafeteria and joining a group of students who will certainly remember when they were going through the same process, making it quite likely that they will spend whatever time they can with you. (For more about visiting schools, see Appendix II in this chapter.)

4. Most important, if you know what field you intend to enter, contact the leading employers in it. Be sure to include the organizations you would most like to work for: Ask their human resource people (those responsible for hiring) which are the schools where they actively recruit. Have them explain why they choose these schools, their impressions of strengths and weaknesses of the respective programs, what types of people they choose from each (to the extent

---

WHAT TO DO IF YOU WILL BE UNABLE TO GET INTO THE RIGHT LEVEL OF SCHOOL

Your analysis of the appropriate schools for you, given the type of employer you favor, may reveal something distressing. You may not be able to get into the schools from which these employers recruit, effectively foreclosing the possibility of working for them. For instance, a leading New York corporate firm (or public interest firm) may recruit actively only at Columbia, NYU, Harvard, and Penn, and accept résumés only from the remaining "top ten" schools. The reason for not visiting other schools for on-campus recruiting may be that it has never been able to get enough serious applicants from them to warrant the expense involved. (This is particularly true for a small, distant school such as Stanford.) You have several choices:

➤ Revise your employment goals. Maybe you are being unrealistic about your talents in general. Maybe you are trying to please someone else who wants you to have the most prestigious employment possible, whereas you may not actually value it. Be sure to examine your own motivations in real depth.

➤ Take another job upon graduation from law school and hope to move laterally after several years. Perhaps your chosen employers hire people not just straight from law school but also laterally (with some years of experience). If so, your best bet may be to get a job with an appropriate feeder organization. If you excel there, you can hold out hope of making the jump to whichever employer you most value.

➤ Go to a slightly "lesser" school and hope. You can always try to excel at a school with a reputation just below those at which your chosen employers recruit in hopes that a sterling résumé will be enough. This is highly risky, however, and sets you up for a long period of anxiety and disappointment.

➤ Wait to apply to law schools. You can improve your marketability dramatically if you excel in a demanding and interesting job or jobs over the next few years, as much of the rest of this book discusses.

that this differs by school), and how many individuals they generally hire from each school. Ask them from which other schools they would be particularly happy to receive résumés. (They might not recruit at some schools for logistical reasons, but would be glad to hear from students at those schools. Similarly, they might be glad to hear from the best students at certain schools that they feel produce strong graduates, but in too small a number to warrant proactive recruiting efforts.)

This is a critical step to finding the right school for yourself, but the one most frequently skipped because it involves a bit of honest effort. By the way, the connection you make with these firms' human resource people should be viewed as an advance marketing effort, so treat these folks well and keep in touch with them.

Do not start your law school research efforts with the human resource professions, because you will be imposing upon their time as it is, and to do so without knowing anything about schools will prove embarrassing. Approach them for such a favor when you have some reasonable idea of what's what in JD programs and can thus use their time efficiently.

5. Do not overreact to the online chat room discussions in which applicants discuss their concerns and opinions. The ratio of ignorant statements and misconceptions to helpful comments is very high.

DETERMINE HOW MANY SCHOOLS TO APPLY TO

Some people want to go to a specific school and would not even think about going to one of its rivals—perhaps due to geographic constraints, such as a spouse attending medical school in the location of the law school. Those who feel this way do not face any problem in determining how many schools they should consider. On the other hand, you should be content to attend one of a number of schools. If so, you must consider how many applications to file. This will depend upon several factors:

- Are you determined to go this year? If so, you must apply to enough schools to be sure of getting into at least one of them.

- What are your chances at the schools you favor? If your credentials are better across the board than those of the average student accepted at these schools, and you can present yourself very well, you need not do a great number of applications. (Do not limit yourself to consideration of just the quantitative credentials, though. As chapters 5, 7, and 8 discuss, consider, too, the rest of what you have to offer, including in particular your career experience and success to date.) If your credentials are not superior, however, be prepared to do more applications.

■ How many applications can you do without sacrificing the quality of essays, the visiting of schools, the interviewing opportunities, and so on? Note, by the way, that there is a large fixed cost to starting the application process, but additional applications tend to take less and less time. Conscientious applicants who prepare for the first application by gathering the necessary information about themselves and establishing how to market themselves effectively generally find that the first application takes about the same time and effort as the next five or more applications altogether.

Many serious applicants apply to about six to ten schools. For all but the very strongest candidates (who will apply only to the most demanding programs), it is appropriate to spread your applications across a range of schools. Thus, you can apply to one or two "likely" schools, several "possible" schools, and a number of "stretches." "Likelies" are schools to which you are likely to be admitted. These are schools at which admittees have substantially lesser credentials than you possess. For example, your LSAT score is four to five points higher than the school's average, your undergraduate grade-point average is 0.3 points higher, your undergraduate college and curriculum more demanding, and your career more interesting and successful than others of similar age. "Possibles" are schools where your credentials are about equal to the average for

---

CHOOSING A PART-TIME PROGRAM

Choosing a part-time JD program is necessarily somewhat different from choosing a full-time program. Your choice of program will probably be limited to those within your immediate area. Therefore, some of the criteria used for determining the most appropriate full-time program, such as available housing, will no longer be relevant because you will probably not be moving. Some of the other criteria may be less important than would be the case if you were to attend a full-time program. The career services office may be unimportant for you if you intend to remain with the same employer after you complete your degree. Other criteria are likely to become more important. A program's schedule may not fit within your own, thereby eliminating it as a possibility.

In spite of these differences, choosing a part-time program still resembles the selection process for a full-time program. The courses must be of value to you, with an academic atmosphere suited to your desires. When you are choosing among several schools that offer what you want, reputation is still likely to be the most important criterion. (Remember, of course, that a part-time program often does not command the same reputation as the university's full-time program.)

those admitted. "Stretches" are the flip side of "likelies": Your credentials are substantially lower than those of the average person admitted.

Why separate schools into these three categories and apply to some in each category? If you apply only to schools in one category, you are likely to miss out on an opportunity. If you do not apply to some "stretches," you may not get into the highest quality school possible. If, on the other hand, you do not apply to a "likely" or two, you risk not getting into any school at all.

AVOID THE LIKELY PITFALLS IN CHOOSING A SCHOOL

Some warnings to keep in mind as you go through the search process:

- Start the process early. You need to gather a lot of information and you should give yourself time to reflect on what you learn at each step.
- Do not take the rankings too seriously. They are no better than rough proxies for a school's quality and reputation. (See Chapter 4 for more on the limitations of business school rankings.) They obviously do not account of your specific set of key criteria. Look for high-quality programs that will satisfy your needs.
- Be wary of schools with learning environments that are not hospitable to you. Do not put yourself through months of hell and the disappointment of performing poorly due to a bad match between you and a school's learning environment.
- Be aware that your interests may change as you go through both the self-evaluation and search processes. You can alter what you want to do and better understand what would help you. As a result, your criteria for schools should change to reflect your changed interests.
- Do not be swayed by spiffy school brochures. The quality of a school is not directly related to the quality of the pictures in its publications.
- Do not be swayed by warm (or cold, or inefficient) admissions people. They are not the ones who will be teaching you or helping you to get a job upon graduation.
- Do pay attention to the quality of the careers service. Your job fate can be dramatically improved by a top-notch department.
- Remember: Eliminate schools that do not offer the program you need.

    —Eliminate those with inappropriate learning atmospheres.

 —Eliminate those with other important negatives for you, such as location and size.

 —Include the highest quality schools you believe you can get into (and, yes, pay attention to the consensus views of the rankings).

■ Ultimately, any number of schools can give you a great learning experience and help your career prospects dramatically, but it is up to you to take advantage of the opportunities afforded you.

FINAL-DECISION CRITERIA

The most important criteria for each applicant will, of course, differ substantially. Some applicants will be greatly cost-constrained, leading them to choose schools that have lower tuition or offer financial aid. Others will choose schools only in a given area. Others will look for the school with the best course offerings on taxation they can get into.

 No matter which criteria are relevant to you, it would be highly appropriate to determine which schools will give you the courses you most want, in an atmosphere in which you think you could thrive (collegial versus competitive, faculty open door versus isolated, etc.), and in a location that is appropriate to your current circumstances and future goals. Having taken account of these and the other criteria most important to you, the final choice should generally come down to the school's reputation. If you were intending to do international corporate law and were admitted to both NYU and Miami, for instance, it would be peculiar to choose Miami. Although Miami is a fine school with a substantial international program, it is not generally regarded as one of the top half dozen or dozen schools in the country, as is NYU. Reputation is not everything, but among schools that do not differ dramatically in their ability to deliver what you are looking for, reputation should ordinarily be the critical factor.

RECOMMENDED READINGS

American Bar Association, *ABA Official Guide to Approved Law Schools.* Provides essentially only statistical information, but is highly informative in this regard. Detailed breakdowns of: employment (by geography, type of employment), financial aid, informational and library resources, student body and faculty ethnicity and sex, and curriculum. The curriculum description is particularly valuable: It includes the typical first-year section size; number of courses offered for second- and third-year students; number of seminars offered, and number of positions available in the seminars (along with the number filled); number of positions available in simulation courses (and the number filled); number of positions available in faculty-supervised clinical courses (and the number filled); and the number involved in field placements and law journals.

Law School Admissions Council, *The Official Guide to U.S. Law Schools.* Describes special programs at the school, such as joint degrees on offer. Lists scholarly journals published by the school. Gives statistical data in various categories: expenses, library and physical facilities, student body and faculty, applicant group (and admitted students), employment. Provides application deadlines and fees.

ADMISSIONS DIRECTORS DISCUSS
CHOOSING THE RIGHT SCHOOL

DETERMINING YOUR OWN NEEDS

Know yourself and have the confidence to act on it. The first step is to decide what's important to you. Too few candidates ask: What do I need to thrive, in terms of location, size, high-tech (or whatever) emphasis, friendliness of faculty members, etc.? Obviously the best thing is to visit. Do it on your own— don't just go on an official tour. Poke your head into a professor's office, hang out in the cafeteria, bump into four or five students and talk with them. Ask students if they are really glad to be at that law school. They'll be honest about the quality and nature of the experience. Then spend some time in the environment around the campus. Do this at some very different schools to learn what you want.   Dennis Shields, Assistant Dean for Admissions and Financial Aid, Duke

There are some applicants for whom academics will be most important, others for whom publications, student groups, and a host of other activities will be. Joyce Curll, Assistant Dean for Admissions and Financial Aid, Harvard

It's critically important, even before applying, to visit schools. Explore, preferably in person, or at least on the Web, the scope of the law school. Read what they say about themselves. Think about how you learn best and work best. Do you take the initiative and thrive on finding things out for yourself, choosing among a wide variety of options, or do you want to have a set menu of what you can do put in front of you?   Joyce Curll, Assistant Dean for Admissions and Financial Aid, Harvard

The local environment matters a lot. For instance, urban versus country—which one is a plus for you? The kind of person who's happy at a rural school may be the kind of person who relieves stress by going out to visit a waterfall; at an urban school it'll be someone who does so by enjoying the nightlife, for example. Joyce Curll, Assistant Dean for Admissions and Financial Aid, Harvard

Begin with a self-evaluation. You can make some broad cuts regarding the type of geographic setting you want, etc. The top schools differ somewhat in geography, size, culture, and mission or philosophy. Some key questions are: Where will you feel comfortable; who is at the school; where is the school located? The number of volumes in the library is irrelevant. The way to get at this is to visit the school, sit in on a class, perhaps come to an open house, information session, or admitted students day. At a minimum you should at least access the relevant Web sites, CD/ROMs, and the like. Personally, I cannot imagine investing three years and so much money without at least visiting the school.   Kenneth Kleinrock, Assistant Dean for Admissions, NYU

Admissions Directors Discuss Their Own Schools

Admitted applicants generally choose to enroll at that law school where they believe they will feel most "comfortable." Well, admitted students choosing Columbia are men and women who are most comfortable when they are uncomfortable—when they are engaging a community of classmates who are quite different than themselves—in terms of their backgrounds, perspectives, experiences, and developing professional ambition. With one of the very largest percentages of students of color, the largest percentage of international students in our JD student body (and by integrating our LLM students, eighty percent of whom are international lawyers), by attracting students from an extraordinary range of professions and careers, by enrolling entering classes the majority of whom realistically aspire to international careers, Columbia is truly, wonderfully diverse.   Jim Milligan, Dean of Admissions, Columbia

Our students are somewhat older and more experienced than those at peer schools. We try from the get-go to look for diversity of experience. This makes for a better education for everybody, including the faculty.   Jim Milligan, Dean of Admissions, Columbia

George Washington is a large urban law school. The positive is that we offer a lot of courses in a variety of fields. The negative is that you could get a little lost if you wanted to; no one holds your hand to guide you.   Robert Stanek, Director for Admissions, George Washington

I would find it hard to put together as diverse and interesting a group of people if the class were much smaller.   Joyce Curll, Assistant Dean for Admissions and Financial Aid, Harvard

We're a larger law school, allowing us to offer a lot of courses, seminars, lectures, and extracurricular activities. On the other hand, if you cannot handle choice, this is probably not the right place for you.   Kenneth Kleinrock, Assistant Dean for Admissions, NYU

Students here are happier than students at other top schools. The faculty is very accessible, always around the courtyard chatting with students. The law review does not just take the students ranked in the top ten percent after first year; there is a write-on competition. In general, we have taken away many of the reasons for competitiveness. The presence of so many chessboards in the library shows the relaxed atmosphere here.   Michael Rappoport, Dean of Admissions, UCLA

Not everyone is comfortable with a small, Ivy League, urban school. Some people will have trouble with each of these three components.   Janice Austin, Assistant Dean for Admissions, University of Pennsylvania

One of the advantages here is that you can take up to four classes at Wharton, the Center for Bio-Ethics, etc. All are within three blocks of the law school. Janice Austin, Assistant Dean for Admissions, University of Pennsylvania

Ours is a school at which people who need a lot of guidance don't prosper. Jean Webb, Director of Admissions, Yale

INVESTIGATING SCHOOLS

There is currently an illusion that a great deal more information is now available about schools, but it's not true. The resources that undergraduate colleges devote to pre-law advising vary dramatically from one school to another, although, for budgetary reasons, most schools have diluted their support for it. When college juniors or seniors do not have a good resource, they turn to one another and share misconceptions. They and others may also visit online chat rooms, where applicants in a state of high anxiety share misinformation or incomplete information.   Jim Milligan, Dean of Admissions, Columbia

When choosing among roughly comparable schools, it should not be a matter of just going on what *U.S. News* tells you, or what a school's reputation is, or what the family attorney tells you.   Michael Rappoport, Dean of Admissions, UCLA

Be as aggressive as possible: Use the Internet, check out the Websites, talk to colleagues who have been through it, and definitely visit. I can't imagine choosing a law school without experiencing the culture for as long as possible. Anne Brandt, Director of Admissions, Vanderbilt

It's unfortunate, but the reference books are often quite out of date.   William Hoye, Dean for Admissions, USC

You have to visit schools and talk to students. Students are brutally honest about their schools. Internet chat groups don't substitute for these visits: The threads take on lives of their own, not closely connected to the realities of the schools.   Elizabeth Rosselot, Director of Admissions, Boston College

Either before or after applying (and being admitted), those with the resources to do so really should visit the school. They should not just talk to the administration and faculty; they should find students in the lounge, etc. Students love to talk about what is good and bad at their schools. This is the only way to get the necessary understanding of what a school is really like.   Michael Rappoport, Dean of Admissions, UCLA

How Different Are the Schools?

You should visit every school you apply to, or at least those you are admitted to. Top schools tend to feature identical salaries and placement statistics, strong professors, etc. Thus the nonquantitative factors are especially important. These include whether a school is urban or rural, large or small, competitive or not. The result can be very different atmospheres at the various top schools. Ask yourself how you want to develop as a person over three years. Similarly, where the school is headed is critical. What changes are planned? What changes have recently taken place? What is the attitude of the school regarding adapting to change?   Don Rebstock, Associate Dean of Admissions and Financial Aid, Northwestern

City schools often don't feel like a college, with important school activities, etc. This can be a problem for those who are going straight from undergrad and want a real college feeling.   Michael Rappoport, Dean of Admissions, UCLA

Some schools have started to specialize in one or another specific field, but sometimes that's more a matter of marketing than of substance.   William Hoye, Dean for Admissions, USC

Some law schools are continuations of undergraduate experiences: They have a small-town atmosphere and most of the students are straight out of college. On the other hand, some applicants may want something very different than what they wanted or liked in college.   Jim Milligan, Dean of Admissions, Columbia

Students should select a law school where they feel they will get the best general legal education. It is not necessarily a good strategy to select a school solely based on one specialization which the school may be marketing. Your interests may very well change in law school.   Kenneth Kleinrock, Assistant Dean for Admissions, NYU

Appendix I

CRITERIA FOR
ASSESSING SCHOOLS

Few people will consider all of the following criteria to be important, but they are listed here to spur your thinking about what you would most like in a program. The most important criteria will depend upon your specific needs, but on average they include course offerings, school reputation, location, academic and political atmospheres, school size, facilities, and teaching quality. The two items applicants tend not to weight heavily enough are the learning atmosphere, for reasons discussed in the body of the chapter, and the quality of the career services function, because schools of equal quality and reputation tend to have very different rates of success in placing their graduates in desirable positions.

GENERAL

Reputation. Is the school considered one of the best schools in the country? Is it particularly well known and respected where you would most like to work? Is it highly regarded in your chosen specialty? Are professors in that specialty highly regarded? As Chapter 4 discusses in detail, the various school rankings should not be considered definitive. Pay at least as much attention to the opinions of those in charge of hiring as employers of the type for whom you wish to work.

Size. Smaller schools often engender a friendly, family atmosphere, with relatively close contact between professors and students. Large schools, on the other hand, are able to provide large numbers of elective courses, activities, and publications.

Location. What part of the country would you prefer to be in for three years? New York is exciting, but expensive and no one's idea of charming. Charlottesville is charming and inexpensive, but not exciting. Do not ignore the fact that you are about to spend three years of your life in law school; try to spend it somewhere you will appreciate.

The location of a school helps determine its social environment. Schools in large cities tend not to foster the degree of social bonding among classmates that schools in small towns do, largely due to the lack of other entertainment options in the latter.

Where do you intend to practice? A "national" school, of course, is termed national because it is well known across the country and able to place its graduates around the country. This does not, however, gainsay the benefits of attending school where you wish to practice. A school will tend to do very well placing its graduates in local firms and agencies. (For any given quality of school, it is easier to get a job in the nearby region than elsewhere.) More than that, you will have the chance to get to know the local legal scene well. Local practitioners will be frequent guest speakers at classes, colloquia, and brown-bag lunches devoted to various employment options. You and your classmates will share knowledge about local employers based upon summer and part-time work for them. This will afford you an understanding of the local scene far beyond what you could get from a distant school, however good it might be. The value of networking, moreover, will be greatest for those intending a very local practice. (Family law specialists need to know, and be known by, the judge and other practitioners in their jurisdiction whereas international corporate lawyers do not.)

Do not be concerned about where you will take the bar exam. You do not need to be at an Illinois law school simply because you intend to take the Illinois bar exam. The top law schools do not teach the laws of their home state, so you will be equally prepared (or unprepared) for Illinois's bar exam after attending Columbia or NYU rather than Chicago or Northwestern.

The school's location will have a major impact upon your spouse's (or significant other's) employment options. A corporate strategy consultant will have a relatively easy time finding appropriate employment in a major city but not in a small town. Similarly, your spouse's educational options are likely to be greatest in a city with numerous major universities rather than in a one-university town. By the same token, your children might have a tougher time socially and educationally in a large city than in a small town, or vice versa.

One additional locational factor to consider: How important is it to be close enough to your former home to allow easy visits?

Safety. Related to the location issue is the question of safety. Be sure that the school environment is, and feels, safe. In assessing safety, make sure you see the school and its environs (wherever students spend time), and do not assume that what appears safe at noon will also be safe at midnight. Discuss the matter with school officials, of course, but do not take their comments on faith. Be sure to discuss your concerns with students physically most like you. (Your notion of a safe environment will not necessarily be the same as that held by a 250-pound world karate champion or a tiny, fragile arthritis sufferer.)

Facilities. Check to be sure the library and computer facilities are top-notch. In particular, note whether they are comfortable for extended work efforts.

Housing. Housing can be a major concern, especially in your first year. Look at the law school dorms and apartments (where married students are generally housed). Examine the price and availability of off-campus housing. Note what transportation options you will have (and their safety implications).

Mission. Schools vary in the extent to which they wish to educate legal generalists versus legal specialists, those who will actually practice law versus those who will use legal training as a springboard for another profession, and those who will practice corporate law versus those who will work in the public interest sector. These differences can have a major affect upon your fit with a program and the students who have chosen to attend it.

PROGRAM

Term length. Long semesters lift the pressure of constant examinations and papers, but quarters make it possible to sample a wider variety of courses.

Program length and timing. Several schools offer the chance to take sufficient courses during summers that it is possible to graduate in just over two years. Michigan offers the chance to start in late May and finish at Christmas (rather than in late spring). Northwestern offers an extended, four-year program for those whose family obligations make a three-year program too intensive.

Courses in other departments. Those studying many different fields of law can benefit from courses in related areas. Thus, someone studying antitrust law might wish to take courses in economics; someone studying taxation might wish to take accounting courses; family law, psychology and finance; and so on. In some cases, this might call for doing a joint degree, but often the needs can be met through just a handful of courses, rather than adding a year to one's program. The problem is that most law schools permit only two, perhaps three, courses to be taken elsewhere in the university. (Penn is a rarity in allowing four courses to be taken elsewhere in the university.) Some schools, however, have brought many such courses within their own program. Thus, some offer multiple courses in accounting, economics, finance, statistics, and so on as part of the regular law school program, thereby obviating the need to take as many courses outside the law school itself. If you will want to take such courses, check to see how many are offered within the law school itself. If you will need other courses, check to be sure that they are open to law students, and that you will be allowed (by the law school) to take the number you need.

Joint degrees. The number and variety of joint-degree programs on offer at the top schools is spectacular. If you want a joint law and forestry degree, contact Yale; law and information science, Michigan; law and bioethics or city planning, Penn. The most popular option remains the JD–MBA, which accounts for nearly half of those doing joint degrees. Joint law and master's degree programs generally require four years of study, thereby decreasing the amount of time that would be required to do each degree independently by one year. (A new exception to this is Northwestern's JD–MBA program, which can be completed in three calendar years rather than four.) Joint law and doctoral programs operate similarly, cutting about one year from the required study time.

The reputation of the "other" degree program may be vitally important down the road. If you intend to teach law and economics in an economics department, for example, the quality of the economics degree you get may matter

---

DO NOT RUSH INTO A JOINT-DEGREE PROGRAM

Some employers cherish those having joint degrees. Thus, law schools love to hire professors with both a JD and a Ph.D. and many Wall Street firms love JD–MBA holders. In some cases, however, the value of a joint degree will not manifest itself for some time. If you are headed into a corporate legal practice, for example, the full value of the MBA may not be apparent until you are advising clients on complex matters (rather than researching issues at the behest of the partner in charge of the client relationship) or managing some aspect of the practice.

Before opting for a joint degree, however, consider whether your needs could be met simply by taking a few courses in the relevant department (or in the law school). Given that law school, at three years, is longer than most knowledgeable observers consider necessary, and most law students tune out from their studies by the end of the second year, it is not clear that adding another year of study makes a lot of sense. You might be better off just taking a few courses in the relevant department. Indeed, adding a year of study for a master's degree is going to be worthwhile for only a modest percentage of those who first contemplate it.

Conversely, you may not need to get a law degree, either. For example, if you intend to open your own business (one unrelated to law), it would be silly to think you should get a law degree so as to eliminate the need for lawyers to help you incorporate, negotiate with your employers, and so on. Even if law school were free, the extra two years you would spend in school would be too high a price to pay. In fact, if you did do a law degree, your failure to practice in the profession on a daily basis would mean that your knowledge and skills, far from improving, would atrophy. As a result, even with a law degree in your pocket, you would find yourself calling in lawyers nearly as often as you would without a law degree. A better solution is to take one or two law courses in the business school aimed at people in your position; then, as appropriate, consider taking another one or two in the law school.

more in your job hunt than does the quality of the law degree. For a JD–MBA, the MBA portion will weigh more heavily if your intended employers are in the business, rather than the legal, sector. Note that although many top law schools are ranked at approximately the same level as their affiliated MBA programs, there are some prominent exceptions. Yale's MBA program is ranked significantly lower than its powerhouse law program (the same is true for NYU), whereas Northwestern and Penn have higher-ranked MBA programs.

ADMISSIONS DIRECTORS DISCUSS JOINT-DEGREE PROGRAMS

The JD–MM (Northwestern's term for what is elsewhere termed an MBA) is really of benefit to them later in their careers, when they are at partner level in a firm, for example, or when they set up their own businesses. The JD/Ph.D. in social sciences is mainly for future law school professors.   Don Rebstock, Associate Dean of Admissions and Financial Aid, Northwestern

We have about 15–16 JD–MBA students enrolled here at a time; i.e., about four per class. They can enroll at one school and apply to the other during their first year of study.   Michael Rappoport, Dean of Admissions, UCLA

People wanting to do a joint degree generally apply to both programs together (although it is possible to apply to one school while in the first year of the program at another). For example, those applying for a JD–MM apply using just the Kellogg (business school) application, which requires more essay-writing and thus shows more about them. Kellogg processes them, then we jointly arrive at a decision. If one of us doesn't want them, the other can accept them, but it's usually all or nothing.   Don Rebstock, Associate Dean of Admissions and Financial Aid, Northwestern

The JD–MSFS is our most popular joint degree. Admissions decisions for each are made separately, although getting into the MSFS might help a little bit in getting into the law school.   Andy Cornblatt, Assistant Dean for Admissions, Georgetown

Plenty of people do JD–MBAs here, a small handful do JD–MDs, and others do one of a whole range of joint degrees. If someone applies to do a joint degree but looks like he or she is simply unable to choose between them and comes up with a vague rationale regarding what sort of policy work might combine the two fields, that won't be enough. It needs to be a clear, convincing argument that they will put both to good use and that both are necessary.   Jean Webb, Director of Admissions, Yale

Internationalization. Law has become a strikingly more global profession in recent years. Law firms in Europe and the United States are merging; other firms are working hand in glove across continents. The Big Five accounting firms are developing massive law practices outside the U.S. (and trying to get regulations changed to permit them to establish practices in the U.S.). These developments mirror the needs of businesses and individuals whose affairs are increasingly international. In numerous practice areas you can now expect to have an international dimension that would not have existed 20 years ago. Most of the top schools, though, have adapted only partially to this new environment. Therefore, if your field has (or will have) such an international dimension, look at schools' programs carefully. Do not just look to see whether some courses on international law are offered. Instead, examine whether courses devoted specifically to the international aspects of your field are offered. Examine, too, whether regular courses (i.e., those not labeled "international") include an international component.

Depending upon your interests, you might wish to do an exchange abroad (see below) or go a large step further and get an American law degree and a foreign degree, too. For instance, both Cornell and Columbia offer the opportunity to do two years of study in the U.S., followed by two years of study in France or Germany, resulting in both a JD and Maitrise en Droit (France) or M.LL.prax. (Germany).

Exchange programs. Those interested in an international dimension to their practice might benefit from a term at another top school, one that offers the opportunity to study in another language or pursue a specialized topic in greater depth. Consider the number and quality of exchanges on offer at a given school, but also make sure your particular interests are catered to. For instance, if you intend to practice international tax law, with a specialization in French taxation, make sure the school has an exchange with a leading French law school. Make sure, as well, that you will have access to the appropriate tax courses in that program. A school like Columbia has established relations with eight programs abroad. UCLA, in contrast, permits no studying abroad during the academic year, just during summers.

CURRICULUM

First-year courses. Nearly all schools require that you take civil procedure, constitutional law, contracts, criminal law, property law, and torts. These are normally taken in the first year, although some schools require that constitutional law be taken in the second year, instead; this difference is not meaningful. Several schools, however, are experimenting with the first-year curriculum, largely to provide a more meaningful context for the study of law. Students have often been mystified at the start of law school insofar as the only overall perspective they have on the study of law, its role in American life, and lawyering in general will have come from the odd political science course they may have taken or the reading they have happened to do on their own. Schools are to be commended for their efforts to dispel these problems. Georgetown, famously, has a special section of its first-year class pursue an alternative approach, examining the economic, historical, and philosophical foundations of law. (Its "Curriculum B" is available to students, but by no means compulsory.) Columbia has a three-week, ungraded introduction to the study of law. William & Mary divides first-year students into law firms that are then tasked to solve legal problems.

Electives. Make sure the school offers sufficient electives in your chosen field. Note, too, whether the course offerings reflect recent developments in the field. Be sure courses listed in the catalogue or on the Website are given annually. Some schools list all the courses they have given at some point in recent years, or hope to give, rather than those that will indeed be offered. Be sure, too, that more than one professor provides them, so that your education will not be savaged by one professor choosing to take a sabbatical during your third year.

Note that some schools have definite specialties (and reputations to match). For example, Tulane is famous for its admiralty and maritime law program, NYU for taxation, Berkeley for law and technology, Chicago for law and economics—and Harvard for too many items to mention.

Clinical courses. Clinical courses offer the opportunity to develop practical lawyering skills and learn what it is like to work for real clients. Internal clinics feature clients coming to the law school for help, with a faculty member on hand to supervise student efforts. External clinics are held away from the law school; a faculty member may or may not directly supervise work done there. In place of a faculty member, the attorneys who regularly work at the institution may be charged with supervisory responsibilities. Mock sessions are the rule in simulated clinics. Sessions are often videotaped, followed by debriefing with a faculty member. Clinical courses are extremely helpful in some fields, such as litigation and family law. In other fields, they are likely to prove useful rather than vital. Check the *ABA Official Guide to Approved Law Schools* for the number of positions available and filled in each type of clinical course. Check the school's Website for listings of the courses on offer for each subject.

Soft skills and law firm management courses. There are many skills essential to successful legal practice that are not learned in a traditional, substantive legal course. Negotiating, public speaking, and other "soft" skills are often critical to success, but some schools offer few opportunities to develop them in a structured class environment (rather than developing them on your own through student organizations and the like). This is a pity. Examine your chosen schools' offerings in areas important to your chosen specialty. For example, if you intend to develop a family law practice on your own, or with one or two others, you may wish to promote yourself by giving speeches to local groups. Public speaking and presentation skills will be important to your success. So, too, will be your knowledge of how to run a practice. Some schools offer courses on law firm management that can be invaluable for you. (If such courses are not on offer, they should be. It is astounding that despite the fact that the business of law has become extremely important, few schools prepare their students for the business side of practice. As a rough and ready substitute, look at the business school's offerings, but be aware that they will not focus on the law firm environment.)

Internships. Nonpaying positions can range from working for a judge to working for a national public interest organization. These placements often offer opportunities that are not readily available via classroom or proper work experiences. As with any good job placement, you have an opportunity to learn about a job at the same time as you are learning how to do it. You can make substantial contacts in your field and your firm or agency. Such placements tend to be particularly important for those not going the standard corporate law firm route. Those headed toward public interest law, for example, will find that an appropriate internship will help them demonstrate their commitment to public interest work (which is critically important in gaining paid employment in this sector).

Externships. Schools increasingly provide real-world placements for which course credit is granted. You can be placed in a private firm, nonprofit organization, government agency, the judiciary, and so on. UCLA, for instance, offers externships at organizations ranging from the Earthjustice Legal Defense Fund to the Directors Guild of America.

Technology. Whether in formal, dedicated courses or ungraded workshops, the school should provide you with ample opportunity to become a proficient user of new technologies.

PEDAGOGICAL ISSUES

Teaching methods. Teachers can use lectures, the case method, simulations, or actual clinics to impart knowledge. Some courses lend themselves to one method rather than another. Unfortunately, all of the top law schools are still overly enamoured of the case method, particularly for the first-year core courses. A mixture of lecture and case analysis would be a better bet for such courses, but the tradition of teaching them via case method is still too strong for most schools even to contemplate a change. Teaching of upper-level courses is nearer the mark. The mixture of case, lecture, and clinic is still being sorted out at most schools, but at least the question of what works best for what subject is under active consideration for these courses.

Teaching quality. Even apart from the question of what would be the best method for teaching a given subject, quality is remarkably uneven and hard to assess (especially from a distance). It varies mightily from school to school and professor to professor, yet few students take enough courses at multiple law schools to be able to render a judgment about the relative merits of the schools' teaching. As a result, the best way to gauge a school's teaching is by examining the ways in which it promotes good teaching. Kellogg (Northwestern University's business school), noted for good teaching, has a number of procedures in place to facilitate good teaching: "Professors are held to high standards in the classroom. Each new faculty member attends an orientation, is assigned a mentor, and is invited to a session on teaching techniques especially designed for Kellogg. New faculty do not teach in their first quarter, so that they may observe more senior colleagues and become familiar with the Kellogg environment. Every class is evaluated by students, and the evaluations are posted publicly. Tenure and promotion decisions are partially based on teaching quality." Compare each law school's efforts against this standard—but expect to be disappointed.

Workload. All of the top schools require substantial work, but there is still a large disparity between the load at the least and the most demanding schools. This is partly a function of the degree of competition (see below) at the school rather than the actual demands of professors. To this extent, it is under your control; you do not have to work 100-hour weeks simply because most people around you are doing so. In fact, as Chapter 16 shows, you can do well in courses (in terms of learning the material and getting good grades) without putting in the ridiculous number of hours most students do.

Still, the more easy-going the academic atmosphere, the less hard you will need to work for a given rank-in-class or possibility to be on law review. Be careful in assessing workload, by the way, because even asking admissions people may mark you as someone insufficiently determined. Pay close attention, instead, at school information sessions when someone else is silly enough to inquire about it. When visiting a school, ask students how hard most people work (and note how many people are still in the library or computer rooms at midnight), but do not take their replies at face value since students love to complain about how hard they have to work.

Class size. During the *first year,* most classes will be quite large, but their exact size is of little consequence. There is little difference between a class of 80 and a class of 125 in terms of the learning experience. In order to provide a more personal, intense learning experience, without blowing the budget, schools generally have one class per term split into smaller sections (with each still taught by a professor). The size of this section can range from about 20 to 50. This size differential can have an impact upon your learning, so prefer schools that have a smaller first-year section size.

During the *second and third years,* classes taken by most students—such as corporations, evidence, and individual taxation—will generally be very large. Other, more advanced or less popular subjects will be taught to much smaller numbers. It is valuable to have available seminars in your field, not just for the in-class attention you can get from professors, but also for the opportunity to get to know professors in your field out of class. (In some fields, such as litigation, the availability of small classes will be less important than the availability of clinics with appropriate professorial supervision.)

Professors. The ideal professor would combine three related activities. She would be dedicated to teaching, and would always be available in her office for conversations and assistance. She would also be a famous lawyer (or consultant on her subject), hired in all manner of controversies. (She might also be a prominent television commentator.) The ideal professor is, moreover, someone who devotes substantial energy to research and publishing, to increase her fame and that of the school.

Although it is impossible to square the circle and have professors both be readily available and be practicing law in important cases *and* be prolific authors, a school can foster an open-door policy that encourages professors to be on campus and readily available to students for at least some portion of each week. Students routinely prefer teachers who teach well over those who do high-quality research at the expense of quality teaching. Some schools have student evaluations of professors printed for student use. You are unlikely to be sent a copy if you request this by mail, but on a school visit you should be able to get a copy from the bookstore or an individual student. Look at this to determine how students really feel about teaching quality at the school.

It is important that a school have full-time professors in your field, not just adjunct professors or lecturers whose full-time occupation is actually practicing in the field. Such adjunct faculty can provide a wonderful view of current issues and the realities of practice, but they are less likely to remain at a school for an extended period (thereby risking leaving you high and dry) and may not be available on campus for out-of-class discussions.

The greatest danger exists for someone who chooses a school because of one or two famous professors. He may be unable to get a class with either of them—perhaps due to their taking a sabbatical year or leaving the school altogether. Or he may change his specific field of interest, negating the value of having these professors at the school. It is also unlikely that a student will develop substantial relationships with these kinds of professors, though there are always exceptions.

SOCIAL ISSUES

Politics. The political leanings of professors can have a major impact upon your experience. Do you want Marxist professors who believe that law is a means of keeping the oppressed people down? Do you want a professoriat that pooh-poohs public interest work in the belief that serious lawyers work in the corporate sector? Most schools have professors representing different points on the political spectrum and, of course, some professors are better than others at keeping their political views from determining how they treat students holding different opinions.

The same is true of the *student body*. Nonetheless, some schools are notably more conservative or liberal (radical?) than others. To get a reading on the political climate, examine the course catalog (are there more courses on corporate taxation than feminist views of the legal process, or vice versa?), check the biographies of the professors (noting whether they have served in Republican or Democratic administrations, the subjects about which they choose to write, and so on), and talk with students at the school.

Even if you are not a particularly political person yourself, a school's political scene can affect you. It can determine what courses are offered, what student groups are active, and whether you will easily make good friends. It can also determine whether you will find professors of like mind with whom you will work closely (and from whom a recommendation will be necessary if you hope to get a judicial clerkship or go into teaching). At its most extreme, a school can be torn apart, as Harvard was in the 1980s, by the battle between left and right.

Student body. The composition of the student body will have a major affect upon your learning experience, your enjoyment of the program, and even your ability to get desirable jobs in the future. The intensity of the law school experience guarantees that much of your time, particularly in the first year and a half, will be spent discussing legal (and societal) issues with other students. You risk being isolated and miserable if you do not fit in with the typical students at a school. Make sure you have spent some time with current students or those who have recently graduated to make sure you will feel comfortable at a school.

You can determine a lot about the nature of a school by looking at the makeup of its student body. Some aspects that might be of interest are the types of jobs people have held before law school; the age range (and, for instance, the percentage of people over 30 or the percentage of married students); the percentage of women students, international students, gay students, and minority students (perhaps including specific minority groups); and the percentage of students coming straight from college. In general, the more experienced the students, the more you stand to learn from them. Conversely, the more students who have come straight from college, the more the school will resemble an extension of college rather than a professional school.

It is, of course, one thing to have a number of students who are like you in some aspect you regard as critical. It is another to see how such people are treated. If you are foreign, for example, you should check to see whether foreigners are well integrated into campus life rather than being a distinct subgroup that mixes little with others.

Competition. Although most students would prefer an atmosphere that emphasizes cooperation more than competition, that is not true for everyone. Some people are inspired to work harder and perform better in a competitive environment. In assessing schools, note that five factors tend to determine the degree of competitiveness among students. Schools that have a high percentage of old-style Socratic method professors are prone to a high degree of competition. On the other hand, the more work that is done in teams (and graded on a team basis), the less competitive the atmosphere is likely to be. If students' grades and class rank are displayed to the class and to potential employers, the atmosphere is likely to be more competitive. The use of a mandated grading curve inspires competition, since an improvement in one student's grade means another's must suffer. Last, the number of students who are flunked out of the school has a large impact. Many, but by no means all, schools try to retain every student they enroll, thereby easing student fears.

Student–faculty relations. The student–faculty ratio, at the extremes, can have an affect upon the relations between the two groups. Thus, at a school with a 20:1 ratio, getting to know professors may be more difficult than at one with a 7:1 ratio. But this simple ratio is likely to conceal as much as it reveals. The relative numbers of students and professors tend to have less impact upon relations between the two groups than do other factors. Most important is the attitude professors have toward students. Some schools have a traditional closeness between students and faculty; faculty routinely invite students around for coffee or drinks, join them for lunches, and so on. At other schools, professors do little more than hold periodic office hours. One determinant of the tradition is the school's geographic situation. Schools that are isolated tend to have closer faculty–student relations than those in the midst of major cities. Another determining factor is the size of the law school. Smaller schools tend to have closer relations than large schools.

Quality of life. Student lifestyles may vary a great deal, of course, depending upon both the program and the student. A program in New York City may influence a student's life less than one in the country. At a school like Duke, in a small city, most student socializing is done with other students, both because the students tend to get on well with one another and because Raleigh-Durham offers limited enticement to pull students away from the law school.

Note that some schools treat spouses and families much better than do other schools. Some allow spouses to sit in on courses as a routine matter, whereas others have never heard of the idea. Again, some but not all schools include families in the school's social life and go to great lengths to help them find jobs, whether in the law school (or university) or in the surrounding area.

Be sure that your favorite activities (including those typically organized as a law school society or club, as discussed below) are available, whether at the school itself or nearby.

JOURNALS AND SOCIETIES

Law review. "Making law review" is important to many people, whether for the prestige it confers or the improved job prospects that result. For those headed into the teaching of law or work at a major law firm, making law review can be critically important. (The law review is invariably the most prestigious of a school's journals.) Law reviews select members on the basis of grades, a writing competition—candidates are given, say, five days to produce an article on an assigned topic, or a mixture of the two. (Several schools permit writing an article on any subject that might prove publishable.) If you are determined to get onto law review and are a particularly strong writer, you might favor a school that uses a writing competition to select members.

Subject-specific journals. The top law schools publish student-edited journals on a wide variety of subjects. Editing such a journal provides you with an opportunity to develop both your writing skill and your knowledge of the field. Some topics are routinely the subject of journals (environmental law, international law), whereas others are quite rare (criminal law, for instance). Even Harvard, with twelve journals, does not cover all fields.

Student societies. A rich and varied offering of student organizations can make law school a fine learning *and* socializing experience. As Chapter 16 discusses, these organizations offer you a chance to develop your skills and legal knowledge, make important contacts, contribute your new-found skills to worthy causes, and have a good time. Remember, of course, that if a certain organization does *not* exist at a target school, you can always plan to take the bull by the horns yourself and create it.

JOBS

Jobs. The more highly employers regard a school's graduates, the more job offers will flow. Specific offers depend upon more, however, than just a school's general reputation. If you hope to practice labor law, for instance, you will certainly want to choose a school that offers numerous courses in the field and has several highly regarded professors who specialize in it. You will also want to make sure other students will be entering the field; otherwise, you can be left out in the cold. A labor law firm will not travel across the country to recruit at Yale, in spite of its high regard for Yale graduates, if it suspects that few if any will venture into labor law.

Check whether people get jobs that you would like to have. In addition, check what credentials they had. In general, distinguish between the job prospects of those at the top of the class and those at the middle and the bottom. With the exception of clerking for the Supreme Court or teaching at a leading law school, the top graduates of the national schools can be expected to get highly desirable jobs. The differences between schools become more marked as you work your way down their class rankings. Those at the bottom of the class at a Harvard or a Yale, for instance tend to do quite well, getting jobs at well-known firms and other highly desirable employers. At less highly regarded schools, this is by no means necessarily the case.

To assess whether a school's degree "travels" to whatever area is of interest to you, consider both where recruiters come from and where graduates end up working. Similarly, to assess the school's overall success in placing graduates, consider not just which jobs graduates take, but also the nature and number of recruiters pursuing graduates (and summer hires). Precise calculations, such as the number of recruiters per student, should not be taken as definitive, just suggestive of the school's success.

Career services. A good career services department will provide in-depth assistance to you at each stage of the career assessment and job search process. Essentially all such departments now offer an opportunity to assess your own skills and interests, but the depth and quality of these assessments are not uniform at even the very top schools. The same is true, albeit to a lesser degree, regarding the following stages: determining precisely which field, then which type of employer, you will first work in; mastering the résumé and cover-letter writing, interviewing, and "call-back" interviewing processes (including those specific to your chosen field, such as public interest); sorting through job offers and negotiating for the best deal; and learning how to succeed in the first months (years) on the job.

Good departments offer presentations—and extensive one-on-one assistance—regarding each step of the process. They also offer brown-bag lunches, for instance, where you can hear from graduates about practice in large firms versus small firms, job opportunities in a given practice area, or how to apply for judicial clerkships. They should have a database of alumni that can be easily searched by location, graduating class, function or specialty, nature of employer, and so on. (Alumni, as discussed below, are potentially highly valuable in your career assessment and search as well as your career success later on.) These services should be available to alums, too, because you may need them more when you are out of law school than when you are in.

To assess a career services department, compare the programs it offers for each of the aspects mentioned above. Note what is available only on a group basis and what is available one-on-one with career service professionals. Good departments will have specialists devoted to each major employment sector. Thus, there will be counselors who deal only with the public interest, the corporate, or the government sector. Discuss the effectiveness of the various programs, and the availability and professionalism of the staff, with a variety of students.

Although the amount of money spent on a service is no better than a rough approximation for the value of the service (see Chapter 4), it can still be helpful to know how much money a career services department has at its disposal. NYU, for instance, has approximately three times as many students as Stanford, but its career services budget is five times that of Stanford. Especially given that there should be some scale economies to such an operation, NYU should be able to provide a more extensive and in-depth service than Stanford can.

Alumni. Alumni can be useful in providing pointers to jobs, or indeed jobs themselves. They can also mentor students while the latter are still in school, offering advice and contacts that can help establish them in their careers. In addition, alumni affect the ranking of the school by virtue of their degree of career success and also by the amount of money they raise for the school. The value of alumni thus resides in their number and their dedication to the school. It is easy for you to determine the number of alums—the bigger the school, the more alums it has. To determine their dedication to the school, look at the amount of money they raise, the percentage of alums who donate, their willingness to come back to the school to sit on panels offering advice to current students, and so on.

Local Connections. Schools tend to do very well in placing their graduates in nearby firms. If you are sure of where you want to practice, consider the extent to which a local school's connections may balance the appeal of a slightly more prestigious but distant rival. Check with the local employers you most value to help you analyze this.

FINANCES

The following provides just a quick glance at key financial issues. See Chapter 17 for an in-depth discussion of these and other financial considerations.

Your costs. Tuition rates vary dramatically from school to school. Public schools charge less than private schools, even for nonresidents. Tuition rates vary across public schools, too, whether for residents or nonresidents. In some states it is relatively easy to become a resident by the second year (or in advance of the first), making the differential in tuition—compared with private schools—all the greater. The cost of living also varies dramatically from school to school. Living in a major city tends to cost almost 50 percent more than living in a small city or rural area.

The cost of attending a school also includes the opportunity cost of what you (or your spouse) might otherwise do during the three years. In other words, you forego income and other opportunities during this time. If your spouse is unable to work at his or her profession, or must take a poorly compensated position, the differential in salary and career advancement is effectively a cost of the program. This differential will vary according to the location of schools, with those in major urban centers generally offering the best employment possibilities for spouses.

Part-time work. Much of the sting can be taken out of the cost of law school through summer employment (between years of law school) and part-time work during the second and third years of law school. You can expect to gross some $25,000–$30,000 for a summer at a top firm. The better the school and the better your grades (and other credentials), the better your chances of landing such a summer job.

Part-time work during law school is different from summer employment insofar as it can only be done near the campus. Whereas you can travel from California to New York for a summer job, if you are in law school at UCLA you can do part-time work only in the greater Los Angeles area. The salaries on offer for such part-time work vary dramatically from one location to another. In rural areas, you might not be able to earn more than 10 or 15 dollars per hour. In the major legal centers, such as New York, District of Columbia, Chicago, Los Angeles, and the Silicon Valley, you might earn 30 to 60 dollars (or even more) per hour. Consequently, your choice of school can have a dramatic affect on the amount of money you can earn during law school. In addition, many schools will ignore what you earn during the school year and not, therefore, alter your financial aid package due to your unexpectedly large yearly earnings. Chat with the career services director, as well as second- and third-year students, to get a sense of the availability of part-time work at local firms, the "going rate" in effect, and the school's treatment of term-time earnings.

Debt load. Calculate the law school debt you will carry upon graduation for each of your chosen schools. Factor in the financial package offered to you, plus your expected summer and term-time earnings. (An average figure as this book is being written is $70,000–$80,000.)

The amount of debt you will carry upon graduation can constrain your actions thereafter. If you have a massive debt load, you may need to work in a field, or for an employer, that you would otherwise avoid. (This can be every bit as constraining upon your career options as would be the case if you went to a lesser school.) If you intend to practice corporate tax law, you may not be concerned if your financial obligations push you toward working for a major firm. If, on the other hand, you want to do education law for a (low-paying) foundation, you might resent being forced to take a high-paying job doing corporate litigation instead.

Appendix II

VISITING LAW SCHOOLS

Visiting a law school is an extremely important part of your research. The visit brings to life a school that has heretofore been only an imaginary place fashioned by rumors, hearsay, Website information, guidebook and brochure blurbs, and statistics. In addition to partaking in the usual tours and information sessions, you should attempt to understand both what daily life is like for students and whether the academic experience is what you seek. Law school visits also offer opportunities to improve your admissions chances: Knowing well the school to which you are marketing yourself, and showing yourself as interested enough in it to have undertaken a substantial visit, are two ways in which you can distinguish yourself.

WHEN TO VISIT

It is best to visit a law school when it is in session so that you can get the right feel for student and academic life. If at all possible, visit when classes are in session, but not during exam period. Attending when school is in session will give you an opportunity to interact with students, who are the best reflection of a school and what it is all about. At exam times, however, students will have little interest in discussing the school (or anything else) with you, so you will be unable to gain an in-depth understanding of the school.

Try to visit a campus on a weekday in order to get the best sense of the school. Weekday visits will allow you to see students interacting and to attend several classes. Visiting Monday through Friday will also ensure an opportunity to visit with admissions staff. Even if the school does not conduct formal interviews, you may be able to leave a favorable impression with admissions officers, which can work to your benefit. (See page 315 for a discussion of "hidden" interviews.)

It is not particularly important that you visit immediately before applying. Even if you visit a year (or two) beforehand, your understanding of the school will stand you in good stead as long as your key criteria for selecting a school have not changed substantially in the interim. By the same token, it is not a bad idea to revisit schools you are seriously considering after you have been accepted in order to arrive at a final decision.

BEFORE THE VISIT

Plan to visit a range of law schools. This is extremely important if you are not certain what you are looking for. Visiting different kinds of schools is a smart move even for those who think they know what they want. You might be certain, for example, that you want to attend a small, suburban law school because you had such a good experience at just such a college. Upon visiting a range of schools, however, you might find that you now would be better served by a much larger environment, both law school and city. Visit small and large, public and private, urban and rural schools. Also, be sure to visit schools that represent a range of selectivity. You need to visit not just your "stretches," but also your "possibles" and "likelies."

Note that you will learn about law schools—and about law school visits—as you tour schools. After you have visited several schools, you will know what items are most crucial for you to investigate as well as how best to gather the information you need. Therefore, do not plan to visit your likely top two choices first. Instead, try to visit several schools about which you are not certain as a means of familiarizing yourself with the visiting process.

Keep these additional guidelines in mind when planning your itinerary:

- Familiarize yourself thoroughly with the law schools you will be visiting. (See this chapter for specific information sources.) You should be familiar with all the basic facts about a school before getting to the campus, where your job is to refine your impressions and conduct a more detailed investigation—not to learn the absolute basics. Start a law school notebook in which you record your data.

- Visit no more than one school per day. The amount you need to do on campus necessitates a full day, not just two or three hours. The more you value a given school, the longer you should plan to spend at it.

- Arrange meetings with individuals in areas of interest to you, whether professors, career service professionals, or financial aid officers.

- Arrange for a formal interview (if this is part of the admissions process for that school).

- Compile a list of the questions you intend to ask at each school, along with any that are specific to this school. (See page 75 for suggestions.)

WHILE ON CAMPUS

Your visit can include general information-gathering and efforts targeted at specific areas of interest or concern to you. Thus, you can take a campus tour or spend time talking with each labor law professor. The time you have available is likely to determine much of what you do. If you have very little time, a great need for financial aid, a keen interest in corporate taxation, and you have already visited a number of other schools, you would be silly to spend most of your time taking a general campus tour. Instead, you would probably want to spend time with a financial aid officer, talk in depth with several tax professors, and discuss the school and the tax department with several students. Given sufficient time, you might want to meet with the career services department as well as sit in on several corporate tax courses.

THE CAMPUS TOUR

You can take a general tour of the university or, perhaps, a tour of just the law school. The former is likely to last up to an hour, whereas the latter is likely to be much shorter. These tours are a pleasant way to get your bearings; they can also give you the chance to size up the atmosphere of the campus. The students who lead such tours are, of course, salespeople for the school, so do not expect to get a forthright perspective on the school's strengths and weaknesses from them.

INFORMATION SESSION

A group information session is essentially a school's sales pitch. It is, however, a useful tool for gaining basic information about a school. These sessions generally give an overview of the school's tradition and philosophy as well as the multitude of academic, extracurricular, and other opportunities available there.

Although admissions officers often lead these sessions, this is seldom a time to try to stand out from the crowd in order to impress them. Those who try to dominate sessions or gain attention with too many questions that are not of interest to other applicants are frowned upon by admissions officers. If you are lucky enough to be one of only a couple attendees, however, keep in mind that your efforts may improve your admissions chances (as the next section discusses).

THE ADMISSIONS OFFICE

At many schools, you can visit the admissions office and ask to speak with an admissions officer, even if you have not arranged an interview. (Do not expect to be given a formal interview, however, unless you have arranged one in advance.) An officer might be willing to give you a few minutes of his or her time to answer questions and address concerns. Express your interest in the school and ask questions that show you to be serious.

You have the chance to impress the admissions officer in a way that might benefit you. Be on your best behavior and be sure your questions and comments show your overall knowledge of the school, your general intelligence, and your poise. Even at schools that do not conduct formal interviews, it is common for admissions officers to make notes of any substantive interactions with applicants. (For more about "hidden interviews" see page 315.)

The Financial Aid Office

If you intend to seek financial aid, you are likely to have numerous questions about how this school handles financial aid matters. Arrange in advance to speak with a financial aid officer; 20 to 30 minutes is likely to be enough time if you are well organized. See Chapter 17 for a discussion of what you will need to know about financial aid.

The Career Services Department

Relatively few applicants pay sufficient attention to the value a good career services department can add to a school—and to their own career prospects. Visiting the career services department at each school you visit will quickly show you which are the most able where your interests are concerned. Take 20 or 30 minutes to discuss what they offer (in light of the discussion on prior pages of what a good career services department can do).

Classes

Upon contacting the admissions office to arrange a visit, ask about the possibility of sitting in on classes. This is your opportunity to get a feel for the professors, students, and the nature and quality of teaching at the school. If you have time, try to sit in on a variety of classes. Consider sitting in on a first-year (core) course as well as an advanced course in a subject of particular interest to you. Try to sit in on a course for which the admissions office does not make the arrangements. Given that the admissions officers want to sell their school, you can expect them to try to route you to the best instructors. To see what an ordinary professor is like, ask students for a suggestion in your chosen field. Then approach the professor of the course and see whether he or she will permit you to sit in. Most will accommodate you without hesitation.

BE AWARE OF YOUR PREJUDICES

Many things can skew your impressions of a school for better or for worse, thereby affecting your ability to evaluate it. Therefore, pay attention to these points.

- Do not let your like or dislike of a single person (admissions officer or other administrator, student, professor) influence your overall impression of a school.

- Bear in mind that weather is a transitory matter and you might be visiting a school on the rare sunny (or rainy) day.

- Depending upon when in the term you visit (i.e., at the beginning of the term or during midterm or final exams), students may be more or less enthusiastic about their choice of school—and about spending time with you. This can vary dramatically from first- to second- to third-year students, by the way, given that each is facing a very different set of factors that will influence their views of life, law, and school.

- If you sit in on an advanced class, do not be surprised if the material and the class discussion are beyond your comprehension. (On the other hand, if the material seems extraordinarily dry, do not be afraid to reexamine whether law school is the right choice for you.)

- Remember that school officials are more likely to try to sell you than are students. Try to talk with as many different types of people as possible to build the most complete and accurate picture of the school.

- Pay particular attention to those students who most resemble you in terms of their background and goals. Whenever you encounter someone who reminds you of you, dig in. Pump her, and all of her friends, for as much information as you can get regarding what they think the school does and does not do well.

- Appreciate and observe the school for what it is rather than obsessing about your chances of admission there. If you focus too much on the latter, you will limit your ability to assess the school.

- Keep in mind that even though a school might have a prestigious name, it is not necessarily the best school or the best school for you. As you carry on your visit, keep in mind the criteria you have established for determining the best school for *you*.

- Remember that choosing a law school is an iterative process—as you visit and examine schools, you should learn more about your own needs; and as you learn more about your own needs, you will refine your criteria regarding which schools are best for you.

THINGS TO NOTE ON YOUR CAMPUS VISIT

➤ Are the students happy or glum? Engaged or apathetic? (Remember, though, that the timing of your visit can affect the ways students are acting.)

➤ Do different ethnic and racial groups interact? On campus and off?

➤ Do professors interact with students? (Look outside of classrooms, especially in cafeterias, the student union, and local watering holes.) Do professors, especially older ones, seem weary and bored with their material—and the prospect of teaching mere law students—or are they energetic and uplifting?

➤ What is the atmosphere like in the classes you sit in on? Are students afraid or engaged?

➤ Are the library and computer facilities well-used? Comfortable? Are there sufficient private carrels and areas for group meetings? Is the atmosphere conducive to studying? (Note that some students work best in absolute quiet, whereas others like to be surrounded by a buzz of noise and activity. Check that the school's facilities meet your own personal requirements for effective study space.)

➤ What is the pulse of the law school? What sorts of activities and events are advertised on bulletin boards? What issues are important to students? (You can discover the latter by talking to students, listening to conversations in eating facilities, and reading the school newspaper.) What is the overall "feel" of the school?

➤ Is there a student course evaluation booklet available?

➤ Where do most law students live? Are there housing options that will fit your needs?

➤ How much interaction is there with other departments and schools of the university? With the surrounding town?

➤ Does the area feel safe, both during the day and the night?

➤ How readily available are restaurants, cafes, bars, theatres, and the like?

➤ Are the athletic facilities of good quality? Available at useful times?

UPON LEAVING CAMPUS

RECORD YOUR IMPRESSIONS

Keep detailed notes of the law schools you visit. During the course of your visits, note what you can. Be sure not to let the day of a visit end without completing your written record. If you visit multiple schools on a single trip, failure to complete your notes on one school before you visit the next will almost surely cause you to

QUESTIONS TO ASK WHILE ON CAMPUS

Do not be merely a silent observer of a law school scene. Instead, ask the people you encounter whatever questions are important to you. Asking the same question of a variety of people will often give you different perspectives on an issue.

➤ What do you particularly like, and what do you particularly dislike, about the school? What do you see as its benefits and shortcomings?

➤ If you could change one thing about your school, what would it be? (This question is especially useful in gauging the honesty—and grip on reality—of the person responding. If the respondent cannot think of anything that she would like to change, assume that you are dealing with a shill for the school or a Pollyanna. In either case, you would do well to spend your precious time questioning others.)

➤ Which professors do essentially no teaching?

➤ Which professors are excellent teachers? Terrible teachers?

➤ How much Socratic Method teaching is there? How strict a version is employed?

➤ Is it common for students to have close relationships with their professors? What opportunities exist for students to foster such relationships?

➤ What do students do for fun?

➤ What campus, legal, and world issues are most important to students?

➤ What are the most popular courses? Which courses are difficult to get into?

➤ What are the strongest and weakest fields?

➤ What are the most popular student societies and clubs?

➤ How competitive are the students?

➤ What do you consider the strengths of this school relative to its competitors? (For students only: Why did you choose this school over others?)

➤ How many students work part-time off campus? What is the usual pay?

➤ What is the quality of the career services department? Are there career services professionals who specialize in (your area of interest)? (Ask the career services people what their backgrounds are. Ask them, too, what their specialties are.)

QUESTIONS NOT TO ASK

➤ Avoid asking questions about admissions requirements or any other questions to which you can find answers on your own by simply reading admissions brochures and standard publications.

➤ Avoid grilling anyone only about the school's weaknesses. Asking about weaknesses shows that you are doing serious investigative work and that you are appropriately concerned about your future, but remember also to be positive and ask about strengths as well.

forget important things about the first or muddle together your impressions of the various schools.

Send Thank-You Notes

Send thank-you notes (or e-mails) to key people with whom you interacted. This can include interviewers, financial aid officers, professors, or other faculty who took time to chat with you. It is not necessary (or worth your time and effort) to send notes to people who conducted large information sessions or tours—these people are not likely to remember you and there is no reason to send a note to thank someone for this kind of routine group treatment. It is the individualized treatments that need to be addressed with letters of appreciation.

Be sure to note the names, titles, and addresses of individuals while on your visits—and be sure to get all the spellings correct. If you are unsure of any spelling details, you can always call the admissions department (for the names of admissions officers), the financial aid office (for the names of financial aid officers), the student telephone directory (for the names of students), or academic department offices (for the names of faculty or administrators) to make sure you are correct. Although sending thank-you notes will not guarantee your admission, it is nevertheless a nice gesture and will be appreciated by the recipients.

4

How to Use
the Rankings

— EXECUTIVE SUMMARY —

Schools are routinely ranked by various authorities (and dilettantes).

■

The rankings provide handy guides to the reputations of different programs,
but are subject to many qualifications.

■

Consult them, but do not rely on them.

■

Recognize their limitations
as well as their strengths.

■

Devise your own rankings to suit your needs.

The purpose of this book is not to rank schools, nor to place school X on a list of "top" schools and relegate school Y to the list of also-rans. Other publications devote substantial effort to doing this; the field will be left to them. This chapter will examine the most influential rankings and discuss the methodologies they employ to reach their conclusions.

For years, the annual ranking put out by *U.S. News and World Report* has been the most important in the field. The decisions of applicants, recruiters, and even the law schools themselves are heavily influenced by the results of the annual *U.S. News* rankings. Consequently, this chapter devotes more attention to the *U.S. News* rankings than to those of its competitors.

The rankings to be discussed in this chapter include:

- *U.S. News & World Report*
- *The American Lawyer*
- *Inside the Law Schools*
- *The National Jurist*
- *The Insider's Guide to the Top Fifteen Law Schools*

USING THE RANKINGS

The ranking of law schools is a very uncertain science. Organizations and individuals undertaking these rankings are confronted by daunting methodological problems. From an immense amount of information, a few factors must necessarily be singled out and calculated—all in order to provide "scores" that allow readers to differentiate among schools that have performed almost identically. For example, how important is it to have a library of 1,000,000 volumes rather than 600,000 volumes, and how does that compare with having a student body LSAT average of 168 rather than 171? Is the school with 1,000,000 volumes and a LSAT average of 168 better than the school with 600,000 and 171, respectively? Or is it equal to it, or worse? It is not obvious how the two schools should be compared, even when two relatively simple quantitative measures are employed. The problem is made infinitely more complicated when numerous other factors are considered, especially because many of these are inherently subjective rather than easily and objectively quantifiable.

Several bypasses are available to the ranking organizations. They can examine the opinions of those doing the hiring at major firms, taking the likely employers of JDs as the ultimate arbiters of worth. (To an extent this is correct, of course, insofar as JDs tend to view the value of their degree in large measure as a matter of what employment doors it opens.) Another possible shortcut is to examine the earnings of the graduates of each school, relying again on the market as the arbiter of the value of the JDs from the various schools. Unfortunately, these shortcuts also suffer from limitations. Some are due to the fact that an overall ranking for a school does not distinguish between how its private-practice graduates do and how its public-interest graduates fare. Nor does it take account of the fact that its graduates may do very well locally but not in another region (or country). Thus, if a school is rated highly because its graduates make a lot of money in private practice, but you intend to work as a public defender, this school may not boost your salary—or employment options—more than another school would.

SOME WARNINGS

Rankings are useful as a very rough guide to the reputation and quality of different programs. Most people take them far too seriously, however, when considering where to apply. It is inappropriate to take the latest *U.S. News* ranking and limit yourself to the top five schools in the list. The schools differ enough in their goals, programs, and atmospheres that a person who will be well served by one may be poorly served by another. To take an obvious example, a person who is determined to study Intellectual Property should be looking at Stanford rather than Chicago. Both are superb, but their missions and offerings are quite different. Stanford, in addition to being located in the hi-tech hotbed of Silicon Valley, offers more than a dozen relevant courses—where Chicago has fewer than a handful.

Chapter 3 lists several dozen criteria that are relevant to choosing the right program. Not all are equally significant, and it is undeniable that reputation is critically important. But it would be foolish to opt for a school ranked fourth by *U.S. News,* rather than one ranked sixth, solely because of these rankings—if the first had an unsuitable atmosphere, had few electives in the aspect of law you want to enter, or suffered from one of a number of other defects that may also be important to you. There is no precision to these rankings; the same publication may reverse the rankings of these same schools next year! The imprecision and variability of the rankings is one reason for being cautious in using them; another reason for caution is that one school will be able to offer you a program geared to your needs whereas another will not.

These concerns give rise to some guidelines for using rankings:

1. Look at as many rankings as possible and consider the consensus rather than any one ranking.

2. Consider even this consensus view as only an approximation of the appropriate tier for a school. Thus, a school ranked about tenth to fifteenth in

various rankings should be regarded as a very fine school, to be taken very seriously, but whether it should be ranked in the top 5 or merely the top 20 is not determinable.

3. Because you should be looking for the best program to meet your specific subject and other needs, with an atmosphere in which you will thrive, the rankings have only a modest part to play in helping you to find this program. They have little to say about which school will provide the courses that will be most useful, the connections that will matter most for the job and region in which you wish to be employed, the academic and social environments at each school, and other key factors.

4. More important than the rankings will be the research you do concerning the details of specific programs, which is discussed in detail in Chapter 3.

THE RANKINGS

The five rankings charted below cover a total of 28 schools out of the 180 law programs currently accredited by the American Bar Association.

	US News & World Report	American Lawyer	Inside the Law Schools	National Jurist	Insider's Guide to the Top 15 Law Schools
Yale	1	5	Top 5	16	1
Stanford	2	7	Top 5	30	4
Harvard	3	4	Top 5	158	2
NYU	4	2	Top 10	34	9
Columbia	5	3	Top 5	140	5
Chicago	6	1	Top 5	59	6
Michigan	7	11	Top 10	63	3
UC Berkeley (Boalt Hall)	8	12	Top 10	153	7
Virginia	8	14	Top 10	9	8
Cornell	10	10	Top 15	33	15
Duke	10	8	Top 15	72	12
Northwestern	12	9	Top 15	30	16
Pennsylvania	12	6	Top 10	44	10
Georgetown	14	13	Top 15	10	13
Texas	15	18	Top 15	37	11
UCLA	16	15		82	14
Southern California	17	16		5	22
Vanderbilt	18	20		13	21
Minnesota	19	55		119	17
Washington & Lee	20			1	

(Continued)

	US News & World Report	American Lawyer	Inside the Law Schools	National Jurist	Insider's Guide to the Top 15 Law Schools
Iowa	21	45		32	30
North Carolina	22			154	24
Boston College	23	19		91	
George Washington	24	23		165	20
Illinois	25	20		129	23
Emory	26	28		107	25
Notre Dame	26	22		7	28
Univ. of Washington	26	71		17	29

There is clearly no agreement as to which school is the best, nor which is the seventeenth best. No school, for example, shows up in the top 10 of all the rankings discussed. There is some reasonable agreement, however, as to which of those schools are considered the real elite. Considering the five sets of rankings above, the following schools were ranked in the top ten more than once:

RANKED IN TOP 10

BY ALL 5	BY 4	BY 3	BY 2
None	Chicago	UC Berkeley (Boalt Hall)	Cornell
	Columbia	Michigan	Duke
	Harvard	Penn	
	NYU		
	Stanford		
	Virginia		
	Yale		

Another quartet was ranked in the top 15 multiple times:

RANKED IN TOP 15

BY 5	BY 3	BY 2
Georgetown	Northwestern	UCLA
	Texas	

These rankings used a variety of methodologies—with some highly anomalous, not to say bizarre, results in the case of the *National Jurist*—yet a clear picture emerges when the whole set of rankings is considered. A dozen schools were considered "top 10" schools by multiple sources and another four were ranked in the top 15 multiple times. Most of the remaining schools received multiple mentions, albeit at somewhat lower levels.

LIMITATIONS OF THE RANKINGS' METHODOLOGIES

Rankings of schools can be based on different factors. Simple rankings may measure nothing more than the vaguely phrased "student selectivity"; others place most importance on the opinions of academics and legal professionals.

These rankings do not provide precise measures of the quality of programs. They do, however, influence both the number and quality of applicants to specific programs, and, as a result, the number and quality of recruiters hiring graduates of the school.

In general it is clear that there are a number of problems any rater of schools must address. What does "best" mean? Is it the school that has the smallest class sizes, is most concerned with clinical training, best prepares students to be litigators, nets graduates the highest salaries, best prepares someone in a particular field, or is the least painful to get through? A rater who chooses any one definition to the exclusion of all others is still faced with potentially insurmountable problems. This is why you owe it to yourself to scrutinize the methodology behind each ranking before assuming its merit.

U.S. NEWS & WORLD REPORT

Methodology. The *U.S. News & World Report* magazine rates law schools each year in March. Its methodology is purported to be quite comprehensive: Each factor considered in the ranking is broken down by score for the reader to examine. These factors, which are broken down into several subcategories, are: reputation (counting for 40%), placement success (20%), student selectivity (25%), faculty resources (15%), and bar passage rate (10%).

Advantages of this approach. The virtues of this approach are clear. By measuring each school on a number of bases, *U.S. News* can claim to have achieved a "depth and breadth" which no other ranking has. Furthermore, the ratings that *U.S. News's* methodology produces are quite stable over time, with no extreme jumps and falls in individual rankings over the years. This is presumably a reflection of reality, as it is rather unlikely that the quality of many law schools would change dramatically in a short period of time.

Limitations of this approach. The *U.S. News* ranking suffers from two problems that face any such survey. For one, innumerable factors that might be relevant to you are not included in this (or any other) ranking. Thus, there is no direct measure, for instance, of the actual quality of teaching or of faculty accessibility at each school.

For another, different applicants want different things in a school. For example, George may prefer a small school with extensive student–faculty interaction and plenty of environmental law courses. Lisa, on the other hand, may prefer a large school in which she can be relatively anonymous and have plenty of electives in intellectual property. Producing one ranking, based upon whatever weighting of these two factors is chosen, cannot do justice to the needs of both George and Lisa. (In point of fact, the *U.S. News* rankings are arbitrary in the weights assigned to the various factors.)

Some of *U.S. News's* categories are clearly relevant to ranking schools but are hard to calculate in a sensible fashion. Other categories can be calculated fairly easily but fail to produce useful information.

Thus, school ***reputation*** is highly relevant to the ranking of schools and to candidates' decision-making. The problem is in measuring it. *U.S. News* uses two separate surveys: a poll of law school deans (and professors) and a poll of judges and lawyers, and combines the responses. Each person polled is asked to rank (on a scale of 1 to 5) the reputation of each of the 179 schools. It is highly unlikely, however, that even a well-informed law school dean will know the operations of other schools so thoroughly that he or she can accurately rate many dozens of them. This is likely to be more true of judges and lawyers, who are not even in the education business. The likely affect of this is that both groups might tend to overrate schools in their region, schools that are already famous, or those that make the biggest splash—or even those they themselves attended.

A potentially larger problem is that one critical group is somewhat overlooked: Employers are not asked about their hiring practices.

The ***selectivity*** measure depends heavily upon the median undergraduate grade-point average of incoming students. This statistic is, remarkably, unadjusted in any way. This assumes that a grade is a grade, regardless of circumstances. At a large number of colleges the median grade point is 3.3–3.5, whereas at the military academies it is below 3.0. The rigor of courses at a community college should hardly be compared with that of courses at Cal Tech, but for the purposes of *U.S. News's* ranking, a GPA is a GPA, no matter where it was earned. The difficulty of getting top grades in hard sciences is generally far greater than that encountered in the liberal arts, yet the rankings do not take this into account. By the same token, a student who took only introductory or low-level courses would be considered on equal footing with someone else who did advanced course work in physics, creative writing, and Mandarin. Consider, too, what this measurement completely ignores. Many of the top schools now accept a substantial number of transfer students, but their undergraduate grades are not considered in this measure. Neither are the graduate results for those who have gone beyond undergraduate studies prior to attending law school.

The measure of so-called ***faculty resources*** (the expenditures per student for instruction, library, and student services) is relatively straightforward; the problem is that it is of extremely dubious value. Let's, consider two schools: Acme University and Garage College. Acme charges $30,000 annual tuition, whereas Garage charges $20,000. If Acme gives $10,000 of financial aid to each student whereas Garage gives no financial aid, students at both schools will pay precisely $20,000 each. Acme, however, will be considered to have "spent" money on its students and Garage will not, resulting in Acme being given a higher ranking in this category.

Another problem arises from the fact that schools are ranked according to how much they spend, not according to the value they get for their expenditures. For example, throughout the 1990s Japan spent a higher percentage of its national income on business investment than did any other developed economy, yet spent virtually the whole decade floundering from recession to recession. This hardly provided other economies with an example to follow. Nonetheless, Japan would have been placed at the top of a *U.S. News* ranking rather than at the bottom as it surely deserved.

The ***placement success*** measurement suffers from both types of problems. It is based in part upon a highly arbitrary formula. *U.S. News* calculates the proportion of the class of 1996 employed full and part time approximately 3 months after graduation but includes one-quarter of those students whose employment status is unknown and excludes those who claim they are not looking for employment. This estimate is obviously flimsy, but it happens to have major consequences. Schools that place most of their graduates locally find it easier to track them, meaning they will have fewer graduates fall into the "unknown" category, thereby giving a boost to these schools that is not readily available to those schools that place their graduates across the world (and thus find it hard to keep such close track of them).

The methodological difficulty in calculating an accurate placement success figure is dwarfed by another consideration: It is not a suitable statistic for distinguishing among the very top schools. This is admittedly a statistic that can be very helpful for applicants choosing between two lower-tier schools. If only 57 percent of Texas Southern University's graduates are employed nine months after graduation but 92 percent of Texas Tech University's are, potential applicants are likely to find this to be very important to their decision-making. On the other hand, if the relevant figures for NYU and Chicago are 100 percent and 99 percent, respectively, it is hard to imagine that anyone should choose NYU over Chicago on this basis.

Each of the other measures used by *U.S. News* also suffers from substantial problems similar to those discussed above. This is not to say that its rankings are valueless; instead, you should be careful not to place undue weight upon them in deciding to which schools you will apply.

OTHER FACTORS *U.S. NEWS & WORLD REPORT* ONCE CONSIDERED

Years ago, *U.S. News* considered the average salaries of graduates. This obviously makes sense, insofar as one of the major reasons many go to law school—and choose one law school over another—is to make as much money as possible. Another related factor is how much of an increase in salaries graduates enjoyed. In other words, what is the difference between the amount they earned prior to law school and the amount they earned after graduation? (This could be expressed as an absolute dollar amount or as a percentage.)

The value of this sort of measurement is subject to many qualifications (see the discussions regarding the *American Lawyer* rankings), but it is more relevant than ever given that more and more applicants are entering law school after substantial prior work experience. As a result, they are inclined to look at financial factors as particularly relevant in their choice of schools.

Rankings of business schools, interestingly, are often based in no small measure upon exactly such calculations. The *Financial Times* and *U.S. News* itself, representing two of the three most important of such rankings, use salary data as important components of their rankings of business schools.

AMERICAN LAWYER

Methodology. In April of 1998, skeptical of the pertinence of the *U.S. News* ranking, *American Lawyer* magazine produced its first ranking of law schools, which it intends to make an annual event. The *American Lawyer* ranking has only one factor: where the nation's highest-grossing law firms go when they are looking for first-year associates. *American Lawyer* contacted the top 100 of these firms (89 responded in 1998) and asked for the tallies of associates hired by the firm per school, per year. This number was then divided by the number of graduates in each school's class. The resulting index is the sole basis of the ranking.

Advantages of this approach. If your primary reason for going to law school is to get a job in one of the country's major law firms, as measured by how much they pay, then this ranking will provide valuable market data.

Limitations of this approach. The major objection to the *American Lawyer* approach is that it ignores all but one reason for which students attend law school. There is no attempt, for instance, to determine where students are happiest or what schools provide the most stimulating education. Instead, *American Lawyer* assumes that all law students desire to join the most lucrative sectors of law practice.

There are, of course, some drawbacks to this approach. For one, it penalizes schools that are attractive to students who plan to take lower-paying—but often equally prestigious—legal employment. For another, it ignores the placement of graduates in nonlegal positions that are at least as lucrative as those in the top law firms. Graduates who go to the top strategy consulting firms and investment banks, for example, could well be included in this listing.

Although the purpose of the *American Lawyer* ranking is to rate schools that place students at the highest-grossing law firms, no attempt to differentiate between these firms is made. Obviously, a school that places 50 students at the Number One firm should score higher than a school that places 50 students at the Number 100 firm. Furthermore, the ranking is biased in favor of urban firms, particularly those in New York City and Silicon Valley. The salary of a first-year associate in Manhattan will be significantly greater than the one of an associate in Austin, Texas. Were a cost-of-living index incorporated into the *American Lawyer* endeavor, the list of the Top 100 would include more firms from different regions in the country, thus influencing the rankings of the law schools themselves.

INSIDE THE LAW SCHOOLS

Methodology. For nearly ten years, Carol-June Cassidy and S. F. Goldfarb have compiled "candid firsthand reports," along with factual data, about each accredited law program in the country. An implied ranking is apparent within the write-ups of the schools: Cassidy and Goldfarb identify various schools as being included within the Top 5, Top 10, and Top 15. These categorizations seem to be based as much on general reputation of a school as on quantifiable factors, but the actual methodology employed is opaque.

Advantages of this approach. The loosely-constructed ranking found in *Inside the Law Schools* is unaffected by many of the overemphasized, easily-calculated factors used in the *U.S. News & World Report* ranking.

Limitations of this approach. The authors do not describe how they ranked schools. There is no discussion of which factors were important, let alone the actual weight accorded to each. Similarly, there is no description of what techniques were used to assess each factor. (In fact, it is difficult to ascertain whether the ranking is based upon anything deeper than hearsay.) Thus, the authors appear to have employed an impressionistic approach, which is not open to serious analysis.

NATIONAL JURIST

Methodology. National Jurist magazine (distributed monthly to law campuses around the country) published a ranking that has garnered much publicity. The ranking was based on a *Princeton Review*-sponsored survey of 18,000 students at

165 law schools nationwide. The ranking attempts to rate "overall student satisfaction." Students were asked to respond to 11 questions regarding the school they were currently attending. The questions addressed three main categories: satisfaction with faculty (36%), school facilities (30%), and quality of life (34%). This rather dated ranking is included here to demonstrate yet another ranking possibility, and to provide guidance in the event that *National Jurist* publishes another ranking in the future.

Advantages of this approach. None of the factors assessed in the *U.S. News & World Report* ranking involve the opinions of students. The *National Jurist* ranking functions under the premise that students—not educators, not employers, not statistics—provide the most valuable assessment of law schools.

Limitations of this approach. This ranking assumes that a law student—who has attended only one law school (his or her own)—has the knowledge and experience to assess the quality of life at all other law schools. This is certainly an heroic assumption.

This survey is also very open to being "gamed." If you were a student at good old Acme Law School, and you knew that your employment options and starting salaries depended to some substantial degree upon the rating of your school, would you not consider rating the school as better than perfect in every survey category so as to improve your employment prospects? This is particularly true of students at schools that are not atop employers' rankings: Those who have limited job prospects are more likely to take this survey seriously than are those at Harvard, Michigan, and so on.

Another potential source of bias concerns the nature of the students who choose to attend different schools. It is quite possible that those attending Harvard are sophisticates who demand the best, who went to Harvard expecting to have the best possible professors for each and every course, and would be disappointed if they did not have the most famous and pedagogically able professor for each course. (Of course, even those who initially had more mundane expectations might have their expectations change upon being immersed in the Harvard atmosphere.) Students who go to Washington & Lee might have very different, very reasonable expectations. Thus, the ratings by these different groups of students might not be readily comparable.

THE INSIDER'S GUIDE TO THE TOP FIFTEEN LAW SCHOOLS

Methodology. The author apparently examined a wide range of other surveys and rankings, ranging from that of *U.S. News* to those of various legal publications and popular journals. The resulting ranking was, presumably, an informed personal opinion rather than a scientific effort of some undisclosed nature.

Advantages of this approach. The strengths of this book are more a matter of its descriptions of the 15 schools it highlights than the order in which it places them. That said, however, the notion of producing a consensus view of other assessments is by no means unreasonable.

Limitations of this approach. As with *Inside the Law Schools,* discussed above, the impressionistic approach to ranking does not allow for a detailed criticism of methodology, except to say that there is no way of knowing how sensible the actual approach employed was (or was not).

THE RANKINGS CONTROVERSY

Several years ago the deans of most of the leading (and also-ran) law schools in the country signed a vicious, and near-hysterical, letter attacking the ranking of law schools. Because the rankings were not perfect, went their argument, no rankings should be published. (*U.S. News* was the intended target of this attack because of its predominance in this field.)

This was hysterical, of course, even in ways they did not intend. First of all, the tone of the letter was a caricature of all the worst qualities of lawyers. It was whining, outraged, and immoderate, the product of downtrodden victims. Second, it treated the users of rankings as small children who would never be able to extract value from a ranking without being misled to their detriment. (What an interesting view these deans have of their future students.) Third, the deans themselves often play up these same rankings whenever they are not about to be quoted in the press. One marvelous example: Stanford's Dean Paul Brest (a signatory of the notorious deans' letter), upon his recent retirement, sent a valedictory letter to Stanford Law alums. His first substantive comment bragged about how well Stanford had recently done in the *U.S. News* rankings, while joking that the rankings were flawed insofar as they had failed to place it first.

A more reasonable response to the *U.S. News* rankings would be to encourage various publications that routinely rank business schools and other educational programs to rank law schools along lines favored by the schools. Having a full set of different rankings available in the marketplace would presumably provide a better rounded view of the schools and lessen the impact of any one approach to rankings. No one at these schools has yet taken such a proactive view of how to respond. Instead, they remain locked in the complaint culture of American law.

In fact, there is an even more troubling aspect to the deans' conduct. They treat the *U.S. News* rankings as though they are a major, avoidable tragedy. Unfortunately, they quite miss the point. Going to Michigan instead of Berkeley— or vice versa—due to a misplaced reliance on some rankings is highly unlikely to destroy someone's life. What is tragic, however, is the dirty little secret the deans fail to acknowledge: So many people who enter law school end up desperately unhappy in the profession. Thus, the critical choice applicants make is not between two high-ranked law schools, but between attending law school and doing something else altogether.

The deans do not wage any protests about this, or write outraged letters to editors. Indeed, they do not even study the fate of their own graduates. What longitudinal studies correlating graduates' happiness with the number of years worked before law school, the nature of that work, the field that the graduates entered after law school, the nature of their employer, and so on have the deans commissioned?

The career services directors at the schools are very clear that a large minority of graduates are sorry that they entered law. Why are they not on the admissions committees at the law schools? Why do the applications not require, as business schools do, that applicants demonstrate that they have explored their career options and thought seriously about them?

It is not *U.S. News* that has a case to answer, it is the deans.

ADMISSIONS DIRECTORS DISCUSS THE "DEANS' LETTER"

Relative to business schools, we rely more on numbers than on qualitative factors. The law school rankings do likewise. How can we throw stones when we live in glass houses   Janice Austin, Assistant Dean for Admissions, University of Pennsylvania

The reality is that they (the rankings) aren't the only sources candidates use in making decisions. The deans' letter was a bit paternalistic in assuming that candidates would use the rankings and no other information.   Don Rebstock, Associate Dean of Admissions and Financial Aid, Northwestern

---

OTHER RANKINGS

Obviously, the published rankings do not necessarily cover all of the issues and concerns you might have about law schools. This leaves you with room to make your own rankings, tailored to whichever criteria you deem to be most important. Following are a few of the "rankings" you might consider helpful.

DEPARTMENTAL RANKINGS

If you are farsighted enough to have decided what type of lawyer you aim to be, it would be wise to consider not only overall school rankings but departmental ones as well. In fact, departmental rankings may well be less subject to the vagaries of imperfect methodologies than are school rankings. This is because professors and employers are likely to have a much better sense of the facilities, teaching standards, and courses within their own specializations. An environmental law professor's assessment of other top schools' environmental programs is likely to be well informed.

Besides consulting published departmental rankings (such as those in *U.S. News*), be sure to talk to employers in the particular field. Ask them to give a rough ranking of schools offering concentrations in that field.

JOINT-DEGREE RANKINGS

If you are considering getting a joint degree, pay attention to the ranking of the other program. Depending on your intended career path, the reputation of the non-law program may be the more important of the two.

LAW SCHOOL HIRING PRACTICES

If you are not planning to waste your time practicing law, but have your heart set on teaching it, you would be wise to formulate your own ranking of law schools. Regardless of what people tell you, the road to a tenured teaching position is very narrow indeed. A professor of law was undoubtedly ranked at the pinnacle of his or her class, and almost certainly attended one of the most exclusive schools in the country. In fact, if you read through the faculty biographies in any Top 40 school's catalog, you will start to notice a trend. Of all tenured professors who received their JDs after 1980 or so, almost all of them come from the same very limited set of schools.

What this should tell you is that if you are absolutely unrelenting in your ambition to teach the law, you should attend one of the very top schools or do not bother at all. Tally up the number of professors according to the schools from which they received their degrees and calculate which programs are the hot spots for future academics.

JUDICIAL CLERKSHIPS

Many law school graduates want to get a judicial clerkship, some for the prestige, others for both the prestige and the learning opportunities. It is clear that Yale sends a much greater percentage of its class to clerkships than do other top schools:

| Yale | 47.5% |
| Harvard | 28.4% |

Stanford	25.8%
Chicago	24.7%
Virginia	21.4%
Columbia	21.1%
Michigan	20.6%
Cornell	17.2%
Penn	16.5%
NYU	16.1%
Berkeley (Boalt Hall)	15.1%
Boston College	13.1%
Duke	12.6%
George Washington	12.3%
Northwestern	11.7%
Hastings	11.7%
Georgetown	11.5%
Texas	10.5%
UC Davis	6.7%
UCLA	6.0%

As is usually the case, however, this data is not unambiguous. Is Yale more successful in garnering clerkship laurels for its graduates, or do its graduates disproportionately seek clerkships? Clerkships are a natural halfway house for those intending to litigate or to teach—or to avoid committing to a real job for another year or two. Those intending to be transactional lawyers, on the other hand, will seldom seek a clerkship because they are likely to learn little that will be of direct relevance to doing deals. Yale certainly produces a lot of graduates who would like to do public interest litigation, work for the government in litigation-related fields, or teach law. They also have a lot of graduates who are still uncertain what they want to do in the long run, which is fitting for a school that prides itself on taking a more intellectual (and thus less pre-professional) approach to the study of law than do most of its counterparts. This attracts a lot of people who want their graduate study to resemble their undergraduate work: to be a continuation of a liberal arts education.

NUMBER OF SUPREME COURT CLERKSHIPS

A Supreme Court clerkship is one of the most prestigious honors to be bestowed on a law student. Open the catalog of any top law program and you will come across the proud statement that, in the most recent graduating class, X number of students are clerking at the Supreme Court. Divide the total number of students in the class by number X and you are on your way to constructing a ranking. One of the problems, of course, is whether to consider only the results of the last year or two, or to look over a much longer period. Given the relatively few clerks chosen each year, the data is "lumpy," meaning that considering only the results of the recent past may overstate the significance of each data point. Going back 20 years, however, risks placing too much emphasis on past reputation.

NUMBER OF RECRUITERS ON CAMPUS

It is a simple matter to divide the number of employers visiting the campus by the number of students graduating. The higher this number, of course, the more employment opportunities are likely to be on offer for the school's students. This is certainly valuable as a very rough and ready guide. If one school has only one-and-a-half employers per student whereas another school has ten employers visit for each graduating student, it is a reasonably safe bet that students at the latter school will have more employment offers from which to choose.

As with most such figures, however, this one should not be pushed too far. The difference between having eight employers and ten employers recruiting each student is hardly likely to be meaningful. After all, you can only work for one. As a means of comparing disparate schools, this too faces limitations. It is not clear whether a school with ten employers per student is twice as good as a school with five employers per student, or just marginally better. For instance, imagine that both you and your closest friend applied to the same ten law schools. You got into all of them and decided to attend Harvard; your friend was accepted only by Harvard (being denied by the other nine), and decided to attend Harvard. Did you do ten times as well as your friend in this situation, somewhat better, or only very marginally better?

NON-LAW EMPLOYERS RECRUITING ON CAMPUS

If you think you might want to work outside of law, you probably should not attend law school. If you remain determined to go to law school, though, you should consider attending a school that has successfully placed graduates in the nonlegal field you are considering. Similarly, you should check to see whether these employers recruit from a given school. For someone interested in strategy consulting, for example, it would be sensible to see how many of the "big four" consulting firms (Bain, Booz-Allen, Boston Consulting Group, McKinsey) recruit on campus. If you are interested in investment banking, check how many of the bulge bracket firms recruit there—and repeat the exercise for whatever boutique firms or specialists are of interest to you. The same exercise can be performed for whatever field or fields interest you.

SHOULD DATA BE GIVEN IN ABSOLUTE OR RELATIVE TERMS?

One of the methodological issues for which there is no definitively "right" answer is whether to adjust data from absolute numbers to per capita—or proportional—figures. For example, should the number of Supreme Court clerks per school be given as a total or adjusted for the number of graduating students per school? Consider a hypothetical example, with only two schools to choose from. If Harvard had 20 clerks and Yale 10, but Harvard had four times the graduating class size of Yale, what would be the "correct" figures?

	TOTAL CLERKS	NUMBER OF CLERKS PER 100 STUDENTS
Harvard	20	3.33
Yale	10	6.67

A case can be made for either measurement. If you want to attend the school with a higher percentage of future clerks, you would opt for Yale (assuming that past performance was an accurate indicator of future results). You might figure that more of your time would be spent around one or another of these paragons than in a school in which they were more dispersed across the student body. Or you might assume that this figure was an indicator of the school's overall quality.

Under some circumstances, however, you might prefer Harvard. You might want to get to know the greatest number of future clerks so as to have the best network later in life, or because you planned to write an exposé of the Supreme Court and wanted the greatest number of sources. You might also believe that future clerks would be likely to identify one another and stick together, thereby giving you the greatest concentration of them at Harvard rather than Yale—presuming, of course, that socializing or intellectualizing with them was your primary goal for law school.

This is by no means the most intractable of methodological problems—that distinction may belong to the question of how different variables should be weighted to produce an overall ranking. But by realizing how a simple matter is open to differing views, you can understand just how complicated ranking schools really is.

OTHER POSSIBLE RANKINGS

The five rankings discussed in the first part of this chapter use various means to arrive at their results. They could use any number of other approaches. Nothing stops you from ranking schools on the basis of what most interests you. For example, you might choose any one or more of the following:

- Percent men (or women, or minorities, or Asian-Americans, or foreigners)
- Percent of incoming students with more than five years' experience (or over the age of 30)
- Number of books used by other top schools produced by faculty of a given school (perhaps adjusted by number of faculty)
- Citation index: number of citations (in the leading journals) of articles written by a school's faculty (perhaps adjusted by number of faculty)
- Number of top 100 (500) firms run by graduates of the school (perhaps adjusted by number of graduates)
- Percent of graduates entering a specific field (public interest, environmental, tax, criminal, and so on)
- Number of courses in your chosen field (or percentage of courses offered in that field)

Each of these could be a valid measure for what you most desire. The first two measures, for instance, are means of determining whether you will have classmates who are most like you—or most unlike you, if you look to learn from those who least resemble you—whereas the next two measures can be used to assess the scholarliness of the faculty. There are innumerable other possible bases for rankings, depending upon what you seek from your law school education.

CONCLUSION

It is impossible for a ranking to assess (accurately or otherwise) the large number of concerns, requirements, and questions that every conscientious law school applicant has. As an *approximate* gauge of a school's reputation, however, the rankings—taken together—can be useful indicators. Their rough and ready nature, however, suggests that they should be indicating the broad class to which a school belongs rather than the precise ranking it should enjoy.

Ultimately, whether the rankings *determine* reputation or *measure* it ceases to be the issue. The school considered "best"—by whatever standards—will generally attract the "best" students and "best" employers. Because you are bound to benefit as much from your peers as your professors, and are undoubtedly concerned primarily about your job opportunities, reputation is an extremely important factor to consider.

ADMISSIONS DIRECTORS DISCUSS THE RANKINGS

What Is Wrong With the Rankings

Most users of the rankings are not sophisticated enough to assess how the rankings have been calculated. The result is a bad combination: unsavvy users plus real problems in measurement.   Janice Austin, Assistant Dean for Admissions, University of Pennsylvania

We analyze undergraduate performance from a multivariate perspective. We consider such factors as grade inflation patterns (which vary significantly across the universe of undergraduate colleges), the rigor of the applicant's course of study, and the selectivity of the college attended. Of the more than two thousand colleges in this country alone, there exists a remarkable range of selectivity (and resultant student quality). That not all colleges are equal in terms of their selectivity and student quality is widely known, but, for reasons I have never been able to understand, an educational reality ignored by many law schools as they undertake their own student selection. Similarly, *U.S. News & World Report* (which accords forty percent of its selectivity to UGPA) fails to recognize these contextual realities in weighing median grade-point average. Jim Milligan, Dean of Admissions, Columbia

Some rankings put inordinate weight on LSAT and GPA numbers, thereby putting pressure on us (via deans wanting to move up in the rankings). Some schools lower down in the rankings have fired their admissions professionals for failing to hit certain GPA and LSAT medians.   Shelli Soto, Dean of Admissions, University of Texas

U.S. News is probably wrong in failing to adjust acceptance rates for class size. The applicant pool for top schools is largely fixed; inevitably, therefore, larger programs accept a higher percentage of applicants. I have recommended to them that they use yield ratios (percent of applicants admitted who actually enroll) instead of acceptance rates, in calculating their selectivity index.   Jim Milligan, Dean of Admissions, Columbia

What Is Right With the Rankings

The rankings perform a useful function by keeping schools from becoming complacent. They need to work hard to keep their rankings.   Don Rebstock, Associate Dean of Admissions and Financial Aid, Northwestern

It's a little too "holier than thou" to object that since we're institutions of higher learning, it's foolhardy, misleading, and sinful to rank us. We have consumers like any other business. It isn't the worst thing possible. It is, for the most part, O.K. and mirrors the reality of law schools' quality.   Andy Cornblatt, Assistant Dean for Admissions, Georgetown

Our dean didn't sign the "deans' letter" protesting the use of rankings because they are a reality of our society and because—if you look at the groupings within those rankings—they tend to be pretty accurate reflections of how the public views the schools, which is highly relevant to the decision of which school to attend.   Don Rebstock, Associate Dean of Admissions and Financial Aid, Northwestern

How You Should Use the Rankings

Don't try to quantify the nonquantifiable; just get a good overview picture of the schools.   Joyce Curll, Assistant Dean for Admissions and Financial Aid, Harvard

The rankings are most useful for applicants at the beginning of the search process, to get the lay of the land regarding what schools are considered most seriously. They can help to develop a general understanding of the law school landscape and applicants can assess their chances of admission to a particular school.   Jim Milligan, Dean of Admissions, Columbia

Too many students make decisions about where to go to law school based on the rankings without finding the right fit for themselves.   Dennis Shields, Assistant Dean for Admissions and Financial Aid, Duke

[I]t's important for people to think about what they consider the factors that are important in a school, and to think about what's behind the rankings. They should recognize what *U.S. News* uses to rank schools. Don't take a numerical ranking as definitive. Instead, consider whether you'd evaluate a school in the same way as the ranking entity did.   Erica Munzel, Director of Admissions, University of Michigan

Most admissions folks find the rankings a bit unfortunate in that applicants take them too seriously. It's very difficult to quantify and portray a large number of relevant factors and combine them into a single measure of quality. William Hoye, Dean for Admissions, USC

To a certain extent, the law school world created the rankings. For a long time we all claimed to be all things to all people. There was thus a need for some reasonably objective approach to give applicants some sense of the relative quality of different programs. The problem is that applicants rely too much on the rankings, which should be no more than a starting point for them.   Elizabeth Rosselot, Director of Admissions, Boston College

Many rankings should be subjected to close scrutiny due to the methodologies they employ. You can and should get a general idea from them of the reputation a school enjoys. Using them to choose between school number fifteen and school number twenty, however, is a problem.   Shelli Soto, Dean of Admissions, University of Texas

How the Rankings Affect What Law Schools Do

Law schools live and die by the rankings. Janice Austin, Assistant Dean for Admissions, University of Pennsylvania

The rankings have changed the admissions profession, perhaps irrevocably. What used to be a private, school-centered, professional practice has become a highly public one. Because the rankings so heavily focus on median LSAT scores, acceptance percentages, and the like, many law schools, regrettably, pay inordinate attention to quantifiable factors. At many American law schools, the role of the admissions professional has changed, sad to say, from one of counselor and student advocate to that of a salesperson or agent. Jim Milligan, Dean of Admissions, Columbia

People "game" the numbers they report to *U.S. News*. This is especially likely to be the case for those schools that move up a lot in one year. Unfortunately there is no effective check on the *U.S. News* numbers. Janice Austin, Assistant Dean for Admissions, University of Pennsylvania

The schools play to the rankings, of course, which then hurts the applicants. Schools now manage their yields, wait-listing qualified students or denying them if it seems that they probably would not attend the school. It means that schools now make the decisions for the applicants rather than letting the applicants themselves decide. For example, I've heard that some Midwestern schools seldom accept Ivy League candidates since they tend not to go to the Midwest rather than the coasts. Because of the way the rankings are constructed, it's hard to reconcile what is best for the institution with what is best for the applicant. Elizabeth Rosselot, Director of Admissions, Boston College

Due to *U.S. News* we [the law schools and admissions offices] are all a little more numbers-driven than we otherwise would be. Dennis Shields, Assistant Dean for Admissions and Financial Aid, Duke

5

THE ADMISSIONS PROCESS

— EXECUTIVE SUMMARY —

Schools put enormous effort into considering each person's application.

■

Most schools use rolling admissions and a fairly standard admissions model.

■

Understand the criteria that law schools evaluate: brains, legal potential, and personal attributes.

—Remember that admissions professionals, mindful of
the need to fill classes with human
beings rather than data points, seek to understand who you are as well as
what you have accomplished.

■

The top schools also value diversity in their classes.

This chapter describes the mechanics of how schools make their admissions decisions and who makes them. In most cases, a school's admissions professionals will determine whether to admit you or not based upon the whole of your application folder—your job histories, educational achievements, extracurricular and community involvements, honors and awards, personal statement and other essays, recommendations, and interview evaluations. Not every admissions officer will weight the different elements in the same way, or for that matter grade them in the same way, but the *process* is consistent for each and every applicant to a school. While the admissions process at different schools varies somewhat, it varies much less than might be expected—partly because admissions officers at the various schools talk with one another about procedures—but probably owing more to the desire schools have to be thorough in their evaluation of candidates. Schools go to great lengths to be sure they have given every applicant a fair chance.

"ROLLING" ADMISSIONS

Most of the top law schools adhere to a rolling admission process, in which applications are evaluated as they are submitted. The school begins to accept applications sometime in the fall (often October 1, but occasionally as early as September 1 or as late as December 1) and will continue to accept them for several months (usually through February 1 or 15). Applicants will generally learn of the school's decision within a month or two (or three) of the completion of their files, although there is considerable difference in the speed at which various schools respond.

Note that your application will receive no attention from admissions officers until it has been completed, meaning that *everything* that is required has been received by the school. Thus, if your second (but still required) recommendation has not yet been submitted, the admissions secretarial staff will keep your file open until they receive the recommendation, at which time they will indicate to the admissions officers that your file is now ready.

THE STANDARD ADMISSIONS MODEL

WHO ARE THE ADMISSIONS DIRECTORS?

The Director of Admissions is typically someone who has worked in law school admissions for some years. At the top schools, this generally means someone who has had at least five years' experience as a more junior admissions officer at the same school, or an equivalent amount of time in charge of admissions at a less prestigious school.

WHO IS ON THE ADMISSIONS COMMITTEE?

Generally, the Admissions Committee includes four to seven faculty members who have been selected either by the Dean or the Director. The appointment of faculty members to the Committee is on a rotational basis. The selected professors are most often tenured, and come from all different fields at the school. The school's admissions director may sit on the committee; if not, he or she will be utilized as a consultant to it. In addition, a number of schools now include students on the admissions committee. They may be voting members or just advisors.

HOW ARE DECISIONS MADE?

There are several models for making admissions decisions. One that is commonly used has the Director of Admissions be the first reader of all files. She will then immediately accept those she feels are outstanding, reject those who are clearly below the school's quality cutoff, and forward a modest number in the "middle group" to the admissions committee. The faculty members on the committee will, among themselves, come to a consensus about which of these files to admit.

A variation on this model has each of several admissions officers give a first reading to various files, with each person having the power to accept or reject the obvious winners and losers but, once again, referring those on the margin to the whole admissions committee (or to other admissions officers). In this variation, it is common for the admissions director to cast a quick glance over the various files he or she has not been assigned, just to make sure that nothing is amiss in the process.

Another approach has two admissions officers give a "blind" reading to an applicant's file, meaning that each one reads without knowing what the other officer has decided. If both admissions officers rate the applicant as an "accept," then no more work needs to be done: The applicant is accepted. Similarly, if both admissions officers rate her as a "reject," the applicant is rejected. On the other hand, if they disagree about her, or both rate her as an "uncertain," then her file will be considered further. At this point most schools have the admissions committee decide as a group.

Thus, the role of the admissions committee is typically to decide the hard cases, generally with the input of the admissions director or other senior admissions officer—or to add perspective to the reading of a file when one or another of its members has specialized knowledge that can help illuminate a candidacy. For example, a faculty member on the committee who has taught in Italy may be able to interpret an Italian academic record more expertly than can an admissions officer.

THE CRITERIA

Chicago has explained what it looks for in candidates: "Our task is to select those candidates who appear to demonstrate exceptional academic and professional promise and, at the same time, put together a stimulating and diverse entering class."

Strong academic promise. "We seek indications that an applicant has the discipline and ability to handle a demanding program. The overall quality of the undergraduate school attended and its grading practices will often be important considerations in interpreting the GPA."

Professional promise. "We will review the transcripts . . . to determine the difficulty of the courses taken and whether the college record has given the applicant an opportunity to demonstrate analytical skills and the ability to speak and write with precision, fluency, and economy."

Diversity among students. "We make special efforts to ensure that each entering class contains students from a variety of racial, ethnic, educational, and geographic backgrounds. Such diversity provides students with new perspectives on the law and promotes informed discussions inside and outside the classroom. We are particularly interested in receiving applications from women and minority candidates, two groups traditionally underrepresented in the law."

Other schools look for similar qualities. One easy way to learn what the top law schools want is to look at the recommendation forms they use. These typically ask a recommender to comment on specific qualities or to check boxes in a grid, indicating whether the applicant's analytical ability, for example, is in the top 2 percent, 5 percent, 10 percent, 25 percent, 50 percent, or bottom half of those the recommender has seen at similar stages in their careers. Leading schools ask recommenders to evaluate similar qualities. The schools in the chart below ask their recommenders to rate or evaluate applicants on the qualities indicated.

	CORNELL	GEORGETOWN	NORTHWESTERN
Maturity	x	x	x
Leadership	x	x	x
Intellectual Ability	x	x	x
Judgment	x	x	
Communication Skills	x	x	x
Character		x	x
Self-Discipline	x	x	x
Concern for Others	x		x

Georgetown and Columbia have particularly detailed forms. Using the Georgetown criteria as a starting point, and "mapping" Columbia's onto it, reveals how similar are their interests:

GEORGETOWN	COLUMBIA

Native Intelligence
  Analytical powers
  Rigor of thought
  Critical facility
  Reasoning ability
	Overall Intelligence
	  Analytical skills
	  Problem-solving skills

Independence of Thought
  Originality
  Imagination
  Creative intelligence
	Independence of Thought
	  Originality

Effectiveness of Communication
  Oral
  Written
	Effectiveness of Communication
	  Oral
	  Written

Industry and Motivation
  Persistence
  Self-discipline
  Study techniques
	Industry and Motivation
	  Academic motivation, industry, persistence
	  Personal initiative

Judgment and Maturity
  Conscientiousness
  Common sense
  Leadership ability
	Judgment and Maturity
	  Personal initiative
	  Judgment
	  Emotional maturity
	  Leadership ability

Personal Attributes
  Ability to relate
	Personal Attributes
	  Concern for others
	  Self-confidence
	  Organizational skills

The picture that emerges suggests that these two schools are looking for candidates who are very similar to the Chicago profile. That profile could be summarized as: brains, demonstrated potential for the rigors of legal study, and outstanding personal characteristics.

THE EVIDENCE SCHOOLS EXAMINE

	PRIMARY SOURCES	SECONDARY SOURCES
BRAINS	Undergraduate record LSAT scores	Work experience Additional coursework Essays
LEGAL POTENTIAL	LSAT scores Work experience	Essays Extracurriculars
PERSONAL ATTRIBUTES	Essays Recommendations Interviews	Extracurriculars Additional materials

THE CRITERIA TRADE-OFF

The question inevitably arises: How do admissions directors determine whom to accept, given that some applicants will have outstanding job records or extracurricular credentials but unimpressive grades and LSAT scores, whereas other applicants will have the reverse set of strengths and weaknesses? In other words, how do admissions directors trade off the different admission criteria? There is no set answer to this. There are, however, three considerations to keep in mind.

First of all, it is important to understand that the top schools do not need to make many such trade-offs. The Yales, Stanfords, and Harvards are in the enviable position of having many applicants with sterling undergraduate records, impressive work experience, and significant extracurricular achievements, which negates the need to trade off criteria.

Second, schools will weight criteria differently depending upon the applicant. For example, someone who is still in college and has had one part-time job at a restaurant can expect to have his undergraduate record, extracurricular activities, and LSAT scores count very heavily. Someone with seven years of work experience can expect that somewhat less weight will be placed on the academic measures; her extensive experience provides a great deal of information about her, making her experience a much more important indicator of her potential than it was for the man still in college.

Third, different schools will have different priorities, causing them to apply a somewhat different set of criteria, and criteria weighting, to the process. Northwestern, for instance, is taking fewer and fewer students straight from college; it values the depth and nature of work experience more than do other schools.

THE IMPORTANCE OF DIVERSITY

Law schools believe strongly in the values of diversity. They feel that a mixture of races, nationalities, educational experiences, and job backgrounds in their student bodies enhances the learning process and also makes for a more attractive group of graduates, given that employers need a wide range of potential recruits. Schools express their desire for diversity partly by marketing intensively to hard-to-attract groups, partly by adjusting admissions standards for those it most desires (especially African-Americans and Latinos). Schools' desire for diversity inevitably influences how they evaluate their applicants.

WHO YOU ARE IS IMPORTANT

Admissions officers have a lot of information about you when it comes time to make their decisions. Most applicants assume that the admissions process is devoted *only* to weighing applicants' grade-point averages and LSAT test scores and they therefore make a fundamental mistake. Admissions offices are made up of human beings, generally those who have chosen to work in a human resources capacity, and consequently they are particularly interested in admitting real human beings rather than a set of statistics. You will find it hard to gain admission if you are just so many data points on a page. Applicants who can make themselves real, that is, human, are more likely to gain supporters among the admissions officers and committee members. You should therefore take every opportunity to distinguish yourself from the mass of the applicant pool and make your human qualities apparent. The reason it takes so much time and effort to accept or reject a given applicant is because admissions officers try very hard to understand the person, not just to glance at the test scores.

THE USE OF INDEX NUMBERS

The most important differences in various schools' decision-making processes concern the use of index numbers. See the sidebar for more information.

INDEX NUMBERS

Many schools use an "index number" to aid their selection process. This number is constructed by applying a formula to an applicant's undergraduate grade-point average and LSAT score. For instance, the University of Virginia's formula recently has been:

$$(4.159 \times UGPA) + (.24 \times LSAT) + 2.0 = Index$$

An applicant with a 3.0 undergraduate GPA and an LSAT score of 170 would have an index number of approximately 55.3. An applicant with a 3.6 and 160 would have a roughly equivalent index number (approximately 55.4). (Thus, within this range, each LSAT point equates to about .06 GPA.)

These formulas are constructed by the Law School Admission Council (also called LSAC or Law Services) for the schools that choose to use them. The schools provide Law Services with the LSAT, undergraduate GPA, and first-year law school grades of the most recent first-year class. Law Services then determines what weighting of the LSAT and undergraduate GPA would have best predicted the first-year law school grades of that year's class. Because the calculations are revised annually, and differ according to school, the weights accorded to the LSAT and GPA results can vary substantially. (The precise weighting of the two inputs is not even uniform for a given school in a given year, due to the fact that the ranges of the LSAT score and the GPA are very different. The technical discussion of this is beyond the scope of this book and, accordingly, will not be included here.) Very roughly, the weighting can vary from about one-third LSAT, two-thirds GPA to the reverse. The vast majority of schools' formulas, however, place no more than 60 percent weight on one of the two factors.

The ways in which schools use index numbers vary almost as much as the formulas they use. The devotees of easy decision-making use it as their primary decision-making tool. Those applicants with index numbers above a chosen cutoff are accepted; those below it are rejected.

Some schools use a refined version of this system. They adjust the GPA component of the index number for such things as the quality of school attended, the grading policy of the school, and the difficulty of the specific curriculum followed. Thus, someone who did mechanical engineering at the United States Military Academy (Army)—a very demanding major, at a top-quality school, with a very tough grading policy—would be treated quite differently from someone who majored in criminal justice at a community college. A 3.0 GPA for the former student would be impressive; a 3.0 for the latter would not be.

Other schools use an index number to select students for part of their class and a file-by-file analysis to fill the rest of it. Hastings, for example, fills approximately half of its class using an unadjusted index number; it fills the other half by looking closely at people's applications, not just their GPA and LSAT data.

A very common way to use index numbers is to consider people above a specified index number to be "presumptive admits"; people below a certain cutoff are considered "presumptive rejects"; and people with scores between these two will require a close, individualized look at their files. The files of the presumptive admits are examined to make sure there is nothing amiss—no trouble-making at college, no choosing the easiest courses on campus, no felony convictions, and so on. The vast majority of those in this category will be accepted. The same is true, in reverse, of those in the presumptive reject category. Their files are examined to see whether there are hidden talents and experiences. If not (true for the vast majority in this category), they are rejected.

Another, very common way to use an index number is to sort people's files by index number, but not to rely on the number for decision-making purposes. Some schools using this approach read all files of a given index number at one time; they are trying to compare "like" with "like." Others assign applicants' files to admissions officers on the basis of their index number. One officer, for instance, will be given the top sixth of files (based, of course, upon their respective index numbers).

Two factors account for most of the variation in the use of index numbers. In general, the more prestigious and higher ranked a school, the less it will rely on an index number in its decision-making. (Many of the top-ranked schools make no use at all of index numbers.) State law schools, by the same token, are more likely to rely on index numbers in their decision-making than are private schools. Given their greater need to justify their decisions—to legislatures as well as applicants—using an index number confers a spurious precision and fairness to their decisions, making them more readily defensible.

Behind the use of index numbers, of course, lurks the specter of the *U.S. News & World Report* rankings, which place such inordinate weight on LSAT and GPA data. (See Chapter 4 for a further discussion of rankings of law schools.)

The grids displayed in *The Official Guide to U.S. Law Schools* (showing what number of students with a given LSAT score and GPA apply, and how many are accepted) give a rough picture of the way various schools value LSAT score relative to GPA.

ADMISSIONS OUTCOMES

There are four different outcomes to admissions deliberations. You can be admitted or rejected, of course. You can also be put on a wait-list. If the committee feels it needs more time in order to accurately assess a specific application, however, it may place the application in a "reserve" or "hold" category. This is most likely to occur to someone who has applied early in the application season and whose credentials put him or her on the margin.

THE LAW SCHOOL DATA
ASSEMBLY SERVICE

Almost all of the American Bar Association-approved law schools require applicants to subscribe to the Law School Data Assembly Service (LSDAS). LSDAS is administered by the Law School Admission Council (LSAC), a non-profit corporation established to coordinate and streamline the law school admission process. All law schools approved by the ABA are LSAC members.

For each law school to which you are applying, LSDAS prepares a uniformly-formatted report. The report contains information that schools use, in conjunction with the individual application and personal statement, to evaluate your file. The information contained in the report includes:

➤ An undergraduate academic summary

➤ Copies of all undergraduate, graduate, and law school/professional transcripts

➤ LSAT scores and writing sample copies

➤ Copies of letters of recommendation processed by LSAC

The Law School Report, compiled by the LSDAS, must be received by law schools in order for your application to be deemed complete. This report provides officers with a standardized version of many elements in your file, including a summary of all academic transcripts (see below) and scores. Additionally, the report contains what is called the admission "index number" (discussed in detail previously).

GRADE CONVERSION

LSDAS simplifies your grades into a standard 4.0 system to make it easy to compare candidates. A common set of numerical values has been selected to represent the various grading systems used by different colleges. LSDAS does not attempt to assess the value of grades earned at each college. Along with the converted grades, copies of all transcripts are included. It is important to note that only undergraduate grades are represented in the index number. Grades received in graduate and other programs do not affect it.

GRADE CONVERSION TABLE*

LSDAS CONVERSION 4.0 SCALE	A TO F	1 TO 5	0–100	GRADES	GRADES
				GRADES AS REPORTED ON TRANSCRIPTS	
4.33	A+	1+	98–100	Highest passing grade (4.0)	Highest passing grade (4.0)
4.00	A	1	93–97		
3.67	A–	1–	90–92		
3.33	B+	2+	87–89	Second highest passing grade (3.0)	Middle passing grade (3.0)
3.00	B	2	83–86		
2.67	B–	2–	80–82		
2.50	BC				
2.33	C+	3+	77–79	Third highest passing grade (2.0)	Lowest passing grade (2.0)
2.00	C	3	73–76		
1.67	C–	3–	70–72		
1.50	CD				
1.33	D+	4+	67–69	Lowest passing grade (1.0)	
1.00	D	4	63–66		
0.67	D–	4–	60–62		
0.50	DE or DF				
.00	E and F	5	Below 60	Failure (0.0)	Failure (0.0)

*Grades Excluded from the Conversion:
- Classes from which you have withdrawn
- Classes receiving an "Incomplete" grade which the school has deemed to be nonpunitive
- Grades awarded after the undergraduate degree was received
- Grades assigned no credit
- Passing grades from systems of one or two passing grades (e.g., Pass/Fail)
- A No Credit grade not signifying failure, and for which no attempt at credit was made

For a complete description of the nuances involved in this conversion process as well as the other elements of the report, consult the information given in the *LSAT & LSDAS Registration & Information Book,* provided by:

Law School Admission Council
Box 2000
661 Penn Street
Newtown, PA 18940–0998
Tel. (215) 968-1001
Fax: (215) 968-1119
Internet: www.lsac.org
E-mail: lsacinfo@lsac.org

ADMISSIONS DIRECTORS DISCUSS ADMISSIONS PROCEDURES

How the Process Works at Their Schools

The admissions staff generally make eighty-plus percent of decisions. Ten to twenty percent go to the admissions committee.   Andy Cornblatt, Assistant Dean for Admissions, Georgetown

Applications are not evaluated by our Admissions Committee until all required materials have been received, and are generally evaluated in the order in which they are completed. All files are read by at least two admissions officers. The Columbia system does not recognize any applicant as either a "presumptive admit" or "presumptive deny" based solely on the quantifiable indices of LSAT score and undergraduate grade-point average.   Jim Milligan, Dean of Admissions, Columbia

We do not use students in the admissions selection process. Files are read initially by admissions officers, then by faculty on the admissions committee. One or another of the readers will bring insight to the specifics of a given file, knowing that X is a hard major at that school (even though it is soft elsewhere), that grading at that school is particularly tough, or that a recommender writes very positive letters for many applicants each year.   Joyce Curll, Assistant Dean for Admissions and Financial Aid, Harvard

We try to make rapid decisions on the clear cases: roughly forty-five percent are handled in one review. In the other fifty-five percent of cases, the initial reader passes on the file, with comments and recommendations, to the faculty. We assign faculty readership by undergraduate institution so that faculty members can develop familiarity with schools, grading, recommenders. We show the faculty reader what happened with, for example, the Princeton pool last year to give them the context for making this year's decisions. We give them the current, weekly statistics regarding the Princeton pool: What actions have already been taken, with index data included for each candidate.   Albert R. Turnbull, Associate Dean for Admissions and Career Services, University of Virginia

The first reader of a file can accept, reject, or pass the file on. If she passes the file on, she can send it to a second reader or to the whole admissions committee, and in either case it can be with or without a recommendation (to admit or deny). Our committee includes professors and five third-year students, who are involved both in making admissions policy and reading and voting on files. Shelli Soto, Dean of Admissions, University of Texas

The file is read first by the dean or director of admissions. All files are read carefully.   Michael Rappoport, Dean of Admissions, UCLA

All files are initially read by me. I will then pass certain files on to the Committee for another review. There are no presumptive admits nor are there presumptive denies. I treat each individual part of an application as a piece of a larger puzzle. A careful read allows me to see how those pieces fit together.   Faye Deal, Associate Dean for Admissions and Financial Aid, Stanford

If we feel that there is a gap in an application, or something that bears further explanation, we may contact the applicant to address it. We might even invite them to write an essay on the matter.   Erica Munzel, Director of Admissions, University of Michigan

Composition of the Admissions Committee

We have a couple third-year students on the faculty admissions committee. There is no risk of a breach of confidentiality since they will have graduated by the time an applicant whose file they read enters law school.   Erica Munzel, Director of Admissions, University of Michigan

The admissions committee consists of five faculty members; we do not involve students in the process.   Anne Brandt, Director of Admissions, Vanderbilt

Faculty are heavily involved in our process, more so than at other schools.   Jean Webb, Director of Admissions, Yale

The Use of Index Numbers

We don't use an index formula for any purpose whatsoever. We read every file. Kenneth Kleinrock, Assistant Dean for Admissions, NYU

We use an index number only as a first look, because it can hide so many things. There are in fact no cutoff points: We give each file a full review. Our process is a very subjective one. Any piece in the file can be more important than another: personal statements, résumés, good (or bad) letters of recommendation, etc. Of course people with higher numbers do have a better chance of being admitted. Shelli Soto, Dean of Admissions, University of Texas

We use an index formula to give a rank ordering to files (for timing of their reading), not for actual decision making. On one day, I'll read high numbers only; another day, I'll read low numbers only. It helps me get through the volume necessary. If we were to use the formula for decisions, we'd have to tweak it endlessly. Janice Austin, Assistant Dean for Admissions, University of Pennsylvania

We use an index formula. We plug data into the computer and out comes an adjusted grade point. We adjust for the quality of the undergraduate school. We give boosts to GPAs at top schools, including the top public schools, such as Virginia, Wisconsin, Berkeley, and UCLA, as well as the Ivies, Stanford, and so on. The impact is greatest in the middle range of GPAs. This adjustment also takes account of the amount of grade inflation at each school. . . . We use an index number to sort files: Those above the requisite number are presumed admissible unless there are problems. Although we use an index, we consider the details for each file. For example, we note whether the overall GPA is accurate, or has been distorted by one bad year; similarly, we look at trends in grades, majors, course selection, and the like. Michael Rappoport, Dean of Admissions, UCLA

There are no index numbers or formulas used in our decisions. I would say that, in general terms, GPA is roughly equal to one-third of the decision (by the way, there are multiple components to a GPA), LSAT is one-third, and personal and other factors are one-third. If each applicant is trying to jump over a bar, the GPA and LSAT together serve to set the height of the bar: The rest of the application needs to be however good or O.K. to get over the bar at that height. Everybody gets to jump; everybody has to jump. Andy Cornblatt, Assistant Dean for Admissions, Georgetown

We have no automatic admits. Ninety-ninth percentile LSAT and top GPAs are still not automatic admits. Faye Deal, Associate Dean for Admissions and Financial Aid, Stanford

Although we do use index numbers, we make subjective adjustments to them. For engineering and science courses, for example, we expect lower GPAs. Thus a 3.6 in Political Science is comparable to a 3.2 or 3.3 in Engineering. People who attended the top colleges get a little added "star"—although you can't quantify it—because they have faced tougher competition. Don Rebstock, Associate Dean of Admissions and Financial Aid, Northwestern

The process is driven by the index numbers. We separate candidates into three groups on the basis of their numbers. The top group is assumed to be admissible. We read their file primarily to see if something is wrong. For example, did they take only soft courses. We examine their personal statements and recommendations, looking less to see if they are academically qualified than to see if there is some other reason to deny them. The bottom group is assumed to be inadmissible, unless something special is found in their application. The middle group is where we put much of our effort. We look here to diversify our class in terms of geography (American and international), undergraduate major, race, ethnicity, and religion.   Elizabeth Rosselot, Director of Admissions, Boston College

We don't use an index formula to make decisions. We read everyone's file, even those that have lower numbers.   Erica Munzel, Director of Admissions, University of Michigan

We do not use an index number. I think an index number can be a bit of a crutch for admissions people. Because we don't use one, we really have to spend more time looking at each individual file.   Anne Brandt, Director of Admissions, Vanderbilt

Our index numbers don't take account of the specific school, the curriculum followed, grade inflation (the middle of the Stanford class applying to law school has a 3.4 GPA, Princeton a 3.2), etc. We use the crude index number as a rough sorting mechanism; we make up for its crudeness by careful review of individual files. We also use it to compare applicant pools from one year to the next and to set presumptive action categories for the current year.   Albert R. Turnbull, Associate Dean for Admissions and Career Services, University of Virginia

INDEX FORMULAS

We use an index number for an initial sorting of files. Our index formula is: $(0.485 \times \text{LSAT score}) + (8.121 \times \text{undergraduate GPA}) - 42.397$.   Elizabeth Rosselot, Director of Admissions, Boston College

Our index number has a sixty-two percent weighting on the LSAT.   Kip Darcy, Director of Admissions, Hastings

Our index number is designed to predict first-year law school performance. It's a regression formula: $(0.044 \times \text{LSAT}) + (0.370 \times \text{GPA}) - 5.328$. We separate candidates into three groups on the basis of their index number. For those at or over 3.3, I can admit them without referring their files to the admissions committee. (I admit at least eighty percent of those in this category.) If I want to reject or wait-list them, I refer their file to the committee. For those at or below 2.9, I can reject them without referring their files to the committee. (I reject at least two-thirds of those in this category.) If I want to admit or wait-list them, I have to refer their files to the committee. Those between 2.9 and 3.3 are automatically referred to the committee, although I do read them first and make a recommendation.   Robert Stanek, Director for Admissions, George Washington

WHAT DIVERSITY MEANS TO THEIR SCHOOLS

By diversity I mean such things as: Educational background (your major); Political views (we mix in people who will challenge everyone else); Age (people over thirty); Gender; Region you are from; An interest in areas that we want to build (intellectual property, human rights, environmental). Janice Austin, Assistant Dean for Admissions, University of Pennsylvania

I try to take into account a whole range of factors in looking for a diverse class. For example, in a class of about 450 students, we have 175 or more undergraduate institutions represented. I also take into account work experience, age, where people grew up (ranch, suburb, inner city), education (public versus private, big school versus small), race, undergrad major, nationality, and more. Robert Stanek, Director for Admissions, George Washington

We want to enroll a diverse class. This can be people with unique traits or experiences, whether this means military experience, being raised by two wheelchair-bound parents, or leaving home at sixteen due to abuse. We want people who have a lot of work experience, a history of public service, and leadership experience. Public service is especially important for us as a public/state school. Shelli Soto, Dean of Admissions, University of Texas

We value people with a different outlook, including a different view of the legal system; for example, someone who worked in the inner city. Similarly, we value people who have grown up in a totalitarian society or worked in law enforcement. Michael Rappoport, Dean of Admissions, UCLA

We hope to achieve a mix of people, with different interests, experiences, backgrounds, and perspectives. They need to be able to listen to other people's views, too. Erica Munzel, Director of Admissions, University of Michigan

THE VALUE OF DIVERSITY

We want people from all over the country, in part to spread our reputation across the country. Don Rebstock, Associate Dean of Admissions and Financial Aid, Northwestern

We value interdisciplinary thinking. We like to get an economist, historian, political theorist, scientist, and manager into a room to focus on a given issue. Out of this comes a rich educational environment. Erica Munzel, Director of Admissions, University of Michigan

6

THE APPLICATION
TIMETABLE

— EXECUTIVE SUMMARY —

Apply as early as you can consistent with doing
the best possible application.

■

Track your progress with the Master Application Organizer.

The top law programs basically use one type of admissions decision format, the "rolling admissions" cycle. With rolling admissions, officers evaluate applicants on a "first-come, first-served" basis. A number of top schools modify this basic format by considering the strongest applications (read: those with the strongest index numbers) first, and then so on down the line, or by offering an Early Application option to applicants. Early Application policies grant early notification of decisions to those applying by, say, December 1. For almost all schools, there is a cutoff date after which no new applications will be read. Be aware that this comes as early as January 15 for some schools.

WHEN SHOULD YOU APPLY—EARLY OR LATE IN AN APPLICATION CYCLE?

The application cycle refers to the period of time during which a school accepts applications for a given class. In other words, a school might accept applications from October 1 through February 15 for the class beginning in September. This raises an important question. Should you apply early (in November, for example) or late (in January or February) if you wish to maximize your chances of getting in?

WHAT ARE THE BENEFITS OF APPLYING EARLY IN THE APPLICATION CYCLE?

There are several benefits to applying early in the application cycle. Assuming that the application is well written, an early application suggests that you are well organized. It also suggests that you are serious about getting into law school rather than applying on a whim. Another benefit can accrue if the school underestimates the number of applications, or quality of applicants, this application season will bring it. If this is the case, early applicants will have the bar over which they must leap set lower than will later applicants.

Certain types of applicants, of course, can benefit (from applying early) more than others. If you are a "cookie-cutter" candidate, with excellent credentials but no unusual qualities or experiences, your file will be less likely to inspire yawns if yours is one of the first of its kind read. For example, the person who is applying direct from college, a political science major with a junior semester abroad in England, will certainly wish to apply very early. A second type of candidate who stands to benefit from applying early is someone who has a complicated message and who therefore must give the admissions committee the time and mental energy to read his or her application carefully. Admissions committees tend to lack this time and lose energy as the application season progresses.

BINDING VERSUS NONBINDING EARLY DECISION

Numerous schools now offer a so-called "early decision" option: Apply, for example, by November 1 and you will be notified of the decision by mid-December. Most of these policies differ little from regular admissions insofar as the acceptance is *nonbinding:* Successful candidates are free to keep open their already submitted applications to other schools or, indeed, to apply to additional schools in the future. Several schools, however, have instituted early-decision policies similar to those used at the undergraduate level. These require that accepted candidates immediately withdraw applications to other schools and forego applying to any additional schools—upon pain of losing their early acceptance. In other words, these programs are *binding*.

The nonbinding programs are well worth noting. Applying early, as described above, offers an improved chance of admission under many circumstances. In addition, early notification for the successful candidate may eliminate the stress of waiting to hear from schools and the need to apply to a greater number of schools, thereby potentially saving time, effort, and money.

The binding programs are not generally so attractive. The schools offering binding early decision have not sweetened the pot by making it substantially easier to get in under this program, unlike the early-decision programs offered at the undergraduate level. As a result, these will not be sensible options for most applicants. The binding early-decision approach should be taken only by those who do not have any doubts as to which school they would like to attend and who will not benefit substantially from being able to compare financial offers from multiple schools.

SOME SCHOOLS OFFERING EARLY *APPLICATION* OPPORTUNITIES

	APPLICATIONS DUE	NOTIFICATION SENT	BINDING?
Boston College	Nov. 26	Dec. 16	No
Chicago	Dec. 1	Jan. 30	No
Duke	Nov. 1	Dec. 15	No
Georgetown	Nov. 10	Dec. 10	No
NYU	Oct. 15	Dec. 1	No
Penn	Nov. 1	Dec. 15	No
Texas	Nov. 1	Jan. 15	No

SOME SCHOOLS OFFERING EARLY *DECISION* OPPORTUNITIES

Columbia	Dec. 1	Dec. 15	Yes
Hastings	Dec. 1	Dec. 31	Yes
Notre Dame	Nov. 1	Dec. 31	Yes

For example, if you left college after your sophomore year to become a stage actress for five years—only to decide that what you *really* wanted to do was finish your degree and become a welfare counselor (your current career), your unique and complex profile needs special attention. Someone in this category should definitely apply early to ensure that his or her application is given appropriate consideration. (International students should seek to apply as early as possible because international credentials may add complexity to their applications.)

WHAT ARE THE BENEFITS OF APPLYING LATE IN THE APPLICATION CYCLE?

There is only one substantial benefit to applying late in the cycle: An applicant has the opportunity to continue to build her credentials during the few months involved. This can be significant for someone with the potential to transform her application. An applicant who expects to finish a major project—and is hoping to achieve impressive results—might wish to apply after the project is finished rather than before. This could provide wonderful material for an optional essay or a glowing recommendation. Similarly, someone still in college who expects fall semester grades to add substantially to the application's appeal should consider waiting to apply until the grades are posted.

A second potential benefit can occur if the school has misjudged its popularity and finds that fewer good applicants have applied than it expected earlier in the cycle, resulting in reduced admissions criteria for those applying later. This is an unpredictable factor and not likely to happen to any substantial degree, however, particularly at the very top schools.

SO, WHAT SHOULD YOU DO?

Most people will benefit, if only slightly, by applying early in the admissions cycle. In general, the most important timing criterion is to get the application done well as soon as is practicable. The earlier it is started, the more opportunity there is to rewrite and reconsider, to allow recommenders to finish their work—and even to have others help out by reading the finished product. The only group that should purposely apply late in the cycle consists of those who can substantially improve their credentials in the meantime.

Apply as soon as you can finish a truly professional application.

HOW LONG WILL IT TAKE TO DO YOUR APPLICATION?

Most applicants underestimate the amount of time that a good application requires, thinking that they can do one in a long weekend or two. The reality is that many of the necessary steps have a long lag built into them. For example, the process of approaching a recommender, briefing her on what you want done, giving her time to do a good recommendation for you, and ensuring that she submits it on time calls for months rather than days of advance notice. This is all the more true when you apply to eight or ten schools rather than one; you have more application forms to get, more essays to write, and more recommendations to request. Although work does not increase proportionally with the number of applications, the increased complexity as well as the number of additional things you need to do will inevitably increase your efforts.

The application process should start at least one and a quarter years in advance of when you would like to start law school. Thus, if you wish to start a program in September, you should start work in May of the preceding year. This may sound excessive, but the timetable in this section makes it clear that this is an appropriate time to get serious about the process. One of the reasons this process takes so long is that schools generally require that applications be submitted six to seven months (at the very minimum) in advance of the start of the program, meaning that you will have about ten months to complete the process if you start at the suggested time.

Starting the application process late, or failing to work seriously at it until deadlines approach, leads to the typical last-minute rush and the inevitable poor marketing job. It could also mean that by the time your application gets to the committee, they have very few spots left to fill. This book presents an enlightened approach devoted to the idea that applicants can dramatically improve their admission chances if they do a professional job of marketing themselves. This timetable is meant to reinforce the message that time is required for a successful marketing effort.

It is useful to establish your own timetable for applying. Ideally, you will be able to start about 15 months before you begin your JD program. Do not panic if you can't, because many people will, like you, need to condense their work efforts. It is useful, however, to make sure you use whatever time you have to your greatest advantage. Be sure you note the dates that are fixed and immutable:

■ LSAT (and TOEFL) registration deadlines and test dates

■ Application deadlines themselves

APPLICATION TIMETABLE

The following is a typical schedule for someone applying to schools that begin in September, with application deadlines in February. It is intended not as an exact timeline for you to follow, but rather as an illustration of the tasks and deadlines you will want to track.

EARLY SPRING

More than 15 months in advance of the program, you should:

- Start considering specifically what you want from a law program, and whether a law degree is indeed appropriate.

- Develop a preliminary list of appropriate schools. Read several of the better guides, look at the most recent surveys printed in the leading law and popular magazines, scrutinize the course catalogues and Web sites of the schools themselves, and talk with people knowledgeable about the schools.

- Send away for the _LSAT & LSDAS Registration & Information Book_ from Law Services.

- Examine several schools' application forms, even if they are a year out of date, to see what the application process will involve.

- Consider who should write recommendations for you (and be sure you treat them particularly well from now on).

- Start putting together a realistic financial plan to pay for school. Research financial aid sources and your likelihood of qualifying for aid. (Identify necessary forms to be completed and their deadline dates.)

- Register for the June LSAT (and TOEFL) exam.

- Consider how you will prepare for the LSAT. Start by getting sample tests from Law Services and subjecting yourself to a sample exam under realistic conditions. If you are not a strong standardized test taker, are unfamiliar with the exam, or just want to save yourself the bother of preparing on your own, figure out which test preparation course you will take and when it will be available. International students will want to do the same regarding the TOEFL exam.

- Start filling out the Personal Organizer in Chapter 8 to get a jump on the essay writing. Glance at the chapters covering what the schools want and how to write the essays so you have some idea of what will be required.

- Start planning school visits.

JUNE

- Take the LSAT.

- Send for the applications now! Requesting one over the Internet (rather than sending a postcard or calling) will get the quickest response. Many schools are inefficient about sending them out, especially to overseas applicants, so be prepared to have every third or fourth one fail to respond. If a school has not yet completed this year's application form, or is temporarily out of them, try to get last year's application form. The application form tends to change very little from one year to the next, so even last year's form will give you a good idea of what to expect from the new application.

- Read the chapters in this book regarding the essay questions, and the essay examples in Part IV.

JULY

- Register for the September LSAT if you are unsatisfied with your June score.

AUGUST

- Develop a basic positioning statement; write a preliminary essay regarding where you are headed and why you want a JD.
- Start visiting school campuses based upon a "short list" of preferred schools.
- Register for LSDAS, notifying them of the schools you will definitely be applying to.

AUGUST/SEPTEMBER

- Take the LSAT again (if necessary).
- Request that transcripts from the relevant schools be sent to LSDAS.
- Establish a file folder system for each school and note specific deadlines for each.
- Approach recommenders. (Assume the average one will take at least one month to submit the recommendations.) The more time you give a recommender, the more willing he will be to support you—and you do not want to get off on the wrong foot here.
- Revise your essays. Have a friend (or your consultant) read them over.

OCTOBER/NOVEMBER

- Attend law school forums.
- Submit completed applications.
- Confirm that your recommenders sent the necessary letters and forms.
- Submit applications for financial aid from third-party institutions (i.e., sources other than the schools themselves).

DECEMBER/JANUARY

- Submit loan applications (for school loans) and any forms necessary for institutionally based scholarships or assistantships.

- Thank your recommenders.

- Contact schools that have not yet acknowledged your complete file.

- Prepare for any potential interviews by reading Chapter 12 and by staging mock interviews with other applicants and friends.

ONCE YOU HAVE BEEN ACCEPTED (OR REJECTED)

- Notify your recommenders of what has happened, and tell them what your plans are. Thank them again for their assistance, perhaps by giving them a small gift.

- Notify the schools of your acceptance or rejection of their admissions offers, and send in your deposit to your school of choice.

- If you have not gotten into your desired school, what should you do? Consider going to your second choice, or perhaps reapplying in the future. (See the discussion in Chapter 13.)

SEPTEMBER

- Enroll.

Each point made above is discussed in detail elsewhere in this book; refer to the in-depth discussions as appropriate. The timing set out in this schedule is of necessity approximate, since everyone's style of working and personal circumstances will vary. For example, if you are working in a liquified natural gas facility on the north shore of Sumatra, you will probably have to allow more time for most of the steps listed here. Using this schedule as a starting point, however, should give you a good idea of the sequence to follow, as well as the approximate timing. It should also go without saying that doing things in advance is always a good idea.

Special Notes for International Students: The application deadlines for the standardized exams (LSAT and TOEFL) are approximately two months in advance of the actual test date. Failure to observe deadlines will result in either an increased fee or the need to take the exam on a later date. LSAT test preparation is not readily available outside the United States, so check carefully to determine where and when you can take a course. Because you must provide official translations or transcripts, recommendations, and the like, you should allow extra time. The slowness and lack of reliability of international mail should also be factored into your timetable, both for tests and for the other elements of the application process.

Also notify the school you have chosen to attend as early as possible so that you can begin the student visa application process. Depending upon your nationality and individual circumstances, this process may be either short and simple or lengthy and complicated.

WHERE ARE THINGS MOST LIKELY TO GO ASTRAY?

You should be aware of two different types of problems. *Problems that are partially outside your control (but not your influence):* (1) Some schools fail to send out a substantial percentage of applications upon a first request, or do so with a lengthy delay. The obvious solution to this is that you start requesting applications early and stay on top of the situation. (2) Your recommenders are another likely source of trouble. They are busy people who, despite their best intentions, are all too likely to need prodding to get the recommendations turned in on time, especially if they elected to write them themselves. As Chapter 11 suggests, you will want to make their job as easy as possible, and then stay on top of the situation.

Major problems that are within your control: (1) The public mails are notoriously unreliable. This can readily be dealt with, however, simply by using Federal Express, UPS, DHL, or another private carrier of greater reliability. (2) Your essay writing is all too likely to fall behind schedule, leading to last-minute rushing and poor writing. Start the whole essay writing process early and continue to give yourself time, on a regular basis, to work on them. You must be disciplined about this if you want to maximize your chances.

ADMISSIONS DIRECTORS DISCUSS APPLICATION TIMING

Early Decision

This year, we offered a binding, early-decision option. If an application was submitted by December 1, the applicant would receive an answer by the end of the month. It was an opportunity to lock in part of our class, even though it was a small number this year.   Kip Darcy, Director of Admissions, Hastings

We have a rolling admissions process. There are enormous benefits to applying early. Our Early Action Process requires that you apply by November 1 and complete every aspect by December 1; we render a decision by mid-December. Applying Early Action enhances your admission chances. It implies an interest in and commitment to Georgetown, and obviously we like that. We find that the sooner we let applicants know that they are admitted, the more likely that they'll attend. This is good for Georgetown.   Andy Cornblatt, Assistant Dean for Admissions, Georgetown

When Applications Are Received

We get one thousand applications in the last week and a half.   Andy Cornblatt, Assistant Dean for Admissions, Georgetown

The majority of our applications arrive within a couple of weeks before our January 15 deadline.   Albert R. Turnbull, Associate Dean for Admissions and Career Services, University of Virginia

About one-third of applications are submitted by December 1, another fifty percent by February 1, and almost twenty percent in the last month. I suggest that people get their applications in before Thanksgiving.   Janice Austin, Assistant Dean for Admissions, University of Pennsylvania

We get about half of our applications by January 1, the rest by our deadline of February 15.   Don Rebstock, Associate Dean of Admissions and Financial Aid, Northwestern

We have really encouraged applicants to get their application in by December 1. We have thus been able to advance our review process by two or three weeks. This year we received almost half of our applications by December 1.   Edward Tom, Director of Admissions, Boalt Hall (Berkeley)

About forty-five to fifty percent of our applicants apply in the last week. William Hoye, Dean for Admissions, USC

The Length of Time It Takes to Render a Decision

We generally mail decisions within one-and-a-half to two months; one month is the minimum.   Don Rebstock, Associate Dean of Admissions and Financial Aid, Northwestern

The Benefits of Applying Early

There can be benefits to applying early. For one thing, you may hear from us early on. For another, if your file turns out to be incomplete, we can notify you that a key piece of information is missing.   Michael Rappoport, Dean of Admissions, UCLA

The standard for admission to Cornell doesn't change over time, but it's still beneficial for a candidate to know what his/her situation is early in the process. Rick Geiger, Dean of Admissions, Cornell

There is a slight advantage to applying Early Decision.   Venetta C. Amory, Assistant Dean of Admissions, Columbia

The benefit to applying early is that we run out of space near the end of the process, so people who would have been admitted only make it onto the wait list. There are also important financial aid considerations. We run out of our limited funds before all people have been admitted.   Don Rebstock, Associate Dean of Admissions and Financial Aid, Northwestern

I think it's a good idea to apply early. When you do, you give me more time to examine your file. In general, admissions people are fresher earlier in the season. Things tend to get compressed towards the end.   Edward Tom, Director of Admissions, Boalt Hall (Berkeley)

The more marginal people's numbers, the longer they should give us to consider their files. For one thing, they are likely to have their folders handed to second and third readers. For another, we are more likely to give the benefit of the doubt to those who have been professional, organized, and on time (versus those who have shown up at the last minute).   William Hoye, Dean for Admissions, USC

There are several benefits to applying early in the process. We are fresher readers early on and more likely to take a generous view. If you are a typical applicant—a poli sci major who did a semester at LSE—it helps if you're the first one of these we see. If financial aid is an issue, the sooner you're admitted, the more likely you are to get aid. In addition, you can visit schools before deposits are due if you are accepted early on. You basically buy yourself time by applying earlier.   Elizabeth Rosselot, Director of Admissions, Boston College

Applying early may be beneficial, because with a process that depends so much on human judgment, the outlook at the beginning will be fresher, not yet jaded.   Kip Darcy, Director of Admissions, Hastings

USING THE MASTER APPLICATION ORGANIZER

The organizers in Appendix III are meant to provide you with a framework for controlling the application process. You may well find that some steps take you a bit more or less time than this timetable allows for; adjust it to your own needs. The important thing is to have a firm schedule and keep to it. The sequence of activities will be approximately the same, no matter how long it takes you to complete them, so be sure you do not skip a step.

Appendix III

APPLICATION ORGANIZERS

MASTER APPLICATION ORGANIZER

SCHOOL	1	2	3	4	5	6	7	8
Applications								
Application Deadline								
Target Mailing Date								
Date Sent								
Target Completion Date								
School Visits/Interviews								
Date of School Visit								
Interview Date								
Application Forms and Brochures								
Date Requested								
Have You Received?								
LSAT Scores								
Date Taken								
Date Requested								
Has School Received Them?								

SCHOOL	1	2	3	4	5	6	7	8
LSDAS								
Date Subscribed								
School Included on List?								
Date Transcripts Requested								
Has School Received Master Report?								
TOEFL Scores								
Date Taken								
Date Requested								
Has School Received Them?								
Essays								
Target Completion of Rough Drafts								
Outside Readings (by friends, etc.) Complete								
Target Completion Date of Final Drafts								
Final Drafts Complete								
Recommendations								
Recommender 1								
Date Requested								
Date Briefing Completed								
Date Finished								
Has School Received?								

(continued)

129

SCHOOL	1	2	3	4	5	6	7	8
Recommender 2								
Date Requested								
Date Briefing Completed								
Date Finished								
Has School Received?								
Recommender 3								
Date Requested								
Date Briefing Completed								
Date Finished								
Has School Received?								
Financial Aid								
Source (If Other Than School)								
Date Information/Forms Requested								
Date Information/Forms Received								
Date Due								
Target Mailing Due								
Date Sent								

APPLICATION ORGANIZER FOR EACH SCHOOL

SCHOOL

ADMISSIONS AND APPLICATIONS DETAILS

Address

Telephone

Fax

E-Mail

Admissions and Information Website

Admissions Director

Admissions Officer Contacted

   Under What Circumstances

Application Fee

Application Deadline Date

Financial Aid/Scholarship Deadline Date

ACTIONS REQUIRED (Make a check when each action is completed.)

- ☐ School's application, course catalog, and publicity materials requested
  - ☐ Received by me
- ☐ Secondary research completed
  - ☐ Website
  - ☐ School Brochure
  - ☐ School Catalogue
  - ☐ Books
  - ☐ Articles
- ☐ Transcripts requested sent to LSDAS
  - ☐ Master Report received by school

☐ Recommenders approached

   ☐ All necessary material sent to them

   ☐ Recommenders' progress checked

   ☐ Recommendation 1 received by school

   ☐ Recommendation 2 received by school

   ☐ Recommendation 3 received by school

☐ Application data form filled in

☐ Application short answers completed

Application essays:

	rough draft completed	*outsider reading completed*	*final draft completed*
Essay 1	☐	☐	☐
Essay 2	☐	☐	☐
Essay 3	☐	☐	☐

☐ Completed application photocopied

☐ Application sent (by Federal Express or similar firm)

   Date

   Routing Number

Interview status

   Required?

   Date requested

   Date of interview

   Interviewer's name

   Interviewer's title

   Interviewer's address (for thank-you notes)

☐ School notified me of file completion

FINANCIAL AID

Financial Aid/Scholarship Form

☐ Requested

☐ Completed

☐ Mailed

☐ Checked with financial aid office and financial aid file is complete

NOTES:

Place this organizer in the folder you keep on each school, showing in detail what is only outlined in the Master Application Organizer.

Part II

Applying to
Law School

7

Making the Most of Your Credentials

— EXECUTIVE SUMMARY —

Although candidates with less than stellar credentials can do well
in admissions by marketing themselves effectively,
the job is much easier for those with excellent credentials.

■

Learn how to maximize the various credentials
that admissions officers will evaluate:

—Your academic record

—Your LSAT score

—Work experience

—Extracurricular, personal, and community activities

■

You can add to the impact of your credentials
by showing that you know where you are headed.

Chapter 5 provides an overview of what the top law schools look for in their candidates: brains, legal potential, and personal attributes. Admissions committees ascertain to what degree you possess these items first and foremost from the credentials you present. Your credentials include the following four items:

- Your academic record
- Your performance on the LSAT (and the TOEFL, for international applicants)
- Your work experience
- Your extracurricular, personal, and community activities

Although even candidates with less than stellar credentials can market themselves effectively—by tweaking essays, getting recommenders to write favorably about them, and interviewing well—you will make the application process easier on yourself if you start out with strong credentials. This chapter will examine each category of credentials to show you how best to shape your profile.

THE ACADEMIC RECORD

WHAT ARE ADMISSIONS COMMITTEES LOOKING FOR?

Your academic record refers not just to the grades you received in college, but also to the quality of your university and the substance of the classes you took. Some law schools rely mostly on the index number (computed using your undergraduate grade-point average and your LSAT score) when looking at your academic credentials, without considering that a GPA can mean many different things depending upon where it was earned and what types of classes were followed. (For more information on index numbers, see Chapter 5.) Most top law schools, however, do indeed take a closer look at your record, considering your college grades in the true context in which they were earned.

Admissions officers are accustomed to examining undergraduate transcripts with a practiced eye. A given grade-point average is more impressive if achieved at a top school in demanding courses, with the better grades received in the junior and senior years. A candidate with high grades in introductory courses and low grades in more advanced courses will be considered less favorably. Similarly, high grades earned at a college (even a top one) notorious for grade inflation will mean less than outstanding marks at a college known for its rigorous grading patterns.

It does not particularly matter what you major in at college. Law schools welcome all undergraduate majors, although there are a few that are most prevalent among accepted law school students. Columbia, for example, states that among recently enrolled students "25 percent have backgrounds in political science, 15 percent in history, 15 percent in economics, 13 percent in literature, 10 percent in pure sciences and engineering, and about 6 percent in philosophy."

It is always a good idea to take undergraduate classes that will provide you with substantive knowledge for use in a future law field. If you intend to practice family law, for example, classes in psychology as well as those in tax and finance will help you down the road. For those planning to practice environmental law, classes in the life sciences and economics are helpful; for commercial litigation or securities law, knowledge of accounting, statistics, finance, and corporate strategy is particularly useful. All future lawyers can benefit from courses that develop writing, research, negotiation, analysis, and public speaking skills.

Perhaps more important than the substance of your classes is that you excel at whatever academic endeavors you pursue. Quality work and serious involvement are the most important things to demonstrate in your university studies. It is best if you also evidence interest in your studies by taking extra courses in your major or in complementary fields, as well as writing a thesis.

The ideal undergraduate record would thus exhibit all of the following:

- Top-quality school
- Demanding courseload
- Top grades throughout, but especially in the junior and senior years
- Courses developing useful substantive knowledge for your future legal field
- Courses requiring exceptional writing ability, good research skills, and analytical prowess

HOW IMPORTANT IS IT?

Admissions officers view your undergraduate record as a key indicator of your intellectual ability and your willingness to work hard. The less work experience you have, the more important your college record will be. A strong undergraduate record earned at a leading university will demonstrate that you can make it through law school, especially if you have had a mixture of political science (or other theoretical) classes and courses demanding substantial amounts of writing. Law schools want people who can cover and quickly absorb an immense amount of material, write well, and are motivated to learn.

IMPROVING YOUR UNDERGRADUATE RECORD AFTER THE FACT

If you have already graduated and do not possess a sterling record, is it too late for you to do something to help your candidacy? Not necessarily. You may not be able to do anything about the grades you got as an undergraduate, but you can always take courses (at night or on weekends, presumably) to provide another set of grades—more recent and potentially more reflective of your current ability—for law schools to consider. Admissions officers call this "building an alternative transcript." Note that there is no unanimity on the effectiveness of this strategy. Some schools will allow positive results from alternative classes to turn an otherwise questionable record into a favorable one; other schools, however, are more reticent to let new grades wipe out the sting of past errors. Check with individual law schools to determine how they regard a second set of grades.

Those schools that are willing to overlook past performances when a new and better transcript is provided will need help in doing so. Although the law schools are capable of interpreting the meaning of good grades received in courses at a well-known, demanding graduate-degree program, they may not know how to interpret your record in coursework from lesser-known programs. Be sure to do all you can to help them understand what your new record means (assuming, of course, that you have performed well in a highly-regarded program). For example, relate to the admissions committees what it takes to get into the program, the program's ranking or standing in its field, the average grades achieved in the program compared with your own grades, or even the average grades achieved course by course, if that helps to show that your record has been superb.

Law schools will value your efforts more highly if you take a series of courses showing in-depth investigation of a subject. Merely sampling a few classes here and there is not as likely to help you in your efforts to redeem an earlier weak undergraduate record. Furthermore, you should try to remedy the specific weaknesses in your original record. For example, if you have not taken any writing or writing-intensive classes, for example (or received poor grades in such classes), you should take expository writing or a writing-intensive course at a local community college or continuing education division of a nearby university. To achieve the maximum possible benefit from these courses, you will have to receive excellent grades in them. Getting mediocre marks may show that you are interested in improving your background, but will arouse serious questions about your ability to do outstanding work in a competitive law program.

Graduate Work

Law schools will want to look at the results of any graduate-degree work you have completed. Serious, well-done graduate work in a Master's or other program—especially if completed in a top discipline at a top university—will always work in your favor. Remember, however, that graduate-level grades are not factored into the index number (see Chapter 5). Furthermore, admissions officers know that the grading in many graduate programs is somewhat lenient, with nearly all students receiving grades higher than a C. Although

ADMISSIONS DIRECTORS DISCUSS THE
ACADEMIC RECORD

WHAT FACTORS DO YOU CONSIDER WHEN EVALUATING AN
UNDERGRADUATE RECORD?

Whatever the major, there should be variety, including some clearly demanding analytical courses. Thus, I'm glad to see a sociology major who has taken some tough statistics courses. There is no set preparation for law school, but some majors may be of less value than others (for example, pre-law). I examine the undergraduate transcript very closely. I look at what an applicant has undertaken in his or her major and I look at what they've done outside of their major.   Faye Deal, Associate Dean for Admissions and Financial Aid, Stanford

What we're looking for is both breadth and depth. We favor applicants who come to us from a broad, liberal arts education. They learn about human vision from the arts, how the world works from math and the sciences, and the human condition from philosophy and history. We hope that they have gained some sense of the world and their place in it. We don't want academic dilettantes, however, so we want applicants to have taken the most analytically rigorous courses in their field—in contrast to descriptive courses such as "Wednesday Night at the Movies." There is nothing I examine more closely than the transcript.   Jim Milligan, Dean of Admissions, Columbia

You may have a person who started out college very ill-prepared, who was coaxed into going the pre-med route, and then halfway through realized he or she was a philosopher and changed majors. In that case, I would pay more attention to later grades. . . . It's not a lock-step kind of analysis we go through. Edward Tom, Director of Admissions, Boalt Hall (Berkeley)

If an applicant has worked successfully for several years—performed well and progressed—and has done well on the LSAT, the undergraduate record will receive much less emphasis.   Don Rebstock, Associate Dean of Admissions and Financial Aid, Northwestern

I do believe in redemption. The trend in grades can be absolutely critical. Anne Brandt, Director of Admissions, Vanderbilt

We take a number of candidates with hard science backgrounds, which are essential for our intellectual property program. We recognize that the grading in the hard sciences is different than in other programs, and adjust for that in making decisions.   Robert Stanek, Director for Admissions, George Washington

Not all UGPAs are created equal. Swarthmore and William & Mary, for instance, have refrained from inflating grades; their averages are between 2.8 and 2.9. At the other end of the spectrum, Stanford and Yeshiva have mean GPAs over 3.4.   Jim Milligan, Dean of Admissions, Columbia

The GPA number is just a starting point. Our first concern is how rigorous the courseload has been. We look at academic letters of recommendation, which are particularly helpful if they address the difficulty of the courseload and, for example, the grading policies of professors from whom the applicant took multiple courses. Another factor we examine is whether there were substantial barriers to performance, such as the need to work many hours per week.   William Hoye, Dean for Admissions, USC

There are a whole host of things that can go wrong in the first year or two of college, such as picking the wrong school or major. Therefore we read transcripts backwards, starting with the most recent work.   Elizabeth Rosselot, Director of Admissions, Boston College

We admit only ten to twenty people each year with GPAs below 3.0. They may be recent immigrants with language disadvantages working full-time and sending money to their families.   Shelli Soto, Dean of Admissions, University of Texas

There is an exception to looking at the whole undergraduate record—someone who went to school for two years at nineteen or twenty and had a 2.0 GPA, then worked for several years, and returned to do the last two years and received a 4.0 GPA then. We would probably ignore the 2.0 in our index calculations. Michael Rappoport, Dean of Admissions, UCLA

To interpret a GPA, we take into account the trend of grades, the quality of the curriculum followed, the school, when the applicant attended school—both because grades have inflated over time and because grades matter less if you went eight years ago, since you have done other things more recently.   Andy Cornblatt, Assistant Dean for Admissions, Georgetown

I know what the strongest and weakest programs are at some fifty to sixty schools. At some smaller, less commonly seen schools (and programs), it can be helpful for students to provide detailed information for me. It helps me evaluate someone if I know, for example, that a new honors program is ungraded, what its selection criteria are, and what is involved in the program in terms of workload, required courses, etc.   Robert Stanek, Director for Admissions, George Washington

It can be useful for us to know about a department or program that consistently issues lower-than-average grades. Send proof that the grading is outside the norm in order to put your performance in the appropriate context.   Don Rebstock, Associate Dean of Admissions and Financial Aid, Northwestern

We see a number of formerly pre-med students who did poorly as pre-meds but then did well in their next field. The key for them is to make sure they get out of pre-med early, so that they can fully demonstrate their talents.   Michael Rappoport, Dean of Admissions, UCLA

In general, we like to see people writing a senior thesis. It requires commitment and self-discipline. It gives them a sense of intellectual ownership of a topic. The process engenders real growth and development. Jim Milligan, Dean of Admissions, Columbia

I'm always impressed when a person has taken upper division electives in other departments; it's a good indication that the person is intellectually curious (and fearless). William Hoye, Dean for Admissions, USC

We want to see that an applicant challenged himself in college. We don't like to see someone taking a lot of introductory courses in the last years of college. Shelli Soto, Dean of Admissions, University of Texas

I like people who've challenged themselves: took the biology course with the pre-meds, took math through several levels, took a foreign language to a serious level. Dennis Shields, Assistant Dean for Admissions and Financial Aid, Duke

We look at undergraduate records to see whether candidates have demonstrated strong performance while taking tough courses and generally challenged themselves. Don Rebstock, Associate Dean of Admissions and Financial Aid, Northwestern

Does It Matter What a Candidate Majors In?

We don't give any advantage to those who major in political science, philosophy, or history. The reason we have a lot with these majors is that they self-select. Jim Milligan, Dean of Admissions, Columbia

I always like to see unusual majors. I like math majors; philosophy majors, because you have to read and think critically, challenge your personal views, and analyze a wide range of materials; engineering and sciences, because these are tough across institutions—you know you're getting someone who's had to work hard and perform well. Dennis Shields, Assistant Dean for Admissions and Financial Aid, Duke

When I see some majors, I shudder: criminal justice, elementary education, music (performance), theater arts (performance), physical education, hotel/restaurant management, and leisure studies. At some schools these are solid programs, but not at many. Robert Stanek, Director for Admissions, George Washington

Certain majors tend to make me leery: criminology, criminal justice (which is not very rigorous at most schools), fine arts, music, dramatic arts. For those in the arts, we look to see how they do in academic coursework, and to see if they took serious academic courses. Shelli Soto, Dean of Admissions, University of Texas

My heart sinks when I see criminal justice majors, pre-law majors. I particularly value interdisciplinary talents and interests; for example, philosophy and biology double majors, or someone with a finance major and a chemistry minor. Janice Austin, Assistant Dean for Admissions, University of Pennsylvania

There's a rebuttable presumption that certain majors are suspect: criminal justice, communications, which is a very popular major for people who don't want to work hard, even though it can be rigorous at some places.   Dennis Shields, Assistant Dean for Admissions and Financial Aid, Duke

Can Post-Graduate Work Make Up for a Relatively Poor Undergraduate Performance?

For someone who has done mediocre undergraduate work, doing excellent Master's degree work can help. We will look very carefully at three items: (1) What is the LSAT score? Does it support the Master's or Bachelor's indication of ability level? (2) What are the letters of recommendation saying? We know graduate grades don't distinguish performance very well, so we rely on recommendations to do this. (3) What is the commentary regarding the undergraduate performance? In other words, what caused it? This sort of applicant is likely to be a better transfer applicant in any event, because he or she will be able to demonstrate through first-year law school performance what his or her ability really is. Jean Webb, Director of Admissions, Yale

I care about what you will do here, and someone who has shown his or her potential, even if not at undergraduate school, helps demonstrate that. Thus, taking a substantial number of courses in a rigorous graduate program can help "rehabilitate" your record. (You don't get any credit with the LSDAS/commercial ranking outfits for additional undergraduate or graduate work, of course.) Erica Munzel, Director of Admissions, University of Michigan

Graduate work can help your cause; any kind of experience that involves analytical thinking and writing is always very important.   Edward Tom, Director of Admissions, Boalt Hall (Berkeley)

Taking courses outside a degree program helps a bit, but I'm looking for some evidence that this person can compete with other students in a demanding program. I need evidence of seriousness, not just of experimenting—taking a course in this and then a course in that.   Robert Stanek, Director for Admissions, George Washington

It's hard to evaluate courses taken in a continuing education program. I don't know who's in the classroom or how stiff the grading might be. As a result, this won't rehabilitate a weak undergraduate record. I have more confidence in the process and product at a serious Master's program. A letter of recommendation from a professor that lets me see the candidate's mind at work, her determination and spirit, and her intellectual curiosity, will be very valuable. Jim Milligan, Dean of Admissions, Columbia

A Master's degree, particularly if it's from a rigorous graduate program, can help make up for lackluster undergraduate results. This is not always the case, of course, but the Master's performance, while not quantified, is at least another element to consider.   Kenneth Kleinrock, Assistant Dean for Admissions, NYU

For someone who is below the twenty-fifth percentile—for example, a 2.85 GPA from Michigan State—there is a need to put together an appropriate package. One option is to go to an outstanding program for additional courses, and to do very well there. For example, a first-class Master's degree program, or a Harvard Extension program. Such a program must have a grading policy we can make sense of. Or he needs to show substantial professional development. After that, he should develop a very thoughtful, reflective application; then he needs to get an interview with me or one of my colleagues.   Janice Austin, Assistant Dean for Admissions, University of Pennsylvania

It is hard to rehabilitate an undergraduate record with later courses or degrees. Everybody does well (grade-wise) in a Master's program, so we don't average in those grades. We might take a Ph.D. into account to a greater extent. Michael Rappoport, Dean of Admissions, UCLA

Taking courses after you have graduated can be beneficial to your admission chances, but it depends heavily upon the rigor of the courses and the grading: graduate courses at a leading institution versus introductory undergraduate courses at a community college.   Andy Cornblatt, Assistant Dean for Admissions, Georgetown

Master's-level performance can make up for mediocre undergraduate performance, but this depends on a number of factors. Take, for example, a candidate with a 2.5 undergrad GPA who then got a Master's with a 3.5 GPA. If this person is twenty-four or twenty-five, I'm not going to be impressed by that record. (After all, everyone at grad school gets at least a 3.0.) Not enough time has passed for that undergrad performance to be overlooked. Every study ever done has concluded that the best way of predicting law school performance is the undergraduate record, not the graduate record. If I've got someone a bit closer to the GPA I'm looking for, or if the person got the degree ten years ago, I'm more likely to ignore the undergrad record.   Robert Stanek, Director for Admissions, George Washington

Overcoming a Weak Undergraduate Record

A person with a mediocre undergraduate record should note two things. First, you'll need solid work experience to rehabilitate your situation. Second, taking additional courses after your undergraduate program can also help. The courses should be part of an in-depth, prolonged program at a serious school. This is usually found with Master's-level (or higher) work but can sometimes include a nondegree program of study.   Faye Deal, Associate Dean for Admissions and Financial Aid, Stanford

A low undergraduate GPA cannot be remedied just by taking a few extension division courses. It's a bit different if the low GPA is old—say, from fifteen years ago. In that case, if the rest of the file says that we'd like to have this person, the real accomplishments after college are what make up for the low grades; taking more courses would not.   Shelli Soto, Dean of Admissions, University of Texas

There are two ways to compensate for a mediocre undergraduate record: an outstanding LSAT and some significant experience out in the world. These can serve as useful counterweights to the college GPA.   Jim Milligan, Dean of Admissions, Columbia

graduate-level grades are not necessarily factored as heavily into the admissions decision as undergraduate marks are, they can still be helpful to your case, especially if earned in a competitive, well-known program. Be sure to do all you can to aid admissions committees in interpreting your marks if they are not earned in a particularly well-known program by giving them as much information as possible about the school.

THE LSAT

WHAT IS IT?

The Law School Admission Test (LSAT) is a four-hour examination created and administered by the Law School Admission Council (also known as Law Services or LSAC) and required by every ABA-approved law school.

There are two closely related purposes of the exam: to predict which candidates will do well in law school and to assist schools in ranking applicants. It is, according to LSAC, a standard measure of acquired reading and verbal reasoning skills. The LSAT does not, however, attempt to measure your legal competence or knowledge.

The test consists of five 35-minute multiple-choice sections, separately timed, followed by a half-hour essay portion that is not scored. A short break is given after the third multiple-choice section. The exam, including preliminary administrative matters, typically lasts from 8:30 A.M. until about noon, making for a very long morning.

The five multiple-choice sections vary in order for each test taker, but they include: one Analytical Reasoning section, two Logical Reasoning sections, one Reading Comprehension section, and a wild card section, which could be any of the above. This (wild card) section is used only to assist LSAC in experimenting with new testing methods and questions and is not scored. (Note that test takers do not know when taking the exam which section is the wild card and will not be scored.)

Analytical reasoning. This section gives questions that require you to make deductions from a set of statements, rules, or conditions. Often called the "games" section, a typical analytical reasoning question would give you information about the eight people seated at a circular table. You might be informed that Harold never sits facing due south, George always sits facing north (including northeast or northwest), Lisa always sits two seats away from Harold, Martha always sits opposite Lisa, and so on. You will be asked, for example, in which seat Harold must sit if Martha is not in a seat facing due north or due south.

Logical reasoning. These questions evaluate your ability to comprehend and analyze arguments that are contained in short passages. Test takers must be able to evaluate the strength of the evidence, and logic of the reasoning, as well as detect the assumptions in these arguments and draw reasonable conclusions from them.

Reading comprehension. These questions are based upon four reading passages, designed to test your reading and reasoning abilities. Passages are drawn from a variety of subjects (some of which you may not be familiar with) but all information needed to answer the questions can be found within the text. These questions require you to analyze the logic, structure, and details of densely written material, and to draw inferences from it.

HOW TO REGISTER FOR THE LSAT

The *LSAT & LSDAS Registration & Information Book* provides a registration worksheet, as well as information about the dates, locations, and price of the exam. It is possible to register by phone, as well as on the Internet. You can obtain a bulletin by contacting:

Law School Admission Council
Box 2000
661 Penn Street
Newton, PA 18940–0998
(215) 968-1001
www.lsac.org

The exam is given in June, September, December, and February of each year. To be sure that you will be able to take the exam at the site you prefer, plan to register several months before the actual exam date.

YOUR SCORE

Your score is now available approximately three weeks after you take the exam by TelScore, for a fee of $10. Otherwise, you will get the score by mail, from Law Services, approximately five weeks after the exam.

Your score is based strictly on the number of questions answered correctly; any incorrect answers will not affect your score. Scores are reported on a scale from 120 to 180. Thus, the lowest you can score is 120, the highest 180. You will also receive a percentile rank, which shows the percentage of test takers who perform (above and) below you. (Remember that the essay you write is not scored, but simply forwarded to your chosen schools.)

WHAT ARE ADMISSIONS COMMITTEES LOOKING FOR?

Top schools have average scores in the mid-to-high 160s, meaning that their students are typically in the top 10 percent of test takers. The range of scores is substantial, however, so a score in the upper 150s need not necessarily be cause for despair. To evaluate yourself, check out where your score falls in relation to those of first-year students at some of the top schools. In the following chart, for example, only 25 percent of NYU's first-year students scored lower than 166 and only 25 percent scored above 171. If your score is a 168, you can infer that, although you are no shoo-in, your LSAT score is unlikely to be a barrier to law school entrance.

	25TH PERCENTILE	75TH PERCENTILE
UC Berkeley (Boalt Hall)	161	169
UCLA	161	166
Chicago	167	171
Columbia	164	171
Cornell	163	166
Duke	161	170
Georgetown	163	168
Harvard	166	173
Hastings	159	164
Michigan	163	168
New York University	166	171
Northwestern	162	167
Pennsylvania	164	168
Stanford	164	170
Texas	158	164
Virginia	163	168
William and Mary	159	164
Yale	168	175

HOW IMPORTANT IS IT?

Admissions officers pay close attention to the LSAT score. Chapter 5 discusses the index number (a combination of the LSAT score and GPA), which, at some schools, is the very first thing a committee member sees and evaluates. There is no getting around it: The LSAT score is important. Yet the degree to which admissions officers rely on it varies according to each particular situation (and school). They tend to rely on it most when analyzing students from unusual backgrounds, or when comparing people from substantially different backgrounds. If you went to a university not well known to the admissions officers, for example, you can expect extra emphasis to be placed on your LSAT score. The LSAT score will likewise be used to compare someone at the top of her class at a weak university with an applicant who did well at a leading university.

The essay portion of the LSAT is read by admissions officers at some schools, and ignored at others. It is worth your while to take it seriously. Not only may it be regarded in its own right, but it may also be used to put your personal statement in context. If your personal statement is a brilliant piece of literature, but your LSAT writing sample is disturbingly shoddy, the discrepancy may be noted by the Committee. They may question whether you actually wrote your personal statement.

HOW TO PREPARE FOR THE LSAT

It is not easy to prepare for the LSAT at the same time you are investigating schools and preparing your applications. To avoid this problem, and to give yourself the time to prepare properly, try to take the exam before you intend to apply. Besides avoiding scheduling conflicts, you will have the chance to prepare better and retake it if necessary.

You have two options if you wish to prepare seriously for the LSAT. You can prepare on your own using specially designed preparatory books or you can take preparatory classes. Self-preparation has several substantial advantages. It is (relatively) low cost, offers complete flexibility of schedule, and allows you to tailor your preparation to suit your own needs. On the other hand, preparatory classes also offer several advantages. They force you to start preparing in earnest well in advance of the exam, they guide you through the mass of potential preparatory material, they offer you an expert on call when you have questions, and they give you the opportunity to study with other people (and compare yourself with them). Finally, their price and inconvenience will be outweighed for some people by the higher scores they are likely to produce as a result.

The appropriate choice for you will depend upon the kind of person you are, your financial resources, your goals, and other variables. Those who almost certainly should take a prep course are those who:

- Have not taken similar tests before, or have not done so in many years
- Tend to test below their overall ability level
- Lack the self-discipline necessary to prepare on an individual basis
- Need substantial help on one or more parts of the exam, such as those who have let their logic muscles atrophy

GETTING THE MOST OUT OF YOUR SELF-PREPARATION

If you decide to follow the self-study route, make sure you do two things. First, buy and use several of the popular prep books, because no one book on its own contains sufficient discussion of the strategies, techniques, and fundamentals required. Second, be sure you practice on past LSAT exams rather than on the very different exams created by the various prep book authors. Old exams are available from Law Services, for $6 each, which you can order when registering. You can also buy one of Law Services's LSAT TriplePrep books, which include three exams and scoring sheets, for $15 each.

You will need to keep to a regular review schedule, such as spending two hours a night twice a week, and six to eight hours on weekends, for six to eight weeks before the exam. Having a study partner can ease the strain and provide you with someone who can explain something that mystifies you (and vice versa). The best partner is likely to be someone with the opposite strengths to yours. Thus, if you are strong in reading comprehension, find someone who is excellent in logical reasoning.

CHOOSING A TEST-PREP COURSE

Test-prep courses tend to cost a lot of money, so be sure you will get what you pay for. The best value, and best instruction, may not come from the nationally known firms. Look carefully at their smaller competitors before handing over the $1,000 or more that the name-brand companies demand.

There are several reasons to look at the full range of test-prep companies rather than opting for the default choice of one of the famous providers. First, the major companies' claims that they have ultra-sophisticated materials, embodying the otherwise unknowable secrets of the exams, are spurious. The fact is that employees of each company, large and small, monitor the efforts of their competitors and readily incorporate their best ideas. Thus, courses are more alike than different. Second, although the major companies can boast enormous libraries of materials on which to practice, few students utilize more than a modest fraction of these materials. Third, the major companies inevitably (given the huge numbers they employ) take on many instructors of average intellect and test-taking talent (including out-of-work actors, waiters, and so on), provide them with limited training, and suffer from high instructor turnover.

The best of the smaller companies can avoid this difficulty. By the same token, if you do opt for one of the major firms, be careful to select the specific course on the basis of the instructor teaching it. To do so, inquire of others who have already taken courses there and check with the firm's clerical staff, too; you are likely to hear that one or two of their instructors are highly sought after.

RETAKING THE EXAM

If, upon completing the LSAT, you are sure you did not perform well, you have the option to cancel your score—either by filling in the score cancellation section on the answer sheet or sending a written cancellation request to Law Services within five days. If you do so, you will not receive a score or your answer sheet.

If you opt to retake the test after receiving your first score, all scores will be reported to schools by LSDAS. Before deciding that this is necessary, however, you should analyze your application to see whether your LSAT score will actually handicap you significantly. Remember that many people with scores in the upper 150s or lower 160s got into top programs because they marketed themselves well (and had something worth marketing). You may be better off applying the time you would otherwise spend studying for the LSAT working on your essay or improving your other credentials.

Ideally, you should take the LSAT only once. A low score will remain with you, regardless of how well you perform the next time. (Additionally, Law Services prohibits you from taking the exam more than three times within a two-year period.) Many schools average the two scores, and very few completely ignore a lower score. The chart gives a sampling of how top law programs treat applicants with multiple LSAT scores.

	HIGHER SCORE	AVERAGE OF SCORES
Berkeley		X
Chicago		X
Harvard		X
Michigan		X
Northwestern	X	
Stanford		X
Texas		X
Wisconsin		X

Most schools are not as kind as Northwestern is—looking only at your highest score. Thus, a candidate who scored 160, followed by a 170, is a very strong candidate at Northwestern, but a weaker one at most other schools. She could have helped herself greatly by preparing better for her first exam. Had she scored

170, for example, on her first try, she would be considered a better candidate at schools that average scores than she currently is. After an initial 170, she might wish to take the exam again (although most people would be advised to leave well enough alone at that point). To avoid harming her chances in case her second score was below 170, she simply would not have listed any schools to receive the score. If she scored above a 170, she could then notify Law Services as to which schools should receive her score.

GENERAL TIPS ON PREPARING TO ACE THE LSAT

➤ Familiarize yourself with the tests by taking plenty of sample exams. Be sure to practice on actual prior LSATs available from LSAC. Review the answers you miss. Make sure, at the very least, you know exactly what to expect in terms of a test's format—what each section asks you to do, how long each section is—before going in. That way you will not waste time reading directions (or panicking), and will be able to concentrate on your performance.

➤ Take care of your health. Get enough rest for at least two nights before taking the exam.

➤ Be organized on the day of the test. Give yourself enough time to have a leisurely breakfast and prepare yourself. If the site is not familiar to you, be sure you have precise directions to it and know exactly how long it will take to get there, allowing for traffic or unexpected delays. Arrive at the testing site ten minutes early so that you have time to go to the restroom and calm yourself down.

➤ Do not wait until the last possible administration of the exam to take it. You may fall ill and be unable to take it, or you may need to retake it to boost your score.

FOR INTERNATIONAL APPLICANTS ONLY: THE TOEFL

The TOEFL (Test of English as a Foreign Language) is a test administered by Educational Testing Service (ETS) to nonnative English speakers to measure English proficiency. Some law schools require TOEFL scores from overseas students (except native English-speaking American citizens living overseas) and those who have lived in the U.S. for fewer than a given number of years. Often, the admission materials do not specify whether or not the test is required, so it is advisable to call and ask.

Unlike the LSAT, the TOEFL is not a complicated test. If you are comfortable speaking and reading English, it should pose little problem for you. The TOEFL consists of three parts: Listening Comprehension; Structure and Written Expression; and Vocabulary and Reading Comprehension. There are two TOEFL formats: the original paper format and the new computer version. The paper format is scored on a scale from 200 to 677, while the computer version is scored on a different scale, with 300 as the best possible score. The top law schools are generally looking for a minimum score of 600 on the standard TOEFL (250 on the new computerized version), but higher scores are preferred.

TO REGISTER FOR THE TOEFL

To find out more about the TOEFL exam or register for it, contact:

TOEFL
Educational Testing Service
P.O. Box 6151
Princeton, NJ 08541-6151
U.S.A.
(609) 951–1100
toefl@ets.org

ADMISSIONS DIRECTORS DISCUSS THE LSAT

HOW MUCH DECISIONAL WEIGHT IS PLACED ON THE LSAT SCORE?

For those with relatively mediocre academic records, a strong LSAT is very important. If we're looking at a candidate with a weak LSAT, we'll only discount it if the rest of the file has no weaknesses. (The same thing is true in general: If any one aspect of the file is weak, the rest of the file should be strong enough to compensate.) Incidentally, in general we care more about the four years of sustained academic work than the LSAT.   Faye Deal, Associate Dean for Admissions and Financial Aid, Stanford

We probably put a little less weight on LSAT scores than our rivals seem to. We weight grades and LSATs about equally. Other schools seem to weight the LSAT more heavily. When we learn from applicants we rejected that they were accepted at other, comparable schools, we very often find that they had so-so grades with high LSAT (over 170) scores.   Michael Rappoport, Dean of Admissions, UCLA

We know there is a small group of people who test poorly but can do excellent work in a rigorous academic setting. They are often the very methodical, organized people, who cannot handle the ambiguity and need-to-move-on on the LSAT. These qualities actually translate well into being good lawyers. It's hard for us to accept many of them, though. It helps greatly if we know the school, the curriculum, and the recommenders.   Albert R. Turnbull, Associate Dean for Admissions and Career Services, University of Virginia

LSAT performance matters most for someone with a GPA below our mid-point. Don Rebstock, Associate Dean of Admissions and Financial Aid, Northwestern

We'll cut second-language English-speakers a bit of slack on the LSAT.   Albert R. Turnbull, Associate Dean for Admissions and Career Services, University of Virginia

If someone has a weak LSAT, he or she needs real strength in other areas. If he has a pattern of poor testing, we will take that into consideration.   Anne Brandt, Director of Admissions, Vanderbilt

How Do You Use the LSAT Writing Sample?

The LSAT writing sample is important in our decision-making. Some members of the admissions committee read it first, to get a clear sense of a candidate's writing ability. We want to know whether you can put together a sentence, a paragraph, an argument.   William Hoye, Dean for Admissions, USC

We do read the LSAT writing samples, but faculty members differ in how much importance they place on them.   Anne Brandt, Director of Admissions, Vanderbilt

It is rare that I read the LSAT essays—only for someone who is absolutely on the borderline.   Janice Austin, Assistant Dean for Admissions, University of Pennsylvania

We do not pay much attention to the LSAT writing sample. Instead, we consider the personal statement to be an applicant's main writing sample.   Don Rebstock, Associate Dean of Admissions and Financial Aid, Northwestern

How Do You Interpret Multiple Scores?

We average LSAT scores if a candidate takes the test more than once. Don't take the exam unless you have prepared for it; it's meant to be taken once. Cancel the score if something goes radically wrong during the exam or if you feel that you haven't been at your best.   Kenneth Kleinrock, Assistant Dean for Admissions, NYU

We ordinarily average LSAT scores; we may overlook the first one if there is a good reason.   Michael Rappoport, Dean of Admissions, UCLA

We use the average of multiple scores. There is one exception, however. If the person took the test before finding out a learning disability, and then took the accommodated test, we would use the second score. We would also, of course, look at the rest of the file to see if they were accommodated in class.   Edward Tom, Director of Admissions, Boalt Hall (Berkeley)

Most applicants submitting multiple LSAT scores have scores that are only a couple of points apart. In those cases, I take the average of the scores. The ones that give me a headache are those that are ten or fifteen points apart. In those cases, I look at the rest of the record to determine which to accept. Taking the exam a third time would help: If you have two strong scores and a weak one, this would establish the strong scores as the relevant ones.   Robert Stanek, Director for Admissions, George Washington

Sometimes there is a very wide discrepancy between the scores, in which case the applicant should provide an explanation for the discrepancy.   Kenneth Kleinrock, Assistant Dean for Admissions, NYU

SHOULD A CANDIDATE TAKE THE LSAT MORE THAN ONCE?

It is a good idea to retake the LSAT if you feel that you underachieved the first time; this shows that you have done everything you can to present the best possible file. This is especially worthwhile if you can improve by more than the standard error of measurement (three points).   Don Rebstock, Associate Dean of Admissions and Financial Aid, Northwestern

WHICH IS MORE IMPORTANT, THE UNDERGRADUATE RECORD OR THE LSAT SCORE?

The top law schools generally consider both academic indicators—the undergraduate record and the LSAT—important. The most competitive schools in fact have so many fantastic applicants that they do not need to make compromises by accepting students who have either excellent grades or excellent scores, but not both. In other words, it is best if you compare favorably with others on both accounts.

Still, the top law schools differ slightly in their messages about which is more crucial, a great undergraduate record or a great LSAT score. The basic story from all of the most competitive schools is that you cannot completely override a poor LSAT score with a great college record, just as you cannot completely compensate for poor college grades with a strong LSAT. Both count for something and, depending upon which schools you apply to, they vary in their value.

You can determine how some law schools value the undergraduate record versus the LSAT score by examining the various formulas they use to calculate index numbers for their applicants. Some formulas assign greater weight to the LSAT whereas other formulas put more emphasis on the GPA.

Even those schools that use index numbers sparingly or do not rely on them at all have philosophical positions on the issue of which element—the LSAT or the GPA—is more critical. Some schools prefer to see exceptional undergraduate grades over an exceptional LSAT score. (This is especially true for those who can show that they tested poorly on the SAT and other college-entry exams, yet still achieved good grades at a strong undergraduate institution.) A poor LSAT and a strong undergraduate record suggest that a student can succeed when he works really hard and that he is indeed willing to work really hard. He has proven that he can do well by applying himself. Strong test scores and a poor college record suggest that, though a student might be intellectually gifted, she is lazy and lacks determination to succeed. No law school is looking for candidates with such apathy. Law schools generally figure that hard-working undergraduates will continue to work as diligently in law school and that students who are lazy in college will continue to be so in law school. Therefore, in many cases they prefer good collegiate performers over good test takers.

But at the same time, other schools see real significance in a strong LSAT score, allowing it to take on more importance than college grades. For one thing, law schools see it as the best indicator (in the absence of anything better) of raw intellectual talent; no school wants students who will have to struggle to do the more demanding work that a rigorous law curriculum requires. For another, law schools know that the public perception of their quality and status rests on several important factors in their profile, one of which is the LSAT scores achieved by their incoming first-year students 1Ls.

At all law schools, generally speaking, the importance of the LSAT score versus the college record changes according to the applicant's age. The longer a candidate has been out of college, the more important the LSAT score becomes; similarly, the significance of one's undergraduate GPA shrinks over time, especially for those with particularly valuable work experience.

**ADMISSIONS DIRECTORS DISCUSS HOW THEY
INTERPRET MIXED (GRADE AND LSAT) DATA**

We look carefully when we see disparate predictors: someone who has a 3.9 but a mediocre LSAT. If they can prove that their SAT score was similarly mediocre, we will put more weight on the GPA. An applicant with a high LSAT but a low GPA, on the other hand, does not have as strong an argument. We know that you can take a prep course, etc.   Edward Tom, Director of Admissions, Boalt Hall (Berkeley)

Someone who is weak in one important area may not be able to make up for it with strength in another area. Thus having good work experience may not make up for a lackluster academic record or LSAT results. Kenneth Kleinrock, Assistant Dean for Admissions, NYU

We've had more success with the person who had a high LSAT and solid but undistinguished grades—who was very busy in college, working full time, editing the paper, doing sports, etc.—than with the reverse. The high LSAT, undistinguished grades type tends to do very well, especially if they've been out of school for at least a few years. Although we've had some success with folks with high GPAs (3.9) and low (for Columbia) LSAT scores, we haven't had as much success with that type of discrepant indicator as the opposite. Jim Milligan, Dean of Admissions, Columbia

For people with a very strong GPA and weak LSAT, we look at their course selection. In particular, we look for academic success in more than one field. For example, does a sociology major do well in economics, statistics, and logic courses. Elizabeth Rosselot, Director of Admissions, Boston College

With a strong LSAT (e.g., 167) but 3.0 (at Michigan State, e.g.), show us that you are very excited about law school and why I should believe that you will engage in intellectual inquiry here when you didn't in college. Erica Munzel, Director of Admissions, University of Michigan

WORK EXPERIENCE

WHAT ARE ADMISSIONS COMMITTEES LOOKING FOR?

Although it is not required for applicants to have had significant work experience, statistics show that rapidly increasing numbers of students are arriving at law schools having already worked full time for a year or more. Many have had accomplished careers, often entirely unrelated to the law. Law schools find this quite appealing. Columbia notes in its admissions materials that, "Our school has been strengthened by a maturity and experiential enrichment that older students bring to their classmates and faculty." Some schools are even willing to deemphasize a less-than-exemplary academic record if an applicant has demonstrated great potential in a demanding—or unusual—industry.

The amount of work experience tends to be much less important than the nature and quality of the experience. Those applicants whose undergraduate performance was comparatively weak, however, should consider working a little longer in order to lessen the currency of grades and course selection, and to increase the amount of positive work-related information to show to the admissions committee.

THE NATURE OF THE EXPERIENCE

Many successful candidates take the tried-and-true path to business school by working as paralegals. Although they get to see what actually goes on in a law firm (thereby learning a bit about law, which many applicants have little or no knowledge of) while simultaneously proving that they truly know what they are getting into, this is not necessarily the best pre-law work route to take. For one, admissions committees know that few paralegals develop real skills; most paralegals spend the majority of their time at the Xerox machine rather than learning anything substantial about the law. It is difficult, in fact, for the law schools to determine whether or not a candidate's paralegal experience was worthwhile or not. For another thing, it is difficult to differentiate yourself from the pool of applicants as a paralegal. You have a far easier time positioning yourself when you have gained substantial and relevant skills in a more unique profession.

Thus, working in a law firm is by no means the best or only route to law school. Accepted students are successful journalists, engineers, playwrights, teachers, businesspeople, and graphic artists. Do not assume that admissions committees will penalize you for having devoted a piece of your life to pursuing an ambition that has little or nothing to do with law. On the contrary, this experience makes you an attractive, unusual candidate—assuming you market yourself well. Remember, too, that there is a big difference between simply doing a job for one to two years and becoming a true professional at something, with three or more years of work experience. This, of course, does not mean you have to work at something for three or more years before going to law school; but your efforts at selling yourself on the basis of your work experience will generally be more easily digested when your commitment to and accomplishments in a field are substantial. Remember, of course, that you must also show that a law degree makes sense in your life and that you have a bright-looking future; in other words, there is a point at which the value of your years of experience begins to decline. Do not squander away time in a job just for the sake of appearing to have career depth in a previous field; gain relevant skills, contacts, and knowledge—and then move on to your law studies.

ACHIEVEMENT AND IMPACT AT WORK

The key to impressing admissions officers with your work experience is not a matter of your specific job or industry, or even of how long you have worked. What you accomplish is the key. Admissions officers want to see people successfully take on responsibility, perform complicated analysis, wrestle with difficult decisions, and bring about change. They want people to progress in their jobs and develop relevant skills, with consequent improvements in responsibilities, salary, and title. People who meet these criteria will be highly valued no matter what industry they come from.

To impress admissions people with your work experience, see that you can demonstrate as many of the following as possible:

- First and foremost, you have been successful at whatever your job involves.
- You have worked well with other people.
- No matter what your job has required of you, you have done more (and exceeded your boss's expectations).
- You have had a wide range of experiences, each one requiring different skills.
- You have acquired substantial skill in your job, which can be applicable to legal study and work.
- You have done a better job than anyone else in a similar position.
- You have achieved meaningful results.
- You have gained in-depth analytical skills.
- You have gained substantial writing experience.

If your work experience gives you little to write about, you face an uphill battle in your applications. If this is the case, consider waiting a year and devoting that year to making an impact in your job. Focus on developing your skills, assuming new and different responsibilities, and impressing one or more potential recommenders to maximize your chances of success when you do apply.

ADMISSIONS DIRECTORS DISCUSS WORK EXPERIENCE

DOES WORK EXPERIENCE "COUNT" IN ADMISSIONS?

Employers love law students who have had real work experience before law school.   Faye Deal, Associate Dean for Admissions and Financial Aid, Stanford

We consider people with two or three years of experience to be quite different than those with ten years. Those with two or three years experience in Washington, for example, are generally dealing with complaints from constituents. Those with ten years may be the top administrative assistant to a representative or senator. We will look more closely at the latter person because he or she is likely to have interesting, substantive work experience that will be valuable once he or she is here. It is the same with any profession.   Michael Rappoport, Dean of Admissions, UCLA

The benefits of having substantial work experience (by which I do not mean waiting tables, etc.) include developing interpersonal and relational skills, the discipline of having to show up and work hard every day, plus learning to juggle multiple tasks. We have found both for the first semester and overall, GPAs were higher for those with substantial work experience than for those without. The additional experience also plays very well with recruiters.   Don Rebstock, Associate Dean of Admissions and Financial Aid, Northwestern

There is probably no professional success that can make up for or outweigh scores and grades that are outside what Dick Badger of Chicago calls the "zone of seriousness" for our school.   Jean Webb, Director of Admissions, Yale

An applicant can offset a lack of extracurricular involvement as an undergrad by having substantial work experience after college. This goes toward demonstrating the maturity of a candidate; it also helps develop critical interpersonal skills.   Don Rebstock, Associate Dean of Admissions and Financial Aid, Northwestern

Those who have worked in jobs that have challenged them bring much more to a class than they otherwise would have had they come directly from college. In addition to working, they may have traveled, practiced their language skills, and developed their people skills. For example, they have learned about leadership, negotiation, and so on.   Kenneth Kleinrock, Assistant Dean for Admissions, NYU

Law interacts with the world, so it is better that someone learn about the world (before coming to law school) than work in law.   Don Rebstock, Associate Dean of Admissions and Financial Aid, Northwestern

There's a disconnect between career services and admissions at most schools. For me, having responsibility for both means that I bring a perspective to the admission process which values maturity, interviewing ability, interpersonal skills and the like as candidates are selected because I will also have some responsibility for assisting them in their efforts to find satisfactory employment. Albert R. Turnbull, Associate Dean for Admissions and Career Services, University of Virginia

We try to put together a group of students who can learn from one another as well as from professors. This can't happen by just taking people on the basis of their GPAs and LSATs. We value having a union organizer with ten years of experience, even if this person might have a mediocre undergraduate record and LSAT relative to some other applicants.   Faye Deal, Associate Dean for Admissions and Financial Aid, Stanford

How Important Is It That Candidates Have Exposure to Legal Work Before Applying?

Exposure to legal practice is important only in the sense that it may convince you not to go to law school, or it may help you decide in which area to specialize. It probably won't help you get into law school. The exception is that we would love to get someone who has worked for some time in a large city police department or sheriff's department.   Michael Rappoport, Dean of Admissions, UCLA

I prefer to see business related experience rather than work in a law firm. In consulting and investment banking, for example, the demands on the person are great, whereas the responsibilities in a law firm tend to be less challenging. Thus the former carries more weight, although we do look at both.   Don Rebstock, Associate Dean of Admissions and Financial Aid, Northwestern

Exposure to law can be very helpful regarding deciding whether to apply, but not in improving the chances of admission.   William Hoye, Dean for Admissions, USC

What Kinds of Work Experience Do You Like to See?

Our public interest program is willing to take people with lesser academics but with a real background in public interest work. This requires demonstrated track records in the field rather than just an expressed interest. For international law, we value experience at the State Department or working abroad as well as possessing several languages. For entertainment law, we value negotiating complex contracts over a period of years.   Michael Rappoport, Dean of Admissions, UCLA

In terms of prior experience, the most common among our admittees are management consulting and financial analyst positions, people who've worked on Capitol Hill, and those who have done short Master's degree programs.   Jean Webb, Director of Admissions, Yale

[Capitol] Hill experience is common here, so I value it less than my colleagues in Chicago or LA do.   Robert Stanek, Director for Admissions, George Washington

I like the Peace Corps, for example. I like things that really challenged the person to think about the world around them.   Dennis Shields, Assistant Dean for Admissions and Financial Aid, Duke

[Categories of applicants who have had interesting jobs or experience that make them highly desirable:]

Olympians: They have shown discipline and commitment; they are interesting as classmates; Military officers: Their comments on international trade and treaties can be valuable; Business owners; Rhodes scholars; Authors of books; Capital Hill people: They can really comment on bills they have worked on. Andy Cornblatt, Assistant Dean for Admissions, Georgetown

We get a lot of twenty-year veterans leaving the military. I like them; they add a lot in the classroom and in the hallway.   Robert Stanek, Director for Admissions, George Washington

WHAT PERCENTAGE OF CANDIDATES NOW HAVE WORK EXPERIENCE BEFORE APPLYING?

Three-fourths of our class has full-time, substantial work experience, not the waiting tables sort. We intend to raise that to at least eighty percent.   Don Rebstock, Associate Dean of Admissions and Financial Aid, Northwestern

Sixty percent of our entering class is not straight from college. Our average age at entry is twenty-five.   Albert R. Turnbull, Associate Dean for Admissions and Career Services, University of Virginia

There is an increasing percentage of applicants with several years of work experience.   Edward Tom, Director of Admissions, Boalt Hall (Berkeley)

HOW IMPORTANT IS IT THAT A CANDIDATE BE SUCCESSFUL IN HIS OR HER JOB?

It's not a matter of what job someone has. Instead, in any field, it's a matter of demonstrating achievement, success, and growth in that field.   Jim Milligan, Dean of Admissions, Columbia

It's important to see success in their jobs; I like to understand why they chose that field. It's also valuable to understand how it led to an interest in law, and how it will benefit a person in studying law.   William Hoye, Dean for Admissions, USC

HOW DO YOU EVALUATE THE QUALITY OF A CANDIDATE'S WORK EXPERIENCE?

One of the key things we look for is the amount of responsibility you have taken on, in whatever position(s) you've had. We prefer you being in the trenches doing real work rather than just Xeroxing files.   Faye Deal, Associate Dean for Admissions and Financial Aid, Stanford

The jobs we like to see are those that help prepare applicants for law school work. For example, some jobs require enormous amounts of analytical effort and training, where the workload is enormous. Some jobs have associated training programs and require a person to make it through one selection process after another. Some jobs are very difficult to get. Some investment banking and consulting jobs, for example, require a person have very good analytical, writing, oral communication, and presentation skills, and handle themselves effectively in person. Other jobs give opportunities to interact with a broad range of constituencies. We take all of this into account in evaluating people. People should do whatever work they are interested in doing. We like a lot of different things; we prefer to have a class with people who have a wide range of background and experience.   Kenneth Kleinrock, Assistant Dean for Admissions, NYU

We look for work experience. When you see someone who is twenty-two and never had a job, it's a bit of a red flag. Additionally, we look for signs of leadership experience.   Anne Brandt, Director of Admissions, Vanderbilt

I worry about people thirty years old who've never done much more than waited tables. They've had an opportunity and not pursued it; I worry whether they have that basic drive that's necessary here.   Robert Stanek, Director for Admissions, George Washington

In general, we believe some time away from formal education between college and law school is a good thing. For many people it offers an opportunity to mature and gain perspective about the direction one's life should take and where law school might fit. While we do not recommend any particular work activity, we do look a bit askance at people who spend years working at frivolous jobs, such as waiting jobs. It's fine to spend a year or two getting away from academe, rubbing shoulders with people who aren't as privileged, paying the bills, having the chance to introspect, but too long at this is problematic. We want to see some get-up-and-go, some initiative.   Albert R. Turnbull, Associate Dean for Admissions and Career Services, University of Virginia

ADMISSIONS DIRECTORS EVALUATE THE IMPACT OF AGE AND EXPERIENCE UPON ADMISSIONS DECISIONS

EVALUATING OLDER APPLICANTS

We don't take academic risks. Everyone taken here is capable of doing very well academically. We are, however, willing to take someone who is at a different level of development than he or she was in college—someone who underperformed years ago but who has accomplished a lot in recent years.   Joyce Curll, Assistant Dean for Admissions and Financial Aid, Harvard

The older someone is, and the longer since he or she went to college, the more weight the LSAT carries and the less the GPA does. For people with a lot of experience, we look at the LSAT score first. We may discount their grades, but the LSAT is helpful in showing that they can compete successfully in law school.   Michael Rappoport, Dean of Admissions, UCLA

The longer someone is away from school, the more the impact of that record is lessened. One can then draw from more than the school record in evaluating the person—the work record and other efforts.   Robert Stanek, Director for Admissions, George Washington

We expect more career focus—a better sense of where they are headed after law school—from older applicants.   Faye Deal, Associate Dean for Admissions and Financial Aid, Stanford

I look at each person as being at a given state of development. The more experience they have, the more you can see where they will get to. For those with real accomplishment, the less you look at the indicators of potential (undergraduate record, LSAT, etc.). Similarly, the less the accomplishment (for older applicants), the more it counts against them, no matter what the initial indicators say. Joyce Curll, Assistant Dean for Admissions and Financial Aid, Harvard

Undergraduate grades are less valuable as predictors after a number of years. With older applicants we look more at the LSAT, graduate work (if any) or additional undergraduate course work undertaken after graduation, and, of course, the nature of his or her work experience.   William Hoye, Dean for Admissions, USC

A twenty-two-year-old poli sci major is likely to have the decision based upon his undergraduate record and LSAT score. But if you're a thirty-year-old, you've been out of school for some time and we'll evaluate your application differently. Your undergrad record will count for less. We will, instead, focus on what you could add to the classroom; we'll consider your motivation for law study carefully. You need to address these matters in your personal statement. Elizabeth Rosselot, Director of Admissions, Boston College

If I'm looking at someone who has already had another career, I'm curious about their interest in law. How did it develop? How do they think their prior work connects to the law? How will their experience enhance their ability to contribute to the intellectual life of the law school? What unique insights and reactions will they be able to share because of their prior experience? While less crucial for younger applicants, they also can benefit by articulating why they are interested in law and how they will contribute to the exchange of ideas and the intellectual life of the law school.   Erica Munzel, Director of Admissions, University of Michigan

EVALUATING COLLEGE SENIORS

For those applying when seniors in college, we generally focus even more on the academic record than for someone who's completed their undergraduate record and been out working.   Kenneth Kleinrock, Assistant Dean for Admissions, NYU

For twenty-one-year-olds right off the college campus, the determining factors are likely to be academic ones. Consequently, they need to choose the schools that offer realistic chances of admission on the basis of these numbers. Michael Rappoport, Dean of Admissions, UCLA

EXTRACURRICULAR, PERSONAL, AND COMMUNITY ACTIVITIES

WHAT ARE ADMISSIONS COMMITTEES LOOKING FOR?

Extracurricular, personal, and community activities include all the nonacademic endeavors to which you have devoted yourself during college and since leaving the academic environment. These include team and individual athletics; artistic, dramatic, or musical performance; private activities such as playing chess or reading; religious activities; involvement in various clubs and organizations; newspaper or other editorial work; and community service.

Extracurricular and community activities are important to admissions officers for many reasons. First, your activity credentials generally show that you interact with others on a regular basis. Law schools generally prefer sociable types (especially leaders) to loners, although most schools will take a few candidates who appear a bit antisocial if they are strong enough in other regards. But the JD is not a degree for people who dislike being involved in group activities. In the same vein, the law profession is not for people who would rather hibernate than interact with varying sorts of people. Extracurricular, personal, and community activities also show how you choose to spend your time away from school and work; demonstrate leadership, initiative, special talents, and honed skills; provide evidence of personality and character traits; and complement ideas presented within your academic profile about how you will fare in a law career. In sum, they give admissions officers an idea about how you might contribute to the law school environment if accepted. Extracurricular achievement is, for obvious reasons, particularly important for those with little or no work experience.

A law school would much rather see that you have put many hours of valuable effort over several years into two activities than joined every group in college, playing very limited roles. Quality matters much more than quantity. In fact, a long list of activities merely dilutes the overall impression that your nonacademic profile gives an admissions officer.

The admissions officers are not looking for any particular activities on a student's palette of involvements. They do not much care whether you are editor-in-chief of the yearbook or director of your company's environmental and recycling team. They are, however, looking for students who have been involved in a few activities for a good length of time, showing commitment and passion. A bit of a balance is usually ideal, so that a student does not appear one-dimensional, but in general commitment and focus is better than being the "all-around" type.

Remember that anything and everything can "count" as part of your profile here. Let us assume, for example, that you are interested in a certain period in American history and have spent time at antique shows and auctions augmenting your collection of furniture and other pieces from the era. This way of spending your Saturdays can certainly become fodder for "extracurricular" material, whether it be merely mentioning it on an activity list or incorporating it into your essays somehow. Be sure to put an appropriate spin on whatever you are claiming as an "activity" to make it a positive credential.

GETTING MAXIMUM VALUE FROM EXTRACURRICULAR AND COMMUNITY ACTIVITIES

Although it does not really matter what activities you choose, keep in mind the following important points about your extracurricular and community record:

➤ *Depth of involvement:* You want to be able to show that you have been committed to one or more activities for a length of time, preferably three or more years. Show that you have advanced within at least one activity and consistently devoted substantial time to it over several years.

➤ *Leadership:* Show that you have taken on an important leadership role in at least one activity. This means founding a club or group, becoming an appointed or elected high officer of a group, or directing a group's efforts in one area. Show that you can motivate others around you to contribute their best efforts to a common cause.

➤ *Something unusual:* Not everyone has the talent or resources to do something really out of the ordinary. But everyone can find a way to use his or her abilities to get involved in something that stands out from the usual student council/yearbook/varsity sports activities that show up frequently on law school applicants' rosters. Doing something a bit unusual can be beneficial because it will expand your own mind, exposing you to something you might not have run into without special effort, as well as make you a bit more memorable to the admissions officers. Training Seeing-Eye dogs, leading nature hikes, becoming a glass-blower, joining a "neighborhood watch" association to fight crime, or playing in a Korean drumming ensemble are examples of activities that are distinctive, but within reach.

➤ *Possession of at least two dimensions:* You want to present yourself as a focused individual with a memorable profile, not someone who dabbles in everything without much commitment to any one particular activity. But avoiding the tag of "well-rounded individual" does not mean you should become one-dimensional. Be sure there is at least one activity you can point to that stands out as not fitting into your main marketing scheme.

THE IMPORTANCE OF COMMUNITY SERVICE

Most law school applicants should be sure to have some sort of volunteer, community, or civic service to show for their four years in college or life beyond academia. As an exception to this general rule, those who come from very low-income families or are required to work a great deal to help support the family should not feel they need to add community service to their activity lists. If it is clear that you spend a substantial amount of energy working for wages necessary for your (or your family's) survival, you will not be expected to have donated your limited free time to charity work.

Other applicants, however, should at the very least have on their activity lists (or work experience lists) a mention of running an event at a Special Olympics function or raising money for a local charity. As with other areas of one's nonacademic profile, more depth in a community service project is always better than these kinds of single instances of volunteerism. Thus, it is much better if you can show that you worked for a cause for a length of time rather than showing up for one Saturday or participating in a single week-long campaign.

WHAT KIND OF COMMUNITY SERVICE?

It is not particularly important what group or cause you help with your time and effort. An admissions committee will be impressed whether you have helped blind children to learn Braille, contributed to an effort to save the seals, helped disadvantaged families with their income tax preparation, or served on the local school board. Of course, committing yourself to a particular activity could substantially help your positioning efforts if you plan to enter a field where your volunteer service could provide you with relevant experience. A candidate proclaiming an interest in family law, for example, would help himself by having worked at a free urban family law clinic for several years.

You should try to be as directly involved in your cause as possible rather than performing work that is only attached to the cause indirectly. Volunteer to work with patients at a hospital rather than shuffling papers in the administrative office, for example. Being directly involved with the people who need your help or in fashioning efforts to solve a community problem will teach you much more (in terms of both hard skills and life lessons) than raising money to support a cause or doing office work for a community organization. Try to allot at least some of your volunteer time for hands-on experience with the "service" component of the work.

Community service can also be used to show leadership, interest in (and aptitude for) the law, initiative, drive, creativity, or an entrepreneurial spirit. Your volunteer efforts in a service project will be that much more powerful and useful to you in law school admissions if you can go beyond the standard effort to contribute more meaningfully to a cause. For example, rather than merely joining a group that protects the natural habitat in your community's park systems, you might consider going one step further by spreading the group's efforts to the next town, thereby becoming the head of the task force for another community. Or you might create a new program for the existing service organization—perhaps a monthly educational meeting for community residents or a kids' task force, to encourage young children to join the service. You might even create an entirely new organization by taking something in which you have helped a single individual and spreading the impact to many others. One applicant we know had helped an elderly woman in the nursing home in which he volunteered learn how to use e-mail to communicate with her grandchildren. When the college applicant saw how effective he had been in helping one woman to improve her life, he decided to take the effort a step further. He founded an organization to teach senior citizens how to use e-mail and make computer systems available for such purposes at libraries, community centers, and nursing homes.

What counts most with community service is that you prove your commitment to caring about something other than yourself. Community service can help demonstrate compassion, appreciation for one's own fortunes, maturity, humanity, and spirit.

USING COMMUNITY SERVICE OUTLETS TO RECRUIT RECOMMENDERS

Doing volunteer work is an excellent way to develop good references. You will be working in a hand-picked activity in which you will be able to control your environment. You can choose a position that is just right for you and your talents, or you can create a position that offers some benefit to an established organization. Charitable organizations know that they are highly dependent upon volunteer workers; consequently, their managers are extremely grateful to anyone who makes a difference. Your involvement in community service can be the ideal place in which to find an appreciative, enthusiastic recommender who can also comment substantively on your talents, initiative, skill, and aptitude for a law career.

THE IMPORTANCE OF COMMUNITY SERVICE
FOR FUTURE PUBLIC INTEREST LAWYERS

If you intend to be a public interest lawyer, or are applying to a school's public interest program, you will be viewed with suspicion if you have not been involved in substantial community activities.

**THE IMPORTANCE OF COMMUNITY SERVICE
FOR ADVANTAGED APPLICANTS**

A commitment to community service is especially important if you come from a wealthy (or even moderately well-off family) and have never had to work for paid wages. If it is evident that you have enjoyed many advantages in your life, you should make an effort to find a service or cause that excites you and devote substantial energy to it before applying to law school.

USE YOUR ACTIVITIES TO HIGHLIGHT YOUR PERSONAL SIDE

Your extracurricular, community, and personal activities can also be used to highlight the personal side of you. As Chapter 5 noted, you should show who you are, not just what you have accomplished. Many applicants use their application essays simply to retell the elements of their professional résumé, or brag about their accomplishments, without ever reaching beyond such matters to let admissions officers understand who they really are. This is generally a mistake. If you come across as just another self-centered, win-at-all-costs individual, your credentials will sell at a substantial discount. No school will go out of its way to take such an individual. Take the opportunity to win over these people-oriented officers; show them you have the warmth, generosity of spirit, and concern for others that will make you a truly valuable member of the incoming class (and of the legal profession thereafter). Show your leadership and team-working skills; show that you have a positive impact that reaches well beyond your own narrow interests. By doing so, you will cause admissions officers to interpret your credentials in a positive light—and your credentials will sell at a premium.

**ADMISSIONS DIRECTORS DISCUSS EXTRACURRICULAR
AND COMMUNITY ACTIVITIES**

GENERAL COMMENTS

I don't care so much what you're interested in, as that you are interested in something—that you are intrigued by it and want to dig into it, that there's an issue you care about or a problem you want to solve. I like it when candidates articulate why they are interested in a particular activity, why it is important to them, what they have learned from it, and/or how their experience in that activity relates to their interests or goals now. If they do this, it often provides further evidence that they are active thinkers who pay attention to the world around them and are thoughtful about their reactions to it.   Erica Munzel, Director of Admissions, University of Michigan

I like to see extracurricular activities that develop writing, debating, and speaking skills. Communication skills in general are crucial in law school. Otherwise, one extracurricular is the same as another. What we see most of is student government, working on the Hill, Habitat for Humanity, working in a prosecutor's office, or some type of government internship.   Robert Stanek, Director for Admissions, George Washington

I value activities that help you develop interpersonal, leadership, and communication skills. I want to see that you have progressed over time.   Janice Austin, Assistant Dean for Admissions, University of Pennsylvania

DEMONSTRATING LEADERSHIP AND TEAMWORK

We want to see leadership and a strong teamwork ethic. Learning how to lead while also being a good team member is important. Community service is one good way of showing this. For example, some of our applicants have received awards for community service leadership.   Joyce Curll, Assistant Dean for Admissions and Financial Aid, Harvard

Leadership skills matter a lot to us. We don't care how many organizations they've joined, for example; we care about the depth of involvement and leadership demonstrated in them (or elsewhere).   Faye Deal, Associate Dean for Admissions and Financial Aid, Stanford

Our "ideal profile" for applicants differs from other schools'. We look for real team players rather than those who will be lone gunslinger litigators. We're a small program so we hope to avoid those who will live on the margins and fail to contribute.   Janice Austin, Assistant Dean for Admissions, University of Pennsylvania

For us, a real sense of ethics and a sense of concern for others, plus a desire to make a real impact in the community, may be more important than raw intellect or academic dedication. When we see someone very decent—with a strong moral compass, compassion and passion, too—this often goes together with a strong sense of leadership. This may be seen in leadership roles or insofar as people look to him or her for leadership. This comes out in the letters of recommendation primarily, but it may come out in the personal statement or even in choices they've made.   Joyce Curll, Assistant Dean for Admissions and Financial Aid, Harvard

I don't care what the activity is as long as you've been involved regarding the direction, focus, mission, and/or creation of it. Being the founder/leader of one activity is more impressive than being a member of ten. We want leaders, not members.   Janice Austin, Assistant Dean for Admissions, University of Pennsylvania

I look above all for two things in extracurricular activities: leadership and commitment to service.   William Hoye, Dean for Admissions, USC

What Particular Activities Do You Value?

I value team sports: being captain in particular. It demonstrates leadership, working in a competitive environment, taking instruction from a coach/mentor. Being a military officer can demonstrate the same. Being recording secretary of your fraternity does not mean much to me.   Janice Austin, Assistant Dean for Admissions, University of Pennsylvania

"Professional joiners" are a turn-off.   Elizabeth Rosselot, Director of Admissions, Boston College

Almost any interest can be helpful in the practice of law, given that law touches on everything. Getting involved in student government is fine, but not necessarily better than getting involved in other matters, which can be every bit as interesting and valuable.   Erica Munzel, Director of Admissions, University of Michigan

As a Jesuit institution, we do like to see humanitarian efforts: the Peace Corps, Teach for America, and so on. Things on the same line at the undergraduate level are also valued highly. Candidates with a demonstrated commitment to public services are the ones that the faculty on the admissions committee are most likely to get excited about.   Elizabeth Rosselot, Director of Admissions, Boston College

What Role Does a Candidate's Roster of Activities Play in the Decision?

If someone is active in student government and in debating, I would take a GPA two-tenths of a point lower than otherwise.   Robert Stanek, Director for Admissions, George Washington

It is really important to us that someone has been active in extracurricular pursuits at college. We look for evidence of well-roundedness and leadership. We are more impressed by leadership of community activities/service organizations, student government, and athletic teams than by leadership of academic organizations, since the latter tend not to involve as much interaction, coordinating of people's efforts, dealing with conflicts, and the like. We are a more cooperative school than most and want to encourage interaction amongst students, so we look for those who won't end up with their noses buried in books in the library.   Don Rebstock, Associate Dean of Admissions and Financial Aid, Northwestern

If someone did community service or part-time work while earning a certain GPA, he achieved more than someone else with that same GPA who didn't simultaneously work.   Erica Munzel, Director of Admissions, University of Michigan

Extracurricular involvement can be important, assuming that someone can articulate in a fresh and compelling way why he/she was involved, how he's grown and learned as a result, and, perhaps, how it's prepared him for law school.   William Hoye, Dean for Admissions, USC

THE IMPORTANCE OF THE PERSONAL SIDE

Admissions is an art, not a science. We're not just looking at people as numbers, letters (i.e., grades), types, or categories.   Joyce Curll, Assistant Dean for Admissions and Financial Aid, Harvard

Our policy states that weight is placed heavily on quantitative measures. But we also hold the belief that numbers don't tell us everything. I admit human beings, not numbers. For this reason, I look at the personal statement first, then at the quantitative measures.   Edward Tom, Director of Admissions, Boalt Hall (Berkeley)

PERSONAL QUALITIES THEY VALUE

I really like optimists, who take whatever happens to them and see it in a positive light. They take real advantage of the opportunities available, or overcome obstacles that would have prevented others from succeeding. I see such people as a good match for this school. They can take advantage of what we have to offer. For example, we have eighty-five student organizations, twelve journals, and a variety of other opportunities of which our students can take good advantage and greatly enhance their experience here.   Joyce Curll, Assistant Dean for Admissions and Financial Aid, Harvard

High intelligence and proven academic skills are not enough. We need to see ample evidence of demonstrated motivation, energy, commitment, perseverance, pride in one's work product and one's self—profoundly human qualities. We seek to admit, enroll, and educate men and women who can and will work collaboratively; who are not selfishly ambitious or competitive in the pejorative sense; and who have developed a sense of responsibility that goes beyond their own individual and material success; and who recognize and accept the responsibilities and not only the benefits of a Columbia legal education.   Jim Milligan, Dean of Admissions, Columbia

We want to see an interest in other people: sincere concern about the well-being of others, maturity, and good listening skills, among other traits. This is important for the fit with Northwestern.   Don Rebstock, Associate Dean of Admissions and Financial Aid, Northwestern

We value "cross cultural" experience. An affluent suburban kid may gain from working in Bedford-Stuyvesant for a year or two. For a kid from Bed-Stuy, it might be working a summer at a major law firm or investment bank. Pursuing such an experience manifests intellectual curiosity and independence of mind and spirit.   Jim Milligan, Dean of Admissions, Columbia

I won't admit anybody who is dishonest or who won't work hard.   Dennis Shields, Assistant Dean for Admissions and Financial Aid, Duke

"Distance traveled" matters a lot to me. Overcoming great adversity and obstacles, perseverance and commitment—all show character.   Faye Deal, Associate Dean for Admissions and Financial Aid, Stanford

I look for superior intellect—it's the engine—and high levels of energy and industry, which are the fuel. I also want people who have values and integrity, some kind of guidance system. Our policy states that weight is placed heavily on quantitative measures. But we also hold the belief that numbers don't tell us everything. I admit human beings, not numbers. For this reason, I look at the personal statement first, then at the quantitative measures.   Edward Tom, Director of Admissions, Boalt Hall (Berkeley)

SHOW WHERE YOU ARE HEADED

If you have a clear idea of where you are headed, and why, you can add substantially to the value of the credentials you possess. Imagine two different candidates. Lisa has a degree in economics and has worked for three years as an analyst in an investment bank. She intends to return to the investment banking world, working in-house as a transactional lawyer. George, on the other hand, has a degree in general studies and has worked a series of odd jobs for the last few years. He states that he wants to be a lawyer in order to help others, although he gives no specifics for how he intends to accomplish this. Imagine that Lisa and George have similar LSAT and GPA results (indeed, their academic records look comparable if you ignore George's lack of focus). Which of the two would you take? In fact, Lisa is surely the stronger candidate. Admissions officers will readily understand her candidacy and implicitly award her "bonus points" for having explored her career options in advance of law school. They know that she will make effective use of the possibilities their school offers because she understands what will be valuable to her in her chosen career. Similarly, her prior work in the field and her continuing career focus suggest that she will be a valuable contributor at law school. In addition, it is clear that she will be readily marketable once she finishes because she has already gotten involved in the field that she intends to work in after law school.

ADMISSIONS DIRECTORS DISCUSS THE CAREER DIMENSION

THE VALUE OF KNOWING WHERE YOU ARE HEADED

It's always good to see an applicant who knows what he or she intends to do in the future, based upon solid evidence. For example, he has already worked in the field he will practice law in. This is certainly of help in gaining admission. Andy Cornblatt, Assistant Dean for Admissions, Georgetown

I don't want to see people who have no idea of what they want to do. They don't need to want to practice law—we're glad if they go into journalism, law, politics, even cartooning, but they should not be clueless about where they're headed. Shelli Soto, Dean of Admissions, University of Texas

The question we're always asking ourselves when we read their files is, "Why law school?" If we don't have a clear understanding of why, it is difficult to make a strong case for admission. Even for older applicants, there can be a lack of a clear reason. If we don't understand why law school, and why now, that admissions offer may not come since we are looking for clarity and focus at this point. This is true even for someone with a very strong undergraduate record and ninety-ninth percentile LSAT scores. Faye Deal, Associate Dean for Admissions and Financial Aid, Stanford

A candidate who fails to demonstrate a serious interest in law will be hurt somewhat in the admissions process. Janice Austin, Assistant Dean for Admissions, University of Pennsylvania

The failure to demonstrate a serious interest in law inevitably hurts applicants' chances a lot. It makes me nervous when people apply simply because it's a professional degree. We ask about this in the interview. If they say, "It's in the family," that is simply not a good enough answer. They should be able to logically project their interests to a field of law, even if they don't know much about the practice of law. They should have at least started to give this serious consideration. Don Rebstock, Associate Dean of Admissions and Financial Aid, Northwestern

We certainly prefer that law not be a default option for an applicant. Jean Webb, Director of Admissions, Yale

EVALUATING CANDIDATES ON THE BASIS OF THEIR CAREER FUTURES

We don't just look at how someone will perform at law school. We're very interested in assessing what people will do after law school, what impact they'll have. For the person to be a leader, a world changer, is very desirable to this law school. Joyce Curll, Assistant Dean for Admissions and Financial Aid, Harvard

We think about an applicant's likelihood of being successful in law school and beyond. Does this person have the ability to be a contributor in law school, to add to the intellectual life of the law school? Is this someone who is engaged, paying attention to what happens around her, thinks a lot about it, and can articulate her responses to it? Will she be successful in practice, and contribute to the community?   Erica Munzel, Director of Admissions, University of Michigan

We look to admit those who will be the best law students. Only a minority of applicants are judged on the basis of what they might accomplish after law school. William Hoye, Dean for Admissions, USC

We're hunting for people who can make a difference in law school and as lawyers. There are three key factors: being able to think clearly, write clearly, and caring passionately about something. If you can do these things, you'll be able to add something to the law school environment.   Dennis Shields, Assistant Dean for Admissions and Financial Aid, Duke

ADMISSIONS DIRECTORS SUMMARIZE
WHAT THEY ARE LOOKING FOR

When I get to the middle of the pool, I'm still looking to find applicants who'll make a difference. They're all pretty bright, so the question is not necessarily who is the brightest. Instead, it's who'll have the biggest impact upon the education others receive. In addition to brains, I look for introspection— someone who has thought about the quality and nature of what they've experienced so far, because that person is most likely to be able to add to the discussion in and out of class.   Dennis Shields, Assistant Dean for Admissions and Financial Aid, Duke

We're looking at many people who are almost indistinguishable in terms of their ability to do the work here. These are people who are truly talented. The key question is who will bring the most to the learning experience of others. Joyce Curll, Assistant Dean for Admissions and Financial Aid, Harvard

We most want people who will engage on more than one front, with both academics and activities. There are many ways for students to excel at Harvard Law School and we look for excellence in a variety of ways.   Joyce Curll, Assistant Dean for Admissions and Financial Aid, Harvard

We rate everyone versus seven categories: Interpersonal and communication skills; Career progression; Intellectual ability; Extracurricular and community involvement; Leadership potential/demonstrated skills; Motivation for Northwestern; Career focus. Although intellectual ability is certainly important, we won't admit someone with very high numbers who lacks the other pieces.   Don Rebstock, Associate Dean of Admissions and Financial Aid, Northwestern

FOR INTERNATIONAL STUDENTS

This section is designed to provide students from outside the United States with information about the special difficulties they face when applying to American law schools.

ADMISSIONS POLICIES

Most of the top law programs require that students have a minimum educational background roughly equivalent to an American Bachelor's degree. The following list gives a rough indication of what level of education is likely to be deemed acceptable. Be sure to double-check with each institution you are interested in, because substantial differences in criteria do exist.

Australia and New Zealand. See United Kingdom and British-styled systems.

Canada. Four-year Bachelor's degree from English-speaking provinces or three-year Bachelor's degree from Quebec are generally acceptable.

Central America. See Spain and Latin America.

China (People's Republic). Bachelor's degree requiring four years of study at a university is generally acceptable.

Denmark. Academingenior or Candidatus are generally acceptable, even in the case of Candidatus degrees requiring only three years of study.

French and French-styled systems. Degrees (diplomes or maitrises) that require a baccalaureate plus four years of further study from a university or grand ecole are generally acceptable.

Germany. Magister Artium, Staatsexamen, or University Diplom are generally acceptable. Fachhochschulen graduates may or may not be eligible.

India, Pakistan, Myanmar, Bangladesh, Nepal. Bachelor's or Master's degrees requiring at least four years of study are generally acceptable, but B.A., B.Com., and B.Sc. degrees alone are often unacceptable.

Indonesia. Sarjana or Sarjana Lengka awarded after five years of study is acceptable, but the Sarjana Muda (requiring only three years of study) is not.

Hungary. Oklevel requiring at least four years of study is generally acceptable.

Mexico. See Spain and Latin America.

Netherlands. The following are generally acceptable: Doctorandus, Ingenieur, or Meester. Kandidaats, Propaeseuse, and H.B.O diplomas are often considered unacceptable.

Philippines. Bachelor's degree requiring either five years of work or four years of work and one year of graduate study is generally acceptable.

Poland. Magister, Dyplom, and Inzynier are generally acceptable.

Russia and former states of the U.S.S.R. Diploma requiring five years at a university or institute is generally acceptable.

Scandinavia. A university diploma awarded for four or more years of study is generally acceptable.

Spain and Latin America. Licenciado, Licenciatura, or Bacharel is generally acceptable.

Switzerland. Diplom, Diplome, and Licence, requiring at least four years of university study, are generally acceptable. The following are often considered unacceptable: Betriebsokonom, HWV, Econ. ESCEA, Ingenieur ETS, Ingenieur HTL and Ingenieur STS.

United Kingdom and British-styled systems. There is no general rule in effect as to British-styled education, although a number of schools require an honours Bachelor's degree.

ACADEMIC RECORDS

American schools almost invariably require that records be translated into English and the translation be officially notarized.

GRADES

The grading systems in use in your country may or may not be familiar to the admissions staff at U.S. law schools to which you are applying. If you have any doubt about this, be sure to have your school send an explanation of the grading system (in English), showing especially the percentage of students who typically get each mark. For example, if your school uses a 20-point system, the top 5 percent of students might have averages of 13–15 points. It is important to point this out, because a poorly informed admissions officer might try to translate your grade of 14 into a 2.8 average in the American style 4.0 system (by simply dividing by 5). The resulting 2.8 is a very mediocre grade, likely to place a student in the bottom half of his or her class. Your 14, on the other hand, might put you in the top 5 percent of your class, something you should want a school to know.

Showing your class rank can thus be very helpful. Another matter of concern to admissions officers is the overall quality of your school. Having your recommenders place it in appropriate context, or having your school note its usual place in the pecking order of local schools, can be helpful, at least if your school is generally well regarded.

8

MARKETING YOURSELF

— EXECUTIVE SUMMARY —

Understand how you compare with the competition.

■

Learn how admissions officers will view your candidacy based upon their expectations of people from your field and educational background.

■

Position yourself well, capitalizing on your strengths
while minimizing your weaknesses, in light of
schools' expectations.

■

Use themes to focus your marketing effort.

■

Learn how to use a special case status to your advantage.

The first part of this chapter shows you how to determine what you should emphasize in your application. Your areas of emphasis depend upon several factors: what the top law schools want, what your competition offers, and your relevant strengths and weaknesses compared with other applicants. The second part of the chapter begins the discussion of how to capitalize on your strengths and make the strongest possible argument for your acceptance. This discussion continues throughout the following chapters, which explore the marketing vehicles you need to master: the essays, recommendations, and interviews.

CREATING A MARKETING STRATEGY

YOUR STRENGTHS AND WEAKNESSES VERSUS THOSE OF THE COMPETITION

Chapter 7 explains what schools seek in their applicants. Reading that chapter will give you a reasonable idea of what your own strengths and weaknesses are. This, however, is not really enough; at this point you should go one step further in determining how you stack up versus the competition.

Start your analysis of the competition you face by getting the summary data schools provide about their entering classes. Columbia, for instance, provides the following information about its entering class:

CLASS OVERVIEW

Applicants	6,743
Matriculants	367
Women	187 (51%)
Men	181 (49%)
Total Minority Enrollment	116 (32%)
Asian	50 (14%)
Black/African-American	40 (11%)
Hispanic	24 (7%)
American Indian	2 (<1%)
International Students	22 (6%)

REGIONAL BREAKDOWN

Mid-Atlantic	45%
West	16%
South	17%
Midwest	11%
New England	7%
International	4%

40 states, District of Columbia, and 13 foreign countries are represented.

AGE BREAKDOWN

20 or younger	4 (1%)
21–24	252 (68%)
25–29	91 (25%)
30–39	20 (5%)
40 or older	1 (<1%)

35% of the entering class came to law school directly from college.

ADVANCED DEGREES

MA	24
PhD	6
MS	5
MEd	3
MBA	2
MPP (Public Policy)	1
MPHL	1
MM (Music)	1
MTS (Theology)	1
MIA	1
MD	1
MSW	1

Matriculants with at Least One Graduate Degree: 47 (13%)

UNDERGRADUATE MAJORS

	NUMBER	PERCENTAGE
Poli. Sci./Government	72	20
Literature	42	11
History	39	10
Economics	31	8
Science/Eng./Mathematics	26	7
International Relations	15	4
Philosophy	14	4
Finance/Accounting/Bus.	13	4
Psychology	10	3
Sociology	7	2
Languages	7	2
Music	5	1
Religion	5	1

LEADING UNDERGRADUATE FEEDER SCHOOLS

Yale	28
Columbia	20
Harvard	18
Brown	17
University of Pennsylvania	13
Stanford	12
Univ. of Calif. (Berkeley)	11
Dartmouth	11
Princeton	10
Cornell	9
University of Michigan	9
Univ. of Texas (Austin)	8
UCLA	7
New York University	7
Duke	6
University of Virginia	6
Brigham Young	5
Barnard	5
Emory	5
Wellesley	5
Georgetown	4
Northwestern	4
Rice	4
Smith	4

Number of Undergraduate Institutions Represented:	*130*
Median LSAT score:	*169*
Median Undergraduate GPA:	*3.63*

You can beef up this profile by adding data from additional sources (see Chapters 3 and 4 for a listing of appropriate readings about the schools). *U.S. News & World Report,* for instance, lists the following for Columbia:

Acceptance rate:		18.7%
LSAT scores:	25th percentile:	166
	75th percentile:	171
GPAs:	25th percentile:	3.43
	75th percentile:	3.75

In addition, you can always ask the school itself for additional information. Many collect and collate more than is provided in the information packages for potential applicants.

Other schools provide data similar to that in the chart above. With these data in hand, it is a simple matter to determine how you stack up relative to the prior year's successful candidates in terms of your academic credentials, LSAT score, amount of experience, and background.

A SHORTCUT TO THE STRENGTHS AND WEAKNESSES ANALYSIS

Each person will be more than just a member of a category; a person who happens to be a paralegal will not—one hopes—be the same as all other paralegals. By the same token, knowing what category you fall into can help you determine how you are likely to be viewed by admissions officers. Admissions officers, like everyone, make various simplifying assumptions about the world. Not all astrophysicists and brain surgeons will be extremely smart, intellectually driven, and so on, but most of us assume this is the case unless given evidence to the contrary. Understanding how your "type" is perceived—absent any other evidence—and about how others in your category will also be perceived is valuable. (Knowing how your most direct competitors—those who most resemble you—will be viewed is an important part of developing your marketing strategy.)

The following chart is intended to make this process of identifying where to focus your efforts a bit easier by showing the presumed strengths and weaknesses of different categories of applicants. If you are a member of one of the most traditional categories of applicants to JD programs—for example, a recent graduate of an undergraduate university with no work experience—recognize that just having the strengths noted here will be insufficient reason to admit you. You may need to be demonstrably stronger than others in the same category (and perhaps even free of the category's typical weaknesses). The chart shows what are presumed to be weaknesses unless evidence proves otherwise.

The first five categories are the broadest, addressing—on the simplest level—the basic "types" of applicants: the 22-year-old, in his last year of college; the graduate student, who has pursued one or more advanced degrees; the "taker of time off," who has been out of college for a year or two, traveling or otherwise soul-searching; the "do-gooder," who has spent her time volunteering for numerous organizations and causes; the experienced professional, who has devoted years to building knowledge and experience in a specific industry. One can, of course, fall into more than one category; be sure to pay attention to the pros and cons of each.

CATEGORY	LIKELY STRENGTHS	LIKELY WEAKNESSES
Applicant Types		
College Student	Still in study mode	Immature
	Energetic	Driven to law school by parents
	Idealistic	Postponing real decisions by getting a JD
		Lacking concrete skills
		Similar to too many other applicants with interchangeable skills!
Graduate Student/PhD	Bright	An ivory-tower thinker
	Accustomed to demanding academic work	Afraid to leave academia
	Possessing knowledge of a field	Possessing limited knowledge of real world
Time Off: Soul-Searcher/ Solitary	Contemplative	A cultural misfit
	Headstrong	Aimless
	Worldly	Lacking drive
	Has thought seriously about future	A romantic dreamer rather than pragmatist
Do-Gooder	Altruistic/Idealistic	Not cut out to be a hardened lawyer
	A "people person"	
		Likely to change career focus upon encountering real world
		Likely to be disappointed with realities of legal practice
Experienced Professional	Possessing knowledge of specific industry	Lacking sincere interest in law
	Hardworking and determined	Lacking patience for serious, independent study
	Willing to share experiences	Unable to work with youngsters as equals
Profession		
Paralegal	Possessing prior exposure to the "dirty work" reality of lawyering	Possibly undynamic
	Possessing sincere interest in law	Possibly possessing little substantive knowledge of any one field
Legislative Aide	Possessing understanding of law	Lacking patience for rigorous study
	Possessing knowledge of substantive field(s)	
	Possessing research skills	
	Possessing communication skills	

Category	Likely Strengths	Likely Weaknesses
Functionary/Secretary	Hard-working Capable of tedious work	Unable to think independently Needing authority Lacking industry knowledge Lacking drive, ambition
Teacher	Hard worker Possessing good social and interpersonal skills Diplomatic, a good negotiator	Overly idealistic Needing constant interaction and feedback Lacking drive, ambition
Public interest	Willing to work hard for low pay Altruistic	Unable to tolerate opposing views Immature, naive
Consultant	Bright Possessing an understanding of business Possessing strong communication skills Possessing strong research and analysis skills Possessing leadership skills	Possessing questionable interest in law Inclined to do deals rather than help others do them Lacking patience for tedious legal study
Finance/Banking	Possessing understanding of business Possessing research and analysis skills	Lacking writing, communication skills
Accountant	Possessing an understanding of accounting Possessing seriousness of purpose Possessing exposure to numerous businesses and industries Possessing quantitative skills	Undynamic; not a leader Lacking writing, communication skills
Computer Programmer	Bright Technologically up-to-date Possessing quantitative skills	Lacking interpersonal skills Lacking leadership skills Unwilling to develop "soft" skills
Engineer	Possessing quantitative skills Technologically up-to-date Used to rigorous academic setting Highly marketable	Lacking outside interests Lacking communication and interpersonal skills Unwilling to joust in class
Military Officer	Possessing good leadership training Determined Team oriented	Unable to think independently A cultural misfit in law school Lacking communication skills

CATEGORY	LIKELY STRENGTHS	LIKELY WEAKNESSES
Scientist	Bright Possessing good analytical skills Very marketable	Possessing questionable interest in law Lacking communication skills Unwilling to joust in class
Human Resources	Social and interpersonal skills Team player	Possessing questionable interest in legal problems (perhaps just interested in people's feelings) Lacking analytical skills
Sales	Possessing communications skills Possessing interpersonal skills	Lacking analytical skills Possessing only short-term focus
Writer, Journalist	Possessing research and writing skills An independent thinker Possessing communication skills	Lacking ability to lead others A romantic dreamer rather than pragmatist
Photographer/Artist	Possessing an unusual perspective Possessing creative problem-solving skills A conceptual thinker	Unable to work with others A cultural misfit Lacking analytical skills
Undergraduate Major		
Political Science	Possessing bona fide interest in law Possessing knowledge of law and government	Similar to too many other applicants Tending to think of law as a grand affair rather than a practical profession Attending law school by default
History	Possessing an understanding of government, the principles behind laws Used to lengthy readings	Similar to too many other applicants Attending law school by default
Economics	Possessing an understanding of business Familiar with key tools for analyzing various areas of law	Lacking patience for "soft skills" Possessing writing skills Possibly preferring business school, but unwilling to work for 3–5 years before applying
Mathematics/Engineering	Disciplined Possessing quantitative skills Extremely marketable	Unable to read between the lines Lacking writing skills Possessing questionable people skills

CATEGORY	LIKELY STRENGTHS	LIKELY WEAKNESSES
Psychology	Possessing knowledge of human behavior	Lacking patience for independent study
	...y people	May place too much emphasis on "soft skills"
Pl...	...inker	Lacking people skills
	...ng formal	Lacking career focus
Li...	...lls	An ivory-tower thinker
	...ing ability	Not used to reading dry texts
	...yze lan-	Particularly lacking in knowledge of law as career
La...	...view-	Lacking analytical skills
		Possessing few scholarly interests
	...urs	
No... *su...* *ex...*	...ate major can change if you have devoted a history major with a math minor, for d set of skills.	
Ag...		
Ol... ...[...rties or older]	Possessing experience and industry knowledge	Lack of energy
		Unable to work with youngsters as equals
	Possessing a calming influence on youngsters in cohort	Impatience with theory
Background		
Disadvantaged	Possessing strong work ethic	Unprepared for rigors of strong academic program
	Possessing underrepresented perspective	Might have difficulty fitting in
Wealthy/Advantaged	Possessing rich experiential knowledge	Arrogant
		Weak work ethic
	Future success all but assured	Spoiled
Recent immigrant	Knowledge-hungry	Grade-grubbing
	Possessing strong work ethic	

CAPITALIZING ON YOUR STRENGTHS; MINIMIZING YOUR WEAKNESSES

Once you have analyzed your situation and recognize where you stand, you should be aware of what an admissions officer is likely to see as your strengths and weaknesses. Your job is now to capitalize on this understanding.

First, you will want to support any of the strengths you do indeed have. You can relate stories in your essays that show you, for example, as an effective leader. Just as important, you can (and should) have your recommenders provide supporting examples.

Second, do whatever you can to minimize your weaknesses, or, better yet, show that you do not suffer from them. Once again, it is a matter of addressing them through each of the vehicles at your disposal: the essays, the recommendations, and (for some schools) interviews. In other words, you should maximize your reward/risk ratio. Schools want students who will make major contributions to their programs—who will provide a reward for accepting them—without involving substantial risks of academic and other types of failure. The higher the reward/risk ratio, the better your chance of appealing to a school.

The tasks facing people with different profiles will, of course, be different. A paralegal at a major law firm faces a very different task from that of a commercial photographer or a recent college graduate in trying to maximize the reward/risk ratio. The paralegal (or law clerk) who has already spent three years working at a top corporate firm is likely to be regarded as being quite bright and determined, with strong research and analysis skills, and a good understanding of law, without being much of a risk to the program. After several years' work as a paralegal, she knows enough about law and the tedium involved in legal practice that there is essentially no danger that she will fail out of the program, or lose interest in law, or be unplaceable in a good job upon graduation. She therefore looks like an easy admit because she brings good experience and qualities to the program without any risk. The problem for her, however, is that she is but one among numerous paralegals, all of whom bring similar qualities. To improve her chances of admission, she must show that she is quite different from those other paralegals in terms of her range of work, the depth of her understanding of a specific area of law (or two or three), her success to date, and how she intends to employ her law degree in the future.

The commercial photographer is in a nearly opposite situation. In his case, the problem is not what he brings to the program. He is likely to be the only photographer applying, so he has considerable uniqueness value to start with. His problems involve the risk side of the ratio. An admissions director is likely to worry that he will be unable to handle the program's grueling academic demands and that he will fail out of the program early on. Similarly, she may worry that he will lose interest in law and simply go back to photography midway through the program. She will probably also worry that his lack of work in a traditional field may make the employers who recruit at the school reluctant to hire him. To improve his chances of admission, he needs to address each concern. He may, for example, want to take several courses that show he has the ability to do analytical, research-intensive work prior to applying . By doing this he also shows that he is sincerely interested in law, is not applying on a whim, and is likely to complete the program. Last, he will want to show where he is headed with his JD and how he intends to get there. This will involve explaining what skills and experiences he already has, plus showing how he will acquire other relevant skills and experiences during the law school program.

The recent college graduate is, of course, a common brand of applicant. She is likely to have excellent grades and scores, and have demonstrated prowess in courses that are at least tangentially related to the study of law. She is likely to be bright and hard working—like the paralegal—and also have strong analytical skills. Although she, too, looks like an easy admit, the recent college graduate is not exempt from the risk factor associated with the commercial photographer.

COMBATING A PRIVILEGED IMAGE

Do:

➤ Participate in/lead substantial community service activities.

➤ Show that you have taken advantage of all opportunities.

➤ Demonstrate that you have crossed social and other divides or experienced the plight of (and sympathize with) others less fortunate.

Do not:

➤ Discuss expensive trips you have taken or glamorous events you have attended.

➤ Describe your parent as managing director of Wall Street's fanciest investment bank—"banker" will do.

➤ Sound arrogant, spoiled, or unappreciative of your opportunities. World-weary cynicism does not play well with admissions directors.

➤ Act as if you hit a triple when you were actually born on third base (as one critic had it of former President Bush). In other words, do not make a big deal out of having gone to a fancy prep school or having managed to make money performing mundane services for your parents' wealthy pals.

An admissions director may wonder about the recent college graduate's motives for obtaining a law degree, and if they are well-founded. Although it is not likely that she will fail out, the bright-eyed 22-year-old may discover that legal study—and, ultimately, a job as a lawyer—is not at all what she had expected. To clinch her chances of admission, then, the recent college graduate needs to show that she is aware of what law school entails and that she understands the almost-inevitable consequence of attending: practicing law.

PERSONAL STATEMENT EXAMPLE

The personal statement written by Heather, below, provides a good example of how to capitalize on a category's strengths and minimize certain obvious weaknesses. Heather graduated from the University of California at Santa Cruz with a degree in Psychology. Although she graduated with honors, Santa Cruz's lack of a grading system leaves her to battle the admissions process without a GPA or an index number. Additionally, an LSAT score of 160—a score below the average of her ideal law schools—is a hindrance. On the surface, Heather is obviously in a precarious position. Her numbers, and the fact that she did not attend a top-flight undergraduate institution, necessitate a strong marketing job. On the other hand, the fact that she spent the last five years working for social service and criminal justice agencies—work she describes intelligently and convincingly—is commendable. She shows that she is truly determined (and, more important, *prepared*) to work for the public interest. She proves herself to be mature: an independent thinker and a persuasive advocate. These are all qualities law schools look for when choosing among applicants.

> Albert was born and raised in California. Our similarities end there. Albert is a crack addict with AIDS who was physically abused and abandoned by his parents at age twelve. He became a sex worker and, when he needed a quick fix, he would burglarize homes. At age 26, he had just been convicted on his third "strike" and was facing 25 years to life in prison.
>
> His public defender had hired me, a sentencing specialist at the Center on Justice, to advocate on Albert's behalf and to develop an Alternative Sentencing Plan. When I first met this client, he was wearing the standard-issue orange sweatsuit provided by the Los Angeles County Jail and he looked relatively healthy. As he told me his life story, including the numerous offenses of which he had been both victim and perpetrator, I began to formulate a strategy to persuade the judge that a rehabilitative sentence was warranted.
>
> I went back to the office to begin my research on the resources available to HIV-positive drug-addicted offenders. I began by looking into the services

offered in the California Department of Corrections (CDC), since the likelihood of my client being sentenced to prison was very high. I learned of the deliberate neglect of HIV-infected prisoners and the dearth of experienced medical staff in the prisons. The situation for the treatment of substance abuse was equally grim: less than 1% of the 105,000 addicts in the CDC receive drug treatment. With this knowledge I began to research community-based alternatives that would address the needs of my client.

Two weeks into my research, my work was interrupted by an emergency. I went to interview Albert a second time, but he was in no condition to talk. His lips were cracked and his face was marked with lesions. Pain radiated from where he had been injected that morning with Pneumovax, a vaccine against pneumonia. The day after my visit, after complaining of a fever and delirium for over twenty hours, the nurse finally felt his forehead. He had a temperature of 105 degrees caused by the contaminated serum the jail medical staff had given him. He was rushed to Los Angeles General Hospital.

One day after he was admitted to the hospital, Albert called me in a panic because his doctor had stopped giving him Indinavir, the protease inhibitor he had been taking for several months to combat his AIDS. From having worked with other clients with AIDS, I recognized the danger of interrupting his medication; he could develop a resistance to this and perhaps other protease inhibitors if his treatment was not resumed immediately. I called San Francisco General Hospital—a leading AIDS research institution—and was told that they did not have Indinavir. I suspected that Albert was being discriminated against due to his inmate status. I contacted his doctor and expressed my concern that it appeared my client's medication had been withheld. Ten minutes later, Albert called to thank me. The nurse had just given his first dose of his medicine. With that obstacle behind us, I resumed the development of my argument to the judge with renewed enthusiasm.

I succeeded in convincing Miller House, a respected substance abuse program for HIV-positive offenders, to accept Albert into their residential care program. In order to dissuade the judge from sentencing Albert to prison, I described in my report the grossly inadequate resources available in the California Department of Corrections to address his needs. I outlined his social history and argued that in order for Albert's cycle of crime to cease, his addiction and medical needs would have to be aggressively treated. I suggested that a term of imprisonment was, in fact, a death sentence. In conclusion, I recommended that the Court strike Albert's priors as permitted under state law, and sentence Albert to the aggravated term, to be suspended with five years of probation and mandatory participation in the Walden House residential program for one and a half years.

The judge accepted my recommendations in full. After the judge announced the sentence, Albert's public defender turned to me and said, "You saved his life." The incredible feeling I get from knowing I have helped alter the course of someone's life in a positive direction is what motivates me to want to practice law.

I have been working for social service and criminal justice agencies for the past five years and I am committed to continuing to serve historically underrepresented individuals in a broader role as an attorney. It is important to me to study law in a school that emphasizes serving the public interest and values diversity. Boalt Hall impressed me as such a school as evidenced by its strong clinical program and the wide range of courses offered that focus on public interest. Thus I apply to become a member of the class of 2001 at Boalt Hall.

Heather is currently attending her first choice, Boalt Hall at UC Berkeley, a school that prides itself on its public interest emphases.

FIT IN–STAND OUT

Another way to think about the reward/risk ratio is, as many admissions directors put it, a "fit in–stand out" problem. *Fitting in* means you are accepted by your classmates as belonging to the program rather than being regarded as an oddity. If you can do the course work, subscribe to the program's goals, and get on well with the other students, you will fit in. *Standing out* means you bring something unique to the program, something that distinguishes you from the other students.

The trick, obviously, is to fit in and stand out at one and the same time. It is not sufficient to do just one of these things. Saying that you really fit in, that you look like a composite of all the other students, gives the school no reason to want you there because you bring nothing different and therefore nothing special. Saying that you really stand out, that you do not resemble any of the other students in any relevant way, is similarly useless because you may be seen as too risky to have in the program. The way to straddle this apparent divide is to fit in regarding certain key dimensions and be different regarding other specifics. Most people will tend to fall more on one side of the divide than the other. The paralegal need not worry that she will fail to fit in; her problem is showing how she stands out. The photographer need not worry about standing out; his problem is showing that he fits in. (The recent college graduate, in contrast, does need to worry a little bit about both.)

FASHIONING YOUR MESSAGE: POSITIONING

Positioning is a marketing concept that is meant to deal with this problem of too many applicants trying to capture the attention of admissions directors who are overwhelmed by the onslaught. To cut through all of this communications haze, you must have a very sharp and clear image that is readily noticed and understood and valued.

Let's look at an example that is dear to my heart. There are many types of whiskey, even of scotch whiskey—and even of single-malt scotch whiskey. Nonetheless, there are a number of products that are distinctively positioned in the market for single-malt scotch. For example, Laphroaig is a single-malt scotch with a peatier, more iodine taste (and "nose") than its competitors. Its unique attributes allow it to market itself to consumers who consider themselves beyond the "beginners'" scotches and who want the strongest possible taste they can find. Macallan, on the other hand, is exceptionally smooth and even bears a certain resemblance to cognac. It tells consumers that its product is aged in old sherry casks, which impart a distinctive hint of sherry in the nose.

These two products compete in the high end of the scotch market, yet each is positioned to be completely unique. Their marketing efforts aim to make it very clear what key attributes they possess, and they are very successful. Both are held in extremely high regard by serious malt scotch whiskey drinkers, although they are considered virtually unrelated to one another. The result is that each can claim a price premium for its distinctiveness that would be impossible were they positioned to compete head-to-head.

APPLYING THE CONCEPT TO YOURSELF

How does this apply to you? You must distinguish yourself from others in the applicant pool who may apply to the same schools you do. Law school applicants are not all the same; your job is to show your uniqueness. You increase your value by appearing unique. After all, if you are the same as 2,500 other applicants, what school will really care if it gets you rather than one of the other 2,499? You also make yourself more memorable by making yourself unique. Remaining anonymous will not help you. Far better if an admissions committee remembers you, perhaps even having a shorthand expression for use in discussing you. Being "the woman who was a private investigator in Miami" means that you are remembered and can be discussed as a unique person. Contrast this with the sort of person who is discussed as "Which one is she? Really? Could I see that file again? I don't remember reading that one before."

GENERAL POSITIONING VERSUS SPECIFIC POSITIONING

To what extent should your positioning be different for each target school? Since no two schools are exactly the same, you might want to position yourself differently for each school. On the other hand, doing markedly different applications for each school is a lot of extra work. Not only do you need to write your essays differently, but you also need to have your recommenders write each recommendation differently. For example, if you intend to apply to Berkeley for its

International and Comparative Legal Studies Program and to Harvard for its Program on Negotiation, you will face the difficulty of being a persuasive applicant for both.

Take a modified approach; have a general positioning strategy that you can fine-tune to fit the needs of specific schools without making major changes in your application. Emphasize different aspects of your experience for a given school; don't try to recreate yourself for it. Obviously, if you have not resolved what you intend to do at law school and afterwards, you may need to do very different applications to each program.

Any positioning approach that you take must be something you can reinforce via specific, powerful examples.

THE MECHANICS OF POSITIONING: USING THEMES

Positioning is meant to provide a method for presenting a very clear picture of you. A simple way to achieve this is to use several themes to organize your material. When writing your essays, for example, relate all or at least most of your material to your chosen themes. Your positioning will be very clear and easy to grasp if your material is organized around three or four themes.

The themes you use will be different from those others will (or should) use. Because law schools are looking for some very definite features in all of their candidates, however, you should have one or two themes that other strong candidates will also use. Chapter 7 shows that schools are always concerned to find people who (1) are motivated to excel in the study of law, and (2) have what it takes to be an effective lawyer.

Law schools want people who will accomplish things, despite the obstacles they will encounter. Success in spite of difficulties is what determination is all about. At age 22 you might have had moderate success without having tried very hard or without having confronted substantial obstacles, but this good fortune is unlikely to continue for your whole career. Thus, you should show that you have accomplished things only after overcoming difficulties placed in your way.

Top schools believe that the education they offer is valuable, and they want to admit students who will get the full measure of this value. Such students are those who want a law degree for the right reasons and who are at the proper point in their lives and careers to get the most out of it. This means they are able to appreciate what a law degree offers them. It also means they will figure out how to maximize the benefit of a program by choosing the appropriate courses and clinics, making the right contacts, and marketing themselves effectively to potential future employers. Those who have not thought through their own futures, or who do not appreciate where their talents and interests lie, are not likely to maximize the benefits of a JD and are thus likely to be rejected by the best schools. This means you are obligated to coherently articulate your desire for a law degree—and why it is best pursued now.

The other organizing themes you choose will be those that are appropriate to you. The essays in Part IV show some examples of what kinds of ideas others have chosen; look at several of them from this perspective. Here are a few of the many possible themes around which one can organize parts of the application, and some idea of who might make use of them.

- *Altruist:* You have spent the last two years working for the Peace Corps, distributing medicine and food in French West Africa.

- *Polyglot:* You speak five languages fluently, with substantial knowledge of multiple cultures.

- *Survivor:* You grew up in a remote, poverty-stricken area of Appalachia, and were the first member of your town to go to college.

- *All-around synthesizer:* As an architect, you have had to bring together the work of various types of engineers, designers, lawyers, accountants, and city planners.

- *Dedicated toiler:* You spent your last year of college holed away in an archive, deciphering the handwritten notes of Alexis de Toqueville.

- *From an unusual background:* Because of your father's job as a jail minister, you grew up on the compound of a notorious prison.

- *Risk taker:* As a journalist, you thrive when culling information from dangerous situations and analyzing it in light of historical fact.

- *Crusader:* In your volunteer work for Planned Parenthood, you have organized a group of abortion-rights activists.

HOW MANY THEMES SHOULD YOU USE?

There are practical limitations to the number of themes that will help you. If you use too few, you have very little maneuvering room in writing your essay(s) because everything has to fit within just one or two organizing themes. If you use too many, you end up doing no organizing whatsoever and your positioning will no longer be clear. The trick is to balance these two factors. Using about three themes is generally appropriate because with that number you do not constrain your efforts so much that you appear boring, but you are focused enough that admissions committees reading your application will know what you are about. The key is that they should be able to summarize your positioning in three or four short phrases. You want to become an individual to them, yet one on whom they can get a handle.

THE MARKETING VEHICLES

You have three primary vehicles for getting your message across to business schools: the essay(s), recommendations, and possible interviews. You will need to be consistent within and across these three vehicles to gain the maximum positive impact. The following chapters will show you how to make the most of them.

CONCLUSION

The penalty for failing to capitalize on your strengths and to prepare a powerful application is, all too often, rejection. Schools have plenty of qualified applicants who took the time to figure out the process and complete a good application. Failure to do these things suggests that you are not able to do so, or at least do not care to. In either case, you are unlikely to be viewed as having top law school potential, at least at the moment.

ADMISSIONS DIRECTORS DISCUSS HOW YOU SHOULD MARKET YOURSELF

THE IMPORTANCE OF MARKETING YOURSELF WELL

Presenting themselves well is most important for that large segment of our applicant pool where selections are difficult. Applicants with decent LSAT scores, good academic records who were active in college and have good work or extracurricular experience—these are the applicants who can help themselves the most with effective presentation.   Erica Munzel, Director of Admissions, University of Michigan

I have been known to say no to applicants with extremely high numbers, simply because they had nothing to say, nothing to offer.   Edward Tom, Director of Admissions, Boalt Hall (Berkeley)

The whole application process is a good test of legal advocacy. You are called upon to marshal evidence and make decisions about what to include or exclude in pleading your case.   William Hoye, Dean for Admissions, USC

Applicants who are at the index number level where we take twenty to fifty percent can help themselves tremendously if they market themselves well. It is especially critical that they show they have special characteristics and experiences to bring, that they are genuinely interesting people.   Albert R. Turnbull, Associate Dean for Admissions and Career Services, University of Virginia

A strong presentation is quite common among those applicants who are admitted. Joyce Curll, Assistant Dean for Admissions and Financial Aid, Harvard

Just the way a person organizes the application materials reveals something, pro or con, about the person.   Elizabeth Rosselot, Director of Admissions, Boston College

Few Applicants Market Themselves Well

Perhaps 100 out of 3,900 applicants do a great job marketing themselves. I would think that there would be more, but unfortunately there aren't.   Janice Austin, Assistant Dean for Admissions, University of Pennsylvania

Few applicants do a first-rate job marketing themselves.   Elizabeth Rosselot, Director of Admissions, Boston College

Show Your Interest In/Fit with the School

If we get the sense that they care about Michigan, having taken the time to do the application well, we are likely to give the person the benefit of the doubt. Erica Munzel, Director of Admissions, University of Michigan

It's easier to submit applications now, so people have taken to just sending them off to a large percentage of the top twenty-five schools. If someone looks like he/she sought out our school and tailored the application to us, that gives the person an edge. We are inevitably impressed by people who have done their homework and determined that our program fits their needs.   Elizabeth Rosselot, Director of Admissions, Boston College

If a person applies to do international human rights here, which is not one of our strengths, I'll question his judgment. It is O.K. if he acknowledges this and shows what program of study he will follow (and note that the overall Penn education, and name, make it worth doing his degree here).   Janice Austin, Assistant Dean for Admissions, University of Pennsylvania

We get lots of people who want to be politicians, theoreticians, and policy makers, but we probably have far fewer people than Stanford would wanting to do patent law, for example.   Jean Webb, Director of Admissions, Yale

We want people for whom Harvard Law School is a good match. Does this look like a candy store (with all its options and possibilities) or a scary place? Someone with real interest and experience in East Asian studies, Islamic law, or alternative dispute resolution, for example, would be of particular interest to us.   Joyce Curll, Assistant Dean for Admissions and Financial Aid, Harvard

Someone who can study something at Michigan that he can't study elsewhere *may* get a bit of an edge in the application process. Similarly, if a person wants to study with a particular professor, that could matter in the admissions process. I might even show the application to that professor and ask if that's the sort of student he'd like in his class. His response may well play into my decision. Erica Munzel, Director of Admissions, University of Michigan

I might give an advantage to someone who can make particularly good use of our key course offerings. This would be true, however, only for someone with specific career experience in a given field, not for someone straight out of undergrad or grad school. Too many students change their minds once they're in the program. A good example of the type of person I might favor would be someone with substantial experience in environmental matters, or from the patent and trademark office.   Robert Stanek, Director for Admissions, George Washington

The Penn Factor certainly counts for you. By this I mean that if you are very specific about Philadelphia, the university, having visited us—which has a high correlation with your coming here, or work by a specific professor.   Janice Austin, Assistant Dean for Admissions, University of Pennsylvania

Be Sure Your Messages Are Consistent

Presenting yourself accurately, honestly, and thoughtfully is critical. It's important that the messages we get from the different pieces of the application are consistent—that the letters of recommendation match the personal statement, which matches the extracurricular profile, etc. This makes the picture comprehensible and credible.   Joyce Curll, Assistant Dean for Admissions and Financial Aid, Harvard

When an applicant mentions the type of law he or she intends to practice in the future, our first instinct is to check the related data. We want to see whether she can back it up—has she been active in groups related to this field, for example. If she can back it up, it's great: She definitely helps her candidacy. At the extreme, this might mean a family therapist intending to practice family law.   Elizabeth Rosselot, Director of Admissions, Boston College

I look for the connection between people's stated interests and their demonstrated commitments and accomplishments.   Kenneth Kleinrock, Assistant Dean for Admissions, NYU

Don't raise questions you fail to answer in the application. We don't have the time to pick up the phone to find out about gaps or inconsistencies in your record.   Elizabeth Rosselot, Director of Admissions, Boston College

Any seasoned admissions officers knows well that any applicant may compose an application essay laying claims to strong character, sound values, noble ideals, and impressive achievements. And many do. At Columbia, however, we are sure to place any professional claims of an application essay in the context of the rest of his/her application . . . indeed, in the context of his/her life. We study how the applicant has actually chosen to use his or her time, energies, and talents. We look at the choices applicants have made in their academic lives, in their work place and in planning their careers, in the communities, in extracurriculars, perhaps in their political and/or religious lives.   Jim Milligan, Dean of Admissions, Columbia

Appendix IV

SPECIAL CASES

RESIDENCY

Public law schools—i.e., law schools at state-funded universities—generally give preferential admissions treatment to their own state's residents. The degree of preference varies from school to school. Hastings, for example, gives no preference, Michigan gives very little, and North Carolina, Texas, and Virginia give substantial preference. Virginia, for instance, appears (on rough calculations) to give residents a preference equal to 0.25–0.3 undergraduate grade points or 4–5 LSAT points. Given the admissions impact—plus the lower tuition at state schools (see the discussion in Chapter 17)—it is well worth exploring the possibilities of becoming a resident, either before or after you apply. If you become a resident before applying, of course, you can reap both the admissions preference benefit and the lower tuition; if you become a resident only after applying, perhaps during a deferral year, you will stand to gain only the tuition advantage.

States generally take a number of factors into account in determining residency. You are likely to be considered a resident if you attended high school in the state, your parents were and remain state residents, and you have not left the state for any substantial, full-time purpose other than education or military service. To become a resident, on the other hand, expect some or all of the following to be considered:

- Where you are registered to vote (and have voted)
- Whether you have a state driver's license (or identity card, if you do not drive)
- Which address you designate on school, employment, and military records
- Where you register your automobile
- Whether you pay state income taxes as a resident

ADMISSIONS DIRECTORS TALK ABOUT RESIDENCY

THE IMPACT OF RESIDENCY UPON ADMISSIONS

Twenty-five to thirty percent of our students are residents, seventy to seventy-five percent nonresidents. We use the same process for both. We give the benefit of the doubt to residents, but the advantage is difficult to quantify.   Erica Munzel, Director of Admissions, University of Michigan

Texas residents tend to have an edge in the admissions process.   Shelli Soto, Dean of Admissions, University of Texas

The differences in admissions standards for residents and nonresidents are sufficient to have separate admissions tracks for the two. For example, consider a 57 (index number) in our system—a 168 LSAT and 3.62 GPA, for instance. We admit eighty percent of residents, but only about thirty-three percent of nonresidents, with 57's.   Albert R. Turnbull, Associate Dean for Admissions and Career Services, University of Virginia

BECOMING A RESIDENT

To become a resident, you need to have lived and worked (and been physically present) in the state for one year without being a student.   Erica Munzel, Director of Admissions, University of Michigan

Becoming a resident after a year is fairly easy. You register to vote, get a California driver's license and a bank account, and establish and maintain physical presence. It's tantamount to giving yourself a $10,000 scholarship.   Edward Tom, Director of Admissions, Boalt Hall (Berkeley)

There are fairly strict rules regarding becoming a Texas resident. You need to live and work within the state for one full year without being a student. You cannot be claimed as a dependent by someone living outside the state. It is O.K. to seek a deferment (from UT Law School) on the basis of wanting to do this during an intervening year.   Shelli Soto, Dean of Admissions, University of Texas

It is now easier to become a Virginia resident, but it's still not as easy as elsewhere. If you enroll at the law school as a first-year student from out of state, there is a strong presumption, which is not easy to overcome, that you came to Virginia for the temporary purpose of education. To become a resident, you can drop out for a year to work in Virginia and pay taxes. You can also convert to resident status if you are married to someone who has been working in Virginia and paying taxes for one year or more.   Albert R. Turnbull, Associate Dean for Admissions and Career Services, University of Virginia

■ Where you reside (and for how long each year), and where your belongings are kept

■ Whether you return to your prior state of residence on a regular basis

It will be necessary to provide documentary evidence of the relevant factors.

You will have difficulty establishing residence in a state if you are considered a dependent of your parents and they live elsewhere, because this single factor will tend to give you the same state residence as they enjoy. To be considered financially independent of your parents requires at a minimum that you not be claimed as an income-tax deduction. Some states will also consider your age, whether you are married, whether you have dependents (other than your spouse), and whether you are financially self-sufficient.

To be sure of your status, check with the law school's admissions department to find out who at the university can advise you. (This is a function generally handled on a university-wide basis.)

Note that in some states it is easy to convert from nonresident to resident status during your time in law school; in other states, this is all but impossible while you remain a student.

LEGACIES

Being a "legacy"—i.e., related to someone who attended a given school—can greatly improve your chances of admission to college. At the graduate-school level, however, the situation is dramatically different. First of all, schools tend to pay little attention to "legacies" from any other school within the university. In other words, if your mother attended Northwestern Medical School, Northwestern Law School will not consider you a "legacy" at all. Even those applicants with relatives who attended the law school itself seldom receive much of a leg up in the admissions process.

There are three factors that tend to determine the affect a legacy will have:

■ The closer the relationship, the better. If one of your parents attended the law school, the impact will tend to be greater than if an uncle were the alum.

■ The more active in alumni and school affairs, and the more the relative has donated to the school, the better. (The standard for giving is very high, indeed. A thousand-dollar annual gift will not qualify someone for development status; a hundred thousand-dollar annual gift might or might not suffice.)

ADMISSIONS DIRECTORS DISCUSS LEGACIES

WHAT COUNTS AS A LEGACY

For us, a legacy is the son or daughter of someone who attended Michigan Law School. It's fine for someone to show a connection to another part of the University if that is an additional reason for wanting to attend Michigan. Legacy status is not very often going to change the outcome of a decision, but I do try to give legacies the benefit of the doubt.   Erica Munzel, Director of Admissions, University of Michigan

The only thing that qualifies as a legacy here is having a parent who attended Boston College Law School.   Elizabeth Rosselot, Director of Admissions, Boston College

THE IMPACT OF LEGACY STATUS

If an applicant's parent is a Columbia Law graduate, the legacy factor serves as a factor in our decision-making but not a highly influential one. Consider it as a feather on the scale, but one significant enough to make a positive difference if the applicant is close to admission based on his/her own merits. The legacy factor plays such a role only a few times each admissions season. The legacy factor exerts considerably less impact on law school admissions decisions than within the undergraduate realm. Expectations to the contrary, when applied to highly selective law schools, are outdated and grounded more in hope than reality. Jim Milligan, Dean of Admissions, Columbia

We are less interested in legacies than many other schools are because we are not a private school.   Shelli Soto, Dean of Admissions, University of Texas

We have a strong "legacy" tradition as a university, but it doesn't matter much if the family is a $50 per year donor.   Janice Austin, Assistant Dean for Admissions, University of Pennsylvania

We pay some attention to "development" cases, but there are very, very few of them. I get some pressure from development staff, but I respond by telling them I'm not qualified to determine the degree of institutional interest represented by that development matter. So I report back to them only on the merits and chances of admission for the applicant in question.   Jim Milligan, Dean of Admissions, Columbia

A legacy matters; it makes up for a point or two (or even more) on the LSAT or a tenth of a point of GPA. (The closer the relationship, the more it affects the decision. "Married to my cousin" doesn't count as a legacy.) In a borderline situation, it definitely tips the balance in the applicant's favor. Legacies are valuable insofar as they give us people who are very happy to be here, and they increase alumni giving.   Robert Stanek, Director for Admissions, George Washington

Being a legacy does not give you a leg up—even if you are the son or daughter of faculty.   Edward Tom, Director of Admissions, Boalt Hall (Berkeley)

Legacy status has essentially no impact upon our decision-making.   William Hoye, Dean for Admissions, USC

Legacies are given a special look and primarily are treated a bit differently (after their applications have been rejected) by our counseling them about possible reapplication or transfer opportunities.   Jim Milligan, Dean of Admissions, Columbia

■ Private schools tend to put slightly more weight on legacy status than do state schools, due largely to the latter relying traditionally on public rather than private funding.

INTERNATIONAL APPLICANTS: JD AND LLM DEGREES

International applicants represent a small but rapidly growing segment of the JD market. As the legal market itself has become more and more global, so too has the admissions game at American law schools. It is, of course, testimony to the positive reputation American law schools enjoy that so many non-Americans are applying. In the past, of course, international applicants generally did a Bachelor of laws degree (a first degree) in their home countries, worked for some years, and then applied to an American school for an LLM. They continue to do so—in larger and larger numbers—but many foreign applicants now look to do a JD in the United States instead of doing a first law degree in their home countries, or in addition to such a first law degree.

The reasons for a foreign applicant to do an LLM are clear. The traditional reason was to learn about American law, so as to go back to the home country and be a better informed lawyer, professor, diplomat, or government administrator. Of course it did not hurt to add the cachet of a Harvard or a Georgetown or a Columbia degree to their curriculum vitae, either. A new reason has been added in recent years. Many international candidates for LLM degrees at the leading American law schools have come intending to practice in America after finishing their degrees. Candidates with just an LLM degree can be admitted to the bar in states such as New York.

Why, then, do foreign applicants consider doing a JD in the U.S.? Some may have done a non-law first degree, thereby necessitating about three years of study, whether in the home country or in the U.S. Similarly, some may want to practice in an American state, such as Illinois, that does not admit candidates to the bar with only an LLM. Others may want to undergo the rigorous training of an American JD degree, preferring it to their home degree options. Still others may wish to have the built-in marketing opportunities afforded by being at an American school for three years (they are able to pitch themselves to potential American employers throughout their stint) or by virtue of earning the most well-understood of American degrees.

Several things are different for international applicants whether applying for a JD or an LLM. American law schools often find it difficult to understand the nature and quality of the high school or university work done by applicants educated abroad. The same is true for work experience, extracurricular and community activities, and so on. As a result, foreign applicants need to make their credentials clear and readily understood. Thus, it can be very helpful to show how exclusive (in meritocratic terms) a given university or high school is; the way a grading system works, in full detail; the hiring policies of a firm; and so on.

Your rationale for studying in the United States will inevitably matter. At the JD level, it is particularly valuable to show that you will be able to handle the rapid flow of idiomatic English, plus the need to read large volumes of detailed materials, and to discuss them in a sophisticated manner.

One curiosity about the international application process: For a JD, a TOEFL score is not generally required but an LSAT score is; the opposite is true for an LLM.

ADMISSIONS DIRECTORS DISCUSS ISSUES RELEVANT TO INTERNATIONAL STUDENTS

THE LSAT

The international applicants tend to be older, with more professional experience. They'll be movers and shakers when they go back home; from an alumni and development perspective, that's great. We look at somewhat lower LSAT scores here. The rough equivalent to an American with a 167 LSAT would be a student from: China: 164; India: 164; Korea: 164; Switzerland: 160–161; Africa: 165 (French West Africa: 162); Former Soviet Union/Eastern Europe: 160; Mexico: 160; Puerto Rico: 155 (We treat them as first-generation Latins, although it is not clear whether they should be regarded as internationals or ethnic minorities.) This assumes that the applicant has not been educated elsewhere in English.   Janice Austin, Assistant Dean for Admissions, University of Pennsylvania

An LSAT score of 162–164 for a Chinese applicant would be fine.   Faye Deal, Associate Dean for Admissions and Financial Aid, Stanford

The rough equivalent to an American scoring 165 on the LSAT would be a German (i.e., someone from a country where English is hardly unknown) scoring 163–164 or a Chinese from interior China (whose exposure to English is very limited) scoring 161–162. (We will look closely at foreigners' essays to see whether they have command of the English language.)   Andy Cornblatt, Assistant Dean for Admissions, Georgetown

International students will be studying in English, in a system that's foreign to them, so I won't bend as much on LSAT scores as some of my colleagues at other schools might.   Robert Stanek, Director for Admissions, George Washington

We don't expect lower LSAT scores from nonnative speakers. Since law school is conducted in English we evaluate their ability to communicate in English.   Erica Munzel, Director of Admissions, University of Michigan

We expect LSAT scores comparable to Americans', but since our LSAT scores cover a very wide range it's not particularly critical in the process.   William Hoye, Dean for Admissions, USC

THE TOEFL AND LSAT

We do not give internationals any break on the LSAT. On the TOEFL, we are uncomfortable with scores below 600 (250 on the new scale).   Elizabeth Rosselot, Director of Admissions, Boston College

We do not require the TOEFL; the LSAT does the same job.   Kip Darcy, Director of Admissions, Hastings

CREDENTIAL EVALUATION

International students: We require they send their transcripts to the UCLA department that analyzes foreign transcripts; we do not accept those from a private service.   Michael Rappoport, Dean of Admissions, UCLA

It can be very difficult to assess the undergraduate records of international applicants. It helps if they provide information regarding the grading system in use. If we can evaluate their performance, and it has been strong, we might give them a bit of a break on the LSAT. On the other hand, lacking good understanding of their undergraduate performance, we'll put a lot of weight on their LSAT score.   Don Rebstock, Associate Dean of Admissions and Financial Aid, Northwestern

The more we can understand about their institution, the better, since we generally don't know the foreign schools particularly well. We welcome getting a good profile of the school.   Robert Stanek, Director for Admissions, George Washington

Some schools require that an international credential evaluation service assess an overseas transcript. We don't require this, but we still find it helpful and therefore welcome it.   William Hoye, Dean for Admissions, USC

GENERAL COMMENTS

It's difficult to get in as an international student. You have to meet the same criteria as everybody else. We may give you a very small break in terms of the LSAT because we know English is your second language, but it's still hard to be admitted as an international student.   Edward Tom, Director of Admissions, Boalt Hall (Berkeley)

International students coming to study in a system that is totally foreign to them have a tough road in front of them in the best of circumstances. Therefore it's helpful for them to show some knowledge of the American legal system. If they demonstrate this in the admission process, I'll be more likely to admit them because I'll know that they won't have to struggle so much (and because it says something about them that they've taken the trouble to learn this). Robert Stanek, Director for Admissions, George Washington

For foreign applicants who haven't done a lot of work in English, we'll check their personal statements carefully no matter how strong their LSAT score is. This is because law school grades are generally based solely upon the performance on a single, time-pressured written exam. Any inability to write English is magnified by that situation.   Faye Deal, Associate Dean for Admissions and Financial Aid, Stanford

ADMISSIONS DIRECTORS DISCUSS THEIR LLM PROGRAMS

Is an LLM Sufficient to Take the Bar in Your State?

International students can earn an LLM here and then practice in New York; they do not need to earn a JD to be admitted to the New York bar.   Jim Milligan, Dean of Admissions, Columbia

For the Pennsylvania bar, an LLM degree is not enough. An LCM, a second graduate degree (done after an LLM), is sufficient, though. Many internationals now do two graduate degrees, using the advanced standing they get from the first to make it possible to complete the second degree quickly.   Janice Austin, Assistant Dean for Admissions, University of Pennsylvania

In Illinois you cannot sit the bar with just an American LLM, although in New York you can.   Don Rebstock, Associate Dean of Admissions and Financial Aid, Northwestern

You may sit for the Virginia bar with just an LLM.   Albert R. Turnbull, Associate Dean for Admissions and Career Services, University of Virginia

The Most Important Credentials for Admission

This degree is designed for foreign attorneys looking to return to their own countries. We do not require the LSAT of them. We look for those who were at the top of their class and have had some solid work experience (at least one year).   Don Rebstock, Associate Dean of Admissions and Financial Aid, Northwestern

Unusual Programs on Offer

We offer an LLM in law and business, which involves two semesters of law and one quarter at Kellogg (the business school).   Don Rebstock, Associate Dean of Admissions and Financial Aid, Northwestern

How International the Program Is

We have 160 LLM students, 140 of whom are foreign-trained lawyers.   Jim Milligan, Dean of Admissions, Columbia

At least half of our LLM students are internationals. In the last year the pool (size) has exploded.   Albert R. Turnbull, Associate Dean for Admissions and Career Services, University of Virginia

Note that LLM students do not have access to all of our placement services (since they are presumed to be headed back to their own countries).   Don Rebstock, Associate Dean of Admissions and Financial Aid, Northwestern

LLM Application Numbers

We have about 1,100 applicants, admit 400, and have 270 enroll.   Andy Cornblatt, Assistant Dean for Admissions, Georgetown

About 400 apply for our LLM, 150 are admitted, and 60 enroll.   Don Rebstock, Associate Dean of Admissions and Financial Aid, Northwestern

Appendix V

PERSONAL ORGANIZER

(Make extra copies of this form to have additional room for describing multiple schools, jobs, or other experiences, as necessary.)

EDUCATION

School:

Degree: Date Received:

Grade-point average: Major/Concentration:

Minor: Relevant additional course work:

Substantial papers written:

Activities:

Offices held/responsibilities/achievements (academic and extracurricular):

Honors and Awards:

Scholarships:

Why did you choose this school? In retrospect, was it a good decision? Why or why not?

(Repeat for choice of major.)

WORK EXPERIENCE

Start with your most recent job and work backward chronologically. If you had more than one job with the same employer, fill out separate data fields for each. Include all part-time as well as full-time jobs.

Employer:

Dates employed: From _____ To _____

Location:

Title/Position:

Beginning salary: Ending salary:

Key responsibilities:

Whom did you manage? To whom did you report?

Key accomplishments (quantify whenever possible):

Key skills that enabled you to accomplish these things:

Superiors' reviews (excerpts):

Reasons superiors feel this way about you (think in terms of your achievements, skills, actions, attitude, etc.):

Reasons for taking the job:

Reasons for leaving the job:

Ways in which the job met your expectations:

Ways in which the job did not meet your expectations:

Important stories illustrating your leadership, teamwork, analytical, and communicative abilities:

What sources (including people) are there for developing further information about each story?

PROFESSIONAL ACCOMPLISHMENTS

Copyrights:
    Title:
    Date:
    Publisher/Publication:

Patents:
    Title:
    Date:
    Number:

Professional certification:
    Organization certifying:
    Date certified:

Professional honors and awards:
    Name:
    Date awarded:
    Organization awarding:
    Reason for the award:

EXTRACURRICULAR (AND POST-GRADUATION) ACTIVITIES (artistic, athletic, community, religious, political, social, etc.)

Activity: Dates of involvement:

Offices held/responsibilities/achievements:

Was this a voluntary position or one to which you were elected/appointed? If elected or appointed, by whom?

Reasons for your involvement:

How does it relate to your other activities and interests?

PERSONAL QUESTIONS

Who are the four or five people who have most influenced you? How?

What are the four or five things you most admire in others? (In whom and why?)

What are your four or five most memorable experiences, whether great or small?

What was your greatest success, and what did you learn from it?

What was your greatest failure, and what did you learn from it?

What fear have you overcome? (How and why?)

What do your friends most like (and dislike) about you?

What are the four or five (or more) key words that would describe you? What on your list demonstrates this?

Do you have a personal motto or something that you frequently quote?

YOUR FUTURE CAREER

How has your interest in this career developed?

What are your career goals? What do you hope to accomplish in your life?

LEISURE TIME

What are your favorite books? Why? What have you read most recently?

(Repeat for favorite movies.)

What do you like to do when given the time? Why? What do you most enjoy about it?

PULLING YOUR INFORMATION TOGETHER

At the conclusion of this exercise, list your major accomplishments in each category.

Work:
1.
2.
3.
4.
5.

Education:
1.
2.
3.
4.
5.

Personal:
1.
2.
3.
4.
5.

Which events or activities represent inflection points in your life (i.e., when you changed direction)?

In what ways are you different from a year ago? Why? (Repeat for five years ago.) Think in terms of your personality, interests, personal and professional goals, and values.

How have your various experiences helped you to grow? What do they show about your abilities? What do they show about your interests?

Which of your experiences demonstrate the following characteristics?

Characteristic	Relevant Experience
Intellectual Ability	
Analytical Ability	
Imagination and Creativity	
Motivation and Initiative	
Maturity	
Organizational Skills	
Ability to Work with Others	
Leadership Potential	
Self-Confidence	
Ability in Oral Expression	
Ability in Written Communication	
Sense of Humor	
Career Potential	

9

UNDERSTANDING YOUR
ESSAY OPTIONS

— EXECUTIVE SUMMARY —

You will be evaluated on your choice of topic as well as
the substance and the style of your writing.

■

Choose your topic carefully.

—Use themes to further your positioning effort through the essays.

■

Learn how the typical applicant approaches an essay topic and how to
develop a more effective approach.

■

Include supplemental essays (if necessary) and a polished résumé,
especially if you have substantial work experience.

Yale Law School's admissions information says of the personal statement requirement: "Faculty readers look to the required short essay to evaluate your writing, thinking, and editing skills, as well as to learn more about such qualities as your intellectual concerns or passions, your humor, or your ability to think across disciplines." And, if you read the fine print, in 250 words or less—no small feat.

With only one or two exceptions, the top law programs in the country require a personal statement from each applicant. The essay offers you the chance to show schools who you really are. Take advantage of this opportunity. Recommenders can show only a *part* of who you are, since most of them are instructors or employers and have thus seen you in only one context. Many schools do not offer everyone the chance to interview as part of the admissions process. In addition, interviews are not under your control to the same extent as the personal statement, which can be rewritten and reexamined to make sure that the "real you" is presented.

Your personal statements can and should present a clear picture of you, but they do not need to tell all. Sketching in the main points with appropriate stories will show who you are. In fact, whenever possible, try to tell a story rather than write an essay. The task will seem lighter.

This is your chance to choose which parts of your past and yourself to highlight, and to determine how people should view them. This is a precious opportunity; take full advantage of the chance to color your readers' interpretations.

CHOICE OF TOPIC

When it comes to the personal statement section of the application, most schools leave the question open-ended. This is Columbia's:

> ". . . a statement may provide the Admissions Committee with information regarding such matters as: personal, family, or educational background; experiences and talents of special interest; one's reasons for applying to law school as they may relate to personal goals and professional expectations; or any other factors which you think should inform the Committee's evaluation of your candidacy for admission."

Often, several topical suggestions will be offered, but even these suggestions will be quite broad, if not exceedingly vague. This open-endedness is both opportunity and trap. The law schools are being deliberately inexplicit. Having left *you* to make the decisions, they expect those who are insightful about themselves, the process, the competition, and the rest of the relevant factors, to make good use of this freedom. By the same token, they expect the average applicant to be upset by the degree of freedom on offer, just as they expect him or her to flub the opportunity.

So don't. Just because you *can* discuss every semi-important aspect of your life containing possible relevancy to the study of law does not mean you *should*. Chicago, which does not require an essay, nevertheless shares this bit of advice in their catalog:

> "It may be helpful to know that essays having a narrow focus are generally more effective than those attempting to make a broad integration of the law with one's general career or scholarly goals."

The next section of this chapter will assist you in breaking apart and analyzing your essay options. After reading the analysis of each topic, it will quickly become apparent which are most suited to you and your application on the whole.

VARIOUS ESSAY TOPICS ANALYZED IN DETAIL

It is often easiest to write a personal statement if you feel you are being asked to answer a specific question rather than to fill up a blank page. Consider what question you wish to answer. For example, what are your greatest strengths and weaknesses? Or, why have you chosen law as a career? These questions represent organizing themes for your essay. The following discussion of typical themes will highlight how others will approach the same topic, as well as what you should do to get the most out of your essay.

DESCRIBE YOUR CURRENT JOB

THE TYPICAL APPLICANT

Most applicants treat a discussion of their jobs as a matter of simply rehashing their résumés, albeit with full sentences in place of phrases. The context in which they perform is absent, making it difficult to understand the significance of what they have done and what talents were required.

A BETTER APPROACH

There are usually numerous elements to a given job. You must figure out and list the many things you do. Next, determine which are the most significant parts of your job and which are most consistent with the position you are attempting to communicate, and then characterize them as favorably as possible. The following should help you with this process.

Is your job important? Most people would say so only if they are egotists or are making a lot of money and enjoying a very impressive title (Senior Executive President for Marketing and Strategy, perhaps).

Assuming you are not in this situation, does this mean your job is unimportant and you will have to be apologizing for it? No, of course not. A job is of real importance under a number of different circumstances. In particular, work gains significance whenever two things are true about it. First, the degree of uncertainty (regarding which course of action would be best) is high, and second, the potential impact upon the firm's success is great. In other words, is there a fair likelihood that an average-quality performer in your job would make a hash of things? If so, would that really affect your firm's performance, or that of one of its components? If the answer to both of these questions is yes, then your job certainly is of importance.

What must you do to perform successfully? In other words, what challenges do you face? For example, if you are an analyst in a consulting firm, you probably work on two different teams. The managers of each team act as if you are meant to devote 100 percent of your time to their respective teams, leaving you to work around the clock or fight the time allocation battle. You are also probably asked to do work that has never been thoroughly explained to you, and for which no formal training was provided, which requires that you seek out the experiences of others who have suffered before you to learn the essentials of what you are meant to do. Thus, in addition to having to do serious analytical work—which might range from in-depth financial analysis to developing sociograms to understand an organization's political dynamics—you have to master the internal politics of your own organization.

Perhaps you are an engineer in a matrix structure, reporting to the regional manager and an engineering director. Your greatest challenge may be satisfying two different bosses with two completely different agendas. The regional manager is probably concerned with making money today, and wants everyone to work as a team without regard to functional specialties. The engineering boss, on the other hand, wants her people to maintain their specialized skills and the prestige of the engineering department. Working on cross-functional teams without taking time out for updating technical skills may strike the former as standard practice and the latter as anathema. To perform your job well may require balancing these conflicting desires.

Or you may be a paralegal in your first job who is effectively being asked to work as the "second chair" in a case that started before you even joined the firm. Not only do you have to learn what a second chair does in litigation, you also have to get up to speed on an involved case—as well as integrate into the firm and learn how to deal with the partner handling this case, who has no time to babysit you as you acclimate.

If the last two occupants of your position were fired, say so. This will make your performance look all the more impressive. On the other hand, the *positive* fate of prior occupants of your job may be relevant. If the last occupants were promoted high in the organization, the job will appear to be one given to high-fliers, thereby increasing its significance. The more senior the person you report to, the more important a job will look.

What is the nature of your work? There are many different types of work. A market researcher is generally doing analytical work. A financial analyst generally does quantitative analysis, although the position may also call for doing extensive write-ups, such as those an equity analyst provides the financial community. A brand manager is likely to be doing a combination of analytical work and influence work insofar as she must analyze the factors for the brand's relative success or failure in different markets and competitive conditions in her country, and then try to influence the manufacturing, packaging, or whatever department, to take the action she wants in order to address these factors. She typically will have no power over these departments and will have to rely on her influence skills (personality, reasoning, expertise, etc.) instead. A restaurant manager will probably be most concerned with managing people, whereas a technical manager may be most concerned with the management of physical processes. An administrative assistant to a senator will have to manage the boss's calendar as well as juggle the competing interests of various constituents, lobbyists, campaign workers, other legislators, the senator's family, and so on.

Many other aspects of your work can also be characterized. Is your job like being in the army: crushing boredom interspersed with brief moments of sheer terror? Are you expected to perform at a steady pace to a predictable schedule or do you work like a tax accountant, 50 percent of whose work may take place in ten weeks of the year? Are you supposed to be the steadying hand for a bunch of youngsters? Are you supposed to be a creative type who will respond flexibly to each new situation rather than simply refer to the corporate manual?

Do you supervise anyone? How many people, of what type, are under your supervision? What does this supervision consist of? For example, are you in charge of direct marketing activities, necessitating that you monitor the phone calls of your direct reports and also analyze their performance versus budget and various economic and industry factors?

Do you have control of a budget? If so, what is the amount you control, and what amount do you influence?

What results have you achieved? Results can be looked at from many different perspectives. From a strategic perspective, what have you achieved regarding the market, customers, and competitors? From a financial perspective, what have you done regarding costs, revenues, and profits (not to mention assets employed, etc.)? From an operational perspective, what have you done regarding productivity of your unit, or of your direct reports, or of yourself? What have you done regarding the percentage of items rejected, or bids that fail, and so on? Similarly, from an organizational perspective, have you taken steps such as altering the formal organization or introducing new integration or coordination mechanisms? Provide numbers and tangible details whenever possible to buttress your claims.

How has your career evolved? Did you have a career plan in place before graduating from college or university or soon thereafter? If so, did you pursue it wholeheartedly? Did it include a focus on developing your skills and responsibilities? What, if anything, has altered your original plan? What was your reaction to events that altered or affirmed this plan? When dealing with the development of your job with a given employer, be sure to note the employer's *reasons* for promoting, transferring, rewarding, or praising you as well as the *fact* of these things.

How does your career progress compare with that of your peers? Sometimes the easiest way to show your success is by comparing your progress with others who entered your firm, or others in the industry, at the same time. Have you reached a more senior position? Been given more responsibilities? Earned a higher salary?

ADVANTAGES OF THIS APPROACH

Your past and current jobs are of inherent interest to law schools. They will want to know what you have done (and are doing), and with what success, because that suggests a great deal about your talents and interests, and the way your employer views your talents and attitude. Taking a broad view of your job enables you to put the best light on your responsibilities and performance.

DESCRIBE YOUR CAREER TO DATE

THE TYPICAL APPLICANT

Most applicants simply list what they have done in the past without showing what has driven their career choices and changes. The result is a list in which the elements appear nearly unrelated to one another. This is what admissions directors term the "résumé" approach.

A BETTER APPROACH

Look at our discussion of the "Job Description" essay. Then think in terms of telling stories rather than simply listing events dryly. A good story has conflict; that is, it has obstacles placed in the way of the hero. The hero may be unable to overcome each obstacle, but she tries hard and is unwilling to give up.

One possible approach is as follows. Find a theme that unites the elements of your job history. For instance, you show how you responded to challenges that were initially daunting. You tried hard and learned how to do what was required. You started to take more initiative as you learned better how to do the job. In fact, once you mastered your initial responsibilities, you understood them in a broader context. Having done so, you moved up to the next level of responsibility.

The telling of your career story should focus upon where you have come from and where you are now headed. If you have changed your direction, explain what happened to change your direction. If you have had your decisions reaffirmed by experience, describe them and how they convinced you that you were on the right track.

(This essay is closely related to the "Reasons for Getting a Law Degree" essay.)

ADVANTAGES OF THIS APPROACH

Telling stories that focus on obstacles and the attempt to overcome them makes this essay interesting to read. Focusing on your personal development in response to challenges is well aimed for an audience of educators. They are preconditioned to appreciate your developmental capabilities.

This approach also sets up your need for a law degree. You have been overcoming obstacles by learning how to perform new jobs, and you have acquired new skills and knowledge; now you need to take another step up.

WHAT ARE YOUR STRENGTHS AND WEAKNESSES?

This question is meant to elicit your opinion of yourself. Modest people, and people from cultures less egocentric than that of the United States, have a hard time responding because it apparently asks you to brag a little. Less self-assured applicants find it hard to be honest and to mention their shortcomings. This topic provides a good gauge of how self confident (or arrogant), accomplished (or boastful), decent (or manipulative), mature, self-aware, and honest you are.

THE TYPICAL APPLICANT

Most applicants list a large number of strengths and no weaknesses. If they do include a weakness, it is generally a strength dressed up as a weakness ("I am too much of a perfectionist." "I work too hard.").

A BETTER APPROACH

Start by choosing two or three primary strengths. Use these to organize your essay by grouping other strengths around them. For example, if you claim you are very *determined,* you might discuss your *patience* in working hard for a long time in order to achieve something important as related to this determination. The problem is not generally finding something good to say about yourself. Usually the problem is limiting yourself to a manageable number of strengths. You want to have few enough that you can discuss them in a persuasive fashion rather than just list them. Using two or three as central organizing devices (i.e., themes) helps to achieve this.

Remember that simply listing strengths is a very weak way of writing. Use illustrations to make your strengths credible and memorable. Instead of bragging about being determined, note your five-year battle to overcome childhood leukemia.

The bigger problem, however, is deciding which weakness to discuss. Simply calling a strength a weakness is not sufficient. This tactic is used by countless applicants, and its insincerity is nearly guaranteed to repel those reading your essays. Instead, discuss an actual weakness that will make your discussion of your strengths more believable, show you to be mature enough to admit your lack of perfection, or present you with an opportunity to show how you have worked to reduce the impact of that weakness or eliminate it altogether. (Do not carry a good thing too far, though, and discuss huge flaws such as your drug addictions.)

Allocate space on a three- or four-to-one basis, strengths to weakness. You will note that I say "weakness," because you should discuss only one or two weaknesses. When doing so, do not dwell on your descriptions of it, or of the problems it has caused you. Do so briefly, thereby limiting the affect the specifics will have upon admissions officers. Then note what steps you take, or have taken, to overcome it.

You want to describe yourself as having numerous strengths that relate well to your positioning effort, without sounding arrogant.

ADVANTAGES OF THIS APPROACH

Grouping your strengths in an organized fashion will give you the chance to cover a lot of ground without taking a scattershot approach. Emphasizing strengths is obviously appropriate, but discussing a weakness may be a good idea, too. Writing with appropriate illustrations will make your strengths memorable; this will also make your claims realistic rather than boastful.

WHAT ARE YOUR MOST SUBSTANTIAL ACCOMPLISHMENTS?

This obviously gives you a chance to "blow your own horn." You can brag a bit about what you have accomplished in life. Moreover, you have the chance to put your own spin on what you have done. A particular accomplishment is all the more impressive when you explain the obstacles you had to overcome in order to succeed.

The topic also allows schools to learn more about you insofar as you discuss why you consider something to have been a substantial accomplishment. Some accomplishments are of obvious significance. Winning the American Book Award for History is obviously significant; you probably do not need to elaborate on the fact of having won it. Other accomplishments are much more personal. For example, if you had stuttered as a youth and finally ended your stuttering in your twenties, this might be an extremely significant accomplishment for you personally. You have probably done things that have had more impact upon the rest of the world, but for you this accomplishment looms larger. You may well want to talk about it as an example of your determination and desire to improve yourself.

This topic gives you an opportunity to discuss matters that are unlikely to be listed on your data sheets or mentioned by your recommenders. Even if you just discuss accomplishments of a more public nature, you can personalize them in a way in which just listing them on a data sheet (or having a recommender talk about them) does not do.

THE TYPICAL APPLICANT

Most applicants use the whole of their personal statement to demonstrate that their accomplishments are impressive; they focus on their accomplishments and not on themselves. Another mistaken tendency is to list a string of things rather than to explain one or two in detail.

A BETTER APPROACH

The first step is to determine which accomplishments you will discuss. Your criteria for choosing appropriate accomplishments will be familiar. Which ones will help your positioning effort? Which will be unusual and interesting for admissions committees to read about? Was this accomplishment truly important to you?

The following criteria are also helpful guides:

- You had to overcome major obstacles, showing real determination in doing so.
- You learned more about yourself.
- You came to understand the need for further skill development and thus, perhaps, a JD.
- You used real initiative, perhaps by pushing a bureaucracy to respond or bypassing one altogether.
- Your success was unexpected.
- You worked extremely hard toward a clear goal.

■   Your impact can be clearly seen (i.e., you were not simply tagging along with someone else who did the real work).

If you are trying to show that you have had relevant real-world experience despite being only 23, you will probably want one (or preferably more) of these accomplishments to concern your post-college life, especially your professional life. Not every accomplishment will fulfill all of our criteria, but you should be able to include most of them in the course of the full essay.

A PROFESSIONAL PROJECT THAT CHALLENGED YOUR SKILLS

To write about your professional accomplishments, consider discussing a project you have undertaken. Projects lend themselves to essays insofar as they tend to have definite starting and end points, specific goals, and so on. Follow this approach to develop your essay:

1. Start by determining what your professional skills are.

2. Look at the most challenging professional project you have faced, preferably one that was successful for you, or one that taught you valuable lessons.

3. After trying to remember it in real detail, abstract exactly which skills you used (or should have used, but have only come to appreciate since then).

4. Remember the attributes your readers are looking for: analytical ability, communication skills, interpersonal skills, leadership ability, dedication, integrity, and so on.

5. Which of these attributes can you illustrate via one of your projects? Which are most important to your positioning effort? Which will be the most interesting to read about? Which can you get someone else to back up in a recommendation?

In writing the essay, go into sufficient detail to bring the events to life, but do not stop there. Discuss why you consider this a substantial achievement, why you take pride in it, and what you learned from it. Did you change and grow as a result of this? Did you find that you approached other matters differently after accomplishing this?

The admissions committee will read this for more than a brief description of the items you list on your data sheet. It will want to learn more about these and the private you, if you discuss significant accomplishments of a personal nature here. It will want to know what motivates you and what you value. It will also want to see how you have developed as a person and as a professional.

ADVANTAGES OF THIS APPROACH

This topic gives you a lot of latitude, as our criteria suggest. Using it to show more of the real you will help you to avoid the usual problems people create for themselves on this essay. You do not want to restate the facts you have already listed on your data sheet; you want to show that you have been ready to face challenges, determined to overcome obstacles, and able to accomplish things that have mattered to you.

WHAT HAVE YOU DONE THAT DEMONSTRATES YOUR LEADERSHIP POTENTIAL?

Top schools expect to produce leaders in law and other fields. They are looking for applicants who have already distinguished themselves as leaders, since past performance is the best indicator of what people will be like in the future.

THE TYPICAL APPLICANT

All too often, applicants discuss being part of a group that achieved something noteworthy without making it clear that they themselves were truly leaders in this effort.

A BETTER APPROACH

This question is deceptively similar to the "Substantial Accomplishment" topic, which, as explained earlier, asks you to describe a real achievement (and what it means to you). The "Leadership" essay, on the other hand, is not looking so much for an "achievement" as it is for an understanding of how you led an effort to achieve something. In other words, your emphasis should be upon your leadership rather than the achievement.

To write this essay, you must understand what leadership is. One obvious example is managing people who report directly to you. Less obvious examples involve pushing or inspiring nonsubordinates to do what you want done. This could be a matter of leading by example, using your influence as a perceived expert in a relevant field, influencing through moral suasion, or influencing by personal friendship. You might have led people through direct management or through influence. Describe your methodology. What strategy did you employ? Why? You may not have been deliberate or extremely self-aware in your actions, of course, in which case you might wish to discuss what you did and why it was or was not a good choice. What problems did you confront? What did you learn about managing or influencing people? Would another strategy, or different actions, have been better choices? Why? Do you have a philosophy of leadership?

You should emphasize that your leadership qualities are the sort that describe a future Attorney General or CEO rather than a high school football hero. Thus, such qualities as maturity, thoughtfulness, empathy, determination, valuing other people's input, the ability to influence or manage very different types of people, the ability to integrate disparate inputs into a unified perspective, and integrity are highly desirable.

You are free to choose something from your professional career, but you might wish to choose something from your extracurricular or private life, too.

ADVANTAGES OF THIS APPROACH

Viewing this topic as concerning your understanding of leadership, and the ways in which you yourself lead, will result in an essay with the appropriate approach. It is not your achievement that is paramount here; it is your method of approaching and resolving leadership issues that concerns the admissions committee. If you show yourself to be aware of the leadership issues inherent in your situation and extract some suitable comments regarding what worked or did not work, and why, you will have the core of a good essay.

DESCRIBE AN EXPERIENCE IN WHICH YOU DID NOT REACH YOUR OBJECTIVES (AND WHAT YOU LEARNED FROM THIS)

THE TYPICAL APPLICANT

Most applicants focus on the mistake they made, or failure they suffered, rather than what they learned from it. Similarly, they fail to recount any more recent successes to show they have indeed benefited from an earlier mistake.

A BETTER APPROACH

You have a great deal of latitude in choosing your failure or mistake. Several factors should govern your response. (1) Try to further your positioning effort. If you are trying to present yourself as a worldly international negotiator, you might wish to show how you flubbed your first negotiations with people from another culture due to your lack of understanding of how they valued different components of a deal. (You can then go on to explain that this started you on the path of investigating the values and beliefs of your negotiating partners and opponents in all future deals, something you believe has underpinned much of your success since then.) (2) Show that you have truly learned from your mistake. One implication of this may be that you will want to choose a failure from your more distant past, not last week. You will not have had much of an opportunity to learn from a recent failure, whereas a failure from two or three years ago may have afforded plenty of opportunity to learn (and to have compiled a run of relevant successes bearing this out). The reason is that you generally need some time to reflect upon matters in order to benefit fully from them. (3) If you choose a distant failure, you are not saying that you are currently making such mistakes.

Having chosen your failure, do not belabor your description of it. Remember that it is what you learned from this failure that is critical here, not the failure itself. Consider what you learned from the experience concerning yourself, your job, your company, your industry, how to manage people, and so on.

ADVANTAGES OF THIS APPROACH

The emphasis here should be upon your development. We learn more from our mistakes than from our successes. A willingness to admit mistakes and then try to learn from them is one hallmark of a mature adult. It is also the trait of someone who will benefit from more formal education.

DISCUSS AN ETHICAL DILEMMA YOU HAVE FACED

The ongoing debate over the proper role of lawyers in society means that ethics is an important issue in a lawyer's training, as well as in the admissions decision.

THE TYPICAL APPLICANT

Most applicants tackling an "ethical dilemma" preach about the virtues of their position rather than recognizing that both sides may have much to offer. The stridency of their approach makes it look as though they are unable to analyze issues with finesse and subtlety.

A BETTER APPROACH

The toughest part of this is to find a suitable subject. Here are some possible topics:

- *People versus profit.* For example, should you fire the Hispanic researchers working for your firm now that the initial products aimed at the Hispanic market have been launched? What were their expectations in taking the job initially? What promises were made to them? What other jobs will be open to them if they are fired? What will be the consequences to the firm if they are retained (or if they are fired)?

- *Your career versus someone else's.* When your thesis advisor publishes your work under her name, what should you do? What were your expectations? Was there an explicit (or implicit) agreement that in return for sponsoring your work, your advisor could take credit in public for the results? Did you lose opportunities for failing to get credit? Or did your protests over the injustice cost you in some other fashion?

- *Taking advantage of someone's lack of knowledge or opportunities.* Should you sell a product to someone who does not know that it will be inappropriate for his needs? By the time he figures this out, you may have moved on to a new division in the company so you will not face his fury or the long-term consequences of having an angry customer.

TIPS ON CHOOSING A PERSONAL STATEMENT TOPIC

Remember that an essay does not exist in a vacuum. Instead, it is part of the whole application and should be answered in the context of how you wish the whole application package to read, and, thus, how you will maximize your reward risk ratio (see Chapter 8). Your choice of topic for a personal statement for a given school will therefore depend upon these factors:

➤ *Your desired positioning.* (For a discussion of this and the following points, see Chapter 8.)

➤ *Your choice of organizing themes.*

➤ *Circumstances specific to a given school.* For example, the University of Pennsylvania currently asks you to write two essays, one of your choosing and one about your reasons for wanting to attend Penn. Under this circumstance, it would be peculiar to write both essays on the subject of "Why Penn?" By the same token, if your usual personal statement discusses how you will contribute marvelously to courses about health law, you will probably want to change topics if this particular school offers no courses on the subject.

➤ *The subject about which you are asked to write.* A given school may constrain your choice by specifying a subject.

➤ *The number of essays you are invited to write.* For example, if Michigan offers you the chance to write two optional, shorter essays (about how you will contribute to the school's diversity, for one, and something that reveals how you think, for another), you will want to consider how best to balance the impression the whole set of essays will make.

➤ *Permitted length.* Some topics can be handled in 250 words; others need much more space.

➤ *The stories you have to tell.* If you have filled out the Personal Organizer (see Appendix V), you will know what sort of material is available to you. Be sure to examine the personal statements in Part IV to see what your competition writes about in order to generate your own ideas. In choosing stories, try for those that:

—Are interesting

—Are unusual (and thus memorable)

—Reveal something not fully described elsewhere in your application

—Show you to have leadership skills and experience

—Make clear your analytical and/or communication abilities

—Demonstrate your mastery of a subject or field

—Are ones that you should tell, rather than those a recommender should tell

—Can be backed up by a recommender

> ➤ *Your age and experience.* Few candidates who are still in college will benefit from writing about why they want to be a lawyer, whereas few older candidates at mid-career will be able to avoid discussing this. In the former situation, few college seniors can say anything both interesting and new. Nearly all college seniors reveal themselves to be naive about the law and lacking in real self-knowledge, particularly concerning career direction, when writing about this topic. In the latter situation, admissions directors will consider it crucial to understand why someone wants to change careers. In particular, you will be expected to show that you know well what you expect to find in a legal career that you have not found in your current career. (See the discussion regarding "Why do I want to be a lawyer?")

Note that you can also write about something that happened in your private rather than your professional life. In fact, such dilemmas are common, so you probably have a wealth of material available.

You will want to show that there was truly a dilemma, at least on the surface. You will probably want to show that you explored and investigated the nature of the problem, since you were no doubt reluctant to make a snap decision when it appeared that any decision would have substantial adverse consequences. In describing what you did, show that you explored every option and did your best to minimize the adverse consequences.

The tone of your essay is another minefield. If you sound like an innocent seven-year-old who believes that it is always wrong to lie, you will not fit in a world of tough senior managers and lawyers who constantly need to make hard decisions with rotten consequences for somebody. On the other hand, if you sound like Machiavelli, for whom the only calculus depends upon personal advantage, and for whom the potential suffering of other people is irrelevant, you will be rejected as a moral monster. You need to be somewhere in the middle, someone who recognizes that the world and the decisions it requires are seldom perfect, but that it is appropriate to try to minimize adverse consequences as best one can. Only in extreme circumstances would it be appropriate to walk away from the decision (and the job).

ADVANTAGES OF THIS APPROACH

It is critical to find a subject you can get your teeth into. Our examples may help you find a subject, one with layers of detail and dilemma. If you go into depth in exploring it (without sounding like a naive child or a cynical manipulator), turn it about and examine it from different angles, and weigh the various options thoughtfully, you will show yourself to be serious lawyer material.

WHY DO I WANT TO BE A LAWYER (OR, WHY DO I WANT TO GO TO LAW SCHOOL)?

THE TYPICAL APPLICANT

Too many people write on this topic. *Young applicants,* especially those still in college, have little to say that will not sound naive to a hardened admissions officer. This is particularly true for those essays devoted to how you will save the environment, represent society's unfortunates, help your ethnic group (which up until now has been woefully underrepresented), and so on. Admissions officers know how easy it is to say—and even to believe—such things at 21; they also know that the majority of the people espousing such views in the admissions process head off to corporate law firms upon graduation.

Another losing approach is to show how much you look forward to attending law school, making it sound as if law school is going to be merely a continuation of your liberal arts education, rather than preparation for a serious career. Once again, this is a hallmark of a young applicant—and one who has yet to think carefully about her future career.

The typical *mid-career applicant* applies to law school because he is desperately unhappy with his current job. Too many of these applicants have no idea of where they are going, just what they are running from or avoiding. Consequently, their approach to this topic tends to show that they do not have a realistic career plan. They describe their hoped-for job in vague, rosy terms, saying they hope to fight for the rights of the people or they look forward to an intellectual career. They often demonstrate as little knowledge of law as the applicant still in college.

A BETTER APPROACH

College-aged applicants seldom have an in-depth understanding of law, so they should generally avoid this topic. (Exceptions are those who have done substantial part-time work in a legal environment.) They should look for topics that will allow them to show themselves in a positive light, rather than parading their ignorance. The top schools' admissions directors are remarkably unanimous on this point.

Mid-career applicants, however, will need to address the question of why they want to be lawyers. They may do so in any number of different ways.

1. *Fixing the Legal System/Public Interest Law.* If, and only if, you have substantial personal experience with some portion of the legal system—or have worked in a field related to your future law career—should you even consider writing about a failing of the legal system and how you will help to remedy it. Similarly, you should proclaim your interest in public interest law only if your employment and personal histories provide abundant support for your claim

that you will go this route. If you wish to represent battered women in custody fights, for example, you will sound like a marvelous candidate if you have been working for years as a counselor in a battered women's home. If you have merely volunteered once a month for the last six months (about the time you have been thinking about putting together law school applications, perhaps?), your essay will fall flat. For this essay, the context is everything. You need to demonstrate convincingly that you have a very substantial, ongoing connection with your chosen field to address this topic convincingly.

2. *Law as a Natural Career Progression.* Another favorite topic within this category concerns why law (school) represents a natural progression for the applicant. All too often, a political science major still in college writes that law school is exactly what he has been aiming for his entire college career. This is simply to state the obvious, of course; this applicant would be better off choosing another topic. This topic is a good one, on the other hand, for someone who has already had substantial career experience in a field related to law. For example, look at the personal statement in Part IV written by Sacha M. Coupet, who worked as a psychological consultant for the Michigan Child Welfare Law Resource Center at the University of Michigan Law School prior to law school. Such an applicant can be very convincing about why law school truly is right for her.

To the extent possible, show that you are not running away from your prior job. Doing so suggests that you are desperate and therefore not in a suitable frame of mind to make a sensible decision about your next career. It also suggests you may have failed at this career insofar as people tend to like jobs they are good at, and dislike jobs they do not do well. If you can, show how law represents simply a further step in a process that is already well under way. Talk about your future job as being clearly related to your experiences, strengths and weaknesses, likes and dislikes. In other words, your future is based solidly upon the foundation of your prior job.

This is a particularly easy essay to write for someone, like Sacha, who has had directly relevant experience for the career she envisions, knows well what lawyers in the field actually do, and has worked with such lawyers. The same would be true for an analyst in an investment bank who works with securities lawyers, or an accountant who handles tax matters alongside tax attorneys.

ADVANTAGES OF THIS APPROACH

Young applicants, especially those still in college, are likely to fare better by writing about another subject. Mid-career applicants, though, can potentially use this topic to their advantage.

Law schools want to make sure you have given substantial thought to your future career. They want to see that a JD fits with the future you envision for yourself. Tackling the subject of "career objectives" in your essay shows that, unlike many applicants, you are aware that law school is not an end in itself.

BRIEF NOTES ON ADDITIONAL TOPICS

FORMATION OF CHARACTER ESSAYS

Because many applicants to the top schools have similar credentials and few experiences that directly indicate a passion or qualification to study law, essays that discuss aspects of the applicant's character and background are often suggested, by the law schools, as the most helpful.

The *typical applicant,* however, fails to isolate which facets of his life (and character) are distinctive. First, he claims that his parents have instilled in him a strong work ethic. Next, he says this is bolstered by an unquenchable desire to learn everything he possibly can. He concludes by proclaiming, suddenly, that only at Harvard Law School will he be able to satisfy this hunger for knowledge. Ultimately, the typical applicant does little to distinguish himself from the crowd of other applicants.

To succeed with this type of personal statement, the applicant must step back and take a good, objective look at his life. Of the qualities he would like to emphasize, which can be linked to his background, to the influence of mentors, to circumstantial events? How is he different from his peers? How would he be valuable to a top school's student body?

Everyone knows we are shaped by where, and who, we came from. Law schools, especially, know this. They want to learn how you have been affected by all sorts of circumstances, even (or especially) those that are out of your control. That does not mean, however, there are no dangers in using personal background as the sole factor in distinguishing oneself. The typical applicant holds it up like a red flag and expects the waters will part for him. This is not so. Certain backgrounds can be advantageous to have, but you need to show you are more than just a category.

The Hard-Luck Story

Although the members of any admissions committee are a jaded bunch, numbed by thousands of pleading personal statements, they are still human. So do not assume they will immediately scrap your application because you have chosen to discuss unfortunate circumstances that formed your life. This category of essay, however, is for applicants who have encountered supreme disadvantage—whether it be poverty, a tragedy, or a life-altering accident. Yet, even more than this, the applicant has overcome it. The hard-luck story can be used to demonstrate stamina, perseverance, and savvy. You (if this is you) have worked harder than most other applicants and are more likely to continue to do so. It may also explain certain weaknesses in your application.

The risk is that you will end up sounding plaintive, self-righteous, and stuck in the past. For this essay to be successful, you must show that this disadvantage was not something that happened to you, but something that you conquered. How is it an inextricable part of you? What are the long-term (positive!) results of this travail?

ETHNIC BACKGROUND

The same is true for personal statements about one's ethnic background. Be sure to do more than claim membership in a group, even if that group is much sought-after by the school to which you are applying. Make your story interesting and detailed. Show that you have ultimately gained something important—and which will be of value in law school and beyond—from your upbringing or later circumstances.)

HANDICAPPED

Applicants who are (or were) physically or otherwise handicapped should follow the same approach as suggested above. There are two potential problems of which you need to be aware. You will face a backlash if you overplay your hand. Do not exaggerate the problems you faced. For example, if you walk with a limp, do not make your tale into a grand tragedy. Approaching your story in a very matter-of-fact, even understated, fashion, will tend to work best. The other potential problem is that you may (inadvertently) suggest you will be unable to get through law school. If this is a problem, attach whatever documentation (or recommendations) necessary to dispel this notion.

UNUSUAL CHILDHOOD OR BACKGROUND

If you had an unusual childhood—lived on an American naval base in the Indian Ocean until you were ten; or you spoke Polish to your mother, German to your father, French at school, and English in the neighborhood; or you were raised by a lesbian couple—you have an opportunity to show you have been shaped by highly unusual factors of locale, language, or circumstance. The committee will notice and remember you, particularly if you show how this unusual start to your life has had an important affect upon your current capability, character, goals, and so on.

Similarly, if you have another unusual dimension to your life, consider whether it should be highlighted in your application. For example:

- Are you from an unusual part of the world: Ajaccio, Chengdu, Luxor, Tampere?

- Have you worked with unusual people? (If you are an opera singer, your work colleagues probably qualify as unusual by law school standards.)

- Do you have knowledge of an unusual industry? (The circus, for example, or the biotechnology industry.)

- Have you been employed in unusual work conditions? (If you, an American, managed a Tex-Mex restaurant in Paris, supervising Albanian and Greek chefs, reporting to a Dutch owner who makes his real money from running drugs, and trying to satisfy a persnickety French crowd, you have the makings of an interesting essay about organizational dynamics, influence strategies, and so on, in a highly unusual situation.)

- Have you performed an unusual job? (Responsible for preventing the theft of fuel from tankers in southeast Asia, for example.)

- Do you have rare personal qualities?

- Do you have unusual outside interests? (A person who has published a successful book, been nationally ranked in squash, started a successful part-time business, or whatever, has something unusual to talk about.)

Note that you will not want to discuss your unusual dimension simply because it is unusual. Instead, you will want to discuss it if you can make yourself interesting, appealing, and meritorious in some fashion. For example, if you are talking about your job (trying to prevent the theft of tanker fuel), do more than describe the job. Show how it requires you to deal with some of the world's savviest and most dangerous thieves, in a culture that is not your own, and thus in a situation in which you could make a truly fatal mistake all too easily. Show the data gathering you did and how you did it. Show the analyses you performed in trying to understand who was involved in the thievery—your company's ship captains, contract employees working the fueling operations in Singapore, the financial controller, or someone else? And so on. In other words, get more mileage out of the situation than just showing that your job is out of the ordinary. (If you are unable to do so, consider trying a different topic.)

ESSAYS ON AN IMMERSION IN THE UNKNOWN

For applicants who have lived/studied/worked in a "foreign" environment, an essay about what they learned may be valuable. The term "foreign" in this context need not be confined to another country. A rich suburbanite who has spent several years teaching in a downtrodden, dangerous public high school can take the same approach as someone who has worked in Bangkok. Similarly, a poor urban kid who has just managed the kitchen or taught tennis in a wealthy country club has also been in a foreign environment.

Be leery of choosing this topic, however, because it backfires on the vast majority of those who write about it. If you have spent a junior semester or year abroad, for example, you almost certainly will write a disastrous, simple-minded, only-scratching-the-surface, personal statement about your learning that people are really the same everywhere despite their superficial differences. Or you will exclaim that you now have an in-depth knowledge of this second culture (despite, perhaps, attending classes in a program designed solely for Americans, or despite failing to become truly fluent in a second language). The same danger exists for others who failed to get to grips with this other culture. Backpacking through Europe or India may have been fun, but you are not likely to get much mileage out of your experiences unless you can bring a sophisticated sensibility to bear. In fact, an additional risk you run is that you will come across as a spoiled brat rather than one who offers real value in a law school setting.

The kind of experience that is likely to prove much more valuable is akin to the urban kid working in the wealthy country club. For example, if you worked for two years in a tire factory outside Clermont-Ferrand alongside French and Algerian workers, speaking only French (or Arabic) with them, you will have a much more interesting story to tell than does the applicant who did her semester at LSE and was so mesmerized by pubs, the changing of the guard, and the fact that the English drive on the other side of the road (!).

The deeper your understanding of the other language and culture, the more extensive your experience, and the more you got off the beaten path followed by well-to-do American dilettantes abroad, the better your chances of success with this topic.

ESSAYS ON A RELATIONSHIP WITH A MENTOR

For applicants who feel a great debt to a mentor (or even an historical figure), an essay about what they learned from this relationship may be a good topic. There are potential advantages to this choice of topic. Given that law schools are in the education business, it does not hurt to show that you are an active learner. Demonstrating yourself to be mature enough to be receptive to the knowledge of those (presumably) senior to you is a nice touch, particularly for younger applicants. You can also show a real warmth to your personality via your relationship with this other person.

The danger inherent in this topic is that you may end up talking more about this influential person than about *you*. Use this person as a foil—the person should, ideally, reflect what is most impressive about your interests, your achievements, and your goals. Or show that you developed as a result of your interaction with this person, but keep the focus on *your* development.

ESSAYS THAT SHOW HOW YOU THINK

Each year a small number of applicants choose to write personal statements that make absolutely no claims, no clarifications, and no declarations of intent. Instead, they hope to demonstrate excellent writing skills and sensitively (if obscurely) chosen themes to imply who they are. Often, the essays have nothing to do with law or the applicant's credentials. Essays that fall into this category can be philosophical, anecdotal, or analytical. In the best of these essays, the reader comes away with a strong sense of the applicant, but the reader arrives at these conclusions himself. The writer skillfully articulates himself indirectly and subtly, rather than in an expository manner.

> *"The personal statement can be an opportunity to illuminate your intellectual background and interests. You might do this by writing about a course, academic project, book, artistic or cultural experience that has been important to you."* (Harvard)

These are high-risk essays by their very nature. Admissions officers are very busy and have a limited amount of time to devote to an individual applicant's file. They are also unlikely to share a passion for whatever specific matter you are exploring in your essay. These factors make it clear that if the piece is not particularly well-written, you risk a very negative evaluation, indeed. Do not choose this strategy unless you are sure of your writing ability. Similarly, make sure several other people, including virtual strangers to you, read it. If people who do not know you understand the (indirect) point you are trying to make, then you at least have a fighting chance of this working.

EXPLANATIONS OF POOR PERFORMANCE: ADDENDA ONLY!

Many applicants use their personal statement to address a shortcoming in their application. They attempt to explain why their LSAT is not a true indicator of their ability, for example, or why they have not been promoted in the last four years. It may make sense to explain such matters, but it seldom makes sense to use the personal statement to do so.

Virtually every school will accept a brief addendum in which you explain a gap or weakness in your record. They strongly prefer that you *not* use your all-too-valuable personal statement to do so. (Instead, use your personal statement to highlight positive aspects of your candidacy.)

The rules are very simple in writing an addendum to address a gap or weakness. Explain the circumstances briefly, in a matter-of-fact way. Do not whine or complain. Offer any supporting proof, if necessary, such as the fact that you were indeed hospitalized with a high fever for three days preceding the LSAT exam. If you think better indicators of your performance exist, cite them. For example, if you had weak grades in your first three semesters, but strong

ADMISSIONS DIRECTORS TALK ABOUT
PERSONAL STATEMENTS

THE ROLE OF THE PERSONAL STATEMENT

The personal statement frames the application. It's the one opportunity for people to tell me their story, to show me the voice they've developed, what they bring to the table.   Edward Tom, Director of Admissions, Boalt Hall (Berkeley)

Good writing gives us confidence that a candidate can write well; that she can handle the work in law school; and, that she can and will contribute to the intellectual life and diversity of the school.   William Hoye, Dean for Admissions, USC

We value freedom so highly that the Law School is basically anarchic. The people who are good candidates for us see our unstructured essay and are challenged, energized, and excited rather than threatened or unsure or frightened. We're looking for people who can respond creatively and independently to our essay.   Jean Webb, Director of Admissions, Yale

The applicant's personal statement is accorded significant decisional weight. In the absence of evaluative interviews, it is the opportunity for a candidate to:

> Educate or inform our Admissions Committee why they have chosen to pursue legal training; show that this choice is consonant with their personal values and professional goals; demonstrate, if their record does not do so itself, that they possess the intellectual power and have developed the academic skills necessary to negotiate well the exceptional rigor of our program; describe how various conditions and experiences in their lives—advantages as well as disadvantages, opportunities as well as obstacles—have combined to shape their view of the world and a sense of their place in it; to communicate to us how and to what extent they have strengthened (through exercise) their values and achieved their personal, academic, and professional objectives; to share with our Committee their understanding of the responsibilities, not only of the benefits, that obtain to membership in the legal profession.   Jim Milligan, Dean of Admissions, Columbia

THE IMPORTANCE OF THE PERSONAL STATEMENT

A personal statement is often a make-or-break component of an application. It should add a dimension to an application; however, it cannot add all dimensions. In other words, it should be focused rather than try to do too much. Longer does not usually make it better.   Joyce Curll, Assistant Dean for Admissions and Financial Aid, Harvard

The bottom line is that people can write their way into law school—or out of it. Elizabeth Rosselot, Director of Admissions, Boston College

It's often not what someone has done; rather, it's the way that he talks about it. Demonstrating an ability to communicate to those around them what they learned, how they think, is important.   Dennis Shields, Assistant Dean for Admissions and Financial Aid, Duke

If people work hard at their personal statements, they can really make a difference.   Erica Munzel, Director of Admissions, University of Michigan

What I do is tantamount to building a new family each year: would you want to know about their backgrounds, their failures? Yes, you would.   Edward Tom, Director of Admissions, Boalt Hall (Berkeley)

Crafting the essay well, giving insight into the candidate, is critical.   Albert R. Turnbull, Associate Dean for Admissions and Career Services, University of Virginia

GENERAL ADVICE ABOUT PERSONAL STATEMENTS

When I read an essay I ask myself, "What does the applicant know about himself and about law that leads him to think that this is the direction he wants to go in?" I want to be sure that choosing law has been a thoughtful decision, not a reflexive one ("I don't know what I'll be doing with my life so I guess I'll apply to law school").   Jim Milligan, Dean of Admissions, Columbia

In marketing yourself to schools, be positive, don't whine. Showing how you have overcome substantial disadvantages can be a key factor. Similarly, put your academic record in context. Show what it means to have something published in your school magazine, for example.   Michael Rappoport, Dean of Admissions, UCLA

It used to be the rage to send in personal statements on blue-backed paper in the manner of a legal summons: "In re applicant X vs. UCLA." I don't miss those.   Andrea Sossin-Bergman, Director of Admissions, UCLA

The personal statement has a different role for us since we interview. Applicants can use it a bit differently: to push their accomplishments, leadership, work experience, motivation, and to show that they have done their homework and know the school well.   Don Rebstock, Associate Dean of Admissions and Financial Aid, Northwestern

Think about what you've done; what's been most meaningful to you, and why; what has had the biggest impact on you. Show that you can be an analytical thinker, not just a reporter. It's important that you write well, effectively communicate your ideas, and say something interesting. Do not, however, do something really "creative" or out in left field just to be different. A well-written, thoughtful statement is what counts.   Erica Munzel, Director of Admissions, University of Michigan

The first test of a personal statement is whether it rings true—is it an accurate portrayal of the applicant. Others include: whether I understand their motivations, why he'll be fun to teach, and how he'll be a good student.   William Hoye, Dean for Admissions, USC

CHOOSING A TOPIC

Don't think in terms of covering the waterfront. Consider the personal statement like an interview that you control: Ask a question that you want to answer. Use one organizing theme to pull together your material; keep it focused. Avoid artifice and any kind of gimmick. A simple, straightforward statement that gets across your message is fine.   Joyce Curll, Assistant Dean for Admissions and Financial Aid, Harvard

We are most interested in what they've done and accomplished. It's also good to see what's impacted them, helped them develop as a person, what struggles they've had. It's appropriate to focus on one item from the data forms—flesh out its significance, demonstrate what they achieved. The most important thing is that it's well written.   Don Rebstock, Associate Dean of Admissions and Financial Aid, Northwestern

I want to see some passion in the personal statement. And, given that we are trying to get a sense of people, it's also important that your personality project. One of the best personal statements that I've seen was about sailing, of all things. The applicant discussed the skills he developed as well as how he developed them, and discussed their relationship to the study of law.   Elizabeth Rosselot, Director of Admissions, Boston College

Don't be redundant: try to choose something that reveals what you haven't already shown us.   Anne Brandt, Director of Admissions, Vanderbilt

Be clear about what a school wants. The topic an applicant chooses reveals a lot about his or her judgment.   Shelli Soto, Dean of Admissions, University of Texas

We don't have anything particular in mind. We want to learn about the applicant. The best essays resonate with the rest of the application. It could be about a cathartic experience, a relationship, even a poem. Sometimes it fits with the reasons for attending law school, but only sometimes.   Albert R. Turnbull, Associate Dean for Admissions and Career Services, University of Virginia

TOPICS TO AVOID

If you are *passionate* about abortion, don't write about it. You are likely to offend someone, whichever position you take.   Janice Austin, Assistant Dean for Admissions, University of Pennsylvania

Essay topics that seldom work well: "I've wanted to be a lawyer since the attorney helped my mother in the divorce." Janice Austin, Assistant Dean for Admissions, University of Pennsylvania

Use good judgment in personal statements. It is inappropriate for an applicant to describe how some man took her diaper off when she was three years old; describing what happened next was far more detail than I needed to know. Similarly, it was inappropriate for someone to give a graphic description of the diarrhea he suffered in traveling the third world. Michael Rappoport, Dean of Admissions, UCLA

Certain topics make us groan: "My grandfather was an attorney." "Why I want to go to law school." Michael Rappoport, Dean of Admissions, UCLA

A number of essay approaches are best avoided: Starting with quotations; "I want to be a lawyer because . . ."; talking about every aspect of your resume rather than focusing on one or two things that would show something interesting about you; satire; poetry. Dennis Shields, Assistant Dean for Admissions and Financial Aid, Duke

One topic that never works is a chronology which repeats what is in the data forms: it's a waste of time. Don Rebstock, Associate Dean of Admissions and Financial Aid, Northwestern

Chronological reports of what they've done tend to be the least helpful of essay approaches. Erica Munzel, Director of Admissions, University of Michigan

The snapshot approach—writing about one incident—seldom works. Elizabeth Rosselot, Director of Admissions, Boston College

Certain essay approaches are usually not successful. Sometimes applicants try to be very creative or cute, but this seldom works. Poetry is not usually a good idea. Humor is good only if a wide variety of people will appreciate it. Giving a litany of excuses for poor academic performance never works. Do not use the personal statement for cathartic purposes; use judgment regarding what personal details you share with someone who does not know you, and then do so in a dignified way. Kenneth Kleinrock, Assistant Dean for Admissions, NYU

Some topics seldom work well. For example, travelogues (my summer vacation on a train across Europe), epic poems, or a list of activities. Be careful about "creative" approaches, too. They get my attention, but not in a good way. William Hoye, Dean for Admissions, USC

For undergrads, I would rather not read about why they want to go to law school. Their comments may be accurate, but they are all the same. For people who are mid-career, the question is a lively one and one that needs to be answered. Jean Webb, Director of Admissions, Yale

Select a topic more interesting than "why I want to go to law school." It's O.K. to connect your topic, in the conclusion, with why you want to attend law school. Kenneth Kleinrock, Assistant Dean for Admissions, NYU

Family stories tend to be highly insightful and useful to us. Overdone topics, which work only occasionally, include things like the value of having studied abroad: "It opened my eyes, taught me to be open-minded, tolerant of other cultures, etc."—ugh. Also, I have yet to see a "brief to the court" on behalf of the applicant done well. They're trying to show a cute connection to the law, but generally get even the terminology wrong. Shelli Soto, Dean of Admissions, University of Texas

We found that our old essay topic, about why you want to go to law school, didn't work well. Candidates wrote about what they figured we wanted to hear. It seldom rang true. It was just repetitive pap: "aid society," "help people," etc. We didn't learn about the individual candidates. Albert R. Turnbull, Associate Dean for Admissions and Career Services, University of Virginia

Avoid the words "LA Law" or "Perry Mason." Do not do a paragraph form of your résumé. Do not explain every weakness: just playing "good defense" will not cut it. In fact, it's better to submit a separate essay regarding weaknesses rather than use the personal statement for that purpose. Andy Cornblatt, Assistant Dean for Admissions, Georgetown

TAILORING YOUR STATEMENT TO A SCHOOL

I can usually tell if I'm reading the same essay as my peers at other schools. Take the time to craft each statement for the specific school you're applying to. I really appreciate when people do that. Applicants on the margin should take particular care to do so. Dennis Shields, Assistant Dean for Admissions and Financial Aid, Duke

My pet peeve is generic personal statements clearly sent off to a bunch of schools. I like to see that a statement has been tailored to us. Don Rebstock, Associate Dean of Admissions and Financial Aid, Northwestern

I like it when an applicant shows that he or she knows what GW does. It's not crucial; we admit some people with generic personal essays—but in spite of those essays, not because of them. If applicants do some homework regarding what we're about it, shows they went the extra mile, which gives them points in my book. Robert Stanek, Director for Admissions, George Washington

Plenty of people make obvious mistakes. They assume we offer a course we don't, for instance. Elizabeth Rosselot, Director of Admissions, Boston College grades for the following five semesters, note this. Explain that you did not enjoy chemistry (your initial major), but "found" yourself when you switched to physics.

Do not gild the lily: Going on too long risks calling overly much attention to your weakness.

UNDERGRADUATE PERFORMANCE

Feel free to point to your grade trend, strong performance in your major, good performance for all but one term, and so on. Do not offer your immaturity as an explanation for poor performance. Limit such explanations to stronger stuff: your need to work nearly full time while carrying a full load, tragedy in the family, or your lack of recognition of your dyslexia.

LSAT SCORE

This is a tricky matter, since law school is full of tests. If you were very ill during the test, consider discussing the matter. Better yet, discuss it in the context of why a later LSAT score is a better indicator of your actual ability. If you had low SAT scores relative to your college performance, note this.

GAPS IN EMPLOYMENT HISTORY

Law schools are not generally very concerned with how you have spent every week of your adult life. If you spent three months after college hitchhiking across Canada, do not feel you should apologize for this. On the other hand, if you are an older applicant, be sure to indicate why you have substantial gaps in your employment history. Similarly, be sure to explain any career shifts you have made.

OPTIONAL ESSAYS

As the sidebar "Extra Essay Opportunities" demonstrates, the majority of the country's top law programs require one personal statement. There is generally no specified topic. Consequently, an applicant can produce one good essay and, with a minimal amount of tailoring, use it for all his or her applications.

If you read your chosen schools' admissions information with a fine-toothed comb, however, you will notice that there do exist numerous opportunities for you to provide additional information. A large number of the top programs state directly that one or two optional essays may be submitted, hint that in certain situations it may be appropriate to include information not found elsewhere, or allow that an attached sheet may be used to answer a short-answer question. All of these are opportunities best taken advantage of. Rather

EXTRA ESSAY OPPORTUNITIES

	1	2 OR MORE	ADDITIONAL MATERIALS (INCLUDING RÉSUMÉ)
Cornell		x	
Duke	x		x
Fordham	x		
Georgetown		x	
Michigan		x	x
Northwestern		x	
NYU	x		
Penn	x		
Stanford	x		
Texas		x	x
Tulane		x	
UCLA		x	x
USC	x		
Vanderbilt	x		
William & Mary	x		
Yale	x		

than cramming as many topics as possible into one, densely-packed two-page statement, you can—and should—use these hidden essay opportunities. The benefits are clear: First, you demonstrate to admissions officers that you are motivated and perceptive; and second, you show that you are a multidimensional person. Using the extra essays allows you to increase the number, or enhance the quality, of themes (and stories) in your application.

Writing optional essays is especially advantageous for schools that severely restrict the length of the *required* personal statement—such as Yale. In 250 words, you can effectively address only one or two themes; it is almost impossible to discuss your character, your uniqueness, your ambition, the reasons why Yale Law School is a good match for you, and other matters all at the same time. Fortunately, there are two other opportunities to articulate yourself. Question 10 in Yale's application, which has no length restriction, provides some hints:

"*Optional:* Please add to this application whatever additional material you believe will enable admissions readers to make a fully informed judgment on your application. Many applicants include the personal statement they have prepared for other law school applications. Examples of issues you might choose to address are: personal goals, history of standardized testing, or special circumstances involving your educational development and achievement. The admissions file readers especially welcome statements that enable them to understand the contribution your personal background would make to the student body at Yale Law School; such statements might concern, for example, your racial or ethnic identity and your socioeconomic background."

Obviously, to ignore this question would be to imply to the Admissions Committee that you have either very little to say about yourself, you are lazy, or that getting into Yale is not your top priority.

ADVICE TO KEEP IN MIND

- In the short-answer section of a school's application, notice when you are asked to "list and describe" something—rather than just "list." If you are allowed to answer the question on a separate sheet of paper, this can be transformed from a spartan 20 words into a paragraph—i.e., a short essay.

- Read applications very carefully. Often, tucked inconspicuously into the last page of a brochure somewhere, you will read that "additional information may be provided" if the applicant strongly feels an issue needs to be addressed.

- Save negative subjects (your performance in a particular semester, etc.) for an addendum.

- Do not write an optional essay simply for the sake of doing it. Unless you have something pertinent and important to say, Admissions Officers will feel you are wasting their time.

- Be respectful of schools, such as Michigan, that permit you to submit additional materials—such as synopses of publications, theses, or dissertations. Be considerate and concise. Do not send in 100 pages of your dissertation on the Civil War. You will be remembered—but not appreciated.

ADMISSIONS DIRECTORS DISCUSS WRITING
OPTIONAL ESSAYS AND ADDENDA

If anything, I look for an addendum explaining key points; people don't use them enough. Janice Austin, Assistant Dean for Admissions, University of Pennsylvania

If you think there's a blip or gap in your history, take the time to address and explain it (in a separate paragraph). This eliminates having the whole admissions committee wonder about it and spend all their energy contemplating why you flunked that course and then took the next semester off. Show us why that shouldn't be a concern. You are even welcome to explain why your LSAT is not reflective of your abilities. Be professional and succinct about it, of course, rather than whining. Erica Munzel, Director of Admissions, University of Michigan

I don't mind an addendum, a paragraph to give some sort of explanation for something. Anne Brandt, Director of Admissions, Vanderbilt

The personal statement is not the place to explain your poor testing history. We do want to know if the SAT dramatically underestimated your college performance, but this does not belong in the personal statement but rather in an addendum. Kenneth Kleinrock, Assistant Dean for Admissions, NYU

We allow several optional statements. Shelli Soto, Dean of Admissions, University of Texas

We welcome an addendum, especially from those with more life experience and/or work experience to communicate. It is fine to bifurcate the two—life and work—with one being the subject of the personal statement and the other of the addendum. Albert R. Turnbull, Associate Dean for Admissions and Career Services, University of Virginia

It's fine to write an additional essay. This is particularly appropriate if you want to explain a personal situation affecting your performance, your reasons for wanting USC, how you became interested in law, or your involvement in community service. William Hoye, Dean for Admissions, USC

You want me to understand how you're presenting yourself. You don't want me wasting time "finding the answers" or deciphering the gaps in your record. It frustrates me and gives me less time to read the essays. Erica Munzel, Director of Admissions, University of Michigan

We're surprised that so few applicants take advantage of our offering them the opportunity to explain their GPAs and LSATs. William Hoye, Dean for Admissions, USC

If your undergraduate performance was undistinguished, it's helpful to explain why. Jim Milligan, Dean of Admissions, Columbia

10

WRITING
PERSUASIVE ESSAYS

— EXECUTIVE SUMMARY —

Plan before beginning to write.

■

Follow this chapter's advice in order to maximize the impact of your essays.

■

There is no excuse for basic foul-ups: misspellings,
grammatical mistakes, factual
errors, or inserting the wrong school's name into an essay.

■

Allot substantial time to reorganizing and redrafting. Remember,
"There is no such thing as good writing, just good rewriting."

■

See Part IV for 30 actual application essays written by a
variety of candidates to the top schools.

In the words of Yale Law School's brochure: "Faculty readers look to the required essay to evaluate your writing, thinking, and editing skills, as well as to learn more about such qualities as your intellectual concerns or passions, your humor, or your ability to think across disciplines." If you intend to rely on your "numbers" to get you admitted, you will be missing the opportunity to dramatically improve your chances. In fact, the better the school, the more likely it is that the objective data in your application will not determine your fate and that the essays in particular will weigh heavily in the decision.

Admissions officers will judge you on the basis of what your essays reveal about your writing ability (including your ability to persuade, structure, and maintain a well-reasoned argument, and communicate in an interesting and professional manner), honesty and maturity, understanding of what the program offers and requires and how well you would contribute to it, and clear ideas about where you are headed. They will want to learn what you have accomplished, who you are as a person, and how well you can communicate. Admissions officers never take the approach of teachers who said, "I'll grade this on the basis of the content, not your writing style."

This chapter is designed to help you actually write your essays. You have learned from prior chapters the types of things you are likely to want to say, but not how to say it; this chapter addresses that need. In addition to reading this chapter, however, learn about successful essay writing by examining some of the many examples contained in this book (see Chapter 8 and Part IV).

GETTING STARTED

SAVING TIME: APPLICATIONS ON DISK

One of the pains of applying to schools is filling in the finicky little boxes on the application forms. (Who still has an old typewriter around for completing them?) Fortunately, a good alternative now exists. A firm called Multi-App has produced software that allows you to replicate admissions forms on your computer. The information that is common to all applications—such as your name and address, undergraduate university, etc.—needs to be inserted only once. The software then places this in the correct blanks on each application form. Sixty-three law schools subscribe to Multi-App; all of the leading programs do. For information, contact:

Law Multi-App
740 South Chester Road, Suite F
Swarthmore, PA 19081
(800) 515-2927
mcs@multi-app.com
www.multi-app.com

The price for Multi-App's complete set of materials is $59; it can be easily down-loaded from the Internet.

Admissions directors seem quite happy to get the information in this format, so do not be concerned that your application will be at a disadvantage if you use this procedure.

BEFORE WRITING

Before starting to write, let's review what we know about your audience and its decision criteria.

Who is your audience? Your audience is the set of admissions officers who will read your application. They are conscientious but nearly overwhelmed by the volume of material they are required to read. They are highly familiar with the determinants of law school and career success. Thus, they will examine your application for convincing evidence of your intellectual ability, potential in the field of law, and individual personal characteristics. Being in the education business, they want applicants who clearly value learning and education. They will also like evidence that a person makes the most of opportunities, whether these be great or small.

By communicating effectively—presenting your material in an organized and concise fashion, and not exaggerating or lying—you will gain credibility as a reliable source of information about yourself and as an appropriate candidate. Remember that as important as it is to be sure you are addressing the committee's concerns, your essays should reveal yourself and convey a true sense of who you are as a person. This may, in fact, be your only chance to do so.

What are the top law schools looking for? The three principle criteria mentioned earlier—your intellectual ability, professional promise, and personal characteristics—are commonly sought by all of the top schools. (For more detailed information, see Chapter 5.)

What does a particular school look for? All schools look for certain traits, such as analytical ability. Yet not every school is looking for exactly the same sort of candidate. Some will concentrate slightly on finding applicants focused on public service, for example, whereas others want those who are technologically oriented. If you are aware of what a given school is looking for, you can emphasize those aspects of your candidacy that are most suited to its needs. The starting point for learning about a school's specific interests, as discussed in Chapter 3, is to read the material it publishes about itself and speak with its current students and recent graduates.

This chapter focuses on writing individual essays successfully, but bear in mind that each essay is part of a whole application package, consisting of required and optional essays, résumé data, recommendations, and possibly an interview evaluation. To ensure that you put together a well-integrated, consistent package, do not try to finish any one essay until you have done at least a rough draft of all the essays for a given school, and planned the other parts of your package as well.

PLANNING

It is important to plan your writing. Planning forces you to think about what you will write before you get tied up in the actual process. Too many people take the opposite approach, writing random paragraphs, hoping to be able to glue them together later, or trying to write the whole of an essay before thinking about it. The results of these approaches are all too predictable. The material included is a haphazard selection of what might be presented and the writing is not necessarily organized and coherent. No amount of editing will cure this problem, which is not merely a problem of word choice or transitions. The greatest problem with the write-before-thinking approach is that, after expending great efforts, writers are disappointed with the results and must go back to what should have been the starting point—thinking about what they should say.

DEVELOPING YOUR MATERIAL

All too many essays sound the same. The poor admissions officer who has to read 5,000 essays, or many more, gains no understanding of an applicant who writes a personal statement that could have been written by any of another 500 applicants to the same school. Few applicants take the time to ask what makes them unusual or unique (or valuable). *Your goal is to develop materials that will help you write stories unique to you, which no one but you could tell.*

Failing to develop your material or examine yourself thoroughly will lead to dull generalities and mark your application with a deathly sense of unsophistication. You will not do yourself any favors by writing, "My travels broadened my horizons by exposing me to different cultures" or "The experience taught me that with hard work and determination I can reach my goals." Statements like these do not merit space in your essays if you want to dazzle the admissions committee.

Pulling together the relevant material for your application essay (or essays, depending on what your particular case may be) will take substantial effort, especially if you have been working for a number of years at different jobs. The material that might be relevant to the essays could come from virtually any time in your life, and be from any episode or experience.

The best way to start the process of generating material is to fill out the "Personal Organizer" in Appendix V in Chapter 8. As you can see at a glance, there are numerous things to note. Try to fill this out over a period of time, because you will be unlikely to remember everything this calls for in one sitting. Referring to your résumé should be helpful. In fact, you might find it helpful to refer back to earlier versions of your résumé, if you still have them. You may also want to look at your transcripts to refresh your memory.

Consider keeping a notebook handy for jotting down ideas, stories, or details about your past or your goals for the future. Reading this book and the many examples in it may also spur your memory. I encourage you to take personal notes in the margins regarding your own experiences.

When you have completed the Personal Organizer, you should have far too much material to use in your essay(s). This is as it should be. You should feel that you have a wealth of material from which you can pick the most appropriate items.

ORGANIZING YOUR MATERIAL

Once you have generated your raw material, what will you actually say? If you have already read Chapter 8, you may have determined what your main themes will be. Now is a good time to recheck that they still make sense in light of the information you have available. Do you have good stories to tell that illustrate your being a fervent historian? Have you the right grades in the most closely related courses to claim this? If not, now is the right time to reconsider your positioning. Think in terms of what would be appropriate organizing themes given the information you do have.

After you have generated your information, you must organize it. There are many methods for doing so. One is to determine the core of your messages. In other words, what key points are you trying to make? If you can state these, the next step is to group your supporting material according to the appropriate points.

To organize your thinking effectively, it is generally a good idea to outline your essay. This will save you time because the outline will make it clear whether you have too much or too little material. It will also allow you to make changes early in the process rather than work on something that will be eliminated because it does not belong. In other words, it is a check on your thinking.

HOW TO MAKE AN OUTLINE

There are several outlining methods commonly used, including the following:

INFORMAL OUTLINE, USING BULLETS AND DASHES:

➤ Primary idea

  —Subordinate idea

  —Subordinate idea

   —Sub subordinate idea

➤ Primary idea

  —Subordinate idea

  —Sub subordinate idea

FORMAL OUTLINE, USING ROMAN NUMERALS, LETTERS, AND NUMBERS:

  I. Primary idea

   A. Subordinate idea

   B. Subordinate idea

     1. Sub subordinate idea

     2. Sub subordinate idea

       a. Sub sub subordinate idea

       b. Sub sub subordinate idea

     3. Sub subordinate idea

 II. Primary Idea

   A. Subordinate idea

It does not particularly matter which outlining method you use. It only matters that it can perform the important functions needed: pulling together related material, showing how idea groups relate to one another, and showing which ideas are primary and in what ways supporting ideas are to be subordinated. You may find that you start with an informal outline and progress to a more formal one as your ideas become clearer.

REVIEWING THE ELEMENTS OF GOOD WRITING

It is usually a good idea, especially for those who are not accustomed to writing anything more than short memos, to review the elements of good writing style.

Peruse Strunk & White's *The Elements of Style,* paying special attention to the stylistic principles in Part V. It is a good idea to have a book like this on hand as you write and rewrite, in case you need to check up on your grammar or word usage.

In particular, note the following tenets of good writing:

- *Simplicity.* Every sentence should be stripped down to its basic components. Every word that is redundant or does not add meaning should be removed. Writing improves when you pare it down and eliminate unnecessary words or phrases. For example, "a very good friend of my mother's" is better as "my mother's friend." "Hideously ugly" is better as simply "ugly" or "hideous."

- *Precision.* Be as detailed and specific as possible at all times. Details bring authenticity to your writing. If your readers see the word "car," their minds are left with a fuzzy, forgettable image. But if they read "rusted-out, pea green '78 Dodge," they are left with an indelible picture.

- *Show rather than tell.* Rather than tell readers what a situation is like, show them the situation (i.e., describe it in detail) and they will sense on their own what you want them to feel. For example, do not tell readers, "I was very sad when my older brother moved to Bangkok." Instead, describe the twisted feeling you had in your stomach as you sat on his bed while he packed his things; recall the last few minutes of nervous conversation the two of you had before he slipped out the back door; describe the tears you shed as you watched the car pull away for the airport; talk about sitting at the breakfast table all alone with your parents after his departure; explore the feelings of abandonment you sensed when he called home but never asked to speak to you. By showing the situation, you will more powerfully convey to your readers how lonely and sad you really were.

- *Choose your words carefully.* Do not follow the masses; avoid clichés and common phrases whose "understood" meanings could be conveyed more effectively using different words. Clichés will dull your reader and make you sound unimaginative or lazy. Phrases such as "blind as a bat" or "it was like looking for a needle in a haystack" can be better and more precisely conveyed in your own original words.

- *Stick to one style and tone.* Decide before writing what kind of style and tone you will employ, and stay with it throughout the entire essay. If your tone at the beginning of an essay is light-natured and humorous, do not switch to a somber or stern voice midway through the piece. If your essay is meant to be fashioned as a personal diary entry, do not suddenly start preaching to an outside audience.

- *Alter the lengths, styles, and rhythms of your sentences for variety.* Your writing should contain some very long sentences as well as some especially short ones for greatest effect. You should not rely too heavily on any one or two sentence constructions, but weave many different sentence forms and structures into your essays.

■ *Forget what you learned in grade school.* Every essay does not have to have the kind of "introduction," "body," and "conclusion" that you learned about as a kid. Your writing does need to be organized and unified, but organization and the development of ideas take on more sophisticated meanings once you have mastered the basics of writing. Your introduction does not have to have one single "topic sentence," nor does it have to summarize everything that will follow in the body of the essay. Your conclusion does not have to restate the topic sentence. Using the first person ("I") is entirely appropriate and necessary for law school essays. Throw out the old rules of thumb if you have not already done so.

GET YOUR CREATIVE JUICES FLOWING

There are many ways of triggering your creativity if you know you have trouble writing crisp and energetic prose. First and foremost, you must read! Reading the works of talented authors, especially those who have produced what we might call "creative nonfiction," will prepare you to let loose your own creative juices for the sake of writing your college essays. Here are a few suggestions if you would like to read brilliant personal memoirs or autobiographical accounts: Ernest Hemingway's *A Moveable Feast*; Zora Neale Hurston's *Dust Tracks on a Road*; Jill Ker Conway's *The Road from Coorain*; Vladimir Nabokov's *Speak, Memory*; Penelope Lively's *Oleander, Jacaranda*; Maxine Hong Kingston's *The Woman Warrior*; Andre Aciman's *Out of Egypt*; Vivian Gornick's *Fierce Attachments*; any autobiographical essay by Calvin Trillin or John McPhee.

There are many books on writing that can suggest a variety of exercises and strategies for unleashing your creativity. Consult, for example, Natalie Goldberg's *Writing Down the Bones* or Anne Lamott's *Bird by Bird* for ideas.

THE ROUGH DRAFT

The next step in the writing process is to produce a rough draft. Be sure you are not too demanding of yourself at this point. Even though you want to do a good job, here "the perfect is the enemy of the good." If you are unwilling to write down anything that is less than final-draft quality, you are highly likely to be unable to write anything at all. Rather than take this perfectionist approach, be sure to limit your goal to that of producing a rough draft that incorporates most of the basic points you want to make. Do not be concerned if the order you had planned to follow no longer seems to work well, or if you cannot quite express your thoughts, or if your word choice is awkward. Get something reasonable down on paper as a starting point.

Writers use any number of different strategies when they start writing. No one method is recommended above others. This is very much a matter of personal preference. You can use any of the following methods. Choose the one (or invent one of your own) that gets you started on the road to producing a reasonably complete draft.

■ *Start with the conclusion.* Writers who use this method feel they cannot write the body of the essay until they know what they are leading up to.

TWO WAYS TO AVOID WRITER'S BLOCK

Many people find themselves "blocked" when they try to write. They sit and stare at the paper or computer, and it stares back at them. To avoid this, do not put pressure on yourself to do too much at once. When you are in the early part of the writing process, try simply to get the basic elements of your thinking about each subtopic down on paper. Do not worry about the quality of what you are writing until you are editing.

Technique One. After you have thought about an essay, try to write down on index cards phrases that convey your various ideas. (Or, of course, use a computer to do the same thing.) Don't plan for too long; just write down the phrases as they occur to you. Then organize the cards into related groups of ideas. Write paragraphs expressing these ideas, perhaps trying to link the related ones together. Then see if you can place these paragraphs into a reasonably logical order. Next, put this structure into a proper outline to see if it makes sense. If it does, link the paragraphs with appropriate transitions. If it doesn't, try reordering the paragraphs.

Technique Two. Involve a friend in the process if it is still too difficult to get rolling with this method. Explain to your pal what you are trying to convey. Have her take notes on what you are saying. Organize those notes into a logical order, with her help, and then explain yourself to her again, being sure to follow your notes to keep things in order. If you can record this, and transcribe your recording, you will have a solid rough draft, which you can start to edit.

■ *Start with the introduction.* When an introduction lays out clearly what will follow, it in effect controls the body of the paper. Some writers like to start with the introduction in order to make sure they have a grip on the body of the paper before trying to write it.

■ *Start with any of the paragraphs of the body.* Some writers like to pick any self-contained part of the body of the paper and write it up, them move on to another part, and then another. These writers like to build the substantive parts of the paper first, and then provide an introduction and conclusion based upon this substance.

■ *Write several different drafts, starting in different places.* This approach involves taking one perspective or starting point for writing a draft, plowing through the entirety, then doing the same thing from another perspective or starting point. Later, the writer can choose one draft or another, or cut and paste using pieces of each.

A majority of people use the third method—writing paragraphs of the body of the paper. They typically write them individually, then place them together in their predetermined order, and only then develop an introduction and conclusion. They take this approach because they know certain aspects of the subject well and can write about them easily, but require more thought to fill in the remaining pieces, such as the introduction and conclusion.

EDITING YOUR ROUGH DRAFT

Remember that "the only good writing is rewriting." You are doing your first part of this rewriting when you start to edit your rough draft.

One of the most important aspects of the editing stage is its timing. Editing without a break between the drafting and the editing stages will limit your insight into the flaws of your draft. You will not see where you skipped a needed transition or explanation because you are too close to the original writing. If you can take a break, preferably at least a night, or better yet, a week, you will be better able to read your draft from the perspective of an outsider.

Make sure you have edited your draft for substance—for what points will remain and what points will be eliminated—before you start editing the language. Otherwise, you will devote time and effort to improving the wording of material that might be discarded. (Even worse, you are likely to keep it in your draft if you have gone to the trouble of making it sound good.) This section assumes that you will revise your essay three times. In fact, if you are a good writer and have taken the time to think through an essay before doing your first draft, you might well need to edit it only once or, more likely, twice. By the same token, if you are struggling with an essay, it might require more than three revisions to sort out the problems.

One warning: Do not view editing as taking the life out of your essay. Editing's role is to eliminate the dead wood, making your points stand out as clearly as possible.

REVISING YOUR FIRST DRAFT

The initial revision should focus on the essay as a whole.

Do you accomplish your objective? Does your essay directly answer the question? Is your main idea clear?

Revise for content. The typical rough draft may have too little and too much material, all at the same time. It will have touched the surface of some portions of the essay, without providing explanation or convincing detail. At the same time, it may have discussed things that do not contribute significantly to your major points.

A good essay eliminates extraneous material while including all the information necessary to your point. Your reader needs sufficient evidence to accept what you are saying, so be sure you have adequately developed and supported your main idea. Material that does this belongs, but material that is unrelated to the main idea should be eliminated.

Revise for organization. A well-organized essay will group similar ideas together and put them in the proper order. If it is easy to produce an outline from the draft, and there is a clear logic to the flow of the material, you can be reasonably certain that you have a well-ordered essay. Otherwise, reorder your material.

Revise for length. Is your essay approximately the right length? If it is substantially longer than the stated limit, consider how to reduce the supporting material. Many schools leave the issue of length up to the applicant's discretion—but be wary of this freedom, especially if you have the tendency to write verbose, rambling manifestos. Adhere to a self-imposed limit and, unless addressing a topic that needs lengthy explanation, stick to it. You probably need more depth if the essay is significantly shorter than the suggested length. You might consider rethinking your choice of topic if you feel you have nothing more to say.

REVISING YOUR SECOND DRAFT

Assuming you have successfully revised the first draft of the essay and the content is as you wish it to be, turn your attention to the components of the essay: the paragraphs, sentences, and individual words.

Revise paragraphs. A paragraph should not be an arbitrarily formed entity. It should, to some extent, revolve around an idea, a central point, a theme. Isolate a paragraph at a time and make sure it sticks together and is not merely a bunch of unrelated statements slapped together.

Look next at the length of your paragraphs. Most writers tend to one extreme or the other: Either all their paragraphs are very short or all are very long. A mixture of lengths is a good idea. The occasional paragraph that is substantially shorter or longer is fine, but they should be the exception rather than the rule. The reasons for this are simple: Too many short paragraphs make you look simple-minded, unable to put together a complex idea or group related ideas together, whereas absurdly long paragraphs will discourage reading by any but the most conscientious reader. Use short paragraphs for emphasis; use long paragraphs for discussion of complicated points or examples.

The three methods you can use to develop your main idea are to provide examples, explanation, or details. Writing without these three components tends to be unsatisfying and unconvincing. Generalities ("I am a morally-driven person") are unconvincing unless supported with specific examples and explanations.

Revise for flow. Even when you have well-written paragraphs placed in the correct order, your writing may still be difficult to read because it lacks suitable transitions between ideas or other means of showing how the ideas relate. For our purposes, the most important method of relating ideas will be using transition words and phrases. Some typical transitions include:

PURPOSE	TYPICAL TRANSITIONS
Amplification	besides, furthermore, moreover, in addition
Cause and effect	therefore, consequently, as a result, accordingly
Conclusion	as a result, therefore, thus, in conclusion
Contrast	although, but, despite, however, on the one hand, on the other hand
Example	for example, for instance, specifically
Sequence	first, second; former, latter; first of all

One other easy way to connect paragraphs is to have the beginning of one paragraph follow directly from the end of the prior paragraph. For example, if you have just said "I needed the chance to show what I could do without overbearing supervision" at the end of one paragraph, the next one could start out "My opportunity to prove myself came with the founding of a new office in Toronto." In this example the relationship between the two paragraphs is ensured by having the second grow organically from the end of the first.

Be sure each sentence follows logically from the prior sentence.

Check your introduction. Make sure it not only introduces your subject but also grabs the audience. A good introduction is interesting as well as successful at conveying your main points. It should appeal to the reader and set the tone for the whole essay. There are many effective openings. You can state an important and interesting fact, refer to something currently in the news, refer to a personal experience, ask a question that you will answer in your essay, or simply state your general point of view. Do not restate the question, if there is one; it wastes valuable space and is a weak, plodding way to begin.

Check your conclusion. A good conclusion does one or more of the following:

- pulls together different parts of the essay
- rephrases your main ideas (without repeating anything word for word)
- shows the importance of the material
- makes a recommendation
- makes a forecast
- points toward the future—showing, for example, how you will make use of something you have learned
- gives a sense of completion

It should not make a new point that belongs in the body rather than the conclusion, nor should it sound tacked on. The concluding paragraph should develop "organically," if you wish, from the material that preceded it.

Revise sentences and words. Most essay writers pile on one long sentence after another. Avoid this by breaking up some of the longer sentences to provide variety. Use short sentences to make important points; long sentences to explain complex ideas or develop examples. Also use a variety of sentence structures to maintain reader interest. Do not, for example, use a "not only . . . but also . . ." structure in every other sentence. Eliminate sentences that sound awkward or choppy when read aloud.

Edit your sentences to eliminate imprecise or wordy language. For example, use "although" instead of "despite the fact that." Add vigor to your writing by eliminating clichés, using fresh and interesting descriptions. Try to write as much as possible with nouns and verbs, rather than primarily with adjectives (which slow the pace and reduce impact). Similarly, write in the active, not the passive, voice.

Revise for tone. Your tone can be assertive without being arrogant. Your essays should sound confident, enthusiastic, and friendly. Be sure to avoid pleading ("I'd give anything if you would just let me in") and whining ("I never do well on those awful standardized tests; it's so unfair that schools even look at the results").

One way to check the tone of your paper is to read it aloud. Read it first to yourself and then, once it sounds appropriate to you, try reading it to a friend. Ask him how easy it is to understand what the strong and weak points are, whether there are any mistakes in it, and whether it sounds like you. Does it reflect your personal style? The ideal essay should sound just like your voice, but with repetitious and awkward phrasings and use of such filler as "you know" and "like" eliminated. It should sound relaxed rather than formal, but still flow smoothly.

Some applicants, remembering a high school textbook, try to avoid writing in the first person. In fact, it is not only appropriate to use "I" when writing your essays, it is essential that you do so. You are being asked to give personal statements, so do not write in the distant and aloof third person.

REVISING YOUR THIRD DRAFT

Three revisions is not a magic number, but will be a minimum for most people. There is nothing wrong with putting your work through more revisions.

Revise again for style. See the earlier comments.

Revise for grammar, punctuation, and spelling. The way to spot grammatical mistakes and faulty punctuation is to read your essays slowly, preferably after having put them aside for some time. Reading them aloud can also help this process. Even if your sense of grammar is keen, however, consider having a friend whose grasp of grammar is extremely good read each essay. Spellcheck the final product.

Check the length (again). One of the key factors affecting most of the essays you will write is that the law schools generally prescribe their maximum length. Failing to observe this constraint raises questions about your willingness to pay attention to the rules that will apply in other situations, so avoid going over the limit. They have established these limits to provide a level playing field for the applicants; someone who exceeds the limits is trying to assert an unfair advantage.

GIVING YOUR ESSAYS TO SOMEONE ELSE TO CRITIQUE

After you have edited the essays to your own satisfaction, or gotten stuck, hand them to several people whose views on writing you respect. They can provide you with an objective view you may not be able to bring to the essays yourself. They can be particularly useful in determining whether your attempts at humor are working, whether the essays convey a true sense of who you are, and whether you have left out important connections or explanations.

Make sure, too, you have people who do not know you well read your essays; they will be able to tell you if something is clear or not. Pay attention to your readers' opinions, but do not give up control of what are, after all, your essays, not theirs. Do not let them remove the life from your essays.

PROOFREADING

Why proofread your paper if you have been careful in composing the final draft? No matter how careful you have been, errors are still likely to crop up. Taking a last look at the essay is a sensible precaution.

What are you looking for? Basically, the task at this point is no longer to make sure the structure is correct; it is to spot any errors or omissions in your sentences and individual words. Errors tend to show up most often where prior changes were made. Combining two paragraphs into one, for example, may have resulted in the loss of a necessary transition phrase. Grammatical mistakes can also live on.

As with any task that is essentially a matter of editing, your timing is of the essence. Wait until you have already finished what you consider to be your final draft. If you can then put down this draft for a few days, you will be able to give it an effective last look. If not, you risk being unable to see mistakes because you are still too close to the writing. Another useful precaution is to have a friend proofread your essays.

SOME TIPS FOR GOOD WRITING

Do:

➤ *Give yourself the time to do the essays right.* Start early; it will take time to do the essays. The results will also be better if you take time between steps rather than try to finish an application in a hurry. Expect to spend 10 to 20 hours getting organized for the effort, and then averaging perhaps 5 to 10 hours per essay, with the most difficult (and first) efforts taking longer.

➤ *Use humor, but only if it works.* Few people can write humorous prose, or recount humorous stories effectively, but if you can manage it, you will definitely distinguish yourself. To check whether you are succeeding, have several people of different ages and backgrounds read your material to make sure it works on paper as well as it would if you were to tell it. Be sure it is not vicious or off-color humor, as this has no place in a law school essay.

➤ *Keep the focus on you.* For example, do not get carried away in describing a particular facet of an unsavory law without showing how this relates to you and your efforts.

➤ *Explain events whenever appropriate.* Many of the things you have done are mainly of interest because of what you learned from them, what you thought about them, and why you did them.

➤ *Favor a full description of one event rather than a listing of several.* It is generally better to describe one event or accomplishment at some length rather than mention a number of them without explaining why you undertook something, what it meant to you, and what you learned from it.

➤ *Be specific.* The more specific you make your writing, the more you personalize it and the better the chance that it will be interesting. Generalizations, without specific information and examples, are weak and not necessarily believable.

➤ *Find someone to edit your work.* Explain what you are trying to accomplish and who will be reading your essays, so that your "editor" can both determine whether you are meeting your objectives and correct your grammar. The test of your writing is what the reader understands, not what your intent may have been.

Do Not:

➤ *Start to write until you have determined what your most important contributions to this program will be.* Reread the school's brochure and the other materials you have gathered on it and remind yourself of why you are applying to it (beyond its high ranking or reputation). Read the recommendation forms the school uses to see specifically what this school wants in its applicants.

➤ *Use limited space to recite information that is available elsewhere* in the application, such as listing your part-time jobs or mentioning your LSAT results.

➤ *Give superficial answers.* Take this application seriously and work accordingly.

➤ *Pretend to be someone other than yourself.* It will not be supportable with your own history and will sound phony.

➤ *Lie or exaggerate.* Doing so causes all of your assertions to be doubted.

➤ *Think that a personal statement limit also defines the required amount to write.* No one has failed to get into a law school for failure to write the maximum number of words on a personal statement. When you have said all that you intend to say, stop.

➤ *Use a miniscule type size or borders to shrink a personal statement to a given space.* Remember that your readers have to read literally thousands of essays and will not appreciate being forced to squint or use a magnifying glass.

➤ *Start by saying,* "In this essay I will write about . . ."

➤ *Use cute or "meaningful" quotations* unless they fit perfectly and do not make people wince when they read them. Too many people seem to have been taught to start everything they write with a cute epigram, regardless of the fact that it may not fit the subject well and all too often does not match the desired tone of the essay. Shakespeare, Napoleon, Churchill, and Twain all said a lot of marvelous things, but that does not necessarily mean you should quote them.

➤ *Use a definition to begin your essay.* This is too often a sophomoric way to begin, so avoid using this crutch.

➤ *Use only bullet points.* Writing an essay requires that you use full sentences.

➤ *Discuss your low grades,* poor LSAT score, or other weak aspects of your record here, unless you have a very good reason for doing so. In general, these explanations are likely to be best placed in a separate addendum rather than in your personal statement.

➤ *Bore the reader.* A fresh and well-written personal statement will aid your application effort.

➤ *Use fancy vocabulary for its own sake.* Use the simplest possible language to explain your meaning precisely. Using "legalese," unless you are already working in a legal field, is particularly likely to strike admissions officers as presumptuous and arrogant.

ADMISSIONS DIRECTORS DISCUSS HOW
TO WRITE THE ESSAYS

WHAT CONSTITUTES EFFECTIVE WRITING

If the first paragraph can pull me in, it helps. I like to be touched—to laugh, cry, have my heart beat faster, etc. I seldom read a full three pages word for word.   Janice Austin, Assistant Dean for Admissions, University of Pennsylvania

They need to grab our attention in the first paragraph. If the first sentence is, "I have always wanted to be a lawyer since I was five years old," I realize that they will have little to say of interest thereafter.   Michael Rappoport, Dean of Admissions, UCLA

Use active voice primarily. Develop an appropriate rhythm, mixing shorter sentences with longer sentences. Don't overdo it: Don't make it overly dense, with inappropriately complicated vocabulary. I don't want to have to reread it to figure out what was intended. There is certainly no room for grammatical errors or typos. Don't substitute "Cornell" for Northwestern. If they do this, my response is to wish them well at Cornell.   Don Rebstock, Associate Dean of Admissions and Financial Aid, Northwestern

Too many personal statements lose you after the first paragraph; they're not organized, they ramble on—we don't know what you're writing about. We deliberately have many of the legal research and writing faculty on the admissions committee, because we want applicants who have a true facility with the language and care about how they craft their written work. After all, the study of law is in some sense the study of language.   Elizabeth Rosselot, Director of Admissions, Boston College

Trying to use every big word you've ever learned doesn't necessarily work; it comes off as affected.   Kenneth Kleinrock, Assistant Dean for Admissions, NYU

Some storytelling or anecdotes within an essay appeals to me.   Shelli Soto, Dean of Admissions, University of Texas

TONE

We consider personal statements (and the whole application process) very seriously. Mocking the process doesn't help, so applicants need to be careful if they are attempting to be humorous.   Erica Munzel, Director of Admissions, University of Michigan

Display a sense of humor if you have one, but don't force it.   Elizabeth Rosselot, Director of Admissions, Boston College

Be honest, but not too controversial.   Janice Austin, Assistant Dean for Admissions, University of Pennsylvania

ATTENTION TO DETAIL

We want people who are bright, well-rounded, and able to write. You would not believe how poorly written many personal statements are: full of grammatical errors and wrong law school names (Harvard rather than Stanford, for example). Remember that this is an application for graduate work and forget the cutesy gimmicks—no green ink, please.   Faye Deal, Associate Dean for Admissions and Financial Aid, Stanford

A trained file reader will tend to spend about twenty minutes with an application. Grab that reader's attention, then don't blow it with grammatical and spelling errors, and so on. Attention to detail shows whether you are serious about the school.   Elizabeth Rosselot, Director of Admissions, Boston College

One of the biggest mistakes in a personal statement is failing to proofread and spellcheck it. Grammar, punctuation, and spelling all count.   Shelli Soto, Dean of Admissions, University of Texas

The personal statement is assumed to be the best work an applicant is capable of. Lots of mistakes in it indicate inattention to detail, which will be a major problem for a lawyer. Don't substitute Michigan for USC in the concluding "I very much want to attend _____" sentence.   William Hoye, Dean for Admissions, USC

Paying attention to detail is important for success in law. If you can't take the time to get the application right—to eliminate typos, grammatical errors, and missing or misspelled words—what will you do when you're practicing law? They need to read it carefully and make sure someone else does, too. I certainly see many mistakes that computers don't catch.   Erica Munzel, Director of Admissions, University of Michigan

There is nothing better than being able to write well, to form a good sentence. Common mistakes are grammatical errors, misspellings, bad sentence structure. The misplacement of a comma even can make a big difference.   Edward Tom, Director of Admissions, Boalt Hall (Berkeley)

People are often sloppy: incorrect information, misspellings, grammatical errors. They often put too much fluff on something. I've read 100,000 essays, so I really don't have much patience for sloppiness.   Janice Austin, Assistant Dean for Admissions, University of Pennsylvania

Using bad language or inappropriate slang is a problem. Spelling and grammar are certainly important. I remember one essay that started "Education is a priviledge." Another person mentioned "vollunteering at a literacy program." Oops. Having coffee stains on the application never helps, either.   Michael Rappoport, Dean of Admissions, UCLA

We ask for 500 words on a topic important to you. It is O.K. to go beyond this, but not pages and pages' worth. Five hundred words is about enough for most people. Don't truncate, warp, and distort by cutting to 500 words.   Albert R. Turnbull, Associate Dean for Admissions and Career Services, University of Virginia

It is not a problem if the person exceeds the 750-word limit.   Janice Austin, Assistant Dean for Admissions, University of Pennsylvania

We don't specify a page limit to the personal statement, but the focus should be on quality, not quantity. (Of course, someone who's led a long and full life should probably write a longer essay than someone fresh from college.) Elizabeth Rosselot, Director of Admissions, Boston College

Be the audience and the writer at the same time. I read 8,000 of these so length matters: Say what you have to say and then be quiet. For most people two pages will do the trick.   Andy Cornblatt, Assistant Dean for Admissions, Georgetown

We have no limit to the length of personal statements, but extraordinarily lengthy statements seldom show good judgment. Two to three pages would be typical.   Kenneth Kleinrock, Assistant Dean for Admissions, NYU

Adhere to the requirements. We say three pages maximum for your personal statement and mean it. It need not be three pages, either; it can be one and a half pages and be great, too.   Michael Rappoport, Dean of Admissions, UCLA

A Last Word

Try giving a draft of your statement to someone who doesn't know you. Have him describe you back to you. If the person has a hard time articulating much, you've got work to do.   William Hoye, Dean for Admissions, USC

REUSING YOUR PERSONAL STATEMENTS

Law schools want to learn similar things about their applicants, so a personal statement written for one may provide the basis for an essay for other schools. This is good for you to the extent that you can reuse your essays and cut down on the amount of work you have to devote to additional applications.

   On the other hand, few things annoy admissions officers more than to receive personal statements that were obviously written for another school, particularly if the other school's name was left in them. It is possible to recycle your essays as long as you do so intelligently. The reason for doing so—to save time and effort—is compelling enough that almost everyone will try to use the best material in more than one application.

Expect to make more changes than just switching school names. This will be especially true in the following situations:

- Your positioning for a particular school is different from your usual positioning.

- You are applying to schools with various numbers of allowed essays. Applying to a school that permitted just one personal statement may have required you to pack brief descriptions of several events into that essay. When writing for a school that has more essay questions, you may want to spread out these events and use them in several essays. This could also involve lengthening your description of the events. (The reverse process would be appropriate when changing from an application with several questions to an application with just one.)

- You are applying to schools with very different essay length requirements or expectations.

  —To lengthen an essay, you may wish to include more examples, elaborate the examples you have already used, or even add additional points.

  —To shorten a long essay, keep your major points but reduce your elaboration of them.

FURTHER READING

Stuart Berg Flexner, ed., *The Random House Dictionary of the English Language*

William Zinsser, *On Writing Well*

William Strunk, Jr., and E. B. White, *The Elements of Style*

William Safire, *Fumblerules*

Patricia T. O'Conner, *Woe Is I*

The Chicago Manual of Style

Appendix VI

WRITING RÉSUMÉS, FILLING OUT FORMS, INCLUDING EXTRA MATERIALS

WRITING RÉSUMÉS

Some schools, including Chicago, Duke, and Texas, require a résumé; most of the others welcome one. It is generally advisable that you submit one, particularly if you have had substantial work experience. A résumé allows you to frame how your experience and progress are viewed, so take advantage of the opportunity. For law school purposes, there is nothing magical about one style of résumé versus another. As long as you convey the right information in easily readable (and skimmable) form, you will be fine. Keep a few rules in mind, then examine the two examples that follow for further tips.

BASIC RÉSUMÉ RULES

- Assume that people will spend only 30 seconds on your résumé. Therefore, keep to one page, unless you are an academician doing a C.V. or have already been Secretary of State.

- Emphasize important points rather than try to list everything you have ever done. Less tends to be more for résumé purposes; it shows that you can prioritize and organize.

- Emphasize achievements, providing quantitative or tangible proof of your results whenever possible.

■ For jobs you wish to describe in detail, consider separating responsibilities (which you can put in an introductory paragraph form) from your achievements (which you can list as bullet points).

■ Use "résumé-speak"—phrases rather than full sentences.

■ Make sure your résumé is visually appealing: It should not be so crammed with material that it puts someone off.

■ Your résumé should be skimmable for main points, including career progress and interests, within 15 to 30 seconds.

■ The space devoted to a topic should reflect its importance.

SAMPLE RÉSUMÉS

Examine carefully the two résumés that follow. Both do a good job: The essential information is readily apparent in each. It is easy for a reader to pick out what elements are of interest to her. Note the stylistic similarities first. The relevant categories, such as education and experience, are easy to pick out. The schools and employers are emphasized more than are the jobs or degrees, yet each element is readily spotted. The flow of each person's career to date is easily tracked, given the clear posting of the relevant dates. (I prefer the overall layout Garth uses because it is so easy to spot the dates and locations of jobs and education.)

The substantive differences of the two résumés, on the other hand, are even more instructive:

■ Garth puts education first, which is generally appropriate only for those who have limited full-time experience. This is indeed the case with Garth. Paul leads with experience, which is highly appropriate for someone with seven years' experience, all of it impressive.

■ Garth devotes substantial space to education, even including his high school record. Only when a high school record is truly impressive, as is the case here, does it belong on a professional school application. Paul, on the other hand, limits his discussion of education, but does note his professional development efforts.

■ Garth, who had only two years of work experience prior to law school, devotes substantial space to his part-time jobs, whereas Paul, with seven years of experience, does not even bother to list his. Once again, given the difference in their situations, each one made the correct choice.

■ Garth lumps all of his jobs—in education as well as urban economic development, part-time as well as full-time—in one category. Paul, in contrast, splits his work into manufacturing and military categories. Within each of these, he sets up two subcategories: manufacturing and engineering for the former, peacekeeping and combat operations for the latter.

- Garth could have improved his résumé somewhat by providing several missing pieces of data. His years of involvement on the varsity soccer team and as a tutor while at Yale should be included. His work for the Democratic Coordinated Campaign should highlight any budget control he exercised. Similarly, his work for the Philadelphia Empowerment Zone should have included tangible demonstration of his successes. Paul, on the other, does a very effective job of making clear his success in tangible, quantitative fashion.

- Garth emphasizes his academic achievements; Paul, his work achievements. Garth is easily able to show outstanding academic work by noting his honors and awards, but has relatively few concrete work achievements of similar strength. The opposite is true for Paul, who has very substantial and easily demonstrated work achievements, but fewer academic honors to note. In other words, each applicant did a fine job emphasizing his strongest suits.

Although both of these are fine examples, Garth does a better job of formatting his material whereas Paul gets more mileage out of his substantive achievements.

GARTH HARRIES   101 Main St., Menlo Park, CA, 90000

(415) 555-5555 gharries@xxx.com

Education

1991-1995   **YALE UNIVERSITY**   New Haven, CT
B.A. in Ethics, Politics and Economics; focus on Urban Affairs. Course work included
multivariable calculus, intermediate physics, data analysis, and corporate strategy.
Honors: *Summa Cum Laude* with Distinction in Major
             Phi Beta Kappa (elected junior year)
             Heinz Fellow and Richter Fellow (summer 1994)
             Men's Soccer Academic All-Ivy Team (1994)
Activities: Men's Varsity Soccer. Tutoring and classroom assistance. Ultimate
             Frisbee, Northeast regional champions (1995). Research assistant to
             School of Management professor (Fall 1995).

1987-1991   **PHILLIPS EXETER ACADEMY**   Exeter, NH
Honors: Awarded the Yale Cup for general excellence, a Coxe Medal for top five
             scholastic rank, a National Merit Scholarship, and other academic
             prizes.
Activities: Student Judiciary Committee (chair). *Exonian* Editorials Editor.

Experience

1997   **PHILADELPHIA EMPOWERMENT ZONE**   Pescadero, PA
Special Projects Coordinator, Economic Development Office. Facilitated, designed
and/or directed a variety of high-priority economic development projects in
disadvantaged neighborhoods of Philadelphia. Significant projects included:
             —Planning for a worker-owned apparel factory, including creating a successful
               $500,000 grant application with business plan
             —Initial analysis of a major retail/entertainment development proposal
             —Research into the economic development programs of comparable and/or
               competing cities and new business creation in the Zone
             —Program design for a Zone-wide job matching and counseling system

1996   **DEMOCRATIC COORDINATED CAMPAIGN**   Scranton, PA
Field Coordinator. Responsible for Democratic Presidential and State Party campaign
activities in the 10th Congressional District. Directed campaign office, recruited
and managed over 200 volunteers, organized events and voter outreach, and
coordinated with other campaign organizations.

1995-1996   **VAIL MOUNTAIN SCHOOL**   Vail, CO
Teacher. Coed K-12 private day school. Taught Algebra and History to 9th, 10th, and
11th graders. Advised 10th grade homeroom and high school backcountry club.
Coached 7-12 boys' soccer team to an undefeated season.

Spring 1994 **OFFICE OF BUSINESS DEVELOPMENT**   New Haven, CT
Part-time intern. Helped rejuvenate and organize merchants' association along
commuter corridor.

Summer 1994 **DEPT. OF HOUSING AND URBAN DEVELOPMENT**   Washington, DC
Intern, Empowerment Zone/Enterprise Community Taskforce. Policy interpretation
and implementation, office coordination and management, and review of urban
applications.

Personal   Avid soccer player, telemark skier, and hiker. Backpacked through Africa and
              Australia.

Paul Simpson

123 Center Ave., Long Beach, CA 91234   (310) 555-0000   ps@isp.com

MANUFACTURING EXPERIENCE

LEVI-STRAUSS   Los Angeles, CA   1997-Present
Supervisor/Project Engineer—Responsible for manufacturing operations. Manage capital projects for world's third largest blue jeans assembly plant.

Manufacturing
—Supervise 100 employees from three unions; represented Company during union negotiations, which resulted in a four-year contract.
—Reduced inventory levels by 60% through automation of materials management system, with cost savings of $1.5 million per year.
—Partnered with outside vendors to improve cleaning system efficiency by 15%.
—Implemented operator maintenance program that increased production efficiency, resulting in a $1.5 million annual revenue increase.

Engineering
—Designed and supervised installation of two production lines, increasing output by 15%.
—Implemented strategy that ensured Year 2000 compliance six months ahead of target date.
—Led process improvement team that reduced water usage by 30,000 gallons/day, saving over $130,000 annually.

MILITARY EXPERIENCE

US ARMY CORPS OF ENGINEERS   Bosnia & Los Angeles, CA   1993-1997
Captain—Coordinated a range of projects for construction and combat applications. Responsible for the deployment readiness of engineering equipment and the combat training for 60 soldiers.

United Nations Peacekeepers
—Initiated a Civic Assistance program while in Bosnia. Completed 24 projects by working with the Bosnian gov't, humanitarian groups, and military personnel from six countries.
—Directed the construction of a multilane bridge, which enabled the UN access to southern Bosnia in order to deliver emergency medical and food supplies.
—Supervised construction of living quarters for 1200-member, multinational UN organization.

Combat Operations/Readiness
—Integrated engineering strategy into overall combat operations plans for a 1500-soldier interdisciplinary force.
—Developed and implemented a program to monitor equipment readiness and repair status for 415-vehicle fleet; decreasing processing time by 60%, and clerical errors by 75%.
—Supervised on-time rail transportation of 600 vehicles during base deployment to Bosnia.

EDUCATION

DARTMOUTH COLLEGE   *Bachelor of Science in Civil Engineering*   1989-1993
—Captain of ice hockey team (1992–1993); selected to All-Ivy Team.
—Ranked in top 10% nationally in ROTC class; supervised training program for 250 cadets.
—Designed and fabricated Formula 1 car as part of an independent project team.

PROFESSIONAL DEVELOPMENT

—Licensed Professional Engineer in California.
—Additional coursework (Financial Accounting, Managerial Finance, Negotiations, Leadership Communication Strategies) at the UCLA Extension School.

PERSONAL

—Mediator and Project Coordinator, Orange County Community Mediation Program.
—Led United Way fundraising drive; doubled annual contributions.
—Married; enjoy furniture restoration, sky diving, golf, and reading early detective novels.

ADMISSIONS DIRECTORS DISCUSS THE
USEFULNESS OF RÉSUMÉS

It never hurts to send in a résumé. In fact, I think that it's very helpful if someone has been working for some time. I would particularly encourage such people to submit a résumé. Albert R. Turnbull, Associate Dean for Admissions and Career Services, University of Virginia

I like to see a résumé. Often someone has organized the information there in such a way as to show what is important to them, what they are most proud of, or that demonstrates how the pieces of their life or career fit together. Erica Munzel, Director of Admissions, University of Michigan

I'll often read a résumé first, if one has been included, to get an overall sense of an applicant. William Hoye, Dean for Admissions, USC

ADMISSIONS DIRECTORS DISCUSS FILLING
OUT THE APPLICATION FORMS

People shouldn't feel compelled to fill out every blank in the application. We don't expect someone to be president of the student body, editor-in-chief of the school newspaper, have done multiple internships, have a 4.0 GPA, and work thirty-five hours a week during college. Kenneth Kleinrock, Assistant Dean for Admissions, NYU

I'm often surprised that so many applicants simply fail to follow directions. They'll not answer a question and say, "see attachment," despite being told not to do this. Kenneth Kleinrock, Assistant Dean for Admissions, NYU

Be sure to read the instructions on our forms carefully. There are only a few questions, but we want them filled in carefully. Don't just say, "see résumé." William Hoye, Dean for Admissions, USC

You get one opportunity to present yourself. If you don't do it in a thoughtful, careful manner—and the file is laden with cross-outs, typos, misspellings, etc.—what does that say about you? Kenneth Kleinrock, Assistant Dean for Admissions, NYU

Any unexplained gaps in an applicant's history raise red flags. You need to show what you were doing at each point. It's O.K. if you spent the year traveling the world, but it needs to be stated. Kenneth Kleinrock, Assistant Dean for Admissions, NYU

ADMISSIONS DIRECTORS DISCUSS WHAT OTHER MATERIALS YOU SHOULD SUBMIT

Don't send in the life preserver with "save me" on it.   Janice Austin, Assistant Dean for Admissions, University of Pennsylvania

If you are submitting a lengthy piece of writing, write a paragraph introducing it and directing us to a couple of pages that are a good sample of your work, since we may not have time to read the whole thing.   Erica Munzel, Director of Admissions, University of Michigan

We don't have time to read lengthy materials. If you send a one-page CV or résumé, and two or three letters of recommendation, that's fine. If someone sends in an article just because their name is on the masthead, or a CD of their band . . . I just don't have time.   Edward Tom, Director of Admissions, Boalt Hall (Berkeley)

By all means, submit a résumé—it's a useful shorthand way of presenting your career. Don't submit other, fluffy items, though; we don't have the time to spend hours on one file. Forget about submitting a thesis, given how unreal many are and how long they take to get through.   Robert Stanek, Director for Admissions, George Washington

We get people sending in videotapes, dissertations, pictures, etc.; we don't have room for these—they're not read or examined.   Michael Rappoport, Dean of Admissions, UCLA

It's a good idea to include a résumé, whether one-page or two. Applicants are free to provide other items, but they should recognize we have a lot to read. Therefore, it's an advocacy challenge to determine how much information, and of what type, to include. At a minimum it should be clear, concise, and compelling. It's impressive when someone achieves the right balance.   William Hoye, Dean for Admissions, USC

Applicants should understand that the admissions committee will evaluate them on the basis of all that they choose to submit. I think that applicants who submit an eighty-page thesis are making a mistake of judgment. I would not necessarily object to reading a thesis abstract if a person felt that it was vital to understanding what they've done. A one-page summary would be fine. Sometimes less is more.   Kenneth Kleinrock, Assistant Dean for Admissions, NYU

Submitting a résumé makes sense, but submitting a thesis probably does not. A thesis synopsis, along with a letter of recommendation evaluating it, would be a better choice.   Elizabeth Rosselot, Director of Admissions, Boston College

11

RECOMMENDATIONS

— EXECUTIVE SUMMARY —

Choosing the right recommenders—whether they be professors, employers, or other types—is critically important.

■

Approaching potential recommenders must be done carefully.

—Give them a chance to say no.

—Explain why you want a law degree, and why you have

chosen the schools you have.

—Explain how important their recommendations will be.

—Brief them fully regarding what they should write.

—Emphasize telling relevant, rich stories.

■

Make their job as easy as possible.

■

Consider whether you will benefit from supplemental recommendations.

For those of you who view the recommendations as little more than a bothersome formality—akin to the Deans' letter—this chapter should quickly convince you otherwise. Applicants complain that recommendations are a waste of time because "all applicants can find someone to say something good about them." These applicants are right to believe that most people can find a supporter, but they are wrong about the importance of the recommendations.

WHY ARE RECOMMENDATIONS REQUIRED?

To understand how crucial a recommendation can be, let us compare two applicants, John and Laura. They both went to well-known schools of Ivy League caliber and have high LSAT scores. Both are 25 and have been working for three years. Both presented solid essays; both are in the running for admission. As is often the case in law school admissions, officers might be faced with two such students but only one slot. In such a situation, when all else is equal, a recommendation can be the distinguishing factor in an acceptance. Compare and contrast these two letters of recommendation:

Recommendation for John:

I had the pleasure of teaching John two different classes: his freshman writing seminar (required of all students at the college) and a course on Southern African-American authors that he took during his junior year. I occasionally had coffee with John during his years as an undergraduate here and have kept in touch with him since he has left. I thus feel well qualified to address his candidacy to your law school.

One look at John's grades (and his LSAT score) and you will see why he graduated in the top 10% of his class. He is bright, thoughtful, and articulate; he often stimulated discussion in the classroom; he has a wonderful command of language. He never received below a B+ on a paper in my class (I am considered the toughest grader in the English department). I feel confident in John's

Recommendation for Laura:

Laura undoubtedly belongs in your next class of promising future lawyers.

A student like Laura comes around only once or twice in a professor's entire career. I have been teaching at the college level for 21 years and have seen such a student only once before I met Laura. (That former student, by the way, is now on the Philosophy faculty at UC Berkeley, a star in his field, and also sits on several boards of directors of major corporations. If my view of Laura is anywhere near correct, you can assume that she is also headed toward great successes in life.) I taught two classes to Laura before becoming her senior thesis advisor, for which I spent the better part of an academic year working closely with her. We keep in close touch today, even seeing each other occasionally. I feel well qualified to write this recommendation on her behalf.

Recommendation for John:

ability to succeed academically at a law school such as yours. Knowing how active and curious he is, I'm sure he will contribute to your various journals and even make law review.

John is also quite a soccer player. Although I don't follow soccer very closely (fencing is my thing), I went to a few games when John was on the team here, and was always impressed with his athletic prowess and his team cooperation skills. I know that he was highly regarded by his teammates and coaches while here; in fact, he even won the "Spirit Award" during his senior year.

Truly, I can't say enough good things about John. He would be a wonderful addition to your school.

Recommendation for Laura:

Laura excelled well beyond other students in both classes I taught her. In the first, "The History of the Industrial Revolution in America," she wrote with such extraordinary insight on a number of topics in the mid-term exam that I approached her about the possibility of her doing research for me on an upcoming book. (This kind of thing is all too rare. Never before had I sought out a particular student to perform research for me before.) Accordingly, Laura did a superb job collecting and analyzing materials for me on western railroad development and its affect on Native peoples. She unearthed several unstudied documents showing that seven members of a particular tribe in Wyoming were actually *promoters* of the railroad companies and their plans for expansion. Always curious and up for a challenge, Laura chose Indian collaboration with white settlers on rail development as the topic of her thesis. I applauded her choice; it was novel and would require much original research, not something that every college senior is ready or able to tackle.

As soon as she began her preliminary studies, Laura ran up against two enormous obstacles, which I believed even she would not be able to surmount. First, the Library of Congress had not declassified certain documents that Laura needed to access in order to complete her study successfully. Second, a well-known Native American professor in our department heard of Laura's research and tried to persuade her against pursuing it, believing that her findings might jeopardize the strong perception that the particular tribe under study was particularly recalcitrant, often able to halt or even reverse the white man's progress. This particular professor,

Recommendation for Laura:

as part of the History Department's thesis committee, would be one of the faculty members responsible for reviewing and approving Laura's thesis at the end of her senior year. Although I obviously disagreed with my colleague's position—I was in fact outraged that a faculty member would try to stop honest and valuable research from taking place because of his own contemporary agenda—I also believed that, realistically speaking, going against his wishes was ill-advised. Looking at these two ominous obstacles, I actually suggested to Laura that we find another topic. But she decided, against all odds, to persist with her original topic.

Laura managed to overcome both problems thrown in her way, although neither was easy to do. First, she petitioned the Library of Congress to declassify the specific documents she needed. She wrote a persuasive letter explaining the historical value of her research and the new light it could shed upon many different aspects of America's past. The maturity she demonstrated in writing her plea and then campaigning about the campus to get prominent research faculty (as well as students and administration members) to sign the petition on her behalf was remarkable. I have never seen someone go after a goal with such ardor. She eventually accumulated over 1,000 signatures before she set off for Washington, D.C. to present the petition in person and argue her case, if necessary. The student newspaper wrote a feature article, and several updates, on Laura and her cause. The entire campus was impressed by her efforts. The Library consented and she was allowed access to the documents she wanted to study.

Recommendation for Laura:

In the second case, Laura played her cards well and, again, showed great maturity in dealing with my colleague. She wrote him a letter laying out the reasons she believed her topic to be worthy of study. She also explained that she was personally a defender of Native rights and culture, in no way wanting or intending to do harm to the tribe's legacy. By highlighting her own contributions to Native study, she showed my colleague that she indeed had no evil agenda to pursue. She convinced him that the research was merely in pursuit of the truth, and convinced him that it was unlikely it would harm the reputation of contemporary Natives. My colleague, though of course still wary, appreciated Laura's attention to his concerns. Although a tough questioner in all thesis presentations, he judged her fairly. In the end, he was very impressed and pleased with her work. He even showed up at the graduation party her parents gave for her, indicating that the two had indeed become friends after the disagreement. Laura's interpersonal skills are clearly well developed. She holds her own, yet is appreciative of others' opinions and stakes, always giving attention where it is due. She is certainly stubborn, but she is also sensitive.

Laura's thesis was the best I have ever supervised. Although she entered a completely new area of study, meaning that there will long be unanswered questions and more room for research, she covered a lot of territory. She made convincing conjectures about the motives of the seven natives who supported the expansion of the western line, the exact nature of their collaboration with the white

Recommendation for Laura:

man, how their collaboration with the enemy affected their relations with fellow tribe members, and how it affected the future of the tribe. Her thesis required both an enormous amount of original research and a keen ability to analyze sparsely recorded data to come up with an accurate picture of history. Her writing, too, is better than that of most of our junior faculty. Moreover, and particularly important to her future in a law career, her passions about Native rights and culture today did not cloud her judgment or her ability to look accurately at the historical record. She was an impartial historian, willing to face up to evidence that she would have preferred to have been different.

Laura is not just an intellectual powerhouse (though that she is). She is also simply one of the finest young people I have ever had the pleasure of knowing. Her fire and enthusiasm in academics is matched by a similar zest for life in her other endeavors. She is thoughtful and warm, ready to share her emotions or lend an ear when it is needed. She became a very close friend of my family's during her senior year, and my kids (who still see Laura now and then) miss her baked treats and her skill as the best kick-the-can player they've ever known. She became so endeared to my wife and me that we used to leave our children with Laura when we went away. I miss being able to go on vacation knowing that my children are with someone responsible, mature, fun, and smart.

Please do not hesitate to contact me if you need any more information about this wonderful candidate.

Which one—John or Laura—would you select? Laura wins out easily, appearing to be the stronger candidate if we compare the two letters of recommendation. She may not even, in fact, be the stronger candidate, but this finely executed recommendation tips the balance well in her favor. Although John got his recommender to say good things about him, Laura got a lot more mileage out of her recommendation. She chose the right person—someone who could share classroom as well as personal experiences about her, and offer compelling as well as interesting anecdotes. Furthermore, Laura influenced the professor to include the right information to support her own positioning effort. The letter offers insight that goes well beyond regurgitating already known facts and assumptions.

The rest of this chapter is devoted to analyzing how to get your best supporters to do the same for you.

WHAT ADMISSIONS DIRECTORS SAY ABOUT
THE IMPORTANCE OF RECOMMENDATIONS

Most letters will be positive, but not many will be substantive. On the other hand, a very large percentage of successful applicants will have had substantive letters of recommendation.   Joyce Curll, Assistant Dean for Admissions and Financial Aid, Harvard

Recommendation letters can be *very* helpful at the margin. Be careful who you ask: A negative recommendation is a real problem.   Michael Rappoport, Dean of Admissions, UCLA

WHAT ADMISSIONS COMMITTEES LEARN
FROM RECOMMENDATIONS

Your Claims Are True

Recommendations are examined first for the extent to which they confirm and support your claims and your positioning. If your essay states that you are an indefatigable scholar, tirelessly researching both sides of an issue, the admissions officers reading your file will look closely to see if your Philosophy professor backs this up.

You Have Many Qualifications

Recommenders are asked to rate you in many areas, from written expression to initiative, from analytical thinking to maturity. Recommendations are an opportunity to provide more information about you, preferably illustrative rather than merely factual. Ideally, they function as a mirror image of the personal statement—a different (but equally positive) view of the same person.

There Is More to Learn About You Than What Is Covered in the Essays

Because you are limited in what you can include in your personal statement, it is difficult to present everything that might make you a desirable candidate. Therefore, it is important that your recommendations fill in the gap. By collaborating with your recommenders, you can use their letters to elaborate on areas of your candidacy that you were not able to cover in your portion of the application.

Your Accomplishments Have Impressed Others

A recommender's positive comments show the admissions office that you have made an impression on others and ensure that your own self-descriptions are valid.

You Can Get What You Want—Subtly

You must decide who should write on your behalf, determine what you want said about you, and get your recommenders to say what it is that you want said. Furthermore, you must make sure the letters are sent in on time. Typically, these are people over whom you have no authority, so you will have to use influence rather than command. The recommendation process, therefore, is a test of your ability to persuade.

There Are Special Circumstances That Influence Your Academic or Extracurricular Performance

Recommendations are a good place for shedding light on certain anomalies or special circumstances that might negatively influence your record. A professor can note that you are the only person in his tenure at the college successfully to handle taking a difficult language from scratch while also playing varsity sports and majoring in mechanical engineering. Thus your modest GPA should be viewed in this abnormal context.

You Can Accurately Evaluate Others and Their Perceptions of You

If you end up choosing someone who writes a mediocre recommendation, you will be doubted on many counts—including your judgment. It may even be assumed that you simply could not find two people who would say something good about you. This assumption is likely to kill your chances of admission.

> *One of the telltale signs that an applicant is not strong enough, or has too little experience, is that the recommenders and the applicant himself all tell the same stories. This suggests that the applicant has had only limited success.*

WHO SHOULD WRITE YOUR RECOMMENDATIONS?

Selecting appropriate recommenders involves sifting many factors. In general, you will be expected to submit recommendations from people who know you and are well placed to address the key issues concerning your candidacy. You will want them to state that you have the appropriate intellectual ability, self-discipline, and character to succeed at School X. The obvious choice—which any school's admission information will quickly tell you—is a professor who knows you well. (There are exceptions to this rule, which will be discussed in the next section.)

If there is not a wealth of obvious candidates, then your choice is relatively easy. However, it is to your advantage to be able to pick and choose. For those of you who are reading this ahead of the game, and have not yet forged relationships with two or three talented professors, start now. After selecting a professor as an ideal supporter for you, make sure to be in several of his or her classes over a period of time. Sign up for office hours. Make yourself known as an intelligent—but not obnoxious—presence in class.

> ### AN ADMISSIONS DIRECTOR DISCUSSES CULTIVATING RECOMMENDERS
>
> If it's not too late, you should identify a professor who's inspired you and take more courses from her in order to build the basis for the strongest possible recommendation.   Erica Munzel, Director of Admissions, University of Michigan

Having done this, it should be simple to follow these rules:

1. ***Choose people who know you well.*** Do not choose the Nobel Prize-winning Chair of the English Department if all he is going to say is that you sat in the front row and seemed to be paying attention. Instead, choose people who can make the recommendation credible and powerful by illustrating the points they make with anecdotes that show you at your best. Need we say it? The people who will be able to do this are those who know you well.

2. ***Choose people who genuinely like you.*** Why? People who like you will take the time to write you a good recommendation. This is impressive in its own right. A recommendation that looks as though it took only five minutes to write suggests that that is exactly how much time the recommender felt you deserved. In contrast, a recommendation that looks carefully done and well thought out suggests that the recommender is committed to helping you. One other reason for choosing someone who likes you: She or he will try to put a positive spin on things, choosing examples that show you in a good light and describing them as positively as possible. Someone who does not much care may well write the first thing that comes to mind.

3. ***Choose people who can write well.*** Do not assume that all professors are created equal, particularly when it comes to articulating themselves. Pay attention, for example, to the written comments your professors leave on your papers. How eloquent—and pertinent—are their critiques? The last thing you want is a recommender who, being unable to perfectly express himself, is consequently unable to convey you.

4. ***Choose people from a range of fields and backgrounds.*** If you are sending schools more than one recommendation letter, be sure to choose people who will be able to provide different—complementary—profiles of you. Selecting two English professors who specialized in Chaucerian literature, for example, will very likely make for two dangerously similar letters. Law schools will wonder about the depth and breadth of your skills and interests, and if you are capable of interacting with more than one type of person.

   If you have been out of school for some time, consider submitting a combination of professorial and employer recommendations.

5. ***Choose people of different genders.*** This is particularly true if you look like someone who may not do well under the supervision of people of a certain gender (if you are a male army Lieutenant, for example, consider having the female Captain write a letter of recommendation). This rule is not hard and fast, however; only select on the basis of gender if it is otherwise a close call.

Brains. The ideal person can address the following:

- Academic achievement
- Analytical ability
- Quantitative skills
- Originality
- Healthy skepticism
- Imagination and creativity
- Communication skills (written and oral)

- Capacity for independent work
- Research skills
- Effectiveness in class discussions, debates, meetings, and so on
- Problem-solving skills
- Thoroughness
- Ability to synthesize material

6. ***Choose people who can address one or more of the key subjects: your brains, your character, your professional success, or your leadership skills.***

Obviously, not just any professor or employer will do. Choose someone who has seen your abilities in more than one format. A thesis advisor, for example, fits the bill perfectly—someone who knows your writing intimately, and has heard you defend it verbally; someone who has watched you pull together a brilliant project; someone who knows your ability to digest a large amount of material. If it has been a long time since you have been in school, or your thesis advisor disliked you or passed away, you may have to find a substitute. Anyone who has seen you work on difficult intellectual challenges is a possible recommender. This might

Character. The ideal person can address the following:

- Dependability
- Motivation and sense of initiative
- Honesty and integrity
- Sense of humor
- Self-discipline
- Energy
- Perseverance and work ethic
- Independence
- Potential for growth

- Open-mindedness
- Responsibility
- Leadership
- Maturity
- Judgment
- Concern for others
- Social commitment
- Concern for justice
- Interpersonal relations

be someone who taught several courses you have recently taken to improve your knowledge in a field related to your career, someone who has taught seminars to your department, or even a manager under whom you have done intellectually challenging work.

One or both of the people you have chosen to recommend you on issues of professional success and brains should be able to address the character issue, too. In other words, you do not need a spiritual or moral leader to address issues of character. The person you select, however, must have seen you in a large number of different circumstances to be able to address these broad issues; his or her knowledge of you may have to be deeper than that required to address your intellectual abilities, for example.

Professional success. The ideal person can address the following:

- Overall work habits
- Self-confidence and poise
- Creativity
- Thoughtfulness
- Ability to acknowledge valuable inputs
- Ability to work with others
- Ability to motivate others
- Ability to make wise decisions
- Ability to retain self-control under stressful conditions

- Communication skills
- Negotiation skills
- Conflict-resolution skills
- Organizational and planning abilities
- Ability to manage a budget
- Leadership qualities
- Ability to analyze difficult problems
- Overall potential for a career in law

The person most likely to be able to assess your professional success—and therefore potential—is your current employer, preferably one who has seen you in operation over a period of time. You may not be able to use your current employer, however. If not, your next best choice might be a prior employer, someone to whom your boss reports (and who has seen your work on a number of occasions), a client, or even a competitor or rival (such as one of your peers). If you do not choose your current boss, or someone else who is an obvious choice, it will be helpful for you to explain why you have chosen not to have the obvious choice write on your behalf.

Leadership skills. These may be evident from your professional success, as highlighted above, or in a school or extracurricular setting.

- ➤ Achievement in elected or appointed positions
- ➤ Ability to motivate others
- ➤ Decision-making ability
- ➤ Team-building ability
- ➤ Responsibility to subordinates
- ➤ Priority-setting ability
- ➤ Goal-setting ability
- ➤ Ability to adapt to and lead change
- ➤ Ability to develop subordinates (and others)

- ➤ Embodiment (and encouragement) of values
- ➤ Ability to develop a sense of value and purpose in work
- ➤ Commitment to a vision
- ➤ Integrity
- ➤ Internal drive
- ➤ Maturity

The leadership attributes might be evident in your professional success, as highlighted above, or in another setting. Thus, you might choose to have an employer, head of a charitable organization for which you volunteer, or faculty advisor to a club you ran at college emphasize your leadership qualities.

IS IT ACCEPTABLE TO USE EMPLOYERS AS RECOMMENDERS?

Yes. Although admissions directors often state that they prefer to receive letters of recommendation written by professors, law schools are shifting towards a professionally-oriented model. More than half of the top schools state very explicitly in their admissions information that they accept, and find value in, recommendations from employers. Columbia, for instance, requires that those working full-time submit a letter from their employer (or commanding officer). Given that law is much more of a *business* than ever before—in conjunction with the fact that the age of the average law student is rising—an applicant's professional success is highly relevant. Firms desire mature people with real-world experience and savvy; consequently, law schools are seeking older applicants who possess these qualities and experiences. What all of this amounts to is an increase in the value of employer recommendations. More and more applicants are using employers to illustrate the intellectual abilities that would otherwise have been described by a professor.

MAKING THE MOST OF AN
EMPLOYER RECOMMENDATION

Employer recommendations are particularly valuable when they address what law schools value most: analytical skills, as well as written and oral communication skills.

Depending on the results you have achieved in your line of work, a recommendation written by an employer may very well be superb—and, in some cases, necessary. There are two reasons for this. First, your most recent accomplishments can lessen the sting from undergraduate mistakes. Second, you **want** to highlight a job that provided excellent preparation for a legal career. If you feel your employer has a keen understanding of your intellectual abilities and capacity for law school work, then his or her recommendation may make all the difference in your application.

There are other notable reasons why a letter by an employer may be necessary. The older you are, the less likely a professor will remember you enough— if at all—to write a detailed, sensitive critique of your intellect, analytical skills, and potential as a lawyer. Additionally, the greater the breach between college and law school, the more likely it is that you will have matured into a very different person, with honed skills and altered goals. In fact, if you have worked for five or more years outside of college, and have no letter from an employer regarding that part of your life, it is likely to look suspicious.

OTHER CRITERIA IN CHOOSING A RECOMMENDER

1. *Choose someone able to support your positioning.* If you claim to be a hardcore philanthropist and public interest advocate, at least one of your recommenders should be able to discuss your serious commitment to the public good. Failure to choose an employer, colleague, or client who has seen this type of work over a reasonable period of time would raise a major red flag.

2. *Choose someone able to address any potential weak spot in your application.* If you are an engineer worried that the admissions committee will presume you to be humorless, as we discussed earlier in the book, this is your chance to prove what an engaging and funny fellow you really are.

3. *Beware the naysayers!* Certain personal characteristics suggest that a person will be effective in their support. Someone who is exuberant about life in general will be a good choice as she is likely to describe an average

---

THE DEAN'S LETTER

A throwback to the time when college deans were expected to know a good deal about the students assigned to them, the "dean's letter" is still required by some law schools. They do not expect to learn much from it, given that deans seldom know much of value about their students; instead, schools generally use it to make sure applicants have not misbehaved at college.

ADMISSIONS DIRECTORS COMMENT ON DEANS' LETTERS

Often a registrar fills this out. We want to make sure that there has been no trouble during college. It's also meant to be a check on what applicants say about their record. It's rarely a detailed letter based upon close knowledge of the applicant.   Faye Deal, Associate Dean for Admissions and Financial Aid, Stanford

We don't require a dean's letter unless there has been an academic or disciplinary problem. In such a case, we need to understand what happened. We also require a statement from the applicant about it in addition to the dean's letter. William Hoye, Dean for Admissions, USC

We want a dean's letter to make sure that there have been no disciplinary issues, or what they have been and how they have been resolved. Of course, recommendations from the dean (or a class ranking) are helpful when we get them. At large schools deans seldom know individual applicants. We understand that that's a reality at such schools. Applicants shouldn't be concerned if that is the case.   Albert R. Turnbull, Associate Dean for Admissions and Career Services, University of Virginia

We don't require a dean's letter.   Michael Rappoport, Dean of Admissions, UCLA

---

performer as marvelous, whereas a dour complainer might describe the performer as terrible. Similarly, an articulate person is likely to write a more impressive recommendation than a poorly spoken one.

4. ***Seek out the voice of experience.*** Be wary about choosing someone who is not obviously more senior, since it will look strange to have someone junior to you writing on your behalf.

5. ***Timeliness counts.*** Choose someone who is reliable and therefore likely to complete your recommendations on time.

6. ***Where did the recommenders go to school?*** People who themselves graduated from a top college and, preferably, a top graduate or professional school as well can speak convincingly about your relative abilities.

ADMISSIONS DIRECTORS GIVE ADVICE ON
WHOM YOU SHOULD CHOOSE AS A RECOMMENDER

GENERAL COMMENTS

Recommendations from employers are useful after a couple of years of work, not after six months.   Joyce Curll, Assistant Dean for Admissions and Financial Aid, Harvard

We require two letters. We prefer one to be from an academic; if someone is coming straight from college, then both can be from professors. If someone has been out of school five-plus years, it's O.K. to submit only (or primarily) work-related ones. Most applicants, by the way, submit three recommendations. Faye Deal, Associated Dean for Admissions and Financial Aid, Stanford

The best recommender is likely to be a professor or someone who has attended a strong law school. I do like to see serious letters from business people, of course, which is to say letters that are detailed in regard to the candidate's analytical and business prowess.   Elizabeth Rosselot, Director of Admissions, Boston College

Academic letters, for the most part, carry more weight than letters from attorneys.   Michael Rappoport, Dean of Admissions, UCLA

I like to get letters from BC law students. This is more powerful than having a student just drop by to praise someone, given that it takes more time and effort to write a letter—and these students have precious little time.   Elizabeth Rosselot, Director of Admissions, Boston College

We get a lot of letters from politicians. It's more helpful if a person you worked for directly on the politician's staff can comment. Similarly, in a large course a graduate assistant who knows your work well from a recitation section is sometimes a better choice than the course professor might be.   Kenneth Kleinrock, Assistant Dean for Admissions, NYU

MUST YOU USE A PROFESSOR?

You can get a recommendation from a professor or from a TA. We realize that at large schools it can be hard to get a professor to know you well enough to write an informative recommendation. The problem with a TA, though, is that his experience is inevitably limited. He can say that you were in the top five percent of his students this year, but not that you were among the top five percent of the last thirty years.   Erica Munzel, Director of Admissions, University of Michigan

We require a professorial recommendation. This reflects our emphasis on academics.   Albert R. Turnbull, Associate Dean for Admissions and Career Services, University of Virginia

In theory, professors are the ones who should know your intellectual abilities best, who can address such issues as analysis, fresh thought, and creativity. Kip Darcy, Director of Admissions, Hastings

We'd rather have a teaching assistant than a prominent professor write if the professor doesn't really know the applicant. Albert R. Turnbull, Associate Dean for Admissions and Career Services, University of Virginia

ADVICE FOR OLDER APPLICANTS

If someone has been out of college for only a few years it is usually still possible to get an academic recommendation, although it's not absolutely critical. For someone who has been out longer, I would expect a letter from a current employer—or former supervisor if you can't reveal that you're thinking of leaving. Kenneth Kleinrock, Assistant Dean for Admissions, NYU

If someone has been out of school for a long time, it is O.K. to tell us it's impossible to provide a meaningful academic recommendation, but we don't like it very much. Albert R. Turnbull, Associate Dean for Admissions and Career Services, University of Virginia

Letters from professors are preferred; the second best are from employers or colleagues. The balance shifts the older someone is. Edward Tom, Director of Admissions, Boalt Hall (Berkeley)

For older applicants—ten to twenty years out—we obviously expect letters from employers rather than academics. This is especially true if we're looking to admit them on the basis of their work experience. Michael Rappoport, Dean of Admissions, UCLA

It is not at all necessary that a thirty-year-old applicant submit a recommendation from an undergraduate professor. Don Rebstock, Associate Dean of Admissions and Financial Aid, Northwestern

For someone who has been out of college for a while, we're willing to look at professors' recommendations written five years ago. Some schools maintain such files. We will also accept a recommendation from someone who has been exposed to your critical thinking, analytical, and other key skills since college. Erica Munzel, Director of Admissions, University of Michigan

RECOMMENDERS TO BE AVOIDED

Getting a recommendation from a neighbor who happens to be a judge—"he's played with my kid for years and is wonderful"—isn't much use. Erica Munzel, Director of Admissions, University of Michigan

People assume that the bigger the name, the better the recommender. This is by no means true. We want to see the nitty-gritty details of what he/she knows about you. Faye Deal, Associate Dean for Admissions and Financial Aid, Stanford

It's a rare circumstance when a high school teacher's recommendation will help you. Your relatives have to like you, so their comments are also seldom of much value.   Kenneth Kleinrock, Assistant Dean for Admissions, NYU

We're pretty good at reading between the lines—when recommenders have felt compelled to write on someone's behalf without being able to really support them.   William Hoye, Dean for Admissions, USC

Regrettably, a common mistake made by applicants is to solicit recommendations from individuals, often in high place in the worlds of business, politics and academe, who are unable to comment meaningfully about the applicant because their relationship with the applicant has been limited in time and by little direct contact, much less real interaction with the candidate. Often, in fact, the "celebrity" recommender knows the applicant's family better than the applicant himself or herself.   Jim Milligan, Dean of Admissions, Columbia

Applicants need to choose recommenders carefully. For example, I see a lot of letters saying that the applicant should apply to a school a tier below Stanford, or that Stanford would be a real stretch for him. There are also quite a few saying that they don't recommend the applicant.   Faye Deal, Associate Dean for Admissions and Financial Aid, Stanford

HOW MANY RECOMMENDERS?

Most of the top law programs in the country require two letters of recommendation. (See chart on following page.) Michigan, NYU, and UCLA require one; George Washington, Hastings, and Texas do not require any. Numerous programs state both the required and the maximum number. Chicago, for example, requires two but will accept as many as four. Thus, almost every program encourages recommendations, extra or otherwise. If you are applying to Hastings, by all means submit one or two letters. It would be a missed opportunity if you did not do so—unless you really have no one to say something positive about you.

Of course, it can be dangerous to go overboard. If the extra recommendation you are considering reiterates points that have been made elsewhere, do not submit it. On the other hand, if your recommender can add a truly different and important perspective on your candidacy, consider submitting it, but only if it is done in the right way. Approach your extra recommender and explain the circumstances. Then ask that he include with his recommendation a letter that you have written stating clearly that the other recommendations are meant to be read first, and that this additional recommendation is to be considered only if the school would consider it appropriate. In other words, you offer this recommendation as helpful additional material to be consulted at the discretion of the admissions committee.

	RECOMMENDATION REQUIREMENTS		
	0	1	2
Boston College			X
Boston University			X
UC Berkeley (Boalt Hall)			X
UC Davis			X
UCLA		X	
Chicago			X
Columbia			X
Cornell			X
Duke			X
Georgetown			X
George Washington	X		
Harvard			X
Hastings	X		
Illinois			X
Michigan		X	
Minnesota			X
New York University		X	
Notre Dame			X
Northwestern			X
Pennsylvania			X
Southern California			X
Stanford			X
Texas	X		
Vanderbilt			X
Virginia			X
Wisconsin	X		
Yale			X

ADMISSIONS DIRECTORS CONSIDER HOW MANY RECOMMENDATIONS YOU SHOULD SUBMIT

We welcome more than our required two letters, especially if they have two from professors and one from an employer. The number of recommendations is a judgment matter for the applicant. There should not be too much repetition of views, nor abusing the time of the admissions committee, but important perspectives should be communicated fully.   Albert R. Turnbull, Associate Dean for Admissions and Career Services, University of Virginia

We require two, and will accept as many as four. We really want the first two to be academic. The exception would be someone who's been out of college for some years.   Anne Brandt, Director of Admissions, Vanderbilt

If someone is submitting three, two academic and one work-related is optimal. Kip Darcy, Director of Admissions, Hastings

A twenty-two-year-old applicant would be wise to keep to two recommendations. Someone who has been working for three or four years might want to give us three if, for example, he or she has two faculty recommendations on file and also submits one from an employer.   Elizabeth Rosselot, Director of Admissions, Boston College

We require one letter; people often give us two or three. But, there is a point at which you may be demonstrating poor judgment in submitting too many. Kenneth Kleinrock, Assistant Dean for Admissions, NYU

APPROACHING A POTENTIAL RECOMMENDER

Ideally, you should start the process about three months before the recommendation deadline. Begin your overture to a potential supporter by scheduling a 30- to 45-minute conference with her. (You will get a better response by having this meeting in person rather than by telephone.) Run it as a proper business meeting, with a typed agenda and outline of each matter you want to share. Explain briefly where you wish to go in your career and what it will take to get there. Explain how you plan to fully take advantage of a law degree. Then tell her what is required in the application process, being careful to explain how important the applications are, including the recommendations. Tell her that you have been considering having her write on your behalf.

Now comes one of the critical parts of the recommendation process. Make sure each recommender is going to write a very favorable recommendation for you. The way to be sure of this is by giving the person a chance to beg off if she is unable to write on your behalf. If she is uncomfortable about writing for you, because she knows that honesty would require her to be less than highly favorable, she will take this opportunity to suggest that someone else might be more appropriate. If she gives this kind of answer, do not press her. Thank her for her time and move on.

If, on the other hand, she is encouraging, give her a further briefing. Tell her how much work will be involved, noting that you will make the process as painless as possible for her, thereby limiting her involvement to something under three hours. (If time is a major issue for her, suggest that you write a first draft that she can then quickly "adapt." See the discussion below in this regard.) Tell her which schools you are considering, and the reasons for each. Explain how you are trying to position yourself in general, and note any differences as to positioning for particular schools if necessary. Show her what questions she will need to answer about you, and how these relate to your desired positioning. Suggest stories she can tell about you, and how these will fit in with the questions. Provide her with plenty of detail.

MAKING YOUR RECOMMENDER'S JOB EASY

Try to do as much of the work as you can, since your recommender is undoubtedly busy. Give her plenty of time to write the recommendation. Be sure to give her:

- ➤ The deadline for each application.
- ➤ Stamped, addressed envelopes.
- ➤ Several copies of each form, with the objective data (your name, address, etc.) already filled in.
- ➤ Copies of your own essays, and a description of your positioning strategy.
- ➤ If she is writing recommendations for all of your target schools, tell her which main points to discuss to satisfy the requirements for each school in one general letter (although she will still need to fill in the grid ratings for each school). Note that this requires you to know precisely to which schools you are applying.
- ➤ Samples of the work you did for her.
- ➤ A list of your recent (and past!) activities, including why you undertook them, in light of your interest in and suitability for law school.
- ➤ An outline of what you wish to discuss.
- ➤ "Canned" descriptions of the stories you want to tell.
- ➤ Your résumé (CV).
- ➤ Your transcript(s).

Be sure the recommender understands what is important and how to write convincingly—i.e., using appropriate stories.

Suggest that the recommender write a general letter addressing each question asked by the schools to which you are applying. Your outline material should provide her with the basis for writing this letter; leave this material with her. You will have thus saved her a great deal of work. The letter can be made user-friendly by placing the topic addressed in each paragraph in bold print, so that readers can quickly pick out the points that are of greatest interest to them. Hint that it would be beneficial for your recommender to explicitly compare you with others who have gone to this or another comparable school. Have her quantify her claims whenever possible. For example, instead of "intelligent," have her write "one of the three most intelligent people I've ever taught."

If your recommender is extremely busy, yet another possibility exists for you. She may suggest that you do a first draft of the recommendation, which she will presumably alter to her taste later on—or she may ask that you write it, and she will simply sign it. This technique, however, can be risky. To assume the perspective and tone of someone in your recommender's position—whether that be academic or professional—requires experience and perspicacity. Chances are, you will end up sounding timid, stilted, and totally one-dimensional.

Generally, writing your own recommendations is safe only if you have a thorough understanding of what your recommender's expectations were, and why you fulfilled them. You are more likely to possess this knowledge if you have been out in the "real world" for a year or two. It is easier to step into the shoes of an employer than a professor; the former's expectations, standards, and judgments are more self-apparent. Penetrating the world of academia is a difficult task, particularly while you are still in it.

Whether your recommender writes your recommendation or has you do it, this well-thought-out approach to the matter will prove helpful in a number of ways. First, this approach minimizes the chance that you will end up with a lukewarm recommender. Second, your approach will have been highly organized and professional. If you had followed the nervous, pleading approach, why should she tell Harvard that you are an effective communicator, destined for litigating greatness? Third, you know in advance what stories she will tell. This means you will retain control of the admissions process insofar as you have a number of stories you want told about yourself, without undue repetition. Fourth, following this process means you will have a well-written recommendation. If your recommender writes it, she will almost certainly use your outline, just as she will treat the matter seriously because you have done so. If you write the recommendation, you can certainly manage to put together a good statement. Fifth, your professional approach means your recommender is likely to improve her opinion of you, meaning she will be a better resource for your future career than she otherwise would have been.

TIPS ON HANDLING DIFFICULT ISSUES

➤ If you find yourself in the position of writing all your own recommendations, formatting them differently and making them sound as if each recommender was the actual author will help camouflage their authorship. For example, you can format one as a letter and another in the question-and-answer format. Similarly, you can use different typefaces and font sizes.

➤ If you went to a second-rate or unknown university, or had mediocre grades even at a top school, you should have recommenders take every opportunity to discuss your analytical skills and intellectual leanings.

➤ If you are unable to get a recommendation from someone the admissions committee would expect to write on your behalf, be sure to explain why either in the optional essay question or in a separate note.

➤ Schools are required to allow applicants to see the recommendations written on their behalf unless the applicants waive that right. You should waive that right: Schools will interpret this as a move on your part to encourage honest expression. In fact, you should work together with your recommender on the recommendation, so you will be privy to it as it is being created, meaning that you have little to gain in any event by having the right to get the school to furnish a copy.

ADMISSIONS DIRECTORS DISCUSS HOW YOU SHOULD HANDLE YOUR RECOMMENDERS

There are three things you should give a recommender: time, a copy of your transcript, and a résumé. In addition, let them know what you are trying to do and how you are going to do it.   Joyce Curll, Assistant Dean for Admissions and Financial Aid, Harvard

Give the recommender a lot of lead time; otherwise they can't do a thoughtful job and resort to boiler plate. Just because it's your deadline doesn't mean it's their deadline.   Kenneth Kleinrock, Assistant Dean for Admissions, NYU

We place more faith in recommendations when applicants have waived their rights to see them (and nearly all do waive their rights).   William Hoye, Dean for Admissions, USC

You have the duty to help a recommender remember why you are so impressive. Give your recommender whatever help you can, including information regarding the context in which you performed. You might photocopy the top page of a paper (containing the professor's comments) and provide a copy of your résumé and your transcript.   Kenneth Kleinrock, Assistant Dean for Admissions, NYU

INCREASING THE VALUE OF YOUR RECOMMENDATIONS

A good recommendation should show you are an outstanding individual, one who is an appropriate candidate for a top law school by virtue of having the appropriate intellectual potential. It should also support your individual positioning strategy.

The following are true of an effective recommendation:

- It is well written. It is grammatically correct and reflects the thinking of a well-educated person.

- It reflects substantial thought and effort. In other words, the person cares enough about you to spend the time to be as helpful as possible.

- It shows you to be a distinctive candidate. The use of examples will aid this considerably.

- The writer knows you well enough to provide several highly specific examples to illustrate her points. These should not be the same examples you use in your essays or that other recommenders note. As with your essays, the use of illustrative stories and examples will make the recommendation credible and memorable. This will also show that the recommender knows you well, thereby showing that you did not have to "shop" for one.

- The recommender does not mention things best handled elsewhere in your application, such as your LSAT score.

- The writer discusses your growth and development over time. Your drive to improve yourself, in particular, is worth comment because your interest in learning and improving is part of what will make you a desirable student.

- The recommender explicitly compares you with others who have gone to this or another comparable school. Have her quantify her claims whenever possible. For example, instead of "intelligent," have her write "one of the three most intelligent people ever to work for me" (or, even better, "one of the three most intelligent of over one hundred grads of Ivy League schools to work for me").

- The person shows how you meet the requirements, as she sees them, of a top lawyer.

The general impression should be that a person of a very high caliber wrote a well-thought-out, enthusiastic recommendation for you.

ONE-SIZE-FITS-ALL RECOMMENDATIONS

In an ideal world, all recommenders would take the time and energy to fill out each recommendation form for applicants' many target schools. Of course, in an ideal world, each day would contain 36 hours and each week eight days. Thus, reality dictates that many recommenders simply write one comprehensive letter to be sent to all of an applicant's target schools.

For the sake of efficiency, it is generally fine for a recommender to write a single letter of recommendation and attach it to the recommendation form for each school, *as long as it answers all of the questions that a school poses.* In other words, recommenders should not feel they have to reinvent the wheel for each of your target schools, but they must be thorough and complete in performing their task. It is important that all recommenders realize the importance of explicitly answering all questions asked by each school. They must also fill out any required grids or checklists (concerning your qualities and abilities) that a school provides as part of its recommendation form if they choose to attach a one-size-fits-all recommendation letter.

In addition, there may be special cases in which a particular school should receive a slightly modified or amplified version of a recommendation letter. For example, if your positioning efforts are different for one of your target schools, you will want to ask your recommenders to keep this in mind (if it is appropriate, given their knowledge about you) for that school. Or if your recommender herself attended one of your target schools, she will want to make note of that in the recommendation.

**AN ADMISSIONS DIRECTOR DISCUSSES
ONE-SIZE-FITS-ALL RECOMMENDATIONS**

It is absolutely acceptable for a recommender simply to check the grid and attach a general letter. Andy Cornblatt, Assistant Dean for Admissions, Georgetown

---

HOW LONG SHOULD THE RECOMMENDATION LETTER BE?

The recommendation forms may provide limited space for a given response, but your recommender may want to write more. Should you or your recommender treat such space limitations as the ultimate authority? No. Recommenders are

ADMISSIONS DIRECTORS DESCRIBE WHAT
A GOOD RECOMMENDATION DOES

Frankly, I like a detailed recommendation. A flat recommendation, such as the following, is of no value. "John Smith received the highest grade in my class. He appears to be very bright. I know of no problems in his record. I think that he would make a very good lawyer." In this case, it's like not having a recommendation. This student clearly asked the wrong person for a recommendation. Faye Deal, Associate Dean for Admissions and Financial Aid, Stanford

People mistakenly think recommendations are about adjectives: he's great, smart, etc. The information contained often matters more than the description. With mixed indicators, show why the positive one is the better indicator. For example, if someone has a strong LSAT and mediocre grades, show why grades were lower because of the applicant's excellent extracurricular efforts—and therefore that the LSAT is the better indicator. Andy Cornblatt, Assistant Dean for Admissions, Georgetown

Relatively few recommendations are good, detailed letters that cause me to see candidates differently. Elizabeth Rosselot, Director of Admissions, Boston College

Recommendation letters tend to be very similar: Ninety-seven percent say the person did good work, etc. What do the really terrific ones that grab your attention do?

—They are read by academics, so letters from academics tend to be the most influential.

—It's excellent for a professor to discuss a person's academic ability, especially if it's not completely reflected in their grade-point average.

—It carries a lot of weight when a professor says "this is one of the top two or three students I've had in twenty years of teaching." Or, "this is the brightest person I've ever met."

—Letters that confirm what a person did can be very helpful, too. For example, to confirm that someone worked thirty hours per week, cared for his invalid mother, and so on.

—Talking about a particular academic program at a school can help; for example, noting that the applied mathematics department is more rigorous than others at the school in terms of grading. Or, discussing what departmental honors mean in that program. Or, explaining that she needed to be one of the top ten in the school to get into his class on X. Or, he got an A in an ultra-competitive setting that included strong graduate students. Michael Rappoport, Dean of Admissions, UCLA

Most recommendations aren't very helpful because they are so general. They should be backed up with examples and specifics, yet only ten to fifteen percent are. Don Rebstock, Associate Dean of Admissions and Financial Aid, Northwestern

A good letter may include weaknesses, and especially how they were overcome. Faye Deal, Associate Dean for Admissions and Financial Aid, Stanford

Through recommendations we hope to learn how well the applicant learns and works collaboratively. This proven ability to learn from and teach one's peers, to appreciate as well as challenge others' points of view, to know how and when to lead a discussion, or to allow (indeed, encourage) others to lead are traits our Committee values highly in a candidate because they are indispensable to enriching learning while in law school, and to working effectively thereafter. Jim Milligan, Dean of Admissions, Columbia

Recommenders can help a candidate by showing that he is a special person, someone who affects people positively. A professor can show that even though an applicant's numbers (LSAT, GPA) are weak, he has the potential to be a great lawyer. The professor will need to give the reasons he believes that, of course. It helps to show how the person thought, how he/she is respectful of others' ideas, drew other people out, added to the educational experience of classmates (and the professor), was thoughtful in handling ideas and people, etc. Rating the applicant as one of the top five he's ever taught in terms of intellect, creativity, leadership, and articulateness would also help. Erica Munzel, Director of Admissions, University of Michigan

The letter of recommendation that is most helpful to our Committee and to an applicant's candidacy is one where the author can speak meaningfully about the applicant, because the author has been in a position, over a significant period of time, to personally observe the applicant's intellect, character, and personality in action, and perhaps in different settings (e.g., work, play, athletics, individual or group tasks), and perhaps in the same setting but under various conditions (e.g., stress, pressure of deadlines, dealing with difficult peers or clients, or with situations requiring subtlety, tact, diplomacy, discretion). Jim Milligan, Dean of Admissions, Columbia

I wish more people would compare candidates with others who have attended the law school. If the comparison is to a recent enough student, it's really helpful because we'll remember that student. This also says something about the recommender, that he/she knows his/her students well. It's also helpful if a professor ranks a student versus all students taught—for example, "this is one of the top ten students I've taught in twenty-three years." Faye Deal, Associate Dean for Admissions and Financial Aid, Stanford

It's great if recommenders can compare an applicant with others attending top schools. Elizabeth Rosselot, Director of Admissions, Boston College

We like detail, context, and, for those with a relationship to Virginia, comparisons with applicants over the years—with others that have come before them. Generalized but bland endorsements aren't helpful. Albert R. Turnbull, Associate Dean for Admissions and Career Services, University of Virginia given some latitude in choosing how best to write a recommendation. This is one reason why it is perfectly appropriate to use the one-size-fits-all recommendation, which does not even try to fit into the provided format.

Typically, single-spaced letters of recommendation are at least one page in length, more often two or three—sometimes even longer.

MAKING SURE RECOMMENDATIONS ARE SUBMITTED ON TIME

The schools can keep you informed as to whether a given recommendation has arrived. If it has not arrived and time is getting short, contact your recommender and ask very politely how her effort is progressing and whether you can be helpful by giving her more information. This will tend to prod her into action without being annoying.

THE FOLLOW-UP

Be sure to send your recommender a thank-you note for her efforts and state that you will keep her informed as to your progress. This is simply good manners. If you need extra encouragement to do so, remember that you may need her services again if schools turn you down this time.

If you manage your recommender well, the chances are that she will submit your recommendations not long after. What should you do, however, if you call your schools and learn that a recommendation is missing? You can certainly call your recommender to encourage her to submit it soon. On the other hand, you can take a subtler approach and send her a follow-up note explaining that you have completed the application process and are currently awaiting schools' decisions. If she has not yet submitted the recommendation, this should spur her into action. If this does not work, contact her again and see if you can help the process along in some way, such as by writing a draft of what she might say.

Keep her informed as to each school's decision. Also be sure to tell her at the end of the process what you have decided to do, such as attend school X and turn down school Y, and why. At this point it would be highly appropriate to send her a small thank-you gift. Very few people do this. It is not a terribly expensive gesture, but you can be sure that you will gain greatly in her estimation for having done it.

Do your best to stay in touch with her as you go through law school, even if this means nothing more than dropping a short postcard or e-mail to her with a few comments about your progress. Staying in contact shows further sincerity in your appreciation of her efforts, and also assures that you maintain contact with a supporter and possible lifetime career advisor.

Remember that your recommender is in a position to help your career for years to come and has already shown a distinct willingness to do so. You should do your best to reward her helpfulness. One sound reason for going to a top law program is to take advantage of the networking possibilities it offers. It would be silly to throw away a very good contact prior to arriving at law school by failing to treat your recommender appropriately.

SPECIAL NOTE FOR INTERNATIONAL STUDENTS

If you have a potential recommender who is not able to write well in English, you can help matters greatly by writing up some stories or even the full draft of a recommendation for her. To the extent that you write well in English, your recommender will be all the more likely to use what you have written rather than struggling with the language on her own. Be sure, also, to provide the recommender with an appropriate editor who is a fluent, native speaker of English. This can be a colleague with whom you are both acquainted, or anyone else about whose editing and grammar skills you feel confident.

EMPLOYER RECOMMENDATION EXAMPLE

The beginning of this chapter features a valuable, well-written academic recommendation by a professor for Laura. The following is yet another example of a successful recommendation, this time from an employer.

Recommendation for Steve:

I enthusiastically recommend Steve for X Law School. I believe that he has high potential for achievement in your program and that he will go on to be an exceptional corporate lawyer.

I hired Steve as an analyst to the media division of SB Bank (for which I am Managing Director) four years ago and I have worked with him daily since that time. Steve has taken initiative in his own career and has matured into an accomplished self-educator, finance analyst, "intra-preneur," and project manager.

In fact, he has become the one person I rely on most to help me manage my division of our company.

I hired Steve because of his academic success, particularly in economics, and his intense desire to come to Wall Street in order to decide whether he wanted to follow a path in corporate law or corporate finance. He was honest with me from the beginning about the fact that he was not certain whether his talents and interests would push him farther into business or eventually to corporate law. I appreciated his honesty. I did not see a problem with this kind of ambiguity from a youngster, since a stint as an analyst at our bank is compatible with both goals. As Steve's inclination toward law has grown, he has taken several measures to ensure that he remains as tuned in to legal matters as possible. He has befriended our in-house counsel, having lunch with her often and even moonlighting for her as a research assistant on several occasions. He tries, when his time allows, to attend all of our drafting sessions with lawyers, even though it is not routine for those at the analyst level to be at such meetings. As a result, he has gained a fine command of much of the legal code (and thinking) involved in M & A, IPO, private equity, and LBO transactions.

As with most of my assistants, I gave Steve a trial by fire when he first arrived four years ago. I put him in charge of running my prospective client operations without giving him any training. I do this as a way to test a new hire's raw intellectual firepower and ability to think on his feet and deal with the unexpected. I was more than pleased with Steve's performance. He immediately figured out that the key to any busy corporate employee's job is prioritization. He developed his own system for handling our pitch calls by the target companies' sizes, time zones, financing needs, and levels of previous contact with us. The immediate result of his effort was an incredible 30% increase in new deal work; we began to acquire one new deal per month, each bringing in anywhere from $40,000 to several million dollars in fees. Steve's system was so effective that I asked him to make it a formality, incorporating it into our best practices efforts and teaching everyone in the office what it was all about. This system—which we nicknamed "SS" for "Steve's System"—still helps us to get appointed as the lead bank in deals. Our income generation has continued to set new records, due in no small measure to his brilliant plan.

Once Steve saw the power that he had to get things done and make improvements, he asked me if he could investigate the possibility of developing an intranet (i.e., an in-house network) that would give every employee at-a-glance information at a moment's notice, keeping everyone up to date and also allowing employees to communicate via chat-rooms and intranet meeting centers on important issues and problems. I gave him my approval; we met weekly for the next seven months so that Steve could update me on his progress.

At our first meeting, it looked as if he had lost some steam on the idea, probably a result of being thrown too many tedious projects during that particular week, which had sapped all of his time and given him little of a personal life. But within a few more weeks, it looked as if he had again mastered the art of survival in our demanding environment. He had again recaptured his enthusiasm for the project, first researching our needs by interviewing everyone in the office. He then made himself an expert on the possibilities of an in-house net by doing extensive research, including conducting meetings with the leading providers and consultants in the field. Steve then presented his plan for an intranet, in a three-hour meeting, to myself and the other principals of the bank. His plan included all of the relevant details, including a realistic budget and projections of how the tool would eventually improve our efficiency and the bottom line. After the meeting, several of my colleagues asked me where they, too, could find analysts like Steve to work for them—everyone was impressed with his knowledge, confidence in front of a roomful of senior executives, and oral presentation skills. We unanimously approved his plan, and he moved right ahead to hire engineers and other relevant technical staff to implement the project. Steve was the de facto project manager of this very involved effort, a task no one I know envied. This required that he sort out the usual sorts of difficulties among the various subcontractors as well as soothe the ruffled feathers of those of us whose ongoing activities were intruded upon. He managed to complete the project on schedule and on budget.

Seven months later, our intranet was ready for use. Although we have not yet been able to study its effect on our business (it has been up and running only a few short months as of this writing), I am confident that the results will be very positive. Although Steve was not the first person at SB to vocalize the idea of an intranet, he was certainly the first actually to do something about it. He has an amazing sense of initiative and perseverance. I would commend any co-worker for having implemented such a huge, new project—but from someone at the analyst entry level, this kind of thing is unheard of.

Steve is not just excellent at managerial tasks: He is also a superb financial analyst. His M & A work, for example, is characterized by a thoroughness that exceeds that demonstrated by our MBA hires. He understands and applies the relevant financial theory, whether that be simple Capital Asset Pricing Model use of comparables or sophisticated valuation of real options. Similarly, he has a useful understanding of the accounting and tax treatment of business combinations. Finding a young analyst with this range of understanding is a treat, but Steve actually goes far beyond this in his work. He routinely excels in understanding the likely operational difficulties that will be experienced by a combined entity. For instance, one bank acquisition was initially pitched on the basis of proposed cost savings that would be made possible by combining systems and reducing retail branches. Steve's highly detailed analysis, based upon an in-depth understanding of the actual costs of combining the specific systems the two banks had in place and the locations of their branches, showed that the likely cost savings would be only 50–60% of the total and would take an extra eighteen months to be realized. This changed our advice to our client and dramatically altered the actual purchase price.

Steve's value has extended beyond our local office, too. Since realizing Steve's public speaking capabilities, I have taken him on the road with me when

I deliver seminars to investment banking employees in other branches of SB (we have branches in San Francisco, London, Singapore, Shanghai, and Buenos Aires). I have shared the floor with him on numerous occasions; his contributions have always been well prepared and his answers to spontaneous questions insightful. He was once pressed by an important high-level executive attending one of our sessions to admit that the reason our media division is so financially successful is that we aim to become the secondary (rather than the lead) bank on most of our transactions. This type of practice concerns many executives of SB Bank because, although it may help the bank's finances in the short term, it jeopardizes our reputation in the banking world, making it a bad long-term strategy. SB has been warning all of our divisions to stay away from developing this kind of reputation, and has thus encouraged our division to take on more lead banking positions; we have often been scrutinized on this account. Steve handled the man's questioning exceptionally well, explaining our particular difficulties in securing the lead position on media deals (which represent a relatively new field for us), and the ways in which media banking is different from banking in other industries. Even at only twenty-five years of age, Steve has remarkable composure.

Steve is one of our firm's best assets. As I think you can see from the stories I have recounted here, he has intellectual smarts, sales ability, project-management ability, interpersonal skills, oral and written communication skills, creativity, and initiative. He is also a good guy, very well liked by everyone. Much of this is because he is humble about his talents and often tries to include others in his successes, so that they may benefit and grow and share the glory with him. In my experience, when a new, hotshot youngster joins a firm and starts making waves with all of his accomplishments, others tend to form a backlash against the person, perhaps in jealousy but also perhaps due to the newcomer's own inability to deal well with success. This is certainly not the case with Steve.

I wholeheartedly recommend Steve for your program. Please do not hesitate to call me if you have any questions or want to discuss his candidacy further.

Appendix VII

RECOMMENDATION ORGANIZER

Name _____

Title _____

Organization/Department

Mailing Address

Telephone   (office)   (home)

Fax   (office)   (home)

E-mail

Planned Date for Contact

Date Contact Made

Schools He/She Is Writing For

Materials Given/Explained (and Date)

Further Materials to Be Supplied

Progress Checks to Be Made

     —Date/School

     —Date/School

Schools That Confirm Recommendation Receipt

Note: This form can be copied, or you can generate your own version by computer, and use it for each recommender.

Appendix VIII

RECOMMENDATION BRIEFING OUTLINE

(The material below is meant to provide an outline to illustrate how you can structure briefing sessions with your recommenders to get them to provide you with the kind of recommendations you need.)

- My ultimate goals:
- How a law degree would help me to reach these goals:
- Why I should get a law degree now:
- Which law programs best suit me:
  —Why/how:
- My positioning/marketing for these schools:
- How he/she can help me:
  —Does he/she want to help me?
  —Total time required:
- Show application forms/explain that only "ticking the boxes" and writing a general letter is required.
  —Show that the objective information has already been filled in, letters stamped, and so on.
- Take recommenders through outline of an appropriate letter.
  —Include details of stories, copies of reports, and so forth.
- Discuss style and form of the master letter.
- Deadlines:

12

INTERVIEWS

— EXECUTIVE SUMMARY —

Establish your objectives:
—Convey a good impression.

—Impart your strengths.

—Demonstrate your knowledge.

—Gain information.

■

Prepare yourself:
—Learn the most likely questions.

—Know yourself and your qualifications vis-a-vis
those of others.

—Know the school.

—Formulate your own questions.

■

Know what to expect from different types of interviewers:
—Admissions officers

—Alums

—Students

■

Practice via mock interviews, videotaping them if possible.

■

Familiarize yourself with the "dos" and "don'ts" of interviewing.

More and more schools are interviewing a significant number of the applicants they seriously consider admitting. One reason for this is that a person's interviewing ability is a very good indicator of how attractive he or she will be to employers during and after law school. An applicant with good "paper" credentials will be unattractive to a school to the extent that he or she is likely to be regarded negatively by employers later on. Another reason for interviewing is that schools can market themselves better by meeting individually with applicants. This is particularly relevant for the elite schools, which tend to feel that they are all chasing the same few thousand absolutely outstanding candidates. These schools welcome the chance to get a jump on their rivals by better assessing candidates and by promoting themselves to their top choices.

Interviews offer schools the chance to learn much more about applicants. Some things are not readily determinable without a face-to-face meeting. These include your appearance, charm, persuasiveness, presence, and potential as an attorney. Interviews also provide an opportunity to probe areas insufficiently explained in the application.

ADMISSIONS DIRECTORS DISCUSS WHOM THEY INTERVIEW

We offer and sincerely encourage interviews as an option for anyone interested. In addition, there are a number of people we'll call—if we want more information regarding any part of the file. It may also be that we're unsure of their awareness about the school. (We want people to apply as informed consumers. There is a tendency in the law school process for applicants to just ship off a bunch of applications without researching or thinking about each.) For some top candidates it may be that we want to undertake some pro-active marketing to them. Don Rebstock, Associate Dean of Admissions and Financial Aid, Northwestern

We interviewed 1,750 candidates out of 4,100. Don Rebstock, Associate Dean of Admissions and Financial Aid, Northwestern

We interview maybe two percent of applicants; the numbers are expanding. We interview the children of alums, children of big donors or people they are sponsoring, people I call in who present particular issues (English ability, contradictory quantitative data), and people who successfully appeal to me as interesting. Janice Austin, Assistant Dean for Admissions, University of Pennsylvania

We interview three different groups of students. The first group consists of about fifty students we have specific questions about. These interviews focus on the particular matter that concerns us. The second group consists of about one hundred fifty candidates that we select as a random cross-section of the group of promising applicants. We want to get a "flavor" or "feel" from them rather than more information on a specific, preselected topic of concern. The third group consists of wait-listed applicants. All wait-listed applicants are entitled to an interview, which is provided at their request. About one-third to one-half of our one hundred fifty to two hundred wait-listed applicants request interviews.   Rick Geiger, Dean of Admissions, Cornell

We recently started to interview those on the wait-list. Each interview is held on campus and lasts for twenty-five minutes. The interviewer has read the candidate's file thoroughly and focuses the interview on the critical issues facing his or her candidacy.   Elizabeth Rosselot, Director of Admissions, Boston College

We started interviewing several years ago. Last year we did two hundred fifty; this year three hundred fifty. We'll probably increase the amount of interviewing we do. We invite about one-third of the Texas resident applicant pool to interview—those competitive applicants for whom a decision isn't obvious. We also accommodate every request for an interview, whether from a resident or nonresident. (We've also experimented with post-acceptance interviews for scholarship selection, and with interviews of top candidates for our own marketing purposes.)   Shelli Soto, Dean of Admissions, University of Texas

I interview a very small number of applicants a year, usually at the request of the admissions committee. Most often it's to have the candidate explain a specific issue from the past raised in the application, to make sure that it's been overcome.   Kenneth Kleinrock, Assistant Dean for Admissions, New York University

"HIDDEN" INTERVIEWS

The party line is that we are not doing evaluative interviews. But like most law schools, if we have a conversation or informational interview with an applicant, it can affect his or her chances.   Dennis Shields, Assistant Dean for Admissions and Financial Aid, Duke

Applicants call all the time. If they speak with me, I may put a notation regarding my impressions of that conversation in their files.   Faye Deal, Associate Dean for Admissions and Financial Aid, Stanford

We do not interview. We have considered doing so but the logistical constraints are substantial. On the other hand, if you stop by (for an informational interview) and the staffer likes you, he or she may make a note. This becomes a part of your file and will be taken into account in our decision-making.   Andy Kornblatt, Assistant Dean for Admissions, Georgetown

A lot of law schools are looking at interviewing and we may end up going down this road in the near future. For the moment, it's unusual for us to conduct a formal interview. On the other hand, I do meet a lot of candidates and keep what I've learned about each candidate in mind when reading his or her file. William Hoye, Dean for Admissions, USC

Nevertheless, the interviewing policy of schools is not uniform. Northwestern and Virginia, for example, allow their applicants to request an interview, whereas Harvard and Michigan interview none of theirs. Other schools interview only those applicants who are borderline candidates—with strong enough numbers that they warrant a close look, but not so strong that they will be admitted without an interview.

Some schools use only admissions officers to conduct their interviews, whereas others use alumni extensively, and still others use third-year students. The schools that rely on admissions officers alone are obviously unable to do in-person interviews with all the applicants they might otherwise wish, due to the time and logistical constraints. For example, there is the problem of interviewing the candidate who is immersed in a round-the-clock project at a remote site in Alaska. Some get around this by doing telephone interviews; others simply evaluate the candidate on the basis of the file alone.

SHOULD YOU INTERVIEW IF GIVEN THE CHOICE?

Most people feel they interview quite well, but the reality is that most do not. To become a good interviewee, you need to understand in advance what points you want to put across, what questions you are likely to be asked, and how to maximize your presentation to satisfy your needs and those of your interviewer. The keys to doing this are to analyze what you will confront and then to practice performing under realistic conditions. Doing this will help you to avoid going blank, letting slip things you intended to avoid, forgetting to mention important points, or being unable to keep the interview flowing in a comfortable fashion.

If a school permits you to request an interview, it is generally to your advantage to do so: You demonstrate initiative and show yourself to be a serious, conscientious applicant. Obviously, you go the extra mile and have nothing to hide in your background.

SHOULD YOU INTERVIEW IF REQUESTED TO?

If a school requests that you interview with it, it is in almost all cases a mistake not to do so. Failing to interview may be taken as an indication of a lack of interest in the school or a tacit acknowledgment of the weak points in your application. It is also an indication that you do poorly in one-on-one situations due to shyness or nervousness (or worse). There are often logistical considerations, of course, and schools are aware that it may not be realistic to expect you to travel 3,000 miles for a Wednesday morning interview, since it might necessitate your missing several days of work or class. The logistical barrier is not as great as it once was, however, now that schools have their representatives travel to most major cities and regions on a regular basis, or occasionally use alumni representatives on their behalf.

Although it is generally appropriate to interview, if you are sure to make a poor impression, either improve your interviewing abilities or maneuver to avoid an interview. The people who should avoid an interview are those who

---

ADMISSIONS DIRECTORS CONSIDER WHETHER YOU SHOULD INTERVIEW IF GIVEN THE OPPORTUNITY

We think that interviewing is critical when it comes to applicants on the borderline. The same is true for those on the wait-list: We tend to admit only those who interviewed really well.   Don Rebstock, Associate Dean of Admissions and Financial Aid, Northwestern

Some applicants think that an interview will surely help them; that is by no means the case. At a minimum you need to be able to express yourself well and show your educated curiosity about the school.   Kenneth Kleinrock, Assistant Dean for Admissions, NYU

Requesting an interview shows a serious interest in UT, initiative, and confidence.   Shelli Soto, Dean of Admissions, University of Texas

For regular applicants we do informational interviews only—no notes are put in an applicant's file. We do evaluative interviews of wait-list applicants only. For them, it's optional; about five to ten take us up on this. It can help advance their candidacies substantively. Going to the effort to interview also shows their desire to come here.   Jean Webb, Director of Admissions, Yale

If an applicant lives in close proximity to Northwestern and doesn't choose to interview, a red flag goes up.   Don Rebstock, Associate Dean of Admissions and Financial Aid, Northwestern

People who have difficulty interacting one on one maybe should avoid interviewing. But if that's the case, you should think about something other than law—reconsider the whole enterprise.   Albert R. Turnbull, Associate Dean for Admissions and Career Services, University of Virginia

The people who interview are more likely to enroll here; it indicates serious focus on the University of Virginia.   Albert R. Turnbull, Associate Dean for Admissions and Career Services, University of Virginia are pathologically shy, whose language abilities will crack under the strain, or who are so contentious that they will inevitably get into a verbal battle with their interviewers.

BEFORE THE INTERVIEW

ESTABLISHING YOUR OBJECTIVES FOR THE INTERVIEW

The interview is important for all-too-obvious reasons. The fact that the school emphasizes the interview means that you have the opportunity to market yourself in a format in which most people do very little good for themselves. Some candidates are afraid of the interview and set themselves hopelessly limited objectives for it. They hope to get through it without embarrassing themselves. Or they hope that the interviewer likes them. You have the chance to make a very positive impression that will further your marketing efforts, so it is up to you to seize it. Do not simply hope to survive the interview; be determined to achieve positive results. Use it to reinforce all of your other positioning efforts.

You already have a marketing strategy in place, so go back to it when you are considering what you hope to accomplish in the interview. If you have positioned yourself as a civil rights crusader, for example, this positioning strategy will help you think through the interview and how to prepare for it.

Ask yourself the following questions at the start of your preparations:

1. How do you want the interviewer to think of you? What specific impressions, and information, do you want her to carry away from the interview?

2. How can you reinforce your strengths and address your key weaknesses?

3. How can you convey any important pieces of information that may not receive full attention (or any attention at all) in the written application?

4. How can you show that you know a great deal about the school—that you are well prepared for the interview?

5. How can you learn whatever you need to know to decide which school to attend?

PREPARING FOR THE INTERVIEW

You should be mentally prepared to deal with four aspects of any interview. The first is understanding the format of a typical meeting as well as what to expect of your interviewer. You also must know what your objectives are, what the school offers, and what questions your interviewer is likely to ask.

TYPICAL FORMAT

No matter what type of interview is involved, the format is likely to include:

- Welcome
- A few easy "ice-breaker" questions, perhaps about how you are, whether it was easy to find the location, and so forth
- Some comments about the school
- Detailed questions, tracking your educational and then work history, or your responses on the school's application form
- The chance to ask questions
- Conclusion

THE INTERVIEW FORMAT

A typical interview will last between 30 and 60 minutes, although if it is with an alum it may be even longer. The first few minutes of an interview may not involve substantive discussion, but they are still important in forming the interviewer's general impression of you. Therefore, do your best to appear confident and relaxed when answering these questions, before reaching the heart of the interview. Doing so will give you confidence and momentum to carry you through the following parts of the interview.

THE INTERVIEWER

You can expect different things of an interviewer depending on whether he is an admissions officer, an alum, or a student. Here are some guidelines on what you are likely to encounter with each type of interviewer.

INTERVIEWS WITH ADMISSIONS OFFICERS

An interview with an admissions officer is likely to be the most formal, although not necessarily the most difficult, of the three types of meetings. Admissions officers will conduct themselves in a gracious and poised manner—their job is not only to find out more about you, but also to leave you with positive impressions of their schools. They are thus likely to consider an interview as much a public relations opportunity as anything else. Admissions officers have plenty of experience interviewing and socializing, so they should not leave you feeling uncomfortable or lead you astray in your discussions.

**ADMISSIONS DIRECTORS DISCUSS THEIR
INTERVIEW FORMATS**

The length varies from fifteen to forty-five-plus minutes, depending upon the quality of the conversation. If someone flies in from Chicago just for this interview and I end it after fifteen minutes (because he's unable to engage me or make his case), it is obviously a failure.   Janice Austin, Assistant Dean for Admissions, University of Pennsylvania

Telephone interviews are for about thirty minutes, in-person interviews for about forty-five minutes.   Rick Geiger, Dean of Admissions, Cornell

Our interviews are thirty minutes long.   Albert R. Turnbull, Associate Dean for Admissions and Career Services, University of Virginia

---

Because interviewing applicants is a significant part of an admissions officer's job, you can be sure he will be extremely well-prepared and thorough. This does not mean, however, that he will spend a great deal of time with you. On the contrary, an admissions staffer's busy schedule will probably keep an interview short rather than allowing it to run overtime, whereas alums and students may have more leisure time to spend with you.

An admissions officer will want to gain some definite opinions about how your past experience and career goals suit you for his school's program, but that does not mean he will be uninterested in your personal life or in getting a feel for your general demeanor. Do not become a straight-and-narrow bore in front of the admissions folks! Be serious, but not overly so. They are concerned about filling their programs with lively candidates who offer more than just good grades and admirable future goals.

An admissions representative will obviously have the most thorough knowledge of the "official" aspects of the school, such as its strongest fields of law. But he will not necessarily know much about what life in the graduate dorms is all about.

INTERVIEWS WITH ALUMNI

An interview with an alum is likely to be the most relaxed and easiest of the three kinds of meetings. (Obviously, this is not *always* the case. An occasional alum will approach her role with a hard-nosed determination to let only the best applicants shine—perhaps she is one of those who remembers "the halcyon days" of her alma mater with pride and wants to ensure that her school maintains high standards. Similarly, you may simply run into a personality clash with an alum, as with any other type of interviewer.) In most cases, however, alums who volunteer their time to interview applicants do so because they are personable, friendly types who like to meet new people and are basically interested in promoting their schools.

Alumni interviews generally take place in the alum's home, in the alum's office, or at a public meeting space such as a coffee shop. Interviews that are conducted in an alum's home tend to be more relaxed and perhaps a bit longer than those that take place outside the home. Interviews with alums in their offices might seem more formal because of the setting and the interviewer's naturally more serious demeanor while at the workplace (especially if it is a law firm).

You can bet that the alum will have received some limited information about you, but her knowledge of you and your candidacy will almost surely be sparse. You should inquire of her or of the school's admissions office before the interview exactly what information she will have received so that you can bring appropriate materials with you to the interview to share and leave with her. You might want to bring a copy of your application or your résumé for her. She will probably not have seen enough of your application to know what your weaknesses are, and thus will not challenge you on these points. By the same token, she will not know your strengths and positive attributes, so to make a good impression you might have to talk at length about ideas you have already expressed in your essays and supporting materials. It is certainly fine to ask your interviewer, if she does not offer the information herself, how much background material she has been given so you know what to talk about and what not to repeat.

Alumni interviewers are instructed to follow certain guidelines, so they will definitely ask some crucial questions—but most will not be as meticulous or sharpshooting as an admissions officer or student interviewer. Alums tend to be chattier, more relaxed, and more interested in selling their beloved schools (or recounting their glory days for you) than they are in grilling you or using hardball tactics. Alums will tend to give you more of their time than an officer of the school would, making it a more relaxed, unrushed conversation.

One drawback of having an alumni interview is that your interviewer will not be present in admissions committee meetings to push your case personally and, furthermore, might not know how to formulate a winning position to support your application. Although schools that use alumni interviewers take their opinions seriously, an alum can convey his opinion about you only through a written evaluation that he sends to the admissions office after your meeting. Even with a favorable impression of you, if he is not an effective or convincing writer, his evaluation might not exude the necessary enthusiasm to make a serious impact upon the admissions committee when it sits down to review your file. He may be relatively unpracticed in the art of admissions and might not know what it takes to push an applicant from reject to wait-list status, or from wait-list to admit status. A professional admissions officer interviewer, on the contrary, will not only know how to convey a proper argument for a candidate, but might also be able to argue her case in person at an admissions committee session.

Another drawback of having an alumni interview is that those who have not been part of the school for some time will know the least about it. In other words, if you are hoping that your interview will provide a great opportunity to learn more about a school's program and how it compares with others, an interview with an alum who has been out of law school five years or more might leave you unsatisfied. Even if an alum graduated fairly recently, it is likely that certain aspects of the school have changed since her time or are currently in the process of revision. If the alum graduated quite some time ago, she probably understands the current atmosphere and curriculum very little, even if she is active in the alumni association and tries to keep up to date from the outside.

INTERVIEWS WITH CURRENT STUDENTS

Student-led interviews are not yet common, but several schools are using them (and several more look likely to begin using them). As rookies, students tend to be less smooth in their interviewing tactics. They may or may not be well prepared, despite training in interviewing techniques. (If the busy law school student is faced with the choice of finishing her moot court brief or preparing for an interview of a prospective student, how do you think she will spend her time?) A student interviewer may have trouble keeping the conversation flowing or thinking of things to say, in which case your job will be that much more difficult. She may even be just as nervous and ill-at-ease as you are (!) because of the responsibility and newness of her role. Of course, this is not usually the case. The students whom admissions offices recruit to conduct interviews of applicants are selected in part for their good communication skills and comfort acting as representatives of the school.

Students often ask applicants very tough questions. Sometimes they simply do not have enough perspective and life experience to realize what is and is not important. Furthermore, because they are so steeped in the intricacies of the law school experience, they naturally have a lot of interview material at their immediate disposal. They know what life at the school is like, and thus can come up with very directed questions, maybe even ones that are so specific that they seem useless for obtaining relevant "big picture" information about you. This might especially be true if you and your interviewer have something in common, such as an interest in environmental law. When this is the case, your interviewer has even more interview material at her disposal. She might thus be tempted to ask you an extraordinary question such as, "Our renowned Professor So-and-So, as you probably know, just argued a major case before the Supreme Court. Do you agree with his principal arguments?"

There is no way to prepare for this kind of treatment. If this happens in your interview, just try to relax, appear calm and confident, and probe the interviewer for further explanation if the question is confusing or entails an understanding of theories or issues about which you know nothing. The interviewer is probably just trying to impress you (or herself) with her seasoned knowledge. Do not let it get to you; just tackle it as best you can and move on.

This, of course, does not always occur. Some student interviewers are likely to be as bouncy, friendly, and relaxed as alums—people with whom you will feel at home, with whom you could imagine becoming friends. You are fortunate if this is the case, but remember to be alert and serious; do not let your guard down just because you see a friendly and welcoming face in front of you. You want to match your interviewer's demeanor, but do not forget that this interview "counts," which means that you must sell yourself and why you should be admitted to the school. Selling yourself to a current student is a bit tricky, because you do not want to appear cocky or obnoxious. It is easier to market yourself aggressively with a more official administrator whose job it is to be impressed with you than it is to someone on a peer level. (This is somewhat like being able to proudly share good grades with your parents in a way that might be inappropriate with your best friend, who would find you arrogant and conceited for bragging to her about your success.)

An interview with a student is likely to be the most useful for your own fact-finding purposes. Because students are themselves involved in the day-to-day operations of the school, they will be able to give accurate answers to many of your most detailed questions. You will probably feel more at ease asking them about the nonacademic side of law school life as well, thus discovering more than you might have wanted to know about the quality of the food in the cafeteria or how often you can expect to get away to hit the ski slopes. But be astute about the types of questions you ask—by the end of the interview you will probably be able to sense whether or not your student interviewer will welcome the kinds of casual or odd inquiries that you would probably not dare to ask an admissions officer. If a student interviewer, for example, jokes with you about how wonderful he found the Pass–Fail option to be when he realized he was not doing well in a Contracts class, it is probably fine to ask him how many times a student is allowed to use the Pass–Fail option; on the other hand, if your interviewer seems particularly serious about academics or mentions that he thinks the grading scale is too lax, it is not a good idea to ask him this kind of thing.

ADMISSIONS DIRECTORS TALK ABOUT THE
VARIOUS KINDS OF INTERVIEWERS

Either I, Jerry Stokes (director of financial aid and director of admissions), Karen Anderson (special assistant to the Dean and a law school graduate), or Sara Parker Johnson (a law school graduate who does interviews on a contract basis) do the interviewing. Albert R. Turnbull, Associate Dean for Admissions and Career Services, University of Virginia

We hired a full-time admissions person, a UT law graduate, to be Director of Interviewing. She conducts all of the interviews; each interview is held on campus and is twenty minutes long. The interviews are generally done "blind"—she does not read the file in advance of the interview. Shelli Soto, Dean of Admissions, University of Texas

Ninety percent of our interviews are done by me or my associate director. Perhaps ten percent are done by an admissions committee member. Rick Geiger, Dean of Admissions, Cornell

Our interviewer might be me or another admissions officer, one of twenty current students, or one of two hundred fifty alumni volunteers. There is no need to seek an admissions officer, let alone me, as the interviewer because all interviews are accorded equal weight in the admissions process. Don Rebstock, Associate Dean of Admissions and Financial Aid, Northwestern

INTERVIEW EVALUATION FORMS

Northwestern uses the interview evaluation form on pages 325–326. It lays out the areas that are of interest to the school and thus the qualities you will want to show. This evaluation form may not capture everything that could be relevant in a candidate, but certainly captures enough to show you the way in which a school will assess you. Other schools, of course, have their own approaches, but they tend to be similar to the one shown here. The primary differences are that some schools use much briefer forms.

KNOWING THE SCHOOL

Chapter 3 examines criteria relevant to choosing the right school for you. It also detailes how to find the information necessary for making a well-informed

NORTHWESTERN UNIVERSITY'S INTERVIEW
EVALUATION FORM

Applicant's Name: _____ Date of Interview: _____

SS No.: _____ LSAT Score & Date: _____

Undergraduate/Graduate Institution(s): _____

Undergraduate GPA: _____ Degree(s) & Major(s): _____

Please complete the applicant evaluation grid below.
Using a sliding scale, position an "X" in the appropriate box
within each category.

	Outstanding	Strong	Average	Below Average	Poor
N/A	Top 5%	Top 25%	Middle 50%	Bottom 25%	Bottom 5%

M _____

SCFO _____

LS _____

IA _____

CP _____

CF _____

XC _____

LP _____

NUM _____

OVERALL _____

Interviewer's Name: _____ NUSL Class: _____

Daytime Phone: _____ E-Mail: _____

Employer and Position: _____

Interview Quality (Check appropriate box.): Good _____ Fair _____ Poor _____

If fair or poor, please elaborate: _____

The Admissions Committee is concerned with assessing the candidate's interpersonal skills, intellectual ability, career progress, clarity of post-degree career plans, extracurricular involvement, leadership potential, and interest in Northwestern University School of Law. Using the space below, please comment on these characteristics as well as any other observations which may be of interest to the Committee. Cite specific examples if possible.

M—MATURITY (poise, confidence, presence, self-awareness)_____

SCFO—SINCERITY & CONCERN FOR OTHERS (politeness, interest in well being of others, not self-centered)_____

LS—LISTENING SKILLS (attentiveness, pertinence of responses, appropriate length of responses) _____

IA—INTELLECTUAL ABILITY (analytical skills, communication, creativity, curiosity, thinks well on feet)_____

CP—CAREER PROGRESSION (professional, career-oriented internships or post-undergraduate experience) _____

CF—CAREER FOCUS (motivation for law school, clarity of post-degree goals)_____

XC—EXTRACURRICULAR BREADTH (well-roundedness of interests and activities) _____

LP—LEADERSHIP POTENTIAL (initiative, contribution beyond expected responsibilities in extracurricular and/or work activities) _____

NUM—MOTIVATION FOR NORTHWESTERN (knowledge of and enthusiasm for Northwestern University School of Law) _____

OVERALL IMPRESSION/OTHER OBSERVATIONS_____

decision. Let's assume you have read that chapter and followed its advice prior to applying. Now that you are preparing for school interviews, it would be a good idea to review the information you assembled for any school with which you are likely to interview. In particular, you should be extremely familiar with the information that the school publishes about itself. If you tell the interviewer that you plan to specialize in intellectual property law, but the program offers no such specialization, you will look foolish.

If you are going to interview at the school itself, try to spend several hours in advance exploring the school and its environs. Talk with people in the cafeteria or lounge, paying attention to the attitudes they evince. Are they generally pleased with the school? Do they respect most of their professors? Do they think the placement office is doing its job? Are there any particular problems concerning the facility itself, such as crime or lack of late-night restaurants that might matter to you? It always impresses an interviewer to see that you have taken the time and effort to examine the school up close rather than just reading some materials on it. Knowing what type of housing is available, or from which professors students maneuver to take classes, is the sort of thing that shows you to be both determined and resourceful. It also helps you to develop good questions to ask the interviewer without sounding artificial. Even if you are not interviewing on campus, take advantage of any opportunities to visit schools for precisely these reasons. (Interviewers invariably spot the applicants who have done their homework by visiting the school and learning what its program is really like.)

If you find out which specific person will be interviewing you, ask people you know who interviewed with the same school to see how the interview was conducted. How formal or informal was it? How rapid-fire? How long? How much was the interviewee expected to initiate, rather than just respond to, questions? How friendly was the interviewer? You will be able to prepare more specifically if you know how this person likes to conduct interviews.

The advantages of knowing the school thoroughly include:

■ You will know that you are prepared, enabling you to relax somewhat during the interview.

■ You will be able to ask intelligent questions about the school, thereby impressing the interviewer, and helping you to choose the appropriate school for you.

■ You will show yourself as being highly motivated, concerned about your career, and in possession of the right work ethic, which will impress your interviewer.

ANTICIPATING THE QUESTIONS

The interviewer is likely to have two types of questions to ask you. One type is the set of questions she uses for everyone, such as, "Why do you want to attend School X?" The other type will be a direct response to your file. If you have claimed to have had some marvelous successes, she may wish to probe to make sure you have not exaggerated the results. Or she may wish to probe for gaps or weaknesses in your undergraduate education. For example, one of the standard things to seek in a résumé is a period of unaccounted-for time. If such a gap exists in your application, expect to be asked what you were doing then.

THE MOST LIKELY QUESTIONS

➤ Tell me about yourself.

➤ What are your greatest achievements?

➤ What are your strengths? Your weaknesses?

➤ What are your personal and professional goals?

➤ Why do you want to go to law school? (How much do you know about the practice of law?)

➤ To what other schools are you applying?

➤ Why do you want to attend this school?

➤ How have you learned about the program?

➤ Why should we accept you?

➤ What would you add to the program?

➤ Discuss [whatever legal issue is in the news].

➤ What questions do you have?

The easiest question to prepare for is, "Do you have any questions?" Most interviewers will give you the opportunity to ask a few questions. You should be ready with three to five questions that reflect your concerns about the school. Keep these in your head rather than on paper, because having to look at your notes will slow down the interview and make it look as though you cannot remember even a few questions.

THE INTERVIEW QUESTIONS

In general, two types of approaches are common. In the first, you are asked more or less directly about the trait or competence in which the interviewer is interested. For example, when trying to get a handle on your degree of independence, the direct interviewer might ask simply, "How much supervision and direction do you prefer?" The second approach tries to elicit information that will also allow the interviewer to determine whether, for example, you "strive for leadership positions," but in a much less direct fashion. In this case, the interviewer is likely to focus on various aspects of your past and current experience—in terms of your education, career, and personal life—to see how much supervision and direction you have had in various projects and whether that amount suited you. The questions that generate this information are likely to be more general, along the lines of, "Regarding that thesis project, what sort of relationship did you have with your advisor? What did you like and dislike about this relationship?"

These more open-ended questions, in which the focus is not made so obvious, are by now standard interviewing procedure. The more experienced the interviewer, and the more time she has available, the more likely she is to use the indirect approach.

You can prepare for both approaches by examining the following list, which covers the most common questions asked on each major topic—education, career, goals, and personal life. Of course, other questions may be asked, but if you are prepared to respond coherently and consistently to each of the following, you will be ready for just about anything else you will encounter as well. Preparing for the following will force you to think through the main issues that are of interest to law schools.

LEGAL ISSUES

Is the expense of trial by jury sensible for civil trials?

Should the U.S. switch to an English system of civil litigation (where the losing party must pay the attorneys' fees and court costs of the winner)?

When is jury nullification appropriate?

Is capital punishment ever warranted?

What is the relationship between law and morality?

Do you favor euthanasia?

Should criminals be forbidden to sell their stories?

Do you agree with the right to silence? Should it ever be restricted?

Should Britain have extradited General Pinochet to Spain?

Should drugs be legalized?

Under what circumstances should abortion be permitted? Is this a legislative or judicial matter?

What type of affirmative action, if any, should the U.S. adopt? Should this be limited to governmental organs or extended to private concerns as well?

Do you support the recent series of Supreme Court decisions giving more power to the states? To what extent do you believe the federal government has usurped power within what is supposed to be a federal, not centralized, system?

Should Congress or the courts determine gun-control policy for the country? What should that policy be?

At what age should minors be tried as adults for serious crimes? For what crimes?

Should tobacco companies be liable for damages to those who smoke (or once smoked) cigarettes? Does your answer change if the plaintiff began smoking after health warnings were put on cigarette packages?

Or if the plaintiff knew smoking to be dangerous? Should meat packers be liable for obesity?

Should Clinton have been impeached?

Should gays be allowed to marry? To adopt children?

Should internet service providers (ISPs) be held liable for whatever they disseminate over the net?

Should large political donations to candidates be prohibited? To politically active organizations?

Under what circumstances is Congress justified in turning down a Presidential appointee?

How would you define justice?

What is (should be) a lawyer's role in society?

Do you feel a lawyer is obligated to be "moral" or to be impartial?

General Tips Regarding Legal Issues

1. The most likely questions regarding legal issues are either the old standbys, such as abortion or capital punishment, or whatever is in the headlines at the moment.

2. To prepare to discuss whatever issues are in the headlines, read *The Economist, The New York Times, The Washington Post, The New Republic, The (London)*

Sunday Times, or other major publications on a regular basis—but particularly for the two months before interviews. (I strongly favor *The Economist;* be sure to read the "leaders" to be ready to discuss current issues, legal and other.)

3. When discussing a legal issue, try to support your point of view while also acknowledging the merits of the opposing viewpoint. This is particularly true regarding the most emotional issues, such as abortion, to demonstrate that you are capable of analyzing any issue dispassionately. You should sound like a reasonable person able to engage in spirited but civilized discussion. In other words, do not just spout your personal beliefs. Instead, discuss the issues in a legal framework.

4. Be ready to discuss the top dozen legal issues in the news; know the main arguments on each side, and be prepared to choose a side.

5. If any of this proposed preparation strikes you as too much trouble, you should forget about law school.

COLLEGE EDUCATION

(Repeat for graduate programs as appropriate.)

Which school did you attend?

Why did you choose that one?

(If you attended a lesser quality school) Don't you worry that you will be overwhelmed by the quality of students attending our program?

What factors most influenced your choice?

In hindsight, are you glad you chose that school? What would you change now if you could? Why?

What was your major? Why?

In hindsight, are you glad you chose that major? What would you choose instead if you could do it over again?

How many hours each week did you study?

In which courses were you most successful? Why?

In which courses were you least successful? Why?

Do your grades reflect your abilities? If not, why did you not do better?

In what ways did your education prepare you, or fail to prepare you, for your career to date?

What did you most enjoy about college?

What did you least enjoy about college?

What extracurricular activities did you participate in? What was your role and contribution in each?

How did you pay for your education?

How would you describe yourself as a college student? Is this still true about you?

GENERAL TIPS REGARDING COLLEGE EDUCATION

1. Avoid portraying your college days as a social experience rather than an intellectual one if at all possible.

2. If your record is poor, show that you have since gotten serious. If there is any acceptable way to explain a poor record without sounding whiny or childish, be prepared to explain briefly.

3. Show that you were committed to learning, whether for its own sake or for the sake of your career.

4. If you changed your goals or interests several times, show that you have been serious about at least one of them while pursuing it.

5. Portray both your academic interests and your extracurricular activities in terms of their contribution to your current (or then current) career interests.

6. Discuss your leadership experiences.

7. If you are interviewing for admission to a part-time program, do not try to excuse a mediocre undergraduate performance by explaining that you were unable to focus well due to the need to work part time as well as study. This combination of work and study will be your fate once again in the part time program, so you will appear unable to handle the responsibilities.

WORK EXPERIENCE

(Repeat as appropriate for different companies and jobs held.)

Why did you choose this profession?

What is your job title? To whom do you report?

What are your key responsibilities?

What have been your major successes?

What resources and whom do you manage directly?

What are the skills required of you in your job?

What are the key challenges of your job?

What do you do best/worst in your job? Why?

How could you have improved your performance?

What have been your major successes?

What have you done that best shows your willingness to work hard/take initiative/innovate/exceed expectations?

Describe a failure on the job.

What are you doing to address your failings?

What do you like most/least about your position? Why?

How do you see this work experience preparing you for the study and practice of law?

General Tips Regarding Work Experience

1. When discussing your boss, your description of what was good and bad about him will probably make it clear what you need, and also what you cannot tolerate, in a boss. This also says a lot about your own strengths and weaknesses, so be careful here.

2. Even when describing what you did not particularly like about your job, try to focus on the positive aspects; otherwise, you risk sounding like a malcontent.

3. Any job change should have been motivated by a desire for more challenges, more responsibility, the chance to grow, and so on. In other words, emphasize the positive, forward-looking reasons for making the change. Avoid the negative, backward-looking reasons for the change, such as being unappreciated, underpaid, or disliked by your boss.

4. If you were fired, confess to this fact if necessary, but be sure to note what you learned from the experience.

5. Working less than 50 hours per week may suggest that you are insufficiently motivated. A good answer will establish that you work as hard as necessary to achieve your objective.

6. Try to bring out the ways in which you demonstrate the key skills and aptitudes valued by law schools: analytical, communication (written and oral), and leadership.

INTEREST IN LAW/YOUR GOALS

What inspired you to apply to law school? How long have you had this in your plans?

What in your experience (educational and professional) has prepared you for legal study?

What interests you about the legal system?

Which undergraduate courses gave you a grounding in legal theory?

What research have you done regarding law school?

What do you expect to be the largest challenges you will face in law school?

What type of law do you want to be practicing in five years? Ten years? Twenty years?

(If you profess an interest in public interest law) How will you reconcile your desire to practice public interest law with your debt repayments and desire to earn a good living when you graduate?

What do you want to accomplish in life?

How have your goals changed in recent years?

What do you expect to learn in law school?

Which other schools are you applying to?

How did you choose these schools?

What will you do if you are not accepted at a top school?

GENERAL TIPS REGARDING YOUR INTEREST IN LAW AND YOUR GOALS

1. Showing that you have thought long and hard about your future career demonstrates your seriousness of purpose.

2. Regarding your long-term goals, do not say that you want to retire as early as possible and lie on a beach in Cancun. Saying this would show you to be lazy or overly stressed, hardly ideal attributes for someone trying to get into a challenging law school. Discuss instead how you arrived at your chosen goal in light of a consideration of your relative strengths and weaknesses, what you most enjoy, your backgrounds and desires, etc.

3. You want to show that you are committed to career success, however you define it.

4. Be sure not to sound as if law school is a default choice rather than something you have actively sought out.

5. If you claim that you will go into public interest law, you will need to do everything possible to sound credible. (A large majority of those who profess this interest do not actually enter the field; this is especially true of those who have not worked for an extended period after college.) If you can support this position with examples of personal sacrifice and work in a relevant field, do so. If you cannot, reconsider your goals—and what you pitch to the law schools.

PERSONAL

Tell me about yourself.

Who most influenced you when you were growing up? How?

What publications do you read regularly? Why?

What books have you read recently? What impressed you about them?

What have you done to keep yourself current, or to develop your skills, in your particular area of interest?

How do you feel about:

—China's advent upon the world stage?

—African internecine warfare?

—(Anything else on the front pages, especially if it relates to your home region or that of the school?)

How do you spend your time outside of work?

Is your current balance among career, family, friends, and interests the right one for you over the long term?

What would you do with the extra time if days were 28 hours long?

What activity do you enjoy the most? Why?

Who are your heroes? Why?

GENERAL TIPS REGARDING PERSONAL QUESTIONS

1. When describing yourself, or what your long-term goals are, be sure a large part of your response focuses upon your career. You want to appear career-oriented, albeit not lacking in personality or other interests.

2. Take every opportunity to show you are highly achievement oriented, and do what you can to develop both personally and professionally.

3. At the same time, show yourself to be a sensible and well-balanced person with compelling outside interests, including (but not limited to) family and friends.

4. When talking about your reading interests, it does not much matter whether you read science fiction, monographs about the Napoleonic wars, or locked-room mysteries, as long as you show that you are knowledgeable and enthusiastic regarding whatever you pursue.

5. These questions provide a natural opportunity to subtly strengthen your chosen positioning.

RECOLLECTING YOUR THOUGHTS DURING THE INTERVIEW

Remember your pre-interview objectives during the interview session. Ask yourself whether you have put across your major points. If you have not, mention briefly but persuasively the points you wished to make, along with the supporting examples or illustrations you intended to use.

GET YOUR GRAMMAR STRAIGHT!

There is nothing more annoying to a highly educated professional than some-one (younger) who fails to use proper English grammar in speech. Many inter-viewers are exasperated by the fact that even the most educated applicants these days cannot seem to put a sentence together without making some un-bearable mistake. Make sure you refine your speech habits before embarking upon your law school interviews, especially regarding the following common (yet not at all excusable) mistakes:

➤ Know the difference between "good" (an adjective) and "well" (an adverb). If you are describing a noun, use "good": "My grades last year were very good." If you are describing a verb or an adjective, use "well": "This year is going really well." Your year cannot ever "go good."

➤ Do not use objective pronouns (as in "me," "her," or "him") as subjects of a sentence. In other words, "Me and my parents went to Italy" is entirely incor-rect. Would you ever say "Me went to Italy"?

➤ Do not use words or phrases if you are not 100 percent certain how to use them correctly. Know the difference between "imply" and "infer." Remem-ber that "irregardless" is not a word. Never use the phrase "I could care less" (unless you actually mean that you care a great deal).

➤ Similarly, expunge "you know," "like," "as if," "uhh," "whatever," and other annoying verbal tics from your conversation.

PREPARING TO DESCRIBE KEY EVENTS

You should be ready to discuss major and minor milestones in your personal, ed-ucational, and professional life. Some interviewers prefer to ask very general, open-ended questions to learn how well you can develop an organized, intelli-gent response. Questions of this nature often revolve around major events inter-viewers glean from your résumé or application. Prepare yourself by reviewing the relevant aspects of each event you expect to discuss. In the case of a suc-cessful business or research project, you would want to recall:

- The project's initial objective
- Who originated it
- Who was in charge
- The resources available
- The timetable

- The activities undertaken
- What you did well and poorly, and why
- What skills you used
- What you would do differently in retrospect
- Other people's roles
- The results
- What went right and what did not, and why

In the case of a successful thesis or advanced study project, you would want to recall these factors:

- The initial proposition or hypothesis that you aimed to prove
- How you formulated the concept
- What research you undertook to prepare
- Who your advisor or mentor was
- The resources available
- The timetable
- The texts consulted
- The activities undertaken
- The methods applied
- The conclusion or results of the project
- What you did well and poorly, and why
- What you would do differently in retrospect

It is a useful exercise to write down on an index card the half dozen most important incidents you expect to discuss, using this sort of approach for each. Carry these cards with you for reading when you are waiting or have a spare moment. Learn them well enough that you can produce a well-organized, apparently spontaneous summary of each of them at the drop of a hat, but do not memorize the stories by rote. Be prepared to be interrupted by the interviewer, and be ready to carry on with the story smoothly once you have answered his question.

WHAT DETERMINES THE LIKELIHOOD OF A GIVEN QUESTION BEING ASKED?

Questions are not generally asked without a reason. Some interviewers believe that certain questions should be asked of anyone, no matter what the person's

ADMISSIONS DIRECTORS DISCUSS HOW THEY
CONDUCT INTERVIEWS

When I interview people, I try to ascertain whether a person has a sense of perspective, is comfortable discussing controversial matters, and does not take criticism of an idea personally. I also want to understand how they will interact with their classmates. I want to be sure that they are comfortable tossing ideas around.   Rick Geiger, Dean of Admissions, Cornell

I sit with their files on my lap and flip through them. I *want* to make them nervous, I want to make them sweat. I'm looking for their answers, but also for their reactions.   Janice Austin, Assistant Dean for Admissions, University of Pennsylvania

My questions are driven by the individual situation, what I find interesting or problematic about the applicant. Of course the academic background for us is critical, so I'll examine it with care. Where the admissions credentials are especially strong we sometimes switch to marketing mode to convince the person to come here.   Albert R. Turnbull, Associate Dean for Admissions and Career Services, University of Virginia

During the second half of the interview, an interviewee is given fifteen minutes to write on a general topic anyone could address. For example, you might be asked to write about your favorite literary character. We give you two topics, and you write about the one you choose. This writing sample is not "graded," just categorized as acceptable or not acceptable. (This is much less important than the actual interview.)   Shelli Soto, Dean of Admissions, University of Texas

Our interviews are thirty minutes. Typical subjects include their educational experience, work experience, goals, what they do in their free time, extracurriculars, nature of their interest in attending school here. We try to do it in a relaxed setting, since that is where you get the most useful perspective on them. We do throw in a few questions to make them think on their feet.   Don Rebstock, Associate Dean of Admissions and Financial Aid, Northwestern

circumstances. In interviewing for law programs, the most likely questions concern why you want to get a law degree, why at this school, what other schools you are considering, what you think you will contribute while at School X, and what you intend to do professionally in the near and long terms.

The other determinant of questions is, of course, you. Your background invites questions that may be quite different from those that would be asked of someone else. If you are in a field that seldom produces JD candidates, you can expect questions concerning why you want a JD. If one of your credentials is relatively weak, you can expect questions about it. If you are the resident of a non–English-speaking country, and attended a foreign institution, you can expect to have your English skills probed.

A good interviewer, and often even a bad interviewer, will try to use the interview to learn as much relevant information as possible about you. Given that most interviewers will not have read your application in depth, you can expect them to ask many of the same basic questions that appear on the various applications. One way to influence the course of an interview with someone who knows little about you is to take a résumé along. Most interviewers will use it as the basis for their questions, so they will ask about the items you choose to list on your résumé. They will also probe for internal inconsistencies as well as checking things that sound inherently unlikely.

The other items an interviewer will probe are things you and she have in common, or about which she is simply curious. ("I see you worked for Senator so-and-so; what do you think of his policy about such-and-such?") The more an interviewer takes this approach, the easier the interview is likely to be. Discussing interests you share is likely to provide an opportunity to share enthusiasms, which is generally easier to handle than responding to probing questions about why you dropped your thesis project after six months. Be sure, however, to keep your own objectives. You can still make the impression you want by being articulate and well organized, even when just discussing your summer in Geneva.

PRACTICE

There are two ways you can practice your interviewing skills and responses. The first is by doing mock interviews with others who are applying, or someone else who appreciates what is involved. This is a good first step to understanding what an interview will be like. The quality of the experience will depend in large part upon how prepared your interviewing partner is. If you can find someone who is willing to read your application carefully, and perhaps even read this chapter, then you are ready to get a good interview. The ideal person to team up with would be someone who is applying to the same schools, but has a very different background from yours, and who is willing to be tough when necessary in the interview. It can be difficult to find the right person, of course. (It is partly for this reason that *Degree of Difference* regularly does mock interviews with clients if necessary by phone or in person, to give them a realistic view of what to expect.) It is not only fair, but also good for you, to switch roles with your partner. If you have to read her essays and data sheets with an eye to seeing what her strengths and weaknesses are, what she will contribute to the program, and the like, you will more readily understand how someone else will do this with you.

Your interview partner can tell you which responses were convincing and which were not (and why). Be persistent and force your interview partner to be specific in noting what worked and what did not. After all, the point is not what you say but *what your interviewer hears* that determines the success of your interview. In fact, simply saying things out loud will often cause you to hear what is not right. Speaking out loud often makes it clear that you are wandering instead of staying focused, trying too hard to excuse some prior mistake, staying too stiff, or pleading rather than convincing. Tape recording your practice sessions will make this apparent.

The second means of practicing is to be sure that, if possible, you interview first with a school that matters less to you. This allows you to develop and refine your pitch and get rid of your first interview nerves without too much at stake.

It is a good idea to use both of these approaches intermittently if you can. Maximize the potential benefits by debriefing your partner after an interview, or reviewing the experience yourself, to be sure that you understand what worked and what needed more thought, and why.

PHYSICAL PREPARATIONS

PHYSICAL ENERGY

- Get plenty of sleep the two nights before the interview.
- Eat a solid breakfast or lunch on the day, so that you do not run out of energy.

APPEARANCE

- Arrive at the actual site slightly before the allotted time so that you do not need to rush and get nervous as a result. Find the restroom and check your appearance.

Men:

- Make sure your hair is combed, and tie is straight and completely covered in back by the collar of your shirt.
- Consider carrying an extra tie or perhaps a shirt, in case something is spilled at lunch.

Women:

- Make sure your lipstick is not smudged or on your teeth.
- Consider carrying extra stockings, in case of a run.

LOCATION

- Be sure you know where the interview will take place and how to get there (and where to park).

OTHER

- Take several copies of your résumé and a copy of your application.
- Take a copy of the law school's brochure and other relevant information about the program to review if you get there early.
- Take the name and telephone number of your interviewer in case you need to telephone her to notify her of a delay in your travel.

STAYING RELAXED

A modest degree of nervousness is good because it gives you the energy to perform at your best. If you tend to be too nervous, try one of these techniques to keep yourself relaxed:

➤ Remind yourself that you have prepared thoroughly (assuming that this is the case) and that this preparation will see you through.

➤ Acting positive, by using the appropriate body language, will help you to feel the way you are acting. Positive body language involves keeping your head up, shoulders square, and eyes forward. Your body should be still (avoid swinging a leg or drumming your hands on the table) but not stiff.

➤ Breathe slowly and deeply.

➤ A great friend of mine, before exams and cross country races, used to go off by himself and keep repeating, with concentration and intensity, "I am King Kong, I am King Kong."

ADMISSIONS DIRECTORS GIVE ADVICE ON
HOW TO PREPARE FOR INTERVIEWS

Make sure that you dress professionally, such as in a suit and tie. (Some fail to do this.) Research the school; be ready to talk about it in a knowledgeable way. Read the admissions catalogue and more. Come prepared to talk about examples of what you have accomplished and how it relates to the qualities you think you have.   Don Rebstock, Associate Dean of Admissions and Financial Aid, Northwestern

If applicants are in college, they should be prepared to talk about what they are doing now—for example, what classes they are taking. . . . In general, they should remember that they will not have the chance to cover everything they want to so they should have in mind a kernel or two that they make sure they leave with us. We do give them the chance to highlight what they wish, so they should have a main theme that they try to develop.   Rick Geiger, Dean of Admissions, Cornell

It's extremely professional to send in a résumé a few days before an interview and then bring one along as well. Read all the pieces that you are submitting as part of the application. Formulate about five minutes of preparation, an argument for your acceptance; the interview will often flow from that. Come in ready to pitch your case. You should have an agenda: An applicant who can't carry the conversation, can't present an argument on his/her behalf, is harming him-herself.   Shelli Soto, Dean of Admissions, University of Texas

Try to look at the landscape of law schools, then look at this particular school. Walk the halls and talk with students; talk with alums, too. I'd develop some questions concerning the primary issues in choosing a school: issues of community—whether it's competitive or not, size, location, etc., are important. I'd have developed a sound understanding of the school (which would reveal that I had done my homework).   Albert R. Turnbull, Associate Dean for Admissions and Career Services, University of Virginia

You should know a lot about the law school—you should do your research. I'll be very candid with them; they should be candid with me, too. My questions will be very pointed. If a recommendation says the person is capable but very quiet in class, I'll ask whether that poses a problem for us. I may ask why you got this C- in class X; why you stopped working at the soup kitchen.   Janice Austin, Assistant Dean for Admissions, University of Pennsylvania

DURING THE INTERVIEW

A considerable degree of the impact you have in an interview is achieved non-verbally; nonverbal messages may constitute over half of the message you deliver. As a result, it is highly appropriate to consider such factors as dress, physical comportment, and the like in order to maximize the chances of interview success.

DRESS

Rules for Men:

- Wear clean, neatly pressed clothes and highly shined black shoes.
- Be sure your clothes fit well. Be sure your clothes do not look as if you are wearing them for the first time, but they should not be so worn that this is noticeable.
- Avoid wild colors or styles.
- Men will never go wrong wearing a conservative dark blue or gray suit with a white or blue shirt, or moderately striped shirt, and a conservative tie.
- Comb your hair and wear no cologne.
- It should go without saying that your shirt should be 100-percent cotton, long-sleeved, professionally cleaned, and heavily starched. The tie should be pure silk and extend to the middle of your belt buckle.
- Be sure your fingernails are cleaned and well groomed.
- You should be clean shaven. If you have a moustache or beard, that is fine; but if not, you should avoid the five o'clock shadow look for formal interviews.

Rules for Women:

- Women should wear a suit (skirt or pants) or a simple dress, and no more than a modest amount of jewelry, makeup, and perfume. Jewelry should not rattle or otherwise distract.
- Women have more leeway than men in choosing appropriate lengths, colors, and cuts of clothing. Your appearance may alter with changing fashion trends but do not go wild; be especially wary of skirts that are too short or blouses that are too low-cut.
- Try not to bring both a briefcase and purse because it is difficult to be graceful when carrying both.
- Wear pantyhose (no matter how hot the weather) and eschew bear arms.

Rules for Men and Women:

- Do not wear such ostentatiously expensive clothes that you might offend your interviewer. For example, leave the Hermes tie in the closet, if it is obvious where it came from.

- Your briefcase should be of good leather, preferably brown, black, or burgundy.

- Be sure you have invested appropriately in mouthwash, deodorant, and other hygienic necessities.

- You want to be remembered for what you said, not for what you wore (or failed to wear).

BEHAVIOR

PHYSICAL BEHAVIOR

Your goal is to be considered self-confident and relaxed. You can show this by remaining poised and thoughtful throughout the interview.

- Greet the interviewer with a smile, an extended hand, and a firm handshake (matching the interviewer's pressure).

- Look the interviewer in the eye.

- Do not sit down until invited to do so.

- Do not put anything on the interviewer's desk.

- Do not smoke, drink, or eat anything even if invited to do so—not even if the interviewer herself does. This can distract either you or the interviewer, perhaps showing you to be clumsy or worse, without any chance of improving her opinion of you. If the interviewer offers you a cigarette, decline politely but not judgmentally by saying, "No, thank you."

- Do not chew gum.

- Maintain a moderate amount of eye contact throughout the interview, perhaps 25–40 percent, but do not stare.

- Gesticulate moderately to make points, but do not go overboard.

- Remain physically stationary, without fidgeting. Interviewers often check your response to a tough question to see if you are exhibiting signs of nervousness (or lying).

- Maintain good rapport with the interviewer by being warm and smiling often. Do not, however, smile idiotically without stopping for the entire interview!

- Sit up straight, but not rigidly, and lean forward slightly. This will show that you are interested in what the interviewer has to say, and that you are professional.

■ Listen carefully, and show that you are listening by nodding, or saying, "uh-huh," "I see," or "right" occasionally.

■ Avoid crossing your arms, or folding your arms behind your head.

■ Keep your voice well modulated, but alive. Speak at a normal speed; do not rush.

ATTITUDES

■ *Be upbeat.* Be sure to emphasize your strengths. Do not discuss your weaknesses in any detail unless pushed to do so. Never complain about anything that has befallen you. No complaint about a low LSAT score, or personality conflict with a boss or professor can improve an interviewer's opinion of you.

■ *Flatter the interviewer, subtly.* Although a good interviewer will have you do 75 to 80 percent of the talking, that does not mean you will be excused for failing to listen to her.

Adopt an attitude similar to the interviewer's. If your interviewer is deadly serious, avoid joking. If your interviewer is lighthearted and jocular, do not sit deadpan. In the first instance jocularity will make you seem frivolous, whereas in the latter instance seriousness will make you seem unintelligent.

Maintain more formality if your interviewer remains behind her desk throughout the interview, without even coming around to greet you initially.

■ *Treat the interviewer respectfully, but not too respectfully.* Treat her as an equal, albeit one who temporarily is allowed to set the direction of the interview. Do not behave submissively. Do not, however, use the interviewer's first name unless and until told to do so.

■ *Relax and enjoy yourself.* The relatively few people who enjoy interviews are those who view them as a chance to discuss important matters with an equal who happens to be interested in the same subjects. They view the interview as a time to learn more about the school as well as a chance to explain themselves.

A little nervousness is to be expected, but exhibiting substantial nervousness works against you insofar as a strong candidate is meant to believe himself well suited to interact at this level.

■ *Make sure it is a conversation.* A good interview resembles nothing so much as a conversation. If there is a pause in the conversation, consider whether:

—You have answered the question fully enough. If you suspect not, ask whether the interviewer would like you to add to the answer.

—You should follow up with a question of your own related to the same subject.

—You should simply sit quietly, without tension, with a pleasant smile.

Ask the interviewer questions to follow up on what she has said. This helps to build rapport and puts you on a more equal footing with her by getting you out of the role of interviewee answering questions. It is also the way normal conversations work, trading back and forth.

- *Avoid sounding like a robot.* If you follow this book's suggestions and prepare thoroughly for your interviews, you run the risk of sounding preprogrammed rather than spontaneous. It is good to sound as though you have given thought to the relevant issues, but not as though you have memorized answers.

   How can you avoid this problem? There are three keys: (1) Avoid a robotic monotone, or appearing to be reaching into your memory for what comes next in your rehearsed response. (2) Focus upon your interviewer. You should be able to remain relaxed, given that you know you are well prepared, and this will allow you to stay focused upon how your interviewer is reacting to you. (3) Occasionally pause before you speak, as if to get organized before starting.

- *Look interested.* Avoid looking at your watch. Do not stretch in your chair. Do not appear bored, no matter how long the interviewer is speaking.

- *Do not ramble on.* If your answer has gone on too long, cut your losses by briefly restating your main points.

HOW TO READ THE INTERVIEWER

The interviewer's demeanor will help to reveal her reactions to the interview. Smiles and nods clearly suggest she agrees with what you are saying, in which case, think about what you are doing right so you can do more of it. Perhaps your interviewer likes the fact that you are backing up your abstractions with solid examples. Maybe you are keeping your cool when being asked very tough questions.

Looking away from you, frowning, or constantly fiddling with papers or pens may reveal disagreement or a lack of interest. If you sense you are losing the interviewer, try to get back on track by asking the interviewer a relevant question or making comments that are sure to be winners, such as some self-deprecating humor or mention of the incidents you feel show you in your best light.

It is important to keep in mind whatever the interviewer says in her opening remarks, because they may give you good clues as to what she values.

If you are talking too much, your interviewer is likely to start looking away, looking at her watch, or asking such questions as "Could you just summarize this part?"

YOUR QUESTION TIME

A failure to ask questions if invited to do so risks leaving the impression that you either did not do your homework or do not particularly care whether the school admits you. Asking questions gives you the opportunity to show how knowledgeable you are about the process and the program as well as that you are taking a proactive approach to your career future.

If you are asked what questions you have, do not rush into asking them. If you have not yet had the opportunity to make one or two key points, ask if it would be acceptable to go back to the earlier question and then mention what you have just accomplished (or whatever). Even if these points are unrelated to any prior question, feel free to say, "I am glad to have the opportunity to ask you a couple of questions, but I hope you will forgive my wanting to mention two things that have come up since I applied. I think they might be relevant to the school's decision making, after which I will continue with my questions." Briefly mention the one or two points. Then go on to your questions.

Try to avoid questions that call for a yes or no response. To understand an area in depth, plan to ask several questions about it. One good way to do so is to ask your interviewer to compare, for example, her school and a major competitor (one that you are actively considering). She will probably mention several points, after which you can ask about one or more of them in greater detail, or ask her why she did not mention subject X.

If you think that the interviewer harbors major objections to you, try to get her to confess what it is she is concerned about, so that you can address her concerns, assuming that you have not yet had the opportunity to do so.

Some appropriate questions, in case you are stuck for something to ask, include:

- How do you expect the school to change in the near future?
- Has the character of the school changed in recent years? How? Why?
- What distinguishes students at this school from those at its principal rivals?

If one reason for attending the school is that a certain professor teaches there, by all means ask whether the interviewer knows him or her, and, if so, what he or she is like as a professor.

Do not try to baffle the interviewer with questions you know she won't be able to answer. If she is an alum of the school, for example, she will not be privy to the school's rationale for its recent decision not to offer tenure to assistant professor X. Similarly, do not ask unintelligent questions, or ones that can be answered with a glance at the school's application materials (such as "What is the usual class size?") just for the sake of asking a question.

After asking several questions, if necessary you can fall back on the old standby: "I had a number of questions when the interview started, but you have covered them all."

Being asked if you have any questions signals that the interview is coming to an end, so do not take too much time.

ENDING THE INTERVIEW

Be sure to smile at the interviewer, shake hands and thank her for seeing you, and leave with an energetic, confident demeanor. (Do not ask your interviewer how you did at the end of the interview. This will put him on the spot and make you seem immature, lacking tact, or unable to wait for a decision to be made in due course. It will not do anything to improve your chances of success.)

Be careful not to be taken in by an old trick. Once you feel the interview is over, you may be asked a potentially revealing question as you are being shown out, on the assumption that you may have let down your guard at this point. Or the office assistant may be instructed to ask a question such as, "How do you think you did?" in hopes of eliciting a telling comment. Assume that the interview is really over only after you have left the premises.

INTERVIEW WRECKERS

➤ Criticizing your undergraduate institution, boss, or company intemperately. (You do not need to be so upbeat as to have no real opinions whatsoever, but negative comments should not evince uncompromising hostility; be sure you have, and express, reasonable grounds for any negative remarks.)

➤ Being too nervous to look the part of a successful, confident lawyer

➤ Appearing blase about attending the school at hand

➤ Asking no questions

➤ Whining about past grades, low LSAT scores, and so on

➤ Blaming others for weaknesses in your profile

GENERAL RULES FOR INTERVIEWS

The following advice is good no matter what type of interview or interviewer you encounter:

Do not criticize others without good reason. Even if you have good reason, do not let the focus of more than a small part of the interview be on your criticisms. Otherwise you may be viewed as a chronic malcontent. Remain positive.

Assume that alumni interviewers do not have your file memorized. In fact, for schools at which you requested the interview, most interviewers will not even have seen your file. You can therefore expect to be able to make good use of the same incidents you discussed in your essays.

Be truthful. Do not lie in answering questions. Being honest, however, does not mean the same thing as being blunt, so do not volunteer negative information if it can be avoided.

Be yourself. Do not pretend to be someone other than yourself to impress your interviewer. Very few people are able to act well enough to carry it off successfully. Focus instead on presenting the best aspects of your own personality.

Never be less than highly courteous and friendly to the staff. The staff is generally in charge of all of the logistical elements of your candidacy, so do not alienate them. The admissions officers may also ask them to give their impression of you, so make sure it is a positive one.

Do not try to take over the interview, but take advantage of opportunities to make your points. Interviewers want to feel they are in charge of an interview, since they need to feel confident that they will be able to get what they consider information relevant to their decision making. Taking over the interview may allow you to make the points you want to make, but the risk is far too great that your interviewer will react very negatively to this and resent your aggressiveness. Use of polite phrases in a confident tone of voice can keep your interviewer from fearing that you are trying to take over the interview: "Perhaps you wouldn't mind . . ."; "I would find it very helpful if you could . . ."

Do not ask the interviewer how you did in the interview. This will put him on the spot and make you sound immature (not to mention lacking confidence). It will not do anything to improve your chances.

Stay relaxed. A good interviewer takes the following as possible indications that you are lying, being evasive, or hoping that he will not follow up on a point:

—Fidgeting (such as twirling your hair, drumming your fingers, bouncing your leg up and down, or picking at a part of your body or clothing. Many people have a tic of which they are completely unaware. Use your mock interview partner or videotape to find yours, and then stop doing it.)

—Speaking much faster or more slowly

—Avoiding eye contact

—Lengthy, convoluted responses

—Desperately looking for a drink of water

—Coughing at length before staring a response

Remain calm even in the face of provocation. An interviewer may be trying to annoy you to see how you respond. A successful litigator, it should go without saying, is unlikely to be easily ruffled.

Answer questions concisely. Do not ramble. Do not take more than two or three minutes for any but the most involved, important questions. In fact, three to five sentences is an appropriate length for the majority of answers.

Structure your responses. Because you have prepared thoroughly (if you have taken this chapter to heart), you are in a position to respond with structured answers to most questions you will be asked. You do not need to start every response by saying "I did such and such for five reasons. Number one was . . . ," but having coherent and well-organized responses will be impressive. Summarize any particularly lengthy answers you give.

Listen well. Be sure you have understood what the interviewer is asking. If uncertain, ask for clarification of the question. Answering the question you thought was being asked, or the one you anticipated being asked, rather than the one she really did ask you, will annoy her and suggest that you are either dim or not paying attention. Listening well means more than paying attention to what is being said. It also requires that you encourage the interviewer by appearing interested. In addition, you should be able to sense the feelings behind the comments made.

Assume that anyone at the office may be an interviewer. Sometimes a junior employee will chat with you while you wait for the real interview to start, trying to get you to give your real reactions to the school or your own qualifications as though a junior person should be on your side rather than the school's. Expect any information you give away to be fed into your file immediately, maybe even given to your real interviewer prior to your upcoming interview.

ADMISSIONS DIRECTORS DISCUSS WHEN INTERVIEWS ARE CONDUCTED—BEFORE OR AFTER FILES ARE COMPLETE

An interview can take place at any point in the process, before or after applying. Don Rebstock, Associate Dean of Admissions and Financial Aid, Northwestern

Our interviewer has generally not read the applicant's file prior to the interview. We ask the applicant to bring a résumé and complete some basic demographic information sheets. We do the interviews "blind" in order to eliminate potential, pre-formed bias.   Don Rebstock, Associate Dean of Admissions and Financial Aid, Northwestern

We conduct interviews whether or not an application has been finished. We interview between October 1 and January 15. Earlier interviewees generally don't have their files complete at the time. I encourage them to send a résumé in advance. Later interviewees often have a complete application. When it is available, we use it as preparation for the interview. All of our interviewers read whatever is available on the applicant.   Albert R. Turnbull, Associate Dean for Admissions and Career Services, University of Virginia

I think that it's optimal to have the file complete. I like to have as much information as possible. I feel that if I know the person a bit better, I get to the meat of the interview faster. Applicants get a benefit from our being able to understand their candidacies well.   Albert R. Turnbull, Associate Dean for Admissions and Career Services, University of Virginia

We interview after the application has been submitted.   Janice Austin, Assistant Dean for Admissions, University of Pennsylvania

In all cases, we have carefully reviewed the file before we interview someone. Rick Geiger, Dean of Admissions, Cornell

SPECIAL TYPES OF INTERVIEWS

STRESS INTERVIEWS

Stress interviews are not much in evidence any more, but they still pop up often enough to merit comment. The idea underlying any form of stress interview is that applying enormous stress to an interviewee will cause him to reveal his true nature and likely performance under stress in the future. A failure to remain poised will reveal a person's supposed lack of confidence in himself.

What exactly is a stress interview? It can take many forms. You may be put in a position in which bright sunlight will be directly in your eyes (think of the movies you have seen in which detectives grill a suspect under a bright light) or your responses may be met by long silences. The tendency in this case is to try to fill up the awkward moments by adding to a response, thereby revealing information you would have been better advised to keep from view.

More likely you will be given too little time to answer questions. This sort of pressure is most readily employed when there are two or more interviewers, one preparing to ask you the next, perhaps follow-up, question while you answer the current one. As you start to answer a question, your response may be ignored or cut short and taken out of context, and the next question tossed at you as fast as possible. The interviewer may dispute what you are saying and challenge you very aggressively. Your weaknesses may be pointed out at every turn. The interviewer can also be obviously hostile and rude. This will continue for some time, until you react, most probably by becoming angry or resentful that you are not being allowed to get your full answers out.

The key to this situation is to recognize it for what it is. If you know that it is a game, you can respond with suitable bits of gamesmanship. Once you know that you are deliberately being pressured, you have the opportunity to take control of the situation. (This is one of the few circumstances in which it is appropriate for you to take control.) If the sun is shining directly into your eyes, excuse yourself and move your chair to a more comfortable location. If you are being subjected to the silent treatment, respond by smiling at the interviewer and simply waiting for her to ask another question. If, on the other hand, you are being pressured verbally, start by leaning back, smiling, and not saying anything for a few seconds. Then restate the last question, "You have asked me whether this project was really successful." Go on to explain that there are, let's say, four parts to your response. Once you have done this it will be all but impossible for the interviewer to interrupt you until you have finished all four. Be sure to start each portion of your response by saying, "first," "second," and so on.

If you are interrupted again, lean back once more, smile again, and say that this approach seems a bit much, and invite the interviewer to share information instead.

FRIENDLY CHATS

One type of interviewer will come on as extremely friendly and casual. She will chat away about recent football results or the interviewee's favorite foods. When she shifts to legal matters, she will be completely unthreatening and will agree with anything and everything you say. The danger is that she will lull you into totally dropping your guard so that you end up volunteering information that you would be better off keeping to yourself. You are inclined to consider a person who finds you agreeable, fascinating, and invariably correct to be on your side. Resist this temptation; your interviewer may just be using a technique to get you to open up about yourself.

SPECIAL INTERVIEW SETTINGS: RESTAURANTS

➤ Do not sit until the interviewer invites you to be seated.

➤ Consider the menu when the interviewer invites you to. Pick something mid-priced, and do so without lengthy deliberations. Make sure you choose something familiar and easy to eat. Avoid things that splatter or require eating with your fingers.

➤ If the interviewer orders a drink or first course, follow suit by ordering at least some mineral water so that you will have something to occupy yourself with while she is drinking or eating.

➤ Do not order too much, since this suggests lack of discipline.

➤ It is usually a good idea not to drink alcohol at all before or during an interview.

➤ Do not criticize the decor or the food.

➤ Treat the servers and busboys very politely.

➤ Wait for the interviewer to begin the "business" end of the discussion. She may prefer to wait until after the drink or first course has been consumed.

HOW TO DEAL WITH THE INCOMPETENT INTERVIEWER

What marks an incompetent interviewer? Examples are: talking too much, going off on tangents, failing to maintain control of the interview, dwelling on inconsequential matters, and failing to pay attention. Here are some tips for dealing with the most common problems:

He talks too much. The more an interviewer talks, the less information he can get about you. Build rapport with him by providing nonverbal encouragement. You do not want to offend him or be rude, but you still want to get some points across. Do so by appearing to agree with him, following up on one of his comments by immediately saying something like, "In fact, one of the things that first got me interested in school X was . . ." And, of course, take advantage of the break he gives you at the end of the interview when he asks you if you have any questions. Phrase your questions as questions, but make sure they are really short advertisements for yourself. For example: "I believe I would be an asset to your program, with my background: a Master's in Psychology and a lot of counseling experience. Can you tell me more about what opportunities I would have to teach (or share) these skills and experiences to (with) others? Would I be able to participate in workshops or counseling internships, for example?"

She goes off on tangents. If you want to get the discussion back on track, use such phrases as: "Let me be sure I understand this correctly" (and then repeat the couple of key points briefly); "Could we go back to that first point, such and such"; "In our remaining time, I hope we will have the chance to touch on the following points that are particularly important for me: X, Y, and Z." Be very friendly and nonconfrontational, showing that you are not trying to take advantage of an opportunity to learn more about the school or sell your own abilities.

She constantly interrupts. Make a note of where you are in a conversation when the interruption occurred and recall this for the interviewer's sake when the interview recommences. She will be impressed that you have kept your focus while she was losing hers.

ADMISSIONS DIRECTORS GIVE ADVICE ON
HOW TO HANDLE YOURSELF IN AN INTERVIEW

Follow general professional etiquette. Make eye contact. Do not fidget. Be comfortable, and appear comfortable: Do not worry about whether to fold your hands or have them at your side.   Don Rebstock, Associate Dean of Admissions and Financial Aid, Northwestern

Use your time wisely. Help me; give me something to hang onto, to overcome your low scores or grades. Either interviewees rise to the challenge or not. Janice Austin, Assistant Dean for Admissions, University of Pennsylvania

Exude energy and enthusiasm; otherwise it can get dry. You need to show that you're very interested in being here.   Don Rebstock, Associate Dean of Admissions and Financial Aid, Northwestern

Be prepared to be proactive; there's too little time for us to work at drawing someone out. You have a limited amount of time to make the argument for why you should be admitted. In fact, my first question is likely to be "give me some sense for why you're here." Elizabeth Rosselot, Director of Admissions, Boston College

During an interview, failure to make eye contact is a frequent mistake.   Shelli Soto, Dean of Admissions, University of Texas

One common mistake interviewees make is not being straightforward—being vague and evasive about a difficulty.   Rick Geiger, Dean of Admissions, Cornell

In the interview itself, allow us to lead the actual interview. One fellow came in and made the mistake of talking for twenty minutes before I got my first question in.   Don Rebstock, Associate Dean of Admissions and Financial Aid, Northwestern

AFTER THE INTERVIEW

First, debrief yourself regarding what went well and what went poorly, and why. This will help you with later interviews for other schools; you will be able to anticipate, for example, what you might be asked concerning an apparent weakness.

INTERVIEW CHECKLIST

- Clothing: My dress was/was not appropriate and comfortable.
- My entrance, including handshake and greeting, was/was not positive.
- My physical actions (smile, eye contact, body language, avoidance of fidgeting) were/were not appropriate.
- Attitude: I did/did not appear confident, enthusiastic, and friendly.
- Questions I handled well (list each, with what was good about your answer):
- Questions I handled poorly (list each, with what was bad about your answer, and suggestions for improvement):
- General Comments:
  - —I spoke too much/too little.
  - —I did/did not establish rapport quickly and easily.
  - —I did/did not stay on a more or less equal footing with the interviewer.
  - —I did/did not impress the interviewer without bragging.
  - —I did/did not balance sincerity and humor appropriately for this interviewer's style.
- My ending questions were/were not appropriate (and sufficient).
- My exit was/was not smooth and upbeat.
- I was/was not appropriately knowledgeable about the program (and the school).
- Interviewer's likely impression of me:
  - —Personal:
  - —Professional:

Second, send a brief thank-you note to your interviewer. Note something that occurred during the interview to make it clear that this is not a form note. You can mention, for example, that you were glad to learn that it will be very easy to get moderately priced housing near the campus. The one absolute requirement of the note is that you get the interviewer's name and title correct, so be sure to get her business card during the interview. If you do not, call the school to determine that you have correct information.

**ADMISSIONS DIRECTORS' FURTHER COMMENTS
ABOUT INTERVIEWING**

WHY DOES YOUR SCHOOL INTERVIEW?

We encourage interviews; we do 600 to 800 in the fall. I find it paradoxical that in general law schools eschew interviews whereas medical schools and business schools make it integral to their processes. My joint responsibility in career services and admissions has had an impact upon my thinking on this issue: Interviewing is critical for job placement so it makes good sense to include it in the admissions process as well.   Albert R. Turnbull, Associate Dean for Admissions and Career Services, University of Virginia

One reason we are interviewing more people is to help identify the applicants who will be what modern law firms want. Our career planning people tell us that firms want rainmakers, people who get on well with other people, etc. Interviewing helps identify various of these crucial characteristics.   Janice Austin, Assistant Dean for Admissions, University of Pennsylvania

We are a small school, so a slight change in the mix of students can be critical to the dynamics of the class. Interviewing helps us to get the right balance. Rick Geiger, Dean of Admissions, Cornell

The law is a very interactive profession; communication skills are critical to succeeding in it. They are number one or two on the list of what is most important. Developing client relationships depends upon communication skills, as does representing a client well. A law firm won't hire someone without an interview, so why should we?   Don Rebstock, Associate Dean of Admissions and Financial Aid, Northwestern

Interviews can yield supplemental information that couldn't be presented, or at least not completely presented, in the application.   Shelli Soto, Dean of Admissions, University of Texas

We have certainly encountered people with very high (LSAT and GPA) numbers who floundered in the interview; we do not admit them.   Don Rebstock, Associate Dean of Admissions and Financial Aid, Northwestern

WHAT INFORMATION DO YOU FIND INTERVIEWS YIELD?

The interview can make a real difference for those with disparate indicators. For example, if someone has mixed grades and a strong LSAT, which should be given more weight? Or if someone has a low LSAT but is not a native English speaker, how well he or she handles the language in a conversation or interview can be important.   Dennis Shields, Assistant Dean for Admissions and Financial Aid, Duke

Where students of color are concerned, I try to determine in interviews how much grit they have. Given the racism they'll face, will they do well in spite of that?   Dennis Shields, Assistant Dean for Admissions and Financial Aid, Duke

We assess maturity, interpersonal communication skills, the way they conduct themselves in a professional setting. This is more of a question for those lacking substantial or impressive work experience after graduation. Another thing we look for is leadership potential, especially for those lacking a leadership track record.   Don Rebstock, Associate Dean of Admissions and Financial Aid, Northwestern

Only ten to fifteen percent of applicants do a really good job in the interview. Perhaps 45 to 50% do an acceptable job, whereas 20 to 25% do a poor job and 15 to 20% do a truly awful job.   Don Rebstock, Associate Dean of Admissions and Financial Aid, Northwestern

COMMENTS FROM SCHOOLS NOT INTERVIEWING ON A LARGE SCALE

Our biggest concern with interviewing is that it's so time consuming. It would help weed out the few people we would just as soon not have gotten, but there are so few that it's not clear interviewing is worth the effort. For example, one recent grad had a very difficult time getting a job. He had an enormous sense of entitlement, he whined, and of course he didn't interview well. He blamed everyone around him instead of himself for his trouble. We don't get many like him, thank goodness, but interviewing might well have eliminated him.   Faye Deal, Associate Dean for Admissions and Financial Aid, Stanford

The legal aspects regarding affirmative action have all law schools thinking about the role of interviewing and other nonquantitative factors in the evaluation process.   Jean Webb, Director of Admissions, Yale

If we could interview the way the Business School does, it would be great, but it would also require more than doubling the staff here, among other things. Joyce Curll, Assistant Dean for Admissions and Financial Aid, Harvard

Part **III**

ON THE ROAD
TO LAW SCHOOL

13

RESPONDING TO WAIT-LISTING, DENIAL, AND OTHER DISAPPOINTMENTS

— EXECUTIVE SUMMARY —

To optimize your chance of being accepted from a wait list,
bring relevant new material to the attention of the admissions office.

■

When reapplying to a school, start by understanding the reasons
for your initial rejection.
—Recognize that you will need to address these deficiencies
to warrant reapplying.

If you have followed our suggested approach, you have applied to six to ten schools. Only one or two of them are in the "likely" category and several others are very likely to turn you down. Prepare yourself for rejection by some of your choices. (In fact, if you get into every school, perhaps you have not aimed high enough.)

Nonacceptance comes in many forms. You may be put on an administrative hold, wait-listed, told to apply again at a later date after you have remedied a specific deficiency, or just rejected outright.

Your reaction should depend upon which of these categories applies and which school is in question. If one of your stretch schools says no, for example, you will probably react differently than if one of your likelies says no. Do not overreact, however, to any single school's decision. The vagaries of the admissions process and the differences between schools mean that one school's decision has limited predictive value in terms of what another school will do. (This is one of the reasons that we suggest applying to so many schools.)

RESPONDING TO AN ADMINISTRATIVE HOLD

An administrative hold means that the school was unable to make a decision on your candidacy within the typical four to eight weeks, so your application will be held over until a later (often, significantly later) date. This suggests that your candidacy is strong, but the school will not know if you are quite strong enough until it has seen more of the applicants.

Take the opportunity to send a short note reaffirming your interest in the program if the delay is scheduled to extend for more than about a month. If you have strong new information available—such as a promotion or a published thesis—by all means, communicate it to the admissions office.

RESPONDING TO WAIT-LISTING

Being wait-listed generally means that you will be admitted to the program only if someone who has been accepted chooses not to come. In fact, schools know that a certain percentage of their admittees will choose other schools or decide to wait a year or two, so they routinely admit more students than they can actually take. The "excess" number admitted, however, is often not sufficient to make up for all those who decline admission. The wait-list is used to manage this situation.

There is an exception to the general rule that a wait-listed candidate will only be admitted if a space in the class opens up. Some schools wait-list candidates they suspect will choose to go to another school. By so doing, the schools eliminate the likely impact on their "yield" statistics—the percentage of people who, having been accepted, actually enroll at the school. (Managing a school's yield is part of playing the rankings game—controlling the school's admissions statistics to get the highest possible *U.S. News & World Report* ranking.) The strongest candidates to the school, along with those whose personal ties or academic interests point to another school, are thus likely to receive wait-list treatment.

Do not despair if you happen to fall into this category. For one thing, schools that play this game are delighted to find that they have been overly cautious and that you actually want to attend their school. By communicating to them that you do indeed wish to attend their school, you are likely to be admitted forthwith. For another, by wait-listing you even though your credentials are strong, the school has indicated that it believes you will get into another top school.

The trouble with being wait-listed is that you may not get off the wait list and into the school until very late in the game. It is not uncommon for schools to call people on the wait list only days before the program's start or, indeed, some days after the start. The lower down the candidate preference (ranking) list a school is, the more it is at the mercy of the wait-list decisions made at other schools, and thus the later it makes its own final decisions. Schools atop the list, such as Harvard, Yale, and Stanford, in effect make the first moves in this game. When they take people off their wait-lists, many of these accepted candidates withdraw from the schools they would otherwise have attended (and at which they had already put down deposits). This second group of schools then goes to their wait-lists, causing the third group of schools to lose some of their accepted candidates. This ripple effect does not conclude until classes are underway in the fall.

Your situation will be complicated by the fact that law schools will give you no indication as to where you fall on the list. In fact, most schools do not rank wait-list candidates. This is because admissions officers realize how many variables will not come into play until later in the game. There is no way for them to accurately assess how many—and which types of—wait-list applicants they will need. Depending on the initial yield, the wait-list may not even be tapped at all. In another scenario, law schools may find that they are "short" in one particular category of student (say, economists or international students) and utilize the wait-list only to fill in such gaps. Another reason wait-lists are not ranked has to do with the priorities of the wait-list candidates themselves. Many will be accepted at other schools and drop completely out of sight. Admissions officers are often uncertain as to how many wait-list candidates are still actively interested.

It is for precisely this reason that you, as a wait-list candidate, must not remain silent. By making yourself a presence to the Admissions Committee, you dramatically increase your chances of being one of the lucky few they "tap" in June, July, or August. As you are likely to continue to augment your list of responsibilities and accomplishments during this lengthy waiting period, you should communicate them to the admissions office.

The information you will want to impart to the admissions officers might become available at different times. Thus, it is acceptable to send them more than one update for your file, but it is wise to limit your contact to two (or three) instances, unless you know for certain that they welcome your constant attention. Find out from the school at which you are wait-listed how it suggests you carry out your contact—whether it wants to receive one or two notices from you or whether it enjoys continuous updates and inquiries from its wait-listed students.

What information will be relevant to this process? How should you communicate your new information? Any new information should show you to be even more the dynamic leader, thoughtful and mature decision maker, and so on, that the earlier chapters showed you how to portray. The one thing that makes your task easier at this point is that, having gone through all of the applications, you probably have a pretty good idea of where your applications were weakest and thus what sort of new information would be most helpful to your case. Knowing where your applications were initially weak means that you can be clever about bolstering these weak points in the months between the initial application and your follow-up communiqués. For example, if you know that one weak point is that your involvement in community and/or extracurricular activities has been virtually nonexistent, there is no time like the present to expand them.

A sound strategy, whether or not you have dramatic new information available, is to send a short letter to the admissions committee that provides any useful additional information you have—and that also restates why you think you would be a valuable contributor to their program, and emphasizes that you still very much wish to attend it. When a law school goes to its wait-list, it wants to be able to make one call per available spot and fill that spot. It does not want to have to contact ten people to find someone still hopeful of attending that school. Neither does it want to have to track someone down, so be sure that you remain readily contactable throughout the summer.

ADMISSIONS DIRECTORS DISCUSS THE KEY ISSUES CONCERNING WAIT LISTS

THE ADDITIONAL MATERIALS YOU SHOULD SUBMIT WHEN WAIT-LISTED

Most helpful are additional letters of recommendation that add to the picture of the applicant.　Jean Webb, Director of Admissions, Yale

Wait-listed applicants definitely should interview if they haven't already. They should also submit a letter of interest, detailing as clearly as possible why they want Northwestern. Additional recommendation letters seldom help because they tend to be pretty redundant. Consider retaking the LSAT in June; we have admitted several applicants due to significant score improvements.　Don Rebstock, Associate Dean of Admissions and Financial Aid, Northwestern

Sometimes I'm swayed by information about what competitors you got into. (We do like to beat them!) Of course, we check this if it's hard to believe, so don't lie to us.　Admissions Director who wishes to remain anonymous

It's helpful if a wait-listed applicant submits a new recommendation that covers recent months.　Elizabeth Rosselot, Director of Admissions, Boston College

If they are seniors in college, for example, we want all their final grades, especially on a senior project, which is, after all, the capstone of a program.　Jean Webb, Director of Admissions, Yale

THE NEED TO STAY IN TOUCH

Write us to show that your file is still "alive," that you are still pursuing admission. Fill us in on any new information pertinent to your candidacy.　Jim Milligan, Dean of Admissions, Columbia

A letter can be very helpful. If we put someone on the list in March and haven't heard from them, we assume they're happy with their situation. When it comes time to pull people off the list, we really focus on the people who've kept in touch.　Anne Brandt, Director of Admissions, Vanderbilt

You have to be positively proactive in your follow-up.　Kip Darcy, Director of Admissions, Hastings

THE IMPORTANCE OF YOUR DESIRE TO ATTEND THEIR SCHOOL

The reasons for wanting to attend Michigan are important. I like to know if someone really wants to come here. This is especially important for candidates on the wait-list, because some stay on it just to get the decision even though they've already decided they'll go elsewhere. Of course, you must be honest about this and not send letters to five schools saying "you are my first choice." Erica Munzel, Director of Admissions, University of Michigan

If your top choice has wait-listed you, inform the school that it is your first choice and that you will unquestionably come if admitted.   Jim Milligan, Dean of Admissions, Columbia

I suggest that you send us a fax or note every three weeks or so. It's never a bad idea to help us understand your continuing interest in attending USC. We review each wait-list candidate periodically, and take into account any new information.   William Hoye, Dean for Admissions, USC

New information is less important than other things:

—Make sure that we know how and where to find you during the summer, even if you are on the road or vacationing. We don't have three weeks to wait to hear from you.

—At that point, we are trying to gauge the level of interest of fifty applicants we are having trouble tracking down. Find a way to let us know that Georgetown is your number-one choice (assuming that it is true). We want to make twenty offers to get twenty students, not sixty offers.   Andy Cornblatt, Assistant Dean for Admissions, Georgetown

No law school wants to extend several offers to fill each remaining spot during the late spring or summer, because it negatively affects their acceptance rates and yield ratios and, as a result, their selectivity profile in the rankings world. And all schools want to enroll students who have manifested a sincere and particular enthusiasm for enriching their community.   Jim Milligan, Dean of Admissions, Columbia

Wait-List Timing

Once we come to August, it's valuable to know that someone will come immediately, without question.   Shelli Soto, Dean of Admissions, University of Texas

It's particularly useful to keep in touch with us—and show that you remain available—at the end of the summer, when things happen quickly but most candidates cannot actually arrange to attend.   William Hoye, Dean for Admissions, USC

Schools have a different sense of time than the candidate does. Serious wait-list activity for us occurs near the start of school. Candidates give up on the process by then, but should stick it out. We're playing musical chairs at this point. Many candidates deposit at more than one institution; summers are the time things are sorted out. We're like the airlines deciding how much to over-book. The closer we get to the time the plane takes off, the more we know about who'll board the plane.   Elizabeth Rosselot, Director of Admissions, Boston College

THE WAIT-LIST NUMBERS GAME

We used to offer 150 to 200 people places on our wait-list; perhaps 125 to 150 would stay on it. Now our goal is to have an active pool of 100 to 125. In recent years we have taken from zero to twenty, most often zero.   Jean Webb, Director of Admissions, Yale

We often accept between a quarter and a half of those we wait-list, but sometimes it's zero and other times it's one hundred percent.   Shelli Soto, Dean of Admissions, University of Texas

We have two wait-lists, our priority list and our regular list. In an average year, 450 to 500 are offered places on our priority list, and twenty-five to fifty are admitted from it. Similarly, 200 are offered places on our regular list, and ten to twenty admitted. Of course, the numbers admitted from our wait-lists vary dramatically from one year to the next.   Andy Cornblatt, Assistant Dean for Admissions, Georgetown

We invite from 200 to 300 to be on our list. We have accepted between ten and fifty in recent years.   William Hoye, Dean for Admissions, USC

We usually have about 300 on the wait list; in recent years, we have accepted between forty-five and fifty.   Don Rebstock, Associate Dean of Admissions and Financial Aid, Northwestern

Last year, we took almost one-third of those who stayed on the list (120+ of 400+). For those on the wait-list, their choice between the day (full-time) and evening (part-time) programs matters because we are trying to get to our target numbers for each. Consequently, if we are looking to add to the evening program we won't take someone who wants to attend the day program.   Robert Stanek, Director for Admissions, George Washington

In recent years, we've had about 150 ask to stay on the wait-list. We cut the list down throughout the summer as the class firms up. At the end of the summer, we might have twenty left on it in case we have to go to the wait-list during the first week of class. (In some years we've taken as few as zero, in other years as many as twenty.)   Faye Deal, Associate Dean for Admissions and Financial Aid, Stanford

RESPONDING TO DENIAL

The first thing to do when confronting a denial is to ask yourself how significant it really is. If you have already been accepted by a school you favor, the rejection is truly insignificant. If this is a school you very much wish to attend, however, a different reaction is appropriate.

The first step is to analyze why you were rejected. You may already know the reason, of course, if you were aware of one or two specific aspects of your application that were likely to keep you from being admitted. If you are not sure, you can always contact the school's admissions office to get their views on why they rejected you. The schools most likely to inform you are the smaller ones that have relatively fewer applications. Schools are most receptive to such inquiries during their slow periods—late spring and summer.

Beware, however, of what even these very helpful schools will say. They will address only substantive matters and will not comment on the actual application. They will not say, "Your essays were so sloppily written, and you revealed yourself to be so arrogant and insensitive, that we never want to deal with the persona you portrayed." For an understanding of the application itself, check it against the relevant chapters and examples of this book and ask an appropriate, objective person to do the same. (Or, call one of us at *Degree of Difference.*)

A school that is willing to discuss your rejection is doing you a real favor, so be ultra-polite in dealing with them. If you are defensive or hostile, which are natural reactions to being told you are less than perfect, you will elicit less useful information from them than you might have if you had been appreciative and welcoming of their inputs.

SHOULD YOU EVER APPEAL A DENIAL?

If you have no truly dramatic new information to bring to the table, do not raise your blood pressure and that of the admissions committee by appealing a rejection. Admissions committees go to great lengths to give applicants a sympathetic reading of their files—with even the most marginal file being read by at least two and often three people—so you can count on the school's having considered your application material fairly.

Some schools, on relatively rare occasions, will be willing to reconsider an application based upon presentation of important new information. If you have such information and wish to appeal, contact the admissions office and explain the situation. See whether they will entertain an appeal. If so, be sure to present convincing new information, reiterating that you do wish to attend this school and will contribute greatly if admitted. (If you are not absolutely certain that this is your number-one choice, do not even consider putting busy admissions people to the trouble an appeal will involve.) Recognize, however, that the odds against being admitted will be very long indeed.

ADMISSIONS DIRECTORS COMMENT ON APPEALS

We have a standard reconsideration process available to people. We have an admissions committee member who hasn't read that specific file look at it. In almost every case the original denial is reaffirmed. Al Turnbull, Dean of Admissions and Placement, University of Virginia

Although it is possible to appeal a rejection, only one percent of the time does it turn out to be worthwhile. If something truly significant has changed since applying, it is possible to turn a rejection into a wait-listing (never an acceptance). Don Rebstock, Associate Dean of Admissions and Financial Aid, Northwestern

---

SHOULD YOU REAPPLY IN THE FUTURE OR SETTLE FOR A LESSER SCHOOL?

Some schools are good enough to tell you that they would be happy to have you reapply if you improve your LSAT score or show that you have benefited from work experience and additional courses in areas pertinent to law study. This is generally a sincere comment on their part, so take it at face value.

The question of whether to reapply is of course a complicated one. If you got into one of your top choices, you might wish to attend it this year, instead of waiting, on the chance that you will get in next year to your very first choice. The situation is more difficult if you got into your eighth choice, but none of your first seven choices. If you realistically think you will be a stronger candidate in the near future, then it might be a good idea to wait and reapply with your improved credentials.

The important thing here is to analyze in what way you will, or could, be a stronger candidate. Cast a critical eye over your file. Look at it from the perspective of this book, analyzing each component fully. Was the component a relative strength or weakness for you at School X, given what the competition was probably like? If it was a glaring weakness, can you do something to improve it? Chapter 7 analyzes in detail what you could do to improve your credentials. If the fault in your application was not the application itself, but your credentials, consider what strategy you will employ to improve them. Ask yourself whether a successful effort will significantly change the nature of your candidacy. Also ask yourself whether you are being realistic in thinking that you can do what you are contemplating.

ADMISSIONS DIRECTORS DISCUSS REAPPLICATIONS

DEBRIEFINGS

If an unsuccessful applicant writes us between June and September, we will discuss the strengths and weaknesses of their files. Don Rebstock, Associate Dean of Admissions and Financial Aid, Northwestern

We do offer a debriefing regarding what was lacking in an application. In most cases, however, a failed applicant can understand where they failed by looking at the profile grid. Al Turnbull, Dean of Admissions and Placement, University of Virginia

I try to help counsel them, especially regarding reapplying. Of course, it's rarely just one thing that was lacking in their application. William Hoye, Dean for Admissions, USC

DOES A REAPPLICANT START WITH A BLANK SLATE?

Reapplicants do not have to overcome a prior application: they simply face a blank slate. Rick Geiger, Dean of Admissions, Cornell

We come to reapplicants' files fresh. We hold the prior files for two years. A reapplicant must supplement his or her file with another letter of recommendation and a statement of what they've done in the meantime. Al Turnbull, Dean of Admissions and Placement, University of Virginia

When looking at a reapplication, we use the original application to help us focus on what has changed in the meantime. For example, perhaps there has been a change in job, title, responsibilities, etc. We keep old files on applicants for three years. Reapplicants should interview if they didn't last time. Don Rebstock, Associate Dean of Admissions and Financial Aid, Northwestern

We don't pull the old application; we just start over from the beginning of the process. Shelli Soto, Dean of Admissions, University of Texas

The decision we make on your file this year has no bearing on future decisions. Most people, however, don't do anything to change their applications. Edward Tom, Director of Admissions, Boalt Hall (Berkeley)

WHAT MUST A REAPPLICANT DO TO SUCCEED?

There are three ways to improve your chances. You need to transform yourself or your application—or apply earlier in the process. Andy Cornblatt, Assistant Dean for Admissions, Georgetown

Sometimes success is just a matter of restructuring and improving the application itself. Typical ways of doing so are adding an improved résumé or including some optional statements and keeping "explanations" for weaknesses or failures out of the personal statement. Shelli Soto, Dean of Admissions, University of Texas

Reapplicants who succeed the second time tend to be those who improved their LSAT scores substantially or have another year of grades to show us—and the grade-point average went up substantially.   Michael Rappoport, Dean of Admissions, UCLA

Reapplication is certainly possible, but it is interesting how few people make major changes to improve their chances. Perhaps five people in this year's first-year class are successful reapplicants.   Don Rebstock, Associate Dean of Admissions and Financial Aid, Northwestern

We receive many reapplications, but few reapplicants have substantially improved their credentials in the interim. Admissions committees are relatively consistent in their judgment, so people who haven't improved their candidacies will again be denied.   Elizabeth Rosselot, Director of Admissions, Boston College

It is rare to go from a "no" to a "yes," not so uncommon to go from wait-list to a "yes."   Andy Cornblatt, Assistant Dean for Admissions, Georgetown

Then consider the application itself. Did you write polished, persuasive essays? Do you have reason to doubt that your recommenders wrote assertively and well on your behalf? If you interviewed, did it go well? If the answer to any of these questions suggests that you have an opportunity to improve your application substantially, what will you do to make the improvements? Are you being realistic in thinking that you will put in the necessary time and effort?

Do not be lazy if you choose to reapply. Rewrite your personal statement(s) and other essays to take advantage of your performance since your initial application, in light of what you have learned was wrong with that application. Consider using new recommenders, based upon their knowledge of your recent performance. If you use the same recommenders, have them rewrite their recommendations, incorporating new information about you to the extent possible.

OTHER OPTIONS

If schools that you want to attend have rejected you (for the moment), do not give up on getting a law degree. If you seriously want a law degree, there are probably a number of schools that can help you meet your needs. Most people who have investigated schools carefully, including those who produce the school guides and rankings discussed in Part I, sincerely believe there are 50+ quality law programs in the country. So even if you applied to an unrealistic set of schools this time around, cast your net a bit wider or reapply to schools you narrowly missed this time.

For those of you who are positively determined to attend your preferred schools—and cannot be convinced to go elsewhere—there are a few other tactics you may wish to employ. The following chapter will discuss them in some depth.

14

TRANSFER AND OTHER OPTIONS

— EXECUTIVE SUMMARY —

If you do not get into one of your top choice schools, consider:
—Transferring to one of your top choices after a year at another law school.

—Attending a foreign law program for one or more years.

—Becoming an exchange student or third-year matriculant at one of your top-choice schools.

—Taking advantage of law schools' reciprocity policies to use another school's career services facilities.

Come summer, you may find that you have been rejected by all of the law programs from which you had most hoped to hear positive feedback. Although this is hardly an ideal situation to be in, there are still several paths—*other than waiting to reapply for entry into the first-year program*—by which the determined applicant can reach her goal: to benefit from the resources of a top program.

TRANSFERRING FROM AN INSTITUTION WHERE YOU *HAVE* BEEN ADMITTED

Each year, the top law programs' admissions offices receive applications from law students wishing to transfer to their institutions. Some of these students have discovered that they are unhappy with their current program—for reasons including unsatisfactory curricula, career services, or location—or have simply realized that their ultimate goals have changed. Most, however, are simply hoping to attend a school with a more impressive reputation than the one at which they first enrolled.

Until recently, most schools took in very few transfers. They did so only to "top up" their second-year classes, to make up for the (minimal) attrition from the first-year class. As the sidebar chart suggests, some schools still operate in this fashion, but others do not. Many top schools have determined that they can profit from a policy of accepting substantial numbers of transfer students—up to 10 percent of their second-year classes. There are several important reasons for these schools' changed policies. There are always some applicants for the first-year class who have substantial strengths but also present substantial academic question marks. These applicants can transform themselves into very attractive candidates, without such weaknesses, upon highly successful completion of a year of law school. Another reason for the schools to have changed policies is that transfer students' GPA and LSAT numbers do not count in the *U.S. News* rankings. Thus, schools can get students whom they value highly (due to their work experience or personal characteristics, for instance) without having to pay a price in terms of their median GPA or LSAT numbers (and thus their *U.S. News* rankings). In addition, transfer applicants function as the ultimate wait-list: Schools can use transfer students to determine in what way they wish to adjust a class's composition after its first year.

	RECENT TRANSFER NUMBERS			
	NUMBER APPLIED	**NUMBER ACCEPTED**	**PERCENT ACCEPTED**	**PERCENT OF 1ST-YEAR APPLICANTS ACCEPTED**
UC Berkeley (Boalt Hall)	200	30	15	18
Columbia	90–100	20–25	c. 25	19
Duke	50	5	10	28
Georgetown	120–130	40–50	c. 36	26
Michigan	70–100	25–30	c. 32	36
Northwestern	85–90	20	35	18
Pennsylvania	65–75	5–15	14	29
Stanford	150	5–10	5	12
Texas	40–70	10–12	20	33
Virginia	80–90	23	27	29
Yale	80–120	10–15	c. 13	8

EVALUATING TRANSFER APPLICANTS

Schools examine one or more of the following when evaluating transfer applicants:

- First-year law school grades
- Quality of the law school
- LSAT score(s)
- Undergraduate performance
- Rationale for transferring:
  —Professional/academic
  —Personal
- Work experience, extracurricular and community pursuits, and so on; i.e., the rest of your file

All schools consider first-year law school grades (better stated as your rank in class) to be the single most important criterion when evaluating transfer applicants. Some, in fact, consider nothing but this one item. Some consider the quality of the law school at which you earn those grades, but others, remarkably, do not.

Some schools take into account one or more of the other criteria listed above. Thus, some schools will consider you in much the same way that they would have (or did) when you first applied to law school. They will consider your undergraduate performance (grades, grade trend, strength of curriculum, quality of school, and so on) as well as your LSAT score. They will also evaluate your professional experience to date, and so on.

Other schools will evaluate your reasons for wishing to transfer. Some demand that you have a professional or academic reason for doing so. For instance, you may have decided that you want to practice international tax law but your current school offers no courses in this, whereas your target school offers several. Other schools care little about such professional interests and require instead that you have personal reasons for wishing to transfer. One such reason would be that your spouse will attend the medical school of your target law school's university, thus requiring that she move to its location.

CHOOSING THE SCHOOL YOU WILL TRANSFER *FROM*

If you intend to go to law school only if you get into a top school, you may wish to avoid over-committing to law at this stage. If you have (or can obtain) a fine job, consider attending law school part time. This will allow you to continue to make money, bolster your nonacademic résumé even as you are attending classes, and even to out-work your classmates for top grades (given that few attending part-time programs will be particularly concerned about maximizing their GPAs). If you decide that law is not for you, or if you do not fare well enough in GPA terms to transfer into a top program, you can walk away from the field without having suffered unduly. After all, your career will not have been on hold and you will have sharpened your reasoning, writing, and research skills while developing some substantive knowledge of law.

If your situation lends itself only to a full-time program, you are faced with a difficult choice. On the one hand, you can select a much lesser school in the knowledge that it will be easier to rank in the top 10 percent of a weak class than of a strong class. This will make it easier to get into schools that consider rank in class of paramount importance. The problem with this is that you risk being saddled with the weak school on your résumé if you fail to transfer to a stronger school. On the other hand, you can opt for the best school you have gotten into. In this case, your chances of finding your way to the top of the class will be diminished, but your résumé will not be a disaster if you end up graduating from this school.

In general, if you feel that you are good enough to merit acceptance at the top schools, you should be able to get top grades at any (lesser) school. Thus, you are likely to favor attending the strongest school to accept you.

RULES FOR PLAYING THE TRANSFER GAME
ONCE YOU ARE IN LAW SCHOOL

➤ Get the most out of your first year.
—Your rank in class will be critically important, so do all that you can to maximize it. (See chapters 15 and 16 for discussions of how best to do so.)
—Be sure to impress two professors deeply, particularly those teaching you in smaller courses or multiple courses. You will want each of them to write highly detailed recommendations about your dynamic class performance, marvelously researched and written papers, and sterling exam. Put your discretionary time into preparing for their classes.
—Pick up any academic awards that you can. For example, moot court at many schools is regarded as something of a chore by most students, but it offers a fine opportunity to bolster your legal résumé.

➤ Analyze your target schools.
—Make sure they admit sufficient numbers of transfer applicants to warrant your efforts.
—Speak with their admissions officers to determine which criteria they employ in evaluating transfer applicants. Do so at the appropriate time— when they are least busy. If you applied for first-year admission, contact them the summer following your application. If you are going to be applying to the school for the first time as a transfer, discuss matters in late spring (when first-year applications have been largely wrapped up).

➤ Analyze your appeal to the school.
—Are their criteria consistent with the profile you can present? For instance, if you have a strong professional reason for wanting to transfer to Boalt Hall, but Boalt values only personal reasons for transferring, you may need to reconsider whether it should be atop your target list.
—Examine information about the first-year class when it becomes available. This will help you to see how you can position yourself to fill gaps and holes in a class's composition.

➤ Upgrade your credentials as appropriate.
—If your target schools will consider your LSAT score(s), you may wish to retake the exam.
—See the discussion in Chapter 7 regarding how to improve your other credentials.

➤ Market yourself according to the advice in this book's second section (chapters 7 through 12).
—Emphasize in particular the work you have done in your first year of law school.
—Emphasize any professional or academic reasons for wanting to transfer. (See Part IV for a sample transfer essay and our critique of it.)

—Do not underestimate the importance of your personal needs. When writing your transfer personal statement, do not hesitate to address personal reasons for your desire to transfer to School X. If, for instance, your spouse is transferred to a location in the vicinity of your dream school—and a long flight from the one you are currently attending—be sure to bring this to the attention of the admissions officers.

➤ Be prepared to wait for an answer on your transfer applications until late in the summer after your first year.

—Schools do not make decisions about transfer applicants until they have second-semester (third-quarter) grades available. As a result, expect to hear no earlier than mid-summer whether you have been admitted.

➤ Recognize that this is a policy area in flux.

—Many schools are likely to increase the number of transfer students they accept. Schools in the midst of such a change are likely to be temporarily easier to get into than would otherwise be the case.

—Most schools are likely to change their admissions policies to a substantial extent over the next few years. For example, fewer schools are likely to consider only first-year law school performance in evaluating transfers. (Schools are likely to make a full file review the standard.) Make sure you know what each school *currently* considers relevant.

Several factors, however, may shift the balance in your decision of what school to attend for your first year:

■ Consider the criteria employed by your likely target schools. If most of them emphasize the quality of law school attended, go to the best school you can. If they do not place much weight on this factor, however, you may still wish to consider a lower-tier option.

■ If you have an inexpensive state school nearby or near where you wish to locate, by all means consider the financial aspects of your decision. In this case, your target transfer schools will understand the financial reasons for your choice of a less-than-stellar initial law school.

■ A school that has one or more very small first-year classes (15 to 30 students, say) makes it easier for you to get to know and impress at least one professor than a school that features only classes of 100 or more. (This will make it easier to get a strong, detailed professorial recommendation when you do your transfer application.)

■ A school that has very limited offerings in an area that is likely to interest you may give you an academic/professional rationale for looking to transfer. (Of course, you will need to show that you discovered this interest after your initial applications to law school.)

PREPARE BEFORE LAW SCHOOL

The importance of your first-year grades and other aspects of your law school performance means that you should do everything possible before school starts to get a jump on the process. See Chapter 15 for a thorough discussion of how best to do so.

Ultimately, it will be up to you to use and adapt the marketing skills you have already learned in this book and apply them to your second application process. All sorts of unpredictable factors may make you a desirable transfer student. If a school yielded an unexpectedly low number of students in a particular category—female students, black students, or students interested in public service, for example—they may see you as a way to boost their poor statistical showing. Use this to your advantage.

ADMISSIONS DIRECTORS DISCUSS TRANSFERRING

EVALUATIVE CRITERIA

A very low LSAT or undergraduate grades, relative to our pool, will still raise questions, especially if the law school isn't particularly strong. First-year law school grades, however, still tend to dwarf these considerations. Jean Webb, Director of Admissions, Yale

Our emphasis is upon how well they've done in law school. We look for stars in other law schools. Our assumption is that they want to move up, not that they are looking to do a specific program. Faye Deal, Associate Dean for Admissions and Financial Aid, Stanford

The eighty-percent weighting given to the LSAT and undergraduate GPA (for regular applicants) is filled by academic performance in the first year of law school. We look for students in the top five percent of their class, or better; we also take into account the quality of the law school attended. Al Turnbull, Dean of Admissions and Placement, University of Virginia

The LSAT is useful only to predict law school performance, so when you have actual law school performance, you ignore the LSAT and pay attention to the law school grades. Doing outstanding work in the first year of even a weak law school program will suffice.   Robert Stanek, Director for Admissions, George Washington

It's important to show why you want to be at Yale Law School, other than our being ranked highly.   Jean Webb, Director of Admissions, Yale

First-year grades and recommendations from their law schools are by far the most important credentials. The LSAT is much less relevant at that point. Andy Cornblatt, Assistant Dean for Admissions, Georgetown

We don't emphasize the LSAT or undergraduate GPA as much as the first- and second-term law school GPA.   Edward Tom, Director of Admissions, Boalt Hall (Berkeley)

GENERAL COMMENTS

Most law schools are now accepting more transfer applicants. They are very enthusiastic members of the community.   Andy Cornblatt, Assistant Dean for Admissions, Georgetown

Ten percent of our second-year class consists of transfers.   Jim Milligan, Dean of Admissions, Columbia

We get from eighty to one hundred twenty transfer applicants and admit ten to fifteen. The number admitted doesn't depend upon attrition in the first-year class. In fact, we want a critical mass of transfer students because they become a sub-group of their own.   Jean Webb, Director of Admissions, Yale

We're not looking to fill empty seats, just to get quality students.   Shelli Soto, Dean of Admissions, University of Texas

We accepted twenty-three out of eighty or ninety transfer applicants last year. Ten years ago we only took five or six, because we were just filling vacated places. Now we are willing to go beyond that.   Al Turnbull, Dean of Admissions and Placement, University of Virginia

We like transfer admits, including those who were turned down the first time. Prove to us that you can do the work and we are happy to accept you. We love it when someone comes back and says, "See, I told you UCLA should accept me." We look at how they did in their law school work rather than the things that kept them out in the first place.   Michael Rappoport, Dean of Admissions, UCLA

Many of those who apply are residents who failed to get into Virginia initially and went instead to Richmond, George Mason, or Washington & Lee for their first year.   Al Turnbull, Dean of Admissions and Placement, University of Virginia

They have the chance to prove, via their first-year grades, what they asserted in their initial applications—that their undergraduate grades and LSATs don't represent their true abilities.   Jean Webb, Director of Admissions, Yale

BEGIN A DEGREE ABROAD

If you are not accepted at a top program of your choice, rather than attend an American law school, you could study law abroad for a year (or more). This could be done in a Commonwealth country, such as England, which enjoys a common law heritage similar to that of the U.S. Or you could study in a very different legal system such as the civil code system of Western Europe and Latin America. (The American system is slowly shifting to incorporate more of the civil code system, just as the civil code systems are incorporating more of the common law approach. Although the two systems are coming closer together, the differences remain marked.)

Studying law abroad offers you the chance to show that you are definitely interested in law. It also gives American schools a set of highly relevant grades to examine to determine whether you are academically up to snuff. In addition, you can add to your admissions profile by learning about a foreign legal system and culture.

As the study of law becomes more and more global, American law schools have placed a higher value on foreign legal study. This can work to your advantage in the admissions game. Note, however, that there is tension between the goal of maximizing your admissions opportunities and getting credit for prior work done.

If you choose to study in a common law system, you will have more limited uniqueness value when it comes time to apply to American programs. (For example, a not insubstantial number of Rhodes, Marshall, Fulbright, Rotary, and other scholarship winners go to England to study law and then enroll in American law schools.) Yet at the same time, it is fairly easy to receive credit for up to one year of course work done abroad due to English (and Commonwealth) common law's similarity to American law.

On the other hand, if you choose to study in another system, such as a civil code system, you will have more uniqueness value when you apply to American programs because such study is less common. (It generally involves studying in a language other than English, making it difficult for many potential applicants to pursue.) The result is that you will improve your admissions chances substantially, but risk not getting credit for as many courses as you might have had you studied in a common law setting.

Studying abroad will appeal most to those who are likely to have a substantial international aspect to their practice. The list of practices involving such an international dimension continues to increase. No longer do just a few people at New York or Washington firms, or working for the State Department need (or wish) to understand foreign law. Even in family law, formerly a true backwater,

---

STUDYING LAW IN BRITAIN

A Bachelor of Laws, the law degree in Britain, is a three-year program. Although the program is geared to prepare students to practice law in England, many of the first-year "common law" courses are similar to American first-year courses. (Foreigners often do just one or two years of study, intending to learn about law but not necessarily wanting to stay the whole three years.) The first year at The London School of Economics, for instance, features these courses:

➤ English Legal System

➤ Public Law

➤ Law of Contracts and Torts

➤ Introduction to Law of the European Union

➤ Property I

   The tuition for LSE, as with other leading British schools such as Oxford and Cambridge, is about $10,000 less expensive than tuition at private law schools in the U.S.

---

there are now attorneys who specialize in divorces for those whose spouse lives abroad or is a foreign national, just as there are attorneys whose practice is devoted to child custody cases involving spouses domiciled abroad. Others who will be attracted to foreign legal study include those who wish simply to have the opportunity to live abroad for the period of study.

   The tuition for foreign schools—not just British schools—is generally substantially less than tuition for American programs.

TRANSFERRING TO AN AMERICAN PROGRAM AFTER A YEAR OR TWO ABROAD

Most American law schools require that those studying law abroad apply for admission as a first-year and, once admitted, petition for advanced standing. The Dean or a faculty committee will evaluate your individual case and decide for which courses to give you credit. (A few schools, including Yale, do not give credit for work done abroad.) Obviously, this can be a slightly risky undertaking, depending upon the policies of the school you ultimately attend. The school in America, after having seen your exemplary performance at a prestigious school such as Oxford, may *admit you*—but may not give you a full year's credit. Check your target school's policies and determine how recent admittees with similar backgrounds have been treated before assuming that your foreign course work will receive full (or any) credit.

**ADMISSIONS DIRECTORS DISCUSS
STUDYING LAW ABROAD**

If someone had done a BA in Law at Oxford, my heart would sing if he/she wanted to do a JD at Penn. He/she would get advanced standing, too, and probably only need two years for the degree.   Janice Austin, Assistant Dean for Admissions, University of Pennsylvania

Those who go abroad to do law in England, such as at Oxford, apply to become first-year students here, but they can get up to one year of credit for a two-year program abroad (and thus graduate from Virginia in two years).   Albert R. Turnbull, Associate Dean for Admissions and Career Services, University of Virginia

We do not give course-for-course credit for those who just did a year of legal study abroad. The only people granted credit are those who do full law degrees: they can get up to one year of credit.   Jean Webb, Director of Admissions, Yale

Doing law in England after your bachelor's degree can help you in two ways: It shows seriousness of purpose and it also gives us a set of relevant grades that will be a factor used in making the admissions decision.   Elizabeth Rosselot, Director of Admissions, Boston College

---

COMPLETE A DEGREE ABROAD

There is another approach available to those intending to study law abroad. You can complete a degree abroad, which will typically take about three years, then apply to an American program for an LLM degree, which can be finished in one year. With an LLM you can practice in some, but not all, states. (See Appendix IV in Chapter 8.)

When it comes time to get a job, however, it may be difficult to convince a top firm, company, or agency that your education stacks up to that of your competition. If your law degree is from a well-known, highly regarded foreign school, you will reduce this risk somewhat. Similarly, if your performance at the American program is compelling, you may make it easier to get a top job. (Some LLM programs require that LLM students do course work separate from JD students. This will work against you. Try, instead, to compete directly—and successfully—with JD students, who are, after all, your competition for jobs.)

This approach to getting a job in the U.S. is so risky that few candidates should consider it. Only those who are likely to practice in both countries, or are considering practicing primarily (or exclusively) in the foreign country, are likely to profit from this.

AN ALTERNATIVE APPROACH

Some foreign law schools permit their students to do a year abroad (and receive full credit for it). This opens up the possibility of doing two years abroad, then a third year in an American JD program—and then an LLM degree at this or another American law school. Doing two years in an American program will basically eliminate the problem of being taken seriously by leading American employers. (Many serious observers of the American legal scene believe that law school need not be more than two years, anyway.) As a result, this approach should appeal to a substantial segment of those intending to become well-versed in international law or hoping to have a practice that focuses on more than one country or region.

PARTICIPATE IN AN EXCHANGE PROGRAM OR BECOME A THIRD-YEAR MATRICULANT

Each year a small number of law students study for one or two semesters at an institution other than their own. The courses they take are credited towards the degree they will receive at their "home" institution. This can be done in one of two ways: as an exchange student or as a "third-year matriculant." A number of schools have established official exchange programs with each other (the Harvard–Berkeley Exchange is one notable example), thereby allowing students at one to take courses at the partner school. The other option is to become a third-year matriculant at a leading school. Most of the top schools permit a handful of third-year matriculants. Columbia, for example, accepts five to ten visiting students each year.

BENEFITS OF BECOMING AN EXCHANGE STUDENT OR THIRD-YEAR MATRICULANT

Job opportunities. Attending a prestigious law school for your second or third year is an excellent way to gain access to recruiters who otherwise might have passed you by. At most schools, exchange students are allowed to use the Career Placement tools, programs, and facilities. Although prospective employers will no doubt notice that you will be receiving your degree from a school other than the one you are now attending, your résumé will nevertheless be substantially enhanced. You can expect prospective employers to take notice if you perform well at the stronger institution.

The improvement in your job prospects may also be a matter of the school's location. If you want to get a job in Chicago but are currently attending a school in Kansas, doing a year at Northwestern could obviously improve your contacts with your desired job market.

Access to influential professors. The professor in your taxation seminar probably will not know—or care—that you are an exchange student or third-year matriculant. Use this to your advantage. Build professional (even personal) relationships with influential professors: Impress them in class, do outstanding papers and exams for them, and so on. If you outperform the students from this school, you may well be able to get recommendations, job referrals, and other professional assistance.

The possibility of getting a degree from your target school. At several schools, there is a tiny loophole that allows some hard-working, ambitious exchange students to earn bona fide degrees. Taking a double load of courses, and thus getting approximately two years' worth of course credit in your one year, may entitle you to a degree from this school rather than your home school. The chances of pulling this off are slim, indeed, but a few people have managed it.

MAXIMIZING YOUR CHANCES

Admission to a prestigious law program as an exchange student or third-year matriculant is highly competitive. Although to some extent dependent on the fluctuation of student body size, your chances of admission will rise dramatically if you can show the committee that you have a genuine need to be at their particular school. Committees are not often swayed, however, by your declaration that you must attend their school because they are the only program on the planet to offer an Abused Animal Clinical Program. They are more likely to treat your application favorably if you demonstrate the necessity of your being in Chicago or Philadelphia or New Haven, rather than your need to attend Chicago, Penn, or Yale Law School. The reason could be a family illness, a spouse's personal situation, or anything else that would have a serious effect on the way you live your life.

AN ADMISSIONS DIRECTOR DISCUSSES
THIRD-YEAR MATRICULANTS

About thirty to forty people apply for five spots. We only admit people with a compelling need to be here. That does not mean a specific kind of law that we offer courses in; it's much more on the personal side, such as having a spouse transferred.   Edward Tom, Director of Admissions, Boalt Hall (Berkeley)

USE ANOTHER LAW SCHOOL'S CAREER PLACEMENT OFFICE

Nearly every ABA-approved law school in the country allows law students from other programs to use its career services facilities (but not to take part in the on-campus recruiting of its students). The practice, referred to by Career Services Directors as "reciprocity," can be useful—especially for those students attending lower-tier schools.

Each school's policy differs slightly from the next. The more rigid policies adhere to a quid pro quo, one-to-one basis. In order for a student at Wisconsin to use the Career Placement office at Harvard, for instance, there must be a Harvard student with a desire to use Wisconsin's. This seems to be a rule that is honored more in the breach than in the observance, however, at least as long as the number of students requesting such service at the given school remains small.

The majority of top law programs are quite generous in granting reciprocity. Many of them, officially or unofficially, have "open-arm" policies. They may state that you will not be allowed to use certain tools, such as the job bank database—but in practice this is often unenforced.

Factors to be aware of:

- Some schools grant reciprocity only to law school graduates, *not* to current law students. This presents a problem, of course, if you are in your first year at School X and are dying to access the career placement office at School Y in order to get a summer job.

- Some schools will not grant reciprocity during the busy months of their on-campus interviewing program.

- A general rule is that students cannot use services of a school within the same area as the one they are currently attending. A George Washington student, therefore, will not be permitted to use Georgetown's career placement office.

15

WHAT TO DO ONCE YOU ARE ACCEPTED

— EXECUTIVE SUMMARY —

Consider deferring law school,
especially if you are not absolutely certain that law is for you

■

Take the necessary steps to reserve your place at your chosen school.

■

Leave your job in a professional manner.

■

Do all that you can to be ready for law school. At a minimum:
—Upgrade your writing skills.

—Learn how to take law school exams.

—Gain a solid understanding of several first-year courses.

■

If you have additional time, upgrade your knowledge in other areas as well.

Two things should be true if you have followed the advice of this book. First of all, you have applied to law school in the knowledge that you are headed in the right career direction. You analyzed your own interests, goals, and talents, and considered them in light of what a career in law involves. Second, you have applied to an appropriate range of schools—and did so in a professional manner. As a result, you now have one or more acceptances in hand.

If both of these are true, you are ready to head to a fine school—so skip the next section concerning "deferral" unless you have a question about when you should attend, now or in the future. On the other hand, you may want to reconsider the whole idea of law school. If so, read the following section with care.

DEFERRAL

Once you have been accepted to one of your top choice schools, you need to decide how to handle the offer. Before sending in your deposit, consider whether you should attend school now, or whether you would be better off postponing it for one or more years.

The majority of schools have generous deferral policies, in part because they recognize that many people who apply to law school should not attend. These policies, however, are by no means uniform. At some schools, it is simply a matter of making your request in a timely fashion. (This basically means applying for a deferral in the spring rather than the summer.) Some other schools grant only a set number of requests, often in the order in which they are received. As a result, the timing of your request may be all important. At still other schools, you will be granted a deferral as long as your reason for wishing one is not regarded as frivolous.

Your reason can be either a personal or professional matter. Gaining a prestigious scholarship for study abroad would certainly suffice; so, too, would the opportunity to manage an important project. Given that your value to law schools and employers will generally increase with development of your skill set and experience, consider carefully what you stand to gain via an opportunity. Most applicants who defer—even for frivolous purposes, frankly—end up glad in retrospect that they did so. On the personal side, taking care of a dying parent would pass muster, as would other, less dramatic matters.

Different schools place the bar you must get over at different heights, so be sure to inquire of your chosen school exactly what its standards are. There are, moreover, a handful of schools that rarely grant deferrals. These do not penalize you, however, if you choose to reapply in the future.

ADMISSIONS DIRECTORS DISCUSS DEFERRALS

How Readily Do You Grant Deferrals?

Columbia automatically grants deferments to all admitted applicants requesting them. Also, we allow prospective students to request a deferment up until July 1, enabling them to have months to carefully consider pursuing other learning and professional opportunities before beginning law school. Moreover, our prospective students can request and be granted deferments for one or two years and we allow them to extend or curtail the length of their deferment, as their circumstances change, as long as they inform us of their revised plans on a timely basis (during February or March).   Jim Milligan, Dean of Admissions, Columbia

We grant one-year deferrals in nearly one hundred percent of cases. For a two-year deferral, we require a structured experience requiring two years: financial analyst, consulting research analyst, Peace Corps, master's degree.   Jean Webb, Director of Admissions, Yale

We generally don't offer deferrals. On the other hand, we don't hold their failure to attend against them if they reapply.   Michael Rappoport, Dean of Admissions, UCLA

We grant only a limited number of one-year deferments—about thirty a year. You should have a LSAT/GPA above the average of the prior year's class, and you should have a good reason.   Kip Darcy, Director of Admissions, Hastings

We only want to enroll people who are ready for law school. In addition, we don't want to lose control of our admissions process. Our standards can change from one year to the next. We give a deferment only if a file is strong enough that even if our applicant pool increases dramatically next year the person would still get in. If someone is denied a deferment and reapplies, we do give substantial preferential weight to that prior admission. In practice it is extremely rare to turn away someone previously admitted; it happens only when standards go up substantially due to the increased size and quality of the pool. Albert R. Turnbull, Associate Dean for Admissions and Career Services, University of Virginia

We're at the liberal end of the spectrum in our willingness to grant deferrals, except for those admitted off the wait-list (because if the applicant pool is a bit stronger the next year it's unclear whether that person would get in). For a one-year deferral, a candidate should write us to tell us what they'll be doing the next year. Anything more than one year, however, is unlikely to be granted. Shelli Soto, Dean of Admissions, University of Texas

For What Purposes (and When) Do You Grant Deferrals?

I'm usually fairly generous, until about June 1. I'm generous with people who have some amazing academic opportunity. If they just want to go to Europe to play, I'll think twice, although I may still grant it. Personal reasons, of course, may also come into play.   Edward Tom, Director of Admissions, Boalt Hall (Berkeley)

We grant two types of deferral requests: for employment opportunities and for personal or family issues the applicant needs to deal with. The request should be made by June. By the way, we strongly prefer that people take time off to get real-world work experience, so having a younger applicant wish to defer to take advantage of a solid job opportunity strikes us as quite sensible.   Don Rebstock, Associate Dean of Admissions and Financial Aid, Northwestern

We are very flexible in granting one-year deferrals, as long as we know by about July 1. After that date, we are a bit tougher. More than one year is a different matter. We'd consider granting a longer deferral for a serious scholarship, but in general, the longer the deferral people want, the less likely they are to come. In fact, only one-half of deferred applicants eventually come.   Andy Cornblatt, Assistant Dean for Admissions, Georgetown

May Deferred Applicants Apply to Other Schools?

We require students to sign a deferment contract, in return for our guaranteeing them a place in a future entering class without requiring them to reapply for admission. The deferment contract stipulates that they are not allowed to apply to any other law school while holding a Columbia deferment. They are allowed to apply to other graduate or professional degree programs.   Jim Milligan, Dean of Admissions, Columbia

We preclude deferred applicants from applying elsewhere during the interim. We don't use deferrals to let a person keep an option open while considering whether law school (or USC) is the right choice for him.   William Hoye, Dean for Admissions, USC

Applicants granted a deferral do not need to agree to forego applying to other schools during their deferral year.   Shelli Soto, Dean of Admissions, University of Texas

Deferred applicants must agree not to apply to other schools in the interim. Andy Cornblatt, Assistant Dean for Admissions, Georgetown

General Comments

Applicants should not apply fully intending to defer their enrollment if they are admitted. Their application may in fact be stronger if submitted in a subsequent year.   Kenneth Kleinrock, Assistant Dean for Admissions, NYU

If you are not entirely certain that law school—and the practice of law—are right for you, by all means defer. If you are unable to defer, trust that you will be able to gain admission again in the future if you so choose—and turn down the offer of admission. *Do not attend law school unless and until* you have ascertained that it is the right career move.

ACCEPTING YOUR OFFER

If you do not face any questions about whether and when to attend law school and you are accepted by your top choice, be sure to send in your deposit to reserve your place in a timely manner. If you are accepted by one of your secondary choices before you have heard from your number-one school, you may face a dilemma if you are required to send in a deposit immediately. Most schools have become so quick about responding to applications, however, that this quandary is no longer common. If you do encounter it, ask the school that has accepted you whether you can delay sending your deposit for a short time, and also ask your first-choice school to speed up its decision making, explaining the situation politely. It is probably wise to refrain from mentioning what your alternate school is, especially if it is of obviously lower caliber or is a very different kind of program.

The one time when this is still likely to be a major problem is if you are accepted by a secondary choice and wait-listed by your first choice. You may not get off the wait-list, or be definitively turned down, until the start of school. You may have to send in a deposit to your second choice, risking losing it if you are eventually accepted by your first-choice school.

International Students. As soon as you have chosen the school you will attend, begin the student visa process. This means getting a Certificate of Eligibility (I-20) form from the school, which verifies that you have the appropriate credentials, language skills, and financial resources to attend the program. This form, along with the accompanying financial documents, must be submitted to the local U.S. Consular office to request the actual visa. This process is all too often delayed by either the school or the consular office, so it is important to begin it as soon as possible.

LEAVING YOUR JOB

Leaving your current job may fill you with joy, sadness, or a mixture of the two. No matter which, it is important to resign in a highly professional manner.

Once you have decided to leave, step carefully. Do not pop into your boss's office and wax ecstatic over your new-found freedom. Instead, think about how much notice you should give. You will obviously give at least as much as is called for in your employment contract. Whether you should give more depends upon a balance of several factors:

■ Are you likely to be regarded as a traitor or spy or bad influence? If so, you may not be welcome; you may be ordered to clean out your desk immediately.

■ How difficult and time-consuming will it be to transfer your knowledge and responsibilities to a replacement? Must you be the one to train your replacement?

—If you will be involved in an in-depth training process, you may want to leave enough time to provide the appropriate support.

■ How has the company treated others at your level who have resigned?

■ What is your relationship with your boss?

—If your boss is truly reliable, perhaps you can tell her in advance of an official announcement in order to give her time to make appropriate adjustments, without jeopardizing your paycheck.

■ Does your company know that you have applied to law schools?

—If so, you should tell them sooner rather than later.

■ How much do you want to continue working?

—If you would just as soon have more time off before starting school, you do not need to worry about being dismissed too quickly.

RESIGNING

Schedule a meeting with your boss on a Friday afternoon, so that she will have the weekend to reconcile herself to your decision. Explain what you have gained from your job and from her. Think in terms of what you have learned about your industry, analytical aspects of your job, written and oral communication skills, and so forth. Then explain why you are going off to get a law degree. (If your boss wrote a recommendation for you, all this can be done briefly, of course.)

To leave the best possible impression, be sure to:

■ Complete any pending projects.

■ Turn over all your files, with detailed explanations regarding how you would suggest your replacement proceed.

■ Train your replacement yourself, if possible.

■ If you have people working under you, give them one last review.

■ Ask for a concluding review of your own performance, assuming that your boss is not angry about your leaving.

■ Consider mentioning what aspects of your position vis-a-vis the company could be improved, but only if you think your boss would be pleased to receive this input.

■ Consider scheduling a telephone call with your replacement one week after she starts work to help her out (and volunteer to call a second time at her discretion).

■ Make every effort to stay on good terms with your former colleagues. Remember that they may well be your future recommenders or clients.

FINISHING COLLEGE

If you still have a few months left of your last semester, do not assume that it is harmless to neglect your courses and party the rest of your time away. Make sure you graduate with the best grades possible, particularly in key classes—those that demand substantial research, analysis, and/or writing. It is not unlikely that, during your search for summer employment after your first or second year of law school, a prospective employer will examine your undergraduate grades along with your first set or two of law school grades. B's and C's in your last term of college give a very different impression to employers than do straight A's. An exemplary record throughout college demonstrates you are self-motivated, that you always give your best. If you have the chance to make phi beta kappa or graduate summa cum laude, do your best to achieve this. Furthermore, get any departmental prizes you can.

If you have a full semester of college left, be sure to take courses that will help you in law school. These include: intensive writing courses, courses in your expected field (Accounting if you are considering Tax Law, Ecology if you are considering Environmental, and so on), and courses that would allow you to complete a second major. Write a thesis or major paper that will give you credibility in the future; in order to enhance your visibility—and your credentials— see if you can get this published in a journal or scholarly magazine, or even a local newspaper.

In addition, start thinking about your future career. How can you best utilize your school's services, organizations, and alumni to get a leg up in advance? Discuss the areas of law you are most interested in with your Career Office's

Dean or pre-law advisor, if there is one. Contact alumni who have attended the law school at which you will matriculate; focus on the ones who practice in your area of interest. These people are a gold mine of networking possibilities. Tell them that you will attend school X in the fall, and that you would love to chat with them about the world of family law or intellectual property law or whatever. When it comes time to search for your first-year summer job, these will be extremely useful contacts.

Think about joining organizations that may be useful to you in terms of developing specific skills. Participating on the debate team, for example, may assist you in conquering some of your fears about the Socratic Method. If another senior is slacking off in the presidency of a relevant organization, volunteer to take over. Approach a professor with whom you have developed a good rapport and find out if she needs any assistance for an article she is working on.

PREPARING FOR LAW SCHOOL

RATIONALE FOR STARTING THE PROGRAM WELL PREPARED

If you are ambitious enough to seek a top law degree, you are probably also eager to do well in the program.

The easiest way to do this is by starting the program well prepared. The student who is poorly prepared will find it difficult to succeed. The poorly prepared student is highly likely to struggle in the crucial first term and barely get through the first set of courses. The redemption process is not likely to start, if ever, until after the core courses have been completed. Only at that point will he be able to compete on somewhat equal ground with other students.

At that point, however, it may be too late to retrieve the situation entirely. After all, the students who performed well initially have been piling up points with professors and students, demonstrating over a lengthy period of time that they are capable analysts and persuasive advocates. This will be reflected in the summer job offers to students. These often lead to permanent offers (i.e., offers for employment upon graduation from law school). In any event, these initial jobs have an impact upon how other law students, professors, and potential future employers perceive you. As if this were not bad enough, at many law schools membership in the law review is partially or totally dependent upon first-year grades.

Starting law school well prepared will not only contribute to a stronger first-year performance; it will also alleviate—if not eliminate—the overwhelming level of stress that takes hold of most 1Ls and refuses to let go.

TRADITIONAL LAW SCHOOL TEACHING ADDS
TO FIRST-YEAR TROUBLES

Many of the top law schools have long been a bastion of poor teaching, especially in first-year courses. Although there are some truly notable exceptions—and some schools are now working hard to improve—the following discussion focuses on the type of institution that a sensible applicant would do well to avoid. Unfortunately, there are still too many schools that meet this description.

At these schools professors operate as if their incoming students are already masters of the material the first-year curriculum purports to teach. Professors plunge immediately into the minutiae of case analysis without ever giving an overview of the course. In fact, they go further in keeping their first-year students in the dark: They wage a campaign to keep them from reading the type of outline and overview material that would reveal the nature and structure of the subject.

The reasons for this are simple. Lawyers were traditionally taught by this case-based, "hide the ball" method. Another, critically important reason, is that teaching in this way is very easy. A professor need only achieve a reasonable familiarity with the courses she chooses to teach; teaching these is very simple insofar as only the professor knows on which items she will focus. The result is that the professor comes across as god-like, without having to put in substantial effort. Furthermore, it is easy to play the traditional Socratic game. Whenever a student poses a question, for example, the professor is ready with the time-honored reply: "I don't know, what do you think?"

Part of the reason for this situation is that top schools have traditionally felt it beneath them to teach "black letter" law. To avoid being considered trade schools, they have tried to teach something grander, at least in the first-year curriculum. Thus they emphasize public policy or "learning to think like a lawyer." This leads, amongst other problems, to professors taking absolutely no responsibility for whether or not students learn the subject. After all, what matters most is not learning the specific subject, but the zeitgeist. Thus, there is no objective way to determine that a given professor has failed to communicate, no appropriate way to judge the professor's teaching effort.

There are several reasons that this situation has continued as long as it has at these schools. Professors have no incentive to devote substantial effort to their teaching. Tenure decisions at top schools are based upon publishing, first and foremost, along with the clients a professor lands, or the publicity he or she garners. Professors need to impress their colleagues rather than the youngsters in the class, both to get tenure and to be respected by those they themselves respect. Nor do schools compete on the basis of teaching quality (as opposed to their unsubstantiated claims about teaching quality). Actual teaching quality has very little impact upon their recruitment of students or professors. It is interesting to note to what extent business schools differ in this regard. The most significant business school ranking is done by *Business Week,* which uses only two criteria for the rankings. One of the two is student ratings of their own business school experience, especially the teaching. Not surprisingly, business schools devote considerable effort to teaching well. Many have new professors team with the best veteran professors so as to learn as much as possible about teaching—and about teaching their specific subject. Those professors who are given low ratings by students are likely to be forced to watch other, better teachers. Those who do not improve sufficiently are unlikely to be given tenure. Law schools, with rare exceptions, have not devoted this level of effort to improving teaching.

The final irony is that one of the great moments for many law students comes when they study for the bar exam after graduation. When taking their bar review courses, these students actually learn each subject (for the first time). This learning occurs in a tiny fraction of the time the students put into studying those same subjects in law school. (Of course, it may be just a coincidence that bar review courses are marketed largely on the basis of student learning, as measured by bar exam pass rates.)

THE ELEMENTS OF GOOD PREPARATION

Learning the law school game is difficult if you have to master every element at one time. You need to learn, among other things:

- Legal writing (of case briefs, memoranda, moot court briefs, and exams)
- Substantive law in a host of fields
- Legal reasoning—i.e., what is relevant and what is not
- Legal research methodology
- A new vocabulary
- How to survive classroom confrontations with professors (when they hold all the cards and, in some cases, believe that threatening you with public humiliation is the hallmark of the caring professor!)

Far better for you if you have familiarized yourself with substantial parts of this game before you have to play it for real.

SKILLS: THE BARE MINIMUM

LEGAL WRITING

Writing is essential to the careers of most lawyers. It is certainly critical to law school performance. Despite this, very few people are good writers when they enter law school. This is as true for the English literature majors as it is for the engineering majors. Frankly, most law schools do a poor job of teaching students to write, despite the schools' protestations to the contrary. Even if they did teach writing well, there is no reason to enter the program as a particularly weak writer. No improvement in writing skills before you enter the program will be wasted.

You have two ways to go about this. First, you can develop your general writing skills. If you are not yet a strong writer, be sure to put in the necessary work before law school. Consider taking a writing course, or a copyediting course, at your local university's extension division. Whereas a writing course will have you doing your own writing, a copyediting course will force you to analyze, critique, and edit other people's writing. Either approach can be very helpful. The key is to take something rigorous.

Second, once your writing is at an appropriate level, you can take a course in legal writing. Harvard Summer School, for example, offers a course called "Legal Writing," described as follows in the course catalog:

> This course is designed for law students, students considering law school, or writers who wish to improve their analytical writing. It is based on the assumption that good legal writing communicates well-considered ideas clearly, concisely, and accurately. Students use the elements of good writing to construct legal arguments, to argue from precedent and principle, and to use facts effectively. They draft a variety of basic legal documents that may include a case brief, a complaint, an answer, an opinion letter, a legal memorandum, and a statute. Course materials are based on contemporary social issues drawing on the areas of constitutional due process, criminal law, domestic relations law, and the right to privacy.

TAKING LEGAL EXAMS

In law school, although other types of writing matter, exams are of ultimate importance. During the first year, in particular, your grade for an entire course will be based solely on the end-of-the-semester exam. Because law school exam performance is so vitally important—and woefully neglected as a part of teaching—you should prepare in advance for it. Some of the general legal writing courses of the type described above may show you how to play the law school exam game. (The UCLA extension course "Writing for Law School," for example, focuses as much on writing legal exams as it does on other types of legal writing.) If you are unable to take such a course, however, consider one of the following strategies during the months prior to matriculation:

Attend an exam-writing seminar. Various companies offer seminars on the skills needed to do well on legal essay exams. You can attend their seminars or buy their seminar tapes. It is actually wiser to buy the recorded tapes because you can listen to them at your own pace, and repeat them as appropriate. These seminars and tapes demystify the all-important law school exams and identify the methods needed to conquer them.

Attend a law camp. Recently, several companies have begun to offer five- to ten-day programs intended to immerse students in all aspects of law school. The structure of the programs is modeled after a first-year curriculum, and the courses are taught by law school professors. These "boot camps" are very expensive affairs (often $2,000 or more) but provide good training in many areas, including that of the essay exam.

SUBSTANTIVE LAW IN A HOST OF FIELDS

So much for the preliminaries; now let's look at the substantive core courses. The key here is to avoid shouldering a full slate of courses for which you are not adequately prepared. If you have no preparation in the basics of at least several of them, you will be in for a tough time. Be sure you have gained a very solid overview of at least two of the fall courses. There are several ways in which you can prepare.

Enroll in a bar review course. Bar review courses are designed to prepare law school graduates to pass the bar exam. More than half of the preparation is devoted to the first-year material, which the bar exam tests heavily. Many of the better bar review courses allow you to enroll for their courses while you are in your first year of law school for a small down payment (approximately $50). You receive a book of outlines for all the subjects you will study during your first year and are allowed to attend the lectures that pertain to first-year subjects. This will consist of approximately ten classes, each two or three hours in length. Additionally, you are permitted to attend the Final Exam Lecture Series. This is a very sensible method of preparation; you will begin law school having already become familiar with each of the first-year subjects. Many of these courses allow you to use tapes of the lectures; this allows you to do the work when your schedule permits. Yet if you are in an area where your chosen course is running at times convenient to you, consider going to the lectures. You will start to soak up the law school atmosphere and law student attitude by being immersed with those facing the bar exam itself. This will likely spur you to greater effort in your own studying.

Read overview materials. One good option is to purchase a commercial outline. *Gilberts, Emanuel,* and the *Sum and Substance* series all produce quality products. Read only the introductory outlines, however, rather than the whole book. These introductions (ranging from 35 to 90 pages!) will provide you with a sense of the subject's structure. Reading the whole outline, totaling several hundred pages, will tend to immerse you in too much detail for your first look at a subject. Another alternative is to read the *Nutshell* books. These are, however, somewhat too long and involved to provide an easy tour of the subject, so they will work best for those prepared to devote substantial effort. You will need to read your chosen material more than once to develop some understanding of how the subject is structured, without which you will not be adequately prepared.

As described above, law camps offer training in various skills necessary for law school success. This includes legal exam writing.

LEGAL REASONING, RESEARCH METHODOLOGY, VOCABULARY, AND CONFRONTATIONS WITH PROFESSORS

The suggestions discussed above will stand you in good stead in many regards. In fact, if you follow them diligently, you will develop at least a reasonable understanding of legal reasoning, research methodology, and, as well, a substantial legal vocabulary. Taken together with your knowledge of the first-semester courses, you will even be well armed for any confrontations with old-style, difficult professors.

ADDITIONAL PREPARATION

If you have extra time, consider developing your knowledge in any of the following areas:

- Courses you will take in the second term.
- Legal research: If you want to learn more about the particulars of legal research, courses are often available at institutes that train paralegals.
- Microeconomics: Microeconomic thinking has become a standard part of the legal toolkit for discussing contracts, torts, antitrust, and a variety of other courses.
- Accounting: Anyone headed into corporate law of any sort will find accounting knowledge invaluable. The same is true, surprisingly enough, in many public interest fields.

■ Whatever will help you in your future career: If you are heading into family law, for example, any course work or reading you undertake in psychology, accounting, taxation, or finance is likely to be very helpful.

Do not undertake these additional preparations, though, until you have readied yourself for the writing you will do in law school and prepared for the (first-term) substantive courses.

**SOME PROSPECTIVE STUDENTS SHOULD
PUT IN EXTRA EFFORT BEFORE SCHOOL STARTS**

Several types of beginning law students should pay particular attention to preparing as well as possible. These include:

➤ Those intending to transfer. Given the importance of first-year grades to their chances of transferring successfully, potential transfers should make every effort to be ahead of the curve upon entering law school.

➤ Those intending to work for employers that demand top law school grades (and law review experience).

➤ Foreign students. Nonnative speakers of English obviously need to get their English language skills up to snuff, preferably by living, working, and studying in an English-speaking environment for an extended period prior to the start of law school. It is especially useful for nonnative speakers to study the material described above, to improve both their grasp of English (including in a legal context) and their understanding of the American legal system. Those raised in the American legal system, and exposed daily to various disputes arising within it, have a substantial advantage over those who assume that the American system is probably much like their own legal system.

➤ Those from weak undergraduate programs and those who are unaccustomed to doing close analysis and writing.

How to Get the Most Out of Law School

— EXECUTIVE SUMMARY —

Understand how best to manage your time.
—Learn how to study for classes and exams without investing too much time.

■

Think broadly about career development.

■

Recognize that law school is about more than class work.

■

Keep stress under control.

■

Take advantage of the networking and social opportunities.

To get the most out of law school, be ready to start working hard—and smart—from the beginning of the first class. There are three keys to this. The first, discussed at length in Chapter 15, is to be up to speed on the basics before you start classes. This means having a good overview knowledge of the courses you will take in the first semester. It also means understanding how to prepare for and take law school exams. The second key is learning how to use your time effectively. To do so requires that you ignore the traditional panic around you during your first terms at law school.

TIME MANAGEMENT IS YOUR BIGGEST RESPONSIBILITY

Law schools deliberately give you more work to do than any human could possibly manage to do thoroughly—at least not without giving up on life as human beings know it. You must learn how to prioritize your assignments. The potential work facing you greatly exceeds your time available to do it. Determine what is most important for each course and focus on precisely that, doing additional work only as time allows.

Falling behind is the biggest trap you face. If you fail to keep up, you will face ever increasing problems. Falling behind results in a downward cycle: You have trouble following today's lecture because you hadn't prepared for it, so you must do extra work to make up for your lack of understanding of the lecture, meaning that you will never have time to get ready for tomorrow's lecture, underpreparation for which will mean that even more work is required to be able to make up for your lack of understanding of it, and so on.

Time management extends to your whole law school experience. You should learn how to do your classwork efficiently, and also decide in advance how you will spend your free time. Arrange your schedule to make time for the key activities you value most highly, and limit your involvement with other matters. You might have time to participate actively in two clubs, a sport, and a volunteer group, along with attending various career services workshops and special lectures that interest you, but you are unlikely to be able to participate in six or eight clubs and play as many sports, too.

CUT TO THE CHASE

There are too many reading assignments in law school, and they are far too long, to do all of them completely and well. The key to keep from being overwhelmed is to learn how to do the essential work first, and the inessential later (or, better yet, not at all).

The typical student. To work effectively, you must learn to see the forest rather than the trees, the big picture rather than only the details. This is contrary to the way that courses are taught, particularly first-year courses. Most students, even those who have been advised by second- and third-year students to get the "big picture," lack the courage of their convictions and spend too much time on the details. They believe the professors who urge them to read the cases (and ignore the commercial outlines and such). They try to read and brief the assigned cases, and may top this up with a look at a commercial outline or other outside material. They end up overwhelmed. As a result, they sacrifice what they regard as the optional efforts—reading the outline for overall perspective and doing practice exams—in order to be able to spend more time reading cases. They work all the time and are consumed by stress.

A better approach. The better approach is a strictly disciplined one. Pick one course for which you will (try to) do the readings, brief each case, and so on. That will be more than enough practice at the traditional law student efforts. (Pay attention to how much more work this requires than do your other courses, without consequent improvement in learning.) For all of your other courses, do not read any cases. Instead, read two other outside materials. Read a canned brief of each case—a summary of the case. *Legalines* and *Casenote* are well-known publishers of such briefs. This will prepare you to follow the day's classroom discussions.

More important, read and re-read a commercial outline. These outlines, from *Gilbert, West, Siegel, Emanuel,* and so on, offer a (relatively) easy-to-understand guide to the important aspects of a subject. As with the canned briefs, they are keyed to the specific casebook you are using, so it is easy to understand which portions will be relevant to the upcoming week's assignment. Read these, and then re-read them. You should make it through the relevant section more than once before a class, and more than once in the weeks immediately after class. (Another possibility is to use a bar review outline.)

A sensible alternative. There is another sensible approach to courses for which a student outline has already been done. Check with second- and third-year students to find out whether anyone in their year produced an outline for any of your first-year courses as taught by the same professor you have. If such an outline is available, highly regarded as an accurate record of the course, and sufficiently detailed (such as 100+ pages, single spaced), feel free to rely on it as your primary source for the course. Make a copy of it to use for your daily notetaking in class. Then, at the end of each day, re-read the relevant parts of the outline and your notes, and put any notes that pass muster onto your master outline (the relatively pristine original).

The bottom line is simple: If you are putting in more than three or four hours a day outside class, you are being inefficient (and possibly wearing yourself down). Stay disciplined; working smart is more valuable than working hard. Extra time spent is unlikely to equate to better grades, just to extra time spent.

PREPARING FOR EXAMS

Take mock exams every several weeks in each course. Pick questions relevant to whatever you have already studied. Have a study partner aid you in assessing your performance; examine, too, the model answer provided by the commercial outline you are using. Doing this will serve many useful functions, among them:

■ You will become accustomed to taking law school "exams," so you will not tend to panic when you must do so for real.

■ You will learn the nature of law school exams. Spotting issues and giving a quick overview of the relevant legal standards, along with a very quick "discussion" of the relevant facts, is far different from the undergraduate exams you remember. (It is also vastly different from other graduate schools' exams.) Taking such exams calls for a different mindset from undergraduate exams.

■ You will understand that a very good overview of a course is critically important, but knowing the details of all the many cases you were assigned is of limited value, indeed. This will cause you not to get overly interested in or overwhelmed by the details of these cases, or by the desire to take excessive notes in class.

MORE EXAMSMANSHIP

Gaining a good understanding of what a professor is likely to test is a valuable skill. Consider four important sources of information:

➤ The emphasis within the course itself. Examine the amount of time devoted to each subject.

➤ Examine the professor's old exams, or ask second- and third-year students what they remember of this professor's exams.

➤ Find out what the professor has written about and is currently researching. Similarly, find out what work he or she is doing on behalf of clients.

➤ Keep an eye on the recent decisions being handed down in the field.

DO NOT COMMIT TO A STUDY GROUP
WITHOUT CAREFUL THOUGHT

Study groups are an important part of law school for many people. Yet all too often they function as a crutch for students who feel they need to maximize the effort they expend studying (rather than their preparedness to take law school exams). Before rushing to form or join a group, decide what you intend to do with one. Most people who join study groups expect to meet with the group for at least one lengthy meeting a week. They also expect to have group members produce an outline of each course and, perhaps, prepare case briefs for assigned readings. This is a major investment; do not undertake it unless you are sure this is how you wish to approach studying.

Instead, do the bulk of your studying on your own, as per the comments in the prior section. The one way in which a study group or study partner can be highly valuable, however, is in critiquing your mock exam performance. When you put yourself through such an effort, have your study partner(s) examine what you have done and suggest ways in which you could have done better. Return the favor, too, of course. Such a study partner can also be a helpful sounding board or reader whenever you need to do a moot court brief or other writing assignments.

Mock exams are available from several sources. The same publishers that offer commercial outlines and canned briefs also offer exam questions, in some cases included in these booklets, in other cases sold separately. The other source of mock exams is the school library. Many schools keep files of prior exams. If your professor's exams are on file, by all means use them. Even if the only examples are from other professors, use them as a viable second choice. Using several sources for exams will keep you from becoming too fixated on any one aspect of the subject.

THINK BROADLY ABOUT YOUR CAREER DEVELOPMENT

Presumably, one of your primary reasons for being at law school is to propel your career forward. If you do nothing other than work hard for your classes, however, you will miss a large part of what law school offers in terms of career advancement potential. Several nonacademic parts of the law school experience are ideal for career enhancement, as are specific courses. Discuss with potential future employers and the career services office which skills you should master and experiences you should gain during the program. Some suggestions:

- Take advantage of the opportunity to get to know your *classmates*. You will learn a lot from the more experienced ones, and will profit from these friendships in the future, including in your career. Staying in touch with them will provide you with important career advice and information.

- Get to know *faculty* members, especially in your chosen field. You will learn a lot more about a field if you spend time with the faculty members who are doing research in it, consulting about it, and so on. They will also be able to put you in touch with good industry sources to discuss the field and potential employers or specific job prospects. You do need to avoid the appearance of trying to cozy up to them simply to improve your grades or to benefit from their largesse without giving back as well. A sincere and active interest in learning about the field, on the other hand, will meet with a positive response.

- Join *student organizations* that are relevant to your likely future career. For example, if you are interested in environmental law, join the environmental law society. You will have a chance to get to know the other members who are themselves interested in environmental law. They will be valuable contacts in the future for information about the industry, job opportunities, and so on. In addition, advocacy organizations and the like, which involve members working on behalf of clients or causes, will give you an opportunity to practice your skills—analysis, presentation, negotiation, communication, and so on—in a relatively relaxed setting.

- Take advantage of the professional services offered by the *career services office*. Take their résumé preparation and interviewing workshops, have them tape a presentation and several mock interviews, and, most important, consult them about your career plans. Take the career assessment tests they give; have them analyze your personal and professional goals; ask for their perspectives on where you are most likely to derive both satisfaction and frustration in your chosen field. These experts are a source of knowledge you would have to pay a great deal to consult outside of law school, so be sure you do not waste an opportunity to get their input free of charge.

- Future employers will value *skills that go beyond substantive knowledge of law.* Your ability to speak in front of large groups, your negotiation skills, your writing abilities, and your knowledge of how to handle clients will, in total, be likely to have as much impact upon your future as will your technical legal knowledge. Therefore, gear your academic efforts to develop a broad range of relevant skills. Consider taking courses outside the law school to do so. In particular, look at the business school's course offerings.

■ Join the local or national *bar association*. Become active on a relevant committee if you wish to meet lawyers active in your field. In order to establish yourself as knowledgeable about your field, contribute to the association's periodical. You have an opportunity to develop your skills and reputation along with your Rolodex (Palm Pilot) without anyone viewing you as a potential rival (yet).

■ Join the local or national *industry association(s)* relevant to your field. For example, if you are a biotech person, joining a relevant biotech association will give you access to people throughout the industry. You can join a relevant committee or help out in some other way. Note, too, that it is particularly easy to get published in most relevant industry periodicals. If you are clever, you can develop relationships with those who will be your future clients (or employers). It is notoriously hard for young associates in law firms to develop their own clientele. This is one way to start the process and get ahead of the game.

■ For those expecting to practice in the same area as the one in which the law school is located, make contact with *practitioners* in your field. Local alums are likely to be the most receptive to your advances. Even before you start school you can solicit their advice regarding which courses and professors to take, what special skills are most likely to be in demand, and so on. If you keep in touch with them as your law school career progresses, you may well find them offering you part-time work, or keeping you in mind when others are looking for help. They will also be helpful after you graduate, when having a strong local network will be of great value to you.

THINK SPECIFICALLY ABOUT YOUR CAREER DEVELOPMENT

Potential employers will compare you with other members of your class, and those at comparable law schools. Before committing yourself to an all-consuming effort to get top grades (and be editor-in-chief of the law review)—which will generally come only at the expense of most of the other benefits and pleasures law school can offer—figure out where you want to go and what it will take to get there. Talk with the career services professionals to determine what GPA, course selection, extracurricular pursuits, and so on will make you an attractive candidate for your chosen (type of) employer. If you intend to work for a major corporate firm, for example, you will need to get better grades than if you intend to open your own firm (where your GPA will be next to irrelevant). But even the most grade-conscious employers do not look just at grades, so make sure you understand how the rest of the package you offer will work for or against you.

The optimal mix of courses, grades, extracurricular pursuits, prior work experience, part-time work experience in law school, and other skills will vary by field. For example, a Ph.D. (in addition to a JD) may be considered all but essential to teach antitrust at a top law school, whereas it may be considered nearly valueless in other arenas. Similarly, being a law review editor will be of great value in going the corporate law firm route, but of modest value in many other contexts. For instance, if you want to practice family law you are almost certainly better off making good connections in the field in your chosen city of practice than writing a law review note.

The better you understand in advance of attending law school what you hope to do afterwards, the better able you will be to chart your law school course effectively. Consider very carefully what will most benefit you in light of your choice of legal field and employer, as well as your background and interests. The following chart looks at where people with different career interests might put their efforts. This is, of course, a very rough-and-ready view, meant more to highlight the fact that people headed in different directions will be wise to emphasize different matters during law school than to prescribe specific activities. In fact, within any field (including those below) there will be substantial variations regarding the specific practice desired, and, as a result, the most appropriate mix of law school efforts. For instance, within the "family law" category, George may want to do international child custody work whereas Martha might want to represent clients in financially complex divorce cases. George will need to take international litigation courses as well as those covering child custody. He may want to take child psychology courses if he has not yet done so. He will also benefit from perfecting his second language, and should consider doing a term or more of legal study abroad. Martha, on the other hand, would benefit little from these courses. She will, instead, focus on developing as much knowledge as possible about accounting and finance (in addition to the typical divorce, litigation, and mediation subjects). For example, she will want to become knowledgeable about forensic accounting—the tracking of assets.

How to Spend Your Energy in Law School, Given Your Specific Career Goals

Activity	Maximize GPA	Law Review	Other Publication	Courses Outside Law School	Local Contacts	Student Organizations	Clinical Courses	Cultivate Relationship with Professors(s)	Part-Time Work
DESIRED EMPLOYMENT									
Litigator (Large corporate firm)	++	+					++		
Family Law (Small specialist firm)			+	+	+	+	+		(+)
Law Professor	++	++	(+)		+	+	+	++	
Public Interest	+	+	+ (public interest focus, preferably specific to desired field)		+	+		(+)	+
Start Own Firm					++		+		++

(+) Potentially important
+ Important
++ Very important

NETWORKING

One of the most valuable assets you will have upon graduation is your network of contacts from your JD program. This network can help you to get jobs and even, through knowing whom to call for information and assistance, help you in your current job. The key to building an appropriate network is of course to make friends, avoid making enemies, be more cooperative than competitive, and impress as many people as possible. The impression you should make is of being clever, hardworking, a great team player, dependable, sensible, and comfortable working under pressure. In other words, your performance at law school will have a major bearing upon the network—as well as the skill base— you develop. Do not go to extremes in trying to network, though, because people trying to curry favor rather than develop relationships will always run the risk of annoying people.

The networking opportunities law students are most likely to overlook, however, are not those within the law school, but those outside: alums, local practitioners (and judges), businesspeople (who hire lawyers), business school students (who will soon be hiring lawyers), and so on.

KEEP STRESS UNDER CONTROL

The first months of law school are loaded with stress. You will probably be in an unfamiliar environment, surrounded by people you do not know, and be expected to produce more work faster than you ever have before. In addition, you may be competing with people of a higher quality than you have ever encountered before. This, combined with your high expectations for your own performance, can generate tremendous pressure.

Such pressure can be good or bad. Pressure can motivate you to work hard in a focused fashion. On the other hand, too much pressure can paralyze you and leave you unable to work or concentrate.

To avoid being overwhelmed by stress, *be aware of the signs.* If you feel panicked about not meeting your goals, or enraged about what is being asked of you, or you are feeling the physical symptoms of stress (such as digestive problems; compulsive consumption of food, alcohol, or cigarettes; or tightness in your neck and shoulders), you may well be suffering from excessive stress.

Then *recognize what is causing your stress.* This is likely to be a combination of two things. First, you are demanding too much of yourself. You are expecting to read each case down to the minutest detail, and be able to respond correctly to each and every interrogation in class. You are also probably expecting to get through the whole program without falling flat on your face a few times. Be realistic; disappointments and mistakes are a normal part of the learning experience. Second, you are failing to appreciate that law school programs deliberately give you more work than anyone can do in the time available.

This can be a rotten combination. You need to learn, as noted earlier, how to digest the important elements of courses without wasting unnecessary amounts of time on them. You must carefully and firmly prioritize what you will do and what you will skip.

In addition, keep your everyday life under suitable control:

- Get regular exercise. Pick a sport you enjoy and devote half an hour or an hour to it at least five days a week. This will provide you with a suitable outlet for your anxiety, anger, and frustration.

- Eat properly. Too many late-night pizzas, or burgers wolfed down minutes before class, will eventually sap your energy and health.

- Get a reasonable amount of sleep, and make sure that once a week you get an extra couple of hours to help make up for your overly-demanding schedule.

- Last, do not let yourself be bothered by trivial annoyances. Learn to kid around with someone about the sillier aspects of your existence, including those that rile you despite their being not worth annoyance, let alone anger. For example, if you are cut off by a driver on the way to school, it is not worth screaming and yelling at him just because you are not suitably relaxed. The more such occurrences bother you, the greater the cumulative level of stress you will feel.

DON'T FORGET THE SOCIAL EXPERIENCE

Get involved in school life. Join several clubs, participate in a sport or two, and get to know your classmates and your professors. If you are married, involve your spouse in as many activities as possible, because it will enrich your experience to be able to share it with someone who truly understands what is involved, and he or she will enjoy the time rather than resenting your new and all-consuming lifestyle.

17

FINANCING YOUR LAW DEGREE

— EXECUTIVE SUMMARY —

Calculate the full cost of a law degree.

■

Consider your options in terms of programs and financing alternatives.
—Schools' aid policies differ dramatically, giving you opportunities
to save a lot of money.

—There are many financing strategies available, but few are realistic
unless you start working on them early in the process.

■

Do not leap to attend a program just because it will save
you money in the short run.

—Law school should be considered a long-term investment:
Look for the best value, not the cheapest option.

Going to law school is a very expensive proposition. Those attending the leading private schools without grant aid can expect to spend over $125,000 for their three years. Even those attending a public school such as the University of Michigan—and paying resident tuition—may spend over $100,000. These figures represent the *direct costs* of the program, but the indirect costs are also important. The *opportunity cost*—or money foregone—is the amount of money you could have earned had you continued working (or begun to work) rather than going to law school. Similarly, if your spouse has to take a lower paying job or change careers, this also represents a potentially substantial opportunity cost.

Despite the size of these sums, the financial consequences of attending a *well-chosen* top school suggest that it can be a very good investment. It has been an extremely good investment historically, and looks to be an even better investment at the moment (given the massive increase in private sector starting salaries).

The question of how you will finance your law degree is nonetheless of critical importance. Whereas the minutiae of filling out financial aid forms is beyond the scope of this book, this chapter will examine the major financing strategies you can employ consistent with your career choices.

CALCULATING THE COST OF LAW SCHOOL

The financial aid you will receive for law school is based upon a simple formula:

Cost of Law School – Expected (Family) Contribution = Financial Need

The cost of attending law school is hardly a mystery. Schools are quite good about providing applicants with information about the cost of attendance (based upon the experiences of their current students) in the application materials they send out. For instance, Duke's 1999–2000 academic year budget for a single student was:

Tuition	$25,500
Hospital Insurance	778
Health Fee (mandatory)	444
Duke Bar Association Dues	60
Government Dues	19
Activity Fee	50
Transcript Fee (one time only)	30

Rent/Room	4,200
Food	3,400
Books/Supplies	1,200
Miscellaneous	2,500
Transportation	1,050
Total	**$39,231**

This estimate will not necessarily be a totally accurate one for you, of course, depending upon such things as how luxuriously you intend to live during law school, how many times you intend to visit home (and how much it will cost for each visit), and so on, so be sure to alter the bottom-line figure to reflect your personal circumstances.

In general, the direct cost of attending a school will depend mainly on its tuition rate, the living expenses in the area, and your chosen lifestyle. Annual tuition and fees can range from about $7,000 to more than $26,000, with the top private schools all charging at the high end of that range. Other costs (housing, food, books, personal expenses, etc.) for a single student can range from $10,000 to more than $16,000, as estimated by the schools themselves. Married students, and those with children, will pay proportionately more. A quick look at two public schools and one private school reveal the range of expense involved:

	TEXAS	BERKELEY (BOALT HALL)	NYU
Resident Tuition and Fees	$7,498	10,864	
Nonresident Tuition and Fees	$15,478	20,668	27,540
Total Budget: Resident	$18,598	24,914	
Total Budget: Nonresident	$26,578	34,718	45,950

As is readily apparent, the total may be as little as $18,000–$20,000 or as much as $45,000 (or more) per year.

YOUR EXPECTED (FAMILY) CONTRIBUTION

HOW YOUR CONTRIBUTION IS DETERMINED

The "sticker price" of law school is one thing; the amount you will actually have to pay is another. You may be given a grant (scholarship), loan, or work-study assistance. Before handing out any money, however, both the law schools and the federal government—the most important sources of financial aid for law students—calculate what they will expect you to contribute.

The law schools expect you to get whatever government loan aid is available before they will kick in any funds themselves (except, in some cases, when they give out merit grants, as discussed below). Thus, the first question is what the *federal government* will lend you. Federal government lending is based upon its calculation of your financial need, which it determines through the use of the Free Application for Federal Student Aid ("FAFSA"; available at www.fafsa.ed.gov), which you may recall from your college applications. Your expected contribution will be calculated by looking at your assets (including bank accounts, home equity, automobile, and so on) and income. Your spouse's assets and earnings are included in these calculations. Annual federal loans up to $18,500 are available—depending, of course, upon your demonstrated financial need.

What if you need more than you can get from the federal government? Law schools still are not ready to help; they expect you to get *private loans* next, from banks or other lenders (see below for a list of possibilities). *Law schools expect you to take on anywhere from $21,000 to $25,000 in annual loans before they will give you need-based grants.* The first $18,500 will come from the federal government, the remaining thousands from private lenders.

Finally, after you have accessed the federal and private loans up to the ceiling amount expected by the particular school, you may qualify for law school grants. Now it is the turn of the *law schools* to assess your expected contribution. They follow much the same approach as the federal government, albeit with two significant differences. First, in many instances they also assess your parents' ability to pay. (In assessing your parents' ability to contribute, however, they are not mandating that your parents pay out any money. Instead, the schools will subtract your parents' expected contribution from what they consider your financial need, allowing you to try to borrow or earn that amount if you so choose in place of having your parents contribute.)

Second, the schools also require an additional application form for their own financial aid. The most commonly used form is the Financial Aid PRO-FILE, developed by the College Board (available at www.collegeboard.org). The other commonly used form is the Need Access application (available at www.accessgroup.org). Both of these operate in a similar fashion: You fill out the form and pay them to send it to your designated schools. As with every other aspect of the financial aid process, be sure that you proceed in a timely fashion. It can take up to one and a half months for these organizations to get your form to all of your schools.

RUN MOCK FAFSA, PROFILE, AND NEED ACCESS CALCULATIONS

The intricacies of the FAFSA, Profile, and Need Access calculations are beyond the scope of this book. Instead, you are urged to gather the information necessary

THE LOGISTICS OF APPLYING
FOR FINANCIAL AID

Apply early for aid. For some schools, fund limitations dictate that financial aid be granted on a first-come, first-served basis. This means that if you submit your forms even a month before the deadline, you may find yourself without much assistance. This is often the case for grants, yet can also be true for need-based loans. Therefore, do not wait until you have been accepted to submit your FAFSA and supplemental forms.

File your income taxes as early as possible after January 1, because schools will require you to send a copy of your actual return and, as well, the FAFSA form requires information that is derived from your tax return. (Keep copies, too.)

Determine whether you need to declare an interest in grant aid. At many schools, all applicants are considered for merit grants. Check at each school to which you are applying, however, whether you need to declare your interest.

Note what is necessary to file for federal and law school aid. Federal funds are available on the basis of what you (and your spouse) need, without regard to your parents' financial situation. Note that your spouse's income and assets will be included in this calculation. School funds, on the other hand, may not only take account of your income and assets, and those of your spouse, but also those of your parents.

To apply for loans only (government or private), expect to submit:

➤ FAFSA form

➤ A signed copy of your most recent federal tax return

➤ A signed copy of your spouse's (if any) most recent federal tax return

To apply for other forms of financial aid, including school grant aid, expect to submit a PROFILE or Need Access report in addition to the other materials.

Expect to refer to numerous other records as well, including:

➤ Current bank statements

➤ Mortgage information

➤ Medical payments

➤ Business financial statements

➤ Stock, bond, and retirement accounts

➤ Loan information (including prior educational loans)

to fill out the practice forms online (at the sites noted above). There are numerous benefits to running these calculations:

- You will learn approximately what contributions are expected of you (and your family).

- You will have gathered the information necessary to fill out these forms "for real."

- You can play "what if" games to determine how to structure your finances before law school. For instance, should you sell stocks to pay down the mortgage on your condo or keep them for law school? Should you give $10,000 to your parents? Or to a sibling? (This is the maximum amount you can transfer absent tax effects.)

The former *asset-shuffling game* (paying down the mortgage) can work because most schools do not assess your primary residence. The latter game (transferring assets within the family) can work because schools assess parents' assets at a lesser rate than they do applicants' assets. These are probably the two most important asset-shuffling games but, of course, there are others. By running mock calculations, you can determine which games are open to you—and which promise the greatest benefits.

TYPES OF FINANCIAL AID

LOANS

The vast bulk of law school financial aid is in the form of loans. As noted earlier, for those who will receive only need-based aid (not merit aid), schools typically require that students take on a set amount of loan—typically between $22,000 and $24,000 per year—before any grant aid or work-study is offered. Given that only a minority of students at the top schools receive merit grants, this means that a substantial majority of students will indeed take on a very substantial debt load to pay for law school. (This is clear from the fact that approximately three-quarters of those who attend the top schools borrow money to do so and, for those who do borrow, the average debt upon graduation is now approaching $80,000.)

For those with good credit histories (see sidebar), it is generally easy to borrow such amounts. Whether you should do so, of course, is another question. After all, borrowing influences not just your financial future, but also your career future. If you graduate with a massive debt load, you will not be able to work for the next years at a community college instructor's salary.

LOAN PROGRAMS

There are four types of loans generally on offer for law school education: Federal Perkins, Federal Subsidized Stafford, Federal Unsubsidized Stafford, and private. American citizens or permanent residents are eligible for the various federal loan programs.

- *Federal Perkins Loan.* Perkins loans are funded through a combination of university and federal funds. These long-term loans generally offer the best terms of any educational loan. They carry an interest rate of 5% and defer the accumulation of interest while students are in law school. (In fact, the loan is free of interest until the repayment point, nine months after the student leaves school.) To be eligible, you must be a full-time student in good standing. The amount of Perkins loan money available to each school, and thus to each student, is limited, causing schools to award Perkins loans to the neediest students. In general, the maximum amount is $5,000.

- *Federal Subsidized Stafford Loan.* These long-term educational loans are underwritten by a government guarantee, but are made by banks, savings and loans, and other lenders. They carry an interest rate of the 90-day Treasury Bill plus 2.5%, capped at 8.25%. There is an origination fee of 3%, and a guarantee fee of 0–1% (based upon the agency). The government pays all interest charges while students are in school and during the six-month grace period thereafter. The maximum amount a law student may borrow in an academic year is $8,500.

- *Federal Unsubsidized Stafford Loan.* The costs of an Unsubsidized Stafford Loan are the same as for a Subsidized Stafford except that the government does not pay interest charges while the student is in school and during the six-month grace period. Law students are eligible for up to $18,500 annually from the Unsubsidized Stafford loan program, minus any amount borrowed through the Subsidized Stafford program.

- *Private Loans.* Various private loans are on offer from well-established educational lenders. These include Citibank, Norwest Bank, Nellie Mae (a largely private loan agency), and the Access Group. Note that all of these involve credit checks and require a satisfactory credit history. One easy way to determine whether you are likely to be approved for a private educational loan is to contact a lender, such as the Access Group, which offers a pre-approval process. Once you have provided your information, they will conduct a credit check and notify you of their decision. If you qualify, you can complete their loan application process, or simply rest assured that you will be able to qualify for a loan when the time comes.

Choosing Loans

Students should borrow from lenders in the order listed above: Federal Perkins first, and to the extent that this does not suffice, Federal Subsidized Stafford. If more is needed, borrow next from the Federal Unsubsidized, and then from private lenders. Because Perkins and Stafford loans will not ordinarily cover tuition fully, students often use private educational loans to complete their funding needs.

When comparing loans, consider both the fees charged for origination or guarantee and the interest rates. Origination or guarantee fees can be charged upon disbursement of your money, or when you go into repayment. In either case, consider these fees in your calculations. Interest rates in private loan programs are seldom flat rates. Instead, they are based upon the Treasury Bill or prime rates, with an additional several percentage points tacked on. This means that the actual interest rate will fluctuate with these market interest rates. It is, of course, easy to determine the cheapest rate if the loans you are examining all use the 90-day T-Bill rate, or all use the prime rate, as the basis of their calculations. It is a bit trickier to compare rates if one lender uses the T-Bill and another the prime rate. To determine what will be cheaper, calculate the current rate in effect by looking up the relevant T-Bill and prime rates and then adding the relevant percent figures. (Although the relationship between the T-Bill and prime rates can change, the former will generally be lower than the latter.)

Try to keep any loans you take out with the same lender as any prior educational loans you have. This will make your record keeping and repayment simple. In fact, even if you take out federal Stafford loans, you will find that most

---

THE IMPLICATIONS OF YOUR CREDIT HISTORY

Note that all student loans, government and private, depend upon your credit history. If you have loans in default, have made late credit card payments, and so on, your ability to borrow may be limited. To make sure that you have a clean credit history, or to start the process of cleaning up your record, obtain a copy of your credit report by contacting one of the following credit-reporting agencies:

➤ Equifax (800) 685-1111

➤ Experian (formerly TRW) (800) 682-7654

➤ Trans Union (800) 916-8800

➤ CSC Credit Services (800) 759-5979

private educational lenders also participate in this federal program. Consequently, you will probably be able to stick to the one-lender policy.

LOAN REPAYMENTS

■ *Grace Periods.* Most private loans, as well as federal Stafford loans, have a six-month period after graduation during which no payments are required. Federal Perkins loans have a nine-month grace period.

■ *Repayment Amounts.* The following chart provides amortization data to help you determine the amount of monthly payment you will make for any given loan. To utilize it, first determine the amount of principal for each loan. (Note that unsubsidized loans will accrue interest during your period of study, meaning that the principal amount to be repaid will have increased.) Once you have the principal amount, check the chart for the duration of the loan and its interest rate. The associated figure in the chart shows how much you will repay monthly *for each one thousand dollars of principal.* For example, if you borrowed $20,000 for 20 years at 10.0%, you will need to repay $9.65 per thousand. Thus, you will need to repay $193.00 per month (i.e., 20 × $9.65). If you borrowed the same amount, at the same interest rate, but for *10* years rather than 20, you would need to repay $264.50 per month.

NUMBER OF YEARS	INTEREST RATE					
	5.0%	8.0%	9.0%	10.0%	11.0%	12.0%
5		20.28	20.76	21.25	21.75	22.25
10	10.61	12.14	12.67	13.22	13.78	14.35
15		9.56	10.15	10.75	11.37	12.01
20		8.37	9.00	9.65	10.33	11.02
25		7.72	8.40	9.09	9.81	10.54
30		7.34	8.05	8.78	9.53	10.29

To calculate the exact loan payments facing you, consult one of the following loan calculators:

www.salliemae.com

www.usagroup.com

LOAN REPAYMENT ASSISTANCE PROGRAMS (LRAPs)

Paying back student loans is no easy feat, particularly if you wish to head into a low-paying field. Because of this, many of the top schools have instituted loan forgiveness programs for students who choose relatively low-paying jobs in one or another of the following sectors: local, state, and federal government; private nonprofit organizations serving the public interest; low-wage private law practices serving underrepresented constituencies; and academe.

The key elements of Stanford's program are set forth below, to provide an overview of a typical program. Following this are a series of charts designed to show the range of differences of top schools' programs on these key points. *A few caveats are called for.* First, in order to simplify a very complex subject, these charts inevitably overlook numerous subtleties. The charts are not designed to show the workings of a specific school; instead, they are meant to show the range of policies at the leading schools in order to highlight the type of information an interested applicant needs to examine for each. Second, some top schools are not included in these charts, either because information was not available prior to this book's publication or because they do not have an LRAP program (Texas, for example). In some cases, the policy of a given school cannot be readily captured by the categories used in a chart, so it has been left out. Third, as is so often the case with financial aid at the moment, the programs are in a state of flux. Expect the weaker programs to be forced, through competition, to improve their terms and conditions.

Stanford's Loan Repayment Assistance Program

Qualifying employment. The employment must be law-related and public interest in spirit and content. The "law-related" requirement means that the position must substantially utilize the legal training and skills of the graduate. Public interest work is defined as working for a tax-exempt organization, a governmental unit (a foreign governmental unit may qualify), or a private employer—as long as at least 50 percent involves providing legal services on a pro bono, reduced, or court-awarded fee basis.

Judicial clerkships do not usually qualify. (The rationale is that the short-term commitment to clerking is designed to lead to a higher paying job after the year or two of clerking.) There is an exception for those who intend to take a public interest position after the clerkship position is completed.

Teaching does not qualify, unless it is clinical teaching (with a practical component).

Income eligibility.

Adjusted Income	LRAP Policy
< $20,000	Loan for all monthly payments provided
$20,000–$52,000	Loan for all monthly payments provided less 15% of income over $20,000
$50,000–$75,000	No loans provided, but payment on prior LRAP loans provided is deferred
$75,000	Benefits not available

Adjustments to income:

- *Spouse's income:* The graduate will be considered as having the higher of his or her individual income or half the joint income.
- *Dependents' allowance:* An exemption of $5,000 for each minor child is allowed.
- *Seniority:* $1,000 is deducted from the graduate's salary for each year in public interest employment.
- *Assets:* Savings up to $20,000, a moderately priced car, and a home with equity up to $100,000 will be excluded from income calculations.
- *Additional income:* Any unearned income is treated as income.
- *Part-time work:* Pro rata adjustment made according to hours worked. Thus, a graduate working half-time would have her salary doubled for purposes of LRAP calculations.

Qualifying loans. Financial assistance is available for need-based educational loans. ("Need-based" excludes loans taken in lieu of "student contribution.") Loans taken to meet undergraduate, law school, and other graduate-school degree requirements, as well as bar examination and bar examination preparation expenses are eligible. Defaulted loans are not eligible for LRAP and will not be considered in determining the graduate's award.

Other eligibility requirements. Graduates cannot participate in the LRAP program if they have defaulted on their original student loans. Once loan accounts have been cleared, however, the law school will process the LRAP application.

Loan cancellation. LRAP-qualifying loans can be cancelled upon sufficient length of public interest employment.

YEARS OF QUALIFYING EMPLOYMENT	PERCENTAGE OF PRINCIPAL CANCELED
1	0%
2	0%
3	25%
4	50%
5	100%

LRAP Programs at a Glance

Qualifying employment

	Legal Service Agencies	Public Defenders	District State/ Attorneys	Nonprofit Organizations	Government	Judicial Clerkships	Private Practice	Other
UC Berkeley (Boalt Hall)	x	x	x	x	x			
Chicago	x	x	x	x	x			
Columbia	x	x	x	x	x	x		
Cornell	x	x	x	x	x			
Duke	x	x	x	x	x			
Georgetown	x	x	x	x	x			
Harvard	x	x	x	x	x	x	x	Academic
Michigan	x	x	x	x	x		x	Academic
Pennsylvania	x	x	x	x	x		x	Nonlegal (some)
Southern California	x	x	x	x	x	x		
Stanford	x	x	x	x	x	Some	x	
Vanderbilt	x	x	x	x	x			
Virginia	x	x	x	x	x			
Yale	x	x	x	x	x	x	x	Nonlegal

Income eligibility

	Income Ceiling
UC Berkeley (Boalt Hall)	$37,500
Cornell	$41,000
Duke	$45,000
Harvard	$72,000
Southern California	$37,500
Stanford	$52,000
Vanderbilt	$35,000

Adjusted incomes above the figures given make a person ineligible for program benefits. Note, however, that the programs differ substantially in two important regards. First, they differ as to how to consider spouse (or domestic partner) income. Some simply average the graduate's income with that of his or her spouse (or domestic partner, in the case of one or two schools). Others take the higher of the graduate's income or the averaged income of the two people. Second, the schools differ as to what they regard as an adjustment (deduction) to income. At issue are such matters as: prior educational debt payments, spouse or domestic partner debt payments, deductions for dependents, child care expenses, cost of living, and medical expenses.

Similarly, some programs increase the income ceiling according to seniority. A typical adjustment is to add $1,000 per year in the program.

Qualifying loans

		LOAN TYPE				
	UNDERGRADUATE	GRADUATE (NON-LAW)	LAW SCHOOL (GOVERNMENT)	LAW SCHOOL (PRIVATE)	BAR EXAM	FAMILY/ FRIENDS
UC Berkeley (Boalt Hall)			x	x		
Chicago			x	x	x	
Columbia	x		x	x		
Cornell			x	x		
Duke			x	x	x	
Georgetown			x	x	x	
Harvard	x		x	x	x	
Michigan			x	x	x	
New York			x	x	x	
Pennsylvania	x		x	x		
Southern California	x	x	x	x	x	
Stanford	x	x	x	x	x	
Vanderbilt			x	x	x	
Virginia			x	x		
Yale	x		x	x	x	

■ Joint-degree candidates should consider whether the loans for the non-law program will be eligible for LRAP treatment.

■ Note that loans from family and friends are never eligible for LRAP treatment.

■ At many schools, graduates are ineligible for the LRAP program if their principal loan balance does not exceed a given total. At Duke, for instance, it must be at least $20,000. To meet this total, educational loans to finance undergraduate or other graduate study might be included (although loan forgiveness may be available only for law school loans).

Loan cancellation

	CANCELLATION BEGINS AFTER	CANCELLATION COMPLETE AFTER
Chicago	3 years	5 years
Columbia	3 years	10 years
Harvard	1 year	10 years
Pennsylvania	3 years	5 years
Southern California	3 years	6 years
Stanford	3 years	5–10 years
Virginia	5 years	8–10 years
Yale	1 year	10 years

Number of graduates currently participating in program

UC Berkeley (Boalt Hall)	11
Columbia	109
Cornell	27
Duke	34
Georgetown	106
Harvard	253
Michigan	55
New York	247
Pennsylvania	35
Southern California	21
Stanford	90
Vanderbilt	4
Virginia	25
Yale	226

The number of LRAP participants at a given school can be very significant for several reasons. A large number of participants suggests that the program is attractive enough to warrant participation. It also suggests that the program has been up and running for some time. In addition, it is a rough indication of the number of people who pursue public interest work upon graduation. At some schools, however, there is a potential downside to having a large number of participants. At Duke, for example, with only about $150,000 available, adding two or three dozen participants would almost surely reduce the support given each participant. At NYU, with a program budget in excess of $1,600,000, the addition of another few dozen participants would not have such an effect.

LRAP Programs: Conclusion

The variation in LRAP policies makes it essential that you know where you are headed (district attorney? private firm with a substantial public interest practice?) in order to know which elements are likely to be most important to you. These variations, and the infinite subtleties accompanying them, obliges you to examine each program carefully, in great detail. The detail can be boggling, but this should not deter you from a proper examination (given that you do intend to be a lawyer, after all).

A note of warning: At many of the top law schools a majority of entering students claim that they will enter public interest law, yet only 5 to 20 percent actually do. Therefore, it is unwise to place too much emphasis upon the quality of LRAP programs when choosing schools, just as it is unwise to load up on debt in the expectation that an LRAP program will rescue you from having to repay it—unless you are dead certain that you are headed into public interest law, and already have the real-world experience to make that belief a reasonable one.

RESOURCES

NAPIL (The National Association for Public Interest Law)
2120 L Street, NW, Suite 450
Washington, D.C. 20037
Tel. (202) 466-3686
Fax (202) 429-9766
www.napil.org

NAPIL, which provided much of the data for the charts concerning LRAP programs, is an organization dedicated to the advancement of public interest

---

HOW MUCH DEBT IS TOO MUCH?

The general rule is that the better the school you attend, the more you are likely to earn, both in your first job out of law school and throughout your career. Attending a better school thus makes a high level of debt more affordable than would be the case if you attended a lesser school.

Nevertheless, the question of how much debt is appropriate for you depends upon your individual circumstances. If you intend to take a relatively low-paying public sector job upon graduation, you may view a $75,000 debt as inconceivable. If you take a job at a leading firm in New York, on the other hand, with total first-year pay of $140,000 or more, the same $75,000 would probably look manageable. This fact could well alter your choice of jobs, which might or might not be a problem. If you have to focus on the salary and bonus of your first year in order to facilitate debt repayment, to the exclusion of all else, you may take a job that is not appealing in terms of the actual work, the particular area of law, the specific firm, the city, or your future prospects. This would be an unfortunate consequence of your debt situation.

Let's put the question of borrowing into perspective. In terms of the amounts you will have to repay, someone who borrows $75,000 for 10 years at 8–10% interest will face a monthly payment of approximately $900–$1,000. This would ordinarily require an annual income of at least $65,000–$70,000. This estimate is well below the starting salaries of most people graduating from top schools, excepting students who take low-paying public sector or public interest jobs. Someone borrowing $50,000 for 10 years at the same 8–10% interest will pay only some $600–$660 per month and needs a salary of only $48,000–$54,000. These figures suggest that the size of a loan necessary to fund an average student will not be large relative to his or her post-JD earning capacity.

law. It is a repository of information about such things as public interest internships and full-time positions in addition to scholarship and loan repayment programs. If you are interested in a public interest career, by all means take advantage of the wealth of information with which they can provide you.

The law schools themselves have, in most cases, separate booklets explaining the details of their LRAP programs.

GRANTS

Law schools offer two types of grants:

■ *Need-based:* These are offered at all of the top schools. Note, however, that they are available only after a student has taken on the requisite amount of loan. Eligibility varies from school to school. For example, wait-listed students may not be eligible at some schools. (See the later discussion, under "Financial Aid Policies," for more about these restrictions.)

■ *Merit:* Many, but not all, of the top schools use merit grants to attract top applicants. Schools obviously differ in what they consider a "top applicant." This will vary according to the relative standing of the schools (a top applicant at North Carolina might not be one at Georgetown), the mix of backgrounds in each school's applicant pool (former foreign service officers might be thick on the ground for Washington, D.C.-based schools but rarities for Chicago schools), the desired types of students (if Michigan were trying to beef up the biotech side of its intellectual property program, it might find a biochemist from a major pharmaceutical company to be worth paying extra for), and a host of other factors.

Many schools have both internal and external constituencies that prevent candid talk about their merit aid policies. The subject of merit aid is complicated by a number of factors:

■ Even the schools that are very active in giving merit aid find it controversial among their own administration and faculty. The idea of competing for students is repugnant to some, as is taking any money out of the pot for the financially needy.

■ It is handy for a school to be able to claim that it is so good, and so attractive to applicants, that it need not enter the competitive fray by offering merit aid.

■ Many schools now mix merit and need-based aid together under the simple heading of "grants," without wishing to describe the extent to which merit aid is included. (This facilitates several schools' saying that they do not actually give merit aid, even though they do indeed.)

■ The merit aid policies of many schools are now very much in flux.

The net result of this situation is that you should not expect to get entirely clear (or straightforward) answers from all of the leading schools about their merit aid policies. Instead, you may learn about some of them only through the actual offers schools make to you. (For more about this, consult the "Bargaining" discussion below.)

A tip concerning merit aid: To maximize your chances of getting a merit grant, be sure that once you are admitted you go to whatever admitted students' days you can in order to demonstrate your keen interest in the school.

OUTSIDE GRANTS

There are numerous organizations that have funded general purpose or specialized grants that may be applied to law studies. These include foundations, clubs, fraternal organizations, labor unions, and churches. (For information about such grants, see the sources listed at the end of the discussion on "Impact of Outside Grants," later in this chapter.)

PUBLIC SERVICE SCHOLARSHIPS

Some schools, such as Columbia, Georgetown, NYU, and Penn, offer public service scholarships in addition to their LRAP programs (see the previous discussion regarding LRAP programs). By making it possible for graduates to incur little debt for law school, these grants facilitate taking low-paying jobs upon graduation. The programs are designed for those who have already demonstrated substantial commitment to public service. Those awarded public service grants are often required to take specific courses and participate in various activities during law school. In addition, these programs generally require a substantial post-graduation commitment to public service, typically for three or more years.

PART-TIME WORK DURING LAW SCHOOL

Students who have demonstrated sufficient financial need are given a package of loans and, often, work-study job opportunities. The jobs on offer often include library work, research for professors, and so on, generally for about $8–$10 per hour. At most schools in major urban centers, however, part-time work for local firms will offer pay that dwarfs the work-study pay. Consequently, it is only at isolated schools that work-study is likely to prove your best option for earning money. (It can be helpful to do research work for a professor, of course, but not for monetary reasons.)

THE LOCATION TRADE-OFF

In general, the schools that offer the lowest cost of living are in locations where it will be hard to earn a great deal of money working part-time during the school year. Charlottesville, for example, is a less expensive place to live than is New York City. By the same token, part-time jobs at local firms pay much better in New York than in Charlottesville. If you intend not to work during law school, you may find the University of Virginia a bargain relative to NYU or Columbia. On the other hand, if you *do* intend to work during your second and third years, Charlottesville may represent a false economy insofar as you could more than make up for a higher cost of living through your earnings elsewhere. This is, of course, yet another example of the fact that your choice of law school is heavily conditioned by the extent to which you already know what you will do during law school.

	PERCENTAGE OF LAW STUDENTS WORKING	PAY RANGE (DOLLARS PER HOUR)
UC Davis	N/A	$12–26
George Washington	75%	$10–45
Georgetown	75–80%	N/A
New York	N/A	$13–60
North Carolina	15–20%	$7–10
Pennsylvania	< 5%	$8–45
Stanford	20%	$30–60
Virginia	< 5%	$14–15
William & Mary	10–15%	$10–25

The differences in this chart are quite marked. The hourly pay garnered by those in New York City, Washington, D.C., and Palo Alto is much greater than that received in Chapel Hill and Williamsburg. Every bit as interesting, however, is the percentage of students who choose to work at the various schools. It may be that those who attend law school in Washington, D.C. are poorer than those attending other schools and thus need to work more. (It may also be that the financial aid policies of these schools are more miserly.) On the other hand, it may be that the opportunities (and pay) for work are greater in Washington than in many other locations, thereby providing temptation to law students there to work as part of their law school experience. Indeed, it is highly possible that students seek out schools in Washington with the intention of taking advantage of the part-time work experience available. It is interesting to compare students at Georgetown and Stanford in this regard. Despite the high pay available at Palo Alto firms, relatively few Stanford students choose to work during law school, unlike students at Georgetown.

LIMITS UPON TERM-TIME WORK

The American Bar Association officially limits full-time law students to 20 hours per week of work. All of the top law schools abide by this restriction and would certainly have a word with you if you were known to be exceeding this total. None of these schools, however, actually monitors the number of hours students log at local firms. In fact, the reason that data from so few schools are included in the chart is because so few schools can even guess at how many students work part-time or what they earn. Thus, the real limitations upon your work hours are your own time and inclinations, not law school or ABA policies.

ADDITIONAL INFORMATION SOURCES

➤ A good place to start your research is at www.finaid.org, which is the most comprehensive financial aid site and also provides links to numerous other resources.

➤ FAFSA (Free Application for Federal Student Aid) may be obtained by writing:

Federal Student Aid Programs
P.O. Box 84
Washington, D.C. 20044
(800) 433-3243
www.fafsa.ed.gov

➤ Loan programs:

Access Group	(800) 282-1550; www.accessgroup.org
LawLoans	(800) 984-0190; www.salliemae.com
Citi Assist	(800) 692-8200; www.studentloan.com
TERI Loan	(800) 367-8848; www.teri.org/loanlink.htm
Key Education Services	(800) 539-5363; www.keybank.com/education

➤ For information on minority scholarship opportunities:

Council on Legal Education Opportunity
1420 N Street NW, #T-1
Washington, D.C. 20005
(202) 785-4840

FINANCIAL AID POLICIES

Financial aid policies are particular to individual schools. These policies, such as whether you are considered a resident for purposes of paying in-state tuition, can have a major impact upon your eligibility for financial aid and the amount of aid you will receive. Whether any given policy will affect you, of course, depends upon your individual circumstances. The following policies have been highlighted because they are the most likely to have a major influence upon your aid awards. Examine them to see which are most likely to affect you, then look more closely at which schools (and how many schools) have policies that might favor you.

IS THE FINANCIAL-AID DECISION INDEPENDENT OF THE ADMISSION DECISION?

No top schools take account of your need for financial aid in making their admissions decisions, unless you are an international. Numerous schools that wish to have foreign students, but lack the funds to sponsor them, do give preference to foreign students able to pay their own way.

ADMISSIONS AND FINANCIAL AID DIRECTORS DISCUSS THE ADMISSIONS
IMPACT OF NEEDING FINANCIAL AID

An applicant's need for financial aid is not relevant to an admissions decision. Shelli Soto, Dean of Admissions, University of Texas

An applicant's financial need is never relevant to an admissions decision. Janice Austin, Assistant Dean for Admissions, University of Pennsylvania

An applicant's financial need, or lack of need, is never taken into account in making admissions decisions.   Albert R. Turnbull, Associate Dean for Admissions and Career Services, University of Virginia

Financial aid is totally separate from admissions. Our office doesn't know an applicant's financial situation.   Erica Munzel, Director of Admissions, University of Michigan

There is a real firewall between need-based aid and admissions.   Katherine Gottschalk, Director of Financial Aid, University of Michigan

CONVERTING TO RESIDENT STATUS FOR THE SECOND YEAR

Given the lower tuition that public schools charge residents, becoming a resident can reduce the tuition burden considerably. At the California schools it is very easy to enter as a nonresident student in the first year, yet be converted to resident status for the second and third years. In other states, this is very difficult to do. In fact, it often requires marrying a state resident to accomplish this conversion. As a result, to get the advantage of Michigan's, Virginia's, or Texas's resident tuition would require becoming a resident prior to law school. (See the discussion concerning residency on pages 199–201.)

PERCENT OF STUDENTS CONVERTED TO RESIDENT STATUS FOR SECOND YEAR	
UC Berkeley (Boalt Hall)	>90%
UCLA	100%
Michigan	< 5%
Texas	< 5% (Note, however, that Texas offers 90 nonresident tuition exemptions—i.e., it considers 90 incoming out of-state students to be "residents.")
Virginia	< 5%

TREATMENT OF PARENTS

WHEN ARE APPLICANTS CONSIDERED INDEPENDENT OF THEIR PARENTS?

Schools traditionally considered law school students to be, at least in part, dependent upon parental support. This was due to the fact that the typical law school student was coming straight from college, or very soon thereafter. Now that the average age at which students start law school is approaching 25, many schools have changed their policies. Some schools always consider students independent, whereas some never consider them independent. Many take an intermediate position, but they apply a dog's breakfast of rules to determine independence. Some consider your age; others consider how many years ago you graduated from college, whether you have dependent children, or whether you have been in the military; still others consider how many years you have gone without being claimed as a tax exemption by your parents. Harvard applies several tests. It considers independent those who, during the last seven years:

- Have not been claimed as income tax exemption by their parents
- Have not lived in their parents' home/household for more than six months
- Have not received more than $10,000 from their parents

DETERMINATION OF APPLICANTS' INDEPENDENCE STATUS

	APPLICANTS NEVER CONSIDERED INDEPENDENT	APPLICANTS ALWAYS CONSIDERED INDEPENDENT	APPLICANTS INDEPENDENT ACCORDING TO CERTAIN AGE	APPLICANTS CONSIDERED INDEPENDENT ACCORDING TO NUMBER OF YEARS OF INDEPENDENCE	COMMENTS
UC Berkeley (Boalt Hall)		(x)			Parents not assessed unless they currently support you
Columbia	x				
Cornell				4	
Duke	x				
Georgetown	x				
Harvard				7	
Michigan				5	
Northwestern				4*	*Measured in terms of years after college graduation
New York	x				Only infrequently is someone considered independent
Pennsylvania			30		
Stanford				6*	*Starting at 3 years, parents' contribution assessed at reduced amounts
Texas		x			
UCLA			30	7	Or being military veteran or having dependent child
Virginia			26		
Yale			29*		*From 27–29, applicants' parents assessed at 50% of otherwise expected contribution

Several schools apply a graduated approach to the contributions they expect from parents. Yale, for instance, requires a full contribution (as calculated by their financial need analysis) from parents of students under 27, a half contribution from parents of students between 27 and 29, and no contribution from parents of students 29 and above. Similarly, at Stanford the parents' expected contribution is 100% at fewer than three years of student independence, 75% at three years, 50% at four years, 25% at five years, and 0% at six years. Northwestern, which prefers candidates to have at least several years' work experience, has an independence policy that encourages those with substantial work experience to apply. At two years after college graduation, a student's parents are required to contribute 50% of the otherwise expected amount; at three years, 25%, and at four years, 0%.

Note that parents need not actually contribute the amount expected: You are always free to borrow or earn the amount yourself.

ASSESSMENT OF NONCUSTODIAL PARENTS

If your parents are divorced, some schools will still assess the noncustodial parent (unless they consider you to be independent of your parents), whereas other schools never assess the noncustodial parent. Some schools are in the middle, assessing noncustodial parents in some cases but not others. Michigan, for instance, assesses them unless the divorce occurred at least ten years ago.

ASSESSMENT OF NONCUSTODIAL PARENTS		
ALWAYS (UNLESS APPLICANT CONSIDERED INDEPENDENT)	**SOMETIMES**	**NEVER**
UC Berkeley (Boalt Hall)	x	
UCLA		x
Columbia x		
Cornell x		
Duke x		
Michigan	x	
Northwestern		x
New York x		
Pennsylvania	x (assess unless divorce at least five years old)	
Stanford		x
Texas		x
Yale x		

IMPACT OF OUTSIDE GRANTS

Scholarships are available from sources other than the law schools. They are most often given on the basis of residence, membership of a specific ethnic group, relationship to a relative who served in the armed forces or is a member of a particular civic organization, or interest in a particular area of law. Do not, however, count on getting an award that will materially affect your options: There are relatively few that pay truly substantial sums. In addition, some law schools deduct part or all of the scholarship from their own grant, meaning that the financial value of the award to you may be limited. Even in this case, though, the nonfinancial value may still make such a scholarship worthwhile. Some of these scholarships will look impressive to future employers, so their résumé value alone is worth the effort of applying.

Do not, however, pay anyone to conduct such a search for you. This field is notoriously loaded with charlatans.

IMPACT OF OUTSIDE GRANT*

	REDUCES LOAN	REDUCES GRANT AND LOAN
UC Berkeley (Boalt Hall)	x	
UCLA	x	
Columbia	x	
Cornell	x	
Duke	x	
Harvard	x	
Michigan	x	
Northwestern	x	
New York	x	
Pennsylvania		x
Stanford	x	
Texas	x	
Virginia		x (75% of amount above $500 deducted from grant)
Yale	x	

*A school's treatment of a grant often depends upon the grant amount. A very small scholarship grant (say, $100) will often be ignored; an immense scholarship (say, $100,000) will cause a school to eliminate all aid, including any grants. For purposes of this chart, an in-between sum of $5,000 was assumed.

To look for outside aid, consult the following Websites for free scholarship searches:

www.finaid.org/finaid/awards.html

http://scholarships.salliemae.com

Or, consult the following:

- Daniel Cassidy, *The Graduate Scholarship Book: The Complete Guide to Scholarships, Fellowships, Grants and Loans for Graduate and Professional Study*
- Debra M. Kirby, *Scholarships, Fellowships and Loans*
- Franklin A. Williams and Mark Fischer, *The Law Student's Guide to Scholarships and Grants*
- Law School Admissions Council, *Financial Aid for Law School: A Preliminary Guide*

FOREIGN EXCHANGE PROGRAMS

If you do an exchange program abroad, for a semester or a full year, you may have to pay tuition to your home (American) school instead of to the foreign school. In some instances, the school you pay depends upon whether you are going to a school with which your home school has an exchange agreement or to a school that you yourself "found." The question of whether your home school's financial aid will "travel with you" is similarly messy—it varies in much the same way. Given that the foreign school's tuition may be higher or lower than your home school's tuition, you may find yourself much better or worse off according to which tuition you are required to pay—and whether suitable financial aid is available. Be sure to examine the fine print of your home institution and whichever exchange programs interest you.

PAYMENT OF TUITION FOR FOREIGN EXCHANGE PROGRAMS

	USUALLY PAY HOME SCHOOL TUITION	USUALLY PAY FOREIGN SCHOOL TUITION	PAY WHICHEVER TUITION IS HIGHER
UC Berkeley (Boalt Hall)	x		
UCLA	N/A (not permitted to go abroad during academic year)		
Columbia	x		
Cornell	(case-by-case decisions—no set pattern)		
Duke	x		
Harvard	x		
New York	x		
Northwestern		x	
Pennsylvania			x
Stanford	N/A (no foreign exchange programs)		
Yale		x	

AMERICAN EXCHANGE PROGRAMS OR THIRD-YEAR MATRICULATION

The same issues that matter when attending a program abroad are present when attending a second law school in the U.S. If, for example, you currently attend Yale but will do a term or year at another American law school, will you pay Yale's tuition or the other school's? Will your Yale financial aid travel to the other school if you pay its tuition?

This situation is most likely to arise if your spouse has a job or educational program that pulls him or her to another location, thereby inspiring you to follow. You might yourself initiate such a change for reason of the program available at the other school, perhaps via an existing exchange relationship (see Chapters 14 and 16 for a fuller discussion of this possibility). Or you might wish to shift schools in part for financial reasons. If you intend to practice law in a state with a very good state law school, which charges a very low tuition for residents (and you could qualify as a resident), you might wish to spend your last term at that school. The potential costs of doing so are clear:

- You might not have access to the same quality professors or courses.

- You might not have access to the same courses, journals, or organizations.

- You might miss your law school friends and feel isolated, in part because few students at the new school will be looking to make new friends in their last term.

- You might miss out on law school merit-based grants.

   The potential benefits, on the other hand, might prove more substantial:

- If you have already exhausted the courses likely to be most valuable to your future career that are offered at Yale, you might benefit from other courses on offer at your new school.

- You may pay much less in tuition (especially if you have relatively few credit hours left to complete and the state school charges by the credit hour, which many do).

- You may be able to work for much higher wages than you could in New Haven.

- You can get a head start on your local networking (especially valuable for those with intensely local practices, such as family law), including building your credibility within your new firm.

- Your degree will still say "Yale."

The most substantial benefits will thus accrue to those able to pay resident tuition at a fine state school and work for their new firm. Those who will be unable to pursue such a strategy are those whose obligations (law review, for example) make it imperative that they remain on campus or whose chosen future requires maintaining contact up until the last moment with the school (such as those who need a great recommendation from a professor for clerkship purposes, both now and in another year or two for a follow-up clerkship, such as at Federal Circuit Court or Supreme Court level).

PAYMENT OF TUITION FOR EXCHANGE PROGRAMS OR TRANSFER TERMS			
	USUALLY PAY ORIGINAL SCHOOL TUITION	USUALLY PAY "NEW" SCHOOL TUITION	PAY WHICHEVER TUITION IS HIGHER
UC Berkeley (Boalt Hall)		x	
UCLA		x	
Columbia		x	
Cornell		x	
Duke			x
Harvard	x		
Michigan		x	
New York		x	
Northwestern	x		
Pennsylvania			x
Stanford		x	
Texas		x	
Yale		x	

ASSESSMENT OF TERM-TIME EARNINGS

Most schools will ignore term-time earnings, especially in the third year, unless they are told explicitly about them. Schools seldom actually learn about part-time earnings unless they involve work at the law school or elsewhere on campus. Michigan, on the other hand, will hold you responsible for any such earnings—if they find out about them—*unless* you tell the school about them prior to their finding you out. (Go figure.) The schools that do not assess term-time earnings at all want to provide an incentive to students to work or they consider that students are sacrificing so much in terms of leisure time and law school activities that they should not be further penalized. The schools that ignore only third-year part-time earnings, on the other hand, generally calculate financial need on the basis of the prior academic year's earnings (so that by the time third-year earnings would be inputted, law school is over for you).

This situation gives rise to interesting possibilities. You can vary the number of course credits you take each term during your second and third years. If you wish to maximize your GPA in the second year, for instance, you could take a slightly lighter courseload, then take a heavier one in the third year. (Firms will have made final offers by December of your third year, so third-year grades

are much less important than second-year grades—and only of critical importance for those going the public interest route [employers hire very late in the
spring] or needing to have their grades examined once they change jobs later
on.) To maximize short-term economic benefit, on the other hand, take the
heaviest possible load second year, and work little or not at all. Third year, take
a light load and work maximum hours (supposedly 20 per week, according to
American Bar Association rules—but no one actually monitors this.) Schools
will already have determined your aid for the whole third year, so your actual
earnings during the year (at most schools) will not subtract from it.

In the case of merit grants, many of the schools that award them do so
without regard to how much you will earn during law school, so your term-time
earnings will be free of financial aid implications.

This is one area in which student practice is rapidly evolving. At Cornell,
for instance, a few students are working during the academic year, while remaining in Ithaca, for firms in New York City and Los Angeles that they had
worked for during the previous summer. (It is not yet clear, however, whether
cyber-commuting will become a regular feature of law school.) Some Penn students, on the other hand, are working part-time in New York City, making sure
not to have any classes on Thursday or Friday so as to facilitate spending those
days in Manhattan. One thing remains constant, however: Yale students seldom
work for local firms, no doubt in part because they do not wish to remain in
New Haven once they finish law school.

ASSESSMENT OF TERM-TIME EARNINGS

	SECOND YEAR ASSESSED	THIRD YEAR ASSESSED	NEITHER YEAR ASSESSED
UC Berkeley (Boalt Hall)	x		
UCLA	x		
Columbia			x
Cornell		x	
Harvard			x
Michigan			x (as long as you declare earnings)
New York			x
Northwestern			x
Penn	x	x	
Stanford	x	x	
Texas	x		
Yale	x	x	

ASSESSMENT OF SUMMER EARNINGS

In calculating aid, many schools factor in a sum of money that you are expected to hand over from your summer jobs during law school. Sometimes this is a flat number, varying from $1,500 to $3,000, which they will impute to you even if (especially if) you have tanned yourself on the beach all summer. Given that it is now possible to make over $30,000 in a summer, this oversight of actual earnings can be very helpful to you. (Similarly, many of the schools that award merit grants do so without regard to how much you will earn during law school, so in such cases your summer earnings are free of financial aid implications.) Sometimes it involves an equation. Virginia, for example, requires that a student contribute 70% of her net salary, minus $1,500. Stanford's contribution formula requires that you contribute at least $1,000, and takes half of whatever you earn above $5,000.

Some schools will "normalize" the time you work. For instance, they will compute your earnings as if you work a 10-week summer. Gross income for the ten weeks is calculated, then taxes and living expenses (based upon a standard student budget) are subtracted. The difference is considered to be savings, applied to law school expenses. Extra weeks of work are not taken into account, but those who work fewer than ten weeks have their salary grossed up to a 10-week total. (Those who do not work at all have an average savings figure imputed to them.)

	SUMMER AFTER FIRST YEAR ASSESSED	SUMMER AFTER SECOND YEAR ASSESSED	NEITHER SUMMER ASSESSED	COMMENTS
ASSESSMENT OF SUMMER EARNINGS				
UC Berkeley (Boalt Hall)	x			
UCLA	x	x		
Columbia			x	
Cornell		x		
Harvard	x	x		(If work more than 12 weeks, "excess" weeks not assessed)
Michigan	x	x		
New York	x	x		(Assess if >$12,000)
Northwestern			x	
Pennsylvania	x	x		
Stanford	x	x		
Texas	x			

TREATMENT OF WAIT-LISTED STUDENTS

The treatment of wait-listed students is by no means uniform. At most of the top schools, they are eligible for both need-based grants and loans (government and private), but at some of these schools there is likely to be little money left for them by the time they are admitted. Many schools have already spent most of their aid resources on applicants they needed to entice away from other schools by the time wait-listed students are admitted.

AID ELIGIBILITY OF WAIT-LISTED STUDENTS

	ELIGIBLE FOR GRANT	ELIGIBLE FOR GRANT BUT MONEY MAY RUN OUT	ELIGIBLE FOR LOAN ONLY
UC Berkeley (Boalt Hall)	x		
UCLA	x		
Columbia		x	
Cornell		x	
Duke		x	
Harvard	x		
Michigan	x		
New York	x		
Northwestern			x
Pennsylvania	x		
Stanford	x		
Texas	x		
Virginia		x	
Yale	x		

TREATMENT OF TRANSFER STUDENTS

Some of the top schools treat transfer students just as they treat regular admits (those admitted for the first rather than second year of the program). This is by no means true, however, across the board. Some schools make no grant aid available, or make it available only in some circumstances. Schools that do not give grants, even on the basis of financial need, do not want to look as though they are luring students from their neighboring schools (many students transfer within a limited region to the best school nearby) and, furthermore, do not need to bid for these students.

The top schools have not competed actively for transfer students up to this point, but expect this to change in the near future, as competition for talent heats up across the board. The bidding war for talent should start to be seen here.

Aɪᴅ Eʟɪɢɪʙɪʟɪᴛʏ ᴏf Tʀᴀɴsꜰᴇʀ Sᴛᴜᴅᴇɴᴛs

	Gʀᴀɴᴛ-Eʟɪɢɪʙʟᴇ	Gʀᴀɴᴛ-Eʟɪɢɪʙʟᴇ, ᴡɪᴛʜ Lɪᴍɪᴛᴀᴛɪᴏɴs	Lᴏᴀɴ-Eʟɪɢɪʙʟᴇ Oɴʟʏ
UC Berkeley (Boalt Hall)	x		
UCLA	x		
Columbia			x
Cornell		x (grant eligible in 3d year)	
Duke			x
Harvard	x		
Michigan	x		
New York		x (need-only, not merit grants)	
Northwestern			x
Pennsylvania	x		
Stanford	x		
Texas			x
Virginia		x (but money seldom remains)	
Yale	x		

TREATMENT OF INTERNATIONAL STUDENTS

International students face a different financial aid situation than do American students. Internationals are not eligible for federal loans, nor can they readily obtain private (American) loans without an American citizen or permanent resident cosigner (guarantor), except in the case of two institutions that have recently established a program with NYU allowing for foreign cosigners. (The private educational loans available to international applicants with an American cosigner include Access Group's Graduate International Student Loan, CitiAssist, LawEXCEL, PEP, and Signature Student Loan programs.) Some American schools will still make grant aid available to internationals, but note that such aid is generally available only after another $20,000-plus of loans (that may not be available) have been factored into the need equation. Only a very few schools have merit aid available for internationals. A few schools will replace the (unavailable) federal loans with their own institutional loans, but that is discouragingly rare. Some schools do have limited aid funds for second- and third-year international students, but not for first-year students.

Thus, international students typically must be able to demonstrate their ability to pay for at least the first year of study and sometimes the whole program before a school will issue a Certificate of Eligibility for the appropriate visa. It is therefore critical that foreign students consider their financial situations carefully, well in advance of applying.

**AVAILABILITY OF INSTITUTIONAL FINANCIAL
AID FOR INTERNATIONAL STUDENTS**

	INSTITUTIONAL GRANTS AVAILABLE	INSTITUTIONAL LOANS AVAILABLE (TO REPLACE FEDERAL LOANS)	PRIVATE LOANS, WITH FOREIGN COSIGNER, AVAILABLE
UCLA	x		
Columbia	x		
Cornell	x		
Duke	x		
Harvard	x	x	
Michigan	x	x	
New York	x		x
Northwestern	x		
Pennsylvania	x		
Stanford	x		
Yale	x	x	

OTHER FINANCIAL-AID POLICIES

Numerous other law school policies can affect your financial aid. For instance, some schools impute earnings (and thus a required contribution) to spouses, whether or not the spouse actually works. This can be particularly tricky if the spouse is remaining home with a preschooler rather than working outside the home. Another example actually concerns child-rearing expenses: only some schools permit child-care expenses to be deducted. These are not the only such examples of other financial aid policies, but the lesson should be clear: Whatever your own situation is, be sure you understand the policies that can affect you at your chosen schools.

EVALUATING FINANCIAL PACKAGES—AND TRYING FOR MORE

EVALUATING AND COMPARING AWARD PACKAGES

Be ready to evaluate, compare, and perhaps negotiate financial-aid packages at different schools. When evaluating an aid package, or comparing various aid packages that you have received from schools to determine which is best, there are six primary factors to consider:

■ *The portions of grant versus "self-help" funding:* Two schools can offer to fill your financial need in radically different ways. One law school may give you 50% of your $30,000 total need in grant aid whereas another might offer only 15% in grant, forcing you to take on substantial debt.

■ *The terms of the loan repayments:* Not all loans are created equal. Subsidized loans, for which the government or institutional lender will pay interest while you are still in school, are better than unsubsidized ones. Loans without origination fees are preferable to those with fees.

■ *The treatment of outside scholarships:* Compare how each school handles outside scholarships, whether you have gained an outside grant for your first year or are hoping to get one later on.

■ *The treatment of summer and part-time earnings:* Note whether such earnings are considered when granting aid, and whether they serve only to reduce loans or can also reduce grants.

■ *Whether there are performance requirements to retain aid:* Grants and loans that are not fixed for three years are generally less valuable than those that are fixed. In considering the potentially variable awards, take into account the possibility that your award amount may be reduced because you were successful in earning money during law school—or because your spouse or parents were newly successful.

In addition, consider whether a grant that is conditional upon your performance at law school will be readily placed in jeopardy. Examine the grade-point average required to keep it. Do not, however, consider this GPA in light of your college GPA. You are likely to struggle to perform as well at law school as you did in college, given the much stiffer competition, and, oftentimes, the stiffer grading policies. Instead, look at the required GPA in light of the actual distribution of grades at this school. If you are required to maintain a 2.7 GPA at a school with a mandated median of 2.85, you face a very substantial risk of losing your grant.

■ *The treatment of spousal income:* If your spouse is likely not to work for substantial periods during law school, perhaps due to caring for a young child, will the school still impute some earnings to him or her?

BARGAINING

Prior to the mid-1990s, applicants to the top schools could not successfully haggle with schools about their financial-aid offers. If Penn offered you a $2,000 grant and $14,000 in loan, you took it or went elsewhere. Those days are gone.

In the last few years, schools have started to bargain—rather surreptitiously—with the applicants they most wish to catch. This started with schools well below the level of the national schools, but has now reached well up the ladder to the truly top schools. A safe generalization is that any school that dishes out merit aid, rather than aid based solely on financial need, is open to some degree of bargaining. This means that Harvard, Yale, and Stanford are unlikely bargainers (although there are hints that at least one of these has been using its vast resources to pursue a few highly desirable candidates). There are also a couple of other schools that look to be resisting out-and-out bargaining, but it is safe to say that of the top twenty schools (however defined), the vast majority now engage in some degree of bargaining.

There are no rules to this new world of bargaining, except that failure to try results inevitably in failure. If Penn, NYU, Columbia, and Chicago all admit you, take the best offer you have from one and show it to the others to see whether any of them will improve their offer to you. Some of them may try to convince you that you will actually do better, financially and otherwise, with the offer they have already made to you. By all means pay attention to this perspective; it may well be right. But by the same token, see whether you can get more money out of the school (regardless of whether you believe the argument they have made).

Do not expect all schools to be equally interested in you. The higher up the list of admits you find yourself, the greater your bargaining leverage. You might be at the bottom of Penn's list of admits, yet at the top of Boston University's or Vanderbilt's. As a result, Penn would be unlikely to match their offers. In fact, even if you were atop Penn's list, it might not feel compelled to match BU or Vanderbilt because it might well trust that its reputation and/or program specifics would be sufficient to land you without an increase in aid.

The more schools of similar repute that have admitted you, the more your leverage with any one of these schools. (As a result, you should apply to many schools that are similar to one another.) This principle can, however, be taken too far. Do not expect Penn to pursue you avidly if you look like a great fit at another school but a poor one at Penn, because the effort to pursue you would not be worth the time of Penn's financial-aid people. If you have strong ties to

---

The general rules when trying to bargain:

➤ When the school gives no merit grants whatsoever, emphasize your poverty. Note that your expenses (rent, child care, auto repairs, and so on) will run higher—and perhaps your (and your significant other's) earnings will run lower—than the school anticipated in its aid award.

➤ When the school gives merit grants, remember that it is most likely to be willing to match another school's grant the better the other school's reputation/rankings, and the more the two are rivals due to geography or similarity of programs.

Chicago, for example, and no compelling interest in a program done particularly well at Penn, expect Penn's financial-aid people to focus on other people rather than on you. The obvious lesson here is to show how you would be a perfect fit for the program, and vice versa, without foreclosing the reasonable possibility of your going elsewhere.

Bargaining is already important in the law school financial-aid game, but it will certainly increase as more and more schools try to buy talent. Texas is unusually frank (see the sidebar) in its willingness to show not only that it will match or better other schools' offers, but also which other schools it regards as rivals to be matched. The same competitiveness exists in other leading schools, albeit without the frankness. Given the advent of bargaining throughout the undergraduate (college) world, more and more of those applying to law school will expect to haggle over law school financial offers; this will propel the

---

THE TEXAS FINANCIAL-AID MATCHING PROGRAM

The University of Texas School of Law offers a merit-based financial aid matching program for admitted students who have received financial aid packages from selected law schools:

UC Berkeley (Boalt Hall)	University of Michigan at Ann Arbor
UCLA	New York University
University of Chicago	Northwestern University
Columbia University	University of Pennsylvania
Cornell University	Stanford University
Duke University	University of Virginia
Georgetown University	Yale University
Harvard University	

"Through this program, the University of Texas School of Law will award scholarship packages so that the admitted applicant's student contribution and educational loans for attending The University of Texas School of Law are equal to or lower than the amounts offered by the listed law schools. . . . To apply for a scholarship package through this program, please submit a copy of your Financial Aid Notification (FAN) or similar official document that reflects the cost of attendance and the amount of grants, scholarships, and loans offered from one of the law schools to The University of Texas School of Law Scholarships Committee." (*Quoted from the University of Texas's own materials.*)

competition for law student talent even further into the world of bargaining. One last note to the wise: When trying to determine which schools are most likely to put toe (and whole leg) into these waters, note that new deans of law schools are highly likely to try to improve the student profile at their schools by changing the basis for awarding aid.

FINANCIAL STRATEGIES

THE BASIC STRATEGIES

By starting the process early, you make it possible to play the financial-aid game with real cunning. The key is to figure out both your career goals and, correspondingly, how you wish to do law school. Choose the school that best matches these desires. For instance, if you intend to work part time during law school for maximum earnings, try to attend a law school that does not assess term-time earnings and that is located in a city where part-time pay is high. Use the charts on the preceding pages to understand the extent to which the relevant financial policies vary by school and choose accordingly.

Other strategies, based upon the information above, include:

1. Save money before going to school. (This is just one more reason to work seriously before law school.)

2. Shift income away from the base year used to calculate financial-aid awards, especially at the schools that make three-year grants up front. Do what you can to get a Christmas bonus the year before—or New Year's bonus the year after—the critical base year, or get paid in options rather than salary.

3. Consider shuffling your assets by transferring funds, for example, to your parents or siblings.

4. Nail down any outside grants you can.

5. Consider reacquainting yourself with your parents. Their financial aid may involve fewer restrictions and qualifications than other likely sources of financing.

6. If your parents have substantial earnings or assets and you do not, consider becoming independent of your parents, or favoring schools that will consider you to be independent.

7. Become a resident in a state that has a public law school you wish to attend.

8. Attend a state law school that permits students to pay resident tuition in the second and third years.

9. Consider delaying your marriage if your prospective spouse will add to your joint assets and earnings. This is especially likely to be the case during the first years of law school, when you will be studying more than working. (You could even consider divorcing such a person, but I am loathe to advise such a thing.)

10. Live cheaply during law school. You can save several thousand dollars a year by living frugally.

11. Get a grant based upon performance in law school. All of the top schools make awards for "best performance in Corporations I," "best moot court brief," or "highest grades by a first-year student."

12. Work for as many weeks as possible during the summer, especially during your second summer, when law firms will pay you especially handsomely.

13. Given that few schools assess part-time earnings, consider logging as many hours as practicable at the best-paying (local) firms. Note that salaries differ dramatically from one location to another, so if you intend to work part time, consider choosing a school on this basis. You are likely to be paid best for part-time work during your third year, so take a heavier courseload second year, so that you can work more hours during third year.

14. Attend a much cheaper school for your last term, or for a term abroad.

15. Enter a field that makes your law school expenses tax deductible, assuming that you return to it upon graduation (see sidebar).

Despite all of the above advice, do not believe that attending a lesser law school for a reduced price is generally a better idea than paying full freight at a demonstrably better school. You are making a long-term investment, so think in terms of value rather than just in terms of price.

KEEP YOUR SPENDING UNDER CONTROL

BEFORE LAW SCHOOL

Law schools will consider your income, not just your savings, when calculating how much money you should be able to contribute. Therefore, wasting money on frivolous purchases in the years before law school can have unintended consequences. Take a look, well in advance of applying to law school, at how schools calculate your expected contribution (discussed earlier) to make sure your current spending plans will not come back to haunt you.

Be careful, also, not to run up too much credit card or other consumer debt. Not only is it an expensive way to finance your spending, but failure to meet your payments will make it difficult or impossible to gain federal or private law school loans. Make sure, too, that you manage carefully your existing educational debt (taken on for college and, perhaps, graduate school). Defaulting on

THE TAX DEDUCTIBILITY OF LAW SCHOOL

Under the new tax law, everyone can claim a Lifetime Learning Credit for graduate education (up to $1,000 at the moment, and $2,000 after the year 2002). A few people, however, will be able to deduct the full cost of law school. The basic requirement is that you intend to return to the field you were in prior to law school, and then indeed do return to it. Thus, if you were a child advocate for a public interest organization and return to this work (and perhaps the same employer), doing very similar work, albeit at a higher level, you may qualify for a deduction. Similarly, if you work before law school as a foreign trade representative for a state, or as a political science professor, and return to the same field, your payments may be deductible. Be sure that you discuss this with your accountant or tax lawyer. The rules are complicated and the case law is very messy, so you may not get a definitive answer to whether such a deduction will pass IRS muster. In that case, your risk profile may be the determining factor as to whether or not you claim a deduction.

By the way, not only may your law school expenses be deductible, but your expenses incurred getting into law school may also be deductible.

this, or even being late with payments, can also limit or eliminate your ability to get new loans for law school.

During Law School

Live as inexpensive a lifestyle as you can manage. It will allow you to live better upon graduation, when your loan repayments will be lower than they would if you had lived at all extravagantly during law school. In addition, the less debt you have, the more career flexibility you will retain. If your debt is $100,000, you will feel pressured to work in the highest paying corporate environment possible or in a public interest position that qualifies for LRAP treatment.

MAKE SURE YOUR FINANCING STRATEGY IS CONSISTENT WITH YOUR CAREER GOALS

When considering how to finance a law school education, be sure to think through the implications of your financing strategy. Make sure your financing approach is consistent with how you intend to do law school. Do not expect to work 20 hours a week for a local firm while also being on law review. Do not expect your earnings from summer jobs between law school to be massive if you intend to pile up public interest credentials (public interest positions, especially during summer internships, pay poorly). Similarly, make sure your financing

SHOULD YOU TRADE DOWN IN SCHOOL QUALITY TO SAVE MONEY?

When should you take a merit scholarship at a lesser school instead of paying full freight at a better school? When should you go to a state law school with lower tuition than a somewhat better private school (with higher tuition)? There are numerous factors to consider:

➤ How large is the quality (and reputation) difference between the two schools?

➤ To what extent do the two schools offer the courses you want and other elements (such as location and atmosphere) you most value? (See Chapter 3 for a full discussion of these elements.) What are the earnings possibilities during summers and term-time at the two schools?

➤ What amount of scholarship is on offer?

➤ How certain are you that you will be able to keep the aid for all three years?

➤ What field do you intend to enter? How certain are you of this? If you are likely to enter a public interest area, consider the LRAP possibilities at the two schools. For other fields that do not pay much (such as teaching), note that you are unlikely to qualify for LRAP benefits (except at a program like Yale's). Huge debts may constrain your ability to enter such a field, although your attractiveness to such employers may well depend upon the quality of the law school you attend.

➤ The more likely you are to enter a high-paying field, the less importance you should attach to the debt you may carry upon graduation.

➤ Note that performance pressure may be much less at the better school, oddly enough, because your rank in class may not matter much to your employment chances. At Harvard, it may be sufficient to be in the upper two-thirds of your class to get the type of job you want, whereas you may need to make law review at a lesser school to get such a job. Check with your desired employers about what it takes from each school.

approach is consistent with your post-law school goals. Thus, do not pile on $90,000 of debt if you intend to teach law at a community college.

To plan your financing effectively, you therefore need to have a good understanding of where you are headed: how you intend to spend your time in law school, what type of law you will practice, and for what type of employer. Do not leave your financing strategy to chance. Instead, start the process of determining how best you can finance your law school education early in the process.

Part *IV*

APPLICATION ESSAY EXAMPLES

Thirty-one actual applicant essays are included in this book, all but one in Part IV. (The other one is included in Chapter 8.) The majority of these are personal statements. The other essays include those written for scholarships, explanations for past problems (such as brushes with the law or questionable grades), optional pieces written for schools allowing more than one essay, and a transfer essay.

Thus, you have a full menu of essay types in front of you. In fact, the range is even greater than you might yet think. The personal statements and other essays reflect the diverse experiences and interests of the applicants writing them—and a diverse lot they are. There are ten men and ten women. Six are Hispanic or African-American. Several were born and raised abroad. Their experience ranges from zero to ten years of full-time work, at jobs ranging from paralegal to journalist, naval officer to psychologist. Several have done substantial graduate work. They applied to the whole range of leading schools. We did not indicate for which school a given essay was written—since similar essays were generally submitted to multiple schools—except in the case of those written in response to a very specific question. Some of the essays describe applicants' formative experiences, including looks at their families; some discuss their academic interests; others describe what they intend to do after law school; still others provide think-pieces about law, society, citizenship, and the like.

There is no magic essay topic, so do not feel compelled to choose what one of these applicants wrote about. In fact, this wide-ranging selection of essays is meant to send an opposite message: What makes a given topic an excellent choice for one applicant is likely to make it a bad one for another. The comments that follow the essays are meant to provide assistance in this regard, pointing out what did and did not work—and why—for each applicant.

Use this section to help you find what topic will work best for you, given your experiences, interests, strengths, and weaknesses. In other words, consider the lessons from Chapter 8, "Marketing Yourself," and those that follow concerning your desired positioning, your reward-risk ratio, and so on. Keep in mind also that some topics will not need to be covered because they may already feature in your recommendations.

Not all of the essays are brilliantly written, but each demonstrates at least better-than-average writing quality for those admitted to the top schools. If you wish to read particularly well-written essays, regardless of subject matter, consider those of Maura Wilson, Sacha M. Coupet, David P. White, and Bill.

Note how much more interesting the essays become as you proceed through this section. The essays are placed in order of the applicants' experience, with the college seniors' essays coming first, followed by those with more (and more) experience. Even though various of the essays written by inexperienced applicants are good, the lack of experience tends to shine through. The gap in experience, maturity, self-knowledge, and understanding of the career choices available—from the college seniors to those with real career experience—is dramatic.

To get the most out of this section, do three things:

- Read the best examples—those of Maura Wilson, Sacha M. Coupet, David P. White, and Bill—to see how professionally someone can market him- or herself. These are textbook examples of good applications.

- Refer back to the discussion in Chapter 8 of overall marketing principles and the Chapter 9 analysis of specific essay topics, while looking at the essays.

- Then look at the efforts of the people who most resemble you in terms of their backgrounds, their chosen topics, and so on.

You will probably not want to read page by page through this whole section. The charts on the following pages are meant to facilitate your picking and choosing whatever is of greatest interest to you.

One last note: Some of the applicants wanted their full names used whereas others wanted only their first names used, or even wanted their identities lightly disguised by our using a different first name. The first four applicants, in fact, wanted no details given as to their identities. Thus there is no uniform policy followed here, except that of honoring the wishes of the applicants. A minority of the applicants were clients of *Degree of Difference:* I leave it to you to figure out which were and which were not.

Applicant	Job	Years Experience	College	Subject (Major)	GPA	Graduate Education
Lisa	N/A	0	Harvard			
Tuan	N/A	0	Princeton			
Julie	N/A	0				
Lawanda Nowlin	N/A	0	Spelman	English Literature	3.7	
Jarrett Epstein	N/A	0	Univ. of Virginia	American Government	3.5	
Judith	Paralegal	1	Columbia	Philosophy	3.8	
Tori	N/A	2				
Jon Queen	Assistant to handicapped woman	2	Cornell	Economics	3.5	
Antonio	Paralegal college counselor (for Community Organization)	1+ 1+	Yale	Molecular Biophysics and Biochemistry		
Garth Morey	High school teacher, Special projects coordinator, Philadelphia Empowerment Zone Field coordinator, Democratic Party	1 1 ½	Yale	Ethics, Politics, and Economics	(Summa cum Laude)	
Maura Wilson	Program analyst, Office of Inspector General, U.S. Department of Commerce	3	Univ. of Washington	International Studies	3.6	
Brendan	Capital markets analyst	3+	Yale	History	3.3	
Amy Crawford	Legal aide, Equity Derivatives Trade Desk	3 1	Univ. of Virginia	Double Major —Sociology —Afro-American Studies	3.4+	
Sacha M. Coupet	Clinical psychologist	4+	Washington University	Psychology	3.4	M.A., Ph.D., Univ. of Michigan (Psychology)

Applicant	Occupation	Undergraduate	Major	LSAT	Essay Topics	Other
David P. White	Executive director, Community Org.	Grinnell	Political Science	4+		Oxford (Philosophy, Politics, and Economics)
Thomas	Naval officer	Berkeley	Economics	5		3.75
Oluwabunmi Shabi	Journalist, *Business Week*	Univ. of Chicago	History	6		
Bill	Religious meditator	Yale	Philosophy	10		3.6+
Noah Pittard	N/A	Univ. of Georgia	Philosophy	0		3.0 1st year, Hastings Law
APPLICANT				**LSAT**	**ESSAY TOPICS**	**OTHER**
Lisa					Cultural influences	Native of South Africa
Tuan					Immigration and experiences leading to interest in law	Native of Vietnam
Julie					Experiences with injustice leading to interest in law	
Lawanda Nowlin					Family experiences leading to interest in law	African-American
Jarrett Epstein				166	Experiences in Britain's House of Lords and European Parliament leading to interest in law	
Judith				178	Original interest in law confirmed by experience as legal assistant	
Tori					Influence of grandfather	
Jon Queen				168	1) Experience as home aide 2) Public service essay: Interest in public service and Penn	
Antonio				160	Talent and training in science and communications leading to interest in law	Hispanic
Garth Morey				169	Importance of community interaction to success of democracy—and his own experiences with this notion	

Applicant	LSAT	Essay Topics	Other
Maura Wilson	165	1) Interest in internationalism and international law 2) Contribution to diversity essay: Applicant's courage and tenacity evident in breaking traditions at a young age 3) Way-you-think essay: Benefits of "children's" literature for adult readers	
Brendan	168	Interest in Latin America and economic development	
Amy Crawford	165	Observations on discrimination and her civil rights work	
Sacha M. Coupet	161	Experience in psychology and children's advocacy, leading to interest in law	African-American (First language: French)
David P. White	158	Experience in foster parenting and as leader of community agency, tied to his interests in law and urban development	African-American (Rhodes Scholar) (Truman Scholar)
Thomas	164	Experience as Mexican-American beneficiary of Affirmative Action, and as naval officer	Hispanic
Oluwabunmi Shabi		Discussion of candidate's Brooklyn neighborhood as extension of herself	Reapplicant: Wait-listed year before
Bill	176	1) Discussion of applicant's study of meditation and interest in law 2) Way-you-think essay: Examination of Buddhist teaching 3) Note on employment history 4) Note on undergraduate grades 5) Note on arrest history 6) Scholarship essay 7) Scholarship essay 8) Optional essay: Why candidate wants to attend Northwestern	
Noah Pittard	165	Why applicant wants to transfer to Boalt Hall (Berkeley) from Hastings	Transfer Applicant

LISA

The day will stand out in my mind for the rest of my life. I know it will because it was one of those series of moments when past and present fit together with great significance, one of those series of moments when you stop to take mental photographs so as to absorb each minute one at a time. It was at the short acceptance speech delivered by President Nelson Mandela on my campus of Harvard University only a few short weeks ago that the trajectory of my life flashed before me. I shivered with pride when Mandela alluded to his Long Walk to Freedom. Time raced backwards in my head as I thought of the long walk of my own family which began on the same soils of South Africa. As I recalled thoughts of people, places and experiences, I began to think of my life not so much as one linear road, but as a puzzle, a conglomerate of separate pieces which somehow fit together to shape the person I have become . . .

A blurry red haze hangs over the deep clay South African soil, the soil of my birth and the base of my puzzle. Emigrating at the age of one, I would learn to love another distant soil in the United States before I would understand my African roots. Time and distance erased homely smells of milliepap and damp cool air. Yet African rhythms would always ring deep in my soul. I was connected to that land somehow. My parents tried to explain to me why near the red soil of Africa, black pieces did not fit with white pieces. They too struggled to handle the stark separation. To them, Africa meant rolling mountains, blue skies, and green trees—colors and curves, not straight edge monochromatic pieces. One day the pieces would match more smoothly, they told me. Until then, Dallas, Texas would become my new home.

In Dallas, I began to discover the world through my one eyes, and in my spirit grew a Texan pride—a reciprocal love of a new home so welcoming to my family. A warm sunny climate translates to warm friendly people in the southwest, and through my progression from elementary school to high school to university, I have forged friendships of binding ties. This is because people take time for one another in Texas. These days I take time to listen to the fascinating stories of my fellow Harvard students, who come from all over the world and each have their own interesting stories to tell. In Texas I was also exposed to the beautiful Latin culture, to the soft roll of the Spanish language, to spicy Tex/Mex food, to happy mariachi music, and to a light-hearted spirit which seeks only the enjoyment of every precious moment of life!

A soft yellow glow emanates near the center of my puzzle and sheds rays of light over all the other pieces. This is the glow of Judaism represented by a symbolic pair of candles lit in my household each Friday to welcome in the Sabbath. Friday evenings in my home are special times. The house is warm with rich smells of roasted chicken and challah bread toasting in the oven, and the calmly dancing candles spread an aura of peace over the house. It is a family time, when my mom and dad, my brother and I sit round the finely decorated Sabbath table to discuss news, events of the week, our individual hopes and dreams, and our goals we hope to achieve together. Judaism touches all the pieces of my puzzle because it touches every part of my existence. My close family ties, my strong system of values and ethics, my search to elevate my life beyond the trivial and mundane, and my appreciation for beautiful things in nature, art, music and literature, in some way all find their derivation in Judaism.

My heart rang with nostalgia and longing when the full resounding voices of the Harvard Kuumba singers sang Ngosi Sikale le Africa—a song my mom used to sing to me when I was a small girl. Mr. Mandela did not see my mouth, but as his lips formed the shape of the words, so did mine. We were singing together, he and I, and I cried. As Mr. Mandela graciously accepted the award of an honorary doctorate of law with a dignified bow and an elegant smile, I smiled too as he reaffirmed for me that day, that hard work and persistence can bring the sweetest rewards.

COMMENTS

What this candidate achieves here is difficult for most applicants of similarly "exotic" backgrounds. The applicant applies a poet's touch and reveals a believable spirit that is not affected or contrived. Many applicants who might wish to convey a similar message would be unable to pull off this kind of essay, the main idea of which is nothing greater than "I am a product of my diverse inputs." The detail about each of the influences—South Africa, Texas, and Judaism—help to solidify the essay's believability and impact. In fact, it comes as a surprise midway through the essay that the applicant is Jewish; we expect her to be black, and the upsetting of that expectation adds to the essay's multicultural message.

TUAN

In the summer of 1978, on a small, overcrowded ship carrying two hundred Vietnamese refugees, a seven-year-old boy forever lost his innocence. Separated from his parents and alone with his thirteen-year-old cousin on this journey, he stood silently while the ship was attacked by pirates who robbed and raped many of the passengers. Terror struck his soul and tears filled his eyes as he witnessed bodies being thrown overboard. He simply could not comprehend the senseless killings. But the nightmare did not stop; dissatisfied with the gold and jewelry plundered from the passengers, the pirates forced everyone overboard in order to seize the ship. The sea tossed and turned as people panicked and fought one another for empty gasoline tanks and water containers to use as flotation devices—it was a quarter of a kilometer to shore. The young boy and his cousin were fortunate; they both knew how to swim. The sight and sound of desperation and death sent chills down his spine, but all he could do was swim. To this day, the memory of a young girl calling to her drowning mother for help still haunts his dreams; and sometimes a deep sense of guilt overwhelms him for having survived when over half of the passengers perished.

I was this young boy. Two years later, I was reunited with my father and eldest sister in the United States. But life in a new country was terribly difficult. For nine years, my father, sister, cousin and I struggled to earn enough to send home to my mother and two sisters in Vietnam while trying to keep our heads above water. The situation was such that I had to sew piecework for the garment industry after school to supplement my father's small income. As a result of his perceived inability to provide for his family, my father resorted to alcohol to escape the loss of dignity and sense of shame. Racial intolerance also added to our difficulties. Derision such as "chink" and "gook" by fellow classmates induced feelings of inadequacy and self-hatred on my part; and because of my poor English skills, I responded by fighting, which further exacerbated the problem. In addition, an assault on my father by three youths who told him to "go back to China" and the subsequent burning of my sister's car forced us to move from our apartment. Such experiences reinforced my resolve to succeed in school in order to escape both poverty and the stigma of being a foreigner.

With the arrival of my mother and two older sisters to the United States in 1989, after eleven years of separation, my financial obligation to the family was eased slightly, which enabled me to concentrate more on my studies. However, the dual necessity of work and commuting to school did not allow me to take advantage of extracurricular activities provided by organizations on campus. Nevertheless, I did gain extensive experience working as a self-employed commercial artist during my undergraduate years. Unable to find a job suitable to my school schedule, I decided to put my artistic talent to work. I bought ads in local Vietnamese newspapers offering my services of designing and painting posters, signs, and advertisements at half the price of competitors. Most of my jobs are on a small scale that include painting windows and banners, and designing menus and advertisements for Vietnamese businesses. While working within the Vietnamese community, I became aware of the pressing need by small businesses as well as individuals in the community for affordable legal assistance. Because of their immigrant background, many Vietnamese lack an awareness of their rights and obligations in American society, which often lead to misunderstandings, confusion, and insecurity. Given the opportunity to attend law school, I hope to alleviate some of the friction and distrust that Vietnamese immigrants have in the law by broadening their knowledge of the legal system.

COMMENTS

This essay starts off well with a jarring story that emphasizes the applicant's background and the difficulties he has had to overcome to get where he is today. The story of the applicant's struggle against discrimination and insecurity also helps to show his attraction to the legal profession. The essay would have been substantially strengthened, however, if he had gone much further into his current work to show that his sentiments are sincere enough that he will indeed play the role he imagines, helping Vietnamese immigrants deal with the legal system. Not only could he have made stronger, more concrete connections between his experiences and observations and his legal future, but he could also have worked in nonlegal capacities to help fellow immigrants. (The failure to do so is a weakness of his application, albeit not of his essay.)

JULIE

Meet, first, my grandmother, Lea. She's eighty-six now and lives across the street. By leaving Germany in 1935, when the public schools of her hometown were closed to Jewish children, she escaped the Holocaust. She treasures American liberties; her favorite song is "God Bless America"; and she reminds me . . . I don't know how good I have it.

Now let me introduce you to the classmate who changed my high school campaign posters from "Vote Julie" to "No Jews." Then to the Neo-Nazis who sporadically demonstrate in front of the synagogue three blocks from my house. Next to Representative David Duke, selling *The Hoax of the Twentieth Century* in my backyard. These are some of my neighbors, and they have caused me to examine those rights which theoretically will prevent Lea's story from becoming my own.

My focus is the freedom of the press: its allotted latitude and resulting ability to shape social discourse. I observe, for example, in my research for my senior thesis, disturbing trends in the coverage of Mr. Duke's senatorial campaign. *The New Orleans Times Picayune* runs article after article on his growing support, his charisma, his nationwide sources of funding. It is only in mid-August that I read of racist and anti-Semitic comments made as late as 1989. The *Picayune*, I discover, has known of these remarks for ten months. For nine months, as the campaign gained momentum, they weren't considered newsworthy. A staunch opposer of censorship, I wonder: Should there be some guidelines for what is and is not printed?

My own journalistic experience reinforces my concern. I worked as a stringer for the Associated Press. I know that its editors will accept a story on Princeton's nude olympics and reject one on Louis Farrakhan. They realize that Farrakhan has caused one of the largest controversies on campus this year, they say, but he's doing it for the publicity. Don't cover it. I also know that *The Bridgewater Courier-News*, a *USA Today* subsidiary, isn't interested in the speeches of Catharine MacKinnon or of Abba Eban or of the American ambassador to El Salvador, but will pay me for ten to twelve inches on Princeton's cheerleaders.

I complement my interest in the societal influences of the media with close studies of our legal and judicial systems. My junior independent work, awarded more than once and published by the New Jersey Department of Higher Education, concludes that women should not turn to the judicial system for protection from the sadistic sexism of hard-core pornography. This semester I chair a Woodrow Wilson School policy conference that examines alternative means of dispute resolution, asking whether the current system truly provides justice. I direct the efforts of eighteen juniors toward a cohesive policy statement which we will present to the U.S. Senate Judiciary Committee.

I do not confine my analysis of the functioning of the law to the classroom. Summer work with the prosecuting office of the District of Columbia taught me that the system is easily manipulable. I answered motion after motion by defense attorneys who knew that if they delayed long enough, the case would be dropped for want of prosecution. I prepared cases with the knowledge that because they were going before Judge X* instead of Judge Y*, the fifth-offense drunk driver would be dismissed with minor penalty.

Back at Princeton, my term on the University Discipline committee offers a different perspective on justice. Four students, along with a group of faculty and administrators, hear charges of violations ranging from plagiarism to alcohol policy infractions to vandalism. I benefit from a view of, and a say in, yet another level of judicial structure.

Law school is a natural extension of these experiences. My professional goal is both to practice public interest law and to continue as a writer of social commentary. It is a goal that allows me to assure my grandmother: I not only value "what I have," but I aim to protect and to strengthen it.

COMMENTS

This candidate's approach is to paint quick portraits of her experiences with "justice," and then draw the conclusion that she belongs at law school—a natural extension of her interests and pursuits to date. This is a valid strategy. Furthermore, the initial stories she tells grab our attention and sympathy. The problem is that she over-gilds the lily. Even the first two paragraphs are rendered a bit melodramatically; they make a reader feel that the writer might be crassly taking advantage of her Jewish roots, trying to win over the admissions committee with a simplistic claim to felt discrimination. After that, Julie demonstrates a basic intolerance of others, which cannot help her cause. Even though any one of the foes she targets could be lambasted, the net effect of objecting to all of them suggests that she is a shrill, neurasthenic sort. It is one thing to object to Farrakhan, another to insist that you have the only acceptable way of dealing with him. Thus, insisting—as a journalistic intern, no less—that your paper must report his activities in full rather than ignore him sounds a bit strident. Similarly, announcing that any and all speeches of Catherine MacKinnon

---

*Actual names were used in the personal statement, but for legal reasons I have withheld them here.

are newsworthy, and that pornography is sadistic sexism against women, is painting with a very broad brush, indeed.

Julie should have eliminated some of her complaints and tempered her portraits with an admission that she realizes discrimination against Jews is not actually common at Princeton (her current home) or at the top law schools to which she is applying. In addition, she could have altered her tone a bit to sound less naive or incredulous that such acts of discrimination indeed occur to this day.

Julie is all too ready to see injustice and evil everywhere, with herself all too often the victim of it. She comes across as immature and lacking in the perspective that real-world experience would provide. Compare her overdone tone, and the limited nature of what she personally has had to confront, with the personal statements of David P. White and Tuan. They faced much more substantial difficulties, weathered them with more grace, and reported them more matter-of-factly. The results are much greater reader sympathy and respect.

LAWANDA NOWLIN

I consider myself fortunate because I do not suffer from the affliction of uncertainty that plagues so many undergraduate students. There has never been a time in my life, since I have been aware of professional goals, that I have not wanted to be a lawyer. I now search my memories for the answer to the question, *Why law?* Perhaps there was something in my family experience that ignited this flame. . . .

I have many fond and vivid memories of my family gatherings. The smell of southern fried chicken and candy yams simmering in the air, and my mother's laughter bouncing off every wall in the house. At these gatherings, many stories were told about the past, but one story in particular that always seemed to dwell within my memories was the story of when Uncle Jerry was, or how my grandmother labels him, a *hero*. In the early 60's, my uncle had a job at a local gas station as a gas attendant, one of the few jobs available for blacks in Lake City, South Carolina under the strict Jim Crow laws. One day, while he was pumping gas, a middle-class, young white male parked his car at the gas station. A few minutes later, a young black male walked over to his car, and my uncle overheard their conversation. The white driver of the car told the young black male "if you don't stop leaning on my car, I'm gonna shoot you, boy!" At this point in the story, my uncle with excitement flashing in his eyes, would laugh as he saw the anxious faces looking at him. "Then, before I knew it," my uncle would cry, "I heard a gun shot and that black boy was lying on the ground dead as a rooster." As the only witness to the crime, my uncle was subpoenaed to appear in court. Moreover, in order for the white driver to be found guilty, Uncle Jerry had to testify. My grandmother often recalled how frightened she and other members of the family were from the death threats they were receiving from the whites in our town. A white man being sent to jail for killing a black man was absolutely unheard of in the little town of Lake City! Nevertheless, my uncle did testify in court, despite the many death threats, and the driver was indeed sent to jail.

My uncle is a hero, not only in my family's eyes, but also in the eyes of the black community. What was so extraordinary about his actions was that he used the law as an instrument for social change during a time when the law was used as a vehicle for subjugation and social control over blacks. It is because of this experience that I am certain of my life goals: I want to be an attorney. My special interest is in civil rights law. It is an interest grounded in my desire to effect change. As a civil rights lawyer, I will be a living voice for those who have otherwise been mute. I will fight for the child who was discriminated against by his school because he is infected with HIV! I will provide a safe haven for the woman whose human rights were violated by genital mutilation! Moreover, as I work to effect these changes, I will do so with PASSION!

Perhaps, one day at a family gathering when the smell of fried chicken and the sound of my mother's laughter are interlocked in the air, one of my family members will begin to tell stories of my family's experiences. Of course, amongst these tales will be my uncle's story. However, I also hope to be a topic within this discussion—not only as the daughter, the granddaughter, and the niece, but as Lawanda, "the heroine!"

COMMENTS

Here is a well-written piece describing the candidate's reasons for choosing law as a profession. The story of her uncle is compelling and dramatic, although not overdone or lacking in authenticity. Even though another candidate using this kind of story may have been better off bringing herself into the story about a family member, Lawanda used her uncle as a tool to explore her own goals and dreams, explaining how her uncle's use of the law as an instrument for positive change has affected her.

Lawanda's essay, although interesting and well written, is not entirely convincing because she fails to show that she has made a major commitment to civil rights work or something comparable—which, lacking full-time work experience, is very difficult to do. Experienced admissions officers might regard this as a fine essay, and thus evidence of her writing ability, but they would probably give odds of two or three to one against her ever becoming a civil rights lawyer.

JARETT EPSTEIN

I had finished my last final during my second year at University a few days before I arrived in London. I had recovered from jet lag, and even was lucky enough to catch a glimpse of Queen Elizabeth II and her husband, the Duke of Edinburgh, during their procession to Parliament for the Queen's Speech. I woke up early that morning, having been too excited to sleep much the night before. Today was the day prearranged to meet Lord Michael Cocks, whose office I was to be interning in for the next three months. I arrived at the Palace of Westminster early for the appointment, not chancing the London Tube's sporadic schedule. I made a left at the main lobby and was in the Lord ante-Chamber. I did not realize until after I had been working in the Palace for some time that the carpet changed from green to red. Throughout the Palace, I would later learn, the color of carpet signifies whether you are in the House of Lords or the House of Commons.

I sat in the ante-Chamber, waiting for the steward to inform Lord Cocks that I had arrived. While I was waiting, the Lord Chancellor's procession led by Black Rod entered the chamber. As I watched the procession, I failed to see the rather plump, bald-headed gentleman with bushy eyebrows approach me. A cockney accent, from what seemed out of nowhere, said "Mr. Epstein, I presume," startling me. Lord Cocks then gave me a grand tour of the building, introducing me (as his new American slave) to many of the "great and the good" of the United Kingdom.

One of the immediate lessons I learned was that Lord Cocks harbors virulent anti-European Union views, which often bordered on xenophobia. I am a government major, read newspapers regularly, and have been involved in Model United Nations since high school, but all I really knew about the European Union was a vague memory of the French, barely passing the Maastricht Treaty a few years before. Little did I know, I was about to be given a crash course on Britain's relationship with Europe. Lord Cocks, sensing my ignorance on the subject, told me to spend the next few days reading the original transcripts from the debate on Britain's entry to the European Union in 1973. I learned a lot the next few days, both from the Hansards, the official transcripts of parliamentary debates, and from various textbooks. I learned that Lord Cocks was not so xenophobic. Being against the European Union, or Euroskeptic as it is known, is rather popular in Britain.

After Lord Cocks was convinced I was better informed about the European Union, he assigned me to do research on Britain and Europe. One of the manifesto commitments of Britain's newly elected Labour Government was the incorporation of the European Convention of Human Rights into domestic law. Lord Cocks was against the proposal and asked me to do research on the topic. The loss of national sovereignty and erosion of Parliamentary supremacy were the two main arguments I suggested Lord Cocks use, in arguing against the incorporation of the European Convention of Human Rights into domestic law.

I spent the next year doing a lot of reading on the European Union and took the sole course offered at my University, but it really was not enough. Even with the emergence of Economic and Monetary Union this January, and imminent introduction of a single currency in 2002, the European Union is still unfortunately relatively unknown in the United States. For my last University semester, I decided to immerse myself in the topic, by spending the semester interning in the European Parliament.

I considered myself knowledgeable about the European Union by the time I arrived in Brussels (at least more so than when I first encountered Lord Cocks the previous summer). I was assigned to work for Angela Billingham, a British Member of the European Parliament from the Eastern Midlands. My main tasks in the office were drafting responses to constituent queries, and following the Economic, Monetary and Industrial Affairs Committee (EMAC), of which Ms. Billingham is a member. The three months I closely followed EMAC provided me an opportunity to expand my knowledge of the European Union. The gamut of EMAC, luckily for me, coincided with my interests in the European economy and the European Union's relations with the United States. Debates on the birth of the Euro, competition policy and transatlantic relations dominated the agenda during my stay. Though the United States often got bashed in committee debates, most Members of the European Parliament (MEPs) recognized the importance of having a strong relationship with the United States, Europe's largest trading partner.

During my stay in Brussels, Ms. Billingham was appointed rapporteur of the parliamentary report on a proposed Commission Directive updating regulations on car heaters. While the subject of car heaters is rather mundane and technical in nature, I enjoyed the opportunity to see the European Union's legislative process from such an inside perspective. While it is obvious that companies now compete in a global marketplace, it was still surprising to see the number of American companies, such as Ford and Chrysler, attempting to lobby Ms. Billingham. I sat in on meetings with Ms. Billingham and members of the European Commission and even given a chance to meet with a few lobbyists one on one.

My other main responsibility in the office was researching and drafting responses to constituent queries. The most immediate lesson, which should not have been entirely surprising, is that, despite their posh accents, not every one in Britain is entirely normal. The letters that came into the office were not surprisingly an eclectic mix of subjects and requests. From the amount of coca in chocolate to the production of condoms, the letters were rarely boring. By the time the internship was over, I was fairly knowledgeable about a grab bag of subjects affecting the daily life of a Brit.

I am fascinated by the legislative process and am particularly interested in the emerging body of laws of the European Union. My experiences in London, working in the ornate and regal House of Lords with Lord Cocks, introduced me to this emerging government based in Brussels. The time I spent in working for the European Parliament further convinced me I want to continue studying European Law.

COMMENTS

The main benefit of this kind of essay is that the candidate shows himself to have received a taste of a legal system other than our own. Jarrett demonstrates some knowledge gleaned from his internships in Britain's House of Lords and in the European Parliament, useful for positioning himself as a candidate interested in studying European law.

The candidate erred a bit in the second to last paragraph of the essay. First, he misses an opportunity to entertain the reader—he should have expanded on the types of inquiries he was asked to research, thereby giving readers some real "food for thought" on his findings regarding chocolate and condoms. He could have left some memorable trivia with the reader and balanced the relative heaviness of the rest of the material in the essay, giving it the perfect feel. In addition, Jarrett should have avoided the statement that "not everyone in Britain is entirely normal." It makes him look a bit naive (to expect that all Britons are stuffy because of their accents) and immature. Despite this minor shortcoming, the essay works well.

JUDITH

"Then they know for certain that all of us are called, and each of us meditates on the extravagance of having a separate fate."   Czeslaw Milosz, *Capri*

I am spending the year after my graduation from an Ivy League liberal arts college working in a large New York City corporate law firm. While hundreds of recent college graduates accept such positions of indentured servitude in order to taste the expensive pleasures of living in the Big Apple, I did not need to go corporate to experience New York. After four years of living and working in the city, I easily could have found myself a more creative and interesting job; of all the jobs my undergraduate friends managed to obtain post-graduation, mine is by far the most mundane. One might think that I took the job because I had romantic visions of behind-the-scenes Wall Street (I had seen the movie, perhaps, and thought it would be all glitz and glamour and Michael Douglas), but in fact, I knew exactly what the job would entail. My mother works as a corporate securities lawyer, and I had worked the previous summer in a San Francisco corporate law firm, so I knew the work would be largely organizational and detail-oriented and would involve long hours. Knowing this, and knowing too that in this diversity-obsessed age I almost certainly would improve my chances of getting into law schools if I chose to do something a little less typical, I nonetheless decided to work in the Corporate Finance practice group of Shearman & Sterling. What motivated my job choice in these circumstances warrants, I believe, some explanation.

The American liberal arts education prepares its participants for everything and nothing. Unlike European institutes or pre-professional schools, the goal of the American liberal arts education is neither quantifiable knowledge nor a specific technical skill, but rather a necessarily imprecise "ability to learn." Spit out of such a system into the wilderness of American capitalism, the liberal arts college graduate is overwhelmed by career options (if not always opportunities). If one can identify what it is one wants to do and then do it well, there are almost no limitations on the American job market. Thus the post-collegiate assessment of one's future includes not simply availability but possibility. The more options one has, the more flexible a system is, the more personal one's choices become. If one can do anything, then what one chooses to do must be what one wants to do. Obviously, of course, character and circumstance inevitably narrow one's options, and for many, I am sure, defining preference is the least of worries. For myself, however, and for many other recent graduates I know or have encountered, pinpointing what it is that one wants to do is the essential post-graduation issue.

What, then, prompted me to become a legal assistant? Am I mad or was I just too afraid to do something more adventurous? I do not think I am either mad or chicken. It has been my experience that it is when I am least occupied and least challenged that I best know what I want and where I want to be going. In college, I was stimulated, interested and involved; and I probably gave less than two hours thought to what I wanted to do with the rest of my life. I thought I wanted to go to law school. The professor of my senior seminar in philosophy, Akeel Bilgrami, espoused a theory of self-knowledge in which he claimed that persons should not be held responsible for acts committed unknowingly (for example, a son committing acts of hatred against a father he thinks he loves), but should be held responsible for not bothering to acquire the self-knowledge that would explain such acts. I agree, and I think therefore that in applying to law school it is my responsibility to make sure that, to the best I can, I know what I am doing. As a legal assistant, I have had the time to question my college conclusions, to wonder whether I really do want to practice law. As a legal assistant in Corporate Finance (working primarily for a partner with a specialty in enhanced equipment trust certificate offerings), I have had a chance to think about law school in an environment that would turn many off of law entirely: not only is the particular field I work in esoteric, but the hours are long and the work is often tedious. Neither my thinking nor the environment, however, has dissuaded me from applying to law school. In fact, I now feel confident that law school is something I very much want to do.

I have always felt attracted to law as a more practical branch of philosophy, and my time at Shearman & Sterling has served to increase this attraction. As a philosophy major, I loved the logic, the systematic thinking and the precision of my subject, but I was frustrated by the ethereality of its goals. The minutiae of metaphysics, the angels on the head of a pin, I found meaningless. Yet immersed in a similarly esoteric side of law, I find that I do not mind the details. As long as the overall goal is a tangible one, the mechanics, however tedious, are bearable. I find too that I enjoy working within a comprehensive (albeit changeable) system; law is the underlying structure of all civic life in our society, and although my day to day work has little direct influence on this structure, I can at least contextualize and interpret my work against it. Although equipment financing in and of itself is not scintillating stuff, if I can relate particular projects to a larger sense of the influence of corporate law on our economy and everyday lives, the details and the precision and the long hours gain interest and meaning and become almost palatable. Thus my experience as a corporate finance legal assistant has not only allowed me the time to assess my future and reflect on what I wanted to do, but it has reinforced my college intuition that I am actively interested in law. Without elevating this year's work into some pseudo-spiritual search (I did not find "myself" as a legal assistant), I think it is fair to say that I attained enough self-knowledge to know that I want to go to law school and that I want to practice law.

COMMENTS

Anytime a college-aged applicant discusses "why I want to go to law school," she takes a risk. Few inexperienced applicants have anything interesting—or even credible—to offer on this topic. Judith, on the other hand, scores well with her confessional essay. She admits that law is "boring," "unadventurous," and the like, and that she purposefully took a job where she would be "least occupied" and "least challenged." She thus risks offending the admissions committee in the way she discusses the practice of law. Judith's candor and honesty ultimately work to her benefit, however. Her knowledge of the profession is indeed real; her desire to check out her potential future is certainly sensible. The result is an essay that reflects her purposeful career exploration.

TORI

My grandmother says that to the day my grandfather Ted died, she could still see my cousin Anita's pink handprint smeared across his right cheek. After Ted had a stroke and a heart attack in the same week, my family and his doctors decided to let him die a peaceful death staring with a half-opened eye at a silent flickering television hanging from the hospital ceiling. Anita returned early from a European vacation just in time to witness the impending death that the rest of my family had grown to accept, and when she entered Room 204, she walked right over to my grandfather and smacked him in the face. As his face burned, Ted ate food again for the first time in days and decided not to die.

Ted lived twenty years after that slap. My family spent half of every other weekend visiting my grandmother and him, bringing them food. Many of my earliest memories are of the way my face felt against a cold vinyl backseat of a car as I slept through the Lincoln Tunnel on the way back home to New York. I would only be a fraction of the person I am now had Anita not been courageous enough to hit her uncle as the nurses gasped in astonishment.

When I was young, Ted used to tell me all the things we would do together when he recovered from his paralysis. He taught me to imagine the two of us walking through art museums and sharing blankets at cold football games. I always knew that his fierce desire to walk again was what got him out of bed every morning. Bruises and cuts were commonplace as Ted would pull himself up from his chair, take one step, then tumble forward until his face hit the cement floor. I used to wonder what he thought each time in the instant between the fall and the landing, knowing not enough of his limbs worked well enough to break his fall.

As I grew up our conversations gradually shifted from what we would someday do together to what I was doing without him. He taught me to live a life passionate enough for both of us, to perform enough good for both of us, to have enough fun for both of us. When his nightly phone call would interrupt my dinner I'd feel embarrassed if I had nothing noteworthy to tell him. When I left for college, he cried and told me to learn enough for him to feel his own enlightenment.

The summer after I graduated from college, Ted pulled himself up from his bed in his nursing home and tried one last time to walk. He fell sideways to his left, and his paralyzed left arm could not protect him from the floor. His left leg twisted grotesquely but painlessly and one of its bones snapped in half. Lying in the hospital afterwards, he no longer could convince himself that he would be able to walk again. When he died soon after, I realized that after heart attacks and strokes, diabetes and seizures, a broken leg killed my grandfather.

My favorite image of my grandfather is one I've only seen abstractly. When my mother was a girl Ted would bring her to the same park bench every night to stare at the Hudson River. Every night all the other men from their apartment building would hover around him and listen to his jokes and stories. My mother calls those his nights of holding court: they were probably the best times my grandfather ever had. In all the smiles I ever saw on my grandfather's face, the left side of his mouth fails to rise along with the right, but what I actually remember are all of my grandfather's teeth shining, big like an easel, like he smiled by the river as a painless and hopeful young man.

I saw my grandfather hold court in nursing home after nursing home. He'd sit in his wheelchair next to the nurses' station surrounded by other men and women in their wheelchairs. The other residents would hear stories about all the things he and I were going to do when he got well once more. They told me that when I wasn't there he'd talk about all the things I was doing, how I was living a life, in his words, grand enough for both of us.

The day my grandfather died, I went from the hospital to his nursing home to retrieve his belongings. Every person there, from cooks to residents to visiting volunteers, asked me how he was, and it invariably sounded like the most important question they would ask anyone that day. When I told them he died, and I saw their eyes water, I also saw my grandfather's handprint across their cheeks. I realized how profound an impact my grandfather had on everyone he met. As my cousin succeeded in doing twenty years ago, my grandfather tried to slap life into everyone around him, and I lie awake at night hoping he is no longer held captive inside a body.

COMMENTS

This is a nicely wrought essay about a rather ordinary and commonplace influence on a young person: that of a close family member. This essay helps us learn several things about the candidate: She is dedicated to her family, she is compassionate and humane, and she is capable of forging connections with and learning from others. The "handprint" theme (developed in the first paragraph and returned to in the final one) helps make this essay memorable.

The problem with this essay is that the candidate is not center stage; indeed, we can infer only a limited amount about her. If there were serious questions about her compassion and humanity, then this essay will have helped her substantially. Otherwise, she will have done relatively little to advance her positioning efforts. It is a safe conclusion that this topic was chosen for lack of anything better, a sure sign that we have a young, inexperienced applicant.

JON QUEEN

"Why are you not packing up my house? I am leaving tonight, and you have to pack everything up right now," Diane yells at me as I try to fade into the wood floor—not an easy task for someone six foot six and two hundred fifty pounds. Later, I will bathe her and change her clothes after she has another biological accident. It is Sunday night at the Pogson house, and I must remind myself why I remain here.

Not very long ago, I was one of a large pool of ambitious graduates with big dreams of entering law school, learning the necessary tools, and contributing something positive to this world. However, at that time the closest I had come to the pressures of real life was the semester I spent interning on Capitol Hill. I felt ready for new challenges, a proving ground other than the traditional classroom. I opted to make it on my own for a while, prove that I was self-sufficient, and recover my focus as a student. What I never anticipated was that during this time, working as a home aide for a disabled woman, I would face challenges that would define my character and test my dedication to its fullest.

I had little inkling of the emotional commitment necessary to care for an elderly lady with multiple sclerosis. I was unprepared for her dementia, incontinence, or confrontational personality. In fact, her husband had committed suicide two years earlier, and the turnover rate for her home aides was very high. Recently, her son casually mentioned that I am the one thing delaying Diane Williams from entering a home, and that touched me deeply. So every night I clean up her excrement, and listen to her disjointed commands and angry outbursts. To further complicate matters, she has been unable to compensate me for the past week due to her financial situation.

Working with Diane has taught me many important lessons. Through her, I have learned the value of a positive outlook on life. I have also learned that in life, challenges never disappear; they merely change shape. I now regard the world from a different perspective, from the viewpoint of a contributor who has faced life's harsh realities, and has done his best to shield another from them. I feel that this new insight will serve as an excellent complement to the knowledge I will gain in law school. In addition, I have proven that I have the tenacity to overcome adverse and stressful situations, a skill that will help me excel in school as well as in life.

I am two years older and ages wiser than I was as a fresh graduate. Although I found my work as an economics major meaningful, I have grown much since then. I have learned the importance and satisfaction of contributing in a real world, one of poverty and disability. After all, life provides a different kind of education, and such experiential knowledge enriches classroom study and conceptual mastery.

COMMENTS

This essay explains how the applicant has spent his time since college, and helps position him as a compassionate and mature adult with more perspective on life than the usual college graduate. Jon benefits from the uniqueness of his experience as a home aide for a disabled woman, and is wise *not* to try to grope for specific connections between his job duties and his future as a lawyer. An applicant would be hard-pressed to group the two careers into a single framework, unless he or she had had other serious exposure to working with the disabled or disabilities law, and thus was better able to forge a natural link between these pieces.

Jon illustrates that he has both the heart to try to help others and the willingness to work hard at unpleasant tasks. The implicit message is that this combination can be powerful; also, that one can trust that he will indeed enter public interest law practice.

University of Pennsylvania Public Interest Scholarship Essay: To support your application . . . provide the Scholarship Committee with a brief description of any experiences, activities, and/or employment, demonstrating a commitment to public interest work and any other information which you feel would qualify you for the scholarship.

Public service has always played an integral role in my life. From an early age, my parents involved me in community programs. As I grew older, I took the initiative, volunteering one day a week in high school for MANNAH (low income housing provided in Washington, D.C.) and The National Children's Museum. Currently, I assist an elderly handicapped woman with her activities of daily living, and provide physical therapy to a polio survivor. Now that I am in the process of choosing a law school, it is important that the institution have a proactive public service program.

The Public Service Program at Penn Law School is the most credible among all of the schools that I have looked at. The school's urban location in Philadelphia provides students with a unique opportunity for community exposure; this affords the students a multitude of potential fields in which to serve, from child custody cases to drug counseling.

My desire is to serve an important role in the public sector after graduation from law school. My success in achieving this end rests primarily on two factors: the excellence of my law education and the quality of my public legal service up to that point. Penn Law provides the perfect marriage between both.

Although my desire to serve the community is a driving force behind my decision to enter law school, I am not merely some naive philanthropist whose heart is larger than his head. I am fully aware of the academic rigor and high level of performance associated with Penn Law. As my undergraduate record indicates, I can successfully balance the obligations of school, work, and athletics. I relish a full load, and some of my best work has been done under pressure.

In closing, I will firmly posit that Penn is my first choice among all of the schools I am considering. I hope that the admissions department will recognize my tenacity, dedication, and work ethic. The University of Pennsylvania embodies all that I am looking for in a law school, and I know that I am not the only hopeful candidate to share in this sentiment. What sets me apart from my fellow candidates is the quantity of my tangible contributions to society; I practice what I preach. I hope that I have effectively presented the strength of my candidacy through this application, and the reason why I desire to attend Penn Law School through this brief statement.

COMMENTS

Jon was wise to focus on the relative substance of his own "tangible contributions" to public service thus far. The bit of personal history he relates makes even more credible his professed commitment to public service.

ANTONIO

Our family gatherings were always full of entertainment provided by the youngest attendees. Cousin Alby was the magician. His brother Nelson was the contortionist. Our cousin Maria from Hartford was vying to be the next Celia Cruz at nine years old. The family talent shows that would spontaneously erupt at each barbecue, christening, or birthday kept the children occupied and allowed the adults to appreciate the spoils of parenthood. My contributions did not involve pulling a rabbit out of a hat, wrangling my legs behind my head, or singing salsa songs octaves too high. I had the gift of enthralling my family members by answering correctly any scientific question posed to me.

"How many planets are in the solar system?" "Why is the sky blue?" "Name the parts of the human digestive system." These were (and still are!) the classics of my repertoire, and year after year my animated answers became a lot more entertaining than the prosaic explanations offered by textbooks and teachers. I developed a sense of identity around my ability to explain everyday observations and occurrences simply and completely. More education brought increasingly sophisticated answers to the same questions and resulted in my characterization as The Scientist. When important conversations during college invited a perspective from the natural sciences, I reveled in being able to contribute substantively.

These very conversations made me question, among other things, my identity, and compelled me to find answers by continuously striving to build community among Latinos at Yale. Much hard work was involved in overcoming the barriers to sustaining that community, and I developed an ability to assess my surroundings more critically than ever before as I became more committed to student activism. Ultimately, I turned this critical eye to the study of science, and realized the profession would not highly value or productively use some of the personality traits that I would bring to it. While Antonio the Scientist fit in well within the confines of the laboratory, Antonio the Communicator did not.

I saw that, like me, most scientists valued communication, but very few cared to interact with individuals outside their own specialty, much less with non-scientists. I lamented the absence of undergraduate scientists in the broader discourse at Yale, especially in those areas that were most important to me, such as the diversity of Yale's student body. This often made me feel isolated, and the ramifications of that feeling, once understood, prompted self-examination and the exploration of alternative career paths. I left college with a greater appreciation of how important it was for me to communicate science to non-scientists, and to urge those that I left behind in the laboratory to do the same. The maturity I gained during this process made me value the exchange between the lay and technical, not for the validation I could receive from relatives or employers, but rather for the larger impact that I could have by being the intermediary between these two groups.

Although I left Yale with the tools for life-long learning, I did not leave with a crisp personal vision. This has developed during the two years since I finished college, and is due in large part to my experience at [large Wall Street law firm]. Here, I have found that the law will allow me to be the communicator that it is natural for me to be, and that the law provides an audience that is interested in communicating about technology's growing impact beyond the laboratory. I have seen that lawyers employ an even more rigorous standard for truth than scientists that fits in well with my technical background. And I also see that the unexpected ambiguities and unanswerable questions of the law will keep things interesting.

I have not even started working as a lawyer, but I already have the feeling that my impact is significant. I have awoken several mornings in the past eight months to hear the first public announcement of the deal on which I was working the previous evening. As one of a handful of paralegals who work on intellectual property due diligence at the firm, I play a role in most "high-tech" deals for which it is necessary. Assisting with patent prosecution and litigation has given me an inside-out view of the law while enhancing the technical competency of the firm's work product. My internal sense of accomplishment has been reinforced by the feedback I have received from the attorney with whom I work, and I can confidently say that the firm looks at me with an eye to the future.

With this experience has come a renewed confidence and desire for academic success, which, in turn, leaves me with an unclouded vision of the type of impact I can make. I am excited about the prospects of taking a biotechnology start-up public, securing protection for a large pharmaceutical company that allows it to post industry record profits, negotiating licensing contracts for a university that allows it to increase the size of its financial aid awards, or acquiring the international influence to figure prominently in developing countries' enjoyment of the full promise of the AIDS triple therapy. All of these are possible in my lifetime.

To borrow a phrase from microbiology, I am in the "logarithmic-phase" of my career. That is to say, the incremental steps in my development as a lawyer over the next several years will lead to explosive leaps in ability to contribute to the profession. In the process, Antonio the Communicator will become Antonio the Advocate. Three years at [law school X] will be an ideal start to that transformation.

COMMENTS

The majority of law school applicants have backgrounds in the humanities or social sciences. Those with science backgrounds automatically stand out a bit, albeit not always to their advantage if they suffer from the archetypal problems associated with scientists/engineers: poor communication and social skills. Antonio does a fine job in positioning himself: He shows that he is indeed a scientist, whose work makes him a natural for intellectual property law (a very hot field at the time of his application). He avoids the negatives associated with his science background, moreover, by showing his desire to be part of a field that requires substantial communication skill.

Despite this fine effort, however, one major problem remains: It is unclear why Antonio wishes to go to law school. After all, even if he wants a career in which communication skill is crucial, he could more readily choose a field other than law. For example, he could opt for scientific journalism or biotech marketing.

GARTH MOREY

The symbol of modern citizenship is the single voter, alone behind a curtain, silently pulling levers. In the face of a distended society, wrenching economic shifts, and transformed mediums of communication, individuals have become increasingly isolated from each other and from their communities. Citizenship has been divorced from community—we emerge momentarily to vote, to be citizens, and then scurry back to our private lives.

For our democracy to succeed, we must shift its symbolism, understand that citizenship depends not only on the vote, but also on participation, discussion, and debate. The synergy of individuals is one of democracy's greatest assets, and that synergy only develops when citizens actively engage with each other. Through the interchange of ideas, participation gives decisions better direction and credibility. More importantly, participation engenders collective commitment to a community. New outcomes become possible through cooperation, and the political community gains intrinsic value for its residents.

These principles are on display in my own life. At the Empowerment Zone/Enterprise Community Taskforce, applications poured in from around the country, vivid testimony to the deprivation faced by America's inner cities. HUD could never have hoped to fund all the worthy projects. Many of the applications, however, noted a new resource, already in hand, rediscovered through the process of neighborhood strategic planning. This resource was community and a shared commitment to the revitalization of a neighborhood's enduring distress. Communities that failed to earn a cent from the competitive grant process still maintained their planning boards and resident councils, capitalizing on the energy and commitment found in the community. In their newly reactivated citizens, they found a momentum that escapes the dependency on cash and government assistance.

The politics in Scranton, Pennsylvania are similar to the coal industry that established the region: hard, dark and self-consuming. During the Presidential campaign, to bring the divided Democratic Party together, I learned that my greatest assets were my ears and the table in my office. With discussion and honest listening, most constituencies learned to ignore, overcome, or avoid their differences. Pro-life Democrats walked door to door with ardent feminists; environmentalists made phone calls from the Building Trades Union hall. By providing a forum for discussion and encouraging individuals to share their concerns as citizens of the same city, I created a forge of Democratic cooperation.

In my classroom, I let students lead the academic process, let them learn through exploration and discussion. In a circle, they struggled with the twin challenges of algebra and adolescence. Together, they came to understand both the immediate material and the more durable lessons of process, reason and analysis. More importantly, they learned to interact with and rely on each other. Through the academic institution, my students explored the citizenship and community, and they developed a set of common ethics and relationships that will be their foundation for years to come.

Intellectually, I recognize participation as the crucial ingredient of a revitalized political sphere. Personally, I gravitate toward inclusion and engagement, toward the interplay of discussion. So I espouse and encourage active citizenship. If we are bold enough to talk to each other, to sit discussing our plans and our dreams, then we can renew the relevance and the energy of our various democracies.

COMMENTS

This is a nicely done exploration of an intellectual idea—relating to the law and citizenship of the United States—that moves the candidate. It is a relief that Garth does not resort to quoting someone else on the topic, but does all the thinking for himself, showing that he is confident and capable of relying on his own intellectual powers. He also does a nice job of focusing on this one theme while also bringing in a discussion of his experience (at the Empowerment Zone/Enterprise Community Taskforce and for the Democratic presidential campaign).

Garth could have improved this essay by giving the reader more context about the two personal experiences to which he refers. Although he laid out the context of his work experiences in the "data sheets" accompanying his applications, it would have been useful to have this information right here, so that readers could avoid having to flip back to other parts of the application while in the middle of the essay. In reading this essay, an admissions officer might wonder what the Empowerment Zone/Enterprise Community Taskforce is. (Where is it based? Is it a federally funded project? What is its specific mission?) An admissions officer might also wonder for which presidential campaign Garth worked, and what his position on the campaign was.

MAURA WILSON

I shifted my feet uneasily as I listened to President Reagan's "evil empire" speech. That evening my six-year-old world was dark, and the yellow glow of our kitchen light did not dent the long ominous shadows that lurked outside our windows. I slowly continued setting the table, the television flickering, and I learned to fear people half a world away, whom I had never seen. My fear made me angry because I was not used to such feelings. I was an independent, confident child, accustomed to facing my few problems directly. The fact that I could not talk to the leaders and citizens of the Soviet Union, and explain to them that Americans were really very nice, infuriated me. I wanted to make things better. I hated being afraid.

Seven years later, elation pumped my heart as I sat in that same kitchen and watched sections of the Berlin Wall come down. I had never been to Berlin, or touched that wall, but the legacy of the Iron Curtain was burned into me. Every current map that I had ever seen of Europe was half red: half feared, half evil. I never considered that it would be any different in my lifetime. Yet there, right before my eyes, concrete slabs were cut and the world swirled with change.

I became an international studies major because I was so excited by this new world we had entered. I chose to focus on United States diplomacy and security because I was intrigued by the opportunities of the post-Cold War era, and I was concerned by the many knotty problems that had emerged out of the disintegration of the formerly bi-polar world. The rules of the Cold War no longer applied, but what would the new rules be? The legacy of the decades-long standoff allowed the world to return to an era of fragmentation and militant nationalism, yet it also provided an unprecedented chance for countries to join together in positive political and economic agreement.

During college I worked for Gensler, an international architecture firm, to learn about the realities of operating a modern global operation. Gensler faced many challenges with its large Pacific Rim clientele. To open an office in Japan, it had to form a business alliance with a Japanese *keiretsu,* one of the powerful families that control economic operations in Japan. It also had to address corporate culture issues, such as altering marketing presentations for Asian clients, who prefer to see very detailed, full-color mock-ups of buildings before they will agree to close the deal. The company learned to carefully navigate the many obstacles, misunderstandings, and difficulties that are a regular part of operating a successful international operation.

After graduation I chose to work for the Department of Commerce because I wanted to help the American government operate more efficiently, especially on a global scale. Among other issues, the Commerce Department is concerned with international trade, along with world-wide problems such as the maintenance of the oceans and atmosphere. I performed in-depth research and reviews of Commerce agencies and programs to identify any operational deficiencies or violations. I reviewed a program within the International Trade Administration that helps American companies to expand their operations overseas. I also evaluated an agency that performed most of the research on the El Nino phenomenon—a topic that could not be effectively and completely examined without input from scientists around the world.

Our home planet is a much smaller place than it was ten years ago, or even ten months ago. Helping the federal government to react and adapt to the increasingly interlinked world we are creating was a very valuable experience. I now look forward to utilizing that experience in obtaining a legal education and practicing law. To ignore the increasingly international scope that law must encompass is unreasonable.

The uncharted political and economic intricacies of the post-Cold War era have created a cacophony of legal viewpoints. This confusion is compounded by the advent of the Internet age, whose international legal ramifications have barely begun to be addressed. I am so excited by the possibilities of international law. I hope that those who create and enforce it can eventually form a set of regulations, precedents and institutions, where lasting and fruitful political, social and economic understandings (instead of wars or decades-long stand-offs) can be forged.

The University of Michigan Law School offers exactly what I want: an excellent, innovative education in international law. The opportunity to meet and learn from law professors from around the world through the Center for International and Comparative Law is unmatched. The comprehensiveness of the program's curriculum expresses a deep understanding of how the future of society, economics and the law are inextricably moving towards a global society that requires international legal expertise. The University of Michigan Law School would shine with the addition of my experience, intelligence and zeal.

At a very young age, an international conflict touched my life with fear. But as the world left the Cold War behind, I left my fear with it, and emerged with a dedicated interest in international relations. The legacy of that fear sparked my concern for protecting and maintaining our efforts in forming a global community. I do not want to slip back to a time when the menace of an "evil empire" is broadcast into our kitchens. The law is a very important caretaker for this exciting, hyper-linked new world, and I want to be an essential part of shaping and caring for it.

COMMENTS

Maura does an excellent job making sense of her interest in internationalism and the law. Her opening paragraph—showing her as a young child watching Reagan's "evil empire" speech on her kitchen TV—is memorable, and helps her to set up the trajectory that would cause her to become an international studies major, work for an international corporation, perform research for the Department of Commerce, and now prepare for a career in international law. Notice the deft way that she placed her work at Gensler into this "thematic" build up. Rather than writing off that experience as unmentionable here (as some, viewing it as "architecture" or "design" work, might have), Maura realized the potential to utilize that job to further explain her understanding of our globally connected world.

Michigan Optional Essay #1. "This essay should focus on aspects of your background and past experiences that will contribute to the diversity the Law School wishes to foster. This essay should offer information not included in your personal statement."

My stomach felt like it was somewhere in the middle of my chest, and it threatened to move further up at any moment. What had I done? What was I thinking? I had chosen to attend St. Ignatius Prep, a previously all-male institution that had gone co-ed. I would be one of the 175 freshman girls, who would buck an over-century-long tradition, and mingle with the 1000 or so boys that roamed S.I.'s halls. I was terrified.

I had attended an all girls' elementary school, and not had a class with a boy since pre-school. Yet I chose to continue my education with hundreds of them, many of whom did not like the idea of females entering their enclave.

High school is tough, and my decision to go to Saint Ignatius made it tougher, but I have never regretted it. Besides being an excellent school, S.I.

taught me that I could rely on my intelligence, quick instincts, and sense of humor to get me through many difficult situations. The first few weeks were the most awkward. Girls were greeted in the halls with quick, intense gazes that ranged from hostile and affronted, to amused at our novelty. I discovered that meeting these gazes directly would make my male classmates at least stop staring. With that victory, I faced the rest of my time at S.I. in the same direct manner.

I endured cat calls and whispers every time I entered my freshman science class, where, due to a scheduling glitch, I was the only girl. I discovered that consistently doing excellent work, and providing intelligent answers to questions, eventually earned me respect in that class. I had my first surprising encounter with a urinal, in the hastily converted women's bathroom, and decided they were nothing to fear. I was quietly amused that the girls' locker room was painted pink. The transition had its bumps, but by the end of my freshman year, we had smoothed the way for all the other girls to come.

At thirteen years old, I stormed a tradition, and stretched my comfort zone to unprecedented proportions. My high school experience had the usual highs and lows, but I treasure the uniqueness of my four years at Saint Ignatius. The self-confidence and maturity that I gained there will be with me for my entire life.

COMMENTS

For a white "mainstream" applicant who has had a fairly ordinary life, the topic Maura chose works well. Since she has no tales to tell about a harrowing immigration journey to the U.S. and no cultural or ethnic "tags" by which to sell herself, she is smart to focus on her courage and tenacity, especially as they were evident as she "stormed a tradition" by entering the first class of females to attend a formerly all-boys school. The little details—the pink painted walls in the girls' locker room, for example—help to make this effective. So, too, does the sense of perspective she brings to her history—the fact that she can smile about what happened, and see how she benefited from it.

Michigan Optional Essay #2. This essay "should reveal, in a way that an LSAT score or a grade point average cannot, something about the way you think. For example, you might choose to discuss an intellectual or social problem you have faced or a book or film that has particularly affected you."

I disagree with the concept of "children's literature." A book that is well-written and compelling appeals to me, regardless of the section of the book store where one can find it. I can still curl up with E.L. Konigsburg's *From the Mixed-Up Files of Mrs. Basil E. Frankweiler* and thoroughly enjoy myself. I love reading about the exploits of Eloise or Madeline. I still get chills when I revisit *A Wrinkle in Time*. These books were my friends when I was growing up, and as an adult I have not forgotten them. Today, I have an even greater appreciation for the skill and deftness with which my favorite early writers serve their craft.

They never patronize their readers, and with just a few phrases, they can translate complicated ideas and feelings into something equally meaningful to a child or an adult.

These excellent qualities are found in the increasingly popular Harry Potter series. J.K. Rowling has created a wonderful world, with complex and interesting characters. She employed the clever trick of creating a fantasy world that parallels and mixes with the world that we already know. She makes it easy to believe in witches and wizards, flying broomsticks, and a boarding school that teaches magic. Her descriptions are brief and vivid, and she always leaves her reader wanting more.

The media is shocked by how widely embraced Harry is. It is a "children's book" after all. I read a discussion of Harry in which the reviewer admitted embarrassment about reading the book in public. He kept his laptop close at hand to prove to any passers-by that he was working. I would read Harry Potter in public with pride! I have read plenty of recently best-selling, and critically acclaimed books that were boring, awkwardly written, or just plain tedious. Rowling not only entertains but also challenges her reader. Averaging around 300 pages, the books are much longer than most written for kids, the vocabulary is advanced, and the plots are complex "who-done-it puzzles," with wonderfully unexpected twists and turns.

Children and adults love the Harry books because they are exciting and funny. But adults also enjoy them because the books give them access to a kid's world. This is a world no less confusing, complex or heart-wrenching than an adult world—it is often more so—but often out of reach for adults. The fantasy, imagination and pure joy of the series inspires nostalgia in adults for their own childhoods. At the same time, adult readers can create a connection with children who are experiencing Harry Potter.

I hope that those adults who eagerly anticipate and enjoy each new Harry installment will branch out and sample some of the many other quality books that children have loved for years, and that too many adults quickly forget. These books can help adults to connect to their pasts, as well as their present situations.

COMMENTS

This is a refreshing way to write about "the way you think." Maura decided to write not on an international concern or political issue but a fairly simple idea close to her heart: adults' enjoyment of so-called "children's" literature. She is sure to remain memorable with this, since it's highly unlikely any other candidate would have written on this same topic. (On the other hand, applicants who write on the importance of human rights, feminism, and other hot issues are sure to remain unmemorable to admissions officers.) The thoughts laid out here are not particularly complex, but they are fresh and compelling.

BRENDAN

For the past two years I have lived and worked in Latin America. I have seen firsthand both the potential for development that exists throughout the region, and the mistakes that foreigners make in Latin America for lack of local experience. However, I am also deeply attached to my home state, Rhode Island, and I believe in my responsibility to development opportunity locally. My aim is to find a way to connect the opportunities that exist in Latin America to the growth of my home state.

I was one year old when I made my first visit to Latin America—traveling with my parents to Mexico's Yucatan Peninsula. That trip marked the beginning of a lifelong fascination with South America. My formation as a Latin Americanist—my consciousness of the layers of society and history in the region, began within the ambient orientation of my family toward Latin America, and has been informed by my own experiences there since before I can remember.

From my earliest memories the region's language, art, food, and music were part of my growing up. As a teenager, I spent several summers in Mexico: traveling with my parents or staying with family friends in the slow, hot city of Kampuchea. When I was thirteen, my parents adopted my sister Maggie from Honduras and we spent the summer in the rainy, unrelenting poverty of Tegucigalpa. My childhood, in sum, was a steady exposure to the variety and contrasts of Latin American—the wealth of nature and ancient civilization, the poverty of the people, the army, the complexity of feeling towards the United States.

Since finishing college, I have been fortunate to experience unusual successes working in the capital markets at a time when these markets are fueling historic changes throughout the region. In the emerging markets of Latin America, the political, economic, and cultural lives of each country ebb and flow around the markets to a pronounced degree. In Buenos Aires a cab driver can tell you where YPF's stock closed the day before. A waiter in Sao Paulo will know the daily change in the Consumer Price Index. Because of these markets' central importance, I have had a glimpse of both where these countries are coming from, and where they are going.

I have observed that three core misunderstandings mark the missteps that foreigners, particularly Americans, make in Latin America. The first is the most obvious, yet poses continual difficulties for foreigners, especially in business: Latin America is not a monolith—cultures vary as widely between Latin countries as they do between the U.S. and any one Latin country, maybe more. Differences range in subtlety from racial and gender attitudes to simple use of language. Thus, Mitsubishi wasted months of effort and uncountable brand value trying to introduce its Pajero sport utility vehicle, which had enjoyed great success in Brazil, to Argentina. The company, in its monolithic view of Latin

America, didn't know that the word "pajero" has a sexual meaning in Argentine Spanish that it does not in Brazilian Portuguese.

Secondly, foreigners tend to mistake the meaning of their "rights" in Latin America. They often assume that the same ideas of contracts and obligations prevail in Latin America as they do in the first world, and that the courts occupy the same exalted place in society that they do in the U.S. They often fail to realize that in Latin America, possession is the chief determinant of ownership (thus the ferocity of land battles between peasants and landowners throughout Latin America). It follows that the prestige of the courts is often less than in the U.S. Power tends to rest much more directly in the hands of politicians and labor leaders. This has been the source of endless tension between the governments of the U.S. and several Latin countries, arising most recently with regard to the ownership of intellectual property rights. Governments in Chile and Argentina have questioned the American assertion that development of drugs and medicines connotes ownership, and that therefore cheap and easy replication by local firms should be prohibited.

Finally, Sam Rayburn's admonition to "go along to get along" holds special meaning in Latin America. The systemization of relationships that makes the U.S. a very efficient society does not yet exist in Latin America. Personality and background play a very important role in transactions ranging from social to official to professional. The importance of individual relationships, especially those arising from family background, is difficult to overstate. Personal relationships are the lubricant of business and society, and the failure to develop them is a principal mistake made by foreigners.

One of the benefits that I have derived from living and working in Latin America, and witnessing first hand the mistakes made and opportunities missed by others, is that I see how the mistakes can be avoided, and the opportunities seized. I hope that this knowledge will allow me to continue to be a part of the evolution and development of Latin America.

I have Latin America in my heart, and I have no doubt that my professional future lies in the region. However, I am from Providence, R.I., and I am strongly committed to the values of place and home. I feel bound by my family and my upbringing to the place of my childhood, and I believe deeply that opportunity is not to be followed elsewhere, but created locally.

One of the principal challenges that I foresee for myself in my professional life is to connect the dynamism and opportunity that the development of Latin America represents, to the stagnant Rhode Island economy. The way is far from clear. Rhode Island's areas of economic strength, tourism and oceanography, bear little relation to the needs of the Latin countries—infrastructure, telecommunications, financial services. As a market, Rhode Island, with fewer than 1 million inhabitants and little cultural attachment to Latin America, is too small and too remote to represent a great attraction to Latin exporters.

However, I am convinced that the flow of knowledge in the interconnection of the Americas will be two ways. Clearly, the Latin countries can learn much from the U.S. in terms of industrial and social organization, investment, etc. I believe that there are also important lessons that the U.S. can learn from the growth of Latin America as well. Examples abound of lessons learned by Latin countries during the course of their recent development that would be well applied in the U.S.

In the mid 1980s Chile privatized its state-controlled pension system. The result was fiscal havoc for the government for four or five years, but out of the chaos emerged a stable base of local capital that has financed the double-digit growth rates that Chile has experienced through the 1990s.

Similarly, in the early 1990s Mexico decided to finance the replacement of its aged highway infrastructure by selling toll-taking concessions to construction firms. In many ways the effort was disastrous (toll revenues failed to meet expectations for reasons that should have been easily avoided, and the concessionaires received a government bailout). However, a new infrastructure was built, and the government demonstrated that private capital and public need could successfully be joined for the benefit of both.

There are clear lessons for the U.S. to learn from the experience of Latin America during the heady growth of the early 1990s. I would like to see Rhode Island benefit from these lessons, and to begin to look beyond its own beverages for engines of growth. For my part, I intend to continue to seek a way of creating opportunity in my state by linking Rhode Island to the continuing development of Latin America.

COMMENTS

Overall, this is a compelling portrait of both the applicant and his passions, what makes him tick. He demonstrates substantial understanding about several topics: Latin American cultures, economic development, and so on. Similarly, his use of detail—in the discussion of the Pajero sport utility vehicle or his family's trip to Honduras, for example—brings the piece to life and helps to make him memorable. There is no doubt that admissions officers will remember "the candidate from Rhode Island interested in forging connections between his home state and Latin American development." This will likely describe no other candidate in the pool.

There are, however, two fundamental problems with Brendan's personal statement. He should have spelled out how he would attempt to link Rhode Island and Latin America, rather than just express a vague ambition to do so. In addition, he should have made clear that law school is indeed the right place for him. Frankly, from this essay one would think that the candidate should be planning to attend an MBA program instead. He should have explained, even in just a sentence or two, how a law degree would help him achieve his goals.

AMY CRAWFORD

I wish to attend law school in order to practice public interest law. This decision is based upon a number of influences and experiences, some of which go back to my childhood, others of which are of more recent origin.

I grew up in rural Southwestern Virginia, where my father was an attorney. My father's law practice is probably unique. It is not unusual for him to handle a divorce in exchange for a load of wood or to represent a client in a child custody case in return for having our house painted. Although my father has never been very financially successful, his work as a lawyer has always been characterized by a great and abiding generosity. Over these years I have seen in my father a genuine enthusiasm for helping people who would otherwise be shut out from the legal system.

In my hometown I also witnessed the silent divisions of our society along racial and economic lines. Why, for example, was the town's curfew only enforced in a neighborhood where the majority of the black community resided? Why did a public school divide kindergartners by their parents' social position or educational level, rather than by the children's capacities to learn? Why were students at one school offered a choice of four foreign languages for study, and students at another school, in a poorer neighborhood, offered only one? I later came to believe that these once puzzling questions are best addressed through social policy or litigation, and though shifts may seem small they can achieve profound and long-term consequences in a given community.

At the University of Virginia, I majored in Sociology and African-American Studies, with a special emphasis on the dynamic between social policy and law. I saw that the questions which had troubled me as a child in my hometown did indeed involve issues of discrimination and social and economic equality. I think that being one of the few white African-American Studies majors gave me an unusual opportunity to examine institutional biases based upon race, gender and class. While in college, I also worked in an alternative sentencing program which provided education, job training and drug abuse counseling to prison inmates. As an intern case manager, I was responsible for interviewing inmates to determine their eligibility for the program. The program was an innovative one, but it was realistic as well, and I saw the tangible benefits which the men and women who participated in it received. Just prior to graduating from college, I prepared an extensive recidivism study which was used to demonstrate to the Virginia Department of Corrections the real impact the program was having on the lives of the inmates after leaving prison and completing our program.

After graduating from the University of Virginia in 1993, I moved to New York City to work for the Legal Aid Society. For the past three years I have been a paralegal with the Legal Aid Society's Civil Appeals and Law Reform Unit. One of the first cases to which I was assigned at Legal Aid was *Jiggets v. Dowling*, a major affirmative litigation case in which Legal Aid challenged the adequacy of the shelter allowance paid to welfare recipients in New York City. The case has been pending for a number of years and has not yet been decided; however, the presiding judge granted the interim application of one family for preliminary relief while the decision is pending. Since the original grant of preliminary relief to one family, more than 25,000 families have applied for and obtained housing assistance and protection from eviction through this interim preliminary relief system.

A primary part of my work at The Legal Aid Society involves coordinating the efforts of Legal Aid attorneys and their clients to take advantage of this system of preliminary relief created by *Jiggetts* particularly in emergency situations. I am one of the individuals for the litigation team designated to contact New York State officials in Albany to ensure proper and immediate processing for relief in emergency situations. Legal service attorneys throughout New York City often ask me to assist them in applications for relief with evictions as imminent as the next day. I have conducted various seminars for Legal Aid and Legal Services attorneys, law school clinics and community based organizations on the benefits available through *Jiggetts*. I have also intervened on behalf of individual Legal Aid clients. For example, one client I worked with recently was a woman who had been a victim of domestic violence and who consequently needed help obtaining housing. First I advocated on behalf of my client pursuant to *Jiggets v. Dowling* by finding a home for her and her family—safe from the batterer. Then I was able to help her with other issues as well, such as correcting her disability payments and obtaining admission of her child to a gifted student program. I saw how the lives of this client and her children were materially improved, and it was significantly based on the judge's interim order of preliminary relief. My work with *Jiggetts* has confirmed my belief that through the legal process our society can be forced, albeit reluctantly, to confront the issues of injustice and inequality which blight the lives of so many individuals.

Another case I worked on at The Legal Aid Society which has demonstrated to me the power of the law to improve people's lives is *Rivera v. New York City Housing Authority,* an ongoing class action suit on behalf of mobility impaired tenants challenging the New York City Housing Authority's implementation of the Americans with Disabilities Act. In this case, I have been assigned to act as the informal liaison between the defendant's Law Department and Legal Aid's individual clients. I have seen first-hand how the lives of mobility impaired people and their families have been changed for the better by *Rivera*. For example, in the case of one family with a daughter confined to a wheelchair, I successfully argued that the family must be relocated because they lived in an apartment building with no elevator. This family's move to an accessible apartment improved the family dynamic by enabling the daughter to attend school independently and by granting her parents more freedom.

Outside of my work at The Legal Aid Society, I have also had to address issues of race, gender and class as a volunteer teaching a weekly class on Civil Rights and Race Relations to students in New York Civil Rights Coalition, which began in 1989 in the wake of the race riots in the Crown Heights section of Brooklyn. Volunteer teachers like myself go to public high schools in the five boroughs to initiate a dialogue about issues of racial and cultural bias with students. These discussions are frank, and range from specific experiences which students have had (e.g., what it is like to be scrutinized by a security guard in a store or to be ignored by a cab driver) to general concerns about discrimination in employment or housing. My experience as a teacher leading these classes has demonstrated to me that some of the same concerns which I had as a child in Virginia are still troubling the youth today. I hope that I have exposed students to the legal system's role in confronting their concerns.

Year by year, case by case, client by client, my commitment to public interest law has broadened and deepened. My passion is to serve disadvantaged and underrepresented people as an attorney advocating for their interests.

COMMENTS

Amy's approach is simple and direct, yet highly effective. She shows how natural it was for her to become a civil rights advocate by highlighting her interesting family background. Many candidates try to do this, in fact, but few succeed fully. The difference in her case is not that she has *written* more persuasively on this topic, but that she has *lived* more persuasively in this regard. She followed up her father's example by majoring in African-American studies, an unusual choice for a white person, as she notes here. After that, she stopped working in the corporate world after one year at Lehman Brothers in order to pursue her passion for civil rights work. In her case, the passion she expresses in this essay does not lack the necessary correlative for credibility: full-time work in the trenches.

It is easy to claim an interest in civil rights law, or other public interest fields, and even to walk that walk while in college. After all, few college students feel that they are making major sacrifices in college by spending a few hours a week in some volunteer activity. After college is when the crunch comes. Applicants who claim a great interest in lesser-paid public interest work are never entirely believable until they have indeed spent some years in the field.

Amy is particularly effective because she combines a lengthy history of involvement with an essay that conveys the nature of the lessons she has learned. The great detail she brings to the stories about her positions with the Legal Aid Society and teaching for the New York Civil Rights Coalition demonstrate both her commitment and the extent to which she will bring a well-developed perspective to the law school classroom (and clinical programs).

SACHA M. COUPET

Monique is a fourteen-year-old going on forty, a survivor of incest whose delinquent behavior is a plea for help. Jamie, barely five and in foster care, insists that he should be able to take care of himself and his younger siblings as he has done, he says, since he was "little" and living with his "forever mom." Sarah, four, was rushed to the emergency room three years ago, severely bruised and minus several teeth after her mother's boyfriend attempted to "discipline" her. Today, this same mother and boyfriend plead before the court for her return. In our legal system, who speaks for these children, too young to exercise any power or to comprehend the magnitude of the decisions that concern them? What is the fate of these children who face an adolescence in juvenile detention, a childhood in foster care, or worse yet, a childhood cut short? Who acts "in the best interest" of these children in whose faces we may see our own sons and daughters? I believe we are all vested with a moral responsibility to advocate for the needs of children and am eager to lend my voice.

My decision to pursue a legal education has emerged from my collective experiences as a psychologist, an advocate, a scholar, and an observer of society. Contrary to my colleagues in psychology who suggest that my decision to study law is tantamount to a defection to "the other side," I do not feel I am abandoning my field, rather I am incorporating it into another much in the way an artist might combine two media. I am a creative person, intellectually and artistically, whether in a classroom or at a potter's wheel, and welcome the challenge of improving on traditional methods by combining the best elements of many techniques. While the theory, language, and practice of clinical psychology and law differ, I do not believe these disciplines are at odds, but rather complement one another. On a micro level, clinical psychology focuses on the transformation of the individual psyche into a structure of operating and understanding one's world. The law is an expression of a similar process on a broader scale, with a focus on the transformation of societal values into social structures. In my experience, the most rewarding challenge has been examining the interface between psychological and legal issues, identifying the points of convergence and divergence, and integrating the two.

Although I began my undergraduate study with the intention of pursuing a career in medicine and complemented my high school curriculum with a number of medical-related volunteer experiences, I broadened my focus in the helping professions one year into college. After two grueling terms in a pre-med curriculum I declared a major in psychology. The research and practice in this discipline more closely reflected the way in which I understood and preferred to work with people, particularly those with socioeconomically disadvantaged backgrounds. Years later, in my graduate research, clinical work, and teaching, I continue to develop a more comprehensive knowledge of how sociodemographic and psychological factors influence the lives of marginalized, oppressed, or underserved populations.

While I admit to a fair share of idealism, my desire to successfully integrate a background in psychology with the study and practice of law has not developed from a visionary notion to right all injustice and cure every social ill, but from a number of positive experiences I have had in the real world. As a family and child therapist, I have counseled numerous persons whose lives have been profoundly impacted by events in the courtroom. Whether working with victims of domestic violence, child abuse, divorce and contested custody, assisting adults and children during prolonged legal disputes, or serving as a representative of the court, I have learned a great deal from observing and participating in the legal process.

Increasingly, as the court becomes the arbiter of America's most intimate family decisions, judges find themselves in need of input from a number of sources. Information gathered about a variety of psychological issues, including child development, parental capacities, attachment relationships, or family functioning has become critical in such legal decision making. From the beginning of my professional training I have had many opportunities to assist the court in searching for and providing this information. My interest and involvement in the legal process has only deepened since.

As a consultant to law students in the University of Michigan Law School's Child Advocacy Law Clinic, I assisted inexperienced attorneys develop an understanding of the psychological issues inherent in child advocacy, particularly as they relate to child protection, parental termination, permanency planning, and foster care. More recently, my work with the Child Welfare Law Resource Center has afforded me continued opportunities to share a psychological perspective with representatives of other disciplines interested in highlighting the importance of child welfare law. My dissertation research reflects this interdisciplinary theme as it combines legal and psychological issues in an examination of the impact of child welfare and foster care policy on family functioning. In addition, I continue to publish and present professionally in areas related to interdisciplinary work in child abuse and neglect.

I have faced each of these experiences within the legal system with the utmost degree of curiosity, excitement, and enthusiasm. I have grown both personally and professionally, having wrestled with philosophical elements of the law that have challenged me to think critically in my role as a psychologist and to flexibly adapt my skills to a legal context. As a psychologist in a legal arena, I felt at first like a foreigner in a new unfamiliar environment, uncertain of the climate, culture, or language. I developed a psychological index applied to the legal system that included such diagnostic categories as "adversarial angst" and "expert witness hysteria," conditions which I observed to afflict many persons whose professional obligations brought them, often reluctantly, into the courtroom. Fortunately, I was spared from such afflictions and found myself, instead, quite intrigued. While I learn from every new legal experience, each exposure has left me feeling particularly limited in my capacity to effect significant change because of my unfamiliarity with the law. Although cognizant of the changes I have helped to bring about in my work as a psychologist, I feel drawn to the broader level of change that a law degree would permit me. Having developed an extensive background in psychological theory and practice, I am now compelled to turn my efforts towards the pursuit of a legal education.

My long-term objective is to facilitate an integration of psychology and law with the goal of enhancing the lives of children and families. As an African-American female, I feel particularly invested in the plight of the growing number of poor and minority children who are over-represented in the child welfare system and intend to play a key role in developing both legal and psychological strategies to assist them. I have committed myself to remaining involved, as a community volunteer and a professional, with children and families whose opportunities in life have been much more limited than my own. While I am conscious of the fact that the course of my life has been significantly shaped by the privileges of a middle class upbringing, I am not too far removed from the experience of those for whom I seek to advocate. My parents were immigrants who left Haiti over a decade before I was born to find opportunities in the U.S. They arrived with few resources, but much determination to succeed. By their word and their example, they have instilled in me the virtues of compassion and respect for others, the importance of hard work and commitment, and an appreciation for all that I have received. With this, I feel it is incumbent upon me to give back to my community in every manner possible.

As a law student, I seek to be an active participant in an educational setting enriched by more than the practical elements of law, but also the philosophical, contextual, and social dimensions of jurisprudence. The University of Pennsylvania Law School is nationally recognized and respected for providing this kind of dynamic learning environment. My life experience, breadth of knowledge in psychology, and commitment to an interdisciplinary approach and public service would allow me to contribute greatly to the diversity and the strength of the University of Pennsylvania student body. I possess the intellectual capacity, perseverance, and maturity to meet the challenges of a legal education and a professional career and look forward to continued opportunities to work on behalf of children like Monique, Jamie, and Sarah.

COMMENTS

This is a superb essay, created from Sacha's wealth of knowledge about her former field of psychology and extensive experience with child advocacy and family law. In one coherent essay she shows:

- Her passion for serving the interests of children
- How and why she got into psychology
- The evolution of her career

- The depth of her involvement and expertise (she presents and publishes in the field)
- How she will contribute to this field in the future, with the addition of her law degree (She does a particularly good job of showing that she is not so much changing careers as adding another dimension to what she already does.)
- Her reasons for wanting to attend Penn

Her personal statement is well-balanced, giving the right amount of space to each aspect of her presentation. It is also easy to follow her intellectual journey; she uses detail to make her points memorable and believable, without cluttering up the flow of her material.

Sacha's statement shows how convincing an applicant with real expertise in a related field can be. There is no doubt that she really knows her field. Similarly, it is clear that she will stay in this field and make more of a contribution with a law degree than she can without. She will have no trouble finding relevant employment, given her experience to date. In addition, her experience has presented her with ample opportunity to make sure that law is the right field for her.

Not only admissions officers would find her an appealing candidate; so, too, would career services officers. After all, they know that they will not have an unemployable person on their hands in three years and, far more important, they will not have an emotional wreck to handle. Sacha has sufficient relevant experience to know what she is getting into, and to know that it is right for her.

DAVID P. WHITE

My older brother is a drug addict. On April 4, 1995—two months before I took the LSAT—this fact changed my life. After returning from my first vacation in years, I came home to a frantic phone message stating that my brother had disappeared. "What are we going to do with the kids?" my mother's message asked. As a young Executive Director of a youth and family-empowerment organization, my response was immediate: "I have room at my place—I'll take the youngest two." Now 28, I have been the physical and legal guardian to Adam, now eight, and Taylor, now five, ever since.

With the humor and insight that distance provides, those first months with the kids almost seem nostalgic. There were dirty faces to wash, walks in the park to take, stories to read and many lessons to teach to these new little people in my life. But I also remember the trauma. My agency, born of grassroots movement, nearly closed down because of my reduced work schedule. Every day, at 5:30 p.m.,

I went home, no questions asked. I quit playing the saxophone and I resigned from several boards of directors on which I served. Money became a scarce commodity and my non-work life was a blur of cooking, cleaning, laundry and discipline. At times, I was bitterly resentful of my brother and his ex-wife's inability to get their lives together. When asked by others, "how are you handling all this?" I used to tell them, "there are dark nights." Day after day, through laughter and pain, we trudged through.

Now, after nearly two years of heroic effort, my brother has pieced together his life and will regain custody of his children soon. Sometimes, as I sit in the nearby park cheering for Adam's soccer team or as I scold Taylor for practicing her gymnastics on our furniture, I can scarcely believe that time has moved so quickly. Our family has actually benefited from the experience. Through a collective determination to keep our children out of state custody, my oldest brother (who also took two kids), mother and extended family members have become part of a stronger family unit. Following the shock of losing his children, my brother has successfully arrested more than a decade of behavior infested with drugs and violence. Most importantly, four of my nieces and nephews have been given a chance to succeed in life without the fetters of a childhood devoid of love and commitment.

For me, parenting my brother's children has never felt extraordinary. As a student of philosophy, I have the tendency to view life's events as connected to each other, as part of a fuller mosaic where each act is understood only within the context of the whole. This belief, that somehow the storm front of my new parenting responsibilities—and the opportunities in my life which I was subsequently forced to delay—would one day make sense to me when placed within the matrix of my whole life, was often the only thread on which I could hold. This belief was also critical to my success in my first job experience. My position as Director of Y.O.U. was a major undertaking which few of my friends expected me to survive. I was chosen from a national group of 52 candidates and was by far the youngest and least experienced of the group. As it turns out, my selection was due more to my lack of political relationships and connections than to anything else; the previous two years of the agency's history had been filled with tension, closed relationships and a visible lack of progress on any programmatic front. In fact, Y.O.U. was not even an agency at the time but rather a network of community-based organizations and activists who were openly divided along racial, financial and neighborhood lines. Apparently, they wanted a fresh start and, with a 24-year-old, cherub-looking face, I represented that.

The first several months were difficult. Few members of the network showed up for the first steering committee meeting that I organized. Many of them wanted me to visit them on their own turf in order to check my "grassroots credentials" before they would accept me as their new staff person. One of those who did show up brought his morning newspaper, whose pages he flipped and read throughout the meeting. It was the first of many frightening experiences and by the third month I was so demoralized that I was ready to resign.

I did not resign, however, and instead took a bold step: I hired staff and started to construct programs. It occurred to me that we could fulfill the original intent of the grassroots movement that had established the Y.O.U. network by molding the stated priorities of the steering committee into a coherent mission statement and a set of non-traditional services. So we did. The result was both unexpected and remarkable: success. Within a short period of time, and through a combination of politics, begging, will-power and luck, we built an organization that merged together the various agendas of opposing committee members into a full-blown initiative, one that could contribute to the larger system of youth and family services in our area while providing direct services to a number of young people.

I have been with Y.O.U. for nearly four years now. During my tenure, and by working with a host of others, I have overseen the development of the following: an incorporated agency in the state of Kansas; four community-/school-based programs; a core of professionally trained staff; an active Board of Directors; and a budget that has tripled in size and that now includes funding from public, private and contractual sources. In a move that could never have been foreseen before my arrival, the original network of agencies opted to become members of a larger coalition that has grown to over 100 members. In addition to providing services to over 500 youth and families annually, Y.O.U. received an award from the Governor of Kansas in 1994 for "Outstanding Community Service" and in that same year was described by the Kansas Office for Community Service as a "pillar" in the field of service-learning. Our success has included something as large as a transportation project that successfully transported 400 youths to jobs and enrichment-related activities, to something as localized as developing an academically failing, clinically depressed youth into a frequent public speaker and school leader through the sustained guidance of our leadership programs. We have accomplished much with the simple concept that agencies make better decisions regarding their services when they work together, and that our whole community is improved when our agencies make better decisions. Ironically, this is the basic idea that stood behind the establishment of the original network long before I arrived but it took a political novice to help them achieve it.

The past four years have been a time of relentless activity and significant accomplishment. Now, looking towards the future, I believe it is time to move forward and to build new skills. I plan to do this in two phases. First, I have recently accepted a position at the Chapin Hall Center for Children, a research and evaluation agency associated with the University of Chicago, to help initiate a city-wide project that focuses on youth development through large collaborative efforts. The position is for six months only and begins in early 1997; my role will be to develop the strategy by which the sponsor organizations can implement their expansive vision. My time at Chapin Hall will also serve as a period of reflection and transition into the second phase of my plan, which is to attend law school in the fall of 1997. I have looked forward to entering law school for some time now and believe that I can significantly enhance my professional abilities through the process of earning my law degree. The method of thought, the actual content of the information taught and the chance to review the accumulated statutes and thoughts that have shaped our society—all of these are things that excite me and that will improve my ability to bring about positive change in the world around me. In particular, I want to expand my understanding of how laws are constructed, interpreted, enforced, marketed to and understood by the public in urban areas across the country. As one who expects to be intimately involved with children's issues and urban community development throughout the duration of my life, I firmly believe that my experience in law school will help me become a better advocate for issues of concern and, ultimately, a more effective man of action.

Aristotle teaches that there is a path to success in life, one that involves a constant dialogue between hardship and joy, family and career. To date, my experiences have confirmed his teachings; my joy and sense of accomplishment have been the direct fruits of a determined struggle to overcome the obstacles in my family and professional life. Now it is time to take these experiences and build on them so that I can continue to contribute to a society that, I believe, is capable of being a safe, humane place for all of us. It simply needs constant advocacy and pressure from those of us who care. I do and I look forward to the challenge of law school which I believe will provide me with the tools to continue to contribute in ways that make a positive difference in the lives of others.

COMMENTS

This essay is remarkable in several ways. First, of course, the writer's remarkable family tale overwhelms readers. Second, David succeeds in tying together his adult life history with his career to date and his future. Few applicants to law school have as interesting a personal history to relate, or as clear a professional impact to offer, let alone personal histories and professional efforts that work in concert—and that show where they will head after law school. Third, David conveys this in a matter-of-fact tone that does not ask for readers to pity him, or indeed to admit him because of unusual circumstances. His positive, understated approach actually gets the most mileage from his position. Most applicants would overplay their hands, risking a negative reaction from admissions officers in so doing.

This essay "should reveal, in a way that an LSAT score or a grade point average cannot, something about the way you think. For example, you might choose to discuss an intellectual or social problem you have faced or a book or film that has particularly affected you."

In the 1980s, "Africanism" moved again from its position as a social undercurrent to grab the center stage of both intellectual and street culture within Black communities around the world. Broadly defined, the term refers to the efforts made by Black people to reassert the broken ties between the African continent, its people, and its scattered progeny around the globe.

The issue is replete with controversy and more than a few have had their racial identities challenged due to their feelings about the subject. At Oxford, we debated about whether or not non-African Blacks (jokingly referred to as NABs) had any claim whatsoever to Africa. We do, I argued, despite the regrettable fact that most outspoken NABs don't know whether Kenya is on the left or the right side of the continent. Our connection includes a complicated mix of blood lineage, shared cultural characteristics and a common legacy of oppression. Together, these things form a heritage for people of African descent that spans over four centuries, a heritage that is as legitimate as it is profound. It is, admittedly, also more complex than our so-called intellectual movements tend to make it.

No matter. Our failings are superfluous to the essence of what Africanism sets out to accomplish. The mere attempt to connect our origins with those of all Black people represents an effort, sometimes successful, to give strength and comfort to a people who still largely feel as if we are on the outside of society looking in.

COMMENTS

This think-piece on being black and separated from Africa has some positive, and some negative, impacts. It is heartening to read an essay on the topic of blackness without traces of bitterness. Similarly, it is nice to see an international perspective on the topic, along with an admission that most non-African blacks have no understanding of Africa. These positives are partially offset, however, by the irredentist notion that "NABs" have a claim on Africa. By the same token, arguing that blacks feel as if they are still on the outside looking in seems very much at odds with the current African experience, where white colonial rule is certainly a thing of the past. Given that black Africa is ruled by black Africans, isn't the claim that blacks feel like they are not on the inside of society actually evidence that NABs are in fact separate from Africa—that they do not reflect much, or understand much, about the actual African experience?

THOMAS

Though always curious about the law, my keen interest developed out of an undergraduate course I took in law and economics. I was amazed at how the extensive unpredictable social and economic effects of a particular law could be great enough to overshadow the original intentions of that law. This unpredictability is due to the complex nature of the minute-by-minute decision-making process of every American where nearly every decision is made taking the potential legal, and subsequent social and economic ramifications into account. Understanding this process and the factors decision makers weigh is paramount to obtaining the expanded foresight necessary to interpret and design laws more efficient in managing and improving society. The keys to understanding, which I am unique in having, are a diverse background, varied work experiences, and a broad education.

Though my desire to positively impact society is commonplace for my generation, my experience as a student in Mexico and later as a naval officer gives me a unique perspective and insight into the mentality of the average American that most students, scholars, and intellectuals do not have. Living and studying in Mexico as an Hispanic, I was able to genuinely become part of Mexican society. This enabled me to view America and the American people from an outsider's standpoint. For the first time I objectively saw everything strong and beautiful and weak and ugly about American society and realized what aspects of it I wanted to help improve. Motivated, focused, and believing anything was possible, I was still plagued by naivete. This was quickly remedied by the traumas I experienced as a young naval officer.

Serving aboard a very small ship, I led over twenty men for two years and advised and counseled them on every matter from the handling of debt to child care. I had to discern what their desires and motivations were, what brought them to work every day and what sent them home satisfied. It was a slow and very painful process learning that they work to live and not live to work. The difficulty of this realization did however provide me with the understanding of basic American values necessary to interpret laws written for the basic American. Designing policies and managing these men to complete complex tasks within the very restrictive framework of a large bureaucracy tempered my desires to improve society with the realization of what was possible.

Insight into basic American values was particularly important as neither of my parents have traditional American backgrounds. As a teenager, my father and his family emigrated from Canada to the Midwest for religious reasons. My mother, though born in America in a rural Hispanic town in Colorado, did not learn English until she was fifteen. She joined the Air Force at eighteen for the job training and in an attempt to raise her socio-economic standing. Though not wholly meager, my background was not the fast track to a potential opportunity to attend a high caliber law school. I was the beneficiary of an excellent Utah public school system, the NROTC scholarship program (as I did not have the resources to attend Berkeley without it), and the affirmative action program at Berkeley. Though not absolutely certain, I believe I was admitted to Berkeley under this program. My high school GPA and ACT score of 28 would not normally have gained me admission and certainly would not have predicted the academic record and achievements I eventually posted.

Though my above comments and statements are very important and are what guide and affect me, I want to study law because I find it excruciatingly fascinating and overwhelmingly powerful. I feel my background, experience, and sincerity would make a fine contribution to the student body at Stanford.

COMMENTS

This essay certainly gives us meaningful insight into Thomas's life and helps admissions officers put his candidacy and achievements into the proper context. Much of what is compelling here is the writer's truthfulness about the naivete of his initial draw toward the idea of wanting to improve American society, and his admission that, although now more experienced and realistic in his ideas, he is still somewhat naive and hopeful. His sincerity about perhaps being admitted to Berkeley solely because of his race is also compelling, but only because he can note that he did indeed achieve impressive results at Berkeley, thereby removing the potential sting and stigma of being admitted under an affirmative action program.

Thomas's essay could have been improved with a bit more detail—some more tangible material into which readers could sink their teeth. The second paragraph on Mexico, for example, would have more impact with some examples of what he finds "strong and beautiful and weak and ugly" about America, especially from an outsider's perspective. The theme of identifying with the common man in America laid out in the third paragraph is appealing and could have been further built upon.

He could also have improved the essay by a more careful use of language. He is not, in fact, "unique in having . . . a diverse background, varied work experiences, and a broad education." Claiming that he is unique in this regard, which overstates the matter, weakens his case rather than strengthens it. "Paramount to obtaining the expanded foresight necessary" is another example of an awkward phrase that could stand improving.

OLUWABUNMI SHABI

This time I decided to take my usual jog uphill past the tennis courts and the playground and straight to the tall obelisk that sits at the center of Fort Greene Park. Out of breath, I squatted against the monument and thought about how the array of colors of the Brooklyn/Manhattan skyline had never been seen by the soldiers who fought here during the Revolutionary war. I also wondered what the skyline must have looked like when Ralph Ellison sat in this park and crafted his novel *Invisible Man*. Focusing my eyes on the Williamsburg Bank clock tower, I realized that it was nearly 7:00 p.m. I snapped myself out of the daze and started the jog home.

I began thinking about how much the neighborhood and I have changed since my awkward and nerdy days at Brooklyn Technical High School on Fort Greene Place. The blocks that were once filled with dilapidated buildings and crack addicts are now filled with coffee bars and young black professionals. But somehow, the neighborhood has been able to maintain its indelible Brooklyn edge, which consists of one part hospitality and two parts attitude. Maybe that's why someone like Spike Lee—who could afford posh midtown digs—chose Fort Greene as his company's home base.

As for myself, I cannot say that my own transition has been as dramatic. There are the usual superficial changes that accompany the shift from adolescence to adulthood. I went from donning bright green coke-bottle glasses to sporting contact lenses. My 16-year-old size six body has become a svelte size eight (or at least I'd like to think so). And of course there are the obligatory Generation-X transitions from chocolate milk to caffe latte and from being an omnivore to being a vegetarian. But beneath the surface the changes have been much more significant. The sure-footed vigorousness, with which I used to argue black and white ideals on my high school debate team, has become an understanding and an appreciation for the complex nuances that envelop even the smallest of issues. My grasp of world politics has shed some light on why in high school my Muslim Egyptian friend and my Jewish Israeli friend were constantly at each other's throats. And my teenage cockiness and self-congratulatory spirit that were often dependent on making good grades or hanging out with the coolest kids, have transformed themselves into a self-awareness and an inner-confidence that is part of me regardless of how I do on my next exam.

Over the past couple of years, much of my worldly deliberations have taken place at a local Fort Greene coffee shop, the Brooklyn Moon Cafe. When I walk in I am greeted by friends and acquaintances. Everyone from artists and musicians to bankers and lawyers patronize the place. They muse over their existence or take a break from the burdens of work and life that await them outside this safe haven. The burgeoning writer exchanges numbers with the up-and-coming actress, and the recent MBA grad conspires with cohorts about starting up a new business. This, I think to myself as I sip my cappuccino, is the new Harlem Renaissance.

There are even times when Brooklyn Mooners can act as a very opinionated surrogate family. While sitting in the Moon after Sunday brunch, I pull out some of my pictures. I had just returned from an eight-week trip to Paris, Cairo, and Lagos. It was the first time I had left the country since I was ten years old. I talked about how my trip had opened my eyes. I discovered the extent to which millions around the world are suffering. But unlike my old days on the debate team, I had decided that my energized words must be followed by decisive action—hence, my desire to practice international human rights law. I speak about the fact that though I love business journalism, I believe the true vehicle of change lies in the law. This of course begins a dispute among dilettantes. But I can't complain. As much as I enjoyed humus in Cairo and crepes in France, there was something comforting about returning home to heated conversation over spicy fries.

But even Fort Greene is not without its own share of distress and tragedy. The neighborhood is occasionally mentioned in the news. It is the location of the funeral procession of Christopher Wallace, a.k.a. rap artist Biggie Smalls. It is the site of the electronics store that was robbed at gunpoint several times over. Fort Greene is also the neighborhood where a 12-year-old, who was molested by her stepfather, had lived. But it is also where I had my first kiss. It is the neighborhood that has the McDonald's where I spent countless afternoons with classmates. And it is, of course, where I take my daily run.

These days I see many who are fleeing the high costs of the near-by Park Slope and lower Manhattan for the more affordable Fort Greene. This neighborhood may just go from being a tree-lined haven for a young community of artists and professionals to a gentrified, watered down version of Greenwich Village. Who knows? But as with all neighborhoods and people, in another few years both Fort Greene and I will be something else. Maybe something completely unexpected or something highly predictable—but most definitely something else. As I walk home each day and acknowledge this uncontrollable spirit of change, my only hope is that some day someone will stand in front of my building as she takes a breather from her evening run and muse about what my skyline must have looked like.

COMMENTS

The applicant uses her neighborhood of Fort Greene (Brooklyn) as a lens through which to examine herself—an interesting and effective way of discussing one's self and one's own development while also making connections with larger movements and developments of local, national, or international importance.

The weakness of her effort is in claiming that she will practice international human rights law, a future that she apparently discovered during a single trip abroad. This of course is not convincing; in addition, it sits poorly with an essay devoted to her local neighborhood.

BILL

For between five and ten months of each of the past nine years, I have lived in Buddhist monasteries and retreats, devoting myself to the cultivation of insight and moral strength. During these periods, I have maintained silence—speaking, as a rule, only to teachers for ten or fifteen minutes two or three times each week. During these periods, I have given up many pleasures, including movies, television, and music, in order to focus more fully on this contemplative labor. I have sought the kind of wisdom that comes from looking within, from paying attention to and staying aware of the immediate experience of life, of the body, feelings, thoughts, etc. This particular type of introspection, which has been practiced in Buddhist monasteries for more than 2,500 years, has also been taught in medical centers throughout the United States, at Monsanto Company, and to the Chicago Bulls; it will soon be taught at Yale Law School. My goal has been to learn what can be learned, to develop the kind of understanding that comes from a calm and concentrated mind's studying life as it unfolds moment by moment. I have aspired to live, in the words of one famous lawyer, "with malice toward none; with charity for all."

Doing so for so long has not been easy. I have had to find the courage to live by my convictions and to follow a path seldom tread; I have not pursued wealth or prestige. I have had to endure the inconveniences of subsisting on very modest means and not having a home of my own. I have had to persevere without the support of my society's culture, the dominant American culture. I have had to find the strength to face life directly—even when it was unpleasant or boring—without distraction and without the dullness that comes from alcohol, drugs, or refusing to acknowledge the truth.

As a result of my efforts, I now more often feel happy and peaceful, more often feel good, than I did before—even when circumstances were trying. I face adversity with greater strength. Feelings of laziness, fear, and discouragement less often defeat me, less often slow me down or sway me from my course. Less often than before do I find myself the servant of loneliness, envy, or craving, acting at their behest, following their dictates. I more quickly notice my own feelings and less often am driven blindly by anger or ill will to speak or act in harmful ways. Even when provoked or insulted, I am more likely to recognize any feelings of hurt, sadness, or shame, and so retain the freedom to choose how to respond. I am less likely to become a slave of anger, immediately and unthinkingly striking back with spiteful words, for instance, heedless of the consequences. Not only do I enjoy greater self-awareness, but also I observe others more perceptively than I did before. My commitment to acting ethically is stronger than ever, and so is my ability to honor that commitment.

Some who have devoted themselves to seeking wisdom now live as monks. Others, including many Westerners, have married and now work in a wide range of fields, as professors, writers, lawyers, political activists, etc., leading dynamic lives that contribute visibly to society. I have decided to become a lawyer.

Embarking on a voyage of legal education appeals to me. I wish to exercise and further strengthen my powers of precise thinking, analyzing, and reasoning, of careful reading, and of persuasive writing and speaking. I believe that knowledge of the law will aid me greatly. I look forward to the opportunity to study and think about the resolution of conflict and the American legal system.

However, I am applying to [law school X] not only because I want a legal education, but also because I wish to have the professional opportunities that a law degree brings, because I believe that a JD will help me find work that is meaningful and satisfying to me and beneficial to others. I enjoy paying attention to detail and being thorough. I am capable of excellence in analyzing, reasoning, reading, and writing. Working as a lawyer will allow me to use my talent. Though I am not yet sure exactly which of the paths that leads from law school I will choose to take, several of them appeal to me, especially employment in the not-for-profit or government sectors.

Since high school, I have felt a strong pull towards public service. During college and after, I felt drawn in two directions to help prevent and alleviate causes of suffering and happiness, and sharing my understanding with others. In the past, my interest in political matters led to my being elected and serving as Chairman of the Liberal Party of the Yale Political Union. I spent time inviting, listening to, and questioning guest speakers about political issues and exploring and debating policy questions with my fellow students. Also in college, in a spirit of public service, I founded and directed a program to bring Yale student tutors into the New Haven public schools. I learned first-hand about education in the inner cities and succeeded in convincing dozens of Yalies to use their time and intelligence to help poor children learn. After college, I worked for Greenpeace. There I had the opportunity not only to learn to train and manage others, but also to go from door to door, from living room to living room, speaking with strangers about my concerns about the environment, informing and educating them, and persuading them to act by donating money, writing letters to their political representatives, and continuing to learn. I encountered some people who were hostile, and others who were sympathetic; I met some who were interested, and others who were not; I engaged and spoke persuasively even to some of those initially skeptical or unfriendly. More recently, I founded a religious not-for-profit corporation and organized six-week retreats with Sayadaw U Pandita, a highly respected Burmese Buddhist monk. This demanding work allowed me to make available, in the United States, opportunities to cultivate insight under the guidance of one of the world's foremost teachers in this field.

Whatever direction my legal career takes—whether I choose to safeguard the environment, protect children, or help in some other way—I will bring to my work a keen intelligence and a certain eloquence, as well as the qualities developed in my rare training: character, strength, compassion, and awareness. Much of the understanding I have is the result of a sustained encounter with, reflection on, and testing of teachings of the Buddha as well as an extensive observation of the human mind. These teachings and the particular form of introspection that I have engaged in are, to the legal profession, largely unexplored sources of knowledge and wisdom. To the discussions of a profession troubled with relatively high levels of dissatisfaction, depression, and alcoholism, I hope to bring interesting ideas, drawn from these sources among others, about which conduct and mental habits contribute to happiness and which to suffering. In a profession sometimes portrayed as dishonest, greedy, and selfish, I hope to swell by one the ranks of those who live with integrity, kindness, and altruism and inspire or convince others to live likewise. To interaction with clients, negotiations, and attempts to resolve disputes, I hope to bring a valuable sensitivity to unspoken needs and to the inner sources of conflict and disagreement. And in a society and to a profession that lavishes affluence and prominence on those who honor their duty of zealous advocacy on behalf of clients, especially rich clients, even if those advocates neglect their duty to third parties and to society, I hope to bring a strong dedication to justice, fairness, and public service.

My commitment to academic excellence is much stronger now than when I was in college, when much of my time, energy, and interest were drawn to the search that led me after graduation into monasteries and retreats. I feel ready to devote myself to the study of law. And I look forward to developing the skills, acquiring the knowledge, and earning the credential that will help me find a position as a lawyer to help many, to share the fruits of my quiet cultivation of wisdom and virtue in action for the welfare of others.

COMMENTS

Although a bit long—a shorter statement would have been more effective—this does a good job of putting the candidate's "alternative" lifestyle into perspective. It is important for someone with big gaps in his or her employment record—in Bill's case, the result of a commitment to Buddhist retreat practices and his philosophical quest—to explain the record to admissions committees. Bill does so by using his knowledge quest as the single most important theme in his profile. He does a good job of explaining the unique difficulties of his passion while also making it known that he is not "loony"—indeed some corporations and mainstream groups have begun to cultivate similar practices in their ranks. Incorporating his interest in public service (which is backed by significant tangible evidence of that commitment) makes sense because it is somewhat related.

Michigan Optional Essay #2. This essay "should reveal, in a way that an LSAT score or a grade point average cannot, something about the way you think. For example, you might choose to discuss an intellectual or social problem you have faced or a book or film that has particularly affected you."

Pali is the ancient Indian language, closely related to Sanskrit, in which is preserved the oldest extant record of the teachings of the Buddha. The *Dhammapada* is a collection, in Pali, of teachings of the Buddha in poetic form. Verse 348 of the *Dhammapada* contains the lines, "Let go in front, let go of behind." Verse 421 speaks of a person who clings to nothing "in front [or] behind." The ancient commentary explains that, in these instances, "in front" means the past and "behind" the future! Usually we think of the future as in front of us, as what lies ahead, and the past as behind. What might the Buddha or the commentators have been thinking?

We can see what is in front of us. Similarly, we can "see" what has already happened. *Marbury v. Madison* was handed down in 1803. Pearl Harbor was attacked on December 7, 1941. We cannot see what is behind us, and we do not know all the future will bring. Who will be elected President in the year 2000? What will a share of Microsoft cost in 2013? Thinking of the past as in front of us and of the future as behind us, unfamiliar though such thinking may be, thus makes some sense. But can viewing time in this way have any effect?

Thinking of the future as behind us, of ourselves as backing into the future, can remind us of our vulnerability. When walking backwards, we do not always know what we will bump into. Living today, we do not always know what tomorrow will bring. On the evening of April 15, 1986, did the residents of Chernobyl have any idea how the next day would change their lives? On the morning of January 30, 1948, did Mahatma Gandhi know he would be killed? Tragedy can strike at any moment, with little or no warning, just as a child walking backwards can hit herself on a table she does not see.

Is there any benefit to be gained by remembering that life is, in certain ways, unpredictable, that we are, for instance, always vulnerable to sudden changes in fortune? Yes. Such awareness can sometimes help us avoid speaking words and performing deeds that harm others and cause us remorse—can help us find the strength to act considerately. Would we, in a moment of anger, speak hurtfully to someone we loved if we knew that he, she, or we would die that day? Probably not. We would be less likely to do so than if we continued dully in our usual way, forgetting that we might not have the opportunity to apologize later, that our angry words might be the last that our loved one ever hears from us, the last that we ever say to him or her. Even if we had to struggle with the anger, even if we felt like saying the injurious words as much as an exhausted man feels like lying down on a soft bed—even then, if only we remembered the uncertainty of life, we might find the strength to resist the malicious impulse. Might not a political prisoner, scheduled to be executed at noon, act magnanimously towards his cellmate in the morning?

Some who have remembered that death can come at any time have chosen to live in an especially beautiful and noble way. They have endeavored to avoid harming others near or far. They have cared for and tried to assist not only friends and family, but also strangers and even enemies. Verse 6 of the *Dhammapada* reads: "Those who do not remember, 'We in this world must all die" continue to quarrel. Those who do remember cease to quarrel." Quarreling with none—with, in the words of Abraham Lincoln, "malice towards none; with charity for all," some strive to end conflict, to resolve disputes, to bring peace. Whether our compassion extends near or far, whether we struggle against the violence of war or of unkind words in our own families, thinking of the future as behind us, remembering there is much we cannot foresee, can help us act wisely in the present.

COMMENTS

Bill's essay is a risky think-piece that sheds light on his philosophical views while also suggesting that his unusual perspective might be highly valuable in class.

As a full-time meditator for the last decade, Bill has a limited number of potential essay topics available to him. Therefore, writing a thought-piece represents less of a risk than it might for another applicant (who would have other, useful topics available). Bill needed to show himself to be a valuable class participant without seeming too odd to fit in. This essay helps by showing his interest in jurisprudence and international affairs without denying his unusual background, his lengthy pursuit of meditation. The essay is as interesting as can be on such a topic, which helps avoid the worst possible result of a thought-piece: boredom.

Note on Employment History (Added to nearly all applications)

As I mention in my personal statement, I have chosen to spend much of the past decade in Buddhist monasteries and retreats. When not in retreat, I have sometimes worked and sometimes spent time with family and friends. After graduating from college and before heading off to monasteries and retreats, I sometimes chose to work and sometimes chose to take time off to read and think about what my next step would be. Some of these jobs felt significant to me (like working for Greenpeace) and others did not (like chopping vegetables for a French caterer). As a result of my choices, now, even when I list all my jobs, gaps in time remain. And to me it seems that some of my jobs are not worthy of mention. It is not the case that I am trying to conceal any period of my life because I was fired. With the possible exception of the French caterer (who liked me personally, but thought I chopped vegetables a bit too slowly), all of my employers have been quite happy with both my work and my character. (Likewise, I have never served time in prison, and I do not have any other blemishes on my record.) Gaps, even chasms, in my employment history are the innocent result of my search for wisdom, which search I write about in my personal statement.

Note on Undergraduate Grades (Added to nearly all applications)

Although I graduated magna cum laude from Yale, I experienced a "senior slump." Also, I tended to do less well in my major, philosophy, than in other fields. I believe that my undergraduate record neither fully reflects my intellectual strength nor accurately predicts my academic performance in law school.

While an undergraduate, I began to long for a kind of wisdom that I could not find in my classes. My thirst for understanding was strong enough to lead me after college to Buddhist monasteries and retreats for much of a decade. My interest was strong enough during college that I did not devote much time or energy to some of my course work, especially to assignments in my philosophy and senior year classes. I vowed in 1987 not to return to school until I knew clearly why I was going, until my commitment to academic excellence was again strong, and until I was prepared to work diligently. Now, after having spent a considerable amount of time on my quest, I am eager to dedicate myself of the study of the law.

My undergraduate grades are more than ten years old. I attended college in the mid 1980s. Now, in the late 1990s, I am more mature and harder working than I was then.

I believe that my LSAT scores of June 1990 (48/48) and June 1998 (176/180) more accurately predict my law school performance than do my undergraduate philosophy and senior year grades. My February 1998 LSAT (170/180) was my first important academic or intellectual test in eight years; perhaps I was a bit rusty.

Note on Arrest History (Added to nearly all applications)

In 1986, I was arrested in connection with a completely non-violent act of civil disobedience intended to persuade Yale to divest from its portfolio holdings in companies that did business in South Africa. I was one of a group of perhaps 20 or 40 arrested for sitting outside an administration building. I pleaded guilty to a minor violation—probably "simple trespass" or "creating a public disturbance." As punishment, I was required to make a contribution of about $25 to a not-for-profit organization. When a period of about one year elapsed without my being arrested again, the incident was expunged from my record.

COMMENTS

All three of Bill's "notes" provide useful information to the admissions committees, so he was wise to include them. The last (on his "arrest history") is an especially nice touch; because the incident was officially eliminated from his record, he was not required to include this, but it actually helps to position Bill as a passionate, yet nonviolent activist, someone who is willing to sacrifice himself for higher goals and ideals. This bodes well for his claims to a future in public interest law.

NYU Dean's Scholarship Essay

Five of the opportunities available at NYU particularly interest me. First is the opportunity to study with NYU's faculty. NYU seems determined to attract outstanding law professors; I hope to feast at the table that has been—and is being—prepared. Second is the opportunity to study at a school seriously committed to public service. I expect to benefit from the Public Interest Law Center and NYU's excellent public interest faculty. I expect, too, to benefit from my fellow students. Finding like-minded classmates in an environment as demanding as law school can make the experience of school not only more enjoyable, but also richer, as a result of friendly discussion. NYU's commitment to public service, its generosity in supporting those committed to public service, and its reputation as a school dedicated to public interest law insure that NYU's class will contain more than the usual percentage of people dedicated to such work. The third opportunity at NYU that particularly interests me is the opportunity to participate in NYU's excellent clinical education program. I intend to make clinical education an important part of my legal education. Fourth, the opportunity to study the law in New York City interests me greatly. The opportunities in New York for internships and for studying with adjunct professors who are leading practitioners are unsurpassed. Much of my family and many of my friends live in New York. Also, though a JD from NYU should serve me well wherever I go, law degrees seem to be somewhat more geographically sensitive than medical or business degrees. Since I think it likely—though not yet certain—that I will settle in New York, can I do better than attend law school there? Fifth is the opportunity to receive an outstanding legal education. I would rate the likelihood of my seeking a job at Cravath as *extremely* low. Still, I know that such jobs are highly sought after. Some research revealed that an unusually high percentage of Cravath lawyers were NYU alumni. While speaking with an attorney who was once an associate at Cravath, I mentioned my discovery and hypothesized that the NYU network at Cravath was particularly strong. No, he corrected me, it is not just that the NYU network is strong. Rather, the partners found that, as a rule, NYU graduates have been trained exceptionally well. Though I expect to serve different interests than Cravath's lawyers, I do seek excellent training. NYU can provide me with that.

COMMENTS

Bill's Dean's Scholarship Essay for NYU is nicely, albeit simply, constructed. There is no room for creativity here, so it is best to state one's argument clearly and succinctly. A nice touch is Bill's incorporation of the information gleaned from research at Cravath—arguably New York's most prestigious firm—despite the fact that this is a path he personally is unlikely to follow. It shows him to be active in learning about the school. It also shows him to be in touch with the real world of law, which is particularly valuable for someone who has been off meditating for the last decade (and is therefore vulnerable to a charge of not knowing much about the real world, let alone legal practice).

University of Michigan Darrow Scholarship Essay

My personal statement explains more thoroughly than this essay does why I am interested in law school and how I hope to contribute to society. I ask the Darrow Faculty Committee to read carefully that personal statement and to regard it as an essential part of my writing on the Darrow topic. In this essay, I will focus mostly on matters not addressed in that one.

I am interested in law school and have decided to devote three years of my life to the study of the law because I believe that a legal education and a law degree will allow me to put to good use my education, intelligence, and other talents. I am convinced that a JD provides many opportunities and powerful means for helping others. Furthermore, many of the particular opportunities that a law degree offers interest me. For instance, a law degree should help me find work that allows me to use reasoning, persuasive writing, and negotiation to effect change, prevent and resolve disputes, and secure justice. Also, with a law degree, I will be in a good position to protect children or the environment, to name just two possibilities, against unlawful conduct.

My decision to study the law is not a whim. My interest in law school is deeply rooted. In 1982, in my college application essay, I expressed a desire to become a lawyer. In 1990, I first took the LSAT and gathered some of the materials that I would need to apply to law school. Though, until recently, I did not act on my desire to become a lawyer, but pursued another interest first, my present commitment is not a sudden fancy, but a welcome return. Also, my recent decision to apply comes after a period of many years of study, discussion, and reflection about my vocation. I have tested the ideas, the beliefs, which have led me to apply to law school, and the more I read, speak with others, and think about the matter, the more confident I feel about my choice of a professional path.

In an educational environment in which I would thrive, there would be a commitment to intellectual rigor in the service of the prevention and alleviation of suffering. The student body would be bright and interesting, and there would be a relatively friendly atmosphere. The faculty would be excellent and somewhat accessible. (Professors would be outstanding, but not standoffish.) Where appropriate, as in the area of child welfare and advocacy, to name just one example, scholars would seek contributions across the boundaries of academic disciplines. The school would offer good opportunities for clinical education. There would be genuine support for public service. And the school would provide both an excellent professional training and the opportunity—even encouragement—to consider issues such as justice and public policy.

I feel confident that I would receive an excellent legal education at Michigan.

Northwestern Optional Essay

Both the excellence of education available at Northwestern and the quality of the academic community attract me. Clearly Northwestern's law school is one of the finest in the country, and Northwestern itself is one of the finest universities in the country. No law school can enjoy the reputation that Northwestern's does without being endowed with an outstanding community of legal scholars. Yet Northwestern's faculty is not only impressive but also accessible. The low student–faculty ratio contributes to students' having many opportunities to become acquainted with professors. Faculty members' commitment to teaching insures that not only will legal scholarship advance but also students will learn. Northwestern's interviewing applicants and valuing personal qualities besides intelligence increases the likelihood that one will want to meet one's classmates and will benefit from doing so; the small class size increases the likelihood that one will be able to thoroughly enjoy the feast of one's fellow students.

The special opportunities for study at and location of Northwestern's School of Law also appeal to me. I feel drawn to public service and so may not have the same opportunities for training after law school that those who head to wealthy private firms may have; therefore, the strength and size of Northwestern's clinical programs are important to me. The work of the Institute for Policy Research interests me—especially its work in the fields of poverty, race, and inequality and philanthropy, voluntarism, and nonprofit organizations. The various lecture series also attract me. Finally, Chicago is one of the great American cities; so long as one has a warm coat and boots, who wouldn't enjoy living there? For all of the reasons mentioned above, I would consider myself fortunate enough to be able to earn my JD at Northwestern University's School of Law.

COMMENTS

Both the Darrow and Northwestern essays, though perhaps not quite as convincing as the NYU scholarship essay—because of their lesser detail—are nicely wrought.

NOAH PITTARD

Transfer application

While I am pleased with my first-year performance at Hastings and fully aware of the advantages accruing to me as a result of it, I am convinced that transferring to Boalt Hall would create opportunities and yield benefits that are simply not available to me at Hastings.

Primarily, I would prefer to attend a smaller law school with a more intellectually driven student body. I write this not as a first-year applicant filled with brochure ideals, but as a rising "second-year" who has just completed his first year at a large, academically multifarious institution. I do not suggest that Hastings lacks bright, exceptional students; indeed, a substantial portion of my section consistently contributed to a vigorous dialectic, both in and out of class. This notwithstanding, I believe Boalt Hall's higher admissions criteria are bound to produce a materially higher percentage of students who share my interest in legal scholarship.

Secondarily, because I arrived at law school with a successful background in entrepreneurial business, as well as a keen interest in the law of commerce, I cannot over-state the appeal and value of student-level access to Boalt's nationally recognized business faculty. Although I would very much enjoy taking more classes with my first-year Hastings professors, I am more excited by the prospect of enrolling in corporations and international business classes with Professors Mel Eisenberg and Dick Buxbaum, to name but two. Furthermore, Boalt's curriculum includes a number of programs (e.g., financial services) that Hastings' does not.

In sum, my decision to apply to Boalt Hall is compelled by a strong preference to be part of a law school where interested, intelligent students, and a dynamic faculty, are the rule. This past year I learned the difference between mere competitiveness and competition, and it is the latter that I hope to find—and contribute to—at Boalt Hall. If admitted as a transfer student, I am confident that I would make as meaningful a contribution to your second-year class as I made to my own first-year class at Hastings.

COMMENTS

Noah was wise to focus intensely on a few reasons for wanting to transfer, rather than discussing each and every benefit of Boalt. Going overboard—using a laundry list approach—would have diffused his message, making him a less appealing candidate as a result. He is also smart not to insult his current school. It is better to discuss the attractions of your prospective school than to criticize your current school. For one thing, your prospective school wants to believe that you will be a full and enthusiastic supporter of it down the road.

Noah did miss one important trick, however. He is clearly attracted to business and should have used this as part of his rationale for seeking out Boalt. Hastings, his current law school, has no business school affiliated with it whereas Boalt's sister school is Berkeley's highly ranked Haas School of Business. (In fact, he later applied to Haas to do a joint JD–MBA.) His successful entrepreneurial experience would have been especially valuable in this context. He should have elaborated on it and explained exactly how he planned to take advantage of Boalt's and Haas's resources in this regard. This would have fitted well his basic argument that he was hoping to transfer to Boalt because it offered much that Hastings did not.

INDEX

ABA: *see also* American Bar Association
Academic record, making most of, 138–146
  "building an alternative transcript," 140
Academic records for foreign students, 177
Acceptance, what to do after, 387–400
  accepting offer, 391
    Certificate of Eligibility (I-20) for
      international students, 391
    Admission Directors' thoughts on, 389–390
  college, finishing, 393–394
  deferral, 388–391 (*see also* . . . Admission
    Directors' thoughts . . .)
  executive summary, 387
  job, resigning from, 391–393
  preparing for law school, 394–396
    elements, 396
    teaching often poor in first-year courses,
      395–396
  skill development, 397–400
    bar review course, 398–399
    legal exams, taking, 397–398
    legal reasoning, 399
    legal writing, 397
    Nutshell books, 399
    professors, confrontations with, 399
    reading overview materials, 399
    Sum and Substance series, 399
Accounting, learning, 399
Administrative hold, responding to, 362
Access Group:
  Graduate International Student Loan, 443
  loans available from, 419
Admissions Office of school, visiting, 71–72
Admission officers, interviews with, 319–320
Admissions process, 99–113
  Admissions Directors' thoughts on, 109–112
  admissions outcomes, 107–109
  executive summary, 99
  index numbers, use of, 105–107, 108
    Law School Admission Council (LSAC), 105
  Law School Data Assembly Service (LSDAS),
    107–109
  "rolling" admissions, 100
  standard admissions model, 100–105
    Admissions Committee, 101
    Admission Directors, 100–101
    criteria, 102–103
    decision making, 101
    diversity, importance of, 104
    trade-off, 104

value of who you are, not just your scores,
  104–105
Advantaged applicants, commitment to
  community service critical for, 169
Alumni:
  interviews with, 320–322
  network, importance of, 5
  of school, assessing, 66, 67
  speaking with before choosing school, 42
  value of in career search, 66, 67
American Bar Association:
  ABA Official Guide to Approved Law Schools,
    47–48, 59
  career dissatisfaction, survey on, 19
  limits on part-time work of law students, 431
American exchange programs, 438–439
The American Lawyer, 78, 85–86 (*see also*
  Rankings)
Appealing denial, 368–369
Application forms, filling out, 274
  Admission Directors' thoughts on, 274
Application timetable, 115–133 (*see also*
  Timetable)
Applying to law school, 135–357 (*see also* under
  particular heading)
  credentials, 137–177
  essay options, understanding, 215–245
  interviews, 313–357
  marketing yourself, 179–197
  personal organizer, 209–214
  recommendations, 277–311
  resumes, writing, 269–274
  special cases, 199–207
  writing persuasive essays, 247–267
Assessing school, criteria for, 53–58
  alumni, 66, 67
  career services, 66–67
  costs, 67
  courses in other departments, 55
  curriculum, 58–60 (*see also* Curriculum)
  debt load, 68
  exchange programs, 58
  facilities, 55
  finances, 67–68
  housing, 55
  internationalization, 58
  jobs, 65–67
  joint degrees, 55–57 (*see also* Joint degrees)
  journals and societies, 65
  law review, 65

Assessing school, criteria for *(cont.)*
  local connections, 67
  location, 53–54
  mission, 55
  "national"school, 54
  part-time work, 68
  pedagogical issues, 60–62 (*see also* Pedagogical issues)
  program, 55–58
  reputation, 53
  safety, 54
  size, 53
  social issues, 62–64 (*see also* Social issues)
  student societies, 65

Bar association, local/national, joining in law school, 407
Bar review course, taking before beginning law school, 398–399
Bargaining about financial aid offers, 445–448
Behavior during interview, 344–346
Berkeley (Boalt Hall):
  Director of Admissions quoted:
    on academic records, 141, 144
    on application timing, 124, 125
    on deferrals, 390
    on extra material, submitting, 275
    on extracurricular and community activities, 172, 173
    on international students, 206
    on interpretation of mixed (grade and LSAT) data, 156
    on legacies, 203
    on LSATs, 154–155
    on marketing yourself, 195
    on personal statements, 237, 238
    on reapplications, 370
    on recommenders, whom to choose, 293
    on residency, 200
    on third-year matriculation, 384–385
    on transfer, 380
    on work experience, 162
    on writing essays, 265
  exchange program with Harvard, 384
  foreign exchange programs, payment of tuition for, 437
  graduates currently participating in LRAP program, 426
  independence status of applicants, 434
  loan types, 425
  LRAP programs, 424
  noncustodial parents, assessment of, 435
  outside grant, impact of, 436
  rankings of, 80–81, 88, 91
  specialties, 59
  summer earnings, assessment of, 441
  term-time earnings, assessment of, 440
  transfer students, aid eligibility of, 442–443

  tuition payments for exchange programs or transfer terms, 439
  wait-listed students, aid eligibility of, 442
Binding vs. nonbinding early decision, 117
Boston College:
  Director of Admissions quoted:
    on academic records, 142
    on admissions procedures, 111–112
    on application timing, 125
    on choosing right school, 51
    on effects of good recommendations, 302
    on extra material, submitting, 275
    on extracurricular and community activities, 171
    on how to handle oneself in interview, 354
    on impact of age and experience on Admissions process, 164
    on international students, 205
    on interpretation of mixed (grade and LSAT) data, 157
    on legacies, 202
    on marketing yourself, 196, 197
    on number of recommendations, 296
    on personal statements, 237, 239, 240, 241
    on rankings, 96, 97
    on reapplications, 371
    on recommenders, whom to choose, 292
    on studying law abroad, 383
    on waiting to apply, 12
    on wait-listing, 365, 366
    on who is interviewed, 314
    on working as paralegal, 23
    on writing essays, 264, 265, 266
  rankings of, 81, 91
Boston University:
  bargaining for financial aid, 446
  Career Development Office Director quoted on work experience and marketability, 14
"Building an alternative transcript," 140
Business Week, ranking by, 396

California Lawyer, 19
Campus tour, 71
Career, exploring law as: (*see also* Law school: Is it for me?)
  Career Services Directors' thoughts on, 23–24
Career choice as reason to choose top school, 4
Career development, thinking about, 405–410
Career dissatisfaction, 19–20
  Career Services Directors' thoughts on, 20
Career flexibility as reason to choose top school, 4–5
Career Services department of school:
  assessing, 66–67
  using, 406
  visiting, 72
Case method of teaching, 29–30
Casenote, 403

Certificate of Eligibility (I-20) for international students, 391
Chicago:
  admissions criteria, 102–103
  bargaining for financial aid, 446–447
  essay not required, 217
  intellectual property course offerings, 79
  loan types, 425
  LRAP programs, 424
  when LRAP loans cancel, 425
  rankings of, 80–81, 91
  recommendations, number of, 294
  resume required, 269
  specialties, 59
Choosing right school for you, 39–51
  Admission Directors' thoughts on, 48–51
  decisions, two major, 40
  executive summary, 39
  final-decision criteria, 47
  how many to apply to, 44–46
    "likelies," "possibles," and "stretches,"
      45–46
  part-time program, 45
  pitfalls, 46–47
  readings, recommended, 47–48
    ABA Official Guide to Approved Law Schools,
      47–48
    The Official Guide to U.S. Law Schools, 48
  researching schools, 40–44
    alumni, speaking with, 42
    employers in your field, contacting,
      43–44
    inability to get in, how to handle, 43
    programs, general knowledge about, 41
    specific schools, getting information about,
      41–42
    U.S. News & World Report rankings, 41
    visiting school, 42
  self-assessment, 40
CitiAssist, 443
Citibank, loans available from, 419
Class size at school, assessing, 61–62
Classes, visiting, 72
Classmates, getting to know, 406
Clinical courses at school, assessing, 59
Clinical studies method of teaching, 31
College, finishing, 393–394
Columbia:
  admissions criteria, 102–103
  Assistant Dean of Admissions quoted on
    application timing, 124
  backgrounds of admitted students, 138–139
  bargaining for financial aid, 446–447
  curriculum, first-year, 59
  Dean of Admissions quoted:
    on academic records, 141, 143, 144, 146
    on admissions procedures, 109
    on choosing right school, 49, 50, 51

  on deferrals, 389, 390
  on effects of good recommendations, 303
  on essays, optional, and addenda, 245
  on extracurricular and community activities,
    172, 173
  on interpreting mixed (grade and LSAT)
    data, 157
  on legacies, 202, 203
  on LLM programs, 207
  on marketing yourself, 197
  on personal statements, 237, 238
  on rankings, 95, 96, 97
  on recommenders, whom to choose, 294
  on third-year matriculants, 384
  on transfer, 380
  on wait-listing, 365, 366
  on work experience, 162
employer recommendation required for
  students working full time, 289
entering class, summary data for, 180–182
exchange program, 58
foreign degrees, 58
foreign exchange programs, payment of tuition
  for, 437
graduates currently participating in LRAP
  programs, 426
independence status of applicants, 434
international students, institutional financial
  aid eligibility of, 443–444
loan types, 425
LRAP programs, 424
when LRAP loans cancel, 425
noncustodial parents, assessment of, 435
outside grant, impact of, 436
personal statement requirement, 216
public service scholarships, 429
rankings of, 80–81, 91
recruitment at, 43
student body, 37
summer earnings, assessment of, 441
term-time earnings, assessment of, 440
third year matriculants, 385
transfer students, aid eligibility of, 442–443
tuition payment for exchange programs or
  transfer terms, 439
visiting students, acceptance of, 384
wait-listed students, aid eligibility of, 442
work experience, value of, 137
Communicating effectively in essay, 247–267 (*see
  also* Writing persuasive essays)
Community service, importance of, 167–169
  for advantaged applicants, 169
  for future public interest lawyers, 168
  kinds, 167–168
  recruiting recommenders, 168
Competition at school, assessing, 64
Confrontations with professors, preparing for,
  399

Cornell:
  admissions criteria, 102–103
  Dean of Admissions quoted:
    on application timing, 124
    on how Cornell conducts interviews, 338
    on how to handle oneself in interview, 354
    on interviewers, kinds of, 324
    on interview formats, 320
    on preparation for interviews, 342
    on reapplications, 370
    on when to interview, 351
    on who is interviewed, 314–315
    on why interviews are done, 356
  foreign exchange programs, payment of tuition
    for, 437
  graduates currently participating in LRAP
    program, 426
  independence status of applicants, 434
  international students, institutional financial
    aid eligibility of, 443–444
  loan types, 425
  LRAP programs, 424
  noncustodial parents, assessment of, 435
  outside grant, impact of, 436
  rankings of, 80–81, 91
  summer earnings, assessment of, 441
  term-time earnings, assessment of, 440
  transfer students, aid eligibility of, 442–443
  tuition payment for exchange programs or
    transfer terms, 439
  two law degrees, 35, 58
  wait-listed students, aid eligibility of, 442
Costs of school, assessing, 67, 414–418 (*see also*
    Financing)
Courses:
  in other departments, assessing school for,
    55
  outside law school, 34–35
Creativity, triggering, 254
Credentials, making most of, 137–177
  academic record, 138–146
    "building an alternative transcript," 140
    graduate work, 140–146
    undergraduate record or LSAT score—
      which more important? 155–156
  Admissions Directors' thoughts on:
    academic records, 141–146
    career dimension, 174–175
    extracurricular and community activities,
      169–173
    impact of age and experience, 163–164
    LSAT, 153–155
    mixed (grade and LSAT) data, 156–157
    what they are looking for, 175
    work experience, 159–163
  age and experience, impact of upon admissions
    decisions, 163–164 (*see also* . . . Admission
    Directors' thoughts . . .)
  executive summary, 137
    extracurricular, personal, and community
      activities, 138, 165–173
      Admission Directors' quotes, 169–173 (*see
        also* . . . Admission Directors'
        thoughts . . .)
    community service, importance of, 167–169
      (*see also* Community service)
    personal activities, 169
    what Admissions Committees are looking for,
      165–166
  for international students, 176–177
    academic records, 177
    admission policies, 176–177
    grades, 177
  LSAT (Law School Admission Test), 138,
    146–157
    Admission Directors' thoughts, 153–155 (*see
      also* . . . .Admission Directors' thoughts)
    "games" section, 147
    importance of, 149
    preparing for, 149–150
    purposes, two, 146
    registering for, 147
    retaking exam, 151–152
    score, 148
    self-preparation, 149–150
    test-prep course, choosing, 150–151
    tips for preparation, 152
    undergraduate record or LSAT score—which
      more important? 155–156
    what Admission Committees are looking for,
      148
    what it is, 146–147
    wild card section, 146–147
  recommenders, recruiting through community
    service, 168
  show where you are headed, 173
  TOEFL performance for international students,
    138, 152–153
  undergraduate record or LSAT score—which
    more important? 155–156
    Admission Directors' thoughts on, 156–157
      (*see also* . . . Admission Directors'
      thoughts . . .)
  work experience, 138, 157–163
    achievement and impact at work, 158–159
    Admission Directors' thoughts on, 159–163
      (*see also* . . . Admission Directors'
      thoughts . . .)
    nature, 158
    paralegal work, value of, 158
    what Admissions Committees are looking for,
      157–158
Credit history, implications of, 420
Criteria for choosing school, 47 (*see also*
    Choosing)
Curriculum of school, assessing, 58–60
  clinical courses, 59
  electives, 59

externships, 60
first-year, 58–59
internships, 60
law firm management courses, 59–60
soft skills, 59–60
technology, 60

"Deans' Letter," 88–89 (*see also* Rankings)
Admissions Directors' thoughts on, 89
Deans' letters, 291
Debt, figuring how much is too much, 427
Debt load of school, assessing, 68
Degree of Difference, xv–xviii, 339, 368, 455
Denial, responding to, 367–371
Admissions Directors' thoughts on:
appeals, 369
reapplications, 370–371
appealing, 368–369
reason for, analyzing, 368
reapply in future or settle for another school?
369–371
Departmental rankings, 90
Disappointments, responding to, 361–372 (*see also* Rejection)
Diversity, value of to Admissions, 104
Drafts of essay, 254–260 (*see also* Writing)
Dress for interview, 343–344
Duke:
academic year budget for single student, 414–415
Assistant Dean, Admissions/Financial Aid quoted:
on academic records, 143, 144
on career dimension, 175
on choosing right school, 48
on extracurricular and community activities, 173
on personal statements, 238, 240, 241
on rankings, 96, 97
on what they are looking for, 175
on who is interviewed, 315
on why interviews are done, 356–357
on work experience, 161
foreign exchange programs, payment of tuition for, 437
graduates currently participating in LRAP program, 426
independence status of applicants, 434
international students, institutional financial aid eligibility of, 443–444
loan types, 425
LRAP programs, 424
noncustodial parents, assessment of, 435
outside grant, impact of, 436
quality of life, 64
rankings of, 80–81, 91
resume required, 269
transfer students, aid eligibility of, 442–443

tuition payment for exchange programs or transfer terms, 439
wait-listed students, aid eligibility of, 442

Early application option, 116 (*see also* Timetable)
binding vs. nonbinding, 117
Early decision, 117
Editor of law review, 36
Educational Testing Service (ETS), 152
Electives of school, assessing, 59
The Elements of Style, 253
Emory:
rankings of, 81
Employer, using as recommender, 289–290
Employment opportunities, investigating, 17–18
Essay examples, 453–510
Essay options, understanding, 215–245
additional topics, 232–236
Admission Directors' thoughts on:
optional essays and addenda, 245
personal statements, 237–241, 245
advice, 244
Columbia and personal statement requirement, optional essay, allowance for, 243–244
essays, options, 242–244
executive summary, 215
personal statements, 237–241, 245 (*see also* . . . Admission Directors' thoughts . . .)
topic choice, 216–217
tips, 222–229
topics, analysis of, 217–232
accomplishments, substantial, 222–225
career to date, 220–221
ethical dilemma, 227–229
job, current, 217–220
leadership potential, 225–226
objectives not reached, 226–227
strengths and weaknesses, 221–222
why you want to be a lawyer, 230–232
Yale, and personal statement requirement, 216
Exams, preparing for, 404–405
Exam-writing seminars as preparation, 398
Exchange programs, 384–385
at school, assessing, 58
Externships at school, assessing, 60
Extra material, submitting, 275
Admission Directors' thoughts on, 275

Facilities of school, assessing, 55
Faculty members, getting to know, 406
FAFSA (Free Application for Federal Student Aid), 416
Family contribution to financing law degree, 414–418
Federal loans, 416
Federal Perkins Loan, 419
Federal subsidized/unsubsidized Stafford loans, 419

Field placement programs, 31

Financial Aid offices at schools, visiting, 72

Financial aid policies, 432–444 (*see also* Financing)

Financial aid PROFILE, 416
   application, logistics of, 417

Financial considerations in choice of school, 5–6, 67

Financing law degree, 413–451
   Admission Directors' thoughts on financial-aid decision independent of admission decision, 432
   American exchange programs, 438–439
   cost, calculating, 414–418
      Duke Law School's academic year budget for single student, 414–415
      family contribution, 415–418
      Free Application for Federal Student Aid (FAFSA), 416
      from law schools, 416
      Need Access application, 416, 417
      private loans, 416
      PROFILE, 416, 417
   evaluating financial packages, 444–448
      bargaining, 445–448
      factors, six, 444–445
      University of Texas Financial-Aid Matching Program, 447
   executive summary, 413
   financial aid, 416, 417, 418
      credit history, 420
      grant aid, 416, 417
      loan forgiveness programs, 422
      Loan Repayment Assistance Programs (LRAPs), 421–427 (*see also* Loans)
      loans, 418–428 (*see also* Loans)
      logistics of applying for, 417
      policies, 432–444 (*see also* Policies)
      repayment chart for loans, 421
   financial strategies, 448–451
      basic, 448–449
      control spending, 449–450
      in line with career goals, 450–451
   foreign exchange programs, 437
   grants, 416, 417, 428–429, 436–437 (*see also* Grants)
   information sources, 431
   opportunity cost, 414
   outside grants, impact of, 436–437
   part-time work during school, 429–431
      limits by ABA, 431
   policies for financial aid, 432–444
      Admission Directors' thoughts, 432 (*see also . . . Admission Directors' thoughts . . .*)
      American exchange programs, 438–439
      financial aid decision independent of admissions decision, 432
      foreign exchange programs, 437

independence status of applicants, school chart, 434
   for international students, 443–444
   outside grants, impact of, 436–437
   parents, independence from for financial aid, 433–435
   resident status, converting to in second year, 433
   summer earnings, assessment of, 441
   term-time earnings, assessment of, 439–440
   third-year matriculation, 438–439
   for transfer students, 442–443
   for wait-listed students, 442
  public service scholarships, 429
  tax deductibility of law school, 450
  trading down in school quality to save money, 451

Fordham:
  part-time programs, 27

Foreign exchange programs, 437
  tuition payment for, 437

Foreign students, 176–177 (*see also* International students)
  extra preparation for, 400

Forms, filling out, 274

Friendly chat interviews, 352

George Washington:
  Career Development Office Director quoted on knowing reason to attend law school, 22
  Director for Admissions quoted:
    on academic records, 141, 142, 143, 144, 145
    on admissions procedures, 112, 113
    on choosing right school, 49
    on extra material, submitting, 275
    on extracurricular and community activities, 170, 171
    on impact of age and experience on Admissions process, 163
    on international students, 205, 206
    on legacies, 202
    on LSATs, 155
    on marketing yourself, 197
    on personal statements, 241
    on transfer, 379–380
    on wait-listing, 367
    on work experience, 161, 163
    on working as paralegal, 23
  merit aid grants, 428
  no recommendations required, 294
  part-time programs, 27
  part-time work during program, 430
  percentage of law students working, 430
  rankings of, 81, 91

Georgetown:
  admissions criteria, 102–103
  Assistant Dean quoted:
    on poor reasons for entering law, 16
    on value of work experience, 12

Assistant Dean for Admissions quoted:
  on academic records, 142, 145
  on admissions procedures, 109, 111
  on application timing, 123–124
  on career dimension, 174
  on deferrals, 390
  on effects of good recommendations, 302
  on international students, 205
  on joint-degree programs, 57
  on LLM programs, 207
  on one-size-fits-all recommendations, 301
  on personal statements, 241
  on rankings, 95
  on reapplications, 370, 371
  on transfer, 380
  on wait-listing, 366, 367
  on who is interviewed, 315
  on work experience, 161
  on writing essays, 266
curriculum, first-year, 59
graduates currently participating in LRAP
    program, 426
independence status of applicants, 434
"law journal," 36
loan types, 425
LRAP programs, 424
merit aid grants, 428
one-size-fits-all recommendation, 301
part-time programs, 27
part-time work during program, 430
percentage of law students working, 430
placement office, non-students' use of, 386
public service scholarships, 429
publications, 36
rankings of, 80–81, 91
Getting most out of law school, 401–411
  bar association, local/national, joining, 407
  career development, thinking about,
      405–410
  career services office, using, 406
  classmates, getting to know, 406
  exams, preparing for, 404–405
  executive summary, 401
  faculty members, getting to know, 406
  industry association, joining, 407
  networking, 410
  practitioners in your field, contacting, 407
  social experience, importance of, 411
  stress control, 410–411
  student organizations, joining, 406
  study groups, 405
  time management, 402–404
Goals, personal, determining before choosing
    law, 8
Grading in law school, 32–33
Graduate work records, 140–146
Grammar, correct usage of in interview, 336
Grammatical writing, 247–267 (*see also*
    Writing)

Grants to finance law school, 416, 417, 428–429
  merit, 428
  need-based, 428
  outside, 429
    impact of, 436–437
  public service scholarships, 429

Harvard:
  Assistant Dean for Admissions/Financial Aid
      quoted:
    on admissions procedures, 109
    on career dimension, 174
    on choosing right school, 48–49, 50
    on extracurricular and community activities,
        170, 172
    on handling recommenders, 299
    on impact of age and experience on
        Admissions process, 163–164
    on interviews, not usual, 357
    on marketing yourself, 195, 196, 197
    on personal statements, 237, 239
    on rankings, 96
    on recommendations, importance of, 283
    on recommenders, who to choose, 292
    on waiting to apply, 13
    on what they are looking for, 175
  attrition rate under 1%, 9
  bargaining for financial aid, 446
  exchange program with Berkeley, 384
  foreign exchange programs, payment of tuition
      for, 437
  graduates currently participating in LRAP
      program, 426
  independence from parents, test for, 433,
      434
  loan types, 425
  LRAP programs, 424
  when LRAP loans cancel, 425
  Harvard-Berkeley Exchange, 384
  international students, institutional financial
      aid eligibility of, 443–444
  no interviews, 316, 357
  journals, 65
  Legal Writing course, 397
  outside grant, impact of, 436
  pay for first year graduates, 5
  placement office, non-students' use of, 386
  politics, role of, 63
  rankings of, 80–81, 87, 90, 93
  reciprocity, 386
  recruitment at, 43
  specialties, 59
  summer earnings, assessment of, 441
  term-time earnings, assessment of, 440
  transfer students, aid eligibility of, 442–443
  tuition payment for exchange programs or
      transfer terms, 439
  wait-listing, 363
    wait-listed students, aid eligibility of, 442

Hastings:
  Director of Admissions quoted:
    on admissions procedures, 112
    on application timing, 123, 125
    on deferrals, 389
    on international students, 205
    on number of recommendations, 296
    on recommenders, whom to choose, 293
    on wait-listing, 365
  index numbers, use of, 106
  no preference to residents, 199
  no recommendations required, 294
  rankings of, 91
"Hide-the-ball" method of teaching, 395
"Hidden" interview, 69, 72, 315 (*see also* Interviews)
Housing at school, assessing, 55
Human resources staff of potential employer,
  contacting before choosing school, 43–44

Illinois: (*see also* University of Illinois)
Index numbers, use of for admissions, 105–107,
  108 (*see also* Admissions process)
Industry association, joining while in law school,
  407
Inside the Law Schools, 78, 86 (*see also* Rankings)
The Insider's Guide to the Top Fifteen Law Schools, 78,
  87–88 (*see also* Rankings)
Interests, personal, determining before choosing
  law, 8
International students, 176–177
  Admissions Directors thoughts on, 205–206
  aid eligibility for, 443–444
  extra preparation for, 400
  institution financial aid eligibility of, 443–444
  JD and LLM degrees, 203–204
  student visa process, 391
  TOEFL (Test of English as a Foreign
    Language), 152–153
Internationalization of school, assessing, 58
Internships at school, assessing, 60
Interviews, 313–357
  Admission Directors' thoughts on:
    how they conduct interviews, 338
    how to handle oneself in interview, 354
    interview formats, 320
    kinds of interviewers, 324
    options for interview, 317
    preparation for interviews, 342
    when to interview, 351
    whom they interview, 314–315
    why they interview, 356–357
    why they do *not* interview, 357
  after, 355–356
    checklist, 355
    thank-you notes, 355
  before, 318–319
    format, 319
    objectives, establishing, 318
  checklist, post-interview, 355

choice for, 316
during, 343–346
  behavior, 344–346
  dress, 343–344
  recollecting thoughts, 335–336
ending, 348
evaluation forms, 324–326
  at Northwestern, 324–326
executive summary, 313
grammar, importance of, 336
"hidden" interviews, 315
  Admission Directors' thoughts on, 315 (*see
    also* ". . . Admission Directors'
    thoughts . . .)
importance of, 315–316
interviewer, 319–324
  with Admissions officers, 319–320
  with alumni, 320–322
  with current students, 322–323
  incompetent, 353–354
  reading, 346
key events, preparing to describe, 336–337
knowing school, 324–327
physical preparations, 340–342
practice, 339
questions, 329–335
  anticipating, 328
  likelihood of given, 337–339
question time, 347
recollecting thoughts during interview,
  335–336
relaxation, striving for, 341
request for interview, accepting or not,
  316–318
  Admission Directors' thoughts on, 317 (*see
    also* . . . Admission Directors'
    thoughts . . .)
rules, general, 349–350
special types, 351–353
  friendly chats, 352
  in restaurants, 353
  stress, 351–352
when to do interview, 351
wreckers, 348
Introduction to law schools, 1–133 (*see also* under
  particular heading)
  admissions process, 99–113
  assessing schools, criteria for, 53–68
  choosing right school for you, 39–51
  programs at law schools, 25–38
  rankings, how to use, 77–97
  reason for entering law and choosing top
    school, 3–24
  timetable for applications, 115–133
  visiting law schools, 69–76
Iowa: (*see also* University of Iowa)

Job, resigning from, 391–393
Jobs at school, assessing, 65–67

Joint-degree programs, 35–36
  Admissions Directors' thoughts on, 57
  caution regarding, 56
  Georgetown, Assistant Dean for Admissions, 57
  and master's degrees, 55–56
  Northwestern, Associate Dean, Admissions/ Financial Aid, quoted, 57
  rankings, 90
  at school, determining before choosing, 55–57
Journals at schools, assessing, 65
Judicial clerkships, numbers of used for rankings, 90–91

Keirsey Temperament Sorter, 8
Kellogg Business School (of Northwestern University):
  teaching standards, high, 61
Knowing school before interview, 324–327

Law camps, 398, 399
LawEXCEL, 443
Law firm management courses, teaching of, 59–60
Law review, 36
  importance of at school, determining, 65
Law school: is it for me? 6–24 (*see also* Reasons)
  Admissions/Career Services Directors' thoughts on:
    value of life and work experience, 12–14
    waiting to apply, 12–13
  as affirmative, not default, choice, 11
  alternatives, 16, 18–19
  career dissatisfaction, 19–20
  Career Services Directors quoted:
    additional thoughts, 22–24
    on self-assessment, 10–14 (*see also . . .* self-assessment)
  faulty reasons for entering law, 14–16 (*see also* Reasons)
  Keirsey Temperament Sorter, 8
  law degree not general purpose degree, 6
  law field, checking out, 7–9
  legal training valued only in lawyers, 9–10
  Myers-Briggs Type Inventory (MBTI), 8
  paralegal experience, 18
  resources, 20–22
  reversal of decision difficult, 9–10
  school experience, checking out, 6–7
  self-assessment, 6–20
    Career Services Directors' thoughts on, 11
  waiting to apply, 12–13
  work experience, 11–14 (*see also* Work experience)
    Career Services and Admissions Directors' thoughts on, 12–14
    critical to self-assessment, 11, 12
    waiting to apply, 12–14

Law School Admissions Council (LSAC), 105, 109, 147
  LSAT and LSDAS Registration and Information Book, 109, 120, 147
  The Official Guide to U.S. Law Schools, 48
Law School Data Assembly Service (LSDAS), 107–109
  LSAT and LSDAS Registration and Information Book, 109, 120, 147
Law school hiring practices for rankings, 90
Lecture as teaching method, 30–31
Legacies, 201–203
  Admission Directors' thoughts on, 202–203
Legal exams, taking in preparation, 397–398
Legalines, 403
Legal reasoning, learning, 399
Legal training valued only in lawyers, 9–10
Legal writing, 397
Lifetime Learning Credit, 450
Loan forgiveness programs, 422
Loan Repayment Assistance Programs (LRAPs), 421–424 (*see also* Loans)
Loans to finance law school, 418–428
  choosing, 420–421
  credit history, 420
  federal, 416
  Federal Perkins Loan, 419
  Federal Subsidized Stafford Loans, 419
  Federal Unsubsidized Stafford, 419
  how much debt is too much? 427
  Loan Repayment Assistance Programs (LRAPs), 421–427
    loan forgiveness programs, 422
    NAPIL (National Association for Public Interest Law), 427–428
    Stanford Law School LRAP, 422–423, 424
  private loans, 419
  repayments, 421–427
Local connections of school, determining, 67
Location of school, assessing, 53
LRAPs, 421–427 (*see also* Loans)
LSAT (Law School Admission Test), 138, 146–157 (*see also* Credentials)

Marketing yourself, 179–197
  Admission Directors' thoughts on, 195–197
  conclusion, 195
  executive summary, 179
  positioning, 191–193
    general vs. specific, 192–193
    mechanics of, 193–195
    themes, 193–195
    vehicles. 195
  privileged image, how to combat, 188
  strategy, creating, 180–189
    fit in—stand out, 191
    personal statement example, 189–191
    strengths and weaknesses analysis, 180–186
  themes, using, 193–195

MBA as today's multipurpose degree, 6, 10
Miami: (*see also* University of Miami)
Michigan: (*see also* University of Michigan)
Microeconomics, learning, 399
Minnesota: (*see also* University of Minnesota)
Mission of school, assessing, 55
Multi-App, 248–249
Myers-Briggs Type Inventory (MBTI), 8

NAPIL (National Association for Public Interest
    Law), 427–428
The National Jurist, 78, 80–81, 86–87 (*see also*
    Rankings)
"National" school, 54
Need Access application, 416, 417
Needs, personal, determining before choosing
    law, 8
Nellie Mae, loans available from, 419
Networking, 410
New York University: (*see also* NYU)
Nonacceptance, responding to 361–372 (*see also*
    Rejection)
Noncustodial parents, schools' assessment of,
    435
Non-law employers recruiting on campus,
    numbers of as ranking method, 92
Nonbinding early decision option, 117
North Carolina: (*see also* University of North
    Carolina)
Northwestern:
    admissions criteria, 102–103
    Associate Dean, Admissions/Financial Aid,
        quoted:
        on academic records, 141, 142, 143
        on admissions procedures, 111, 113
        on appeals of denial, 369
        on application timing, 124–125
        on career dimension, 174
        on choosing right school, 51
        on conducting interviews, 338
        on "Deans' Letter,"89
        on deferrals, 390
        on effects of good recommendations, 302
        on extracurricular and community activities,
            171, 172
        on how to handle oneself in interview, 354
        on international students, 206
        on interviewers, kinds of, 324
        on interview option, 317
        on joint degree programs, 57
        on LLM programs, 207
        on LSATs, 154, 155
        on personal statements, 238, 239, 240, 241
        on preparation for interview, 342
        on rankings, 95, 96
        on reapplications, 370, 371
        on recommenders, whom to choose, 293
        on wait-listing, 365, 367
        on what they are looking for, 175

    on when to interview, 351
    on who is interviewed, 314
    on why interviews are done, 356, 357
    on work experience, 159–160, 161, 162
    on writing essays, 264
    exchange students, 385
    foreign exchange programs, payment of tuition
        for, 437
    higher score of two LSATs accepted, 151
    independence status of applicants, 434, 435
    international students, institutional financial
        aid eligibility of, 443–444
    interview evaluation form, 324–326
    interview requested, 316
    JD-MBA program, 56
    Kellogg, high teaching standards of, 61
    MBA program, ranking of, 57
    noncustodial parents, assessment of, 435
    outside grant, impact of, 436
    program, assessing, 55
    rankings of, 80–81, 91
    summer earnings, assessment of, 441
    term-time earnings, assessment of, 440
    third year matriculants, 385
    transfer students, aid eligibility of, 442–443
    tuition payment for exchange programs or
        transfer terms, 439
    wait-listed students, aid eligibility of, 442
    work experience, particular value of to
        Admissions, 104, 435
Norwest Bank, loans available from, 419
Notre Dame:
    Career Services Director quoted, 11
    rankings of, 81
Nutshell books, 399
NYU (New York University):
    Assistant Dean for Admissions, quoted:
        on academic record, 145
        on admissions procedures, 110
        on application forms, filling out, 274
        on choosing right school, 49, 50, 51
        on deferrals, 390
        on essays, optional, and addenda, 245
        on extra material, submitting, 275
        on handling recommenders, 299
        on impact of age and experience on
            Admissions process, 164
        on interpretation of mixed (grade and LSAT)
            data, 157
        on interview option, 317
        on LSATs, 154, 155
        on marketing yourself, 197
        on number of recommendations, 296
        on personal statements, 240, 241
        on recommenders, whom to choose, 292, 293,
            294
        on waiting to apply, 13
        on who is interviewed, 315
        on work experience, 160, 162

on working as paralegal, 23
on writing essays, 264, 266
Assistant Dean, Career Counseling/Placement, quoted:
on career dissatisfaction, 20
on exploring law as career, 24
on knowing why you want law school, 22–23
on self-assessment, 11
on value of work experience, 12
bargaining for financial aid, 446
career services, 67
foreign exchange programs, payment of tuition for, 437
graduates currently participating in LRAP program, 426
independence status of applicants, 434
international corporate law, 47
international students, institutional financial aid eligibility of, 443–444
loan type, 425
MBA program, ranking of, 57
noncustodial parents, assessment of, 435
one recommendation required, 294
outside grant, impact of, 436
part-time programs, 27
part-time work during program, 430
percentage of law students working, 430
public service scholarships, 429
rankings of, 80–81, 91
recruitment at, 43
specialities, 59
summer earnings, assessment of, 441
term-time earnings, assessment of, 440
transfer students, aid eligibility of, 442–443
tuition payment for exchange programs or transfer terms, 439
wait-listed students, aid eligibility of, 442

One L, 30
Opportunity cost, 414
Order of the Coif, 32
Outlining essay material, 251–252
Overseas study:
to begin law degree, 381–383
to complete law degree, 383–384

The Paper Chase, 30
Paralegal experience, 18
Boston College, Director of Admissions quoted, 23
George Washington, Director for Admissions quoted, 23
NYU, Assistant Dean for Admissions quoted, 23
Stanford, Associate Dean for Admissions/ Financial Aid quoted, 23
University of Virginia, Associate Dean for Admissions/Career Services quoted, 23
value of as work experience, 158

Parents, independence from for financial aid, 433–435
noncustodial, 435
Part-time program, choosing, 45
Part-time work at school, 429–431
ABA limits, 431
assessing, 68
Pay, increased, for graduates of top schools, 5
Pedagogical issues of school, assessing, 60–62
class size, 61–62
professors, 62
teaching methods, 60
teaching quality, 60–61
workload, 61
Penn: (*see also* University of Pennsylvania)
PEP, 443
Perkins Loans, 419
Personal organizer, 209–214, 251
education, 209
extracurricular/post-graduation activities, 211–212
professional accomplishments, 211
questions, personal, 212
work experience, 210–211
Personal statement:
Admission Directors' thoughts on, 237–241, 245 (*see also* Essay options)
example, 189–191
reusing, 266–267
Pitfalls in choosing school, 46–47
Politics at school, assessing, 62–63
Positioning yourself, 191–193 (*see also* Marketing yourself)
Practitioners in your field, contacting, 407
Prejudices, awareness of your own, 73
Prioritizing assignments, 402
Privileged image, how to combat, 188
Professors:
preparing for confrontation with, 399
at school, assessing, 62
PROFILE, 416, 417 (*see also* Financial aid)
Programs at law schools, 25–38
assessing, 55–58
courses outside law school, 34–35
curricular organization, 33–34
editor of law review, 36
executive summary, 25
for first-year students, 26
grading, 32–33
joint-degree programs, 35–36
at Cornell, two law degrees, 35
disadvantages, 35–36
at University of Pennsylvania, 35
at Yale, 35
law review, 36
organization of curriculum, 33–34
for part-time students, 26–28
prerequisite for admission to bar, 26
publications by students, 36

Programs at law schools *(cont.)*
  at Georgetown, 36
  law review, 36
  required courses, typical, 28–29
  for second and third year students, 26
  social life, 37–38
  specialization, 34
  student body, 37
    at Columbia University Law School, 37
  teaching methods, 29–31
    case method, 29–30
    clinical studies, 31
    field placement programs, 31
    lecture, 30–31
    Socratic Method, 29–30
  two law degrees, obtaining, 35
  workload, 31–32
    Order of the Coif, 32
Public service scholarships, 429

Quality of life at schools, assessing, 64

Rankings, how to use, 77–97
  absolute or relative terms for data, 93
  Admission Directors' thoughts on, 95–97
  conclusion, 94
  controversy, 88–89
  "Deans' Letter," 88–89
    Admissions Directors' thoughts on, 89
  executive summary, 77
  other, 89–94
    departmental, 90
    joint-degree, 90
    judicial clerkships, 90–91
    law school hiring practices, 90
    non-law employers recruiting, 92
    other, 93–94
    recruiters on campus, number of, 92
    Supreme Court clerkships, 91–92
  rankings, 80–89
    The American Lawyer, 78, 85–86
    Inside the Law Schools, 78, 86
    *The Insider's Guide to the Top Fifteen Law
      Schools,* 78, 87–88
    limitations of methodologies, 82
    The National Jurist, 78, 80–81, 86–87
    U.S. News & World Report, 78, 82–85
  only rough proxies, 46
  using, 78–80
    guidelines, 79–80
    uncertainty of, 78–79
    warning, 79–80
Reapplications, 269–371
  Admission Directors' thoughts on, 370–371
Reasons for entering law, 3–24 *(see also* Law
  school: Is it for me?)
  alternatives, 16, 18–19
  career choice, 4
  career flexibility, 4–5

employment opportunities, investigating, 17–18
  executive summary, 3
  faulty, 14–16
    Career Services Directors' thoughts on, 16
  financial considerations, 5–6
  for going to top school, 4–5
  intangibles, 5
  pay, increased, 5
  self-assessment prior to choice, 10–11
  should you go to law school? 6–20 *(see also* Law
    school: Is it for me?)
    Keirsey Temperament Sorter, 8
    Myers-Briggs Type Inventory (MBTI), 8
    resources, 8–9
  status, 4
Reciprocity for career placement services, 386
Recommendations, 277–311
  Admission committees, what they learn from,
    283–285
  Admission Directors' thoughts on:
    importance of, 283
    Deans' letters, 291
    effects of good recommendations, 302–303
    how to handle recommenders, 299
    number of recommendations, 295–294
    whom to choose, 292–294
  approaching potential recommender, 296–299
  briefing outline, 311
  difficult issues, handling, 299
  employer recommendation, 289–290
    sample, 305–308
  executive summary, 277
  follow-up, 304–305
    thank-you note, 304
  how many, 294–296
  increasing value of, 300
  for international students, 305
  length of letter, 301–304
  one-size-fits-all recommendation, 301
    Georgetown, Assistant Dean for Admissions,
      quote, 301
  organizer, 309
  recruiting through community service, 168
  required number, 294–296
  timely, 304
  who should write, 285–291
    criteria, other, 290
    Deans' letters, 291 *(see also . . .* Admission
      Directors' thoughts . . . *)*
    employers, using, 289–290
    University of Michigan, Admissions Director,
      on cultivating recommenders, 285
  why required, 278–283
Recruiters on campus, number of as ranking
  method, 92
Rejection, responding to, 361–372 *(see also* under
  particular heading)
  administrative hold, 362
  denial, 367–371

options, other, 371–372
wait-listing, 361–367
Repayment chart for loans, 421
Reputation, choosing for, 47, 53
Required courses, typical, 28–29
Researching law schools, 40–44 (*see also* Choosing)
Research methodology, learning, 399
Residency, as factor in admissions decisions, 199–201
Resident status, converting to in second year for financial aid, 433
Resigning from job, 391–393
Restaurants for interviews, 353
"Résumé" approach to essay writing, 220
Résumés, writing, 269–274
   Admission Directors' thoughts on usefulness of, 274
   rules, basic, 259–270
   sample, 270–273
"Rolling" admissions, 100
   for top law programs, 116

Safety of schools, assessing, 54
Self-assessment prior to choice, 6–20, 40 (*see also* Law school: Is it for me?)
Signature Student Loan program, 443
Size of schools, assessing, 53
Skills, personal, determining before choosing law, 8
Social issues at school, assessing, 62–64
   competition, 64
   politics, 62–63
   quality of life, 64
   student body, 63
   student-faculty relations, 64
Social life in law school, importance of, 37–38, 411
Societies at schools, assessing, 65
Socratic Method of teaching, 29–30
Soft skills, teaching of, 59–60
Special cases, 199–207
   Admission Directors' thoughts on:
     legacies, 202–203
     LLM programs, 207
     residency, 200
   international applicants for JD and LLM degrees, 203–204 (*see also* International)
   LLM degrees, 203–204, 207
   legacies, 201–203 (*see also* Legacies)
   residency, 199–201
Specialization, 34
   investigating, 17
Specialties at school, assessing, 59
Stafford loans, 419
Stanford:
   Associate Dean for Admissions/Financial Aid quoted:
     on academic record, 141, 145

     on admissions procedures, 110, 111
     on career dimension, 174
     on Deans' letters, 291
     on effects of good recommendations, 302, 303
     on extracurricular and community activities, 170, 173
     on impact of age and experience on Admissions process, 163
     on international students, 205
     on interviews, none, 357
     on LSATs, 153
     on transfers, 379
     on waiting to apply, 12
     on wait-listing, 363, 367
     on ways to learn about law, 23
     on who is interviewed, 315
     on whom to choose as recommender, 292, 293, 294
     on work experience, 159, 160
     on writing essays, 265
   Associate Dean for Career Services quoted:
     on career dissatisfaction, 20
     on exploring law as career, 23–24
     on poor reasons for entering law, 16
     on work experience, 13
   bargaining for financial aid, 446
   Dean Paul Brest, reaction of to rankings, 88
   Director, former, of Career Services Office, quoted:
     on knowing why you want law school, 22
     on work experience and marketability, 14
   foreign exchange programs, payment of tuition for, 437
   graduates currently participating in LRAP programs, 426
   independence status of applicants, 434, 435
   intellectual property course offerings, 79
   Intellectual Property courses, superiority of, 79
   international students, institutional financial aid eligibility of, 443–444
   loan repayment assistance program, 422–423, 424
   loan types, 425
   LRAP programs, 424
   when LRAP loans cancel, 425
   noncustodial parents, assessment of, 435
   outside grant, impact of, 436
   part-time work during program, 430
   percentage of law students working, 430
   rankings of, 80–81, 91
   recruitment at, 43
   summer earnings, assessment of, 441
   term-time earnings, assessment of, 440
   transfer students, aid eligibility of, 442–443
   tuition payment for exchange programs or transfer terms, 439
   wait-listed students, aid eligibility of, 442

Status as reason to choose top school, 4
Stress control in law school, 410–411
Stress interviews, 351–352
Student body of law school, 37
  assessing before choosing school, 63
Student-faculty relations at school, assessing, 64
Student organization(s), joining in law school, 406
Students, current, interviewing with, 322–323
Student societies at school, assessing, 65
Study groups, 405
Sum and Substance series, 399
Supreme Court clerkships as ranking method, 91–92

Tax deductibility of law school, 450
Teaching often poor in first-year courses, 395–396
Teaching methods in law school, 29–31 (*see also* Programs)
  assessing before choosing, 60–61
Term-time earnings, assessment of, 439–440
Test of English as a Foreign Language (TOEFL), 152–153
Texas (*see also* University of Texas)
Thank-you notes:
  after campus visit, 76
  to interviewer, 355–356
  to recommender, 304–305
Themes of marketing strategy, 193–195
Third-year matriculants, 384–385
Time management, 402–404
Timetable for applications, 115–133
  Admission Directors' thoughts on timing of applications, 123–125
  Early Application option, 116, 117
    binding versus nonbinding decision, 117
  executive summary, 115
  for international students, 122–123
  Master Organizer, using, 125–133
  problems, potential, 123
  "rolling" admissions, 116
  sample timetable, 119–123
  time required to complete application, 118–119
  when should you apply, 116–118
    early, 116–118
    late, 118
TOEFL (Test of English as a Foreign Language), 152–153
Trading down in school quality to save money, 451
Transfer and other options, 373–386
  Admission Directors' thoughts on:
    studying law abroad, 383
    transfer, 379–380
  choosing school you will transfer *from*, 376–379
  completing degree abroad, 383–384
  exchange program, 384–385
  executive summary, 373

from institution where you have been admitted, 374–376
  evaluation of transfer applicants, 375–376
  overseas study for beginning, 381–383
    transfer after one year/two, 382
  overseas study to complete degree, 383–384
  reciprocity for career placement offices, 386
  rules, 377–378
  school to attend for first year, factors in choice of, 378–379
    preparation before law school, 379
  third-year matriculation, 384–385
Transfer application essay example, 509–510
Transfer students, aid eligibility for, 442–443
Tulane:
  specialties, 59
Tuition at schools, assessing, 67
Two law degrees, obtaining, 35

UC Davis:
  Director of Career Planning quoted on value of work experience, 12
  part-time work during program, 430
  percentage of law students working, 430
  rankings of, 91
UCLA:
  Dean of Admissions quoted:
    on academic record, 142, 145
    on admissions procedures, 110, 111, 113
    on application timing, 12 4
    on choosing right school, 50
    on Deans' letters, 291
    on deferrals, 389
    on effects of good recommendations, 302
    on extra material, submitting, 275
    on impact of age and experience on Admissions process, 163, 164
    on international students, 206
    on joint-degree programs, 57
    on LSATs, 153, 154
    on personal statements, 238, 240
    on reapplications, 371
    on recommendations, importance of, 283
    on recommenders, whom to choose, 292, 293
    on transfers, 380
    on work experience, 159, 160–161
    on writing essays, 264, 265, 266
  Director of Admissions quoted on personal statements, 238
  exchange programs, 58
  externships, 60
  foreign exchange programs, payment of tuition for, 437
  foreign study, 58
  independence status of applicants, 434
  international students, institutional financial aid eligibility of, 443–444
  noncustodial parents, assessment of, 435
  one recommendation required, 294

outside grant, impact of, 436
rankings of, 80–81, 91
summer earnings, assessment of, 441
term-time earnings, assessment of, 440
transfer students, aid eligibility of, 442–443
tuition payment for exchange programs or
  transfer terms, 439
wait-listed students, aid eligibility of, 442
Writing for Law School course, 398
University of Illinois:
ranking of, 81
University of Iowa:
rankings of, 81
University of Miami:
rankings of, 81
University of Michigan:
allowance for additional essay materials, 244
career dissatisfaction, survey on, 19
Career Services Office Director quoted on work
  experience and marketability, 14
Director of Admissions quoted:
  on academic record, 144
  on admissions procedures, 110, 112, 113
  on career dimension, 174–175
  on cultivating recommenders, 285
  on effects of good recommendations, 303
  on essays, optional, and addenda, 245
  on extra material, submitting, 275
  on extracurricular and community activities,
    169–170, 171–172
  financial aid decision independent of
    admissions decision, 432
  on impact of age and experience on
    Admissions process, 164
  on international students, 205
  on interpretation of mixed (grade and LSAT)
    data, 157
  on legacies, 202
  on marketing yourself, 105, 196
  on personal statements, 238, 240
  on rankings, 96
  on recommenders, whom to choose, 292, 293
  on residency, 200
  on resumes, usefulness of, 274
  on wait-listing, 365
  on writing essays, 264, 265
Director of Financial Aid quoted:
  financial aid decision independent of
    admissions decision, 432
graduates currently participating in LRAP
  program, 426
independence status of applicants, 434, 435
international students, institutional financial
  aid eligibility of, 443–444
joint degrees, 55
little preference to residents, 199
loan types, 425
LRAP programs, 424
merit aid grants, 428

no interviews, 316
noncustodial parents, assessment of, 435
outside grant, impact of, 436
program, assessing, 55
rankings of, 80–81, 87, 88, 91
resident status, converting to as difficult
  process, 433
summer earnings, assessment of, 441
term-time earnings, assessment of, 440
transfer students, aid eligibility of, 442–443
tuition payment for exchange programs or
  transfer terms, 439
wait-listed students, aid eligibility of, 442
University of Minnesota:
rankings of, 80–81
University of North Carolina
Assistant Dean, Career Development/
  Placement, quoted on work experience,
  13
merit aid grants, 428
part-time work during program, 430
percentage of law students working, 430
rankings of, 81
substantial preference to residents, 199
University of Pennsylvania:
Assistant Dean, Admissions, quoted:
  on academic record, 144, 145
  on admissions procedures, 111, 113
  on application timing, 124
  on career dimension, 174
  on choosing right school, 50
  on conducting interview, 338
  on "Deans' Letter," 89
  on essays, optional, and addenda, 245
  on extra material, submitting, 275
  on extracurricular and community activities,
    170–171
  financial aid decision independent of
    admissions decision, 432
  on how to handle oneself in interview, 354
  on international students, 205
  on interview formats, 320
  on legacies, 202
  on LLM programs, 207
  on LSATs, 154
  on marketing yourself, 196, 197
  on personal statements, 239, 240
  on preparation for interviews, 342
  on rankings, 95, 97
  on studying law abroad, 383
  on when to interview, 351
  on who is interviewed, 314
  on why interviews are done, 356
  on writing essays, 264, 265, 266
Assistant Dean, Career Planning/Placement,
  quoted on work experience, 13
bargaining for financial aid, 445–447
courses in other departments, allowance, 55
exchange students, 385

University of Pennsylvania *(cont.)*
  foreign exchange programs, payment of tuition for, 437
  graduates currently participating in LRAP program, 426
  independence status of applicants, 434
  international students, institutional financial aid eligibility of, 443–444
  joint-degree programs, 35, 55
  loan types, 425
  LRAP programs, 424
  when LRAP loans cancel, 425
  MBA program, ranking of, 57
  noncustodial parents, assessment of, 435
  outside grant, impact of, 436
  part-time work during program, 430
  percentage of law students working, 430
  public service scholarships, 429
  rankings of, 80–81, 91
  recruitment at, 43
  summer earnings, assessment of, 441
  term-time earnings, assessment of, 440
  third year matriculants, 385
  transfer students, aid eligibility of, 442–443
  tuition payment for exchange programs or transfer terms, 439
  two essays, requirement for, 228
  wait-listed students, aid eligibility of, 442
University of Texas:
  Dean of Admissions quoted:
    on academic record, 142, 143, 146
    on admissions procedures, 110–111, 113
    on career dimension, 174
    on conducting interview, 338
    on deferrals, 389, 390
    on essays, optional, and addenda, 245
    financial aid decision independent of admissions decision, 432
    on how to handle oneself in interview, 354
    on interviewers, kinds of, 324
    on interview option, 317
    on legacies, 202
    on personal statements, 239, 241
    on preparation for interviews, 342
    on rankings, 95, 96
    on reapplications, 370
    on residency, 200
    on transfers, 380
    on wait-listing, 366, 367
    on who is interviewed, 315
    on why interviews are done, 356
    on writing essays, 264, 265
  Financial-Aid Matching Program, 447
  independence status of applicants, 434
  noncustodial parents, assessment of, 435
  no recommendations required, 294
  outside grant, impact of, 436
  rankings of, 80–81, 91

resident status, converting to as difficult process, 433
resume required, 269
substantial preference to residents, 199
summer earnings, assessment of, 441
term-time earnings, assessment of, 440
tuition payment for exchange programs or transfer terms, 439
wait-listed students, aid eligibility of, 442
University of Virginia:
  Associate Dean, Admissions/Career Services, quoted:
    on admission procedures, 110
    on application timing, 124
    on conducting interview, 338
    on Deans' letters, 291
    on deferrals, 389
    on effects of good recommendations, 303
    on essays, optional, and addenda, 245
    financial aid decision independent of admissions decision, 432
    on interviewers, kinds of, 324
    on interview formats, 320
    on interview option, 317
    on LLM programs, 207
    on LSATs, 153–154
    on marketing yourself, 195
    on number of recommendations, 295–296
    on personal statements, 238, 239, 241
    on preparation for interviews, 342
    on recommenders, whom to choose, 292, 293
    on residency, 200
    on resumes, usefulness of, 274
    on studying law abroad, 383
    on waiting to apply, 13
    on when to interview, 351
    on why interviews are done, 356
    on work experience, 160, 162, 163
    on working as paralegal, 23
    on writing essays, 266
  Career Services Dean, quoted on knowing why you want law school, 22
  Dean of Admissions/Placement, quotes:
    on appeals of denial, 369
    on reapplications, 370
    on transfers, 379, 380
  graduates currently participating in LRAP program, 426
  loan types, 425
  LRAP programs, 424
  when LRAP loans cancel, 425
  independence status of applicants, 434
  index numbers, use of by Admissions, 105
  interviews requested, 316
  outside grant, impact of, 436
  part-time work during program, 430
  rankings of, 80–81, 91
  resident status, converting to as difficult process, 433

substantial preference to residents, 199
wait-listed students, aid eligibility of, 442
University of Washington:
  rankings of, 81
University of Wisconsin
  Assistant Dean, Career Services, quoted on
    value of work experience, 12
  part-time programs, 27
  placement office, non-students' use of, 386
USC:
  Assistant Dean quoted on work experience and
    marketability, 13
  Dean for Admissions quoted:
    on academic record, 142, 143
    on application forms, filling out, 274
    on application timing, 124, 125
    on career dimension, 175
    on choosing right school, 50, 51
    on Deans' letters, 291
    on deferrals, 390
    on essays, optional, and addenda, 245
    on extra material, submitting, 275
    on extracurricular and community activities,
      171, 172
    on handling recommenders, 299
    on impact of age and experience on
      Admissions process, 164
    on international students, 205, 206
    on legacies, 203
    on LSATs, 154
    on personal statements, 237, 239, 240
    on rankings, 96
    on reapplications, 370
    on recommenders, whom to choose, 294
    on resumes, usefulness of, 274
    on waiting to apply, 13
    on wait-listing, 366, 367
    on who is interviewed, 315
    on work experience, 161, 162
    on writing essays, 265, 266
  graduates currently participating in LRAP
    program, 426
  loan types, 425
  LRAP programs, 424
  when LRAP loans cancel, 425
  rankings of, 80
U.S. News & World Report, 41, 78, 82–85, 107 (*see
  also* Rankings)

Values, personal, determining before choosing
  law, 8
Vanderbilt:
  bargaining for financial aid, 446
  Director of Admissions quoted:
    on academic record, 141
    on admissions procedures, 110, 112
    on choosing right school, 50
    on essays, optional, and addenda, 245
    on LSATs, 154

on number of recommendations, 296
on personal statements, 239
on waiting to apply, 12
on wait-listing, 365
on work experience, 162
graduates currently participating in LRAP
  program, 426
loan types, 425
LRAP programs, 424
rankings of, 80
Visiting law schools, 69–76
  after leaving campus, 74–76
    impressions, recording, 74–76
    thank-you notes, 76
  before visit, 70
  "hidden" interviews, 69, 72
  when to visit, 69–70
  while on campus, 71–74, 75
    Admissions Office, 71–72
    campus tour, 71
    career services department, 72
    classes, 72
    Financial Aid office, 72
    information session, 71
    prejudices, personal, awareness of, 73
    questions to ask, 75
    things to note, 74

Wait-listing, responding to, 361–367
  Admission Directors' thoughts on, 365–367
  aid eligibility of, 442
  executive summary, 361
  managing yield, 363
Waiting to apply to law school, 12–14 (*see also*
  Work experience)
  if you can't get in, 43
Washington: (*see also* University of Washington)
Washington and Lee
  rankings of, 80, 87
William and Mary (College of):
  Career Planning/Placement Assistant Dean
    quoted:
    on exploring law as career
    on self-assessment
  curriculum, first-year, 59
  part-time work during program, 430
  percentage of law students working, 430
Wisconsin: (*see also* University of Wisconsin)
Work experience, value of, 11–14, 157–163 (*see
  also* Credentials)
  critical to self-assessment, 11, 12
  Georgetown Assistant Dean quoted, 12
  how much, 13
    Career Services Directors' thoughts on,
      12–13
  and marketability, 14
    Career Services Directors' thoughts on, 14
  New York University, Career Counseling
    Assistant Dean quoted, 12

Work experience, value of *(cont.)*
  UC Davis, Career Planning Director quoted, 12
  waiting to apply, 12–14
  Admissions Directors' thoughts on, 12–13
Workload in law school, 31–32
Writer's block, two ways to avoid, 255
Writing persuasive essays, 247–267
  actual application essays, thirty, 453–510
  Admission Directors' thoughts on, 264–266
  critique by someone else, 260–261
  elements of good writing, 252–254
  executive summary, 247
  importance, 248
  planning, 250–252
    developing material, 250–251
    organizing material, 251–252
    outline, making, 252
  proofreading, 261
  readings, further, 267
  reusing personal statements, 266–267
  rough draft, 254–260
    editing, 256–260
    writer's block, two ways to avoid, 255
  starting, 248–250
    applications on disk, 248–249
  tips for good writing, 261–263

Yale:
  bargaining for financial aid, 446
  Career Development Executive Director quoted
    on poor reasons for entering law, 16
  Director of Admissions quoted:
    on academic record, 144
    on admissions procedures, 110
    on career dimension, 174

  on choosing right school, 50
  on deferrals, 389
  on interview option, 317, 357
  on joint-degree programs, 57
  on personal statements, 237, 240
  on studying law abroad, 383
  on transfers, 379, 380
  on wait-listing, 363, 365, 367
  on work experience, 160, 161
  exchange students, 385
  foreign exchange programs, payment of tuition
    for, 437
  independence status of applicants, 434, 435
  international students, institutional financial
    aid eligibility of, 443–444
  joint-degree programs, 35, 55
  judicial clerkships, highest number of, 90–91
  loan types, 425
  LRAP programs, 424–426
    graduates currently participating in LRAP
      program, 426
    LRAP loans cancel, 425
  MBA program, ranking of, 57
  no credit for studying law abroad, 382
  noncustodial parents, assessment of, 435
  optional essay, allowance for, 243–244
  outside grant, impact of, 436
  personal statement requirement, 216, 243
  rankings of, 80–81, 90, 93
  term-time earnings, assessment of, 440
  third year matriculants, 385
  tuition payment for exchange programs or
    transfer terms, 439
  wait-listed students, eligibility of, 442